DMU 0364471 01 3

KT-451-832

Lincolnshire College of Agriculture and Horticulture
Library
CAYTHORPE

# TRAINING SHOWJUMPERS

# TRAINING SHOW JUMPERS

ANTHONY PAALMAN

J. A. ALLEN : LONDON

*To Sonja,*
*the best wife any man ever had*

British Library Cataloguing in Publication Data

Paalman, Anthony
Training Showjumpers
1. Show jumpers (Horses) 2. Horse training
I. Title II. Holstein, Gisela
636.1'08'88 SF287 77-30100

ISBN 0-85131-260-8

Library of Congress Card No. 77-30100

First published 1978
Reprinted 1984
Reprinted 1986
Reprinted 1988
Reprinted 1989
Reprinted 1992

Published in Great Britain by
J. A. Allen & Company Limited,
1, Lower Grosvenor Place, Buckingham Palace Road,
London, SW1W 0EL

© Anthony Paalman 1984

All rights reserved. No part of this book may be reproduced, stored in a retrieval system, or transmitted, in any form or by any means, electronic, mechanical, photocopying, recording, or otherwise, without the prior permission, in writing, of the publishers.

Book production Bill Ireson
Illustrated by Gisela Holstein

Printed in Great Britain by
The Bath Press, Avon

# FOREWORD

I FIRST met Anthony Paalman when he came to work in Ireland in the 1960s; he was our official national instructor and senior course designer, for many years.

I was privileged to work very closely with him when I was Chairperson of the Training Committee of the Show Jumping Association of Ireland. I saw very quickly the total dedication this man displayed in every job he undertook, whether it was teaching twenty unruly youngsters on equally unruly horses, building a Grand Prix course with minimal material or designing a set of fences that had been sponsored by Sir John Galvin as a result of seeing the effect of his teaching on young riders.

In 1969–1971 Anthony trained the Irish Junior Team, which competed for the European Championships. In each of these years they won an individual medal, culminating in a Team Gold in 1971. In 1969 when I was preparing for the Ladies' European Championship, the variety of courses and problems he set for me was of tremendous benefit and a great confidence builder.

Anthony Paalman's enthusiasm has inspired hundreds of young riders to work towards his high standards, both in his training methods and his stable management. In everything he did, the welfare and proper development of the horse was his first consideration. He was patient and helpful to all his pupils, always taking a deep personal interest in them. During the winter period he gave lectures and training courses at various centres throughout the country. I hardly need to say that his methods are sound, progressive and painstaking. Without doubt, he has raised the whole standard of course building, as well as improving the all-round standard of equitation in this country.

I was delighted when he wrote his book, which has more than lived up to expectations, covering as it does every aspect of the young horse's training, both for jumping and dressage. The book contains many superb photos and drawings to illustrate the text. There are detailed diagrams of how to make gymnastic jumping grids, loose jumping lanes and diagrams for making fences.

I recommend this book to everybody interested or involved in show jumping at whatever level.

IRIS KELLETT
*Kildare*, *Ireland*, 1984

CONTENTS

# INTRODUCTION

THERE is an old saying: "He who teaches the young controls the future". This is particularly true in the world of showjumping. The juniors of today will be the seniors of tomorrow and it is our responsibility to see that they are correctly trained and educated, thereby ensuring the continuing progress of equestrian art for future generations to delight and participate in.

It is this, above all else, which urged me to write this book. I have not set out to write an academic treatise, but to give practical advice in the training of showjumping horses and riders and, as a necessary foundation for that training, the basic schooling of the horse in general. I have also included a chapter on course design and construction as I believe that the rider should have an understanding of the rudiments of this art in order that he will not damage his horse's confidence, especially in the early stages of schooling and jumping training.

Many trainers are convinced that only their own particular methods and principles are sound. They point to their success as proof of this and tend to regard further discussion on the subject as pointless. However, it is possible they may have achieved an even greater success had they been aware of alternative methods. What is and what is not correct is, of course, a matter of opinion. I believe that there are various approaches and that there are some which are better and more effective than others. One must progress beyond mere expansion of a basic technique, or the implementation of what has been handed down by one's predecessors. An ability to isolate the good from the bad and to apply it accordingly in one's own methods is essential. A real horseman will always be alert to suggestions and advice which can improve himself and his horse.

The training technique in which I believe is the Natural Training Method and it is fully explained in this book. It is evolved from the classic principles of the European cavalry schools and to it I have added my own experience as a trainer and course designer in Australia, Central America and Europe. I believe that the Natural Training Method is an excellent method of developing showjumpers.

I hope that the reader of this book will save himself much time and frustration of effort by following the principles I advocate and will thereby develop both himself and his horse to the fullest potential.

ANTHONY PAALMAN
*Dublin*

## HAPPY PERFECTION

*A great deal of happiness in life*
*consists of things which one undertakes to fulfil in perfection,*
*or at least as near as possible.*
*Only when a task is perfected in all ways and exactly rounded off*
*does it give contentment and fulfilment.*
*One who neglects his work*
*and deals carelessly or superficially with it*
*will never know this feeling.*
*The conscious perfection makes out of the work an art.*
*The smallest little things, when in perfection,*
*become a work of art.*

WILLIAM MATHEWS

# THE NATURAL TRAINING METHOD

THE Natural Training Method has evolved from the training principles of the famous European cavalry schools. These classic principles must be preserved and at the same time adapted to the needs of modern showjumping.

The main characteristic of the Natural Training Method is the easy and relaxed manner in which the horse co-operates with the rider's demands. The horse is progressively taught to work without using unnecessary energy and to develop his athletic ability to the utmost degree, the purpose being to encourage the horse to use his own initiative within limits determined by the rider. The horse will become so eager to please, and will gain so much self-confidence, that in a difficult situation he will quickly make the right decision, without any aid from the rider. To most English riders, and those in English-speaking countries, this free forward way of riding and training is routine, as they have learned in the hunting field to trust their horse's own initiative and sense of survival.

The Natural Training Method is the exact opposite of what I call the *unnatural* method. The latter is used by many European riders and is a method where the rider, when jumping, interferes constantly with the horse's natural stride, changing rapidly from overriding to checking backwards and vice versa. This is *especially* harmful as it is done right from the very start of the horse's schooling when, even over small training fences, the rider feels he has to "do something". The rider is convinced that his horse will not be able to approach a fence, or take-off over it, without his direction.

Consequently the horse has no self-confidence because he has never had the chance to jump "under his own steam", and the rider has no trust in his horse.

I cannot believe that this method is the way to train a horse. Controlling a horse's pace and adjusting his stride is, of course, necessary in competition, especially at indoor shows, but even then it should be done as an aid to assist the horse, not to dominate him. A horse ridden in the unnatural method depends totally on his rider. Once the rider makes a mistake – and it sometimes happens to the best of them – the horse is completely lost and has no ability to "save" the situation. This will also be the case should the horse be sold and his new rider does not exercise the same control as his previous one. A horse must, of course, be trained to obey, but this should be done whilst building up the horse's own initiative.

Before training any animal it is necessary that one should make an honest judgement of one's own qualities and deficiencies. To do so is hard but a credit to a horseman when done correctly.

The most important thing to aim for is to be able to control one's temper at *all* times. Keep reminding yourself of this. Unlimited patience is essential to achieve permanent results, and when you know patience is not one of your strongest attributes you must be aware that damage will be done and training rushed if you indulge yourself.

It is impossible to put all horses through a uniform training and it is therefore essential that one develops an understanding of the horse's psychology. Every horse, like every human being, has his own personality and character and needs to be handled accordingly.

Recognising one's own limitations is vital. There are first-class trainers, experts in their own right, who are not very good competitors. Equally, there are riders who are highly successful, have cool nerves, a great sense of timing and the necessary courage and will to win a competition who are unable to train a horse to the same standard as the "made" horse they are accustomed to riding.

Therefore, one must try to improve oneself constantly, but, in the end, must decide what one is best at and excel at it, leaving to others that part of the job which is beyond your own capabilities.

I have given in this book the complete programme of the Natural Training Method. To receive the full benefit from it the trainer must study and put into practise *all* the principles involved. This cannot be too often repeated. If you think you will leave out the dressage, dip into the improvement of style or just forget about the free jumping parts of the programme, then you cannot expect either your horse or yourself to jump as well as would have been the case had the complete programme been followed.

If the programme is followed fully then the horse will develop and mature and serve you willingly – and to the very best of his ability Even a moderately talented horse, when schooled in the Natural Training Method, will surprise and delight you with his performance.

PART ONE

# THEORY

CHAPTER ONE

# PURCHASING A SHOWJUMPER

THERE is no such thing as a "standard pattern" for a good showjumper according to which one could select one's horse.

I have seen horses all over the world, from those with the most beautiful conformation to the most awkward caricatures, who were, in spite of their extraordinary conformation, first-class showjumpers.

There are certain aspects of conformation, bone structure, distribution of muscles and the horse's action one should look for and others one should avoid. One should pay equal attention to the fact that the horse must have courage (heart), be willing to jump (trier), and be a very good free mover.

The horse must have the right temperament, as there is nothing harder to correct than bad temper and cowardice.

A horse can have a perfect conformation, as wanted for a show class, but without the above-mentioned qualities the prettiest one will still not be suitable as a showjumper.

When purchasing a showjumping horse one often has to consider potential and character before beauty to make a decision. Naturally, it would be ideal to find a horse that has a perfect conformation also, but it is not really necessary. He should be well bred, because the qualities required of him in his jumping career are handiness, suppleness, endurance and speed, as in modern showjumping the results are not only judged by good jumping but by speed as well. A horse physically built for speed has necessitated in recent years – in various countries – a systematic breeding for *faster* showjumping horses.

I am not saying that if one finds a horse with all the desired advantages he will definitely make a high class jumper, but at least the chances are better than if one starts off with a horse that has some inborn handicaps.

## CONFORMATION

### *The head*

The appearance of the horse's head does not have much influence on his jumping capabilities, although one prefers a smallish head with an alert, honest and sympathetic expression, full of character.

The head in general should be well proportioned, which shows quality, and broad between the eyes, this, it is said, being a sign of intelligence. The ears should not be too big as this would denote a lack of quality – and not too small, which will denote possible cunning. The eyes should be bold, large and "well set" on the side of the head, which will give almost 180° vision. A good full eye denotes intelligence and honesty. Good nostrils result in the horse having ample scope for intake of air. The gullet should not be too thick and should run into a well developed windpipe, giving good passage for breathing.

A "well set" head (the point where the head joins the neck) is important. This gives not only a harmonious effect, but it also prevents a lot of difficulties throughout the horse's entire training. If the head is wrongly "set", the cheek bones heavy and the lower jaws large and narrow, the horse is difficult to collect, as these jaw bones interfere with the action of the parotid glands (producing saliva). Consequently the horse will have a difficult mouth.

### *The neck*

The ideal neck for a showjumper should be light, fairly long and nicely arched, coming well out of the shoulder. This is important, as the

*Fig. 1*
Well set head and nicely arched neck.

*Fig. 2*
Ewe neck.

*Fig. 3*
Very thick and short neck.

horse needs head and neck to balance himself. It will be more difficult for the horse to keep his balance if his neck is very thick and short. Such a horse requires a lot more specialised training than the average horse in order to become flexible enough for jumping.

One should also avoid a horse with a too high, or ewe, neck. These horses generally carry their head too high and the nose too far in front of the vertical line. They are difficult to control, as, owing to this high head position, the bit is not only resting on the bars but is also pressing against the molars, which results in the horse developing a hard mouth. Due to their head carriage these horses are usually weak in the spine, and when ridden will drop their backs and, to stay in balance, will move with their hocks too far apart. It takes a very long and skilful training to develop the back muscles so that the horse can round his back and bring the hocks closer together and more underneath his body. (One will quickly see the point if one lifts one's own head backwards, feeling the back become hollow and stiff and a pressure on the kidneys.)

Horses who naturally carry their head too low and whose neck comes straight out of the shoulder in one line with the back are mostly overbuilt (higher in the quarters than in the withers). They are also generally too much on the forehand and move, by nature, unbalanced. It takes a long period of schooling for the horse to develop the necessary muscles enabling him to transfer any excess weight from the forehand to the quarters.

*The withers*

The withers should be higher than the quarters, but too high withers need a well fitted saddle as they get easily sore. Too low or flat withers do not give the saddle enough grip, and it might slip. The withers should be well muscled, but not too fleshy, otherwise the saddle might move. Of course, one will have this trouble with most young horses during the first year of training.

If one fears the horse might get sore behind

the elbows (from the girths) I would suggest covering the girths with a motorcycle inner tube. The rubber will get slippy when the horse is sweating and the skin will not get sore. Sometimes sheepskin is used instead, but it makes the skin sore on account of its heat retaining qualities.

*The shoulder*

The horse's natural stride is as long as the imaginary extension of the slope of the shoulder. In other words, the more sloping the shoulder the longer the stride will be. Therefore a long shoulder, sloping from the withers to the point, provides well sprung suspension and free movement covering much ground. A straight shoulder, often in conjunction with too short and straight a pastern, inhibits the horse's movement, gives the rider an unpleasant ride and will make the horse inclined to stumble.

*Fig. 4*
The horse's stride, in relation to the imaginary extension of the shoulder.

*The trunk*

The chest should be deep and broad and the ribs well sprung to give ample room for breathing organs and heart and to carry the girths well. If the trunk is round like a barrel the saddle would tend to slip.

*The back*

It is necessary for the horse to have a good length of back, in correct proportion and balance. Too long a back is mostly weak. A weak back can often be improved by light harrowing work (three times per week for approximately 30 minutes). I emphasise "light" work, as working too hard might develop a roach back. When young horses have to do heavy farmwork (ploughing) for too long, this sometimes happens. I do not really mind horses which are *born* with a roach back, although they are mostly difficult to break, but when schooled correctly they will become strong horses, since they have by nature their hindlegs more underneath their body. But the roach back, which is *developed* through too hard work, makes a horse unsuited and can only be cured by a long rest period.

*Fig. 5*
A nicely made young showjumper, the German-bred Holsteiner. Note the nicely arched neck and the point of the withers higher than the croup.

Horses with too short or too straight a back usually have a very stiff spine and consequently mouth difficulties.

Wide, well rounded and well developed muscles of the loins are essential, especially the part behind the saddle.

*The hindquarters*

Look for large, strong muscular quarters, together with large hips and good length from hip to point of buttock, which denotes power of movement. The tail should be well "set".

*The legs*

Special attention should be paid to the horse's

legs, because in the career of a showjumper they have to withstand a lot. If one leg is unsound the other three do not compensate, as training cannot be continued.

One likes the forearm long and straight and covered with strong muscles. The knees should be low down, large and flat.

The hocks of a showjumper must be perfect, strong and clean, because they are the hardest worked joints of all. They have to work as a spring in the take-off and give full length of stride for impulsion. Therefore one should only choose a horse with a well developed and low hock, which should be neither too straight nor too bent, but set at the correct angle, otherwise it will never stand up to the strain of showjumping.

A hock with windgalls, bog spavin, spavins or stringhalt is unsound. Stringhalt is a convulsive exaggerated lifting movement in one, or both, hindlegs.

Any unsoundness is a reason not to buy a horse.

Avoid horses whose hocks are by nature too wide apart, or horses who turn their hocks sideways and outwards while moving, as this makes the hoof move the same way before lifting off the ground. Some people try to stop this by putting a stud into the outside of the hindshoe. This stops the hoof from turning, but puts twice as much strain on the hock and will do damage. It is very difficult to train such horses to bring their hocks underneath their body. As a result of this natural handicap they carry too much weight on the forehand and will have difficulty getting their forelegs off the ground at take-off. Therefore they are careless with the forelegs, especially at upright fences.

Strong and well developed gaskins denote power. Short cannon bones on the fore and hindlegs reduce strain on tendons and ligaments.

The fetlock joint should be well developed and clean, without windgalls.

Fore and hindpasterns should be clean and sound and set at the correct angle. They ought to be of medium length and medium slope. Not only does too short and straight a pastern give an uncomfortable ride, but it can also be the cause of stumbling. The pastern bone must be sloped enough to ensure that the horse will move with plenty of "spring". This is most important, as we know that the pastern works as a spring and shock absorber, because after the jump the horse lands on *one* foreleg *only*, which, for a split second has to carry the horse's and rider's full weight.

If the pastern is a straight and/or a short one it has not enough "give" and the entire shock will be absorbed by the tendons and the hoof and this could cause dropped sole or even navicular disease.

If the pastern is too sloped – especially in the hindlegs – then it is not strong enough for the hard and strenuous work at the take-off.

*The feet*

The hoof is the part of the horse which is in active use most of the time. Therefore, a good conformation is most important. The hooves should all be of equal size and not *too* large, but above all they should be sound, because the condition of the feet are a common source of lameness.

*The coat*

The coat shows whether a horse is healthy and in good condition. When a horse is well looked after his coat is shiny and fine.

### MOVEMENT

It is essential that a showjumper has loose, free movement and covers a lot of ground. His action should show great mobility. The experienced observer will not judge the movement on first impression, bad or good, as the performance depends a great deal on how the horse is shown. It is advisable to see the horse free, out in the field or in an indoor school, in order to form a clear picture of his true action and movement. When the horse is shown in hand he is often sent on too much with the whip, which may be deceptive. When judging the horse's movement one has to be mindful of his condition. A horse in good condition, fit and

*Fig. 6*
When shown in hand, the horse should move relaxed, freely and regular. The horse should not be sent on extensively with the whip.

with developed muscles, will show better action than a weak one.

The walk should be free and regular, covering much ground; the hindfeet should touch the ground well in front of the hoof marks of the forefeet.

The trot should also be free and active. One does not like too much knee action, nor should the horse move his feet too low over the ground. While maintaining an energetic impulsion and an even cadence the moment of the suspension should be elastic.

The canter is the most important pace for a showjumper. The horse should move with a light "bouncing" stride and in natural balance. When the speed is extended the horse should not change his centre of gravity to the forehand.

It is equally important to judge a horse's movement from the front, and especially from the rear, as well as from the side, to see if the horse moves straight from head to tail. If the horse turns one of his legs in, or out, it is considered to be wrong.

It is recommended that one should see the horse being ridden *first* before riding him oneself. It is extraordinary how many horses give a completely different ride to what one expects, sometimes favourable and sometimes disappointing.

*Balance*

To check a horse's balance, ride him in all three paces on a loose rein, on a circle, alternatively on both reins. The badly balanced horse will point head and neck to the outside to remain balanced; he will try to increase the curvature of the circle to prevent himself from falling in with his shoulder. One can, of course, accept such a display from a green horse, but a well schooled horse must be able to move in a balanced manner on a loose rein – even on a small circle. His entire body must be bent laterally and his paces should not become disunited; the hindfeet must follow in the track of the forefeet.

*Bad co-ordination*

When a horse's movements show symptoms of weakness or are unco-ordinated, the buyer must have the ability to determine the possible causes:

*Physical cause.* The horse can be weak or badly shod; perhaps he is just a bad mover by nature. In these cases the action can be improved by physical training and correct shoeing.

*Psychological cause.* A malfunction in the horse's nervous system can cause badly co-ordinated movements. Just as in a human being, all actions of the horse are controlled by the brain relaying messages to the nervous system (brain, spinal cord and nerve). A nervous state of mind can cause loss of the normal control over the muscular actions. In motion, the horse will show symptoms of stumbling in front or knuckling over with the hind fetlock joints.

In some cases one of the legs fails to function properly. It is then lifted extremely high or dragged over the ground, or it may make longer or shorter strides than normal. Extreme cases are known where a nervous horse suddenly goes lame.

A "wobbler" is a horse also having insufficient control over his muscular actions. The horse lacks the necessary control over the quarters. The rider will notice this, particularly during the transition from a faster into a slower pace, when circling, reining back or when turning on the haunches. The wobbler is not able to round his back or bring his hocks underneath his body. To control his balance the horse will sway his quarters sideways, which gives the rider a most unpleasant feeling. Needless to say, these horses are not suited for showjumping.

One must realise that it is rough and unskilful handling that upsets the horse's nervous system. Therefore, certain riders often have horses which move in a badly co-ordinated manner, stumble or shake their heads. In order to prevent or improve this the trainer has to understand and master the horse's mind.

CHARACTER

In general, a bad temperament and cowardice are hard to correct. Therefore, try to judge the temperament and intelligence of the horse you want to buy. Pay attention to the expression on his face, the action of his ears and the way he takes notice of his surroundings. A good

*Fig. 7*
Attentive and placid expression.

*Fig. 9*
Nervous and sensitive expression.

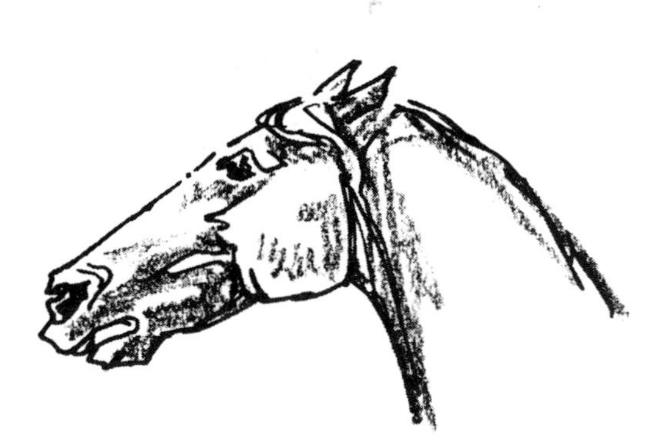

*Fig. 8*
Anxious and timid expression.

*Fig. 10*
Bad tempered expression.

expression of the eyes goes together with a placid disposition. Before buying a young unbroken horse, try, if possible, to watch him in the field, together with other horses, and find out whether he is a "herd leader" or a "follower". One can nearly be sure that a natural "leader" will also be a bold jumper, who is not afraid to go on.

## JUMPING ABILITY

*A green horse*

When one wants to see an unbroken horse jump one should let him jump free over a small fence at the long side of the indoor school, or along the hedge of the field. Approaching the fence the horse should lengthen the last few strides, lower his head and lengthen his neck. He should take-off correctly and round his back as well.

When over the fence the highest point should be the withers, *not* the head.

One should ensure that the horse does not slow down whilst approaching the fence and also that he is not sent on too much with the whip.

*A novice horse*

When approaching the fence the novice horse should not take a stronger hold on the bit when lengthening his strides before take-off.

Place a pole on the ground at a distance of 3 metres in front of a small fence. Approach at

*Fig. 11*
The unbroken horse should jump loose, not on the lunge. It should approach the fence willingly without being sent on too much. The horse should have good "use of himself", whereas the legs of most unbroken horses will hang down rather than be well folded.

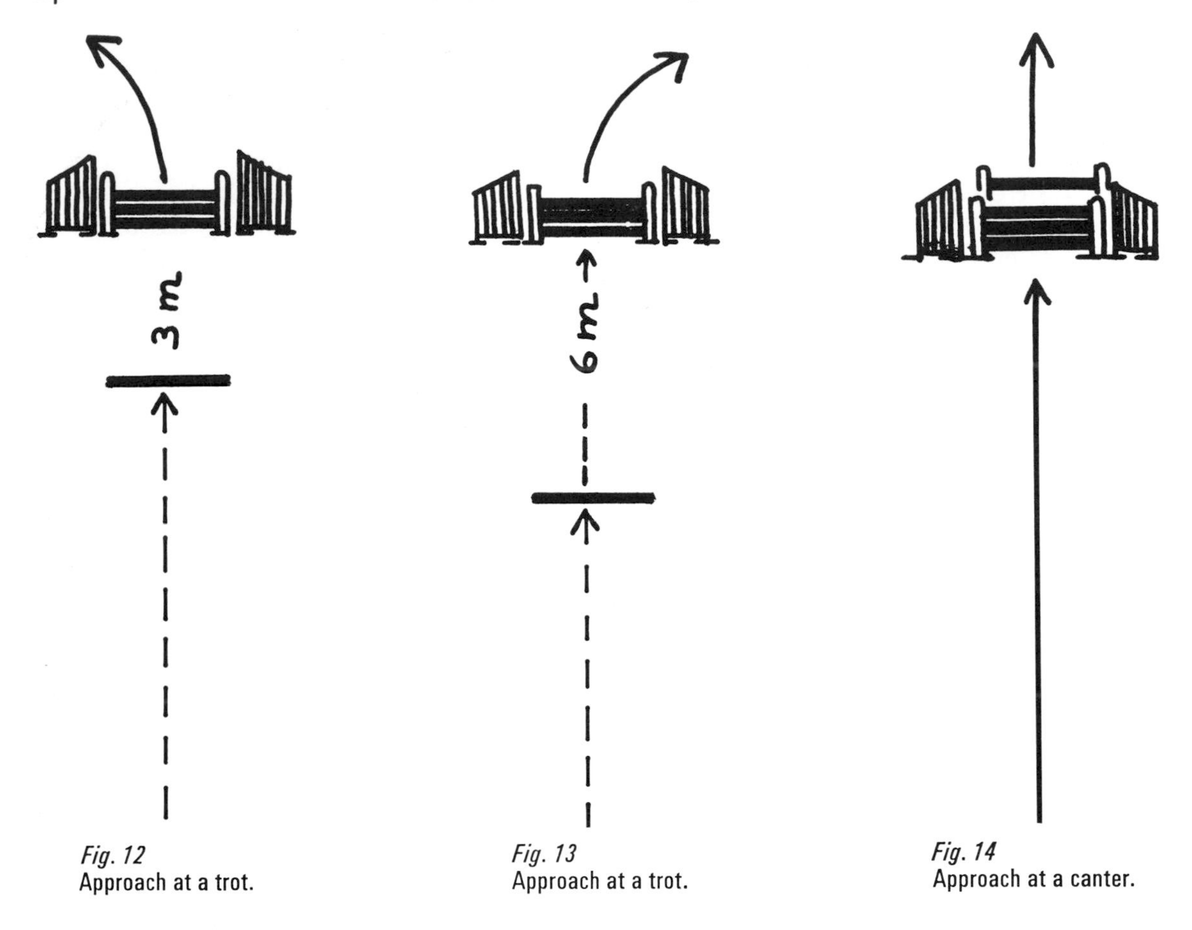


*Fig. 12*
Approach at a trot.

*Fig. 13*
Approach at a trot.

*Fig. 14*
Approach at a canter.

a trot, cross the pole at a trot and take-off, jumping the fence from a trot. Then place the pole at a distance of 6 metres in front of the fence. Again approach at a trot. Over the pole the horse breaks into canter, takes one stride and then takes-off. Having jumped this two or three times, take away the pole. Alter the fence into a small oxer (for safety reasons use only one pole at the far side). Approach this fence at an ordinary canter. Should the horse rush into the fence, approach it out of a figure of eight and the horse should soon settle down.

One should not risk spoiling a young horse's confidence by testing "how high" he can jump. One should realise that it is, at this stage, more important that the horse is not frightened.

*An older horse*

Buying an older and experienced horse is usually very difficult. Although one can check on his official winnings, it is essential that the rider and his new mount will be able to establish a good partnership. This applies particularly to sensitive mares, because one has to "ask" a mare while one can "tell" a gelding. This is one of the reasons why most male riders prefer geldings and why mares work more willingly for a lady rider or children.

A nervous competitor with stage fright, or with little jumping experience, is inclined to become upset and subconsciously stiffens his muscles. The horse will quickly sense this and react by pulling and going panicky because the rider makes him feel insecure. Such a rider

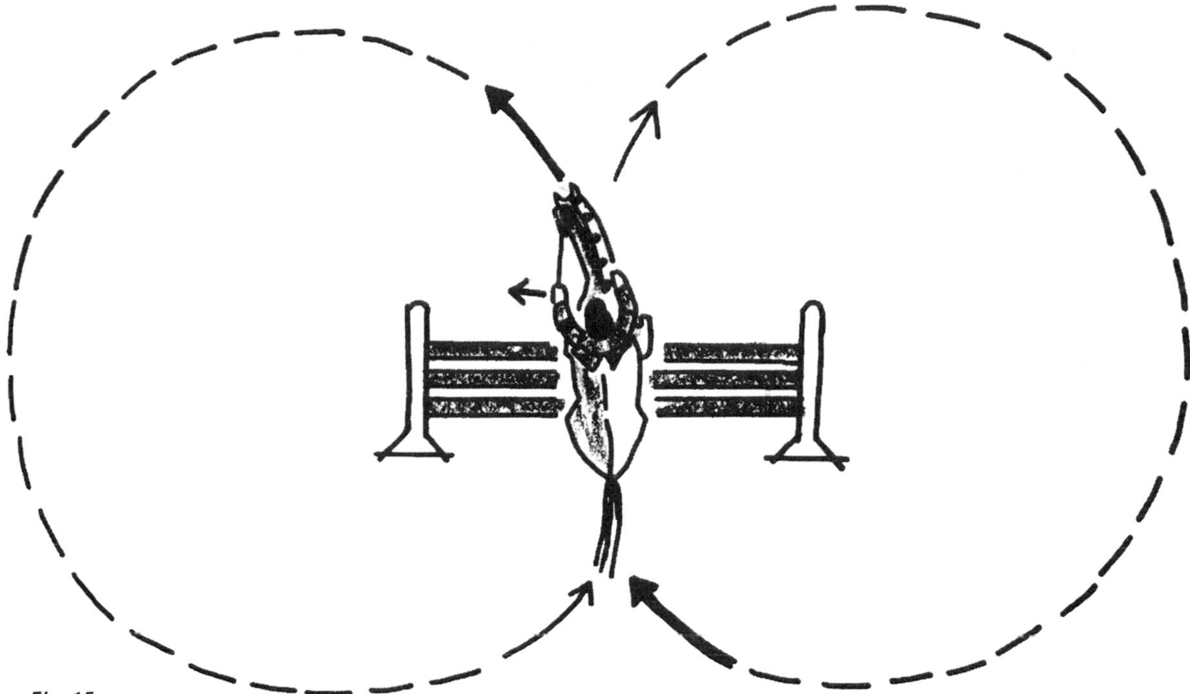

*Fig. 15*
Approach out of a figure of eight, if the horse rushes into the fence.

should buy an older horse with plenty of competition experience and a cool temperament. He is ill-suited to ride thoroughbreds because they are highly sensitive, become upset quickly and need to be ridden by relaxed, cool riders with experience. For a young rider buy an experienced horse which will be his teacher, because it is very hard to train a young rider on a green horse, as one might easily spoil both.

In some cases a highly strung horse might get on very well with a lady rider and form a successful partnership. In general, ladies have sensitive hands, more patience and a sympathetic attitude towards the horse. A bit of caressing and mothering works wonders with a shy or temperamental horse. There are highly experienced riders who are unable to ride every horse, even if the horse is of Olympic standard. The important point is that horse and rider should create a harmonious partnership.

### VETERINARY EXAMINATION

Needless to say one should only consider buying a horse which is sound in every way. It should be examined by a veterinary surgeon. He will pay special attention to the horse's heart and lungs, which undergo extreme stress in jumping competitions. Some limitations of the horse's performance and endurance is frequently mistaken for a lack of physical fitness. It is more often a case of strained heart or lung trouble. Horses have given their last breath in the battle to win and dropped dead from exhaustion in the ring as a result of a heart attack. Therefore the heart and lungs should be examined, not only when buying a horse, but occasionally later on, to check if the horse is not overworked.

Once you have chosen your horse, bear in mind whether the horse also would have chosen you!

CHAPTER TWO

# STABLING

## HANDLING

It is most important that the horse breeder should be familiar with the psychology of the horse and handle him properly from the day he is born. Most horse breeders are horse lovers and do the right thing automatically. However, there are breeders who err in turning out young horses with little handling for far too long. Such horses will grow up in the natural state, estranged from human beings. This provokes many difficulties later on when the horse is being broken. I have witnessed cases where half wild young horses had to be drugged in order to have them shod, a risky treatment, as it is not only dangerous for the heart and lungs, but when the horse is waking up he can injure himself in jumping to his feet.

All these difficulties could be avoided if the horse was handled regularly from the time he is born, developing confidence in human beings. Make a daily habit of lifting up the young horse's feet. This is not very difficult if approached logically. In motion the horse, while lifting up one foreleg, automatically transfers his weight on to the other foreleg. Therefore it is reasonable that if one lifts up one foreleg one should lean against the horse's shoulder, pushing his weight over onto the other foreleg. That way little resistance is encountered. There is also a logical way of lifting a horse's hindleg. In motion the horse lifts up his hindleg in a forward-upwards direction. Knowing this, one starts to lift a hindleg in the same direction. Only if the horse does this relaxed should one gently move the hindleg backwards.

Every four to six weeks the young horse's feet must be rasped down and checked by a blacksmith for hoof deformations or ailments.

When the foal is still with his mother it is advisable to leave the mare without a headcollar as the foal might get caught in it when playing around. The foal, however, should have a headcollar as soon as possible and should be led daily, along with the mare. When the foal is weaned he should be led around on his own. Some breeders take their weanlings around on a lead when herding. This is not a waste of time; the result is seen when one starts to school the horse. Then one will appreciate the benefit of the good relationship between man and horse.

Too often this "pre-training" is neglected. Therefore I emphasise: the first impressions which register in the horse's mind will remain there and influence him throughout his life.

## FEEDING

### *General principles*

It is not my intention to give a feeding schedule as to what and how much a show-jumper should be fed, because every horse must be fed individually and not according to any rule. If in any doubt I recommend one obtains professional advice from a veterinary surgeon. The quantity and kind of food required depends entirely on the horse's digestion, the amount of work on each particular day, the horse's age, size and temperament. Incorrect feeding can seriously affect the horse's health, and his training will then suffer a setback. His physical condition, muscles, wind, temper and his sight are affected by feeding. Therefore there are certain rules one should consider in devising a feeding schedule.

To keep up a horse's appetite he must not be overworked – and the food should not be monotonous. The feed should be rationed into small portions and given four times per day in order not to overload the stomach, which is very sensitive. The horse needs at least two hours rest after each feeding in order that digestion can take place. Neglecting this could cause colic.

A strict parasite control is essential. Worm doses should be given regularly to young, unbroken stock as well.

*Ingredients for a mash*

One needs bran, linseed oil or linseed. Due care should be taken that the linseed is soaked in water the night before and then stewed for a few hours until a jelly is formed and the seeds have become so soft that one can easily squash them between two fingers. Some of this boiled linseed is then poured on to the bran, mixed, covered and left to cool. Additional ingredients vary for each horse: oatmeal, a few handfuls of flaked maize, treacle – and once per week Epsom salts.

*Changing to dry feeding*

Immediately after a horse comes in from grass the veterinary surgeon should give a "physic" to clear the horse's stomach (worms, etc.). The first day after this "physic" the horse's stomach and intestines might be irritated, therefore the horse should get a mash (without Epsom salts and linseed) instead of dry food.

To prevent a horse getting a colic when he is brought in from grass it is essential not to change suddenly to dry feeding. During the first month of schooling the horse should be fed crushed oats (never whole oats), and three or four times per week a warm mash in the evenings, as this will ensure not only good digestion but keep the young horse quiet as well.

When stabled some horses are not over keen to finish their food when used to grass. To compromise and to increase their appetite one should give the horse some freshly cut branches of the willow tree three times a day. The same remedy is recommended for some jumping horses during the show season. A long and tiring journey, stabling in strange stables, or after the excitement of a hard day jumping are all reasons that some horses lose their appetite, just when they need food so badly for their performance. To be on the safe side in such a case one should take along some willow tree branches on the journey and keep them in a bucket of water so that they stay fresh. If not available, find some gorse, cut it into small pieces and soak it in camomile, then mix it with a small amount of oats. Most horses like this mixture, even sick ones. In case a horse might have digestive trouble, camomile will often solve this problem too.

*Variety in feeding*

Nervous and highly strung horses should get their oats ration never as whole oats but crushed or as meal (well dampened). When oats are crushed they lose a great percentage of their protein.

I also suggest replacing half the oats ration by barley. The barley should be lightly crushed, not into meal as this could lead to indigestion. Whole barley should be well boiled or soaked overnight.

As highly strung horses are often poor doers, the fattening potential of barley will improve the horse's condition without making the horse unmanageable. Whole oats increases the horse's explosive temperament and can even be harmful as some horses seem to be allergic to it. Side effects can be filled legs, nettle rash, itchy skin, particularly at the tail, and so on.

For these reasons weak and quiet horses should be fed on whole oats mixed with chopped straw. Never use barley straw but preferably oats straw. Care must be taken that the straw is not chopped too short, as it could then become lodged in the guts and cause colic. The mixture of oats with chopped straw will increase the horse's mastication, consequently the food will be mixed better with saliva, giving more nourishment and stimulating the digestion.

Horses who wear the "coat of poverty" (dull hair) or are in the moulting period (changing their coats) should have added to their bucket of water each morning a few handfuls of linseed meal which has been soaked overnight and is well stirred before use. This speeds up not only the moulting process but gives the horse a shiny and fine coat as well.

Not every horse will be satisfied with the same food all the time without any variety, so now and then, to encourage his appetite, and as an alternative, one should feed: carrots, sugarbeets, a few handfuls of flaked maize, a bit of grass, fresh clover, horsenuts, grassmeal, some molasses, dry bread and/or apples (these should always be cut into pieces, as apples could easily become lodged in the horse's throat).

During the jumping season, when the horse consumes a lot of energy, it is desirable to provide a sugar supplement in addition to the normal food ration. Sugars, like glucose, honey and molasses, all come under the heading of carbohydrates and are a good source of energy.

If one feeds beans, crushed or whole, one should give only very little, soaked overnight. The best time to feed them is in the morning, because then there is more acid present in the stomach, and two hours after this morning meal the horse is usually exercised, which aids the digestion.

All the year round every horse should get a hot mash in the evenings, at least twice per week (one with Epsom salts).

*Hay feeding*

Feeding hay three or four times per day in small quantities is much better than giving it only once or twice per day, as it keeps the horse occupied the whole day and no hay will get spoilt. It should *never* be fed straight from the field, because then there is too much heat in it, which will damage the horse's health; it needs a few months to sweat out. For horses coming in from grass, or those which make a "sound", or are coughing, hay should be soaked with boiling water a few hours before feeding and left covered with sacks. This way hay will not affect the breathing and in many cases the coughing will stop.

Which type of hay one feeds depends on the country one lives in. Of clover and lucerne hay, only about half the quantity should be fed in comparison with white hay, as it contains a much higher percentage of protein and minerals.

When travelling abroad one does well to obtain the same sort of hay one's horse is used to (otherwise one does better to bring one's own). A different sort of hay should be fed soaked. Special care must be taken never to feed mouldy or dusty hay. To keep any dust out of the stable the hay must be shaken up outside the stable in the open air. Hay dust contains vegetable matter, which provokes irritation of the nasal passage and can cause various kinds of lung diseases.

## COLICS

There are different types of colic, mostly caused by an obstruction, and they are extremely painful. In extreme cases they can be the cause of a twisted gut. The experienced horseman will recognise the first symptoms of a colic and put the horse into a large box, with plenty of straw and well banked sides and corners (the horse could easily get cast and injure himself when rolling with pain). As soon as possible professional help should be sought and diagnosis and treatment left to the veterinary surgeon. The sooner he is called the better are his chances of curing the horse. Colic is very often the cause of death. Clinical analysis of the different types of colic is not relevant in this context, but I emphasise that colics could often be prevented, as they are closely connected with wrong feeding or careless treatment of the horse.

*"Day-off" colic*

In most stables on one day per week horses are not exercised. It is dangerous to give a horse the same amount of food as he would get on a normal working day. Owing to the lack of his usual exercise, the normal amount of food can upset the digestive system and cause colic. To prevent this the horse should only be fed half the normal amount on his "day-off". A warm mash is a suitable feed for the preceding night and also for the last meal of the "day-off".

In order not to overload the stomach after colic, it is most important that the horse should frequently be given small quantities of warm food or mash.

The horse has a very small stomach (it is nearly as small as that of a sheep), holding 15 litres approximately.

*Nervous colic*

This term is used deliberately, as this type of colic mostly occurs in highly strung horses. The well bred horse, if handled roughly, becomes easily obstinate and excited, which affects his nervous system and can upset his digestion, often resulting in a nervous colic. The droppings will be very loose; diarrhoea is possible. Then there are horses who are so sensitive by nature that they sense, beforehand, that they are going to a show. On the other hand, some young horses *only* suffer from this nervous complaint during their *first* jumping season. If the show is on a Saturday I give such horses a light meal on Thursday and Friday evenings, otherwise they may well get a colic. There are also horses who will *stop eating* when one makes preparations for going to a show, as they know exactly what is going on in the yard. Other horses, who travel a lot from show to show, do not take the slightest notice and are calm and cool and eat in any and every strange stable.

*Water colic*

It is very important that every rider should know what to do when a horse has to stale while being ridden. Especially on a long trip, the rider can feel his horse slowing down and trying to stop. This might be a sign that the horse has to stale. The horse must be given the chance to come to a halt. The rider lifts his seat out of the saddle and stands in the stirrups while the horse passes water. If the rider does not understand the signs he might force the horse to keep going, which in turn might cause a "water colic".

During my army service I knew of horses who would not stale while mounted, and with others we had to loosen the girths or take the saddle off completely. Some horses would never stale on the road; they had to be led onto the grass by the roadside or straw had to be put under them.

It is a completely different matter when the horse has to defecate while being ridden. The rider should *never* allow his horse to come to a halt, as this teaches the horse a bad habit. The only thing one has to do is to lift one's seat out of the saddle in order to let the horse round his back while he keeps going.

*Windsucking colic*

One frequently meets this type of colic with horses who windsuck or crib-bite. Windsucking colic can also occur if one gallops a horse too fast and for too long against the wind, especially on the beach. This makes the horse swallow the wind, leading to a great amount of air in the tubes, resulting in a colic. This is probably the reason why horses in the field on a stormy day instinctively tail the wind. Therefore it is never an example of good horsemanship to face the wind when standing still, mounted, especially when the horse is warm.

*Sand colic*

Some horses have a habit of pawing the ground and licking the soil while out at grass. This can cause a colic. It is in general a sign of a lack of minerals, which can be given in a block of rocksalts.

## BOREDOM AND STABLE VICES

By nature horses are seldom vicious. Many horses, after coming in from grass and from living in the company of other horses, find it hard to get used to the small surroundings and the loneliness of the box. They get bored, especially when they do not get enough attention and exercise. This boredom can lead to all kinds of stable vices. One must pay attention to the horse's behaviour in the box to prevent or to cure these habits at an early stage before they become permanent.

*Eating the bedding*

Boredom is one of the causes why horses learn the bad habit of eating their bedding. Eating too much straw will make the horse drink too much to keep all this dry matter floating in the stomach. This again is bad for the horse's kidneys and makes him in general weak and could cause leg filling. In some cases the fault may lie in the feed being either inadequate or with insufficient bulk.

Eating mouldy straw can affect the lungs. To stop the horse from eating his bedding one can sprinkle the straw with a little disinfectant diluted with water. Most horses dislike the strong smell and stop eating the straw. An alternative bedding to straw is peat moss or wood shavings.

*Fig. 16*
Crib-biter in action.

*Pawing the door*

Another bad habit is pawing the stable door, which might result in swollen knees or other injuries. Iron bars or a grate on top of the box door will make the horse stand further away from the door and save the knees.

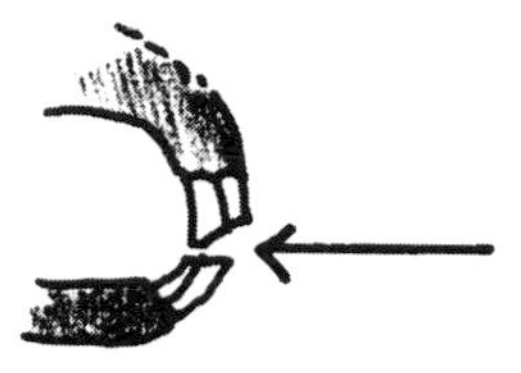

*Fig. 17*
The edges of the upper teeth become severely worn.

*Eating timber*

Eating timber is, for the owner very costly and, for the horse, a very dangerous habit (splinters). Use products such as Formular DC or Cribbox according to instructions, which will stop the horse going near the timber. An alternative: Vaseline mixed with red pepper-powder or the strong smelling Renadine.

*Fig. 18*
Crib-biting strap.

*Eating droppings*

When a horse eats his droppings a mineral deficiency, or worms, can be the cause. There is the risk of bacterial infection and re-infestation with worms from the droppings. The horse should be given a better balanced diet and a block of rocksalts. In many stables I have seen rocksalts hanging on the wall . . . covered in dust. The owner usually complains that his horse just does not care for rocksalts, but if the rocksalt is put into the manger the horse will get the taste of the salt while he is eating and will then start licking.

*Windsucking*

A windsucker repeatedly swallows air, rounding his neck and making a typical sound. If the horse is taking hold on something, or he puts his upper teeth on to anything suitable, the vice is called crib-biting. The edges of the upper front teeth become badly worn, severely in some cases. The horse will markedly lose condition owing to bad indigestion. Precautions, such as Formular DC or an electric wire, are more comfortable for the horse than the usual crib-biting strap or flute bit. Some windsuckers do not bother to take hold of anything with their teeth, in which case the above precautions are of no use.

In some cases windsucking may be caused by internal parasites, which should be cleared from the system. But the main cause is boredom, though giving too many sugar lumps in the stable can be a contributory factor, as many horses lick the box door or feed manger after eating sugar. This habit can easily develop into windsucking. (However, it should be remembered that a sugar lump during schooling can do no harm; on the contrary, the chewing brings the parotid glands into action, making the horse's mouth wet and foaming.)

The horse might also have learned windsucking by copying another horse who already has the vice. Therefore a windsucker must be kept separated from other horses. In most cases of windsucking the Forsell operation is carried out and is normally successful, with the scar hardly noticeable on completion.

*Boxwalking and weaving*

A boxwalker walks around in his box in a circle, at varying speeds, in extreme cases even trotting. The term weaving is given to describe the vice in those horses who extensively weave from side to side with their head, forehand and neck. They mostly do this in a stall or over a box door, or even in a field. The same habit can often be seen in caged animals or in elephants who have been tied up. The horse shifts his weight continuously from one foreleg to another, the continual strain on the tendons – particularly on the forelegs – being so great that it can cause permanent damage. As both vices sometimes continue for a length of time it is abundantly clear that the loss in physical condition and the mental stress is enormous. It is troublesome to school a horse who is afflicted in this way. As these habits are mostly caused by loneliness and boredom, one can give the horse a companion either a dehorned goat or a gelded donkey. This sometimes works wonders. Another popular method is to install a metal grille in the wall between the horses so that they can see each other, which acts as a distracting influence on the horse's mind. Both vices can easily be avoided and it is a great pity that a good showjumper's potential should be devalued by his becoming a box walker or weaver.

*Fig. 19*
**Weaver in action.**

In some cases it helps to cure a weaver if one attaches two ropes to the ceiling of the box, just on the inside of the box door. The two ropes should be fixed 50 centimetres apart, and each should carry a small wooden box in which there is a heavy load. This box should be hung at the height of the horse's knees. Each time the horse weaves, one of the wooden boxes will then touch his legs. Most horses dislike having their legs touched, and thus many will give up the weaving habit. The same remedy can be used in a stall.

## TETANUS (LOCK-JAW)

I find it desirable to inject all horses in the yard against tetanus. Death from tetanus can be eliminated by a course of three injections, which will safeguard the horse for a lifetime. Not only showjumpers, who take the greatest risk of getting injured, but all horses should get these injections fairly early in life, as the germ which causes tetanus (Clostridium Tetani) is common in horse manure. The slightest injury can cause tetanus.

## COUGHING

Coughing should be treated by the veterinary surgeon, as each time a different virus may be the cause. But it should not be forgotten that after

*Fig. 20*
Loose box with raised floor and grooves in the walls to give the horse a grip in case he should get cast. But note haynet is incorrectly positioned.

the horse has recovered from infection it will take him some time to recuperate on account of his muscular weakness and lack of stamina due to his having been laid off. Therefore, strenuous work should be avoided, as it might damage his lungs, strain his heart or cause him to develop broken wind.

### THE STABLE

Most horses stand in their stables 23 hours a day. Many have the bad habit of pawing their straw backwards, so that the forelegs stand much lower than the hindlegs. This downhill position puts a big strain on the foreleg tendons. When standing the forelegs usually carry three-fifths of the horse's weight, but in this downhill position they are carrying much more. The position is also bad for the back muscles and the horse feels pressure on the kidneys, drops and stiffens his back, shoulder and neck muscles.

The horse will take up the same wrong position when the lower half of the box door is too high. Therefore, raise the floor at an angle of 15° (sloping) in the area where the horse is standing most of his time and where he tends to place his forelegs. In a loose box this would be just inside the door, as most horses spend their time looking out over the door itself. In stalls the slope would start from underneath the feed manger, at a height of 0·3 metres, sloping down to floor level. The horse will also find it easier to get up after lying down, as he gets up forelegs *first*, contrary to, for example, a cow.

*Feed manger*

The feed manger should be large, 75 × 30 × 30 centimetres, in order to prevent the horse from nosing out his feed. Placing the feed manger at a height of approximately 65 centimetres will prevent the horse from injuring his forelegs when pawing. It also allows a foal to eat along with the mare, thus getting used to oats at an early stage. The low position while eating also has a good influence on the back muscles of the horse.

*Drinking*

Water is just as important to the horse as food, perhaps even more so. Most horses like a mouthful of water whilst eating so it should be at their disposal close to the feed manger. Automatic drinkers are ideal, especially the ones with a ballcock. To avoid injury to the horse's legs it is recommended that the drinkers are fitted in a corner, boxed in with timber, which should slope backwards down to the ground. Should a horse roll in his box he will then not get caught under the drinker and injure his legs.

In some instances one should turn off the water supply. For example, after a large meal or after training, in case the horse should come in a bit warm and might be inclined therefore to drink too much. The water left in the drinker from earlier will be enough to meet his needs and will be at an equable temperature which cannot do him any harm.

Some people object to automatic drinkers on the grounds that they would be unable to check on the quantity the horse is drinking. In general, only horses with kidney trouble will drink too much. This is easily detected because such horses have very wet beds.

Buckets should never be left in the box, not even when hung on a hook. Horses tend to play with them and can easily injure their legs, especially with metal buckets or when the bucket is tied up. It is much better to offer the horse a bucket of fresh water several times a day. In any case, one should never let the horse drink too much when he is warm; a quarter of a bucket is enough, and one should put a bit of hay on top of the water to prevent him drinking too quickly, which could cause colic.

*Hay racks and nets*

The danger with hay nets is that the horse can too easily get tangled in them with his legs. Hay racks share a similar disadvantage. If they are at the same level as the feed manger the horse can kick, bend the iron bars and get caught with the hoof. If the hay rack is hung too high the horse will get the dust into his eyes while eating. To eat the hay he has to stretch neck and head to reach the hay rack, hence his back will drop, giving him pressure on the kidneys, just the opposite of what we want to achieve when training the horse. The hay rack is a bad invention, as eating with the head up forces the horse into an unnatural position, because in nature the horse eats off the ground, rounding his back. Therefore hay should be fed from the

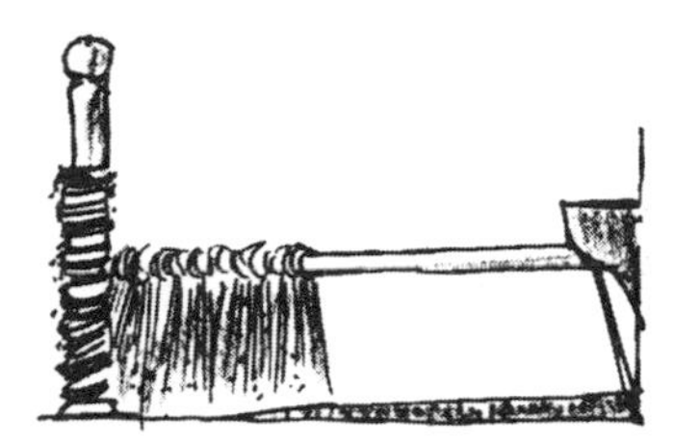

*Fig. 21*
Stall with raised floor.

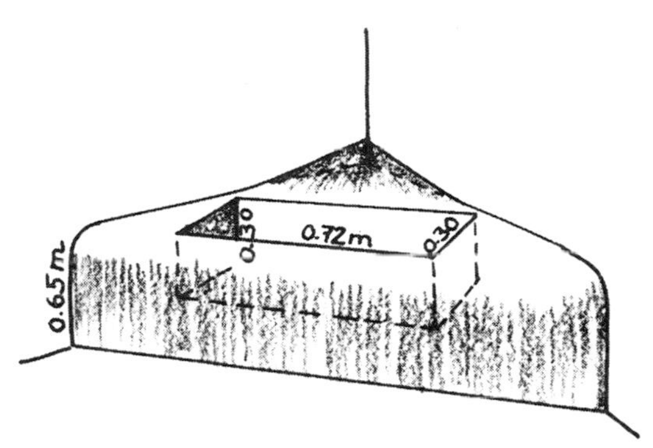


*Fig. 22*
Spacious feedmanger.

*Fig. 23*
The effect of eating hay from an incorrectly positioned hayrack. The horse takes up an unnatural position, drops his back and stands stretched out.

*Fig. 24*
**Eating hay from the ground. The horse takes up a natural position, his back is rounded and his legs normal.**

ground and given frequently, in small quantities, to keep the horse busy and the hay from getting spoilt.

A "specially constructed" hay rack, under the feed manger, has many advantages. The horse eats off floor level and no hay is wasted or spoilt. The iron bars must be strong enough and close together so that there is no danger of the horse's feet getting caught. Hay is put in through the opening from the outside. The floor is sloping towards the horse.

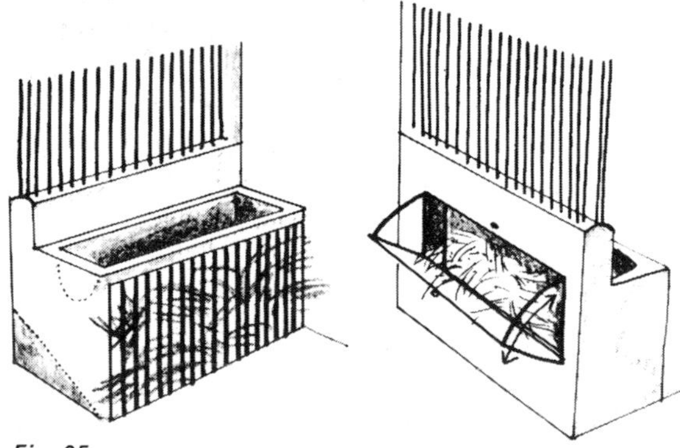

*Fig. 25*
Hayrack under the feedmanger.

*Bedding*

I prefer a deep litter straw bedding, as this mattress saves a lot of straw. The box needs to be mucked out only once or twice a week, depending on the size of the box and the climate. On remaining days only the really wet spots are taken out, the bed is shaken up and fresh straw is added. (Not barley straw. The awns of barley straw may cause eye trouble; it may also cause colic if a horse should eat his bedding.) Always ensure that the sides and corners are banked sufficiently, otherwise the horse might get cast when rolling. This thick mattress encourages the horse to lie down, which is important for a satisfying rest. Unfortunately hocks and elbows are often capped and spoilt and muscles stiffen from lying on insufficient bedding, especially on a concrete floor. To avoid rising damp and cold from a concrete floor, in some luxury stables the floor is paved with timber blocks (hard wood), the size of a normal brick joined together with tar. The floor level is sloped 15% from each corner towards the centre.

If box walls are built of concrete it is advisable to have three horizontal grooves along the sides (height from 1 to 1·3 metres). In the event of a horse being cast he can get a firm grip with his hooves to free himself from the wall. The same effect can be achieved by fixing three strong timber laths along the sides of the wall. Box walls can have timber kicking boards similar to an indoor school. The slope of the kicking boards will give the horse more room to use his legs in the attempt to free himself.

*Ventilation*

Good ventilation in the stable is a must as plenty of fresh air is essential, but it must not be draughty. During the winter the stable should be warm (not over 18°C), but never humid. The windows should be situated high enough so that the horse's legs cannot get caught when he is rolling. The windows of the English loose boxes are too low, and even when covered with a grille they are still dangerous. I have witnessed horses getting caught with their hooves and shoes between the bars. In stalls the windows should never be over the horse's head because the cold breeze coming in can affect the horse's eyes and cause a cold as well.

*Dust*

Good ventilation will reduce the usual amount of dust in the stable. Bad ventilation and dust are responsible for bronchitis, chronic coughing and broken wind. (The latter can be recognised by the characteristic double heaving movement of the flanks when breathing.) Horses with one of these diseases should be stabled in outdoor boxes and be put on peat moss or shavings. These substances do not contain the particles of vegetable dust which are in straw. Shake up the straw bedding while the horses are not in the stable. Hay should also be shaken up outside the stable before feeding. For the same reason it is also important that the surface in the riding school is kcpt damp. If not, this dust will also effect the horse's health and eyes.

RUGS

All horses in training should wear a blanket in the stable. It keeps the muscles warm, the coat shiny and dust free, thus saving labour and shielding the horse from flies. However, the blanket should not be a burden to the horse, but as comfortable to wear as possible. Most blankets do not stay in place, especially when the horse is lying down or rolling. Some people try to keep the rug from slipping by putting on a tight roller, which is most uncomfortable for the horse. No matter which type of roller is used, it will always put pressure on the horse's back and lungs, especially when lying down. Putting a sack or folded blanket on the withers underneath the roller increases this pressure. Easing the pressure can only be achieved by placing a piece of padding on either side of the withers underneath the roller, so that the roller does not touch the withers. The same can be achieved by the "anti-cast roller". But although the pressure on the withers is relieved there will still be an unpleasant and tight feeling all around the horse's body, which is often the reason that a horse eats the rug. Besides, the rug will still shift sideways. Possibly more horses get sore withers from a tight blanket roller than from a saddle.

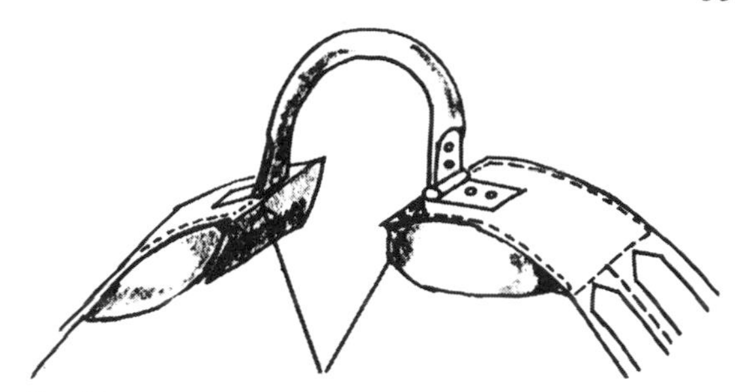

*Fig. 26*
An "anti-cast roller". This one has two hinges and will, therefore, fit every horse.

THE AUSTRALIAN BLANKET

It was during my stay in Australia that I discovered this type of blanket, which I found to be the most efficient one. I have introduced this blanket in several countries, as it is most comfortable for the horse because it has *no* roller but is held in place by adjustable straps. The winter blanket can be made from the same jute material as ordinary blankets, with a woollen lining. The summer blanket is made of strong cotton and for rainy weather the same blanket is made of waterproof material. These waterproof blankets should not be worn in the stable as, apart from Vistran, these materials do not let the warm air – radiating from the horse's body – pass through, and can therefore cause skin irritations, which makes the horse rub against the stable walls. Part of the blanket, like the breast-pieces around the front edges and over the withers, can be lined with sheepskin, as some horses have very tender skin which is easily chaffed.

The blanket is fully washable if one uses a material like padded nylon. The parts, usually made of leather, should then be made of Vistran, and artificial sheepskin is used for lining instead of real sheepskin.

*The straps*

The straps for the Australian blanket need only be bought once, as they can be transferred from one rug to another. At first glance it may look a little complicated, but once practised one will find out how easy the straps are to use.

When putting on the blanket for the first time the straps have to be adjusted so that the blanket will stay in place without hindering the free movement of the horse. The straps underneath the body are joined in ring D, where the girths of the saddle would be when riding. Strap A comes up between the forelegs and ring E is held by the leather strap, closing the front of the blanket. Straps B and C are fed through holes on each side of the blanket and hooked into the side rings. These straps are adjustable to keep the blanket from shifting sideways. If, for instance, the blanket usually slides to the horse's near side, then the side strap on the off-side must be shortened. Do not try to keep the blanket in place by shortening one of the two straps between the hindlegs, as that would make the horse sore.

Straps E and F are adjustable on both sides with a buckle. They should hang fairly loose and are crossed between the hindlegs. For sensitive horses one likes these two straps made of soft nylon. When taking off the blanket one has to open the two hindstraps and *one* of the side-straps. In front the blanket is closed, as are normal blankets (instead of having a fixed buckle it is more practical to have three holes at different heights; this gives a better fitting to the individual horse). As the frontstrap has to withstand additional tension from strap A, it is advisable to reinforce the breastpiece with a piece of fairly stout leather.

When travelling one can attach the tailguard to a ring on top of the rug. If one lives in a very cold climate, or has a cold stable, one can give the horse extra protection with an apron made from the blanket material. It has a strap on both sides which is fed through a buckle attached to each side of the blanket.

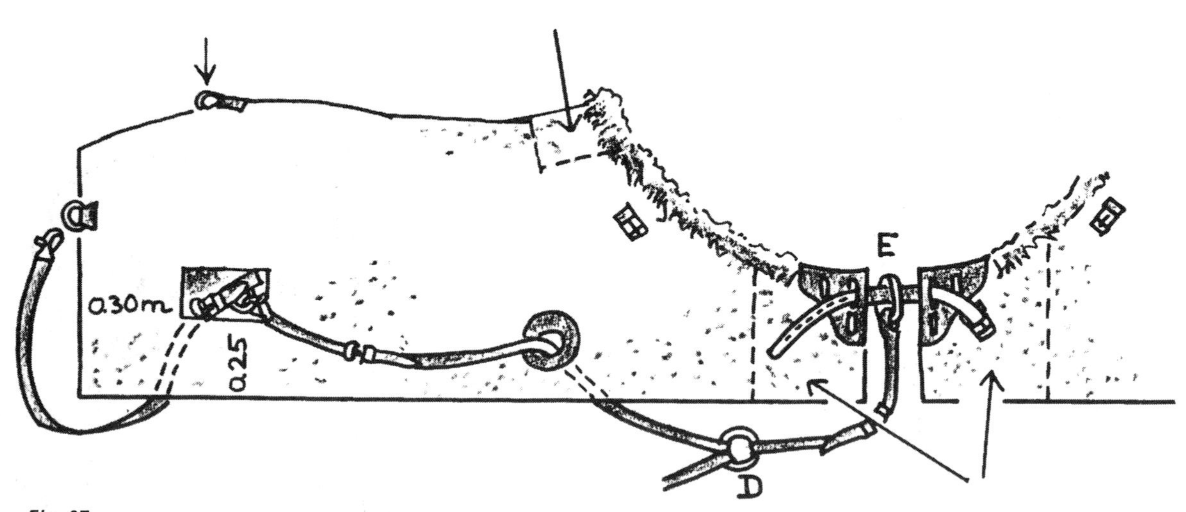


*Fig. 27*
The Australian blanket. Note arrows indicating areas lined with sheepskin and the ring for attaching a tail-guard when travelling.

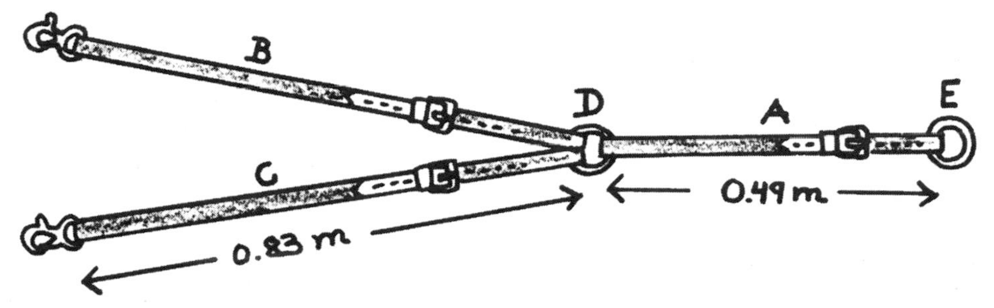


*Fig. 28*
Straps A, B and C, placed underneath the horse.

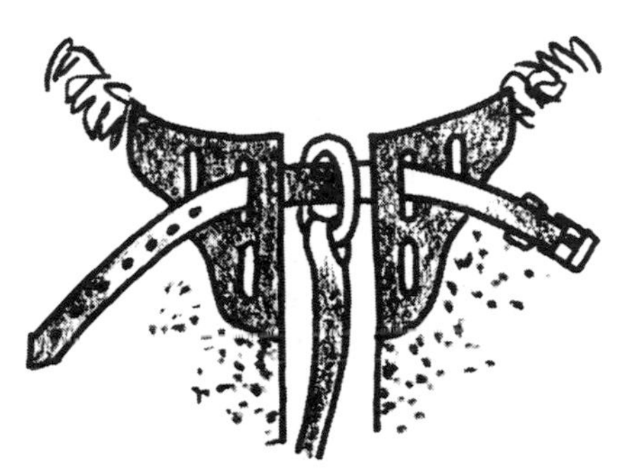

*Fig. 29*
Front strap of the Australian blanket, also holding ring E of underneath strap.

*Fig. 31*
Leatherpatch on the side of the Australian blanket, with a D-ring to hold the end of the underneath strap and buckle, with let-through for the hindstrap.

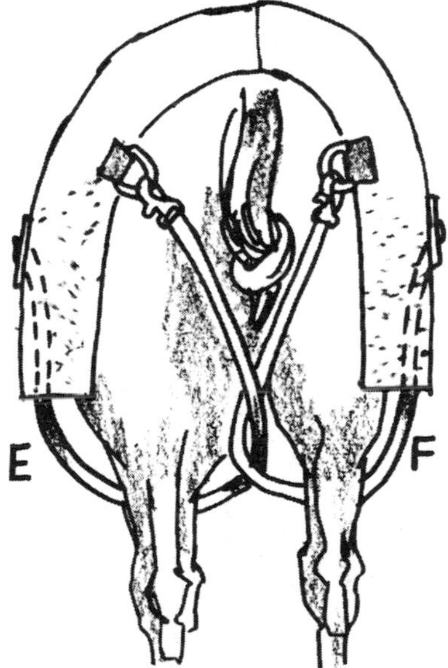


*Fig. 30*
Hindstraps E and F of the Australian blanket are looped one around the other, before being hooked into the D-rings on their own side, on the back of the blanket.

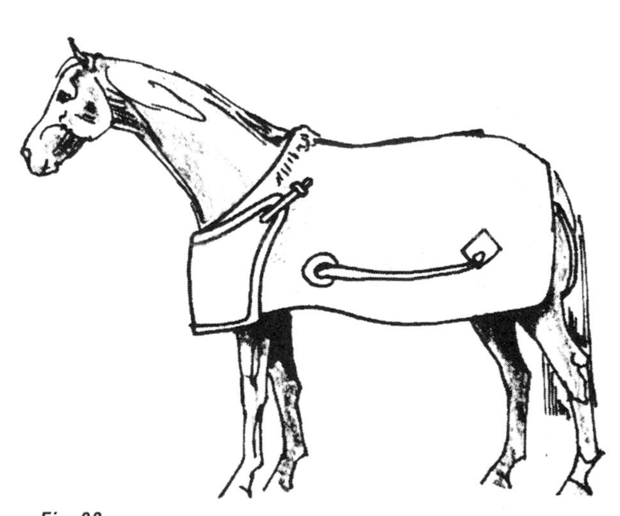

*Fig. 32*
Sheepskin lined apron with Australian blanket for extra warmth in the winter.

*Rug-biter*

Many young horses feel uncomfortable wearing a blanket and roller for the first time. They will try to get rid of it by biting and nibbling at it. Once a horse has acquired this habit there is the risk that he will keep it up – and that can be very expensive.

All kinds of gadgets are on the market which promise to prevent a horse eating his rug. The most terrible one is the wooden neck cradle. It is as uncomfortable for the horse as a straight-jacket for a man. It should only be used to prevent a horse from gnawing at blisters.

The wooden side-bar has nearly the same effect. Both instruments get the required result, but at the same time they stiffen the horse's head and neck. Both are barbarous gadgets.

*Fig. 34*
Wooden side bar. Very uncomfortable for the horse.

*Fig. 33*
A neck cradle is cruel.

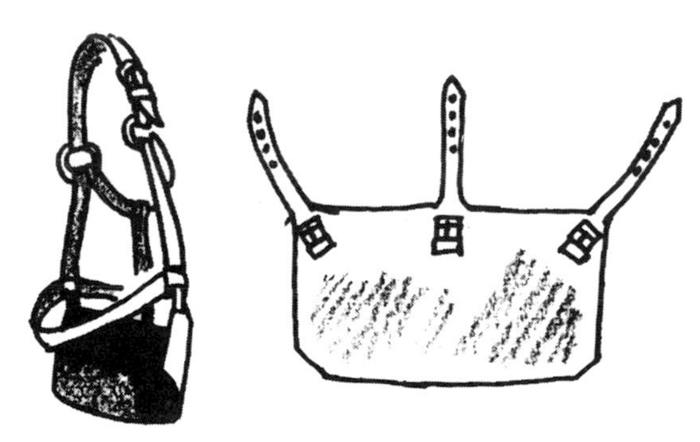

*Fig. 35*
Protective bib, not very effective.

A less severe but also less effective protection is the so-called protective bib made of stout leather. Although a bib does not interfere with the movement of the horse a clever horse will quickly find a way around it and will still tear the blanket. There are different ointments on the market which prevent horses from tearing and biting their rugs. One just has to rub a little of the ointment on to those spots of the blanket the horse likes to get at. If the horse's lips touch the ointment he will get an itching sensation. Most horses are cured after the first try.

CHAPTER THREE

# SHOEING

THERE is an old saying "no foot – no horse", which is very true, because if one single foot is unsound it effects the activity of the horse, in some cases for a long period. Therefore it is necessary to care for the horse's feet, and the earlier one starts to do so the better.

It is especially important that a showjumper is properly shod. A neglected or badly trimmed hoof can cause an unnatural and uneven distribution of the horse's weight on the walls of the hoof. It influences the degree of stress on the tendons and might damage the joints. Horses who have malformed hooves and bad action from birth can have these defects corrected by expert trimming, if started very early.

Opinion on how a showjumper should be shod depends on tradition, climatic conditions and horse breeds of the different countries. In any case, the degree of foot angle has to be correct. In English speaking countries the farriers are inclined to take more off the heel, so that the frog, even with shoes on, nearly touches the ground. This, however, can cause bruising, especially on hard or rocky going. On the European continent it is usual to take more off the toe, leaving the heel as high as possible,

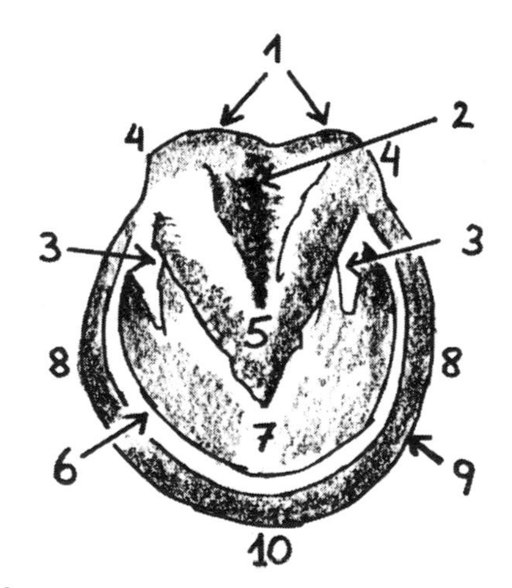


*Fig. 36*
The underside of the hoof.
1 Bulb of heel.
2 Cleft of frog.
3 Bars.
4 Heel.
5 Point of frog.
6 White line.
7 Horny sole.
8 Side wall.
9 Bearing surface of wall.
10 Toe.

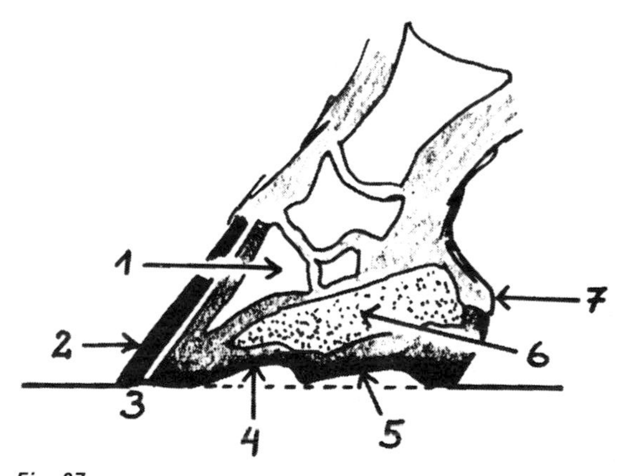


*Fig. 37*
The inside of the hoof.
1 Coffin bone.
2 Outside wall.
3 White line.
4 Sole.
5 Horny frog.
6 Plantar cushion.
7 Bulb of heel.

without changing the degree of foot angle which has to form a continuous straight line with the pastern bone. Continentals believe that a highish heel is most important as it acts as a shock absorber.

Nevertheless, a horse's foot is not designed by nature for jumping, whereas cloven-footed animals are natural jumpers on account of their type of hooves, which give them that extra spring and shock absorbing support.

When a horse is walking and trotting the toe of his foot touches the ground first naturally, whereas in an extended trot and in gallop the heel of the hoof touches down first. When doing roadwork in too fast a trot, damage is being done to the internal hoof structure. In general, the heel of the hoof takes the greatest pressure.

This is shown by the fact that if the horse has not been shod for some time, the bars of the shoe get embedded into the heel of the hoof. The

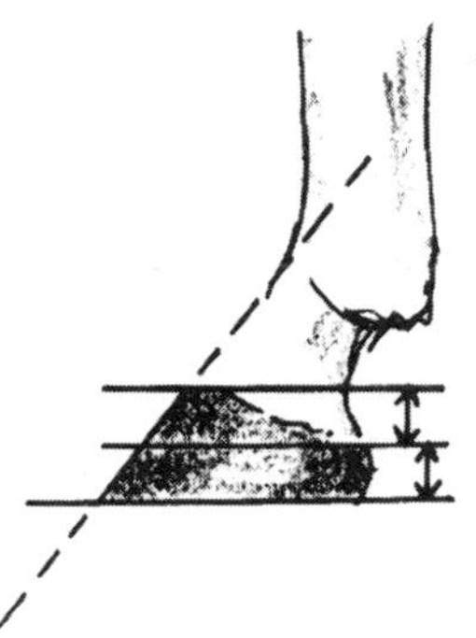

*Fig. 38*
Correct degree of foot angle.

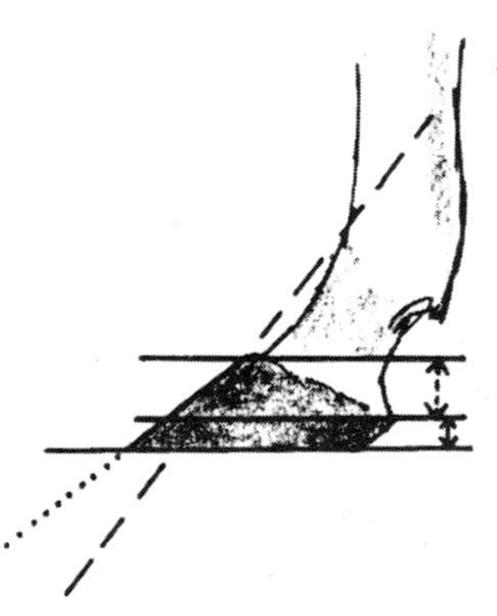

*Fig. 39*
Angle too sloping: heel too low, toe too long and flat.

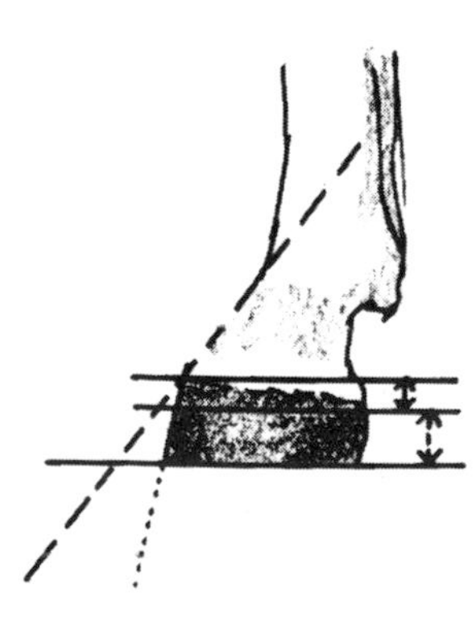

*Fig. 40*
Angle too steep: heel too high, dumped toe.

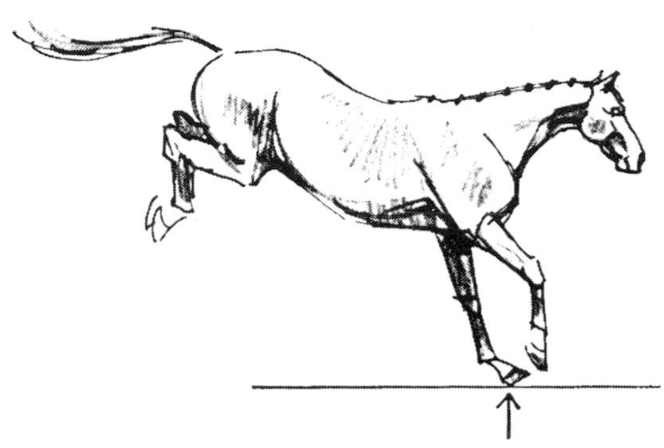

*Fig. 41*
On landing after a jump the horse's weight falls onto the heel of one forefoot.

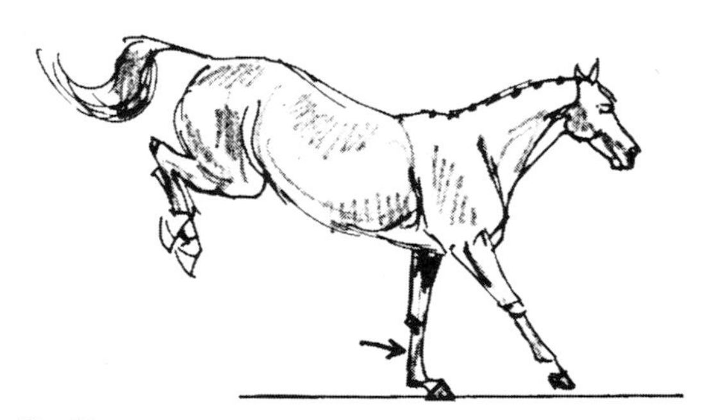

*Fig. 42*
Note the strain on the tendon.

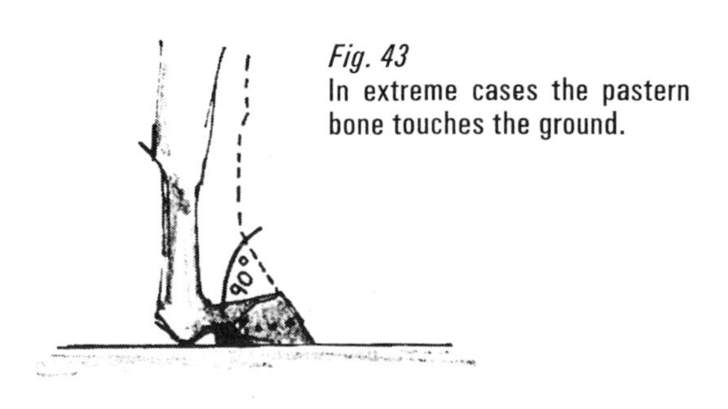


*Fig. 43*
In extreme cases the pastern bone touches the ground.

pressure on the heel is greatest in extended or over extended trot, gallop and when landing after a jump. It is therefore reasonable to leave the heel as high as possible, especially for a showjumper. One can observe that on landing after a jump, the entire weight of the horse falls for a split second on to *one* forehoof only, the heel acting as the shock absorber. Its function is to protect the horse's body from severe jolts. Often the pastern bone touches the ground, it then forms an angle of slope nearly 90° to its normal position. Therefore, if the heel is cut too low, the stress upon the tendons and the internal structure of the hoof is even more severe.

Thoroughbreds have by nature lower heels than plainer horses. The toe should be trimmed more than the heel to achieve the correct degree of foot angle. But thoroughbreds have sometimes very little horn on the toe as well, then the horse should be given shoes with thickened bars in order to obtain the correct degree of foot angle. Better still, and very light, are plastic wedges, which are nailed between shoe and hoof to raise the heel.

On the continent, shoes for showjumpers have a much wider web, which helps to prevent the shoes from pressing into the bearing surface of the hoof wall, causing corns, cracks or bruising. Aluminium shoes are also used. The wider webs give more support when the horse has a lot of roadwork to do and when jumping on hard ground. Also the protection against dropped soles and seedy toes is greatly improved by wide web shoeing, especially when the horn is softened by a wet stable or marshy fields.

Most Continental showjumping horses are shod hot. When this is done one can make the shoe fit the hoof and not the hoof fit the shoe . . . as is necessary when shoeing cold. When shoeing cold it is most difficult to obtain a level bearing surface so that the hoof and shoe meet all round. Usually several gaps remain between hoof and shoe; in extreme cases one can see the daylight shine through. This, of course, can cause corns and cracks, as well as making it easy for gravel to work itself between the hoof and the shoe, developing an under-run sole. A correct fore-

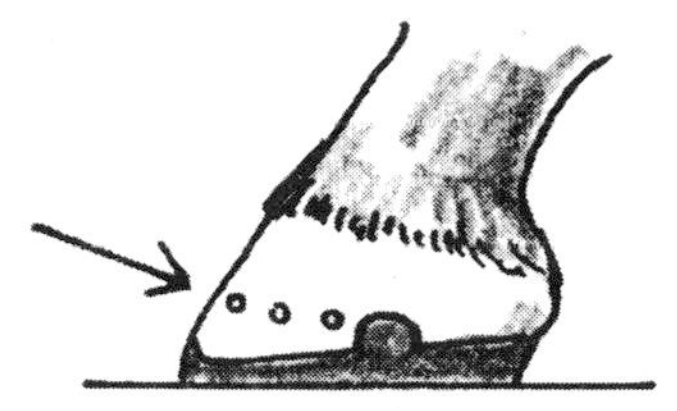

*Fig. 44*
Typical thoroughbred hoof, shoe with thickened bars.

*Fig. 45*
Correctly shod front shoe (full shoeing).

*Fig. 46*
Bars too long.

*Fig. 47*
Bars too short.

*Fig. 48*
Correctly shod hindfoot.

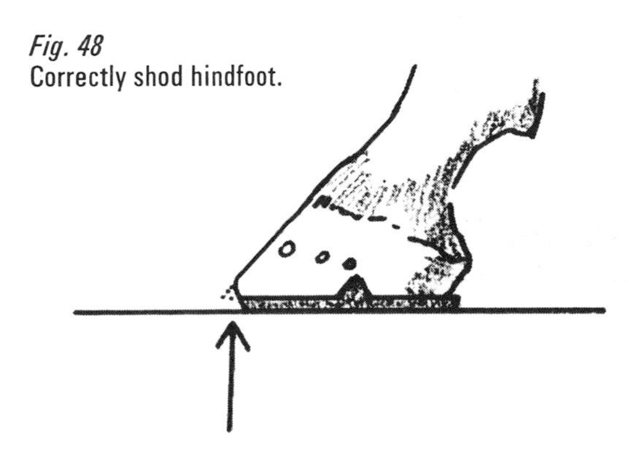

shoe should have the toe rounded off and the rear edges of the bars well levelled to match the slope of the heel, while not standing over (full shoeing). If the bars are left longer the horse might overreach, especially in deep going. If the bars are too short, they do not cover the whole bearing surface and the horse is practically walking on his toes.

The hindhoof has a naturally different degree of slope than the forehoof and has less heel. Nature provides the forehoof with more heel, as it has to do more shock absorbing than the hindfeet. While the hindfoot has a flatter angle of slope, the horse is able to put it further underneath his body, thus acting as a spring to create propulsive force. When going on a longer trip with showjumpers one should always carry a spare set of shoes of one's own blacksmith, for where one is going there might not be a farrier able to make the required shoes at short notice.

### HORSESHOES

People who are particular about how their horses are shod prefer hand-made shoes. They have a wider web and the fullering is wide and shallow and a sufficient distance away from the outer edge.

Factory-made shoes have the disadvantage that their web is commonly not wide enough and that the nail holes are situated slightly too near the outside of the web, consequently the nail cannot be driven up high enough in the white line and cannot get the same proper grip compared to hand-made shoes. Therefore the horn of the wall may crumble away, particularly on hard going, and the shoe might shift or get lost altogether. Only a skilled farrier can make good use of the factory-made shoe, as its groove is very narrow. With a new shoe the nail head might still fit into the groove, but when altering the shoe or re-shoeing the groove might have got too narrow, and unless the farrier is conscious of this and re-opens the groove the nail heads will no longer fit all the way into the groove. The nail head may also get jammed at the top and cannot be driven home, as the neck no longer fits all the way down. The nail head gets worn first, the "clenches" come up and the shoe might shift or get lost. The nails ought to be driven reasonably high, more so at the toe than at the sides, towards the heel, depending of course on the thickness of the wall and according to the varying slope of the wall. This ensures less strain on the wall and less likelihood of the shoe shifting. If all nails are driven equally high all round and generally too low they are at too sharp an angle and do not obtain a firm hold. This can cause cracks and splitting of the edge of the wall, subsequently the shoe being more liable to shift.

In most English speaking countries I have noticed the clenches being turned down and simply hammered flat against the wall, then smoothed over with the rasp. This weakens the clenches, as metal is removed from the bends. In other countries, however, the farrier uses a special tool to make a shallow bed under the bend of the nail. The clenches are then embedded in these grooves instead of being hammered against the wall. This method ensures that the clenches have a better grip, and when smoothing lightly over with the rasp there is less risk of metal being removed from the bend of the clenches. Furthermore, those farriers will also

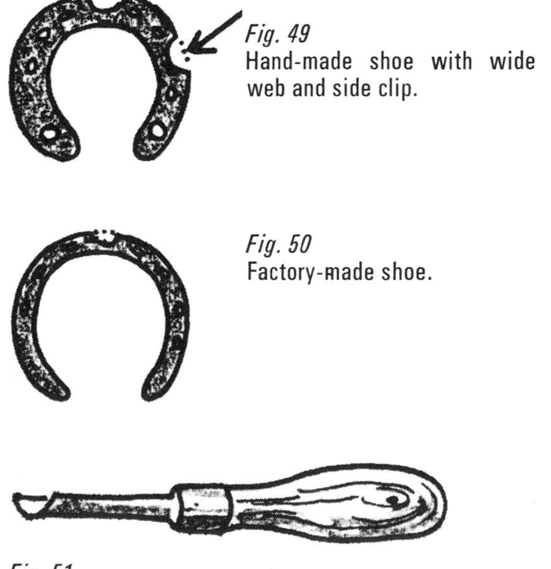

*Fig. 49*
Hand-made shoe with wide web and side clip.

*Fig. 50*
Factory-made shoe.

*Fig. 51*
Tool to make grooves for clenches.

fill the old nail holes with a special putty, using even white putty for white hooves and black putty for black hooves. This not only gives a tasteful and neat looking finish, but also prevents any moisture getting into the old nail holes, preventing rot.

*Clips*

It is important that toe and side clips are large enough (as in continental or aluminium shoes). A small clip gives little support and cannot prevent the shoe from shifting and it occasionally becomes embedded in the hoof, causing cracks or lameness.

On the hindshoe, clips are seldom used on the toe for jumpers, as this tends to make the horse overreach or forge, usually at the trot or when jumping. There is a clip on the inside, kept well forward, and a clip on the outside further back. Horses tending to brush should have no inside clip at all, because if the clip should get worn or bent the horse is liable to hurt himself against the sharp edges, especially when riding sharp turns, as in a speed competition.

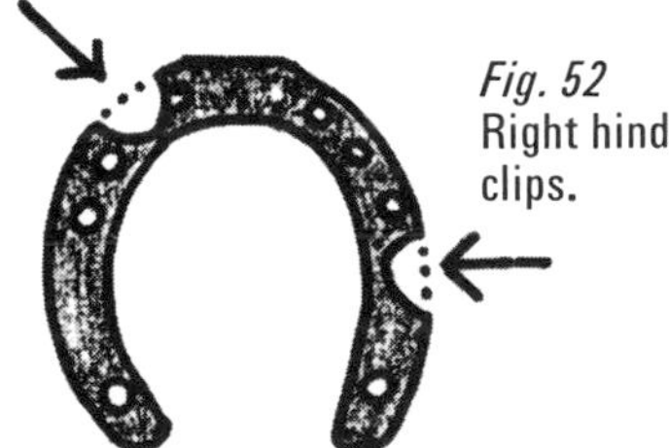

*Fig. 52*
Right hindshoe; note the large clips.

*Studs*

I always obtain my studs from Germany, as the German studs are screw-in studs and bigger and give more effective grip in heavy going. One should always use two studs per shoe to guarantee a horizontal bearing surface. The stud holes on the foreshoe should be placed 1·5 centimetres from the rear end of the bar to prevent the hindshoe overreaching.

It is advisable to use "blanks" (a square stud) on the inside (reducing the risk of the horse injuring himself) and a sharp stud on the outside.

Important: to prevent brushing, the studs must always be in line with the shoe. In deep

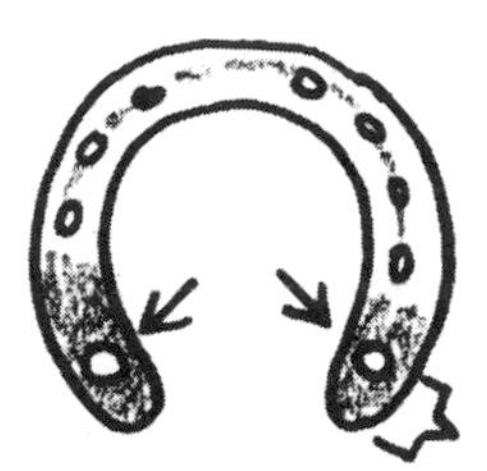

*Fig. 53*
Correct use of studs on a front-shoe, 1.5 cm from end of bars.

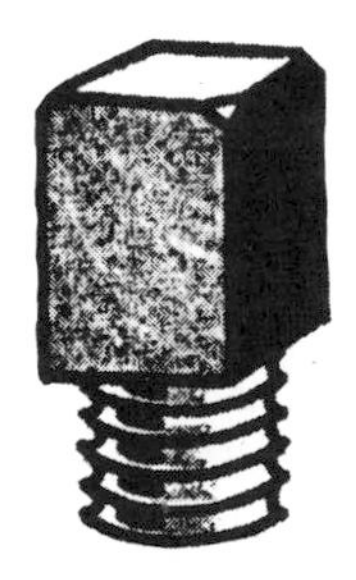

*Fig. 54*
"Blank" for inside of hoof.

*Fig. 55*
Stud for outside of hoof.

*Fig. 56*
Stud for hard going.

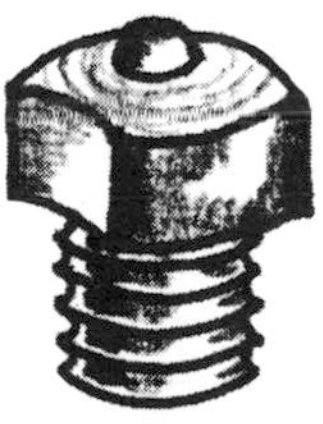

*Fig. 57*
Stud for roadwork.

*Fig. 58*
Irish hindshoe.

going one uses large studs, and when the going is hard one uses H-studs. These cut into the hard ground and act more or less as shock absorbers, thus taking a lot of stress from the tendons, especially when landing after a jump.

Studs with a steel core are excellent to prevent slipping on the road. For light horses and ponies a horseshoe nail with a steel core has the same effect. One or two nails in each shoe are sufficient.

To avoid injuries, studs must be taken out immediately after jumping before the horse is loaded or put back into the stable. The stud holes must be filled with a little grease and then plugged with cotton wool. If the stud holes are kept clean there is no problem in screwing the studs in at any time.

In several English speaking countries only *one* stud is used in the foreshoe, placed in front on the outside. Also on the hindshoe only one stud or calkin is used on the outside. If the shoe is fitted with only one stud or calkin, without the other bar being raised to the same level, then the stud or calkin will meet the ground first, forcing the hoof to knuckle over sideways until the other bar meets the ground. However, the bone structure and the joints of the horse's foot are not made for such sideways movement, but is by nature designed only for an up and down movement. Using only one stud is creating an unnatural, uneven bearing surface, ruining the horse's feet, joints and tendons, and causing stumbling and brushing.

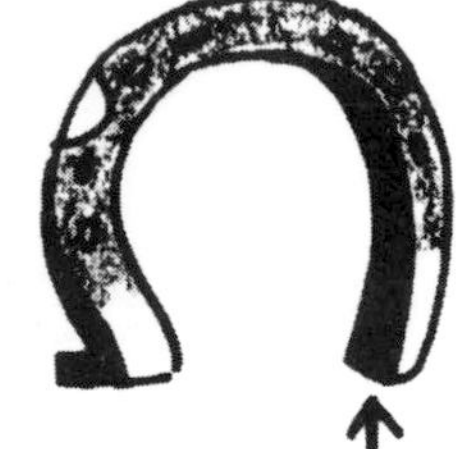

*Fig. 59*
A calkin on the outside and a raised bar on the inside . . .

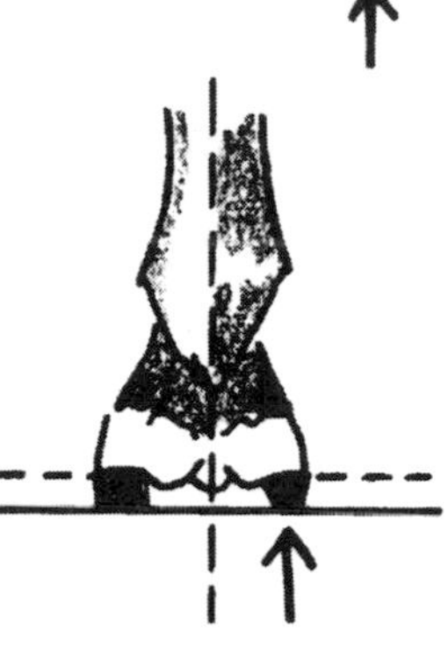

*Fig. 60*
. . . provide a level walking surface.

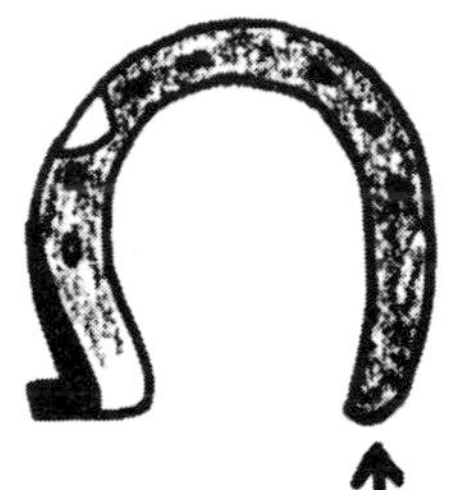

*Fig. 61*
A calkin on the outside, without a raised bar on the inside . . .

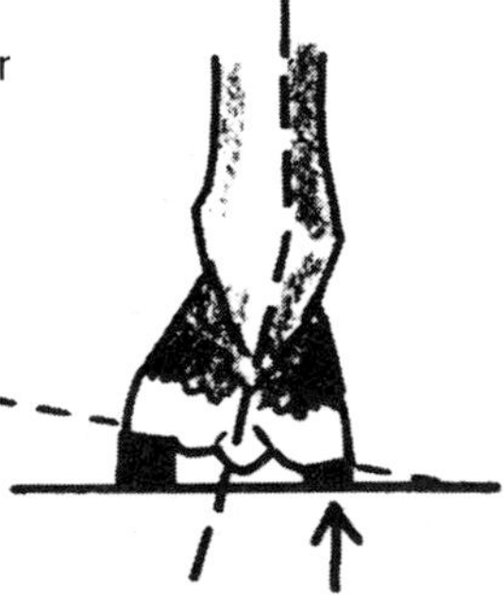

*Fig. 62*
. . . the hoof knuckles over every step.

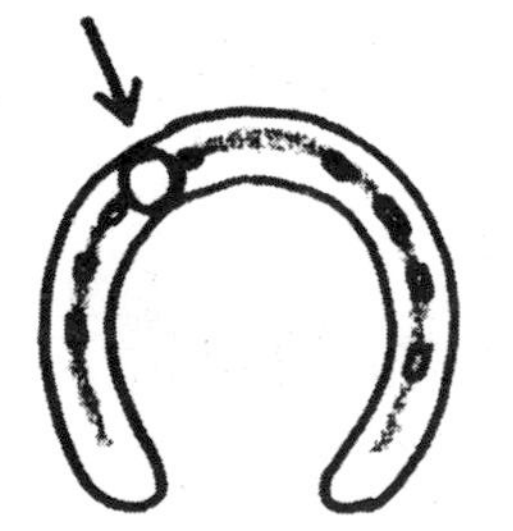

*Fig. 63*
Incorrect use of stud on frontshoe.

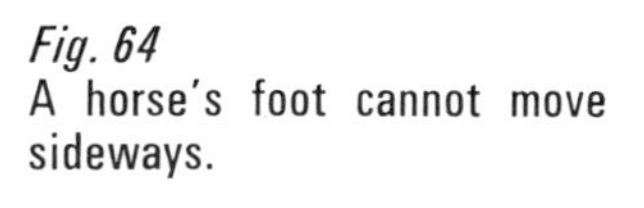

*Fig. 64*
A horse's foot cannot move sideways.

CORRECTING HOOF-DEFORMATIONS

Correcting neglected or deformed hooves is one of the most important tasks for a skilful blacksmith, who can work miracles with pathological shoeing and so on. For instance, horses inclined to stumble should get a shoe with a "rolled toe" or "set up" toe. The toe of the hoof is rasped off fairly upwards and the toe of the shoe is bent up accordingly usually at an angle of approximately 22°. So, lazy horses, tending to drag their toes, won't trip when hitting an unevenness in the ground.

For horses who brush, the "featheredge" shoe is prefered to the three-quarter shoe, as the latter leaves a quarter of the bearing surface unprotected. The featheredge shoe, even with the narrower web on the inside, still protects the bearing surface all round and keeps the hoof level.

For jumpers with very wide, flat feet, a shoe with a bar across is used to give added support to the soles. This bar should not be too near the heel in case the horse should overreach

For horses with thin or dropped soles this same shoe can be used with a piece of hard rubber or plastic added between hoof and shoe. The same type of shoe is also used for horses with a "seedy toe", with the only difference being that the web of this shoe has to be hollowed out as well as the toe. This prevents any pressure on the toe of the hoof, as the horse's weight is now distributed only on the bearing surface of the sides of the hoof and not on the toe. "Seedy toe" is a cavity formed between the hard outer and the soft, sensitive inner layer of the horn inside the hoof. A small secretion of horn is formed and the cavity gives a kind of hollow sound when the hoof is hammered. Also noticeable is the absence of the white line in some places. Seedy toe can arise from laminitis or from pressure of the front clip.

The above mentioned type of shoe should be used for horses whose hooves have been (partly) de-nerved, or who have been suffering from navicular disease or laminitis. These shoes may help the horse to resume work.

Laminitis is likely to be caused by a toxic

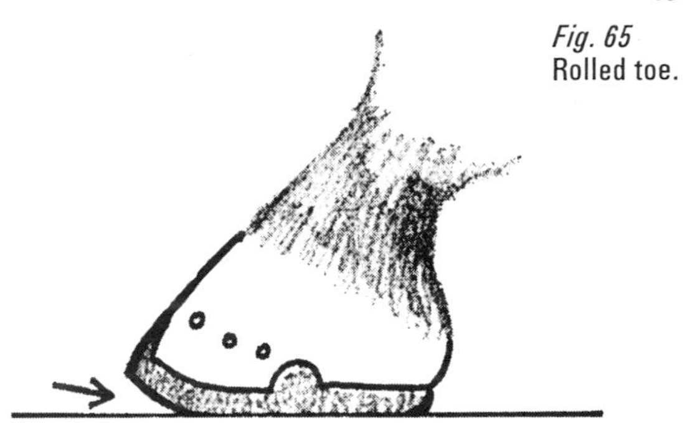

*Fig. 65*
Rolled toe.

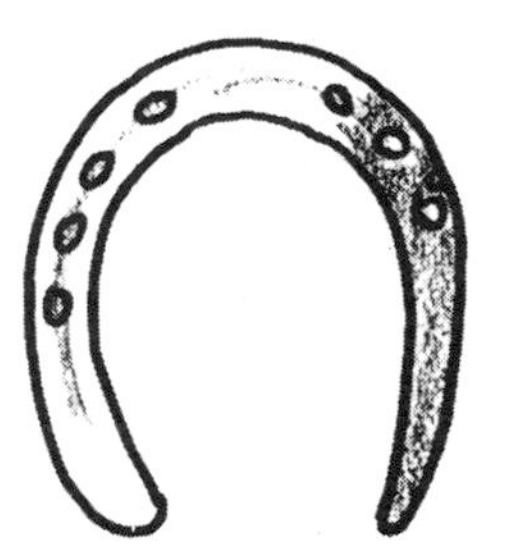

*Fig. 66*
Featheredge shoe.

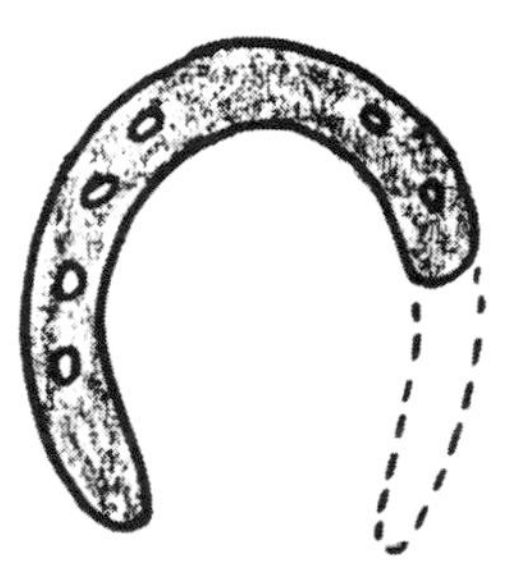

*Fig. 67*
Three-quarter shoe.

*Fig. 68*
Cross bar too near the end of the bars.

*Fig. 69*
Correct position of cross bar.

*Fig. 70*
Sole between hoof and shoe.

*Fig. 71*
Insert of hard rubber . . .

*Fig. 72*
. . . and shoe for a foot affected by seedy-toe.

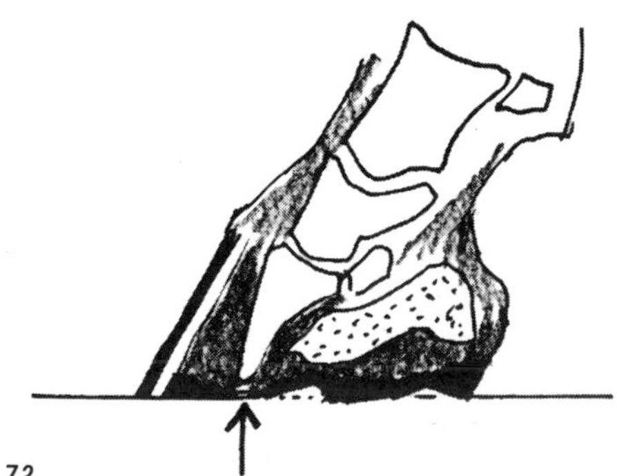
*Fig. 73*
Foot affected by laminitis.

condition or digestive upset. Also dropped sole may be followed by an attack of laminitis. It is an inflammation of the structures between the pedal bone and the hoof. Due to the disturbance of blood supply the foot may feel very hot. If laminitis is diagnosed (X-Ray), pathological shoeing is necessary. Keep the horse off too rich pasture and once cured ration the grazing (a couple of hours per day at the most). Once the horse is off the pasture and stabled, experience has taught us to feed wilted nettles, damped hay, bran mash and a very limited amount of oats. All this in conjunction with careful trimming of the hooves.

The most vulnerable part of the hoof where often damage occurs is the heel. It has less and softer horn protection than the toe. Bruising, overreaching and side bones at the back of the horn wall are the most common damages. Although the toe of the hoof has a much harder horn protection, the coffin bone is often damaged in jumping horses when the hoof knocks a pole hard, or when cracks occur in the horn wall. This can develop into a seedy toe or "dropped sole". Dropped sole is also considered to be a result of navicular disease. These symptoms can be noticed by pointing when the horse is standing still, or in motion when changing from soft going on to hard going or when travelling downhill. Then the horse will move with a short-stepping action.

*The speed flex hoof pad*

On the hard and rocky going of Central America, some showjumpers and racehorses wear a shock absorbing sole between the shoe and the hoof, the speed flex hoof pad, made of a remarkable plastic which cushions the hoof and tendons against strain. The pad will not shift and is unabsorbent. It prevents injuries to sensitive frogs, dropped or thin soles and is ideal when packing is needed.

Packing in hot climates entails that before the shoe is fitted the hollow space between pad and hoof sole is packed with cotton wool and soaked in linseed oil. The oil keeps the horn soft and the packing also prevents dirt or gravel working itself between pad and hoof sole. The packing can also be done using cotton wool soaked in warm tar to prevent moisture entering between pad and hoof sole, keeping the hoof and frog healthy. No matter which type of packing is used, the hoof can still "sweat out" and does not become sticky. The pad stands up to long wearing.

Some horses in Central America are shod in front with rubber shoes. The rubber shoe has an internal steel frame to support the nails. The fullering is quite wide and the nail holes are shallow and cone-shaped. This shoe has a wide web, is thicker than normal shoes and consequently is excellent for horses with flat or dropped soles, giving the horse a firm grip, even on slippery roads. The rubber shoes are ideal for horses which have to do a lot of roadwork.

*Dumped toe*

A hoof with a dumped toe (usually the forefoot) is in some cases created by unskilled trimming and shoeing. The similar "club foot" is believed to be hereditary and is mostly found in horses in countries with a warm climate and hard going. There the horse's hooves develop, in general, with less slope and have narrower higher heels. In countries with a wet climate and soft going the shape of the feet is rather wide with lower heels. In a dumped toe and club foot the hoof is very upright, possibly at an angle of more than 60° with the ground. The sole is extremely vaulted and the frog is pressed in between the bars, tending to rot. Both malformations eliminate shock absorbing and often appear together with the disease of sidebones.

A skilful farrier can improve the shape of the hoof by trimming the bearing surface of the *whole* hoof as much as possible, and of the heel in particular. He must make a special "slipper shoe". The web of this shoe is slightly wider than normal and the surface of the web, facing the hoof, is sloping from a higher inside down to the outside. In time the shape of the shoe will make the hoof expand. The slipper shoe can only have a front clip; it can have no side clips as these would interfere with the expansion of the hoof. The shoe will not have the desired effect if the hoof is not first trimmed down sufficiently, otherwise only the lower part of the horn wall will move outwards while the upper part will grow even steeper. Besides using a slipper shoe, one can also get results by riding the horse unshod if the feet do not meet hard or rocky ground. Or, if one lives in a wet climate and has a particularly wet or boggy field, one can turn the horse out without shoes and let nature help to soften and expand the hooves.

*Fig. 74*
Slipper shoe for a club foot.

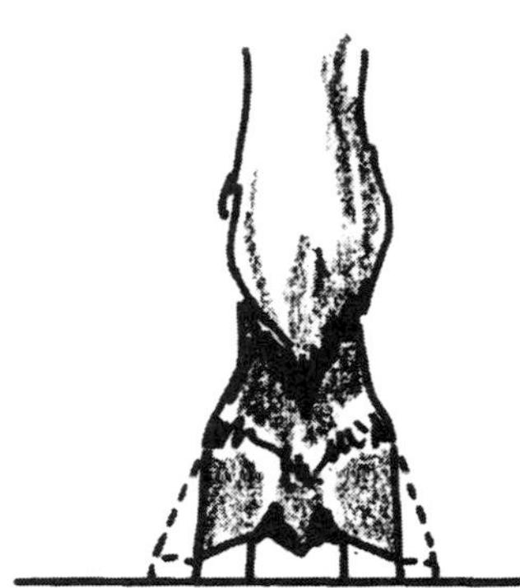

*Fig. 75*
Club foot, trimmed down correctly and fitted with a slipper shoe.

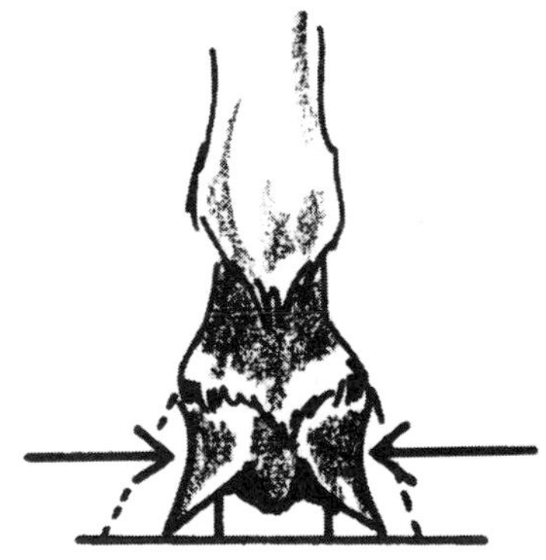

*Fig. 76*
Club foot left too long.

*Fig. 77*
Water-stall for cooling tendons and keeping feet soft.

*Fig. 78*
Poultice in a plastic bag.

*Fig. 79*
Cover with a sack.

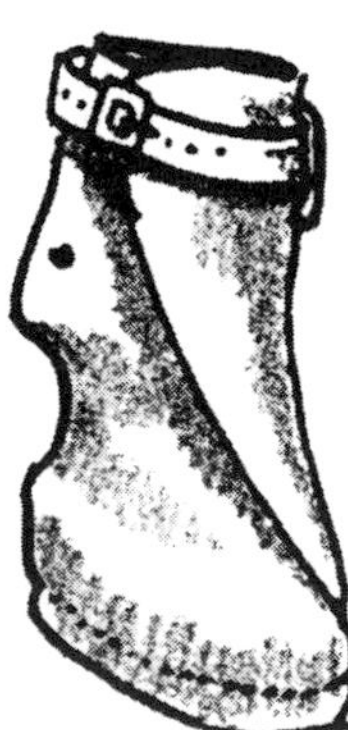

*Fig. 80*
Rubber poultice boot.

*Hard and brittle feet*

This condition can originate from a protein deficiency in the horse's diet. Advice from a veterinary surgeon should be sought in order to establish a diet which will stimulate the horn growth. The condition often develops in the summer on hard going. To prevent this one should ride the horse often into water or swim it. If there is a shallow river or lake nearby one can tie the horse up and leave it for a while standing in the water (also advisable for horses with a club foot).

Today, swimming is used in the training of horses in many countries, and swimming pools specifically for horses are not uncommon. Swimming horses gets them fit whilst at the same time saving their tendons from becoming strained, and helps to keep their feet flexible.

If a horse becomes lame or has corns due to a hard hoof make a poultice from a mixture of cow manure and linseed meal (sloppy) and put it into a plastic bag. Then place the horse's foot into it and put foot and bag into a rubber poultice boot. If a rubber boot is not available an ordinary sack can be used as cover. But when tying the sack, make sure that the string or bandage is not too tight, as that might interfere with the blood circulation. The horse must then be tied up in the stable in order not to pull off the poultice. If the treatment is carried out twice daily then after a few days the horse should be sound again. Afterwards one has to clean the hoof well, inside and out, paint it with hot tar – to keep in the moisture – and so prevent the foot from drying out again.

*Rotted frog or thrush*

Neglect is the common cause for discharge from the cleft. It occurs mostly in horses whose feet are constantly exposed to wet ground (riding outside in the winter, a wet bed, hindfeet of horses stabled in stalls). It can be cured fairly easily by dropping a little hydrogen peroxide, 20%, into the frog grooves (do not let it get near your hands or clothes). After the peroxide has stopped effervescing, sprinkle a little copper sulphate powder on to it and press it well in with a little cotton wool. To seal it off, paint the whole hoof, inside and out with hot tar. This treatment is necessary otherwise the frog decomposes and hoof canker may follow.

*Hoof growth*

For horses with bad hoof growth, or in fact all showjumpers who have to jump continuously, a daily application of Cornucrescine is necessary. Rubbed well into the coronary band of the hoof it is a safeguard against many foot troubles.

I hope that having read all this the reader will appreciate how important it is to have a show-jumper well shod. One should get the best farrier available . . . and get him regularly. Remember: no foot – no horse.

CHAPTER FOUR

# TACK

ONE cannot school a horse correctly without the proper tack. A bridle, a saddle, lungeing equipment and protection for the horse's legs are the basic tack needed for training a showjumper. These are few requirements, but they must fit properly and be of the right type. It is pitiful that so many people use the wrong tack, which makes the training very difficult or nearly impossible. I will explain in detail which sort of tack I think is the most suitable for training a showjumping horse.

## THE BIT

### *The German snaffle*

The bit is one of the most important parts of the tack. The best bit, in general, is the thick, hollow German snaffle. This bit originates from the German Cavalry School in Hanover. It is considered to be the most suitable one for breaking, lungeing and riding. It plays a vital part in "making the mouth" according to the Natural Training Method

The rings are not fixed to the mouthpiece. This has the advantage that the horse, when moving his tongue, has only to lift up the movable mouthpiece and not the entire bit (which he would have to do with, for instance, the egg-butt bit, where the rings are fixed). This will encourage the horse to chew the bit, bringing the parotid glands into action, providing a foaming and sensitive mouth.

The bit should always be used with two rubber side discs. There are soft rubber discs and harder ones. The latter are more effective because they not only stop the bit from slipping through the mouth but also prevent the corners of the horse's mouth getting cut. This often happens with worn-out snaffles with sharp edges.

These rubber discs press, as would a gentle hand, against the side of the horse's mouth when the rein aids are applied. It is not very hard to fit the discs on to the bit. First wet them, then feed two narrow leather straps (two throat lashes) through the hole in the rubber disc. Hold a strap with each hand and pull them apart while somebody else pushes the ring of the bit through. Do not try stretching the rubber with twine, or its like, as this might cut the disc.

*Fig. 81*
Thick German snaffle.

*Fig. 82*
An egg-butt bit is dead in the horse's mouth.

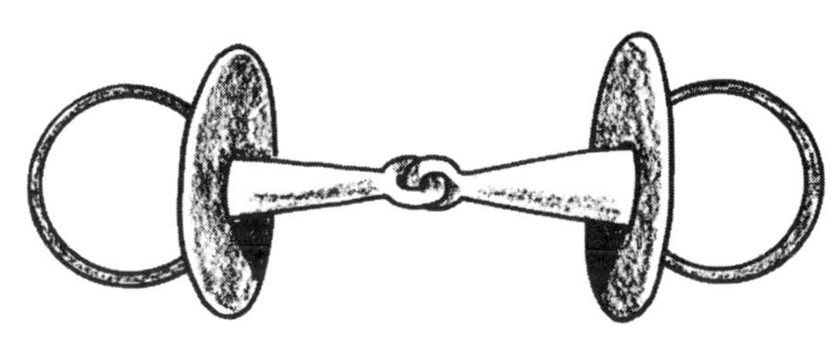

*Fig. 83*
German snaffle fitted with two rubber discs.

*Fig. 84*
How to fit a rubber ring.

It is very important that the snaffle is thick, and therefore "soft". A thin snaffle will act as a nutcracker upon the horse's bars, tongue and the corners of his mouth. It can so bruise and lacerate the bars of a horse's mouth that it not only draws blood but prevents the unfortunate horse from eating properly afterwards.

The bit should not be too narrow either as it then might pinch the horse's lips. Some people think that a thick German snaffle might be too soft for an older horse well used to the bit. This is a misconception because even in a hard or spoilt mouth a thick snaffle can work miracles. If one puts the bit either two holes higher or lower, so that it rests on a "fresh" part of the bars, it will be effective.

*Other bits*

Although I prefer, in general, the thick German snaffle, there are exceptions. For instance, some young horses in the beginning have over-sensitive mouths. For such horses I use a thick rubber bit for the first two months of training. During this time the horse will only be lunged, and while lungeing the rubber bit has the same effect as an ordinary snaffle, while being that little bit softer. Some horses adapt so well to this bit that it is not advisable to change over to the snaffle at all.

The correct rubber bit consists of a flexible rubber mouthpiece and two side rings. These run through a metal insertion to ensure free movement of the mouthpiece.

I advise against using a rubber bit with a chain inside the mouthpiece. Most horses chew the rubber, breaking it in places. Then the chain begins to rust and might break unexpectedly, which can cause an accident. The same bit is available in nylon and Vulcanite (Eldonian). It lasts longer than a rubber bit and is not flexible, which is an advantage, because some rubber bits are too flexible and act in the horse's mouth more like a thick rope. However, most horses are from the beginning very happy with a thick German snaffle. Even the mouths of over-sensitive horses are so well developed after two months of lungeing and ground work that one can change from the nylon bit to the ordinary German snaffle.

If a horse is not happy with an ordinary German snaffle the rider's hands are usually to

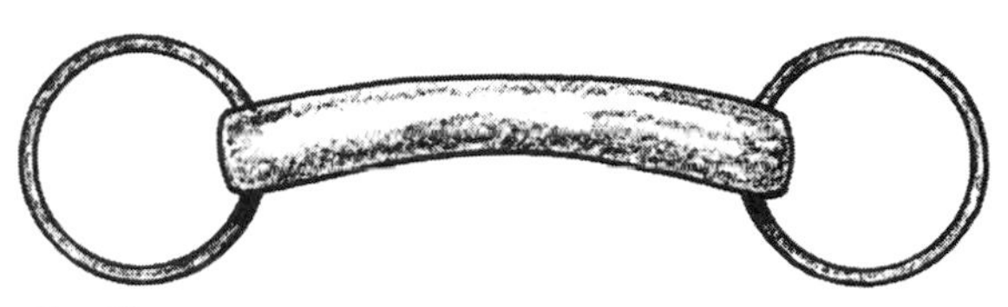

*Fig. 85*
A rubber bit.

blame. If, however, the rider is convinced that he is not at fault, then he must think carefully about why the horse is unhappy with the ordinary snaffle. Many riders do not realise how sensitive a horse's mouth is, and that the bit rests on a particularly sensitive bone which has only a very fine covering of skin tissue. The rider should be aware of this before he considers changing over to a more severe bit.

*Teeth trouble*

When mouth trouble arises always check the horse's teeth first before resorting to a more severe bit. Neglected teeth are often the cause of difficult mouths. The horse's molars should be regularly examined, for sharp edges may cause irritation to the horse's cheeks. They hurt the horse, not only when being ridden and when asked to flex the jaw, but also while eating. Such horses try to avoid chewing and are generally in poor condition. If the manger is examined one

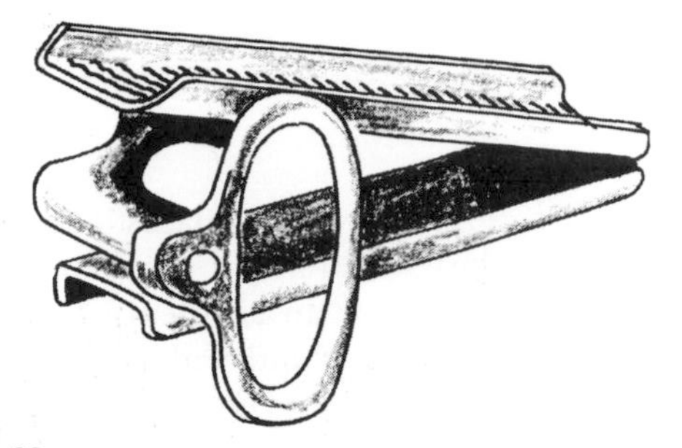

*Fig. 86*
Horse dentist's special tool.

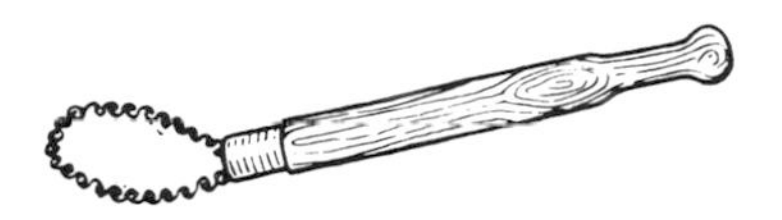

*Fig. 87*
Touch with a chain end loop.

*Fig. 88*
Half-moon bar bit.

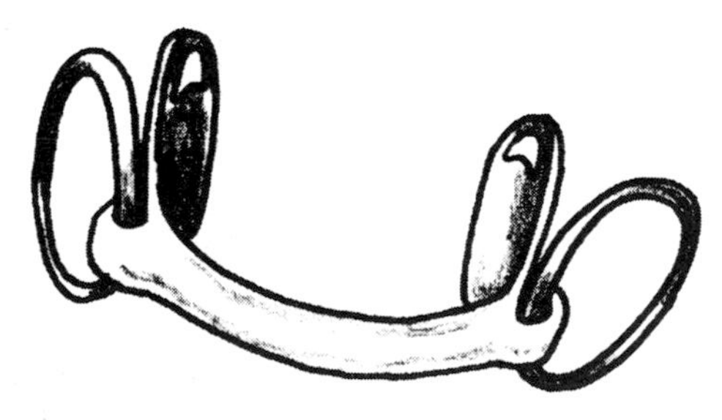

*Fig. 89*
The Italian leather bit.

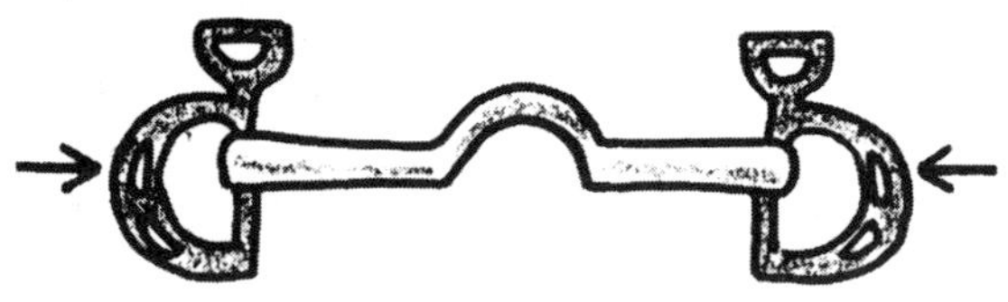

*Fig. 90*
The Uxeter Kimberwicke bit.

*Fig. 91*
The "French" snaffle.

often finds little balls of hay formed by a horse having chewing difficulties. (Another cause of bolting food is lampas.) When checking the manure one will find the whole grain of oats in it. Where these sharp edges on the teeth exist they must be rasped down.

Some mouth troubles are also caused by wolf teeth. On account of their very short roots these wolf teeth can cause severe pain if touched by the bit. They should be removed by a veterinary surgeon immediately.

In America special horse dentists visit stables regularly. It is amazing to see how expertly they treat even highly strung horses. They seldom have trouble making a horse stand still during treatment and many use a method which originated with the Red Indians: they simply blow gently into the horse's nostrils, which makes him "freeze".

To keep the horse's mouth open during treatment, horse dentists use a special tool. This is put between the molars on one side of the horse's mouth, giving the dentists unhampered freedom to work on the other side. The tool cannot hurt the horse as it does not rest on the gums but on the molars.

*The touch*

When filing teeth, and on other occasions, one might have to use a touch to make a horse stand still. Most stables use a stick with a rope loop at one end, which is wound tightly round the horse's nose. This is unnecessarily painful for the horse and less cruel methods are readily available.

The touch with a chain end loop works just as well and does not slip or cut off blood circulation. With the string at the end, one can tie the stick to the head collar, so that, should the horse get loose, he cannot hurt himself.

Another suitable touch is made from light aluminium and looks like a nutcracker. It is easy to put on and, if one lets go of it, it will immediately fall off. Neither horse nor handler can get hurt.

*Low upper palate*

Another peculiarity of the horse's mouth is lampas, where the hard palate swells. It is then sometimes even lower than the upper teeth, making it difficult for the horse to eat or graze. Lampas is due to too much blood in the tissue. One can often observe this when horses come in from grass, but then it will disappear gradually when the horse is changed over to dry feeding. If it does not disappear veterinary assistance should be sought.

When a horse with lampas is ridden in a broken snaffle, the joint of the bit would hit against the low upper palate. Until the lampas has disappeared one should use a "half moon bar bit" (wind wet cotton wool around it and fasten it with cotton thread to make the bit even thicker). Or use the thick Italian half moon bar bit, which is made completely out of leather, except the two normal metal siderings. Joined onto the mouthpiece are two leather discs, a little larger than the metal rings, and positioned between these rings and the side of the horse's mouth. There is a hole in the top part of the disc to let the cheekpiece through, which is then holding the disc and ring together. This holds the mouthpiece up horizontally, making sure that the horse is unable to pull his tongue over the bit and, at the same time, preventing the lip angles from being pinched.

*Sharp and high bars*

The half moon bar bit, with cotton wool covering, should also be used for horses with extra long lip angles, or for horses with sharp and high bars. A jointed snaffle would have a nutcracker effect, pinching severely the lips and bars.

*Flat jawbones and tongue over the bit*

When the tongue groove is of normal shape, then approximately half the tongue is embedded in it. If a horse has a thick or sensitive tongue, or too low or too flat bars, the tongue will lie more or less on top of the tongue groove, taking more pressure from the bit than normal. Therefore an ordinary snaffle would provoke the horse to put his tongue over the bit or try other ways to get relief, such as nervously shaking his head, going behind or over the bit, rearing or opening his mouth, and generally not accepting the bit. So one has to use a bit which gives extra room for the tongue, like, for instance, the Uxeter Kimberwicke bit. The curved bar (high port) leaves adequate room for the tongue. The bit does not rest on the tongue, but on the bars, which do not get pinched. Remove the curb chain and hooks and use the top loops of the rings for the reins. The bit will stay in the correct position causing no lever action – it ensures a comfortable and relaxed mouth. The "French" snaffle can also be used. It is a bit with two joints and, in the middle, a flat metal piece which rests on the tongue. This prevents the tongue being pinched. The extension on the ring, attached to the bridle, keeps the mouthpiece in a steady position at a 90° angle to the tongue. The more tension on the bit, the more freedom the tongue has. If the habit of putting the tongue over the bit is established it will take considerable time before the horse accepts the newly offered freedom for the tongue. So do not expect immediate results. If the horse "persists" then the use of the "tongue spoon" is essential.

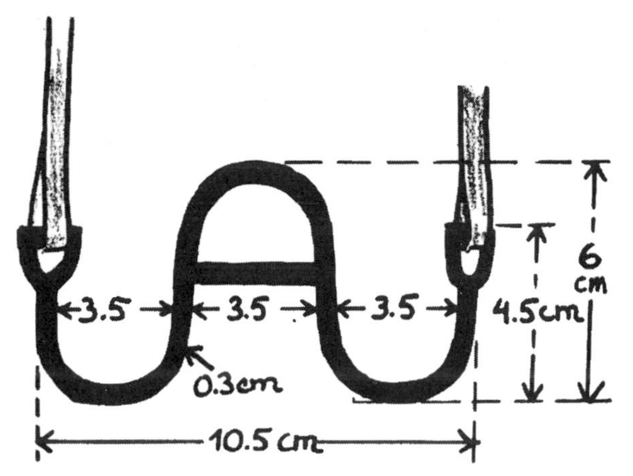

*Fig. 92*
The Australian tongue-spoon.

The "Australian" tongue-spoon has the advantage of being very thin and practically

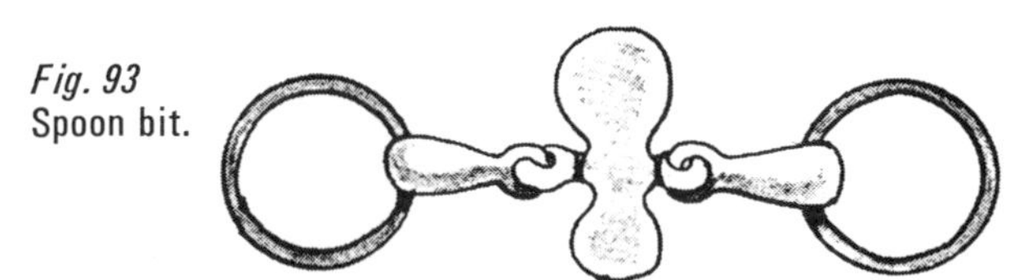
*Fig. 93*
Spoon bit.

unnoticed by the horse. Most other tongue-spoons are much thicker, giving the horse a cumbersome feeling of too much steel in the mouth. The special design of the Australian tongue-spoon brings the spoon very high up on the tongue and makes it absolutely impossible for the horse to pull his tongue up and over the spoon.

I can recommend this tongue-spoon to everyone who is faced with this problem, as it works most efficiently. But it is most important to fit the tongue-spoon first and *higher* than the bit to avoid the lips being pinched between the tongue-spoon and the bit.

The use of the "spoon-bit" is not advisable as it easily hurts the upper palate, which forces the horse to go with an open mouth to avoid pain.

To prevent a young horse from picking up this bad habit, at the beginning, when breaking, I adjust the headpiece so that the snaffle lies a few holes higher than normal. After a while one can let the bit down again to its normal position.

*The Hackamore*

In severe cases of natural mouth difficulties the Hackamore bitless bridle is very useful. It originated in Mexico (the Spanish name is Jaquama) and it is used a lot over there for polo ponies and showjumpers. The Hackamore is ideal for giving the bars a rest during re-training, provided the rider has a very light hand and an independent balanced seat, so that he does not need the reins to balance himself against the horse's mouth. If riding a horse in a Hackamore one must never allow the horse to take a strong hold, as it is then very difficult to control him. Instead, the rider must give and take constantly, so that the horse moves on his own four legs. Occasionally I move the noseband up or down, 1 centimetre at a time, to allow the parts of the nose to rest and prevent hardening, so one always has control on a soft part of the nose.

*The double bit*

I have no objections to a double bit provided it is used only on older, well schooled horses, and only by riders who have an absolutely perfect independent seat in dressage and when jumping. The rider's hands are then independent from his body and he can keep up an even contact with the horse's mouth – in all situations. If the double bit is used by a rider who needs the reins to balance himself, the double bit will be as sharp in the horse's mouth as a razor blade.

The double bit must be fitted properly:

(i) Curb chain at correct length. If the curb chain has the correct length, the side cheek bars of the bit form an angle of 45° with the mouth. Any other way of fitting the curb chain is wrong and painful for the horse and provokes disobedience.

*Fig. 94*
Hackamore, with curb-chain and lever action.

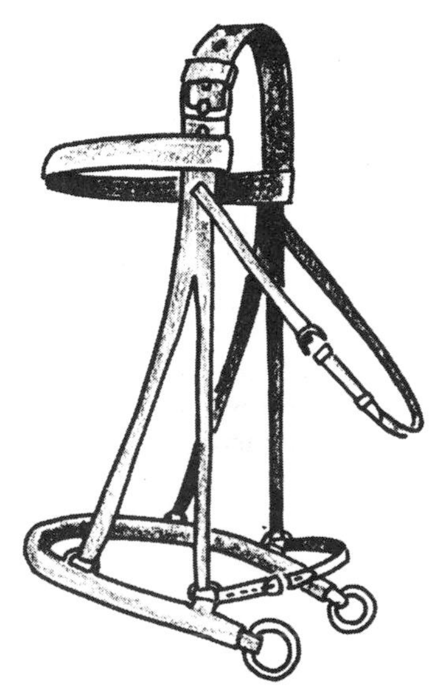

*Fig. 95*
Special jumping Hackamore (no lever action).

*Fig. 96*
The Italian-bred horse Aberali, ridden here in a jumping Hackamore by the brilliant American rider Miss Kathy Kussner. Note the happy and attentive expression on the horse's face.

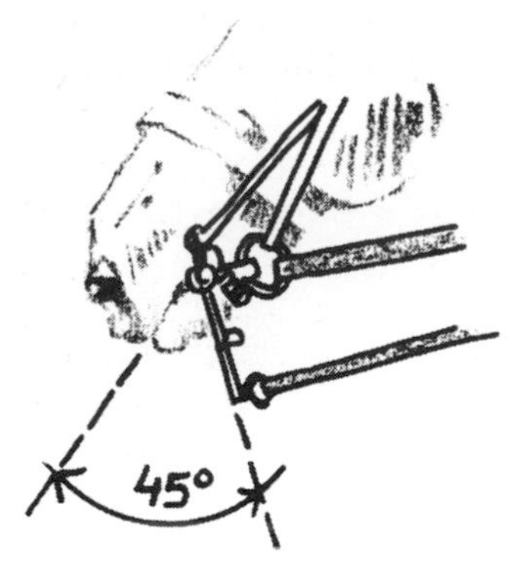

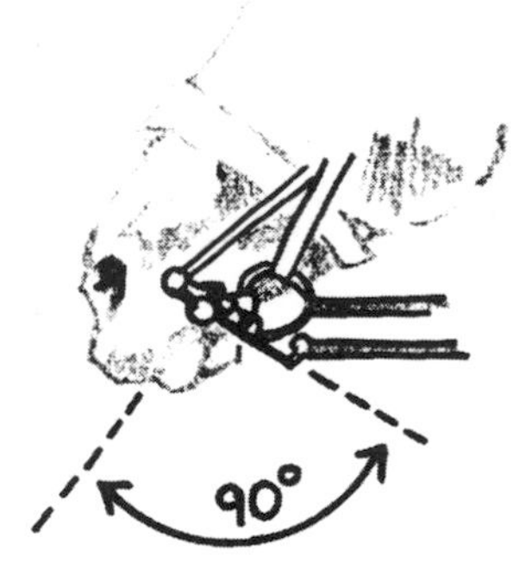

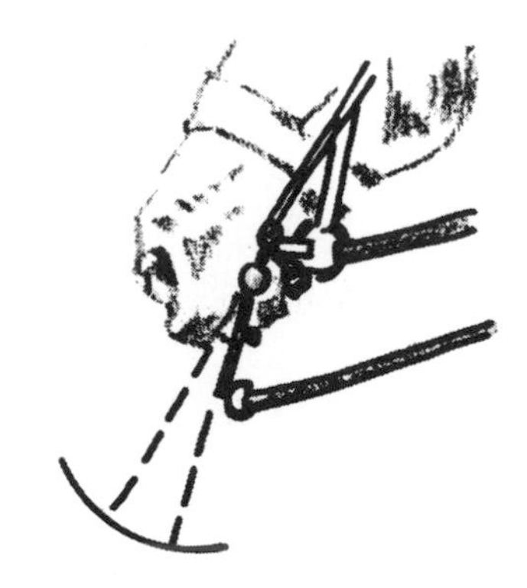

*Fig. 97*
*(Left)* curb chain at correct length; *(centre)* too long; *(right)* too short.

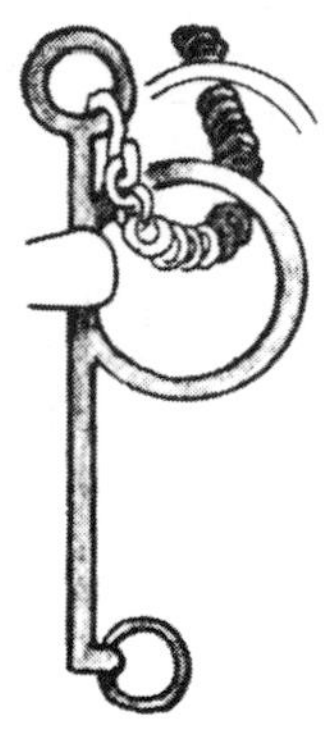
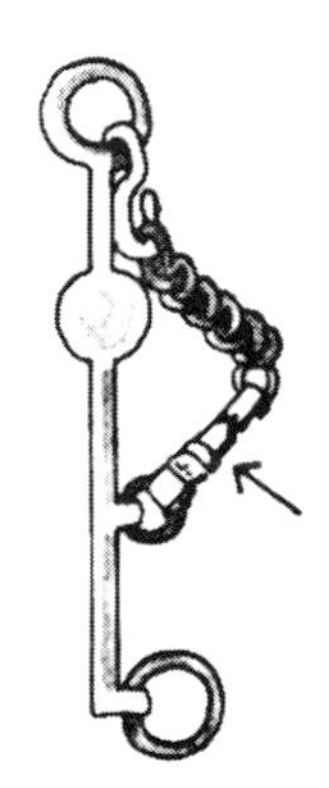

*Fig. 98*
*(Left')* curb chain of a pelham bit threaded through side rings; *(right)* lip strap holding the curb chain in place.

(ii) Curb chain too long. If the curb chain is too long, the cheek bars of the bit will form an angle of nearly 90° with the mouth. On account of this most horses will pull their tongue over the bit to avoid pressure of the mouthpiece; some horses even suffer so much that their tongue becomes blue. The curb chain has to be shortened so that there is less pressure on the tongue and bars and more in the curb chain groove.

(iii) Curb chain too short. This is also very painful for the horse, as there is then too much pressure on the curb chain groove, which becomes sore. To avoid this pressure the horse will move with an open mouth.

When using a pelham bit the curb chain should be threaded through the two side rings of the bit. Then it rests lower and exactly in the curb chain groove.

With a double bit the lip strap should be used to achieve the same effect. It is fitted through the curb chain centre-ring into the lip-strap eyes.

If the curb chain groove is very sensitive or sore one should use a rubber curb chain guard.

I repeat: in most cases the ordinary German snaffle bit should be used.

Only in cases of mouth deformations or tooth trouble may one use another bit. No matter which type of bit is used it should be adjusted so that it touches the corners of the mouth without wrinkling them.

*Fig. 99*
The "German" curb bit, with a thick, hollow mouthpiece.

THE BRIDLE

For the training of the showjumper one needs an ordinary snaffle-bridle without a buckle on top of the headpiece. This might injure the rider's face in the event of a fall. The throat lash should never be too tight; one should be able to put one's fist freely between the lash and the horse's throat. The bit should not be stitched in but buckled-in for easier cleaning. The brow band should not be too short, allowing free movement of the horse's ears. The nose band is part of the bridle. There are different types of nosebands.

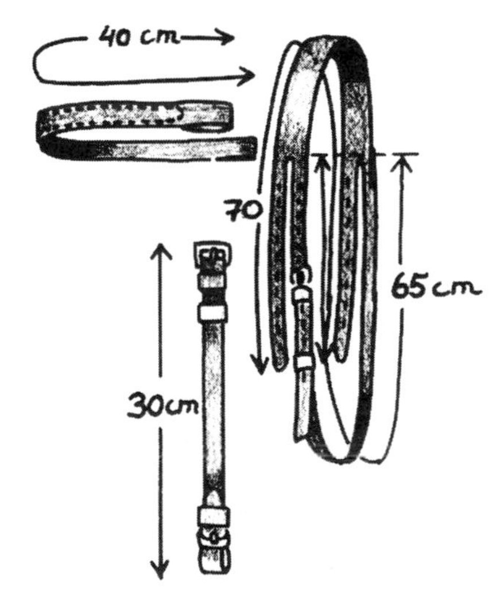


*Fig. 100*
The parts of a bridle, showing measurements to fit a medium size horse.

*The ordinary noseband*

This is a most suitable noseband. If fitted properly it does not hinder the horse in any way and leaves enough room for the bit to move easily without pinching the skin of the horse's lips. Fitted correctly, it should be two fingers below the cheek bone and also loose enough that one can fit two fingers between the nasal bone and the noseband. If fitted too tight it interferes with the relaxation of the lower jaw, causing soreness at the bones. When the noseband is well made then the nose piece should be at an angle of 90° with the cheek straps and the cheek strap of the noseband should be hidden beneath those of the bridle.

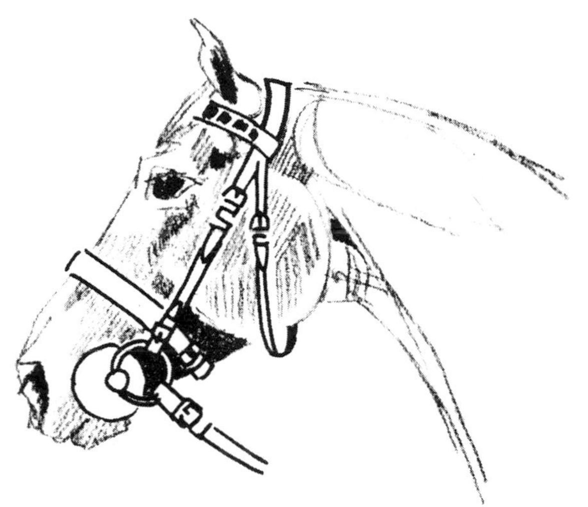

*Fig. 101*
Correctly fitted ordinary noseband.

In *a badly made noseband* the rear straps are too long and the front piece is too short. The cheek straps of the noseband lie in front of those of the bridle. The rear strap of the noseband hangs too low, pinching the skin between noseband and snaffle ring, causing the horse to carry his head too high.

*The drop noseband*

The drop noseband originates from the German Cavalry School in Hanover. It is intended to keep the horse's mouth closed. However, it is wiser to look for, and eliminate, the reason why the horse should need a drop

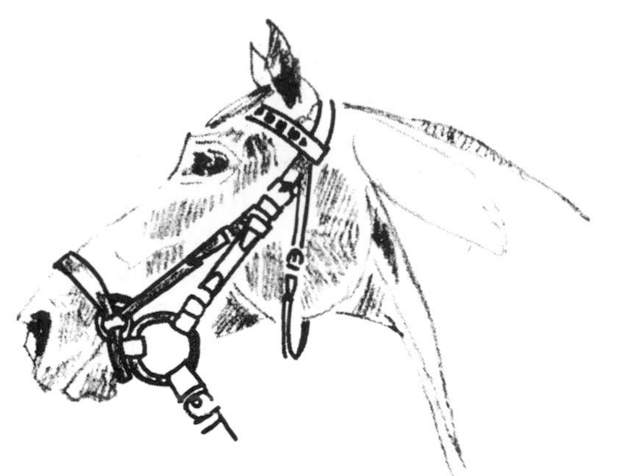

*Fig. 102*
**Correctly fitted drop noseband.**

*Fig. 103* **(right)**
**The measurements to fit a medium sized horse.**

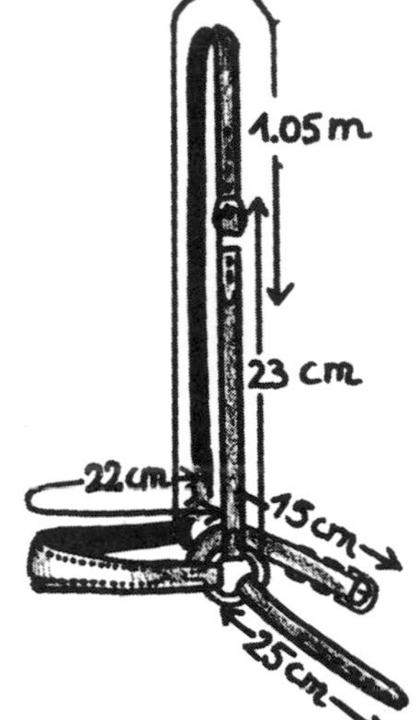

*Fig. 104*
**Drop noseband with curb chain.**

noseband. Besides, the drop noseband is commonly fitted too tight, which prevents the horse from relaxing the lower jaw. One should be able to put at least two fingers between noseband and nasal bone. The cheek strap on the noseband should lie in *front* of those on the bridle.

A fairly common fault in a drop noseband is that the nose piece is far too long and hangs down and the rear strap is too short.

There should be a small leather strap between nosepiece and cheek strap, preventing the noseband from dropping down. The noseband should rest on the base of the nasal bone. If adjusted too high it might push the snaffle up too high and pinch the corners of the lips. If, on the other hand, it lies too low and too close to the nostrils it will interfere with the breathing of the horse. It will then pinch the skin between snaffle and noseband, causing discomfort to the horse. The correct position is approximately 5 centimetres above the nostril. The rear strap should be kept soft, and if the horse has a very sensitive skin thread the strap through a rubber curb chain guard.

For hard-mouthed horses the rear strap may be replaced by a curb *chain*, covered with a rubber curb chain guard, and the noseband covered with sheepskin.

*The Mexican noseband*

During my stay in Mexico I noticed that this noseband was extensively used. It is excellent to re-train a horse which goes with an open mouth or one which does not relax its lower jaw, or one which jars against the bit. The upper rear strap of the noseband gives a gentle pressure on certain muscles, which helps to re-train a horse from those habits, although it is not necessary to adjust it too tight. There is never any danger of the nosepiece dropping and obstructing the nostrils and causing interference with the breathing.

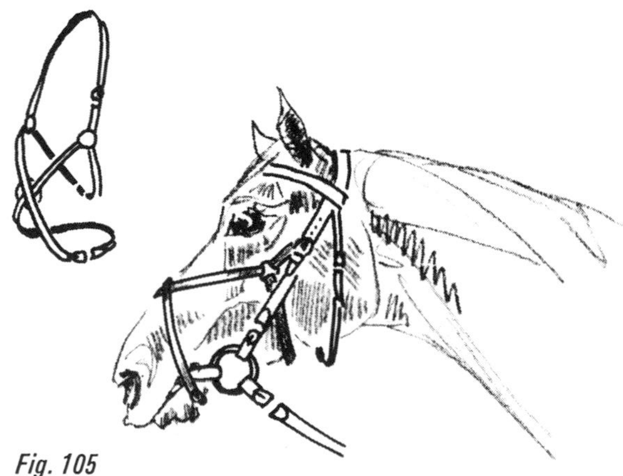
*Fig. 105*
**Mexican noseband.**

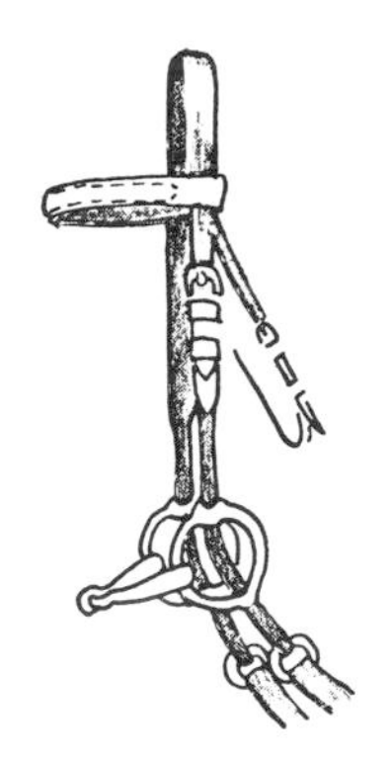

*Fig. 106*
"Gag" bridle.

*The "Gag" bridle*

Some riders use this to try to lift up the head and neck of a horse which is leaning too much on the forehand. This will prove unsuccessful because the increased pressure on the poll works in the opposite direction.

## REINS

*The German web rein*

In my opinion this is the most suited rein for jumping. It is light in the hands and therefore does not tempt the rider to take too strong a hold. It also has small leather anti-slip hand grips. It is very important that the leatherpiece from the snaffle ring to the web is not shorter than 46 centimetres, otherwise the martingale ring has too little room to run and may get caught at the joining of the leather part and web. When using a martingale, stoppers should be stitched on to the reins, as near as possible to the buckle. The leather hand grips make it easy for the rider to maintain the same length of rein. A rider with a firm seat will be able to jump a full course while holding the reins at the same leather grip. (There are, of course, exceptions where every rider has to yield the reins completely, if, for instance, the rider should get left behind or if the horse should make a mistake and need the free use of his neck to re-establish balance.)

*Fig. 107*
German web rein.

*The rubber-covered rein*

This rein is partly covered with rubber to prevent it slipping through the hands. When new it works efficiently, but when it becomes worn or wet the reins become more slippery than ordinary leather reins. They are too long and too thick, tempting the rider to take too strong a hold. Being too long, the reins become dangerous, since the rider's foot may get caught in them, which will jerk the horse in the mouth. The same can happen in case a fall occurs.

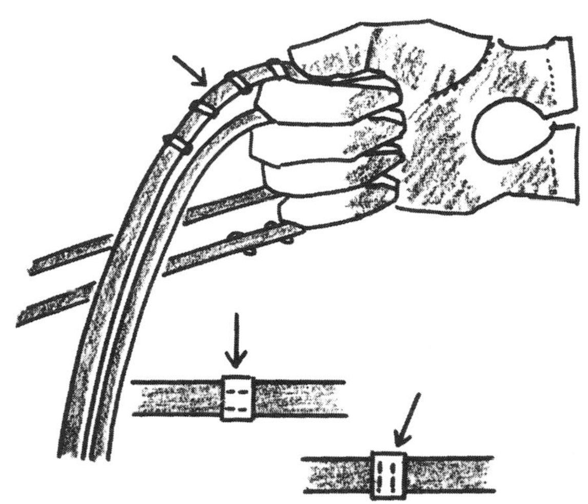

*Fig. 108*
Leather grips on the snaffle rein, stitched on *(top)* correctly; and *(bottom)* incorrectly.

*Double bit reins*

When jumping in a double bridle it may easily happen that one of the reins will slip through the rider's fingers, which is especially painful for the horse if it is the snaffle rein on one side and the curb rein on the other. Slipping of the snaffle reins can be prevented by stitching leather hand grips on to the snaffle rein in the region where one catches the rein while jumping. The stitching should be done lengthwise, with two stitches only (not vertically, as this would weaken the strength of the rein). It is easier to adjust the reins while jumping if the curb bit rein and the snaffle rein are separated by the forefinger. In this position the snaffle rein is always on top, so one cannot get mixed up while shortening the reins.

## THE BREASTPLATE

A breastplate should always be used when jumping, particularly on young horses with fleshy withers, as it keeps the saddle in place over the centre of gravity of the horse. There are two different types of breastplates. There is the ordinary one, lined with soft leather or sheepskin. Then there is the V-type, which holds the saddle in position with two little side straps attached to the rings in front of the saddle. I prefer the first type, as the V-type can become very tight between the horse's forelegs when jumping.

*Breastplate carrying weights*

Lady riders must carry – in jumping competitions – the same minimum weight as gentlemen riders (except when riding sidesaddle or in record breaking attempts). It is advisable to carry the weights (pieces of lead) in the breastplate rather than in the saddlecloth. In the neckstrap of the breastplate the weights are closer to the horse's centre of gravity and therefore more easily carried. The built-in steel frame makes sure that the weights do not press on to the withers. As saddle and bridle are included in the weight there is also the possibility for lady riders to use a saddle with a special heavy tree in case they have difficulties in making the required weight.

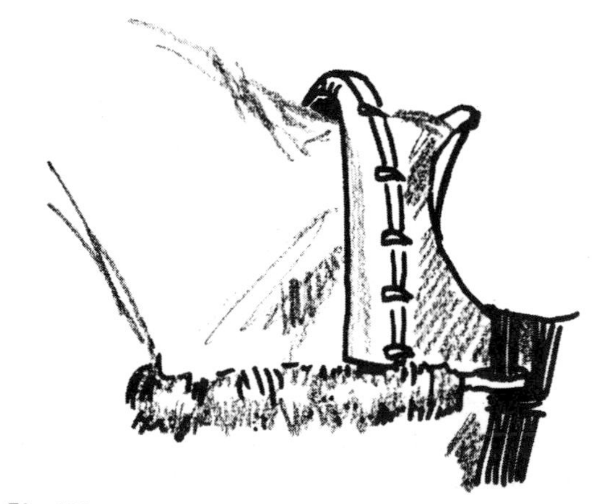

*Fig. 109*
**Breastplate carrying weights.**

## THE SADDLE

A correctly built saddle is the foundation for a correct seat and administration of aids. Without a well-balanced saddle it is impossible to have a balanced seat.

The points of a well-built saddle are better appreciated by an analysis of the French Danloux saddle, which is used in the French Army Equestrian School at Saumur. I have used these saddles for many years and found them to be most satisfying. Such an analysis shows that the pommel is absolutely free of the withers, so that one can see the daylight all the way through (air tunnel). Therefore it will fit every horse, because no pressure will ever fall on the withers, vertebrae or kidneys but will rest on the back muscles and ribs of the horse. It will never move – forward or backwards.

Most important is that the deepest point of the saddle is in the front half. I find that 90% of all saddles are too low at the rear. Most riders have become so used to their saddle that they are not aware of it getting lower at the cantle until the deepest point is really at the rear instead of in the front half of the seat. Once a rider has become used to such a saddle he will find it very hard to adjust himself to a well-balanced saddle.

The reason for saddles being too low at the rear is that they are well worn – probably by riders who sit too far back in the saddle. Such a saddle needs refilling. Alternatively, it could be that the saddle has an outdated tree. This would force a rider, no matter how skilled, to sit too far back in the saddle, causing pressure on the horse's kidneys. The horse will try to avoid this pain by dropping his back, moving with his hocks wide apart and carrying his head too high. Sitting at the rear of the saddle will also make the rider put his legs too far forward, nearly touching the horse's elbows. This makes it impossible to give proper aids.

Only in a well-built saddle, with the deepest point in the front half, is the rider's centre of gravity located vertically above that of the horse and the weight of the rider correctly distributed on to all four legs of the horse. The rider's hip

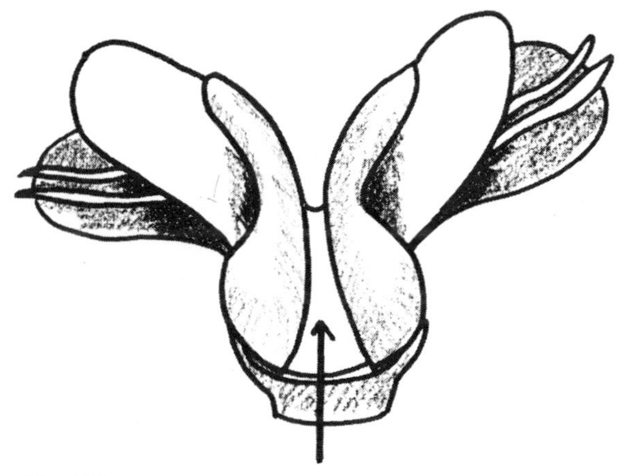

*Fig. 110*
A well padded, French Saumur saddle.

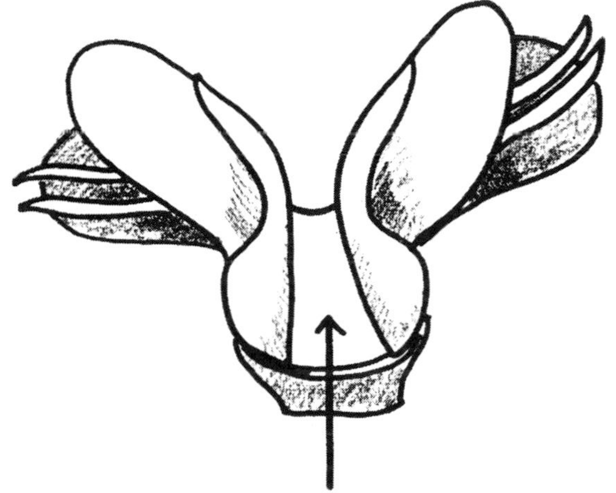

*Fig. 111*
In this saddle the air tunnel is too wide.

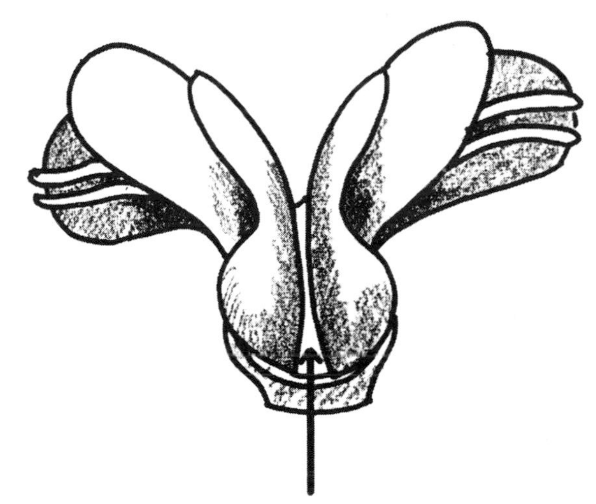

*Fig. 112*
In this saddle the air tunnel is too narrow.

and heel should be on an imaginary vertical line, showing the girths just in front of the rider's leg. Only with this leg position can the rider really feel the horse's body with the calves of his legs and thereby give the correct leg aids.

The Danloux jumping saddle promotes the *forward seat* and prevents the rider from getting left behind and keeps the lower legs in position. The knees are close to the horse as the knee rolls are *above* the knees. If the pads reach down, between knee and horse, the rider cannot get a proper grip or feeling of his horse. Besides, the saddle has a *movable* stirrup leather bar which guarantees utmost safety in case of a fall and also makes it very simple to unhook the leathers. The spring of the stirrup bars should be kept open for safety rearsons. With most other saddles it is extremely difficult to unhook the stirrup leathers, even when the safety catch of the bar is open.

Another favourable point of the French saddle is that the stirrup bar is positioned vertically exactly above the girths, assuring correct seat and leg position, contrary to most other saddles where the stirrup bar is placed in front of the girths.

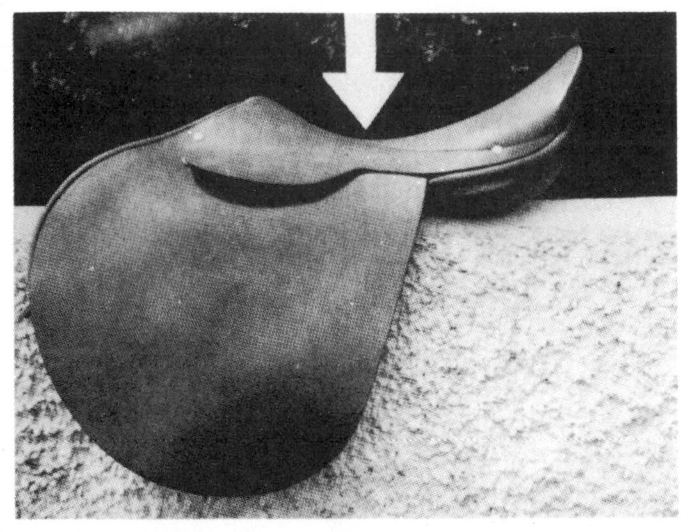

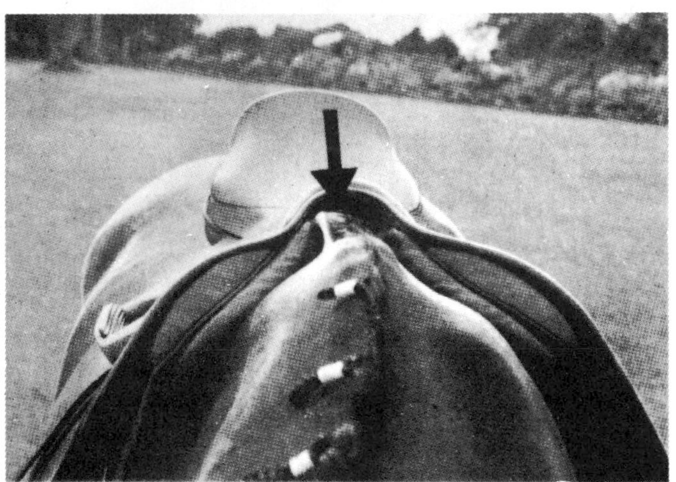

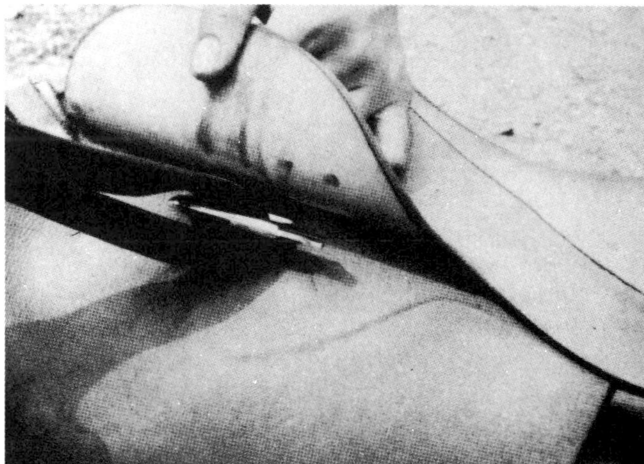

*Fig. 113* (top, left)
The lowest point of the saddle is in the front half.

*Fig. 114* (centre, left)
The Saumur saddle fits every horse. Note the (arrowed) air tunnel.

*Fig. 115* (bottom, left)
A saddle horse, with an adjustable top to hold a saddle upside down for cleaning.

*Fig. 116* (top)
The rider's knees are close to the horse, because the knee rolls (arrowed) are above the knees. The calf roll prevents the rider's leg from slipping backwards.

*Fig. 117* (centre)
The movable stirrup leather bar.

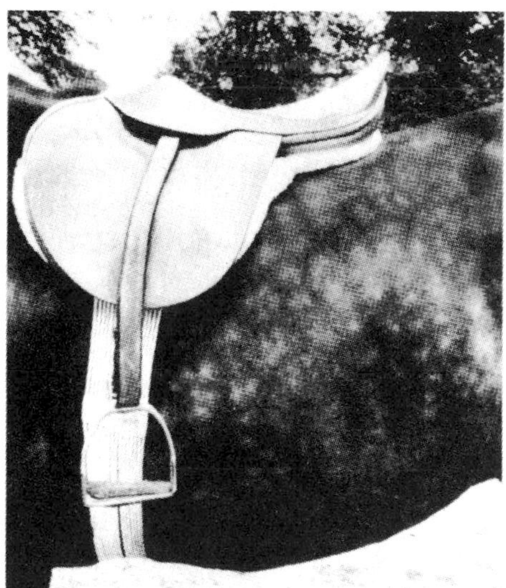

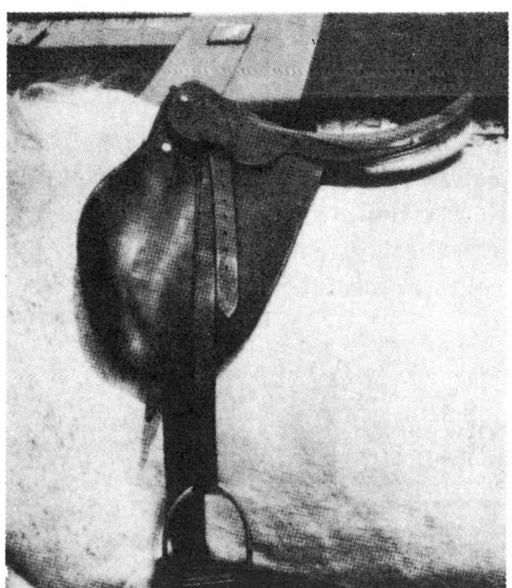

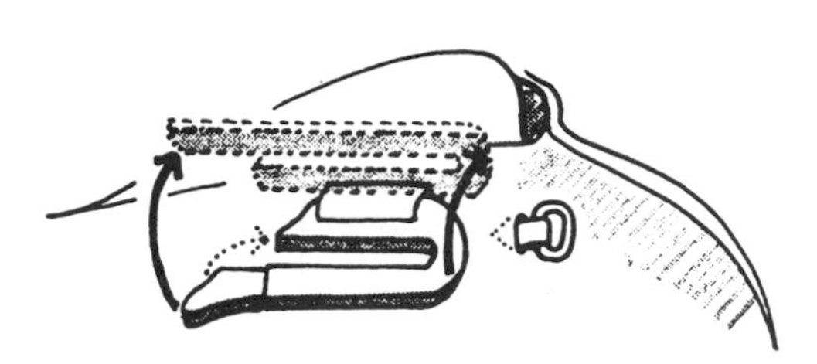

*Fig. 118* (top, left)
Fit the buckle of the leather close to the stirrup.

*Fig. 119* (centre, left)
French saddle with fittings.

*Fig. 120* (bottom, left)
Movable stirrup leather bar.

*Fig. 121* (top)
German saddle showing deepest point near back of saddle, thick knee roll between rider's knee and horse.

*Fig. 122* (centre)
No rider can learn how to ride in this saddle.

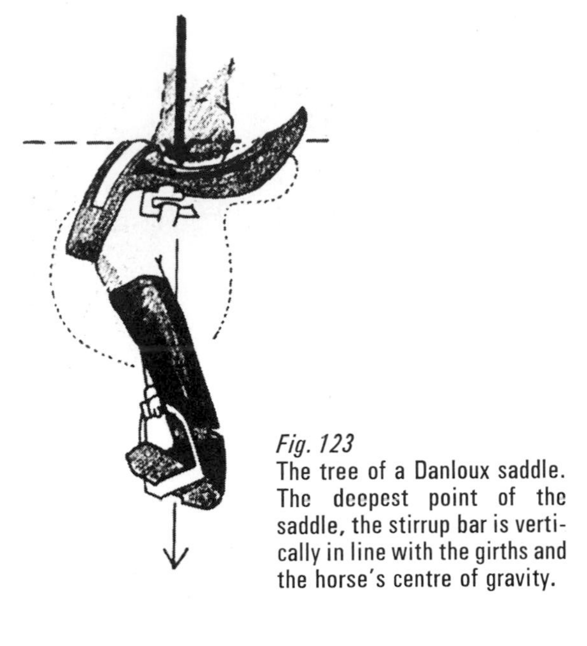

*Fig. 123*
The tree of a Danloux saddle. The deepest point of the saddle, the stirrup bar is vertically in line with the girths and the horse's centre of gravity.

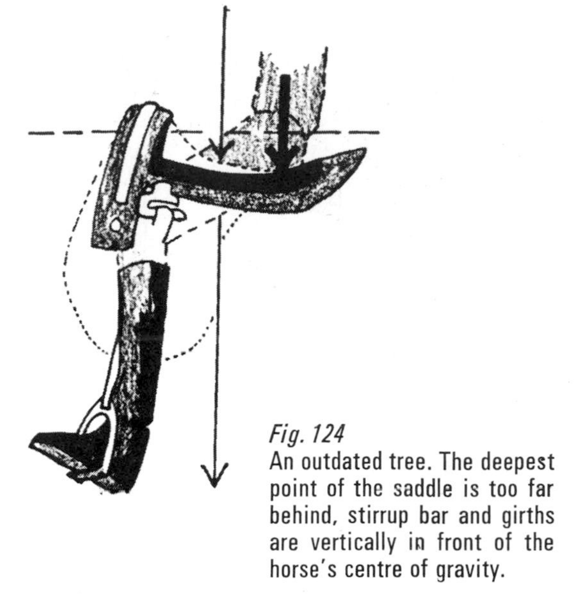

*Fig. 124*
An outdated tree. The deepest point of the saddle is too far behind, stirrup bar and girths are vertically in front of the horse's centre of gravity.

A common fault in other saddles is that they are lopsided, induced by a rider who puts too much weight on *one* seat bone. Many riders do not realise that they are actually sitting this way. Mostly it is the left seat bone that carries too much weight. If one of the hips is collapsed there will be more pressure on one seat bone. There are two reasons for this. Mounting has stretched the left stirrup leather. Stirrup leathers should be changed frequently – from one side to the other – to keep them equally long. Also, many riders mount the wrong way: they take hold of the

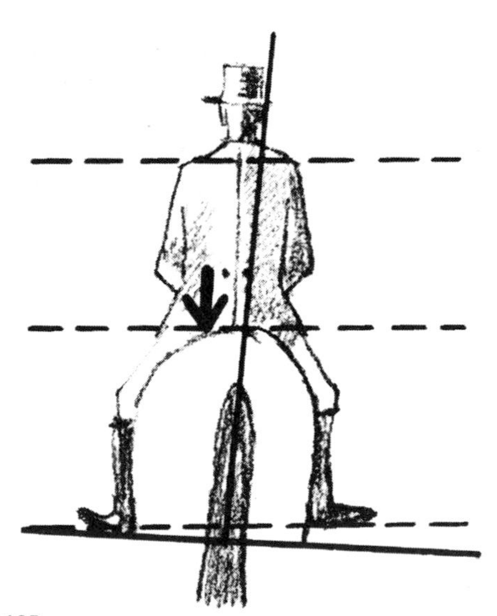

*Fig. 125*
Lopsided saddle. The rider is putting too much weight on his left seat bone.

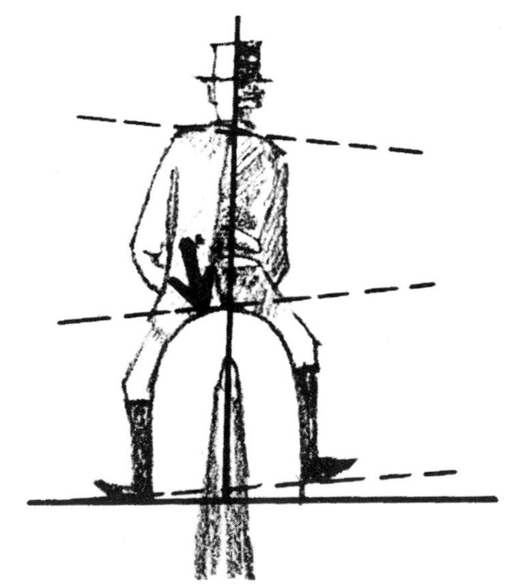

*Fig. 126*
The rider is sitting lopsided, right hip collapsing.

*Fig. 127*
*(Left)* mounting incorrectly (this will make the saddle lopsided); *(right)* mounting correctly.

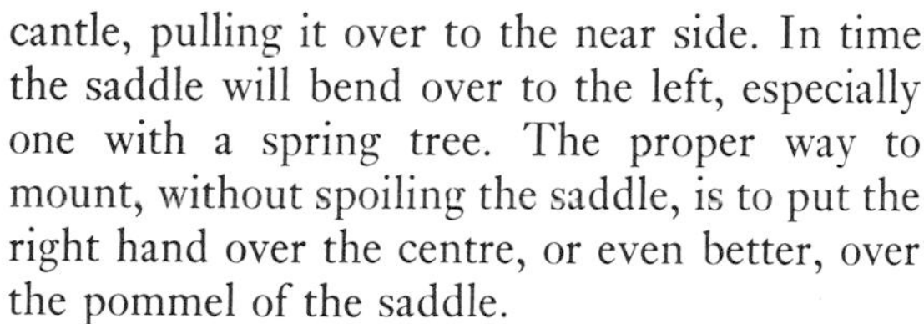

cantle, pulling it over to the near side. In time the saddle will bend over to the left, especially one with a spring tree. The proper way to mount, without spoiling the saddle, is to put the right hand over the centre, or even better, over the pommel of the saddle.

It stands to reason that in a lopsided saddle the rider can only sit lopsided. The displaced weight of the rider makes it impossible for the horse to move straight and to follow with the hindfeet in the tracks of the forefeet. The horse is forced to move more or less like a dog: the near hindfoot steps between the tracks of the front feet (the same can occur when riding side-saddle incorrectly).

When saddling a horse be particularly careful to see that the saddle is placed in the correct position. First, the saddle is placed gently on the withers of the horse, then pushed backwards – the way the hair grows – into its proper position (it should never be pushed forward). If the saddle is put too far forward it interferes with the movement of the shoulders and the girths will pinch the horse's skin causing girth galls.

*Stirrup leathers*

Normally the buckle of the stirrup leather is fitted underneath the shirt, the leather part of the saddle which covers the spring bar. This

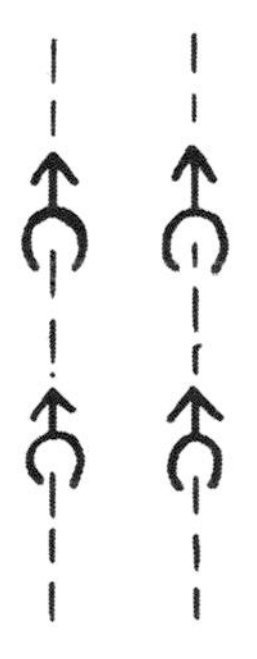

*Fig. 128*
Tracks of a horse which is moving straight.

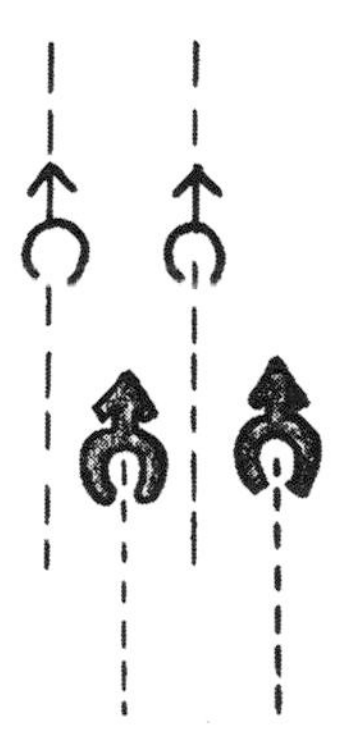

*Fig. 129*
The rider's right hip is collapsing, thus shifting more weight to the left. This forces the horse to move his quarters to the right (on two tracks).

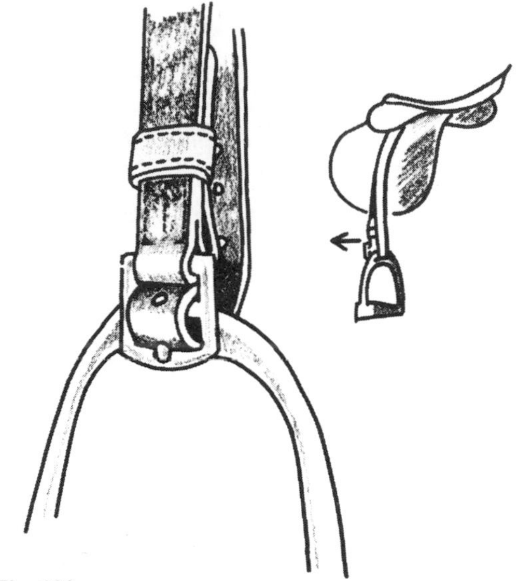

*Fig. 130*
Stirrup leather fitted with buckle at top of stirrup, buckle facing forward.

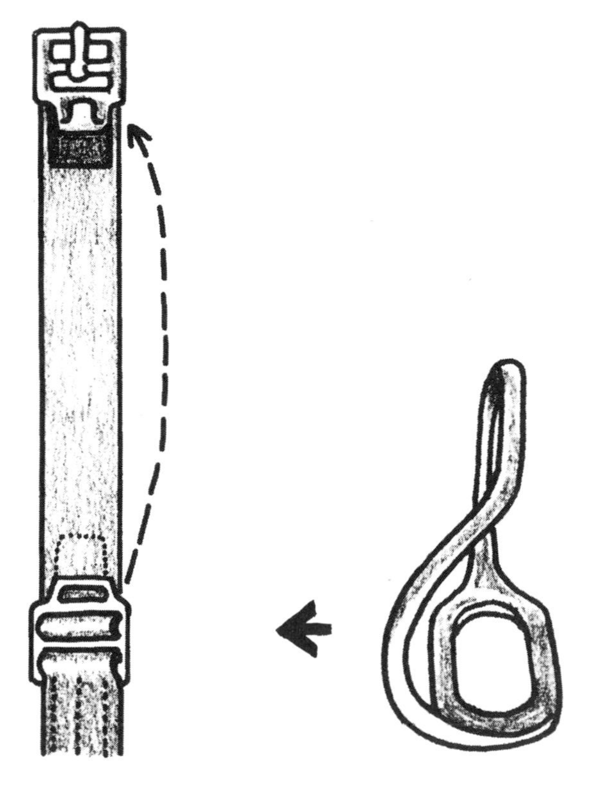

*Fig. 131*
Extension stirrup leather.

*Fig. 132*
Australian safety stirrup.

can be very painful to the rider's legs and wear out the riding breeches, especially when the stirrup leathers are new. It is more comfortable to fit the stirrup leathers upside down, so that the buckle is situated on the outside top part of the stirrup iron (facing forward and not towards the boot). The end of the stirrup leather is threaded back through the buckle and held by a holder. Having allowed three or four extra holes for adjustments, one should cut off the remainder of the stirrup leather, because one never uses this part anymore. (For easy mounting one can use an extension stirrup leather.) When mounted, the rider can alter the length of the leathers easily: leaving the leg in its proper position, slip the foot out of the stirrup, lift the buckle up and alter the length.

## STIRRUPS

The stirrup irons should be heavy and wide enough to slip off the foot easily in case of a fall. On the other hand, the stirrup should not be too wide, as then the rider's foot could slip completely through and get caught. The boot should always rest close to the inside bar of the stirrup, leaving a space of approximately 2·5 centimetres to the outside bar. Very useful, and extremely safe, is the Australian safety stirrup, since the foot can never get caught. The safety stirrup with the rubber ring on the outside is not as good because it is mostly too narrow and could catch the foot, even if the rubber ring is open.

Extremely useful is the ready made "offset" stirrup. It has a slanted sole and an off-centre loop for the stirrup leather, which keeps the knees in and the heels down and the foot at the correct angle. One will achieve the same effect by fitting a home-made sloped wooden wedge into an ordinary stirrup. This also promotes a correct leg position with a bent ankle and deep heel, giving an excellent grip with the knees. The stirrup wedges are also on sale ready-made. A simple way of achieving the same correct foot-angle is to adjust the stirrup leather by winding it once around the outside arm of a stirrup.

*Fig. 133*
This safety stirrup is often too narrow.

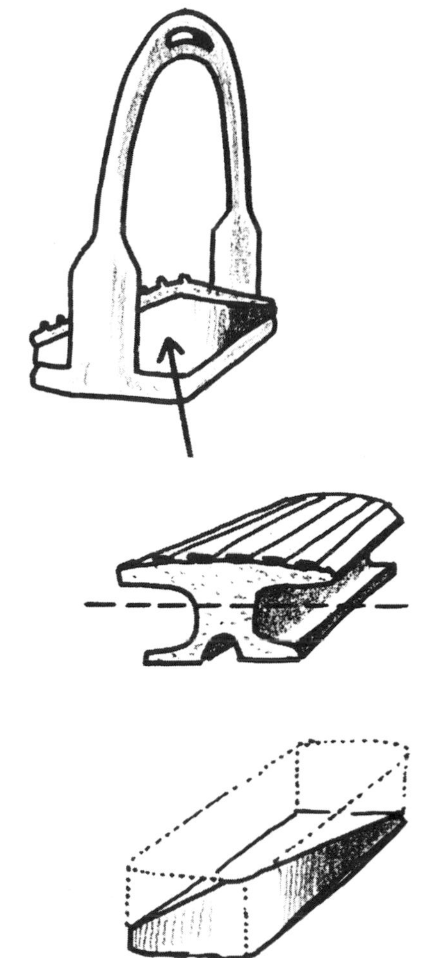

*Fig. 134*
A ready-made offset stirrup.

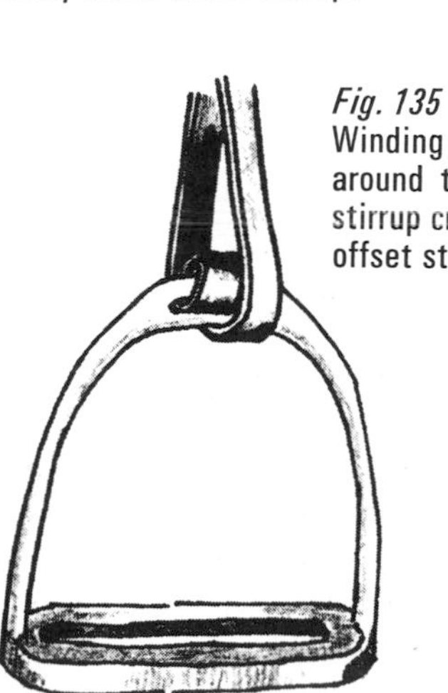

*Fig. 135*
Winding a stirrup leather once around the outside arm of a stirrup creates the effect of an offset stirrup.

*Fig. 136*
An easy way to convert a regular stirrup iron into an offset stirrup. Make a wooden wedge-shaped tread with a rubber cover *(top)*; cut an ordinary rubber tread into top and bottom parts *(centre)*; make a wooden wedge, with the thickest part diagonally opposite the lowest *(bottom)*.

Nail the top of the rubber tread to the top of the wedge, with the bottom part underneath. That way it may then be fitted like an ordinary tread.

CLEANING TACK

Tack should be cleaned at least twice weekly – more often, if time allows – using a bar of glycerine saddle soap. This cleans the leather and leaves it soft. Use lukewarm water and squeeze out the sponge well; rub over the bar of saddle soap and clean all the tack. Dry with a towel and hang. When the leather is dry use Harris' Saddle Paste. Rub this paste well in with your finger tips for best results, because the warmth of your fingers causes the paste to penetrate deep into the leather. Then the leather, when in use, will never feel sticky or dirty your hands and breeches. If the paste is put on with a brush it stays on top of the leather and will crack when the leather is bent in use. Afterwards use a soft brush and cloth to shine all leather work. *Do not* use oil, as this leaves the leather too greasy and sticky and will stain riding breeches. To clean the saddle underneath put it upside down on a special saddle rack.

All nickle should shine like silver and the snaffle should be cleaned after riding each different horse for hygienic reasons. Girths and saddlecloths must be kept immaculately clean to avoid infections.

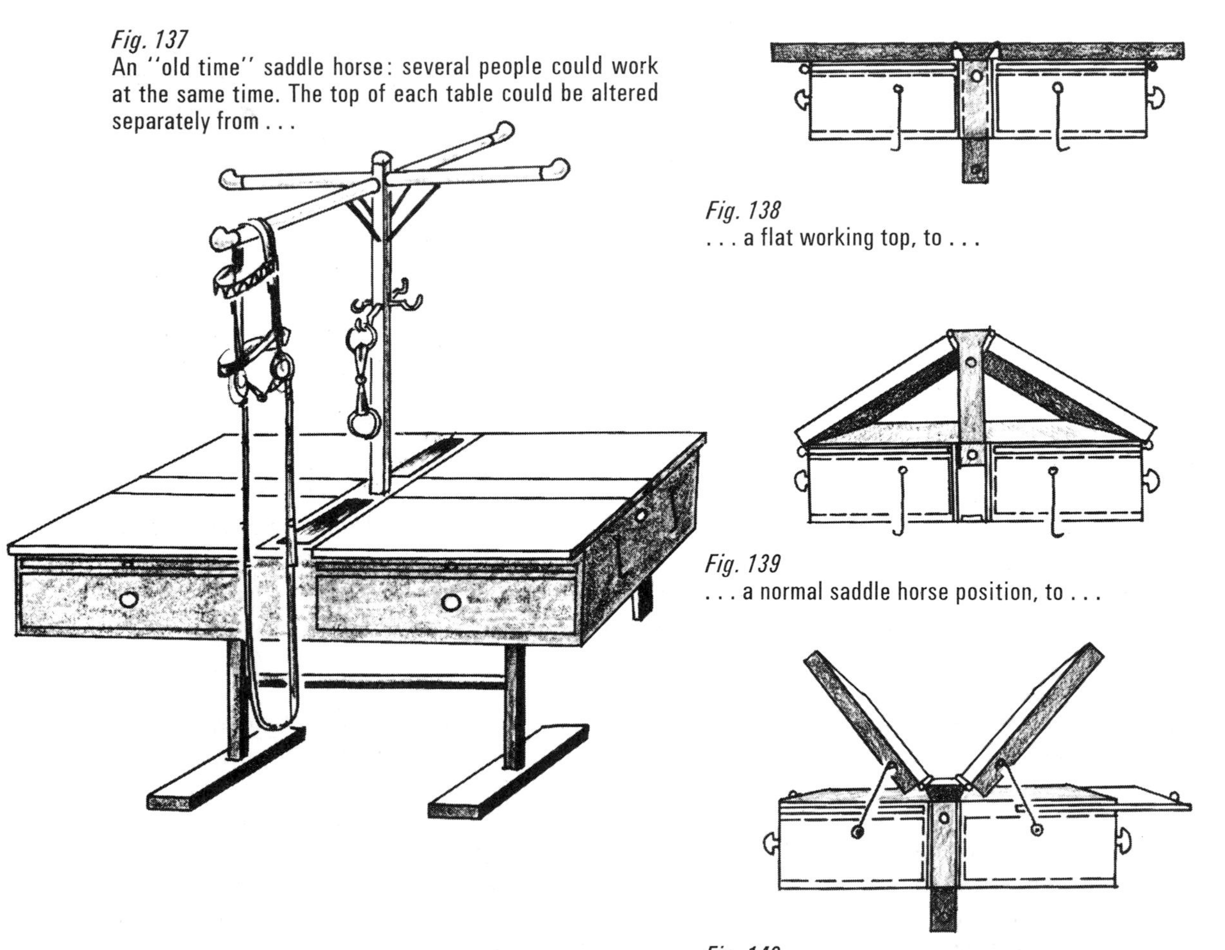

*Fig. 137*
An "old time" saddle horse: several people could work at the same time. The top of each table could be altered separately from . . .

*Fig. 138*
. . . a flat working top, to . . .

*Fig. 139*
. . . a normal saddle horse position, to . . .

*Fig. 140*
. . . a position holding the saddle upside down. Between the two table tops are holders for the bars of saddle soap.

## SADDLECLOTHS

The saddlecloth is to protect the saddle from sweat. It should lie flat without creases and free from the withers. The simplest and most economical is a cotton numnah, with straps to fit the saddle, which can be machine washed. It is thin and gives the rider close contact with the horse.

The felt numnah has many disadvantages. It retains the sweat and loose hair, especially when the horse is changing his coat; it is also difficult to wash and even more difficult to dry. A numnah, completely hard and dirty underneath, is an ideal breeding place for bacteria.

A horse which resents the tightening of the girths is often referred to as having a "cold back". A folded woollen blanket makes a good saddlecloth when breaking young horses, or those who have a cold back. The blanket is soft and warm and will make it easier for the horse to relax. A cold saddle, put on a horse's back without a saddlecloth, makes a young horse buck and move with a hunched back.

## GIRTHS

Of all the girths available, I consider the German cordstring the most suitable. The thick, round strings of these white cotton girths (width 12·5 centimetres and available in three lengths) are held in place by cross weaves, which prevent the girths from getting tangled and give an even pressure all round. The same girths are made from Terylene, which is even softer and easier to wash. Unlike leather girths, this design and material allows the air to circulate through, thereby avoiding chaffing and girth galls, even in a hot climate.

In England and Ireland nylon girths are widely used. Although the cheapest, they have a disadvantage: the strings are supported, if at all, by very weak crossbands. These girths get tangled and often rope behind the horse's elbows, causing sores. Even if you have to use such girths, attach three stout leather straps on the outside which will keep the nylon strings separated.

Crossed leather girths are too narrow behind the elbows and pressure is not evenly spread.

*Fig. 141*
German string girths with elastic (arrowed) extension.

*Fig. 142*
Nylon girths get tangled if not supported by stout leather pieces.

The folded leather girths are very warm and uncomfortable for the horse, because they are made all in one piece and do not allow air to circulate.

Linen girths have sharp edges and will injure the sensitive skin behind the elbows. If one *has* to use these girths one should thread them through a motorcycle tube.

One should always fasten the girths – on each side – at the same height to give the rider an even feel under both legs. Never over-tighten the girths, particularly straight away when saddling, but allow two fingers to pass between them and the horse's body. Too tight a girth gives the horse considerable discomfort. After tightening the girths, put your hand under them and pull them away from the horse to make sure that the skin is not wrinkled.

## SURCINGLE

For safety reasons one should always use a surcingle when jumping or training. It is a great pity that many riders remember the surcingle *after* they have had an unnecessary accident with broken girths. The surcingle is pulled through the loops of the breastplate and must stay at all times over the ordinary girths, with the buckle underneath the horse's body and not behind the elbows, where it could injure the skin.

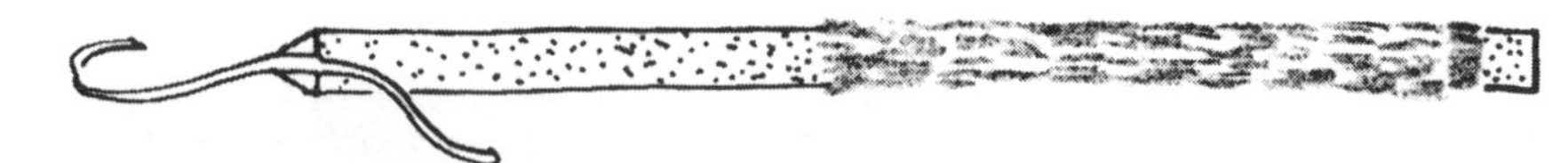

*Fig. 143*
The Sandown bandage.

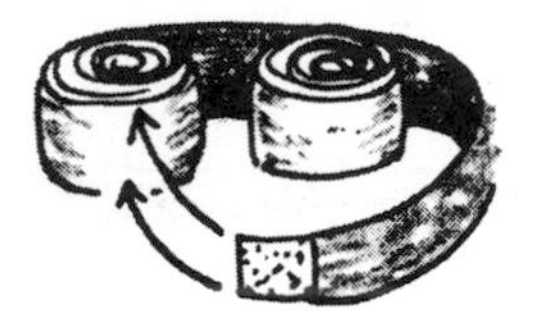

*Fig. 144*
The proper way to roll the bandage up in pairs.

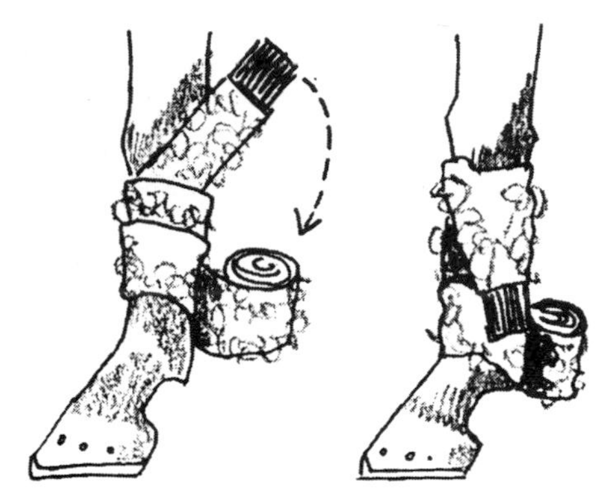

*Fig. 145*
Protecting inside of leg against brushing.

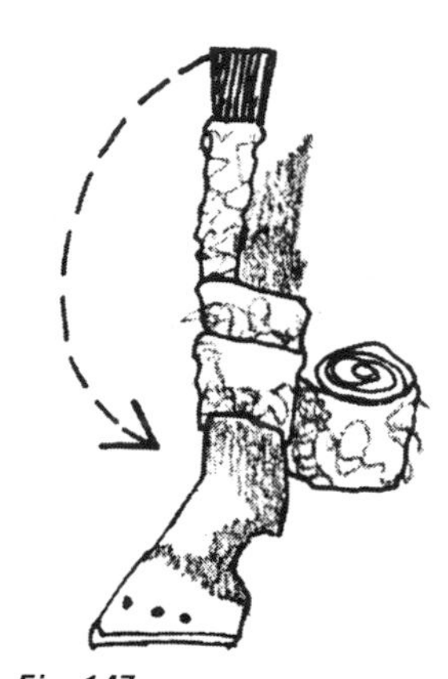

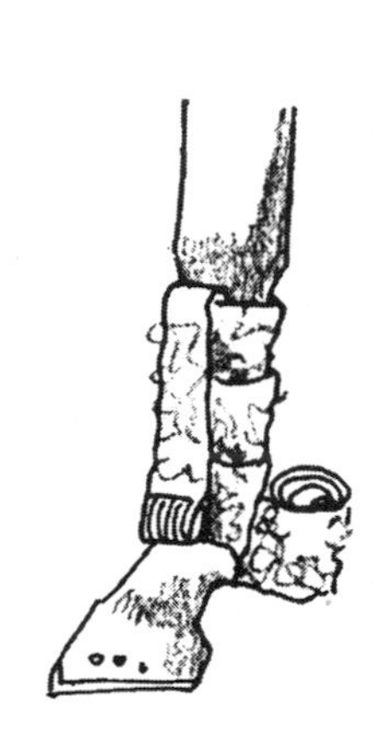

*Fig. 147*
Protecting canonbone.

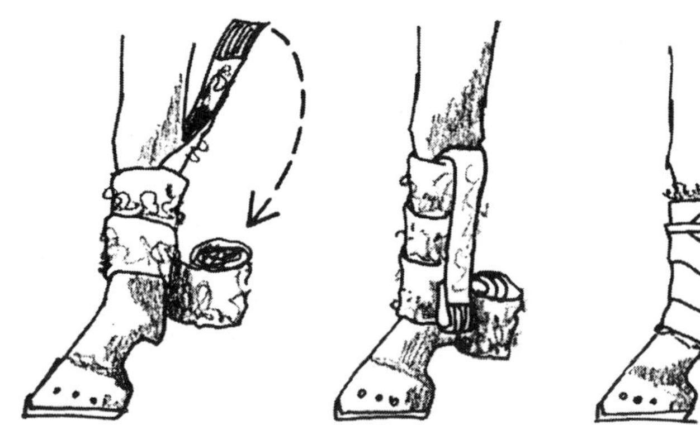

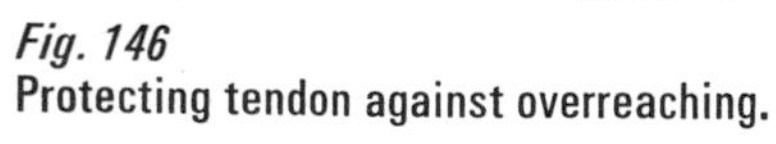

*Fig. 146*
Protecting tendon against overreaching.

*Fig. 148*
Cooling bandage.

## LEG PROTECTION

*Bandages*

When training a showjumper it is imperative to protect his legs, not only when lungeing, jumping or doing cavaletti work, but also when giving the horse free exercise, turning him loose for a short time in the indoor school or in the field, and before loading the horse into the horsebox. Putting on bandages is not pampering a horse (as one can often hear "tough" riders say, who use this excuse because they just don't want to bother to put on bandages).

Leg protection is necessary to prevent injury. After training a horse and putting in a lot of work, one should not take the risk of having the horse damaged or out of training due to carelessness.

However, bandages can be harmful when inexpertly applied and when putting them on it is important that the strings are not too tight (never tighter than the bandage itself), otherwise they interfere with the blood circulation and leave ugly white marks on the horse's legs. The tapes should finish with a secure knot and bow on the outside of the leg, the ends tucked away neatly under the tapes. Never tie the bow on the tendon as this may cause lameness.

*The Sandown bandage*

The English Sandown bandages are most versatile and I have used them for many years. The first half is made of fleecy soft wool and the second half of plain cotton, so that the leg is first padded and then packed slightly tighter, which gives an even support. The bandage is easy to put on, does not slip down and supports the tendons without weakening them.

This bandage should be used not only when training but also *after* training the horse, especially after strenuous work such as lungeing, cavaletti work or jumping. After exercise the bandages are taken off, well shaken out and then re-done, this time a bit looser than in exercise and covering the fetlock joints completely. This prevents the legs filling and encourages blood circulation. The bandages are left on the horse for at least two hours after work. If done regularly the horse will not get any windgalls and existing windgalls will disappear after a time.

A wet Sandown bandage can also be used to cool a horse's leg. It stays cool and wet for approximately 12 hours. One can prolong this time by putting an upside down overreach boot filled with ice cubes above the bandage.

Instead of bandages after exercise another very effective treatment is the use of "Poudre Amoricaine". One can buy this powder ready made and mix it with water, but one can also mix it oneself. The recipe is: 1½ litres of vinegar, 300cc camphorated spirit, 100cc Arnica and 100 grammes copper sulphate powder. These ingredients are mixed with blue clay. The mixture is painted on to the horse's leg with a large brush and a second coat is applied after an hour. Start above the knees and hocks and paint all four legs down to the hooves. Next morning just hose the legs down to clean the clay away – the result is amazing. Any surplus mixture will not dry out if kept in a plastic bucket with an airtight lid, which avoids vaporising.

*Brushing boots*

There are various types of brushing boots on the market made either from leather or from felt. They should have leather protection on the outside and a *rounded* lower part to cover the fetlock joint comfortably. Foam rubber lining is not recommended because it irritates the skin, creating infection.

With all brushing boots the middle buckle or fastening should be closed first, then the top one, and finally the bottom one, which must not be closed tightly in case gravel works itself under the boot making the skin sore.

*Overreach boots*

Overreach boots are very important as injuries from overreaching are extremely slow to heal. Overreach boots also protect the coronary band, because cracks could lead to inflammation of the soft lining of the coffin bone. When unprotected the coronary band easily becomes injured if the hoof knocks a pole hard while jumping.

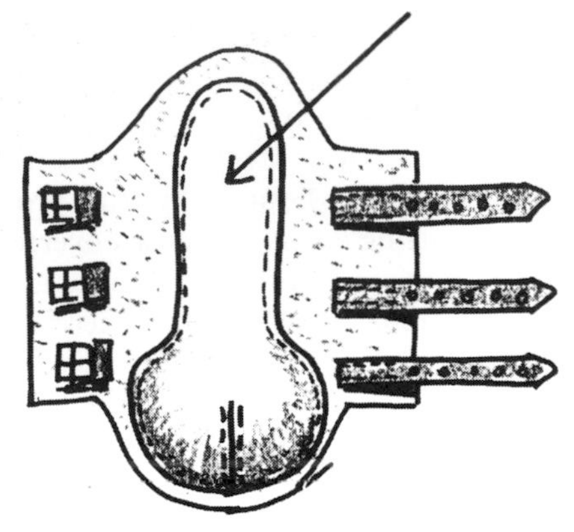

*Fig. 149*
Brushing boots.

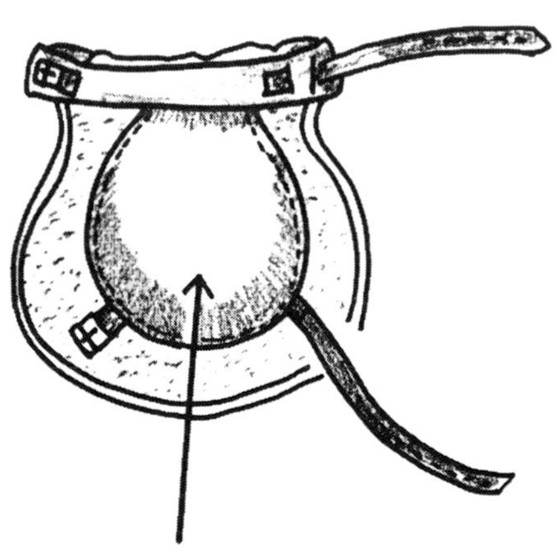

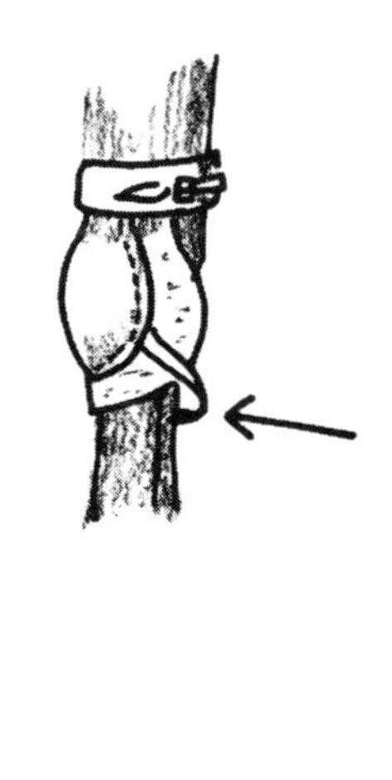

*Fig. 150*
Kneecaps. Note (arrowed) loosely fitted at bottom.

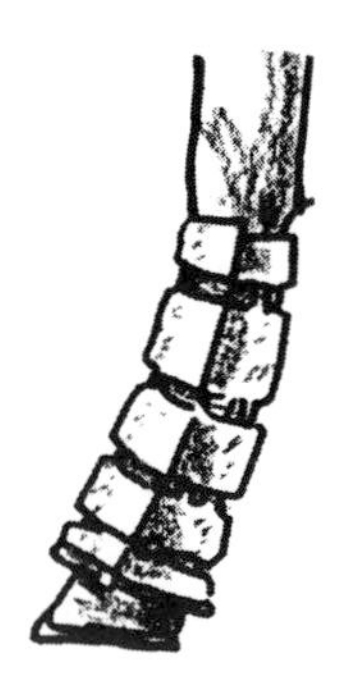

*Fig. 151*
Transport boots.

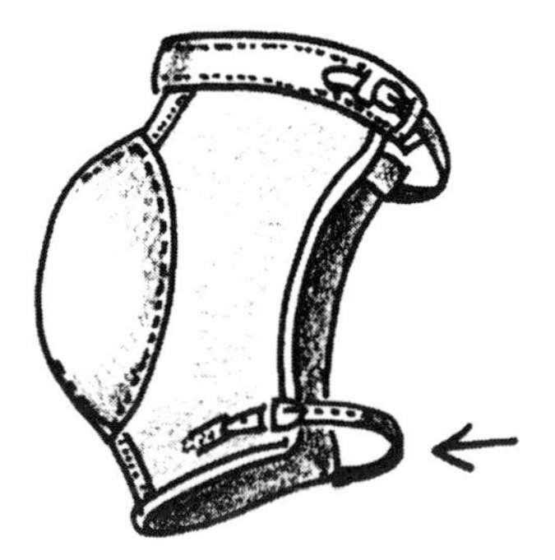

*Fig. 152*
Hock protectors, loosely fitted at bottom (arrowed).

*Kneecaps*

Kneecaps are necessary when transporting horses, when free jumping and in road work. They are made from soft felt with a leather cap. To give extra protection one could have them lined with sheepskin. The bottom strap must be loosely fastened, giving freedom of movement.

*Fig. 153*
Suitable spur.

*Protectors during transport*

There are special leg protectors which are used when transporting horses. These are made from very thick felt, held by several leather buckles and straps, with a leather or plastic hem sewn around the bottom edge. They reach all the way down to the ground. Hock protectors are also advisable during transport, as the horse might kick out behind and get capped hocks. Care should be taken when putting them on for the first time because the horse might kick and hurt himself. Therefore it is advisable to do it out of doors. Tail protectors should also be used.

## SPURS

Spurs should only be used by riders who have perfect leg position at all times. Even experienced riders must be very careful wearing spurs when riding sensitive horses. Only after young horses have been taught in conjunction with the dressage whip to obey the different leg aids should they be ridden with spurs.

Mares in season should not be ridden with spurs. Some highly strung horses are ridden and jumped successfully all their lives without spurs. But lazy horses, when ridden with spurs, will learn to respond quicker to the leg aids. The spurs should not be used to punish the horse, but only with great discretion to complement the normal leg aids, and then should only be applied with a short tap and not constant pressing.

Vague or continuous and unnecessary use of the spurs makes a horse so dull that he will fail to react any longer. Some riders, when wearing spurs, use them constantly, unknown to themselves.

The use of sharp spurs is dangerous and cruel, as they can cut the horse's skin (especially those with the little wheel, which can get stuck with horse hair and then become as sharp as a razor edge).

Sharp spurs will make the horse "sour" and produce swishing tails and grinding teeth. The horse will defend himself by kicking at the spurs, reining back or rearing.

The most suitable spurs are those with no sharp edges or wheels, but extra long, straight necks, so there is no need for the rider to turn his knees away from the saddle in trying to reach the horse with the spur.

PART TWO

# THE FIRST SCHOOLING YEAR

CHAPTER FIVE

# BREAKING

One will probably wonder why in most of the illustrations in this part of the book girls are handling and working the horses. Since I have lived and worked in English speaking countries, I have learned to appreciate the way in which girls treat horses. Highly strung and nervous horses settle down quickly, because girls are more sensitive and have more patience than the average man and are prepared to mother the horse. This personal care is most important.

## TACKING UP

To prevent a lot of trouble when breaking a horse, one should handle and school him as soon as he comes in from grass, as he is then relaxed and generally weak. It is a mistaken policy to bring the horse first into a strong condition by giving him plenty of whole oats, because the stronger the horse becomes the more difficult he will be to handle. Such a horse may easily damage his wind, and while being lunged he may be too fresh. Hence, he will buck and play, damaging his hocks and fetlock joints.

### *Putting on a head collar*

Every young horse feels, more or less, surprised and frightened when being broken. Lack of understanding and impatience on the trainer's side can do permanent damage to the horse's confidence in humans, especially at this early stage of training. To obtain good results the trainer must have unlimited patience.

When trying to halter a shy young horse, one should never walk straight towards his head on entering the box. Instead one should talk gently to the horse, never raising the voice, and avoid making sudden movements with the arms. Walk slowly, step by step, towards the horse's withers and try to pat the horse on the shoulder, at the same time gently putting a rope around his neck with the right hand at the height of the withers. Then try to reach the end of the rope with the left hand. Now, someone else must hold this rope while you put on the head collar. It is advisable, for the time being, to leave the head collar on, even underneath the bridle, if the horse is head shy or difficult to catch.

*Fig. 154*
Putting on a headcollar.

### *Putting on the bridle*

The difficulty in the beginning is that the horse will not open his mouth when one tries to put in the bit. One can trick the horse by putting some oats or carrots in the left hand on top of the bit. The horse will open his mouth to take the reward. At the same time one has the opportunity to put the bit into his mouth. Besides, a good trainer always carries a reward in his pocket. The so-called "training reward system" is a very important part of schooling, as it develops the necessary friendly relationship between horse and trainer.

An extremely head shy horse will become frightened when the bridle is pulled over his eyes and ears. I have successfully practised

*Fig. 155*
A young horse will learn – without any force being required – to stand tied up if the lead to the ring at the wall is tied, not to the ring itself, but to a twine loop which is then knotted into the ring. Should the horse panic, the twine will break and the horse will not get hurt or "hang". Since the horse will not feel frustrated he will give up and stand, maybe after breaking the twine a few times.

*Fig. 157*
Chain lead.

*Fig. 158*
If a horse pulls too much when being led, loop the chain part of the lead around his nose, over the nasal bone.

*Fig. 156*
If a young horse is tied so that the lead is tied directly to the wall, he might shy, or try to free himself for no good reason. The lead, or the halter, may break and the horse will "hang", pull and hurt his legs or damage his nerve centre at the poll and become permanently headshy.

*Fig. 159*
To undo this loop simply ease the lead and the loop will slip off the horse's nose, then pull the lead through fully, back to the normal position.

the following method: position yourself with your back to the horse's breast, with his neck over your right shoulder. For the time being take the brow band off the bridle altogether. Open the buckle of the left cheekpiece. Push the right part of the bridle around the horse's neck, close to the withers. Then gradually move with the bridle in the direction of the horse's head. Put the bit into his mouth, while the right part of the bridle with the headpiece is still in your right hand and around the horse's neck. Now move the bridle gently forward until it is behind the horse's ears, where on the near side it can be buckled. In this manner work the bridle from the withers forward towards the head, without having to pull it over the horse's eyes and ears.

*Fig. 160*
Putting a bridle on a headshy horse.

Special care should be taken when closing and opening the cheekpiece, as the slightest movement next to the horse's head and eyes may upset him. When the buckle of the cheekpiece does not open easily *push* the strap; do not pull it.

After practising this a few times one can leave the brow band *only* on the right-hand side of the bridle while using the same method of putting it on. When the bridle is in its proper position, catch the brow band in as well when closing the buckle of the cheekpiece.

The same technique applies when taking off the bridle if the horse is very head shy. Do not pull off the bridle over the horse's ears, but first open the top buckle of the left cheekpiece. Slip the brow band off on the near side. Wait until the horse opens his mouth, then let the bit slip *gently* out of the mouth.

*Fig. 161*
Later on, also include the browband.

*Taking off the bridle*

When taking off the bridle never act like some people, who do not take the trouble to open the noseband and who merely stand in front of the horse, pull off the bridle with a jerk and chuck the bit out of the horse's mouth. I have seen people do this, even with a double bit, without opening the curb chain, which is very painful to the horse and one of the reasons why a horse becomes head shy.

When taking off a bridle, stand beside the horse under his neck. Catch both cheekpieces,

*Fig. 162*
Before putting on the saddle, get the horse used to a folded woollen blanket placed quietly on his back. After a while put it on with a little more vigour.

*lift* the neckpiece forward over the ears, wait until the horse opens his mouth and then let the bit slide down gently *without* letting it touch the horse's teeth.

This way, one will gain the horse's confidence and never have any problems with head shyness.

*Putting on the saddle*

The first tacking up, and backing should be done in the horse's box, provided the box is large enough and the ceiling not too low. The horse is more relaxed and confident in the security of the familiar surrounding of his box. In the beginning I always use a folded woollen blanket underneath the saddle. Before putting on the saddle one should get the horse used to the folded blanket on his back. It should be put on, and taken off, from both sides a couple of times each day. If the horse accepts this without fuss and stands relaxed one can start putting on the saddle as well.

Carry the saddle over your right arm, holding the girths in your left hand. Approach the horse slowly; keep talking to him and gently put the girths over his withers first. Let them slide down, very gently, the other side and try to avoid touching the horse's right foreleg. If one carelessly should suddenly drop the girths the horse might easily become upset owing to them unexpectedly dangling down. Bend down carefully and fish for the girths, either with one hand, or, to extend the length of your arm, use the hook of a walking stick, avoiding excess movement. All the time keep the other hand on the saddle so it will not slip or fall and frighten the horse.

Be careful not to tighten the girths too much at once, and do it very gradually, as it will slightly interfere with the breathing. Some older horses blow themselves up in self-defence against the girths being tightened with a sudden jerk. By such unskilled handling the horse acquires "saddle and girths force", which is a bad habit and one which can remain indefinitely.

*Fig. 163*
"Fishing" for the girths.

A young horse who has never experienced the girths will usually stand quiet, unaware of the tight feeling that they will give him. But, once the horse starts moving, then he will certainly feel the pressure of the girth on his lungs and may start bucking. For this reason one should use a girth with an elastic *division*. On a young horse one should only fasten the girth fairly loosely, using at first a breastplate to keep the saddle in its proper place. This is very important as a slipping saddle can give the young horse a fright he will not forget for a long time.

Having fastened the girth then leave the horse on his own in the box for 45 minutes or so that he may get used to the saddle and snaffle (both of which should be old, in case the horse might rub them against the wall trying to get rid of them). The reins are removed from the bridle altogether for safety reasons.

Remember, the horse is left in the box loose only with saddle and bridle. *Never* practise the antiquated and harmful technique of tying the horse up with side reins. *No* breaking bit *nor* tying up with cross reins is necessary.

While the horse is loose in the box, after about 15 minutes one should tighten the girth a few more holes – on the *off-side* – in order to prevent the skin from stretching on one side only. Run your fingers downwards between girth and skin, making sure there are no wrinkles.

When taking off the saddle, one must, again, be very careful with the girth. One should always strive to avoid any indelicate movement in order to gain the horse's confidence. Loosen the girth carefully and do not let it slam against the horse's foreleg; it might frighten him and make him jump. Instead, lift your left leg and catch the dropping girths with your foot. (One should, in fact, always use this method.)

This entire procedure I repeat three times per day for about a week before mounting the horse for the first time.

During this week I also carry out another exercise: stand on a wooden box beside the horse, close to the saddle, on the near- as well as on the off-side. This will make the horse familiar with the height of the rider. By nature the horse is more frightened of the unexpected

*Fig. 164*
Never let the girths drop down, but guide them down with the left foot.

*Fig. 165*
Familiarising the horse with the height of a rider.

*Fig. 166*
Lie over the horse's back, petting the horse and talking to him.

*Fig. 167*
The horse feels the rider's weight, spread equally on his back.

height of the rider on his back than of his weight. This dates back to ancient times when horses were running wild and had to be aware of prowling animals who usually attacked by leaping on to the horse's back. This is why most harness horses have to wear blinkers, which prevent them seeing what is happening behind and above them.

BACKING THE HORSE

As soon as the horse is no longer afraid of the height of a rider standing on the wooden box, the trainer may then attempt to get the horse used to weight on his back.

One should get a leg up and lie over the saddle. The horse should stand still and relaxed, held loosely by an assistant. With a highly strung and sensitive animal, first lie over his bare back without using a saddle at all. The horse will then feel the weight of the rider spread more softly all over his back and will accept it more easily, because the pressure of the saddle would only be on both sides of the vertebral column. All the time keep talking to the horse and pat him to relax and distract his mind from what is going on. If the horse does not seem to stiffen up he may be led around in the box, but the assistant should not take too strong a hold of the lead. If the horse shows any signs of resentment to the weight on his back, slide down gently to regain his confidence. After a few minutes one can pursue this exercise and it will not be long before the horse willingly accepts this mounting in the box.

After a little while, with the assistant still in attendance, lift your right leg across the horse's back, taking care not to touch the croup, and slide carefully down into the saddle (of course, the strirrups have been removed). First, sit bent forward, then straighten up slowly and very carefully.

Make the horse acquainted with the tacking up and mounting process for some time before actually starting to ride him in the lungeing ring, held by an assistant on the lungeing rein. The horse will, of course, be schooled throughout this period. One should lunge him daily for 30 minutes with the Chambon and also practise liberty exercises "work on foot". In this way the necessary muscles are developed slowly, enabling the horse to carry the weight of the rider later on without any effort. There are, regrettably, some trainers who are forced to shorten this basic schooling on account of the amount of time and money involved, although it is more often than not because of lack of patience on their part.

To school a horse to perfection one cannot neglect this most important fundamental stage.

## MOUNTING AND DISMOUNTING

As we are now discussing the mounting of a young horse, I will mention a few fundamental points on this subject. When breaking a young horse one should always get a leg up. Later on, when the horse is well used to being mounted and ridden, he has to be made accustomed to being mounted with the rider's foot in the stirrup.

In the beginning this should be done from a mounting block while an assistant holds the horse on the cheek strap of the noseband without interfering with bit or reins. While the rider puts his foot and weight into the left stirrup the assistant should put some weight on to the right stirrup leather. In this manner the horse will not get off balance due to the rider's weight while being mounted.

When mounting, every horse must stand rock-still under all circumstances. The horse should be taught this from the beginning. First the rider should make sure that the horse is standing evenly on all four legs, or with the near fore foot slightly forwards. This is necessary to maintain balance, otherwise the horse has to move forwards or backwards to re-balance himself under the additional weight of the rider.

Nervous and sensitive horses often turn away before the rider gets a chance to put his foot into the stirrup. This is either an example of bad education or of a rider putting his foot too far through the stirrup, irritating the horse with the toe of his boot and causing him to move away.

*Fig. 168*
In the beginning always get a leg up.

Some horses have the bad habit of moving backwards while the rider is mounting. These horses are afraid and should therefore never be punished, as this would do more harm. It is useful to allow the horse to go backwards until he stops by himself. Then rein back the horse a few more steps. If this is done for a few consecutive days the horse will become very reluctant to move backwards, since this is an unnatural movement for horses.

Many horses do not like to stand still when being mounted because they are afraid of being jolted by the rider's weight suddenly dropping with a thud on to their backs, often at the rear of the saddle, which is more painful still. If the rider mounts correctly every horse will stand still, no matter in which environment.

*How to mount correctly*

(i) The horse must stand well on the bit. The rider holds both reins in the left hand, the right rein slightly shorter, bending the head and neck slightly to the off-side. If the horse should then try to move on, his body will be forced to move towards the

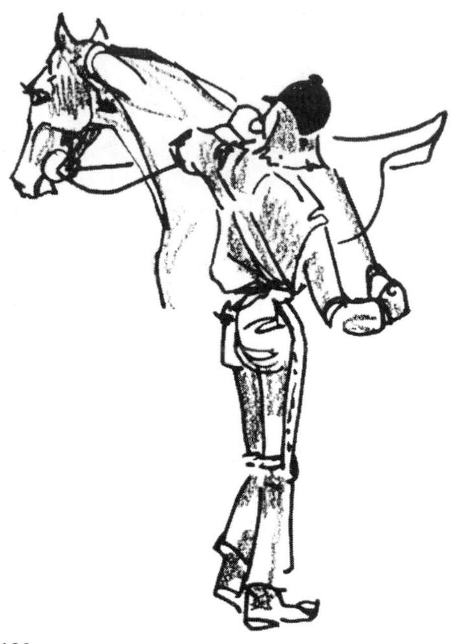

*Fig. 169*
Before mounting a horse, make it stand square and on the bit, right rein tighter.

*Fig. 170*
Mount, without touching the horse with the left toe.

*Fig. 171*
Land on the knees, put the right foot into the stirrup, do not sit down yet, and move off.

*Fig. 172*
After a few strides, gently slide into the saddle.

rider, promoting easy mounting. Should the left rein be shorter the horse would turn his body away from the rider, this being particularly dangerous if the rider has his left foot already in the stirrup, because if the horse should shy away the stirrup leather may get stuck in the spring bar.

(ii) One now swings the right leg high across the croup, without touching it, and puts the right foot into the stirrup, *without* sitting down in the saddle.

(iii) Ride on, standing in *both* stirrups in the forward seat, gripping firmly with the knees.

(iv) After a few strides gently slide into the saddle and straighten up. Using this technique the horse has to carry the rider's weight for the first few strides on his shoulders instead of on his back and loin muscles.

To avoid dropping into the saddle use this technique also when being given a leg up; land on your knees first and sit down only *after* moving on a few strides.

*How to dismount correctly*

Keep the horse on the bit. Take both reins into the left hand, the right rein being slightly shorter than the left one; pat the horse's neck. Place the left hand on to the horse's neck and the right hand on to the pommel of the saddle. At the same time take *both* feet out of the stirrups. (If the left foot is kept in the stirrup, and if the horse should shy away, he could drag the rider with the rider's left foot caught in the stirrup.) Now press up with stretched arms and swing the right leg across the croup (without touching it with the boot) and dismount gently.

One can often see riders dismount in the most dangerous ways. The above-mentioned is not only the correct and safest way to dismount but also the most comfortable one for the horse.

FREE EXERCISE

Horses in training should be turned out loose every day for a short time if there is a suitable field available near the stable. This prevents the horse from getting bored in the stable, improves his appetite, loosens all the muscles naturally (without the rider's weight) and completely refreshes the horse.

After horses are brought in from grass, free exercise is a useful aid in making the transition from the free life out in the field to the isolated stay in the box. Natural exercise makes training much easier and more effective.

However, an hour on grass daily is enough, otherwise the horse will eat too much grass, his stomach will get blown up and this will interfere with the horse's breathing in work.

In winter never turn the horse out early in the morning. At that time of day the grass is still covered with dew or even frost. This could result in colic. In winter and in bad weather one should cover the horse with a waterproof blanket to keep the back muscles warm and the horse dry and clean when rolling. In the summer it is advisable to let the horse out in the early morning or in the evening because midday is usually too warm and there are too many flies which are most unpleasant company for the horse.

Horses who are shod should not be let out with other horses as they might kick and hurt each other.

Although the horse is turned out only for a short time, the grass he will eat will affect the normal amount of stable feeding: how much so will depend on various factors. For example, in the spring and summertime the grass contains a much higher percentage of protein, therefore the normal amount of stable feeding must be cut down to prevent overfeeding of protein. Also, the quality of the grass (depending on climate and soil of each country) and the amount of grazing the horse gets will make a difference, as well as the varying temperaments of horses – some will only graze, others will exercise most of the time.

If a suitable field is not available one can let

the horse run loose in the riding arena before riding. Most horses are so delighted with the freedom that they buck and play around, risking splints or other damage. This can be prevented if the owner bothers to put on four brushing and overreach boots, which takes only a few minutes. It is most annoying if the horse goes lame on account of an injury incurred in the field, especially during the showjumping season.

*Out on grass*

Contrary to the rest of Europe, in several English speaking countries it is customary to turn horses out on grass for a long period. The hunters are let out during the summer (after the hunting season) and the showjumpers during the winter or to recover from an illness. But why is this done, and for what benefit? In my opinion there is no logical reason. I cannot help feeling that this so-called "deserved holiday for the horse" is used, in many cases, as an excuse to avoid the trouble of keeping the horse stabled.

A couple of hours daily on grass, covered with a waterproof blanket, I feel is adequate, because even in the off-season the showjumping horse should be ridden daily to prevent weakening of the muscles and a loss of general physical fitness. Otherwise, if turned out for a few months, the horse will suffer a serious setback in his training and take a long time before he is fit for serious training. That is why at the beginning of the showjumping season so many horses run out of breath half way through the course. To compete with horses in this unfit condition is very bad for their hearts and lungs and their health in general.

But in spite of all this many people still turn out their horses. Horses which were in the summer covered with a blanket in the stable are in some cases suddenly turned out without one, just at the time of year when the weather is getting rougher. Regrettably, some people do not even bother to check on their horses from time to time. It often happens that horses are left alone for months without proper supervision. I have even seen clipped horses in a snowstorm out in the field, day and night, without shelter or blanket and without sufficient water.

Besides, many owners do not realise that the horse feels lonely when completely on his own. When used to the company of humans the horse will pine just like a dog when left alone.

However, people who do decide to turn out their horses for a long period should look after them. Take their hind shoes off and re-shoe their forefeet at least every two months, otherwise the horn will grow too long and the shoe will grow into the horn of the hoof. A neglected hoof will, on account of the unnatural slope of foot-angle, put a disastrous strain upon the tendons. The feet of horses which are turned out on grass should be treated with special care. In the winter the deficiency of protein in the grass should be made up by additional feeding.

CHAPTER SIX

# LUNGEING

CORRECT lungeing with the Chambon improves *every* horse. Lungeing is a necessary, as well as an important, part of the training of a showjumper. But, regrettably, it does more harm than good when executed incorrectly. If the horse is just running around on the lunge, then lungeing is a waste of time. Using side reins, crossed reins or double lunge will have a bad effect on the horse's muscles and mouth. However, with proper equipment and when executed correctly, lungeing is beneficial for the horse.

It is a great pity that some riders are unaware of the fact that lungeing is as much an art as riding. They leave this important part of the training to the groom. Most grooms, however, are overfaced with this task, because one of the most important points of correct lungeing is the contact between the trainer's hand and the horse's mouth. It should be the same as when riding, and can only be achieved if the lungeing whip is used with the same effect as leg aids are used when riding.

Without sending on the horse properly, lungeing is not only a waste of time but can do harm, because the horse will go too much on the forehand, will bend his body too much laterally inwards (more so when lungeing on the easy side), and in doing this will fall over the shoulder to the outside. Horses are easier to bend on one side than on the other, mostly the near-side, depending on the position the embryo took in the mother's womb.

If a horse is *not* sent on to the required degree, even lungeing with the Chambon can not improve the horse.

## THE CHAMBON

The Chambon originates from the French Army Equestrian School at Saumur and is used extensively in France and Italy. The Chambon is, in my opinion, the proper lungeing equipment. It is of vital importance when schooling a horse in the Natural Training Method. It is especially beneficial for the young showjumper, because it develops the muscles needed for jumping, especially in the back and quarters. It helps to make the horse supple and relaxed, corrects ewe necks and hollow backs and activates the hindlegs to establish a natural balance.

The Chambon works naturally without force. If used on nervous and highly strung horses it will make them settle down and enjoy their work. On lazy horses with lack of impulsion, however, it has quite the opposite effect.

### *Equipment*

The Chambon consists of:

(i) the headpiece, which will be fastened under the headpiece of the bridle;

(ii) a side rein or similar leather strap with an inlaid rubber ring for flexibility, passing between the forelegs and fastened to the girths;

(iii) a nylon string 1·35 metres long with a snaphook at each end.

(iv) a bridle with German snaffle and fitted with two rubber discs;

(v) a lungeing rein 6 metres long, having a bolt snaphook *without* a swivel to prevent tangling. (The handpiece of the lunge should have three loops: during the first month put the hand into the first loop, lungeing at full length. During the second month of training use the middle loop, and from then on the third loop.) The lunge is then at its shortest permissible length.

*Fig. 173*
The headpiece of the Chambon.

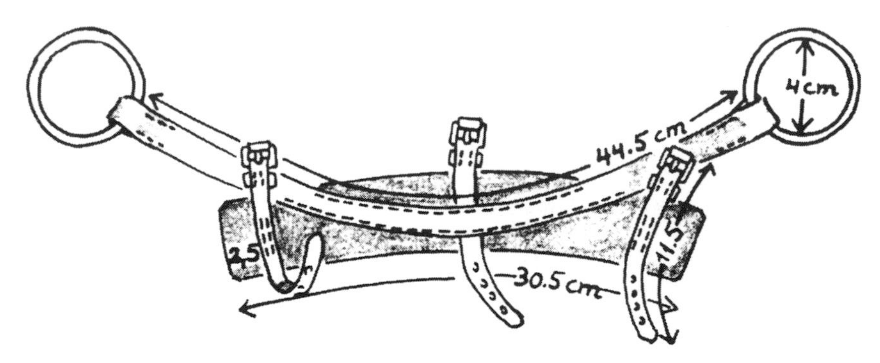


*Fig. 175*
The headpiece showing straps and dimensions.

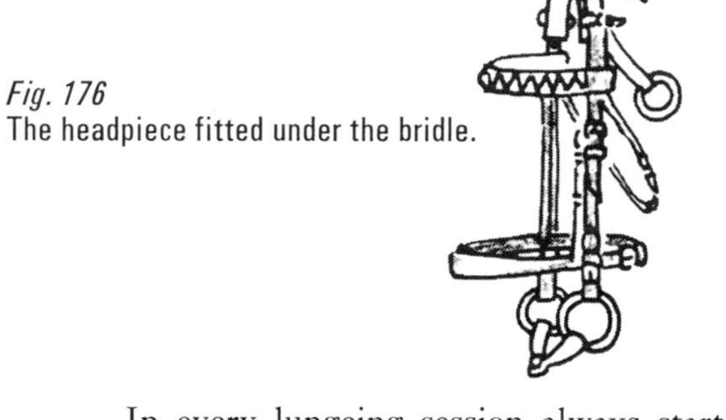

*Fig. 176*
The headpiece fitted under the bridle.

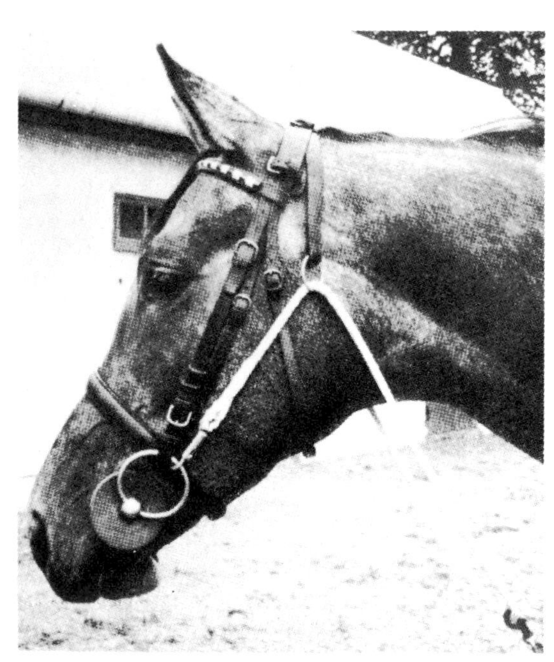

*Fig. 174*
The Chambon fitted.

In every lungeing session always start with the lungeing rein at full length, gradually shortening it to the length required for whatever stage the horse is being schooled;

(vi) a lungeing whip of 2·5 metres in length, with a lash of 1·8 metres. Only then is it possible to reach the horse's hocks with the end of the lash without having to step forward;

(vii) brushing boots on all four legs;

(viii) overreach boots;

(ix) a lungeing ring, diameter 12·5 metres.

When lunged with the Chambon the horse will feel its effect *only* when he tries to lift his head higher than normal, and consequently tightens the string of the Chambon. The

*Fig. 177*
Nylon string with clips (use light ones).

*Fig. 178*
Side rein.

*Fig. 179*
Handpiece of the lunge.

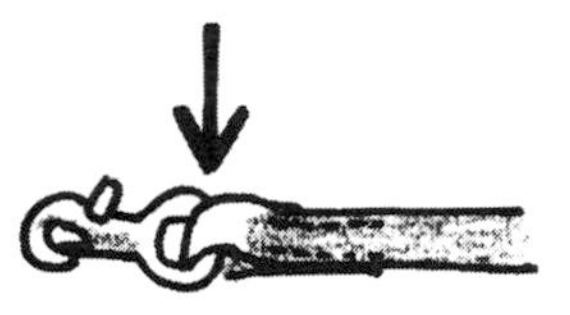

*Fig. 180*
Bolt snap hook without swivel. A buckle and strap is too time consuming when changing rein.

Chambon will only limit the movement of the horse's head and neck in an upwards direction . . . the horse will have every freedom to move head and neck sideways, forwards and downwards.

Even in restricting the upwards movement of the head with the Chambon there will *never* be a *backwards* pressure on the mouth. If the horse lifts his head higher than normal the bit will move higher up into the horse's mouth; simultaneously the horse will feel a gentle pressure on the nerve centre underneath the headpiece of the Chambon. This gentle pressure will not hurt the horse in the least. It is a very gentle aid which most horses accept without resistance. The horse's reaction to this will be that he lowers his head automatically. The snaffle will then slip downwards into its original position. This movement of the bit encourages the horse to chew the bit.

In view of this, one will realise that there can *never* be a backwards pressure on the horse's mouth, no matter whether he is impetuous, plunges about or carries his head too high. One will never need a martingale on a horse schooled with the Chambon, but will have a well-muscled and balanced horse with an easy mouth.

I would like to emphasise: the Chambon is designed for lungeing *only*; it is not suitable to ride with.

The length of the Chambon is altered by making the side rein (or leather strap) shorter or longer. Normally the nylon string of the Chambon should be quite tight when the horse's nose and hip are on the same horizontal level.

On young horses, who have not worn the Chambon before, it is fitted loosely, so that the horse only feels it when carrying his head extremely high. In time the horse will become accustomed to the Chambon, which can then be tightened step-by-step until the horse just about feels it when carrying his ears on a horizontal level with his withers.

Once the horse is used to the Chambon start

the lungeing session (30 minutes) with the Chambon in the normal position. During the last 15 minutes, tighten it slightly so that the horse must really use his back when being sent on.

Only start to canter the horse on the lunge after about two months, never sooner. Loosen the Chambon again, because in the beginning every horse will carry its head high in the canter. In time shorten the Chambon, step-by-step, until it has reached the normal position while cantering.

Later on, however, it is left to the trainer's judgement to find out the suitable length of the Chambon, which will vary for each horse. If the Chambon is not fitted tight enough, after the initial three months, it cannot have the desired result.

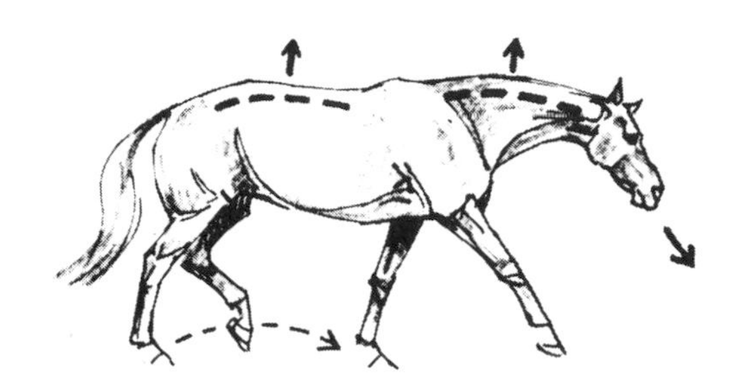

*Fig. 181*
A horse which has been lunged with Chambon. The correct muscles have been developed.

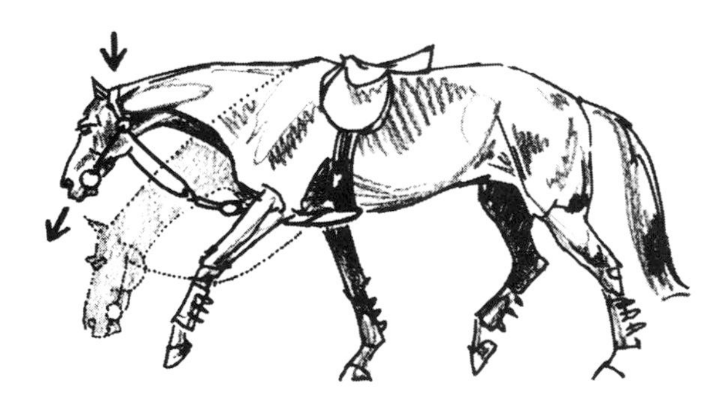

*Fig. 182*
The horse has every freedom to move his head forward-downwards and sideways.

*Fig. 183*
Muscles of a spoiled or badly developed, unbroken horse.

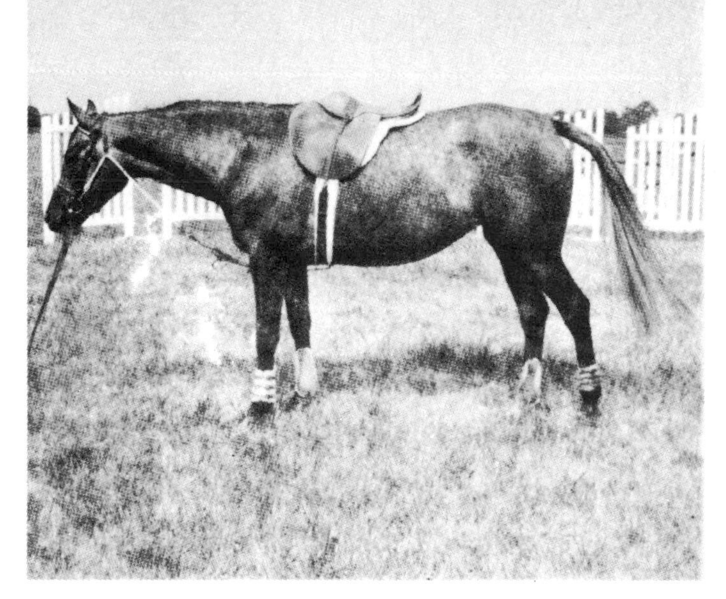

*Fig. 184*
A three-year-old filly at an early stage of training. She has been lunged with the Chambon for about two months. Standing relaxed like this, she does not feel the Chambon.

*Fig. 185*
When she raises her head she feels the restriction of the Chambon.

*Fig. 186*
When she walks forward she is completely relaxed, nose pointing forward-downwards. The Chambon is ineffective. The arrows indicate where the correct muscles are being developed.

THE LUNGEING RING

Having a permanent, or semi-permanent, ring to lunge horses in is of enormous importance, especially for young horses. If possible one should never lunge a young horse in the open as this teaches him to pull and run out. With no barrier the horse will fall out over the shoulder or jump around, hurting his legs and mouth.

The lungeing ring prevents the horse from learning these bad habits, because he is kept within the barrier. The horse will never learn what pulling means, but will move on his own four legs without having a chance to lie on the "fifth" leg – the trainer's hand. Neither will such a horse later on pull on the rider's hand.

A lungeing ring made of poles and barrels is very convenient; it can easily be shifted or removed.

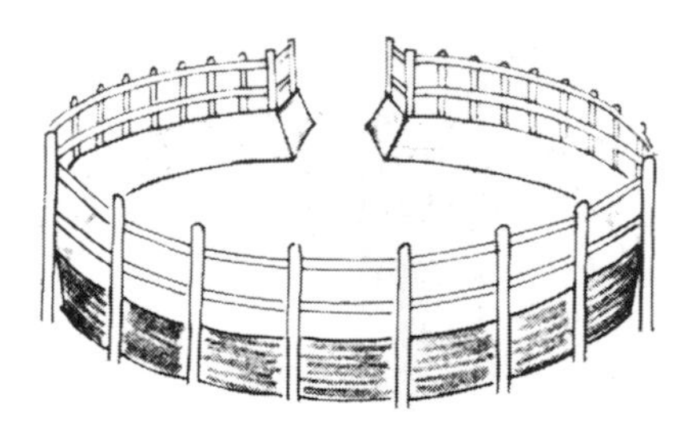

*Fig. 188*
A permanent lungeing ring.

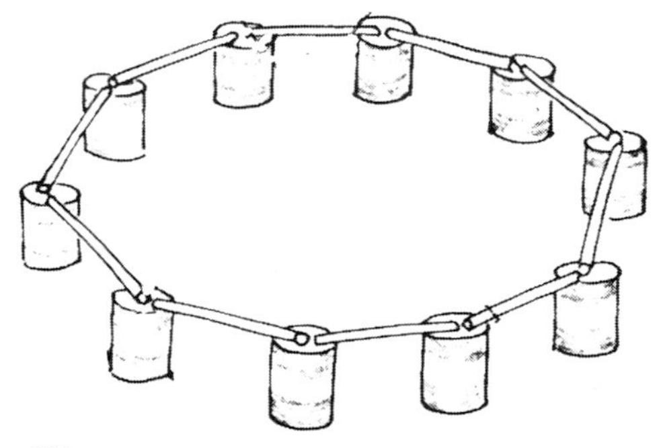

*Fig. 187*
A semi-permanent lungeing ring, average diameter 12·50 metres.

If the lungeing ring cannot be built in an indoor school or outdoor arena, some fine cinders or coarse sand, mixed with shavings, should be put down on the track to save the horse's tendons and to keep him from slipping or injuring his legs.

In Australia most studs and racing stables have a "permanent" lungeing ring. The ground is well drained or the ring is covered. The barrier is usually over 2 metres high to keep the horse from jumping out of the ring. It has sloped timber kicking boards, 1·2 metres high, so that the horse cannot hurt himself and the sand cannot work itself out of the ring.

*Where* one is lungeing the horse is the deciding factor on how to attach the lunge itself. If one is forced to lunge in an open field without a lungeing ring, never use the lunge on the snaffle ring, because when the horse starts pulling – which he certainly will – the snaffle will slide through the mouth and hurt and spoil the bars. Use a cavasson, but make sure to put the lunge into the side ring, never into the centre ring, because the whole cavasson would move around the horse's head and could hurt his eyes.

When lungeing in a lungeing ring one attaches the lunge to the inside (snaffle) ring.

People often attach the lunge to the snaffle ring in the wrong way: they either thread it through the inside snaffle ring and hook it to the outside ring, or hook it on to the centre of the leather strap, joining both snaffle rings. Both methods are incorrect and give a very unpleasant pressure on the horse's tongue, bars and the corners of his mouth. Also the two snaffle rings are pressed together, which forces the snaffle to work as a nutcracker and make the centre joint pinch the palate. This makes the horse move with an open mouth.

*Fig. 189*
(*Left*) when lungeing in a lungeing ring, the lunge is hooked into the inside snaffle ring to start making the horse's mouth; (*centre*) wrong: the joint of the bit hits the upper palate, the horse will go with an open mouth; (*right*) this will have the same effect, also put more pressure onto the outside ring.

THE LUNGEING WHIP

The trainer must realise that the horse will react to the slightest movement of the whip, whether it is intentional or not. Therefore the trainer has to control the action of the whip and be sure that it will only touch the horse where he intends it to do so.

A good way of learning how to use the whip is, for example, to practise against a mark on a tree and check that the end of the lash touches the mark. Bear in mind that using the lungeing whip correctly is an art and one which needs a lot of practise in order not to upset the horse.

The degree of sending on depends largely on the sensitiveness of each horse. Never use the whip on the horse's body, because whip marks are a sign of bad horsemanship.

The horse must be taught to respect the whip and to respond to it. This is *only* possible when the whip is of the required length and the trainer is able to use it correctly, yet delicately. It is imperative to apply the whip aids at the right time and in the appropriate places, because when ridden the horse will be schooled on the same principles when being taught to obey to similar aids: the leg aids.

The rules of using the whip are as follows:

(i) point the whip towards the horse's hip when the horse is circling correctly;

(ii) if the horse makes the circle too small, point the whip towards the shoulder;

(iii) to increase the pace, move the whip from the horse's hocks towards the saddle and if he does not respond touch the hocks gently;

(iv) lower the whip if you want the horse to slow down the pace;

(v) no matter on which rein you are lungeing, always hold the lunge in the left hand and the whip in the right hand. Usually the left hand is not as strong and is, therefore, more sensitive than the right one, allowing a finer contact. When lungeing to the right the whip should cross underneath the lunge;

(vi) to teach the horse to come into the centre of the ring (to change rein or at the end of the lungeing session) use the aid of a soothing voice, saying "whoa, whoa"; lift

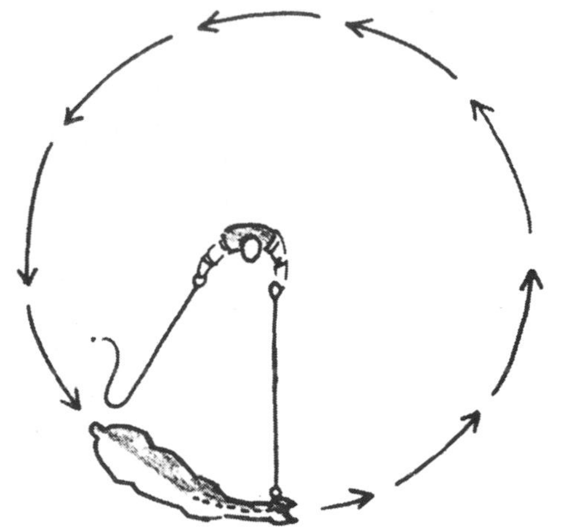

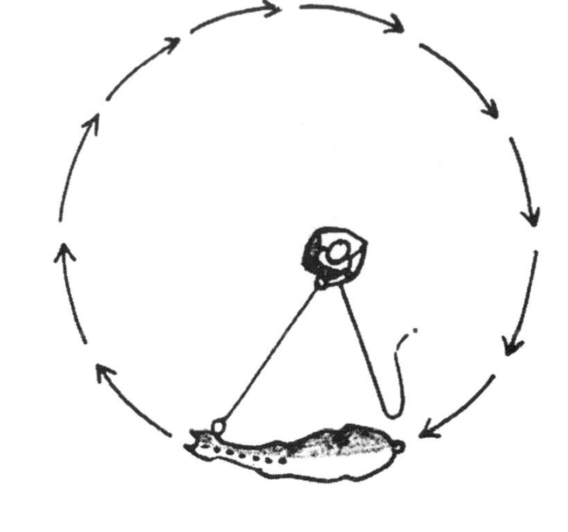

*Fig. 190*
(*Left*) lungeing on the left-hand rein; (*right*) lungeing on the right-hand rein – the lunge is still in the left hand.

up the right elbow with an exaggerated movement and put the whip underneath the left arm. Reward the horse. This movement and the tone of voice is quickly observed and understood by the horse as a signal to come into the centre of the ring. Never pull on the lunge to make the horse come into the centre. Gather the lunge gradually in a couple of big loops and make sure the horse does not step on it;

(vii) while the horse is coming into the centre take care that the whip underneath the left arm does not fall, because then you must bend down to pick it up and this will scare most horses. Besides, the horse might step on the whip and break it;

(viii) still standing on the near side of the horse, hook the lunge into the off-side snaffle ring and only then move over to the other

*Fig. 191*
How to hold the whip when calling the horse into the centre.

*Fig. 192*
How to take over the whip when moving off on the left-hand rein.

side of the horse. Stand still for a little while before allowing the horse to move off on the other rein. This pause is most important to relax the horse. Then let the horse move on quietly in a walk, otherwise you teach him the bad habit of breaking into a trot or even canter. When the horse is moving towards the track yield the lunge gradually and fluently, without interfering with the horse's mouth. At the same time put your right arm behind your back (when lungeing on the left rein) and take the whip from underneath the left arm. This way it becomes a less conspicuous movement.

*Never* move the whip in front of the horse's face as this would frighten him.

## HOW TO LUNGE

### *Preliminary lungeing*

A nervous young horse who has never been lunged before has to learn to go around in a circle. For the first few times use a cavasson (with the lunge fastened on the side ring), because the excited horse might suddenly try to turn or change rein. When moving off, always face in the same direction as the horse and walk on together with him, keeping the whip behind the horse and yielding the lunge very gradually.

Most horses are less flexible on one side (often the off-side). On this stiff side an assistant might have to lead the horse around the circle. If one is working the young horse in a lungeing ring he will, after a couple of days, be confident enough to move out to the track by himself and go around willingly.

Never forget to use the voice, the most powerful medium to improve the co-operation and mutual understanding between horse and trainer. Use the voice in a low tone and make repetitive sounds to calm the horse and make him slow down. Use a higher tone to increase his pace. The horse will soon connect these sounds with a certain task to perform.

Only when the horse has learned these basic rules of lungeing should one start to use the Chambon, adjusted loosely. First try to get the horse lazy and let him move along the circle line in a quiet manner. When lungeing a young horse, a good opportunity presents itself to make the horse used to the saddle. Occasionally one can then also attach the stirrups and let the horse become familiar with the irons dangling against his sides.

### *Using the Chambon*

When the horse is playful and fresh in the beginning of the lungeing session do not interfere with the lunge, as the horse's mouth and/or his legs could get injured. Let the horse play; he will settle down quickly himself. Remember that the horse has been standing in the stable for possibly the last 23 hours. Therefore it is only a natural reaction to play around a bit when finally taken out of the stable. For the first five to ten minutes one should let the horse simply go around without asking for impulsion, lateral bending, etc. First the horse has to loosen his muscles. If that is *not* permitted one creates tension and resistance.

Never lunge for more than 30 minutes at a time. Working in a small circle is very strenuous – especially for the hind fetlocks and hocks, which are the hardest worked joints of all. An overworked hock will become stiff and make it

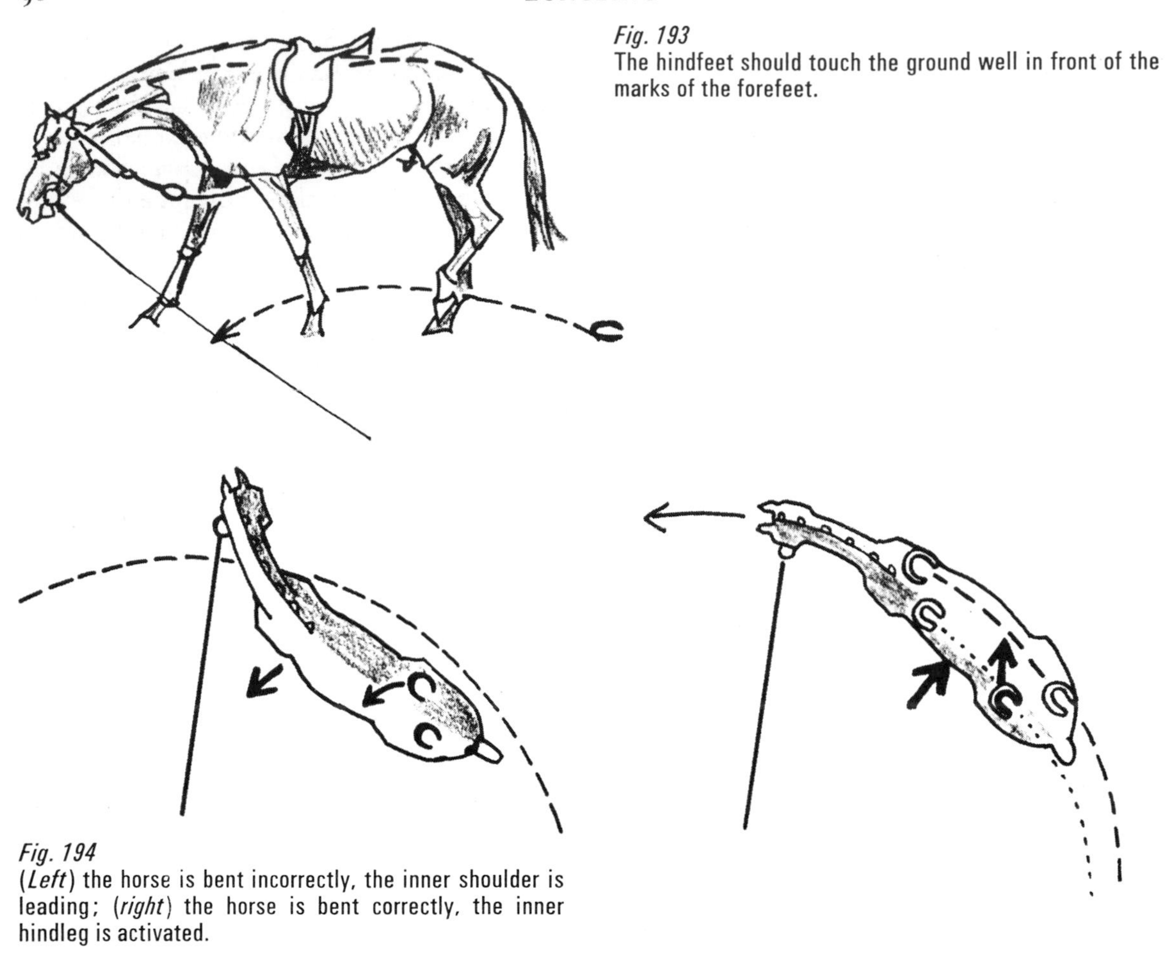

*Fig. 193*
The hindfeet should touch the ground well in front of the marks of the forefeet.

*Fig. 194*
(*Left*) the horse is bent incorrectly, the inner shoulder is leading; (*right*) the horse is bent correctly, the inner hindleg is activated.

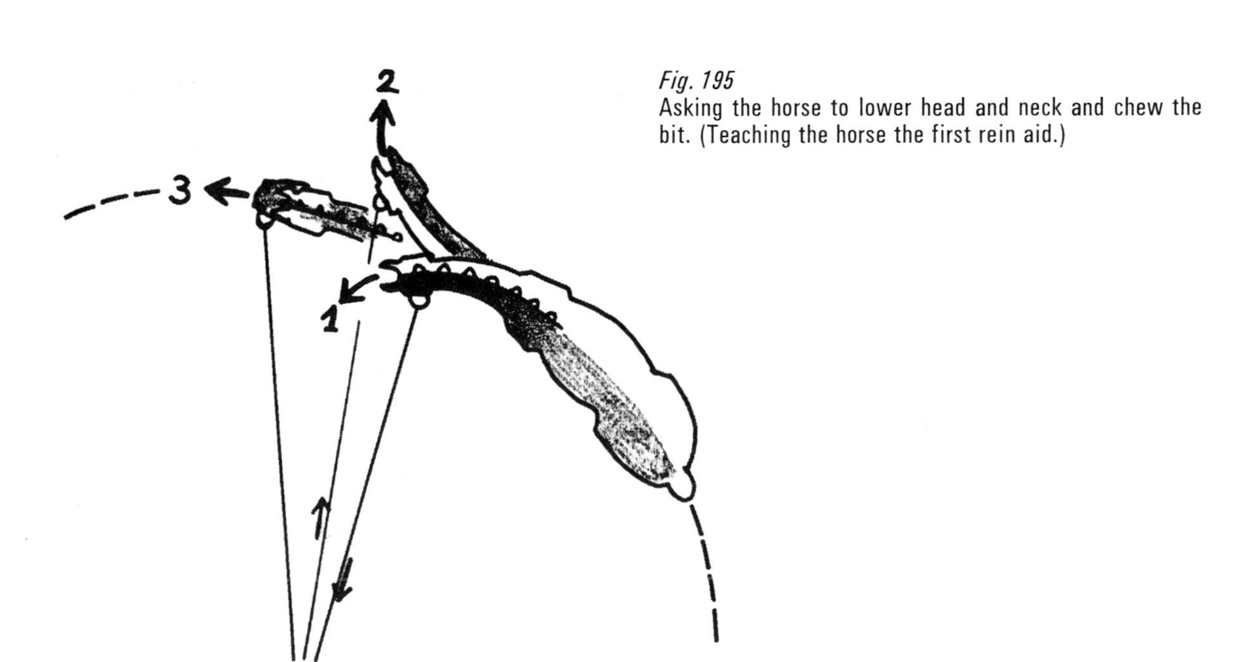


*Fig. 195*
Asking the horse to lower head and neck and chew the bit. (Teaching the horse the first rein aid.)

impossible for the horse to have full use of the hocks at take-off.

By nature most horses are stiffer on the off-side. Therefore always start lungeing on the left-hand rein (near-side). After five minutes change rein and lunge for ten minutes on the right-hand rein (off-side). This is followed by five minutes on the left, and another ten minutes on the right-hand rein. If the horse one is training is stiff on the near-side, the opposite applies. Always start on the weaker side, but work the stiff side more.

Start lungeing at a walk, making sure that the horse walks freely with active hindlegs. The hindfeet should touch the ground in front of the marks of the forefeet. This is essential, not only to improve the walk, but the other paces as well. After a few minutes brisk walking exercise point the whip from the hocks towards the saddle in order to make the horse proceed at a slow trot.

Many horses are unable to bend their body laterally inwards according to the curvature of the circle line on which they are moving, particularly at a trot or canter. They fall over the shoulder into the circle, shifting their centre of gravity to the inner foreleg. Head and neck are bent to the outside and are used as a "rudder" to maintain balance. When the inner shoulder, instead of the head, is leading, it shows that the horse is unable to bring the inner hindleg underneath his body.

However, when a horse is lunged correctly with the Chambon he will be able, in time, to bend his body laterally inwards and lead with head and neck in the direction where he is going. Simultaneously, the inner hindleg is moving closer to the track of the outer foreleg. This is a sign that the inner hindleg is brought more actively underneath the body. The more the hocks are engaged the more the back muscles will develop and make it easier for the horse to round his back. A horse needs to round his back to increase his balance and for jumping as well.

To increase the horse's elasticity the trainer should now and again (not constantly) request the horse to stretch his neck and lower his nose downwards and forward.

When teaching the horse to lower his head and flex the lower jaw the trainer should hold the lunge for a few seconds a little tighter, creating a slight tension on the horse's mouth, The horse will bend his head and neck towards the trainer. This tension causes the snaffle to slide gently across the tongue (as if it was a mouth organ). At the same time the rubber ring on the outside of the snaffle pushes against the angles of the lips. This action provokes the horse to make a submission with the lower jaw, whereupon the trainer releases the tension immediately by yielding the lunge. The horse's instant reaction will be that he lowers his head and stretches his neck and back. At the same time he will champ the bit, which brings the parotid glands (saliva) into action, creating a wet and foaming mouth.

This slight sideways bending of head and neck is the preliminary education of the "first rein-aid" (the loose rein), which the young horse is being taught before he is ever ridden ("making" the horse's mouth).

Note the difference between the old school and the Natural Training Method, where lungeing with the Chambon ensures there is never a backwards pressure on the horse's mouth, giving him every freedom with head and neck in a forward-downwards direction. This position of the horse's posture encourages impulsion. It is the most important point if one is to make the lungeing exercise a success (which would not be the case when side reins are being used). With the Chambon, the horse learns easily and is relaxed enough to bend his entire body laterally inwards, from head to tail. Nevertheless, this is not enough. It is most important that the horse not only stretches his neck and lowers his head but also lengthens his strides. Otherwise one could teach the horse to go on the forehand. Therefore the moment the horse flexes the lower jaw, yield the lunge, while sending on the horse with the whip. The horse must lengthen his strides without increasing the pace. Try to achieve this in all three paces.

*Never* allow the horse to drag his hindlegs over the ground, even though he may be stretching his neck downwards, foaming and champing the bit, *he must maintain active impulsion.* Develop the propulsory force in the quarters. This makes lungeing with the Chambon so valuable for schooling a show jumper.

*Transitions*

Bending the horse's neck laterally inwards and the request to him to stretch his neck is also applied during transitions on the lunge. For example, the transition from trot to walk: use a soothing tonc of voicc and at the same time create a slight tension on the horse's mouth. When the horse flexes the lower jaw, yield the lunge completely. Accepting this freedom, the horse will bend head and neck towards the outside of the lungeing ring while lowering his neck. At the same time he will slow down to a walk. But if the horse is reluctant to obey to the voice and lunge aid and only bends his neck outwards, keeping going around in a "pony trot", do not hesitate, but send him on again. This time use the whip a bit more firmly and take a slightly stronger hold on the mouth. The horse must now bend head and neck more towards the trainer. In this position one keeps the horse going around for a few more times before yielding the lunge. The horse will be so relieved that, again, he will bend his neck to the outside of the ring – but now slows down *willingly* into a walk.

However, if the horse is schooled to use his hindlegs properly one should have no trouble in making the transition into a walk. It is often that the horse is allowed to go around at the same sleepy pace, without using his hindlegs actively, which leads to him resisting the transition into a slower pace.

When the horse has reached a more advanced stage of schooling one can reduce the head and neck bending to a minimum. Only a hint of this lungeing rein aid will then make the horse flex the lower jaw and simultaneously stretch his neck and back. Also later on, when ridden and jumped, a slight sideways movement of the rein will guide the horse to turn in the desired direction and no pulling will be necessary.

*Cantering on the lunge*

During the first two months of lungeing never request the horse to canter. If one asks the horse to canter too soon he will get upset and the canter will become disunited. A good trainer has patience, and one day the horse will be supple enough to offer the canter on his own accord. Schooling the horse to canter on must be done out of a slow trot only, never out of a walk or a halt. For example: suppose the horse is trotting on the left-hand rein – one bends his neck a little more to the left, for a few strides, then yields the lunge suddenly and urges the horse with voice and whip to canter on. The horse's reaction to the sudden yielding of the lunge is to bend his head and neck outwards (to the right), thereby transferring his weight to the off hindleg. The off hindleg starts the left canter, and the sudden freedom of the left shoulder allows the near foreleg to move freely forward. This weight transfer is natural and can be observed when horses running free in fields break into a canter. Do not let the horse canter for more than two or three rounds at this stage of schooling.

Never allow the horse while still in a canter or a trot to move towards the centre of the ring when changing rein or at the end of a lungeing session. When the horse is cantering change into a trot first, let him circle a few times, then change into a walk and again circle a few times in a brisk walk. Only after these two transitions have been executed correctly should one ask the horse to come into the centre.

When lungeing one should make many transitions from walk to trot and from trot to walk. Monotonous trotting around will make the horse bored and tired rather than elastic and flexible. In the beginning request the transitions to be executed always at the same spot in the lungeing circle. This makes it easier for the young horse to remember and to understand the trainer's wishes.

*Even paces*

Not every trainer realises how important the pace of a walk really is. Many do not have the

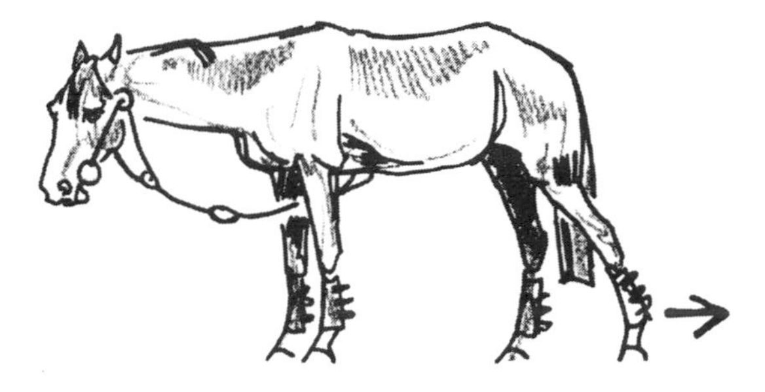

*Fig. 196*
Every horse should be lunged with the Chambon. Improving a weak horse, with a low head carriage, hind-legs trailing . . .

. . . when sent on, the horse will feel the Chambon . . .

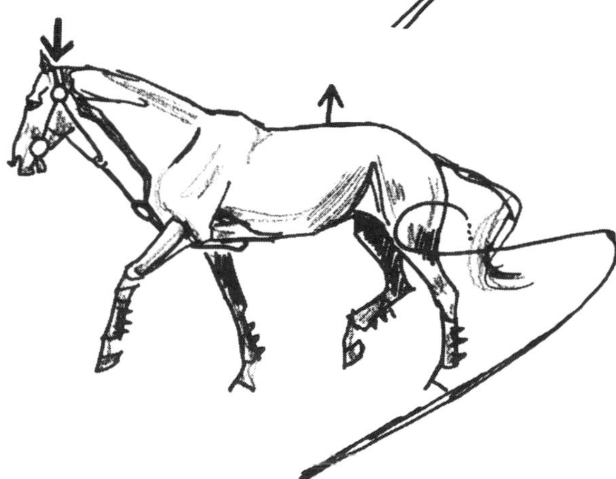

. . . and if increasingly sent on, the horse will have to engage his hocks and his back will come up . . .

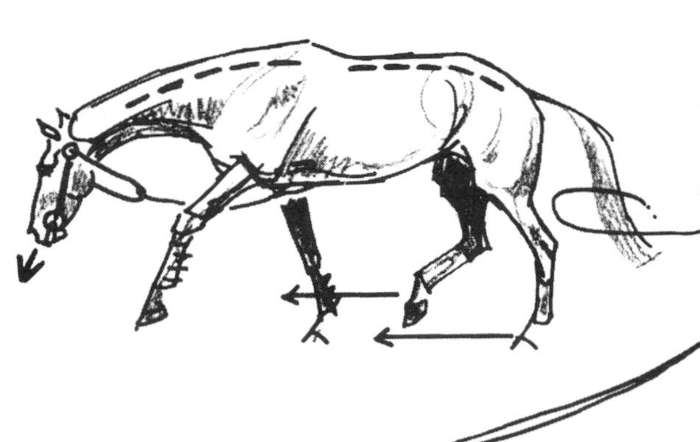

. . . eventually, after the horse has developed the necessary muscles – this may take some time – the same horse will again move with a low head position . . .

. . . but now he will move in balance, with activated quarters, back and neck well rounded.

patience and generally they do not spend enough time on the walk, finding it boring and a waste of time. They are not aware that by neglecting the walk, the elementary pace, they also spoil the free movement of the other two paces. This applies equally to lungeing and riding. When walking the horse must really march on and one should count the rhythm. When trotting the pace must be even, relaxed and slow; the same applies to the canter.

After a couple of weeks lungeing one will notice that the horse goes at an even balanced rhythm, in all paces. In walk he travels at a speed of approximately 100 metres per minute. In trot at about 200 metres per minute and later, in a slow canter, at approximately 250 metres per minute.

If the lungeing has been done correctly, and regularly, the horse will keep an even cadence and pace without rushing or pulling later on when being ridden. This is particularly important for a showjumper.

### THE VALUE OF THE CHAMBON

Trainers who do not have much experience of the Chambon will perhaps ask themselves if the Chambon has any value in schooling those horses who naturally carry their head low, or horses who go too much on the forehand, or if a well-built horse with a good head carriage would not be spoiled when being lunged with the Chambon. To those trainers I can only say: do not hesitate to use the Chambon on *every* horse. Whether it will be a success or not depends entirely on *how* one lunges with the Chambon.

A horse who carries his head very low is often over built, goes too much on the forehand and drags his hindlegs. Such a horse will only benefit from the Chambon if the trainer uses the lungeing whip effectively on the hocks to make the horse use his hindlegs more actively. When a horse is sent on, his immediate reaction is to lift his head, whether he is loose in the field or being lunged. At this moment a horse with a low head carriage will feel the gentle pressure of the Chambon at the poll. He will respond as any other horse by lowering his head and neck, but now he will move in a balanced manner, his pace will become more mobile, with active hindlegs and a rounded back. The hindquarters are strongly engaged, which enables the horse to shift any excessive weight from the forehand to the quarters (this is the main point which has to be improved in such horses). This desired effect of the Chambon can be achieved only if the horse is sent on accurately and in proportion to his degree of sensitivity.

The weakest point in most horses is the back and loins, the reason for many problems. Lungeing with the Chambon will develop the muscles of back, loins and hindquarters, making them supple and strong. It will enable even problem horses to move in balance and so eliminate many difficulties.

Always remember that one of the most essential points of training is *relaxation, while maintaining active impulsion* in all three paces.

After lungeing, when taking off bandages or boots, always take off the overreach boots first. They sometimes are quite difficult to pull off and the horse's hoof might slip, knocking the inside of the other foreleg and may injure it. If the legs are still protected by the bandages nothing can happen. After strenuous work like lungeing the hindlegs should be freshly bandaged with Sandown bandages.

### OTHER LUNGEING TECHNIQUES

There are still many trainers who use different lungeing methods because they are not aware of the advantages of lungeing with the Chambon.

#### *Lungeing with side reins*

This is mostly done to get the horse to "accept the bit" and to "place" his head. This, however, is a grave misconception. No side rein, not even those with inlaid rubber rings, can be as sensitive as a rider's hands. In walk and canter the rider's hands have to follow with every stride the *natural nodding movement* of the horse's head in order to maintain a steady contact. The side reins cannot do this, and therefore interfere at every stride with the mouth, giving a dead, passive pressure on the bars. The horse will try to avoid this by either going behind, by leaning heavily on the bit, or by opening the mouth and stiffening the back and neck muscles. The parotid glands cannot function properly because they get jammed between the cheekbones and the jowl, which can injure them or the salivary ducts, which are positioned under the tongue, and the horse might never foam in his life.

These kind of injuries cannot be avoided by making the side reins a few holes longer. They may be so long as not to interfere with the horse's mouth when carrying his head in the normal position, but should he try to stretch his neck and push his nose forward-downwards – as he should – he certainly will meet the deadening side reins and will be forced to overbend.

Side reins spoil a horse even more when used equally long on both sides because the horse is then forced to go around the circle completely straight from head to tail. Fixed in this uncomfortable position his centre of gravity shifts to the inner shoulder, which is leading instead of head and neck. Consequently, it is impossible for the horse to bring his inner hindleg underneath his body.

*Fig. 197*
Four lungeing methods which, though still widely used, are incorrect and harmful to the horse.

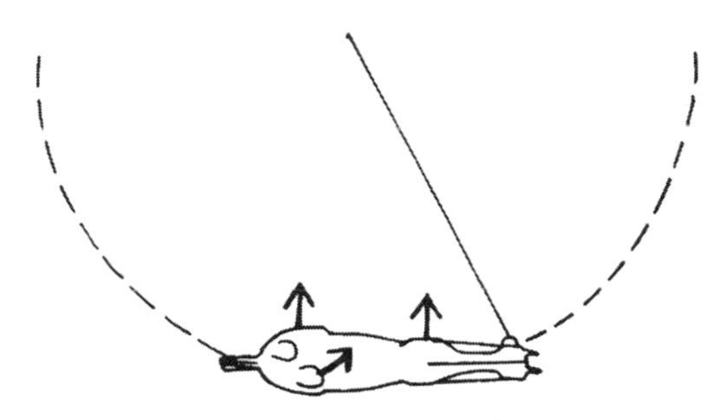

1. With equally long side reins, the horse cannot bend according to the circle line.

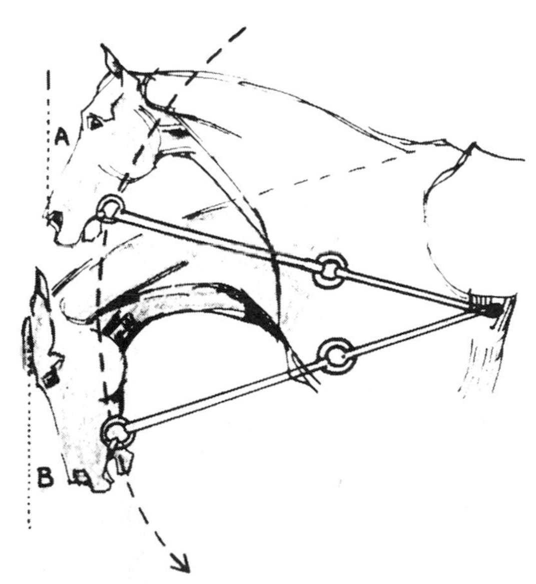


2. With long side reins, the horse can carry his nose (A) correctly in front of the vertical . . . but when he lowers his head (B) and tries to push his nose forward-downwards, as he should, then he is forced to overbend.

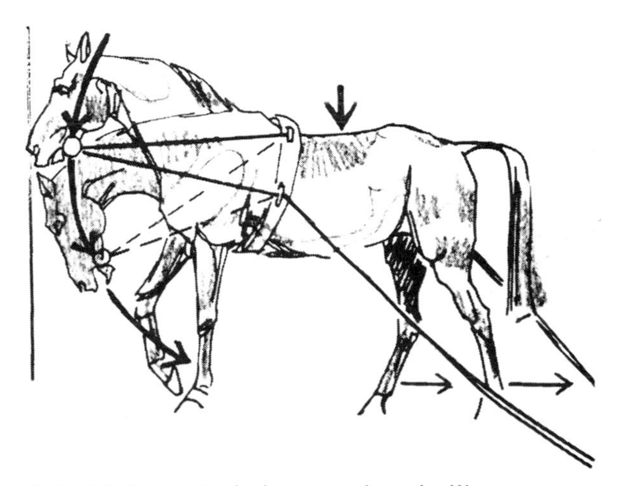

3. Double lunge attached as a running rein. Wrong.

4. Lungeing with the dumb jockey. Worse still.

If side reins are used when lungeing then the inner side rein should be 10 centimetres shorter than the outer one. This will at least allow the horse to bend his body laterally inwards according to the circle line.

Other methods, such as a double lunge, attached as running reins, the crossed side reins and the dumb jockey are antiquated and do not conform with the Natural Training Method. They interfere with the horse's paces, shortening the strides and forcing head and neck into an unnatural position (placing the head). They stiffen the neck and back muscles and make the horse drop his back instead of rounding it and make him move with his hocks wide apart.

Under no circumstances should one use these outdated methods in schooling showjumpers, as they need freedom of movement, and the intelligent and well bred ones especially do not take kindly to force.

### THE GOGUE

Two French cavalry officers, Monsieur Chambon and Monsieur Gogue, were the designers of two items of training equipment to which each of them gave their name. One is called the Gogue and the other the Chambon (the Chambon, with all its advantages, has been described fully in the preceding pages). Between both items there is a fundamental difference as regards to their influence on the horse's mouth. If one should study the action of the two reins only superficially then confusion might arise. Therefore it is necessary to explain the difference in detail.

The Chambon is designed for lungeing only; it is not suitable for riding. It should be used on every horse, young or old, because there is *never* the slightest pressure on the horse's bars. The Chambon only restricts the raising of the head with gentle pressure at the poll. In the various training exercises in the Natural Training Method, including lungeing with the Chambon, the horse's neck and whole body is *first* made flexible *laterally*. When this is achieved the horse will *offer*, on the rider's request, a "direct" bending. On account of this logical developement the horse has a gentle mouth, moves freely and in balance and is easy to collect.

The Gogue, however, should never be used on a young horse, because it imposes, with more or less backward pressure on the bars, a *direct* bending on the horse's neck.

Therefore, I am reluctant to write about the Gogue at all. Nevertheless, I shall compromise for the horse's sake, because I still prefer the Gogue to running reins and side reins. Today so many people seem to be in a hurry while schooling that they have no patience, or probably not the knowledge to school correctly, and try to achieve quick results with running reins. The bad influence of the running reins will be explained in detail in a later chapter. Their main disadvantage is that they impose a solely backwards pressure on the horse's mouth and that they overbend the horse. The Gogue is kinder to the horse's mouth because it has a double action: it exerts a gentle pressure at the poll, and the pressure on the bars depends entirely on how high the horse carries his head. This tension increases, together with the one at the poll, if the horse lifts his head. With the head at medium height and the nose approximately horizontal with the hip the pressure on both the poll and the bars is only very slight. This pressure diminishes to a minimum if the horse lowers his head and stretches his neck downwards.

There are two different ways of attaching the Gogue, either as the Independent or as the Command.

*The Independent*

The design of the Independent is similar to the Chambon, the cord of the Gogue being, at 2 metres in length, longer than that of the Chambon. The ends of the cord are not hooked into the snaffle rings, as with the Chambon, but run through them and back to the snaphook of the side rein, where they are fastened. The cord forms a triangle.

The Independent can be used when lungeing as well as when riding, but when lungeing it should *only* be used on an excitable horse who

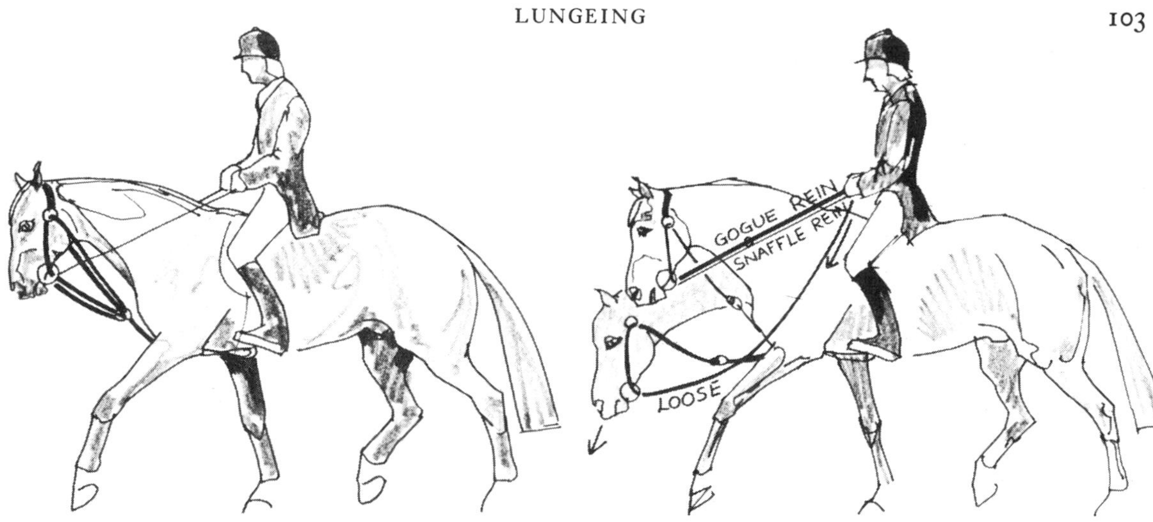


*Fig. 198*
The Independent Gogue.

*Fig. 199*
The Command Gogue.

is inclined to run too fast on the lunge, or on an older horse with a difficult neck.

When instructing mounted beginners, either on the lunge or in a class, I prefer the Independent to side reins as a means of keeping the horse calm. The Independent allows more freedom of the horse's neck and eases the rough rein action of a beginner. Experienced riders will not like to ride with the Independent, however, as the "direct" feeling on the mouth is broken, imposing a "dead" feel in the rider's hands.

*The Command*

Its design is similar to that of the Independent; the cord is also 2 metres long. But each end of the cord, instead of being hooked into the snaphook of the side rein, is attached to an additional pair of reins, which should not be longer than 2 metres.

The Command must never be used solely, as a single rein, but only together with and supporting the normal snaffle reins. Both are used independently.

The Command has an advantage over running reins in that it exerts pressure in two places: the horse's poll and the bars of his mouth. The pressure on the bars is, therefore, milder than one of running reins, and should be manipulated constantly by yielding the Gogue reins more or less. The rider who uses the Command is trying to bend the horse's neck "directly". Once he has achieved this he has to be very quick in yielding the reins suddenly with a pat on the neck. This will prevent the horse overbending.

Nevertheless, before deciding to use one of the Gogues one should contemplate why the use of it seems necessary in the first place. A horse's high head carriage, for instance, or the sensitivity of his mouth, can also be improved by simply lowering the bit temporarily one hole on each side. The bit is then resting on a "fresh" part of the bars and this change of the bit's location mostly works to satisfaction.

CHAPTER SEVEN

# FREE-JUMPING

FREE-JUMPING in the jumping lane is of enormous advantage to every showjumping horse and a *vital* part of the Natural Training Method.

Because we use a jumping lane in which all fences are movable, the distances, heights and types of fences can be altered according to needs and for the individual improvement of a horse. Such specialised and individual training is not possible in a *Couloir*, which is a fenced-in lane with permanent fences and banks and ditches. In a Couloir the fences remain at the same spot and always at the same distances to each other. This is boring for the horse and can even do harm to horses whose stride is not suited to the existing distances.

In the jumping lane *without* permanent fences one can start schooling young horses already before they are broken and ridden. By jumping very small fences in the lane the young horse develops muscles, balance and self-confidence and learns to use himself in a natural manner, because he is not hindered or influenced by a rider. Do not be afraid that this might be too much for a green horse. Because the horse is jumping only on a straight line, the fences are very small and the number of them are adjusted according to the growing strength of the young horse. When galloping with other horses in the field, doing sharp turns and sudden stops, he is putting much more strain on to tendons and joints. Anyway, I suggest that a green horse does not jump more often than twice per week in the lane.

The jumping lane is not only of great advantage in the normal training of the showjumping horse, but especially valuable in re-training troublesome horses who stumble or put in an extra stride before take-off. I shall explain later how to improve a horse's technique by jumping him loose in the lane with special distances.

## SETTING UP THE LANE

This is quite simple, especially if one can use an indoor school or a suitable outdoor arena.

The corners of the school are rounded off with planks and/or barrels to prevent the horse facing into the corners, which would tempt him to stop or turn around. The lane can be built with poles and barrels or uprights. This enables the trainer to reach the horse with the lash of the whip whenever it should become necessary to send the horse on. When the fences, later on, become higher, one should use a wing at the inside of the fence in order not to tempt the horse to jump out of the lane into the arena.

In the beginning one needs, depending on the size of the arena, one to three assistants. They are positioned to keep the horse moving around.

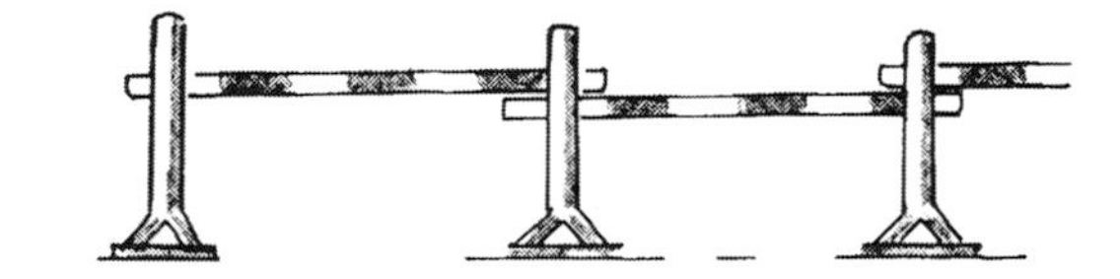

*Fig. 200*
Setting up the jumping lane.

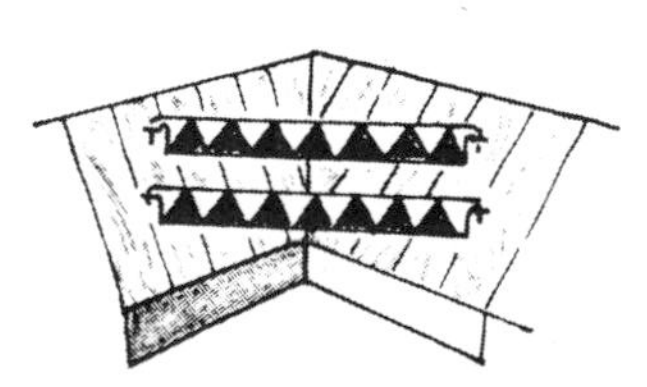

*Fig. 201*
Fencing off the corners of the school.

Later on the horse will enjoy this exercise so much that there will be no need to urge him on; he will go around at an even pace all by himself.

There must be absolute *silence* when a horse is jumping. Nobody should speak or move suddenly because this would definitely disturb the horse, affect his concentration and he would make faults, stop or turn around. The assistants must be qualified to judge the rhythm of the horse and send him on if he is losing impulsion or calm him down when he is going too fast. They must learn to send the horse on only when the horse has passed them, so that they are pushing from "behind", not when the horse is approaching them or level with them. The horse becomes so attentive that one step towards him will cause him to stop. The assistants should be able to judge the horse's pace and when he is approaching the fences in balance not to send him on suddenly before take-off. This would interrupt the horse's own judgement in finding his correct take-off position.

The other task of the assistants is to build and re-adjust the fences quickly and correctly.

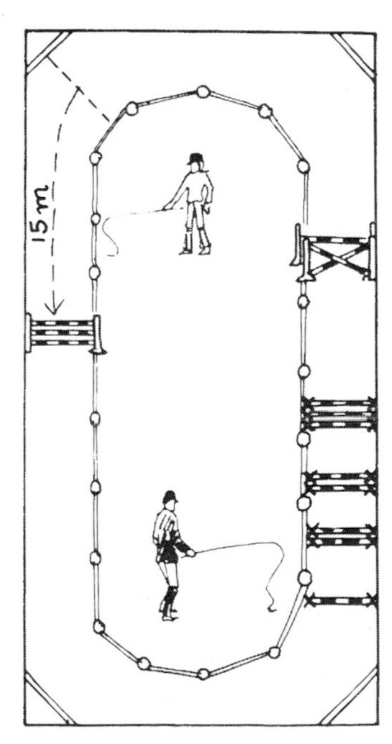


*Fig. 202*
The jumping lane.

*Fig. 203*
A horse tacked up for free-jumping.

BUILDING UP FENCES

Before going into detail I shall explain the tacking up for this exercise. All four legs of the horse must be protected with bandages or brushing boots. Two overreach boots are essential and kneecaps should also be used. The saddle is put on, without stirrups, but with breastplate and surcingle, which will keep the saddle flaps down as they might disturb a young horse. This is an ideal opportunity to accustom a green horse to the "feel" of the saddle and girths while jumping. If a bridle is used instead of a head collar the reins must be taken off.

I have heard people say that horses become careless when jumping with brushing boots on. That is nonsense. With or without protection the horse feels the blow when knocking a pole, but with protection the trainer avoids risking injuries to the horse's legs which could take it out of training for a long time. After such an interruption in the training one has to start all over again, because the horse's muscles become weak and it can take months before the horse is fit again. Therefore there is *no excuse* for not using leg protection.

Before putting any fences into the lane the horse has to learn to go around at an even pace. He will learn to stop and collect his reward when called. Only when the horse does this can one start introducing fences.

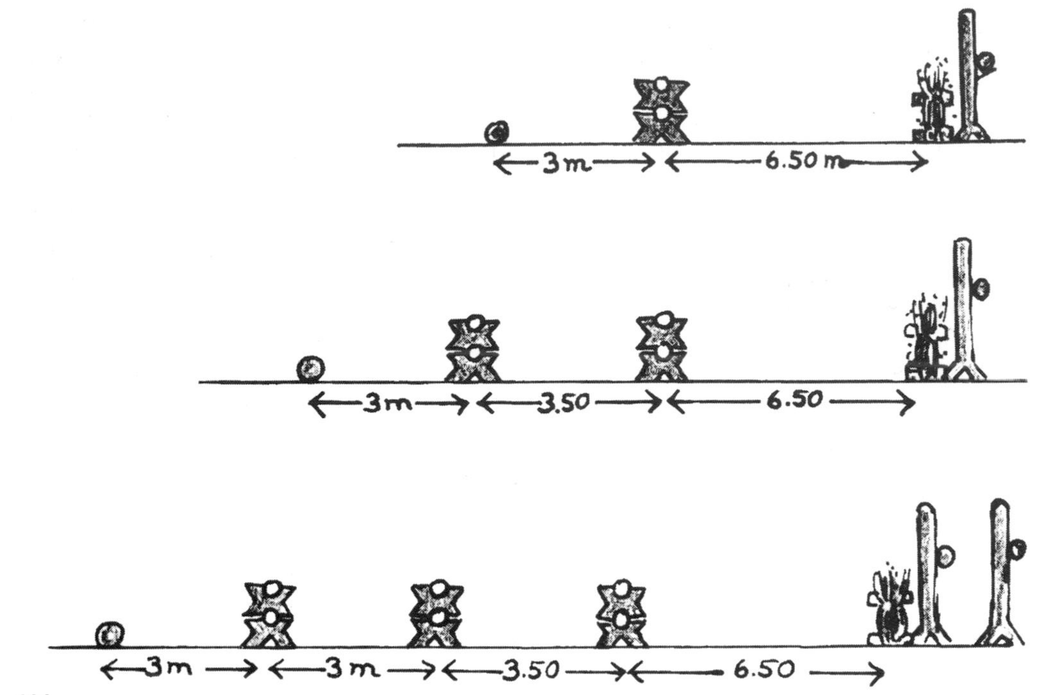


*Fig. 204*
**Start building up the fences in the lane.**

Start on one long side with a brush fence and a rustic pole slightly behind the fence, height 0·6 metres. Begin on the left-hand rein, as this is easier for most horses. Get the horse to canter around the track smoothly without rushing the fence. Then place two cavaletti, one on top of the other, 6·5 metres in front of the brush fence. From now on there should always be a thick, white pole on the ground 3 metres in front of the first obstacle in the row. This teaches the horse to judge the take-off point for the first fence.

When the horse is jumping this well, place another set of two cavaletti 3·5 metres in front of the others. Then add another set of two cavaletti 3 metres in front of the previous set. Only when the horse jumps these fences relaxed should one alter the last fence into a small spread fence.

If there are no cavaletti available one can build these jumps from two crossed poles. For horses who are inclined to jump too close to the kicking boards, therefore risking a fall, I prefer building the fences this way because they make the horse jump in the centre, being the lowest point.

All distances in the jumping lane are shorter than those used in competitions because the speed while schooling is much slower and the fences simpler, therefore the horse's strides are shorter.

The horse should approach the row of fences out of an ordinary trot (approximately 200 metres per minute), or out of a slow canter (250 metres per minute), covering approximately 3 metres with each stride. Very gradually school the horse to a faster speed, at the same time making the fences larger and widening the distances between them. This will bring the horse up to the standard of novice competitions with 300 metres per minute.

Of course, all distances given for the jumping lane are average. They might not be suitable for every young horse in the early stages of schooling. In the beginning the distances have to be adjusted according to the length of the horse's natural stride. The trainer must classify his horses. Start with building long distances and jump all the horses with a naturally long stride, then build equally shorter distances for the young horses with a short stride. If the hooves left their imprints in the centre between an in-and-out jump then the fences have been placed at a suitable distance. The trainer should check on this after the horse has gone through the lane once or twice. It is very discouraging for a *young* horse to be schooled over distances which are not suitable for his natural canter stride, because it will make him rap his legs *constantly*. He will then either start to rush or to refuse.

In time, however, the horse will become more experienced and the trainer will gradually alter the distances to the normal length. After basic schooling *all* horses, no matter how long or short their natural stride is, should be able to jump the fences placed at normal distances. Considering all this one will appreciate the advantages of a jumping lane in which the fences can be moved and altered.

The most important point of training a horse in the jumping lane is to regulate the speed correctly. If this is done all the time, without fail, then one will achieve amazing results. I know from experience that regular and well-planned training in the jumping lane makes *every horse* jump – and like it – but only under the condition that they are taught to go around and jump at a relaxed but active regular pace. This is very difficult because at the beginning some young horses will rush during the approach; others will slow down. Some will pick up too much speed while jumping through the lane, others will lack the power or will to keep going. If the trainer and his assistant have an accurate feeling and an eye for rhythm they will in time school the horse to approach the fences, jump the whole row and continue after the last fence in one uniform and balanced pace.

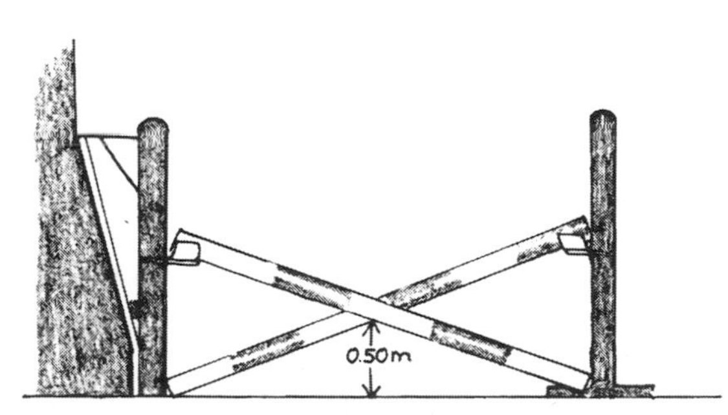


*Fig. 205*
A fence made from crossed poles. On account of the movable wall hanger (constructed to fit the same length poles on top and bottom) the fences can be erected anywhere along the long side of the school.

Send the horse on *only* when he goes too slow. But when necessary react immediately, because if the horse loses impulsion and is not sent on he might land on top of a fence, will learn to put in an extra stride or to refuse. All of this will spoil not only a horse's jumping but his confidence as well. In the beginning one might have to send some young horses on after the first, second or/and every following fence. But they soon will learn that the easiest way to cope with the entire row of obstacles is to maintain an even speed. Build the row for a very reluctant horse in the direction of the stable or exit.

If a horse approaches the row too fast, or accelerates too much while jumping the row, he will flatten or jump in too far over the fences, coming too close to the following element. For such horses build the lane to be jumped away from the exit or stable.

For the horse's sake do not try to jump all fences on the first day. Remember that an ordinary showjumping course has only approximately 15 jumps. Build up the fences in the lane gradually over a period of weeks in order not to overwork the horse and spoil his confidence. Only then will the horse enjoy jumping. Make a break after every third round. Call the horse in and give him his reward. Make much of him, talk to him and give him time to relax completely. Horses learn this very quickly. One word in a soothing voice will make him halt and come in to you. Do not let him always stop at the same spot on the track because the horse will anticipate it and will stop there without being told to do so.

When the horse is completely relaxed, which might take quite some time with excitable horses, the assistant will lead the horse back out into the lane and start him jumping the next three rounds. Do not school a young horse more than three times, three rounds each time. A very fit and experienced horse can do five times three rounds altogether, but never more. Remember that if there are eight fences on the track the horse will then have jumped 120 fences. And consider the distance: in a school of 20 × 60 metres the horse will then have covered 2,400 metres. Therefore only a very fit horse can do five by three rounds in the lane.

Change rein every week in order to develop the horse evenly on both sides.

If a refusal or resistance of any kind occurs – which is most unlikely if the loose jumping was done correctly – it can stem from various causes. The horse may be physically weak; his jumping may be good the first and second round and then deteriorate. The trainer has to realise this and regulate his demands accordingly. Or the horse may not have understood what was demanded of him or was "overfaced". This can happen so easily. Therefore remember: the jumping exercises must be carried out regularly and strictly in *progression*. It is important that each schooling session starts again with a few easy fences – and *not* at the same level at which the horse finished the previous lesson.

When schooling a nervous horse let him first go through the lane with all fences (poles) flat on the ground. When he does this confidently, start building up the last fence, then the second last as well, and so on. After a few weeks the nervous horse will acquire more confidence and enjoy jumping.

A highly strung horse may become excited while he is jumping and will increase his speed too much. Use your voice to calm the horse, and give him more frequent, and much longer, breaks between rounds. Watch the expression on the horse's face and the heaving of his flanks. If he is still heaving he is not ready yet to go on again. After the horse has settled down, lead him into the lane and halt a few lengths before the first fence. Wait there for a few minutes and talk to the horse with a soothing voice until he takes a deep breath. This is the signal that he is relaxed. Then let him move off slowly to do his round.

Some horses rush off after clearing the last fence. If the trainer has progressed as explained here then one word of his will be sufficient to slow the horse down. If the horse does not obey his voice he should place a pole or cavaletti behind the last fence in the row at a distance of approximately 6·5 metres, depending on the height and width of the last obstacle. While airborne over the last fence the horse will notice the pole on the ground and automatically collect himself on landing, shortening his strides, thereby transferring more weight to the quarters, and will slow down. I use the same method for curing older, spoilt horses from taking off after a fence when mounted. It works amazingly quickly and soon the horse will slow down even without the cavaletti on the ground behind the fence.

After the horse is jumping the lane fluently and without any problems, also place a fence on the other, long, side of the school. It should be a straight fence and no higher than 0·9 metres. Place it approximately 15 metres out from the corner. Also place a pole diagonally in the corner to aid the horse in finding the correct take-off place at this, his first single fence. Make sure that all horses come through the corner at the same slow speed, then they will cross the pole and take four more strides before take-off at the single fence. If a horse slows down too much and has to be sent on accordingly, place the single fence a few strides further away from the corner and let him jump towards "home". At this single fence the horse will show what he has learned already on the other long side in the multiple combination and have a look and search for the correct take-off position. But the trainer has to make sure that the horse is maintaining impulsion and rhythm in the approach.

Every person who trains horses regularly in

the jumping lane knows and praises the enormous progress the horses make. The horses learn to *use their brain* when jumping and will, later on in competitions, help their rider in any difficult situation. It is especially then that the rider will realise how well spent the time was in building up the lane and the fences and probably have to clear it all away again. When he is riding the horse over jumps the first time he will feel that power, balance and natural bascule which the horse was allowed to acquire when loose jumping without a rider in the jumping lane.

When schooling young horses in the jumping lane never become too elated or too depressed about a performance. Only in the long term can one judge the horse's true jumping ability. I have often had horses who did not show much potential at the beginning because they were weak or lacked courage. Often they turned out to be very successful showjumpers because they were helped to overcome these initial handicaps and could then show their real ability.

### ADVANCED JUMPING LANE

The design for the advanced jumping lane is an eight row one and is a little more advanced than the elementary one explained on the previous pages. It is suitable for schooling horses loose or mounted. The horse will learn to lengthen or shorten his strides according to the alternately long and short distances between the elements.

When free jumping, the trainer should urge the horse with the long whip to lengthen his strides in between the elements which are placed at a long distance.

When schooling whilst mounted, the rider too should apply forward driving leg aids to encourage the horse to lengthen his strides at the long distances. Occasionally the rider should jump the lane with his eyes closed, counting the varying number of non-jumping strides in between the elements. This method will teach the rider to feel the rhythmic tempo in pace when the horse either lengthens or shortens his stride.

The set-up of rows numbers seven and eight are particularly excellent education for the rider himself in order to school his eye whilst counting the non-jumping strides and calculating the distances when approaching the last element of the lane. I mention again that it should be noted that these distances are different compared to the distances in combinations at shows.

The first element of the lane should be a particularly heavy white pole to catch the horse's attention and to prevent rushing.

When commencing the schooling session it is more inviting if one puts the poles, alternately, up on one end only and slanted onto the ground at the other end. Once the horse jumps freely the poles may be placed level at both ends.

For the in and out elements one should use, intentionally, only *one* single pole to teach the horse to find his take-off point correctly without the aid of a ground line.

The elements which have non-jumping strides in between them should be built compactly.

The last fence in the row, the oxer, is built at first with two crossed poles in front and a single pole at the far side to get the horse used to the fairly short distance.

Then build a proper oxer, well filled up and, later on, if this oxer is built bigger, one should of course also increase the distance in between the last two elements accordingly.

The benefit of learning the technique to

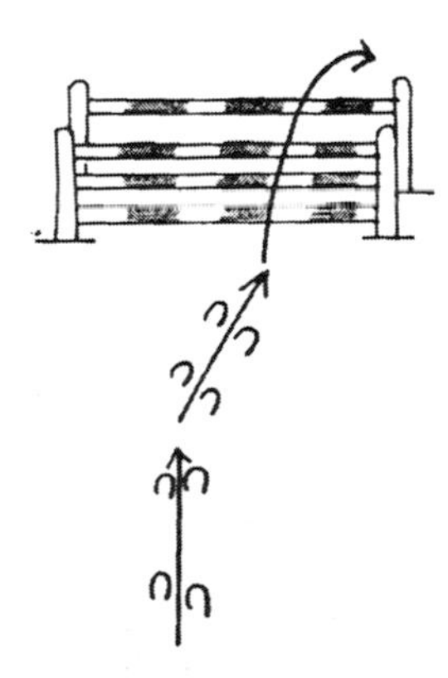

*Fig. 206*
**The horse will progress and learn to lengthen a short distance by moving on a diagonal line.**

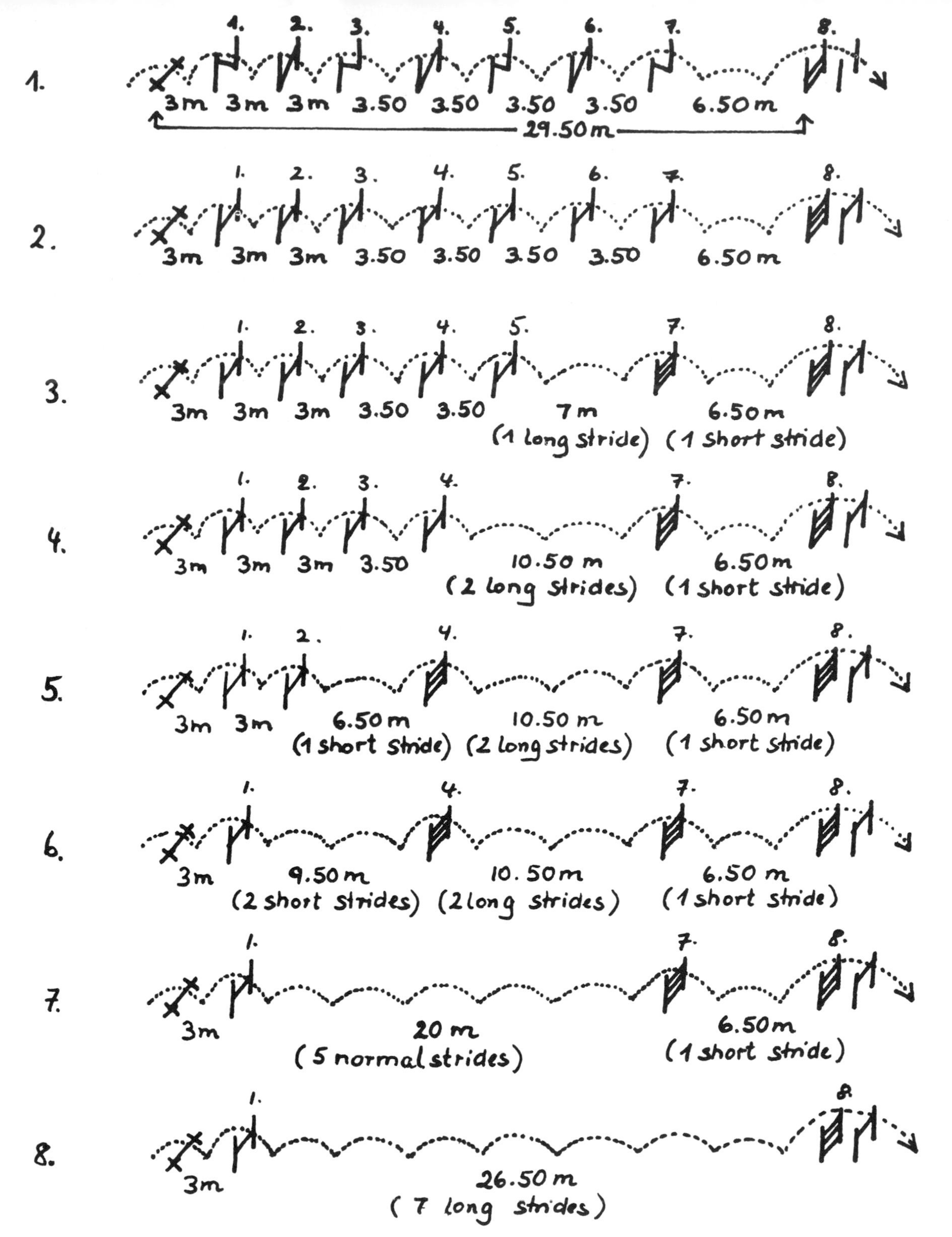


*Fig. 207*
Advanced set-up for free-jumping. It should also be used later on, mounted.

lengthen and shorten the strides will be appreciated later on when the horse is presented with a difficult take-off situation in competitions. The horse will then respond willingly to the rider's aid in approaching a fence in order to take-off at the correct point.

Also in combinations, if the horse should come in too far over the first element, he will be able to shorten the next stride and still meet the correct take-off point for the next element (and vice versa). Another technique the horse might have learned is to lengthen a short distance by moving on a diagonal line.

This education for the horse will definitely reduce the risk of his incurring jumping faults or refusals.

### DISADVANTAGES OF JUMPING ON THE LUNGE

Unfortunately several trainers still have the habit of schooling their horses over single fences on the lunge. They invariably practise this on the left-hand rein, developing further what is already the more flexible side of most horses. The horse thereby becomes unevenly muscled. Later, in competitions, the rider will have serious problems with right-hand turns and with the horse running out to the left.

In general, when jumping on the lunge out of a circle, the horse can bring only *one* hindleg (his inner hindleg) underneath at take-off. This "unnatural" position puts more strain on the inner hock and fetlock joints. Strained hocks, swollen legs and windgalls are the result. The horse is also forced to change his centre of gravity to the inner foreleg, thus having no alternative but to land always in the left canter.

When jumping the horse in the jumping lane, however, he is able to bring *both* hocks simultaneously underneath his body at the take-off, because his body is straight and he is approaching the fences out of a straight line. Therefore the horse's muscles will develop evenly and he will be free to land in either canter.

A further disadvantage of jumping on the lunge is the fact that the trainer is often not

*Fig. 208*
Jumping on the lunge – bad for the horse.

*Fig. 209*
A painful disaster.

quick enough with the lunge in following the horse's head when airborne. The horse receives a sudden painful check in the mouth. This jerk, considered a punishment by the horse, undermines his confidence. The horse will remember this painful experience and become reluctant to repeat it. He will try to break away from the trainer. Should he succeed he may easily step on the trailing lunge and injure his jawbones.

On account of all these disadvantages I am strongly against jumping horses on the lunge. Schooling horses in this way does not conform with the Natural Training Method, in which there is never a backward pull on the horse's mouth.

Jumping mounted out of a circle (*not* on the lunge), or out of short turns and angles, belongs to a much more advanced stage of training. This method is used to school horses for jumping against the clock.

CHAPTER EIGHT

# SCHOOLING "ON FOOT"

THE elementary schooling "on foot" is to make the horse familiar with the rein aids (making the mouth), with the rider's leg aids (on two tracks) and with reining back.

The horse is learning these fairly advanced exercises in liberty with the careful aid of the dressage whip. The horse is not overfaced in doing these exercises at such an early stage, even before being mounted, because he only has to balance himself without the encumberance of the rider's weight.

On foot the horse is taught the whip aid as an auxiliary leg aid. Later on, when mounted, the same whip aid is used in conjunction with the leg aid and is finally replaced by the leg aid.

Also in re-training older or spoilt horses the work on foot is of great value. Every day, before mounting, practise a few liberty exercises with horses who are too much on the forehand, behind or over the bit, have difficulties when reining back or are particularly stiff laterally on one side.

The liberty exercises (work on foot) are based on classic European training principles, used for generations in all former European continental cavalry schools.

The schooling methods used by these cavalry schools were considered and accepted by everybody (cavalryman and civilian) as equestrian law. Nobody would think of questioning their methods.

Today, however, since the cavalry has ceased to exist in most European countries, their training methods are not taught as widely and as precisely and have therefore lost much of their dogmatic force. There are not many trainers left who inherited this knowledge and who are able to pass it on. The lack of this knowledge causes many trainers to regard, for instance, the work on foot, amongst other things, as outdated and unnecessary. They are convinced that this pre-training is a waste of time and that it could be practised more efficiently (with engaged quarters) when mounted. They are of this opinion because they did not have the opportunity to learn these training methods properly. Or perhaps they tried the liberty exercises incorrectly and, as the required results could not be achieved, the principles involved were blamed. These trainers can be assured that this pretraining is *not* a waste of time, as the horse learns to perform advanced movements correctly during the first two months of schooling before being mounted.

The trainer will undoubtedly benefit later on from it and save time by obtaining quicker results when practising these same exercises mounted.

The work on foot promotes the physical and psychological development of the horse, thus gaining a mutual understanding between horse and trainer.

Fortunately I was in a position to study for many years the classic training principles and got to appreciate the value of the liberty exercises, amongst other things. I will explain these in as great a detail as possible to remove any misconception existing on this subject.

### THE FIRST EXERCISE

It is the main purpose of this (and the following) exercise to bend the horse's body laterally without any influence from the reins. Horses whose muscles are made supple and flexible on either side will have no problem in bending their entire body laterally inwards from head to tail. A horse *first* has to become *laterally* flexible. When this is accomplished sufficiently the horse will have no problems in bending *directly*, rounding his back and neck effortlessly, with engaged quarters.

Many trainers do not realise how necessary

this succession is. They start bending the horse's neck "directly" (placing the head) using running reins, martingales and side reins. They do not realise that by doing this the rest of the horse's body stays stiff as a stick, becoming even stiffer in time.

The trainer takes both reins in the left hand (the buckle on his little finger to prevent the horse from stepping on the reins). He places himself on the near side next to the horse's shoulder. He touches the near hock gently with the dressage whip. The horse should lift his near hindleg and cross it forward-sideways in *front* of the off hindleg. Touching the hock of the *near* hindleg, just before the horse lifts it up, encourages him to lift up this leg higher and bring it further underneath his body. If the trainer touches the hock at the wrong moment the horse might drag his hindleg over the ground or become excited and obstinate.

This is the first exercise, teaching the horse to bring *one* hindleg well underneath his body. This hindleg *must* cross in *front* of the other hindleg, and *not* behind it, which would be a grave mistake and fail the purpose of the exercise.

The sideways movement of the horse's quarters should be performed slowly, step by step, to prevent rushing and brushing of the legs (brushing and overreach boots should be used).

The horse should be allowed to move slightly *forward*-sideways. Do not try to keep the horse back with the reins because the forward impulsion must be maintained and encouraged under all circumstances, in spite of the lateral flexion of the horse's body. If the horse should try to move backwards, stop the exercise immediately and move the horse a few strides forward and start the exercise again. If the horse moves back-

*Fig. 210*
The first exercise "on foot".

wards during this sideways movement the quarters will not be engaged. An assistant should stand behind the horse at a certain distance, and while talking quietly prevent the horse from moving backwards.

When doing this exercise for the first few times be satisfied with two or three strides, as it is a pre-schooling for the turn "around" the forehand.

Before doing the exercise on the other rein it is important, at each interval, to move the horse forward. Never practise this exercise more than twice on each rein. As soon as the horse has learned to respond to the aids of the dressage whip, and moves his quarters willingly sideways, one can then start to use the dressage whip from the hocks gradually along the horse's body until approximately one hand behind the girths, which is the region where, later on, the rider's leg applies the lateral leg aid. In this manner the whip acts as an auxiliary leg aid. Later on when the horse is being ridden he will already understand and respond to the sideways driving aids of the dressage whip. He has developed the necessary muscles and will, while mounted, easily move his quarters sideways, bringing *one* hindleg further underneath his body.

THE SECOND EXERCISE

As soon as the horse can do the first exercise effortlessly and in a relaxed manner one can start on the second exercise. In this exercise the horse moves on two tracks facing the kicking boards. The support of the kicking boards of the indoor school plays a very important part as an aid to prevent the horse from moving too much forwards, thereby avoiding the engagement of his quarters. (In case there is not an indoor school available, the railing surrounding the field can be used for the same purpose.)

The trainer stands with his back to the kicking boards on the near side of the horse next to his shoulder. He takes both reins in the left hand and the dressage whip in his right hand. While moving along the track in this position he touches the horse's near hock – at each stride – just before the horse lifts his near hindleg.

It is essential that the trainer moves along the track, *keeping up with the horse.* If the trainer moves slower than the horse, he risks the horse moving his quarters too much to the side or coming to a halt and making a complete turn on the forehand instead of moving forward on two tracks, thereby injuring the coronary band of the hooves or brushing the legs. For this reason never interrupt the free forward impulsion and the regular balanced rhythm of the strides. The forehand must always precede the quarters, while the inner lateral pair of legs cross in front of the outer lateral pair of legs.

This exercise on two tracks should be practised daily on *both* reins, but for the first few weeks the horse should do no more than four to six strides, because this liberty exercise is very tiring for the young horse.

It is quite possible that when beginning to teach this exercise the horse may offer some

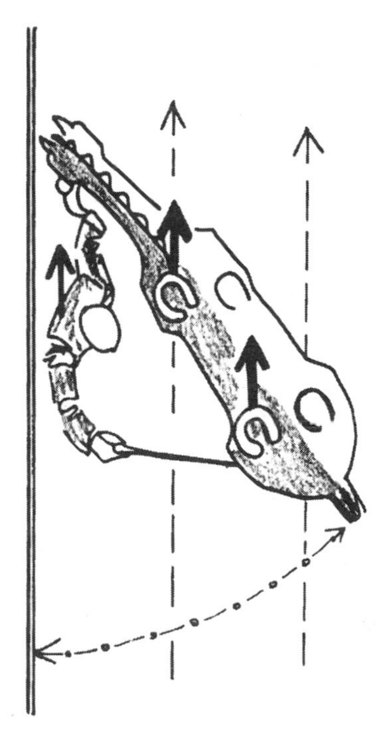

*Fig. 211*
The second exercise "on foot".

resistance by means of moving backwards. In such a case the assistant should follow behind the horse and send him gently forward without upsetting him.

Caution must be taken in the use of the dressage whip because unskilled handling of the whip will make every horse nervous, upset and disobedient. The horse will contract and stiffen his muscles. He may break away from the trainer or make a vigorous turn with the quarters. Such an unexpected movement can make a horse lame at once. (The same applies when showing a horse in hand; one should never turn the horse on the spot to the left, but first change into a walk and then make a large right-hand turn.)

When a horse is stiff on one particular side one should practise these liberty exercises more often on this side to bring the horse's stiffer hindleg further underneath his body.

How important the lateral flexibility is for a showjumper can often be noticed at indoor showjumping competitions. The well-schooled horse, under an experienced rider, takes the corners bent laterally inwards (horse's body is laterally bent around the rider's inner leg), head and neck pointing in the direction in which he is moving. In this position the horse is able, when coming out of a corner, to approach the next fence in a straight line, engaging both hindlegs at take-off. A stiff or unbalanced horse will go through the turns bent laterally to the outer side. The horse is unable to engage the inner hindleg and is therefore forced to change his centre of gravity to the inner foreleg, falling into the turn. The horse is unbalanced, cannot engage his quarters and has no time to straighten his body in approaching the next fence. He will refuse, run out or knock a pole.

When a horse advances in his liberty exercises one should practise this two track movement in a very slow trot. The trainer must have absolute feeling for rhythm and cadence in order to follow the horse's pace exactly, otherwise the trot becomes hurried or disunited and the horse may become upset and could turn around and injure himself.

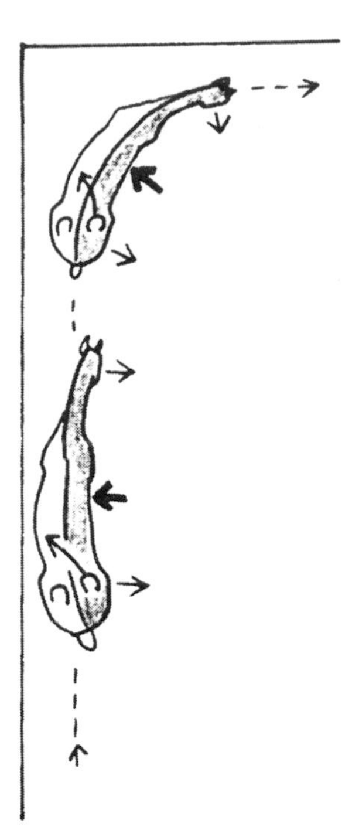

*Fig. 212*
A well schooled horse in a turn, bent laterally inwards.

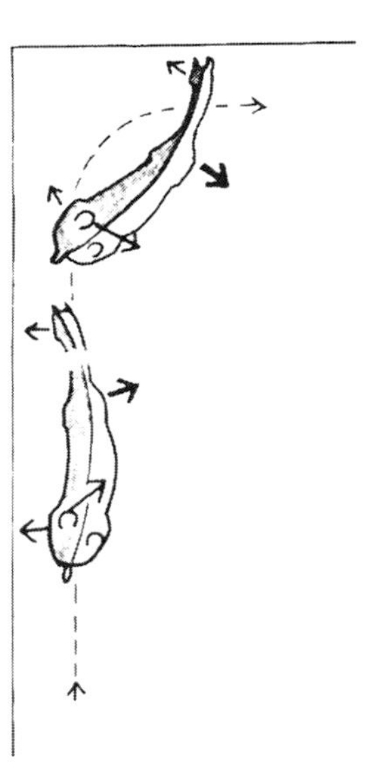

*Fig. 213*
A badly schooled horse in a turn, bent to the outside and falling into the turn.

THE THIRD (REIN BACK) EXERCISE

Reining back is an unnatural movement for the horse; his natural movement is *forwards*. Therefore the rein back mounted may only be exercised at an advanced stage of schooling, after the horse has developed the necessary muscles and responds to the rider's forward and lateral driving leg aids.

Nevertheless, unmounted rein back can be exercised at an early stage and so prepare the horse's appropriate muscles. It will eliminate many difficulties which arise when schooling the reining back *mounted* without this pre-training on foot.

When re-training older horses, or ones who are too much on the forehand and have a stiff back, this backing on foot works wonders. One will notice that the horse learns, in time, to move backwards with regular, consecutive strides, transfers any excess weight from the forehand to the quarters, lowers the quarters and engages his hocks. This is achieved without any backwards pressure on his mouth and without any kind of force.

(Caution must be taken that one never stands straight in front of the horse, as he might strike out suddenly with one of his forelegs.)

The rein back should be practised on both reins. Start on the left-hand rein on the track. Take both reins into the left hand *without* putting any pressure on the bit. With the whip, touch the coronet band of the hoof which is placed most forward. Touching the forefeet alternately will teach the horse to move backwards in diagonal pairs with long, even strides. The horse will round his back and the hocks will become engaged and be brought well underneath his body. Under no circumstances should the horse be pushed backwards with the reins, because this would teach him to rear or to drop his back and drag his hindlegs over the ground.

Most young horses, or those with a weak back, will, while reining back, round their back excessively, lower their head and neck and make exaggerated high steps with the hindlegs. The reason for all this is that the young horse's back muscles are not developed and that the horse tries to ease the pressure on the kidneys. Therefore do not interfere with this low head and neck position by lifting the horse's head with the reins, as this could cause severe pain in his spine. After developing the correct muscles the horse will be able to carry head and neck in the correct position (nose and hip at the same height). The horse will then be able to move backwards in the same balanced manner

*Fig. 214*
The correct rein back "on foot".

*Fig. 215*
Most young horses start the rein back like this.

as if he was moving forward. He will flex his jaw and champ the bit.

In order not to strain the joints of the hind-legs one should not ask for more than four to six backing strides at a time. The rein back must be done gently, otherwise the horse might easily injure the coronet band of his hindfeet with the front shoes.

After having reined back a few strides, reward the horse and *lead him forward* in order to maintain the forward impulsion before one continues the exercise. Change rein frequently.

Horses with one stiff hock have the habit of moving their quarters sideways while reining back to avoid engaging that particular hock. To prevent this and to make the stiff side of the horse supple practise the rein back with his stiff side along the kicking boards, eliminating any deviation of the quarters. But do it very gently. because using force would make the horse tense and stiffen his muscles.

In the more advanced stage of reining back, or while re-training an older horse, the whip could gently touch the croup while the horse is moving backwards. This indicates to the horse which muscles should become extra active and will make him lower and engage the quarters. Then the horse will round his back extensively while head and neck will be raised slightly higher. Should the horse move his quarters sideways, avoiding this "collection", one should touch the sides of the horse's flanks with the whip.

If this method of reining back on foot is done correctly one will benefit enormously later on when riding the horse. There will then be no need to take an extra strong hold on the bit when reining back. When starting later on to rein back, mounted, an assistant should stand

*Fig. 216*
Emphasise the lowering and engaging of the quarters.

*Fig. 217*
Incorrect reining back. The horse is pulled backwards with the reins.

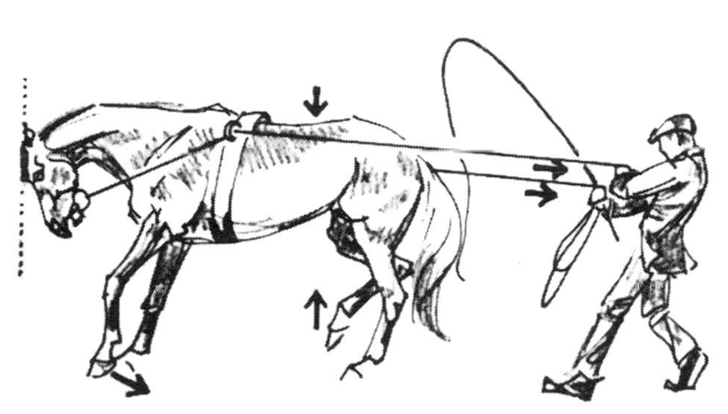

*Fig. 218*
The rein back when long reining. The horse with a long back drops it, overbends and drags his forefeet.

*Fig. 219*
The horse, again, will drop its back and overbend and drag its forefeet if pulled back under the rider.

in front of the horse and, if necessary, touch the forefeet with the dressage whip whilst at the same time the rider is applying the normal rein back aids. The horse remembers the rein back on foot and will rein back willingly when the assistant only makes a step forward towards the horse. Therefore there is no need for the rider to pull on the reins, not even when the horse is only learning the rein back aids mounted.

*Incorrect reining back*

Teaching the horse to rein back by pulling on the reins will spoil the horse's mouth. Sore bars are inflicted by hard and pulling hands of ignorant trainers.

Years ago it was common on the European continent, when schooling horses, to rein back with long reins. Unfortunately for a young horse, this method is not outdated yet, because in many countries the same old fashioned breaking tack is still used, more by tradition than by common sense.

Reining back with long reins can only be done by pulling on the bit. The same mistake is made if the trainer tries to rein back on foot by pulling the reins instead of using the dressage whip. When pulled back with long reins, horses who have a long or weak back and/or a long or weak neck perform badly. Because of the pressure on the bit the horse goes with an open mouth behind the bit (overbent). The parotid glands become jammed between the jawbones and the jowl. The neck is bent wrongly in the third vertebra. The nose, which should be on a horizontal level with the horse's hip, is carried much too low.

The horse is unable to move backwards diagonally and drags his forelegs over the ground and makes lofty high short steps with the hind-legs. The horse cannot use his loin muscles sufficiently, therefore he drops his back, subsequently the quarters are not engaged.

Horses who have a short and/or stiff back, or a short or stiff neck, act differently according to their different conformation. When pulled backwards these horses go *over* the bit with an open mouth. The nose is on a much higher level than

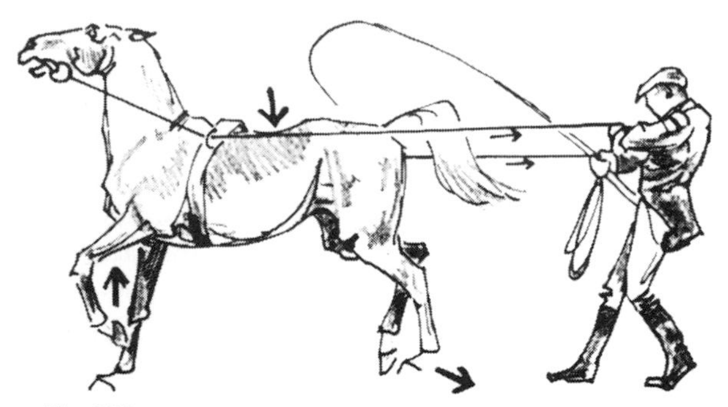

*Fig. 220*
A horse with a short back will react like this, when pulled back in long reins.

the hip. With this ewe neck position the horse is forced to drop his back, inflicting pressure on the kidneys. This painful experience prevents him bringing his hocks close together and underneath his body as he should. The horse makes high and lofty short steps with the forelegs and drags his hindlegs over the ground.

Practising this antiquated and wrong method provokes all kinds of trouble (rearing, pulling and so on).

*Fig. 221*
He will do the same under the rider.

## REIN AIDS (ON FOOT)

In the Natural Training Method "making the mouth" is practised on foot during the first two months before mounting the horse. The expression "making the mouth" means to make the horse understand how to react upon the rein aids and how to accept the bit.

The rein aids are applied without hardening the bars. The horse learns to bend head and neck in alternate sideways directions and to flex the lower jaw and champ the bit without any pressure on the bars. One preserves an unspoilt mouth. There are three different rein aids: first, the "loose" rein; second the "long" rein; and third, the "collected" rein (on the bit).

The first and second rein aid are practised on foot. The third rein aid is practised only when mounted.

*Fig. 222*
The first "loose" rein aid "on foot".

## FIRST ("LOOSE") REIN AID

Stand on the near side of the horse, close to the withers with the right arm across the horse's neck. Hold the left rein in the left hand and the right rein in the right hand. Keeping the same distance between both hands, move the reins alternately sideways *out* from the horse's neck, to the left and to the right, while maintaining with both hands an equal contact with the bit. This is most important. The snaffle will slide sideways over the tongue and bars (like a mouth organ). The movement of the bit is limited by the rubber discs pushing alternately against the lip angles.

Remember, to move the hands *only* sideways, *never* backwards . . . which might happen unbeknown to the trainer.

Having carried out this sideways motion of the bit once or twice, one will feel a slight flexion of the horse's lower jaw. The *immediate* reaction must be to drop the reins *completely*. This sudden freedom will tempt the horse to lower his head and to stretch his neck down and forward, at the same time to round his back.

One must have the necessary feeling for a steady contact with the mouth and never miss the exact moment to release the reins when the horse flexes his jaw. If one's reaction comes too late the horse will learn to pull on the reins, especially when one makes this mistake too often.

If this exercise is carried out correctly on both sides of the horse, in approximately one week he will have gained confidence in the trainer's hands and will understand the first rein aid.

The horse will remember this aid later on when being ridden. It will then be applied first at a halt, later in all three paces. It is called "showing the horse the way to the ground".

### SECOND ("LONG") REIN AID

If the horse has understood the first rein aid then start practising the second rein aid. Carry out the first rein aid a few times, and after the horse flexes the lower jaw and champs the bit *do not* drop the reins (as in the first rein aid), but instead follow with both hands the downwards-forward movement, maintaining the same feeling with the horse's mouth while he lowers head and neck.

Every horse who has gained confidence in the trainer's hands will stretch his neck and lower his head as confidently as in the first rein aid, but will now take the rider's hands with him. After the submission of the horse's lower jaw, follow with the hands without interference, maintaining the same tension on the bit, just as one will have to do when clearing a fence.

As time goes by there will be no need to keep the hands so wide apart, or to move the bit as much sideways as in the beginning when practising these two rein aids. The more the horse understands the action of these rein aids the closer one can bring the hands together. The horse will then respond if the trainer *only turns* his wrists alternately sideways – outwards.

If the two months of early training are actually followed as explained, with regular lungeing with Chambon and work on foot, in conjunction with free jumping and backing in his box, then

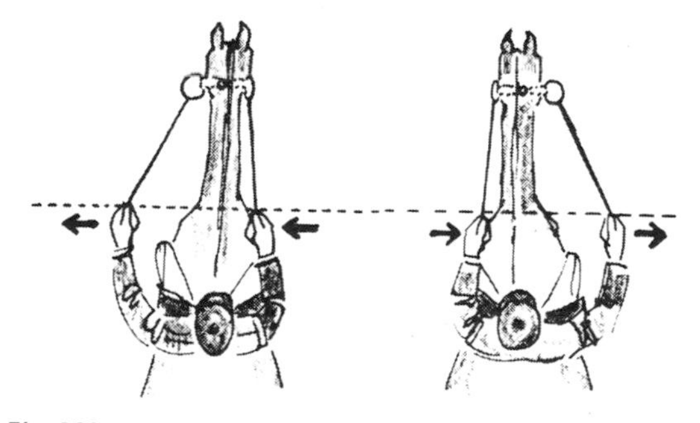

*Fig. 223*
The first "loose" rein aid mounted. The rider moves the bit alternately sideways. *(Left)* Phase I; *(right)* Phase II.

*Fig. 224*
Phase III. Drop the reins immediately the horse makes a submission.

*Fig. 225*
The second "long" rein aid "on foot".

*Fig. 226*
The second "long" rein aid when mounted.

*Fig. 227*
When clearing a fence the rider maintains the same tension on the bit – and the horse the same posture.

one will *not* have a weak, nervous young horse when one finally starts riding him. The horse will be well muscled and confident. He will understand the rein aids, will turn easily – in any direction, which he learned while lungeing – and will obey the rider's voice. One should, therefore, have *no problems* and one will be compensated for the time spent on proper pre-schooling. It stands to reason a horse schooled in the Natural Training Method gains a great advantage indeed in comparison to a weak, young and timid horse, who is mounted straight away without having had any pre-schooling.

### THIRD ("ON THE BIT") REIN AID

The third rein aid can only be practised mounted. It is an advanced movement and is explained later.

### "MAKING THE MOUTH"

It is a fact that pre-training makes breaking a horse easier. But over the years the methods of pre-schooling have changed and been improved, especially in regard to making the mouth.

Many years ago most horses were broken with the double lunge, breaking tack or with the dumb jockey. Some people still use these old-fashioned methods. The disadvantages are so many and so grave that comparison with the Natural Training Method is useful.

Part of the old method is the "breaking bit", or as it is sometimes known the "key bit". This is a very thick, straight, hollow bit with holes in it and has three hanging keys which are supposed to make the horse chew the bit and

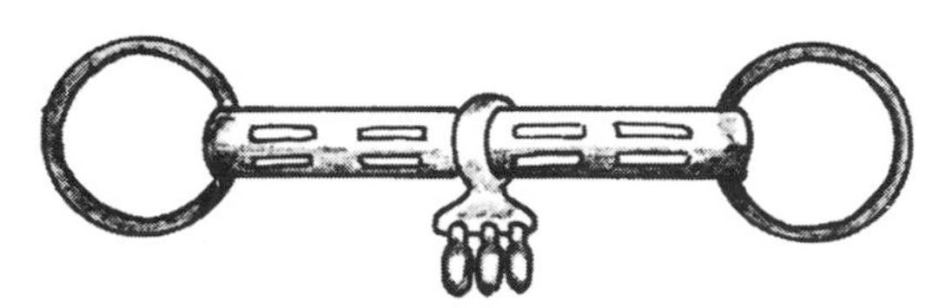

*Fig. 228*
Old fashioned breaking bit with keys.

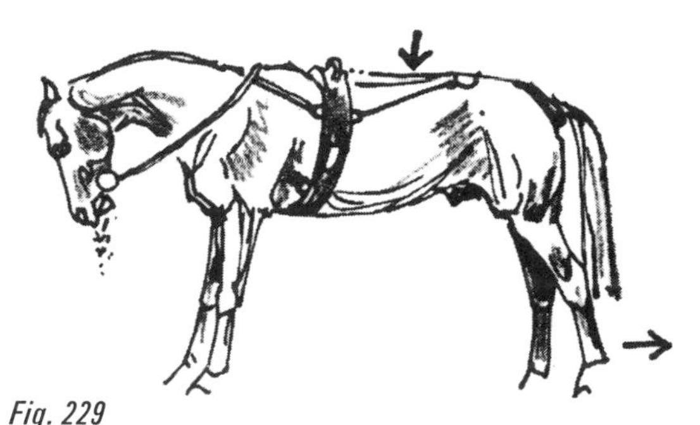

*Fig. 229*
The breaking tack is brutal and has a bad effect on the horse's physique.

produce a foaming mouth. In some cases the bit is filled with cotton wool soaked in sugar or honey. This breaking bit is placed in the mouth daily – for quite some time – to "make" the mouth. The horse is usually tied up with crossed side reins. Unfortunately this not only stiffens the neck muscles but hardens the bars and makes many young horses go *behind* the bit. Other horses learn to lean on the bit in trying to deaden the pain on the bars. Some horses will never relax the lower jaw but are constantly flapping with the lower lip.

This bad habit is continued later on when being ridden. Many horses acquire stable vices: weaving, putting the tongue over the bit, wind-sucking or cribbiting and pawing.

By using the breaking bit and crossed side reins the horse is unable to move head and neck, being fixed in an unnatural position. Not only the neck becomes stiff, but also the back and the loin muscles, which is very painful for the horse. He will have great difficulty standing in a comfortable position. In an attempt to ease the deadening pressure on his tender and unspoilt bars and on his back he adopts unusual positions to stand, stretching all four legs as far in front or behind as possible and dropping his back. Once a horse has learned that a certain position gives him at least some relief from his frustration and suffering he will be very reluctant to move. Of course, this is against the Natural Training Method, because instead of rounding his back and bringing his hocks underneath his body, the opposite is achieved.

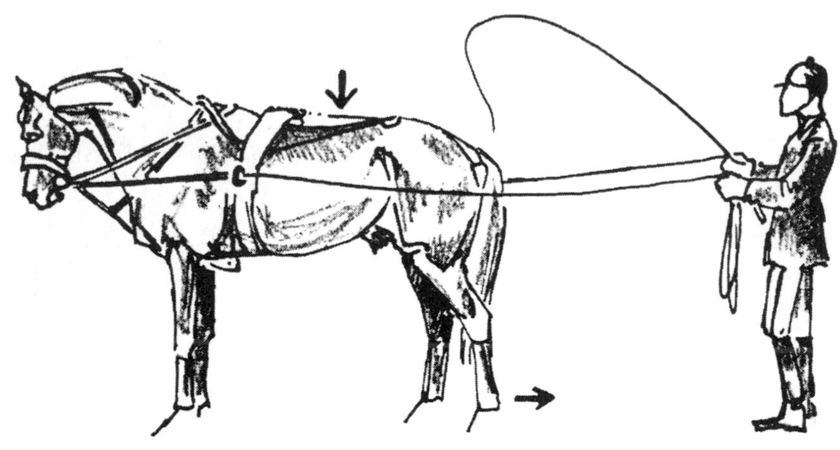

*Fig. 230*
Driving a horse in long reins continues the bad effects caused by the breaking tack while making the mouth. The horse's head is "placed", the back is dropped, the hindlegs are trailing.

When taking out the breaking bit it may be noticed that the bars and tongue are red and blue and the salivary ducts under the tongue are injured. Therefore, obviously, it will create an apprehensive horse who will not easily accept the action of the bit when being ridden later on. The horse's frame of mind is affected because he will fret under such pre-training methods.

The second phase in the old schooling method was to "drive" the horse in long-reins, sometimes even in conjunction with crossed side reins and standing martingale. In Europe, the old method of driving horses in long-reins is practised sometimes for harness horses. The mouths of harness horses are, on account of the specialised rein aids in coaching, developed completely differently to those of riding horses.

The coachman is only able to use two aids – *pulling* the reins and sending the horse on with the *whip*. This also applies to long reining. Therefore, to make a right-hand turn, the coachman pulls on the right rein and eases the left rein and vice versa.

I practised in Germany Die Achenbach'sche Fahrlehre, the method which is used in most countries when driving harness horses single, tandem, four, or even more, in hand. Therefore I know from experience, that the coachman, no matter how skilled, must *always pull backwards* when changing direction. The same thing happens when turning with long-reins: the hands move forward and backwards like steering a bicycle.

It is logical that this old-fashioned method of making the mouth must be catastrophic for a riding horse.

It is not often realised how particularly vulnerable the bars are. The sensitive and sharp bone can, to a certain extent, be compared to the human shinbone. It is covered only with fine tissue and nerves. Therefore there is almost no cushion between the skin and jawbone where the bit lies. Regrettably, people make the mistake when schooling of being too rough on the bars. The young horse develops a sore mouth from being jerked and snatched around, and rather than giving in to that sore spot the horse will push against it. He learns that if he pushes hard enough it deadens the pain and so the trainer has developed a bigger problem than he

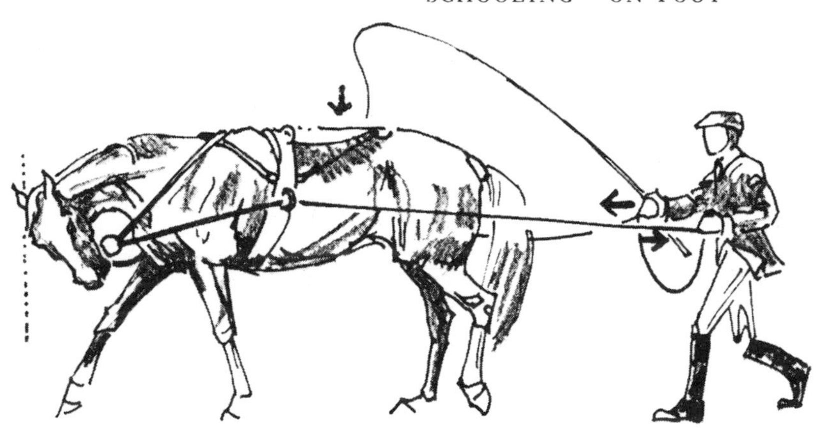

*Fig. 231*
When turning, the trainer has to use coachman's aids and pull the inner rein backwards, the horse is behind the bit, leaning over the shoulder.

*Fig. 232*
Some harness horses have such a hard mouth that they pull the carriage more with the reins than with the traces.

*Fig. 233*
A turn on a bicycle and a turn with long reins are done with the same movement.

had at the start. Before the horse has even been ridden he has already been taught to pull against the rider's hands. Every horse before he is broken and ridden has an unspoilt mouth; he will feel the slightest tension of the reins. Therefore the rein aids should be used merely to guide the horse. Even the *weight* of the long reins is too heavy and hardens the bars. If, later on, a horse is found to have a hard and difficult mouth, it is because it was created by unskilled treatment. In such a case, not the horse but his trainer is to blame.

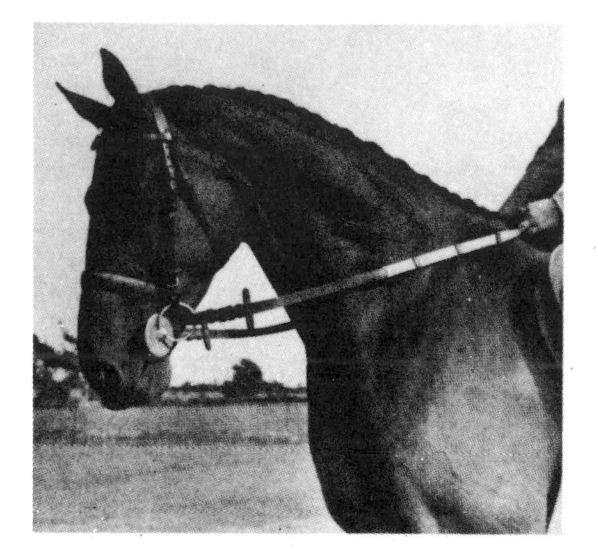

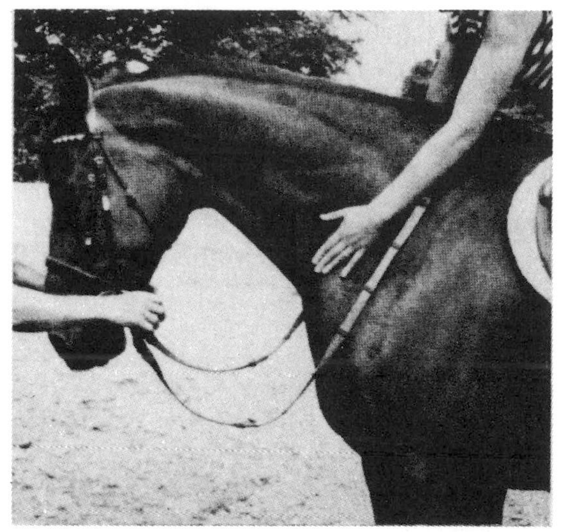

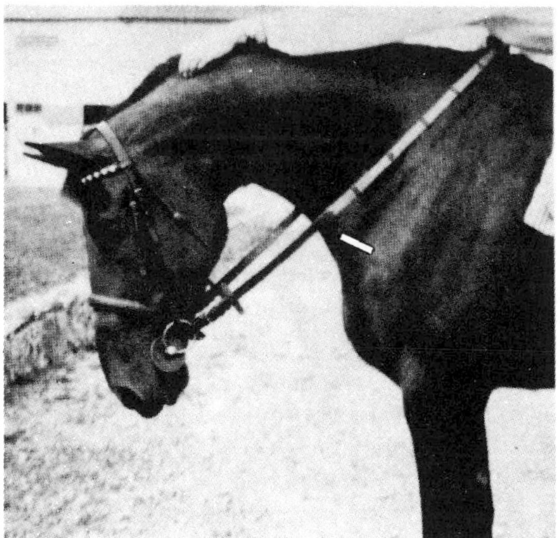

*Fig. 234* (top)
The upper neck muscles should be well developed.

*Fig. 235* (centre)
If they are squeezed, the horse bends his neck directly.

*Fig. 236* (top, right)
The underneck muscles should be thin and loose.

*Fig. 237* (centre, right)
They thicken and stiffen when the horse is above the bit.

*Fig. 238* (right)
When the muscles are squeezed, the horse bends his neck laterally.

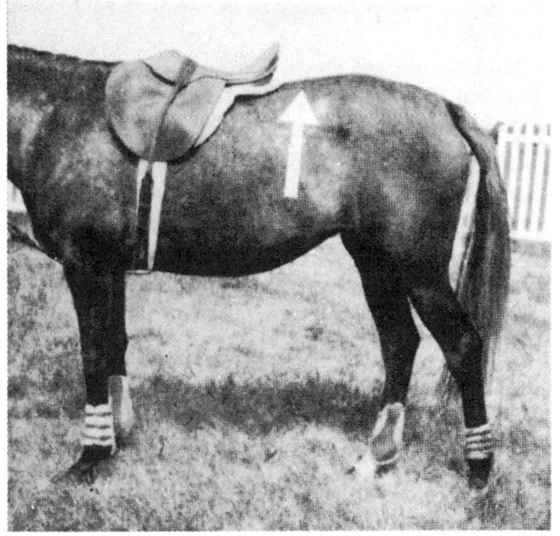

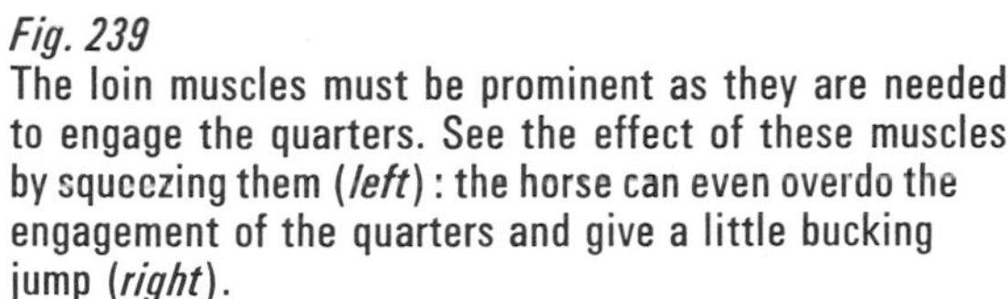

*Fig. 239*
The loin muscles must be prominent as they are needed to engage the quarters. See the effect of these muscles by squeezing them (*left*): the horse can even overdo the engagement of the quarters and give a little bucking jump (*right*).

## THE MUSCLES

To school a showjumper correctly it is essential that the trainer knows exactly *which* muscles have to be developed and *why*.

For every branch of equitation the horse has to develop particular muscles. That is why a horse which has to perform in various branches of the sport can hardly be expected to beat a specialist in one particular field. An event horse, for instance, must be versatile, disciplined to do dressage, fit to do the endurance and cross-country section and accurate to do a show-jumping course.

Therefore it is not an example of good horsemanship to compete with a promising young showjumping horse in all kinds of events. A potential showjumping horse needs specialised training to build up muscles that enable him to shift weight suddenly from the forehand to the quarters and to lower and engage the quarters. All his muscles and joints have to act as a spring in "shooting" the horse like a rocket forward-upwards and take-off. The horse must be so elastic and athletic that he can bascule effortless over enormous obstacles, either out of a collected canter or out of a gallop.

Such muscle development takes a long time and can only be achieved by progressive and continual training. Only then will the horse jump with comparatively little effort and last a lifetime. Regrettably, promising young horses are often pushed too fast because people are over anxious to see quick results. They are rushed through a two-year training programme in half a year. The horse is then actually running before he learned to walk. He will not be the horse who keeps winning year after year until he is retired.

The "upper" neck muscles, in the region close to the atlas, should be well developed. If the horse is on the bit then these muscles are prominent, while the "under" neck muscles, on either side of the neck in front of the shoulder, should be relaxed and hardly visible.

If the horse carries his head too high these under neck muscles will stiffen and become clearly visible. One can, in fact, feel this part of the neck becoming thick and stiff if one places both hands on either side of the neck base while an assistant pushes up the horse's head. If one squeezes these under neck muscles gently with thumb and forefinger on the one side, one will notice that the horse bends his neck and head to this side, while making a submission with the lower jaw. This indicates how important the flexibility of these muscles is in the "lateral" and consequently the "direct" bending of the neck. Horses who contract their upper neck muscles and therefore lean on the bit, or poke their nose forwards, can be corrected at a halt by squeezing these muscles at the atlas. This, in conjunction with forward-driving leg aids, creates a "direct" flexion at the poll and the horse bends his head towards his chest. At the same time the horse will make a submission with the lower jaw.

The muscles of the shoulder and forearms should be strong and well developed and clearly visible when standing close to the horse's shoulder and looking down.

The back, loin and quarter muscles are very important for a showjumper. It is essential that they should be strongly developed, including the buttocks (if one lifts up the tail, the buttock muscles are clearly noticeable) and the second thighs, because this part of the horse is the "power station", creating the propulsive force. Straight behind the saddle, on either side of the loin vertebra, one should actually feel two large bundles of muscles which come into full power and action when needed at take-off and to round the back.

Well developed back and loin muscles strengthen the weakest region of the horse's body: the connection between the quarters, the middle part and the forehand. One can actually see these loin muscles move at every stride, while lungeing with the Chambon, when the horse rounds his back. Or one can feel them move (with one's hand) when riding at walk up and downhill (an excellent exercise to build up these muscles).

In young or badly schooled horses the lumbar vertebra is higher than the muscles on either side. One can hardly expect that such a horse will give the rider a pleasant ride or will be able to jump correctly.

When mounted one can see the effect of these muscles by squeezing them (as done with the neck muscles), again in conjunction with strong forward driving seat and leg aids. The horse will engage his quarters actively, in fact so much that he will be even "overdoing" it, giving a little forward bucking jump at the same time. The horse feels the squeeze along the entire spinal cord reacting upon the atlas joint; he will lift up his head and put his nose forward. Such a squeeze, now and again, can be quite effective on horses who carry their head too low, are overbent and go behind the bit.

During the entire schooling in the Natural Training Method the slow development of the muscles is carefully planned. The tendons and ligaments will also become strong and guarantee a long and active career of the horse.

CHAPTER NINE

# JUMPING-DRESSAGE

I HAVE deliberately chosen the term *jumping-dressage* in the hope of creating greater interest among showjumping riders in practising gymnastic exercises while schooling their jumping horses.

This book is mainly concerned with the training of showjumping horses and riders, nevertheless we have to talk about dressage, because it is impossible to school a showjumper correctly without using jumping-dressage.

It is regrettable that some showjumping riders consider dressage as unnatural. They talk about it as if it were some peculiar form of foreign riding and not really necessary for schooling showjumping horses. This is a *grave* mistake because to school and improve a showjumping performance it is essential to carry out a systematic training on the flat, which is dressage. However, it is not quite the same as for a dressage test, but it involves the same *principles*.

Jumping-dressage is a long series of progressive gymnastic exercises which develop the horse's movements, obedience, balance and jumping ability to the utmost degree. It is pleasant for a rider to jump such a horse, as it will respond quickly to the rider's aids. For these reasons I feel no showjumping rider should overlook this chapter by telling himself that he knows all about dressage and prefers to read only about jumping.

I am aware that I touch on a delicate subject when saying that jumping-dressage is more productive for the showjumping horse than is classic dressage.

The differences between classic dressage and jumping-dressage are that in the latter the impulsion, accumulated in the collection, is used to propel the horse not only forward but *upwards* as well to clear fences. In classic dressage, however, this propulsive force is used in a forward direction.

The important difference is that a showjumper needs complete freedom of head and neck to be able to *bascule* over large obstacles. A showjumper must be able to change fluently from a high degree of collection to an elastic degree of expansion in order to cope with spread fences. He must respond to the minimum use of aids in turning quickly and fluently and have enough initiative and "heart" to attempt all obstacles. Therefore dressage for a jumpėr cannot possibly be the same as for a dressage horse.

*Fig. 240*
In a dressage horse the accumulated impulsion is used in a forward direction only.

*Fig. 241*
In a jumping horse the impulsion is used in an upwards-forward movement.

THE SEAT

Not all riders are fully aware that in various branches of equitation different seat positions are required. In order to acquire good results in schooling horses it is important for the rider to practise and perfect these different seat positions.

*The forward seat*

The founder of the forward seat was the late Captain Caprilli, instructor at the famous Italian Cavalry School at Tor di Quinto, near Rome, and at Pinerolo.

The Caprilli system advocates the preservation of the natural balance of horse and rider. Before Caprilli introduced the forward seat position the technique used was quite the opposite, preventing the horse from using his full strength and jumping ability.

The forward seat was demonstrated for the first time in 1901 at the International Horse Show in Turin. In spite of the fact that there was at first strong opposition, Caprilli's method became a phenomenal success. Cavalry officers from all parts of the world came to Italy to study his system and in later years the forward seat was adopted by all cavalry schools. Unfortunately the great master met with a fatal fall in 1908.

A showjumper can only be schooled successfully in the Natural Training Method, based on the Caprilli principles, if the rider completely masters the independent balanced forward seat.

The forward seat is used when jumping, when riding in hilly country and when riding over cavaletti. It is used in all three paces. Walk and trot are most suitable to practise the forward (light) seat, especially when riding over cavaletti in these paces.

The most important point of the forward seat is that the seat is positioned very close "over" the saddle – but never *in* the saddle. The rider is riding "on the fork", even when landing after a jump or riding downhill.

This is only possible if the rider has a very *firm* grip with his knees; they must be immovable at the same place on the saddle. The stirrup leathers have to be shortened sufficiently to give the rider a definite "feel" of the stirrups. The lower leg is positioned slightly behind the

*Fig. 242*
Perfect forward seat. American rider Carol Hoffman riding Salem to victory at the Dublin International Horse Show.

*Fig. 243*
Beautiful style. The American Bill Steinkraus.

girths. The heel is well pushed down, the foot slightly bent outwards at the ankle, so that the sole can be seen from the side. The stirrup is situated under the ball of the foot and the foot rests on the inner side of the stirrup. If the stirrup is positioned too close to the heel it eliminates the elasticity of the ankle. The ankles do not touch the horse's sides. Because the foot is slightly at an angle the calf and knee get closer to the horse, ensuring a firm grip. This grip is vital for an independent balanced seat in jumping.

The leg aids are given with the inner side of the calves. Only if the horse does not obey is a short active tap with the spur applied. (Some riders make the mistake of pressing with their ankles, therefore having to turn out their knees and calves, losing grip and dropping their seat into the saddle.)

The rider should always keep his head up; in looking down he tends to round his shoulders and stiffen his back. The shoulders should not be too far in front of his knees, as that would mean loss of balance. By straightening the shoulders and broadening the chest the rider will slightly hollow his back without stiffening it. This way the rider's centre of gravity is located vertically above his knees and above that of the horse.

A firm grip with the knees ensures independent hands and rein aids in all situations. The hands are always carried *free* from the horse's neck, ready at any time to follow the movement of head and mouth smoothly and without disturbance. The reins are held *shorter* than normal according to the forward position of the rider's upper body. The elbows are kept close to the body and the lower arm should be on a straight line from the elbow to the horse's mouth. Shoulders, elbows and wrists must be supple to ensure a sensitive, steady contact with the horse's mouth.

Riders who do not master this forward seat proclaim that it is impossible to apply correct leg aids and half-halt aids in the forward seat position. They are of this opinion because they lose balance when applying leg aids and are

*Fig. 244*
The balanced forward seat.

therefore forced to sit down in the saddle. This disturbs the balance and rhythm of the horse's movements. Once a rider has established a firm forward seat he will certainly have *no* problem in applying the aids in all three paces without loosing balance.

*Incorrect forward seat*

Although there is no controversy about the fact that the forward seat should be used for jumping, one can often see it practised incorrectly.

*Too long stirrup leathers*

These are often the reasons for a rider losing his balance in the forward seat while jumping. The rider's lower leg is positioned *in front* of the girths, the toe is pushed down and the heel pulled up. The knees, being in the wrong position, cannot find a firm grip and the rider does not get a definite "feel" of the stirrups. The rider gets left behind, dropping into the saddle, while airborne, (especially over spread fences), and balances himself on the reins, thus pulling the horse's head and neck up.

*Fig. 245*
Too long stirrup leathers.

*Fig. 246*
Too short stirrup leathers.

The rider's sudden change of balance in mid-air, and the high head and neck carriage of the horse, will cause him to drop his back and to shift the centre of gravity to the quarters. The horse is likely to make faults with the hindlegs, especially on the far pole of spread fences.

*Too short stirrup leathers*

These will also unbalance the rider's forward seat. When jumping the rider's lower leg will swing backwards and upwards, forcing the rider to change his centre of gravity too much to the forehand. This sudden change disturbs the balance of the horse. The rider is forced to seek support by resting his hands on the horse's neck or taking a hold of the mane. In any case, the rider drops the reins, losing contact with the horse's mouth.

The horse misses the contact with the reins and at the same time becomes disturbed by the rider's sudden change of balance. The horse will come on to the forehand and most certainly make faults with the forelegs. He will knock the top front pole of a fence.

*The remount seat*

The name originates from the vocabulary of former cavalry schools. This seat was practised when breaking and schooling young horses.

In the remount seat the rider's seat is always in the saddle, in contrast to the forward seat where the rider's seat should never be *in* the saddle, but *on* the saddle.

The upper part of the rider's body is bent slightly forward and his shoulders are just in front of the imaginary vertical line going from the rider's hip to his heel. The rider holds his hip bones slightly forward, putting more weight on to his thighs and stirrups than on his seat bones.

When riding in this seat position the rider brings his weight closer to the horse's withers, thus avoiding any excess weight on to the young horse's weak and undeveloped loin muscles.

*Fig. 247*
The remount seat.

*Fig. 248*
A rider showing a hunter at full gallop. A showjumping trainer cannot use such a style of riding. It would lead to disaster when riding a showjumper, which can only produce its best if it is trained and ridden in a style suitable to its purpose.

The remount seat allows the horse to round his back and should be used not only for *young horses*, but also for horses who have a *sensitive* or "cold" back, as it prevents the usual bucking after mounting. In the remount seat the rider rides with shorter reins than in the dressage seat because the distance from his hands to the horse's mouth is shorter on account of the forward position of his upper body. The hands are carried low and free of the horse on either side of the withers to be able to follow the movement of head and neck. The rider's lower leg position and the length of the stirrup leathers is the same as in the forward seat.

*Rising trot*

Rising trot can be ridden in two different seat positions. Firstly, in the remount seat, which is used when riding showjumpers, young horses, and when practising *jumping-dressage;* and secondly, in the dressage seat. This is done only in *classic dressage* and on trained horses.

*The parade seat*

In the parade seat the rider is "at ease" and he relaxes his muscles, while the upper part of the body is kept erect and the head well up. The rider holds his hip bones vertically and sits close to the front of the saddle. The rider's ears, shoulders, hips and heels should be on an imaginary vertical line; the girths can be seen slightly in front of the lower leg.

*Fig. 249*
The parade seat.

*The deep seat*

In the deep seat the rider turns his hip bones (pelvic structure) slightly backwards, tilting the pelvis and tucking the seat under. At the same time the rider pushes his seat bones forward – in conjunction with forward driving leg aids. This increases the horse's action and forward impulsion, sending him into the rider's hands: "riding him from the rear to the front" (one makes, to a certain extent, the same movements with the seat as when sitting on a swing).

In spite of the rider's strong muscular seat and leg actions, his seat should be positioned close to the front of the saddle. When riding turns, stronger actions are applied on the inner side, with the outer leg supporting behind the girths to prevent the quarters from deviating sideways. The rider's upper body is in the same vertical position as in the parade seat. Even when contracting his seat and loin muscles the rider should not round or stiffen his back.

The position of the lower arms depends on the movement of the horse, the degree of collection and the arching of the horses' neck. The rider's hands must be held free of the horse's neck at all times. Arms, wrists and fingers should maintain flexibility in order to follow smoothly the horse's movements of head and neck.

The stirrup leathers should be approximately three holes longer than in the forward seat, otherwise the rider's seat would be pushed too far back in the saddle. The foot position is parallel with the horse's body, holding the stirrups slightly in *front* of the ball of the foot. Less weight is put on to the stirrups in comparison to the remount or the forward seat.

*Fig. 250*
The deep seat.

## GYMNASTIC EXERCISES

Exercises which develop the muscles and balance of the horse are explained in previous chapters and will continue throughout the book.

It is equally vital that the *rider* pays attention to his own physical fitness, otherwise he cannot learn to jump correctly. A stiff rider does not have the flexibility needed when jumping and will be unable to follow quickly enough with his upper body the change of balance of the horse. A rider who is not "with" the horse's movements gets left behind, will automatically take a tight hold of the reins and hinder the horse. The horse feels uncomfortable because his balance is disturbed; he will become nervous and unco-operative.

The following gymnastic exercises originate from the former European cavalry schools, where they were called "physical drill". In those days not only the recruits were ordered to undergo a course of physical training but senior cavalry men joined in as well – voluntarily.

These training courses were especially planned for the rider in order to make his muscles supple and to improve his balance, freedom of action and strength to stand the strain of daily riding. The emphasis was put not only on strength but on controlling and co-ordinating the muscular action as well. This cavalry training was considered to give the rider the cavalry spirit, discipline, sense of reflex and "boldness". For example, when a young man joined the cavalry he may have been clumsy with rounded shoulders, not knowing how to hold himself. After a basic physical training course the same young man walked tall, looked slim and had mental control over his muscular actions.

Some riders not only sit slackly on a horse but also walk like that. For this reason I feel it is necessary to recall these physical drill exercises so that the rider of today may also benefit from their influence.

One of the fundamental principles is breathing correctly – under all circumstances.

What happens when one breathes? One takes in oxygen, which is the body's most vital necessity. It is the driving power behind all our physical and mental processes. One could live for three days without water, three weeks without food, but no more than three minutes without oxygen.

Breathing in should always be done through the nose. Most medical men think that how one breathes is more important than how deeply one breathes. There is really no need to throw the chest out and to pull the tummy in sergeant major style, but if one does not hold oneself correctly one cannot breathe properly. Bad posture, hunched shoulders and a rigid back inhibits natural breathing movements. It is rather like sucking orange juice through a bent straw. Correct breathing decreases the adrenalin output, which increases when one is nervous and which can then constrict breathing.

Many competitors use far too much energy, not because they have to work so hard while jumping but simply because they do not breathe correctly. Their normal steady rate of breathing may change completely. Tension and nervousness makes one hold one's breath or breathe too quickly and the result is breathlessness and lack of oxygen. Some riders have to struggle with this problem by the time they are halfway through a competition course (which normally doesn't take longer than two minutes). There are riders who, prior to entering the arena, get so worked up that they are nearly breathless. Needless to say riders in such a condition influence their horses and such tense partnerships are not capable of giving harmonious performances.

A rider who is not breathing normally is no longer supple and his centre of gravity will not be in accordance with the natural balance of his horse in all movements. The rider's hands will also become less flexible and this will prevent the horse from using his neck to *bascule* over the fences. This in turn will make the horse obstinate and unwilling to obey his rider's demands.

All this can be avoided if the rider practises gymnastic exercises. Some suitable ones are described. The exercises should be done at least three times a week for some 30 minutes each time.

*Fig. 251*
Riding without stirrups is useless, unless the correct leg and heel position is maintained.

One should use a quiet horse and, for safety's sake, one tacked up with the Gogue Independent (I am opposed in principle to the use of side reins) and a rubber snaffle is preferable. The end of the reins should be fastened to the neck strap of the breastplate in order to prevent the horse from stepping on them when he stretches his neck to the ground.

All the gymnastic exercises should be first practised when the horse is standing still and also later on during all the three paces.

The rider's leg position is most important, particularly when doing these exercises without stirrups. The knees and calves should be placed against the saddle in the *same position* as if riding with stirrups: heels well down and toes up. This position will ensure that the leg muscles become stronger, to such an extent that one will be able to ride as easily without stirrups as with them, even in rising trot. The benefit of this will be shown later on when a rider may lose his stirrups during a jumping competition and may have to jump without them.

There are riders who, for one reason or other, frequently lose their stirrups. In such cases use of a thin elastic band fastened on to the stirrups and around the rider's feet is advised. This prevents the rider from losing his stirrups and at the same time it is not dangerous because if a fall occurs the elastic band will break easily.

However, to the well-educated rider, losing one, or even both, stirrups makes no difference because he has developed muscles to ensure the proper firm grip. This is why I am so strongly against those riding schools, where, although riding without stirrups is taught, they neglect the correct leg and heel position. Their pupils have their legs hanging down from the hips in a sloppy fashion. This forces the rider to turn his hips forward and to sit in front of his seat bones. Such a rider will never achieve a correct independent balanced seat and rounded shoulders and rigid back, again, leads to bad breathing.

The exercises, all in dressage seat position, are:

*Exercise 1*

The basic seat position is the "deep" dressage seat, where stirrups should not be used. The rider leans slightly backwards, placing both hands onto the cantle of the saddle. The heels are then pressed down with the toes turned upwards. He now lifts both knees as high as possible and wide apart, turning his hip bones into a backward direction and pulling the tummy in consciously. At the same time he should expand his chest by breathing in deeply. He then lowers both knees again, bringing his legs back into the original position while breathing out. Repeat this exercise 20 times while breathing rhythmically. This exercise strengthens and makes the abdomen supple, the back muscles and particularly the tummy muscles firm and promote the correct "deep" dressage seat.

*Fig. 252*
First exercise.

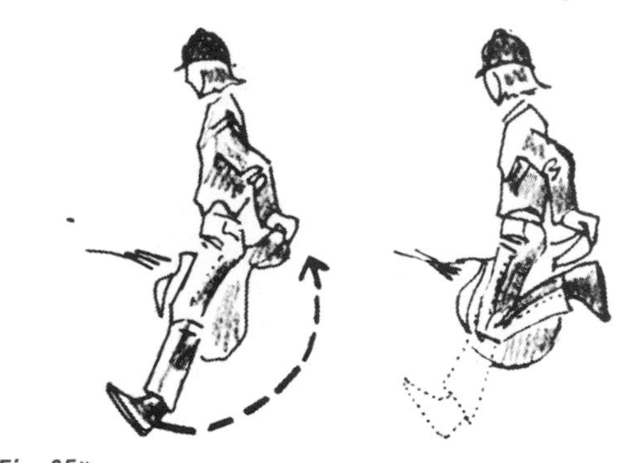

*Fig. 253*
Second exercise.

*Exercise 2*

The basic seat position is the same as in Exercise 1. The rider places both hands onto the cantle of the saddle. Breathing rhythmically he should swing his left lower leg out from the knee in a back and upwards direction, touching the saddle with his left ankle. At the same time he swings his right lower leg out from the knee in a forward direction with heels down and toes up. Both knees should be kept static and a firm grip maintained. During this exercise, with alternate forwards and backwards swinging of the lower legs in either direction, the rider should push his seat deeply into the front part of the saddle and keep his head well up. Repeat 20 times. This exercise makes the hip and leg muscles, and in particular the calf muscles, supple.

*Fig. 254*
Third exercise.

*Exercise 3*

The seat position is again the same. Place both hands onto the cantle of the saddle. While breathing rhythmically make a circling movement with the toes of both feet, from the outside towards the horse. The knees and lower legs should at the same time be maintained in their normal position. This exercise makes the ankle joint supple and flexible and the calf muscles are used as well; it will also enable the rider to press his heels further downwards, thus giving him a stronger grip and better leg position. Repeat 20 times.

*Fig. 255*
Fourth exercise.

*Exercise 4*

The basic seat position is again the same as in the previous exercises. Place both hands onto the cantle of the saddle. While breathing properly the upper body remains motionless. Close the eyes, drop chin onto chest and make a circling movement with the head. Roll the head a few times so that the ears touch the shoulders. Let the head roll as far back as possible. Repeat ten times, alternately in either direction.

Although this is an excellent exercise to make the neck muscles supple and to establish the rider's balance, great care must be taken when first practising this exercise, especially during sitting trot and catner, because a dizzy spell could arise and this could easily lead to a fall.

*Exercise 5*

The basic seat position is again maintained, but stirrups should now be used. Place only one hand on the cantle. Using the free hand to catch the ankle on that same side and pull it up as high as possible, while keeping the other leg in its normal position, *both* knees should be maintained in a firm grip. Then release the foot and with the toes pointing inward find the stirrup without looking down. Practise ten times on each side. If this exercise is practised later on during trot and canter it will be more difficult, but it will teach the rider to find his stirrups quickly in any situation.

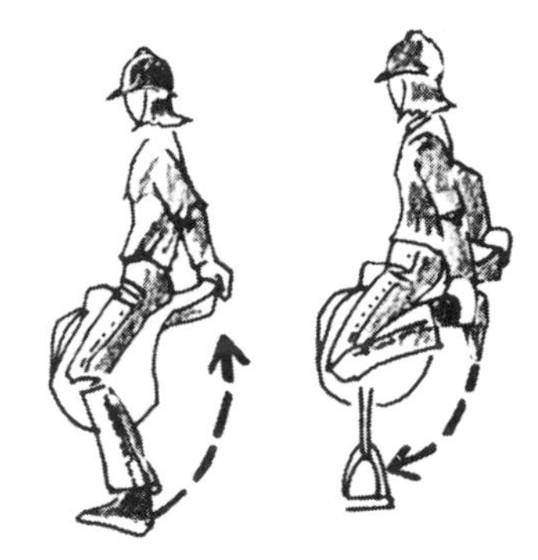

*Fig. 256*
Fifth exercise.

*Exercise 6*

The basic position is again the dressage seat. *No* stirrups are used. Stretch both arms to the fingertips sideways. Maintaining this position swivel the trunk around sideways to the back and forward as far as possible, and follow this movement with the head. The seat remains in the saddle. While breathing rhythmically, the upper part of the body and midriff will become very supple. The exercise is excellent for the balance, especially when it in practised is sitting trot and canter, because to maintain balance the rider is forced to take a strong grip with his legs. Repeat ten times.

*Fig. 257*
Sixth exercise.

*Exercise 7*

Again the dressage seat is the basic position. *No* stirrups are used. The heels should be pressed downwards very firmly otherwise balance may be lost. With both arms stretched forward, bend the upper body forward and downwards (breathing out) until the fingertips touch the toes. Then slowly raise both arms high up and bend over backwards (breathing in) until head and arms touch the croup, breath out and relax. Then slowly raise arms and body (breathing in) until one sits up straight again. Repeat ten times. This exercise can only be done on a very quiet horse. Not only the back muscles but the entire body will become supple and strong. One will feel the calf muscles contracting if the heels are kept well down.

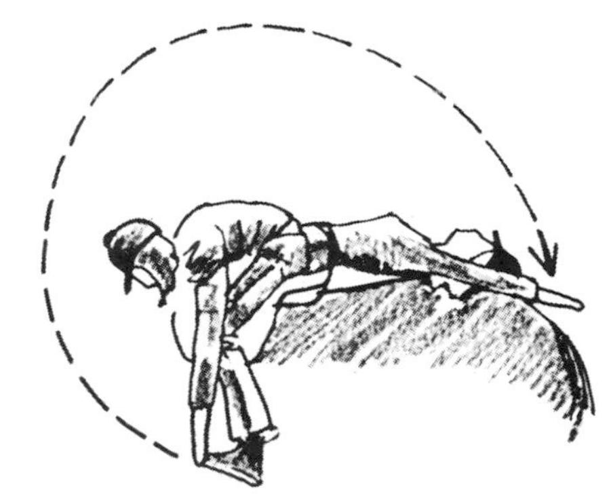

*Fig. 258*
Seventh exercise.

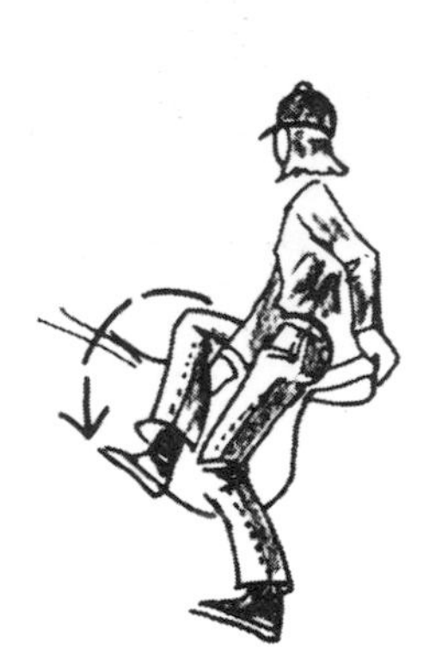

*Fig. 259*
Eighth exercise.

*Exercise 8*

Sit in the dressage seat with both hands on the cantle. *No* stirrups are used. Place the left hand on the cantle and the right hand on the pommel. While breathing in lift up the right knee (heel pressed down) and swing the right leg over the horse's neck without touching it, breathing out while lowering the right leg on the horse's near shoulder. Now (breathing in) lift up the right knee and bring it over the horse's neck. Lower it into its original position (breathing out). When this exercise is executed with the left leg, place the hands vice versa. Repeat ten times with each leg. This exericse will not only improve the balance of the rider but will also make his hip and abdominal muscles supple.

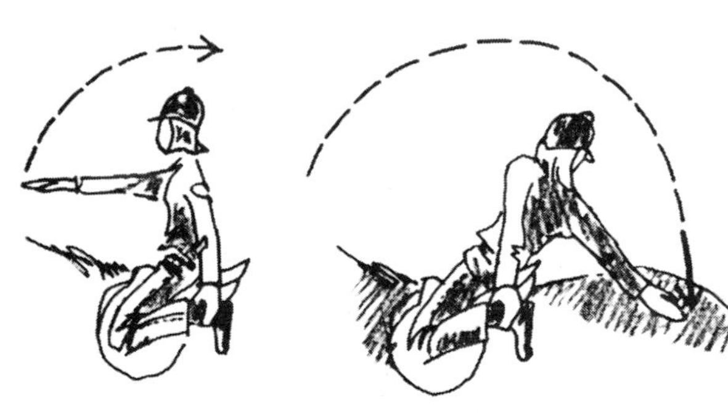

*Fig. 260*
Ninth exercise.

*Exercise 9*

Stirrups are *not* used. Take the left ankle in the left hand and pull it as high as possible upwards (both knees remain in the normal position). Now stretch the right arm straight forward and lift it (breathing in). With a sudden jerk turn the palm of the hand outwards (if this movement is done quickly one will feel the muscles of the shoulders, arms, wrists and hands come into action). Move the hand backwards and place it on the left hip of the horse (slowly breathing out). Then the stretched arm is brought downwards and forwards again, completing the lower half of the circle, passing the rider's knee, while breathing in. This exercise should be practised ten times with each arm as it is a perfect breathing exercise which broadens the chest and expands the lungs while absorbing air. It also strengthens the midriff muscles, which enhances the rider's ability to stay in balance.

Additional exercises, all in the forward seat position, are:

*Fig. 261*
Tenth exercise.

*Exercise 10*

Stirrups should be used. The purpose of this exercise is to acquire a better balance, which is essential for an independent forward seat. The basic position is the forward seat (shorten the stirrup leathers accordingly). Push both stretched arms forward with a vigorous movement in the direction of the horse's mouth while breathing out. Then bending both arms bring the elbows as far as possible into a backward direction without raising the shoulders while breathing in. This vigorous stretching and bending of the arms to and fro is of great value when quick reaction in jumping is necessary (following the horse's head and neck). Repeat ten times.

*Exercise 11*

Remain in the forward seat and cross the arms behind the back. Do rising trot, breathing in while rising and breathing out while touching down. Practise this exercise when trotting without stirrups. It strengthens one's leg muscles and it also greatly improves the forward seat grip and stamina as well. The seat should not be lifted so high that one can see daylight between seat and saddle, instead the hips should be brought more forward than upwards. Practise this for a few minutes.

*Fig. 262*
Eleventh exercise.

*Exercise 12*

Stretch the arms as explained in Exercise 6, but now practise it in the forward seat. The seat should be out of the saddle but at the same time close to the saddle in all three paces. Use stirrups and breathe rhythmically. This exercise is particularly good for improving the independent balanced forward seat.

*Fig. 263*
Twelfth exercise.

*Exercise 13*

Practise this in the forward seat using the stirrups. Bend forward and breathe out. Touch the toe of the left boot with the fingertips of the right hand. Keeping the head well up and the seat out of the saddle, repeat the same movement with the left arm, touching the toe of the right boot; when the body is raised breathe in. Repeat ten times on both sides. It is excellent for the improvement of the stomach and back muscles. Experienced riders may practise this in trot and canter as well.

*Fig. 264*
Thirteenth exercise.

The following exercise is practised *unmounted* and is very beneficial for accomplishing both the dressage seat and the forward seat.

*Exercise 14*

Each foot is placed in either corner of a door frame (approximately 1·2 metres wide), that is, in the same position as if they were placed in the stirrups, with the ball of the foot on the threshold, the heel on the floor and the little toe against the jamb of the door. A stick is then placed across the small of the back and held firmly on the inside of the elbows, thereby

*Fig. 265*
Fourteenth exercise.

pulling back the shoulders and expanding the chest. Keep the upper part of the body erect with the head well up. While breathing out bend the knees slowly, pushing them down towards each other until they nearly reach the floor. While breathing in straighten the legs. Repeat this exercise 20 times. This splendid exercise has a tremendous effect on firming the calf, ankle and upper leg muscles. It will also help develop a strong grip for an independent balanced forward seat.

## BALANCE

Grave mistakes can be made in the schooling of horses if one is uncertain about the natural balance of the horse in motion and in jumping.

By nature every young horse moves in balance. From the first weeks of his life he canters in the field without losing his balance or stumbling. Nevertheless, during the first few months of riding the young horse has great difficulties in maintaining his balance due to the additional force of gravity of the rider's weight. To appreciate how difficult it is for the young horse to re-establish his natural balance while carrying the burden of a rider, imagine a burden on one's own back. One automatically places the burden above one's centre of gravity, which is between the shoulders. This is the easiest way to carry it. One reacts the same way as does a young horse trying to re-balance himself. One rounds the back and pushes the head and neck downwards and forward. The weight would be twice as heavy if carried lower down on the small of the back.

It is more or less the same for the horse. When the rider distributes his weight closer to the withers he makes it easier and more comfortable for the horse to carry. If the rider sits too far back near the cantle of the saddle his centre of gravity is not distributed *above* that of the horse but over the weaker part of the horse's back – the sensitive spine and loin. This disturbs the free use of muscles which cover the loin and vertebrae. The horse cannot round his back or bring his hind legs underneath. Both are most important for a showjumper to propel himself forward and upward.

In the early stages of schooling the young horse should therefore never be ridden on the bit but *only* on a loose or long rein, held finger-tight. Only then the horse has the opportunity to regain his natural balance carrying a rider because he can move with a low head and neck carriage. This enables him to use his back and quarters freely.

Once the horse has re-established his natural balance on level ground start riding him in hilly terrain in a forward seat on a loose rein. This is excellent pre-training for the balance of a future showjumper. It is difficult for the young horse to carry the rider's weight, but when this weight is shifted about as well then it is nearly impossible for the horse to move in balance. The horse relates his paces to the centre of gravity of his rider. For this reason it is absolutely necessary that the rider on a young horse sits as still as possible.

For example, imagine again a heavy burden on one's own back. If somebody gives it a sudden pull or push one's "natural" reaction would be to move either forward or backwards in an attempt to keep one's balance by trying to stay under the centre of gravity of the shifting load. The horse's balance is affected in the same way, especially when jumping, with a rider falling backwards and forward, shifting his weight excessively. If the rider brings his upper body when jumping very suddenly and exaggeratedly

*Fig. 266*
Carrying a weight easily and in balance above one's own centre of gravity.

*Fig. 268*
Compare the weight carrying man with a horse, who carries his rider in balance above his centre of gravity.

forward, or if he is left behind, or if he shifts his weight extremely to one side of the horse, then the horse is forced to change his centre of gravity accordingly. It will disturb the horse's balance and affect his performance seriously. When the horse has re-established his balance whilst being ridden in all three paces in both flat and hilly country on a loose rein without increasing his pace, only then can one start to ride the horse more towards the bit. It is very regrettable to see so many horses not being given the time to first develop their muscles and balance before being pushed onto the bit and asked to move in a collected manner.

*Fig. 267*
The weight is twice as heavy when carried lower down with a hollow back.

*Fig. 269*
Compare the weight carrying man with a horse, whose rider throws his weight into the back of the saddle. The horse will drop his back and feel the weight twice as heavy.

*Fig. 270*
To experience the force of gravity inherent in a tall burden which shifts its weight, carry a person on your shoulders. Any movement he makes will unbalance you considerably. The horse experiences very much the same effect if its rider moves about too much and is "all over the horse".

## HANDLING REINS

### *Taking up and shortening reins*

This action seems so simple, nevertheless many riders do it wrongly. They take up the reins too hastily and too roughly, alarming and upsetting the horse. The horse then reacts by increasing his pace. Some riders shorten the reins rather roughly and the horse's head is then pulled from one side to the other and equal contact with the mouth is lost. Other riders make the mistake of looking down at their hands whilst shortening the reins. They then unconsciously bend their bodies forward. This causes the horse to increase his pace as he tries to remain under the rider's centre of gravity.

The correct method is to take up the reins and shorten them gradually and gently without upsetting the horse. Before even touching the reins lift up the head, straighten the shoulders and shift the weight slightly backwards. The horse will adjust himself accordingly by bringing his hindlegs further underneath his body. Take up the reins and shorten them as follows: whilst moving the right hand over the left hand, take with the right thumb and forefinger the left rein and pull *a small piece* through the left hand, keeping the left fist closed. Then do the same with the left hand and shorten the right rein. Both reins should be shortened alternately until they have reached the desired length. At the same time make sure that contact with the horse's mouth is not lost – at any time.

*Fig. 271*
Shortening reins.

### *Both reins in one hand*

For example, if both reins are to be taken in the left hand: the left thumb is lifted and the right rein is then placed between the thumb and index finger of the left hand, with this same right rein then leaving the left hand between the fourth finger and the little finger.

To take both reins over in the right hand, place the right hand in front of the left one (with the knuckles in horizontal position). With the index, middle and fourth finger between the reins and the thumb and little finger spread out, take both reins over into the right hand.

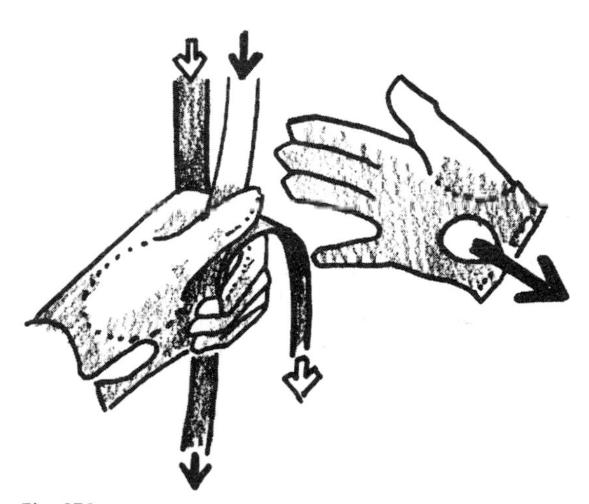

*Fig. 272*
Both reins in one hand.

To take one rein in each hand again: open the

thumb and little finger of the left hand and place the three middle fingers of the left hand on the left rein, in front of the right hand. Lift up the right thumb and the left hand takes over the left rein. When this is done gently and correctly the contact and feeling with the horse's mouth will not be disturbed. Both reins should always be in the left hand when riding with one hand; the right hand must be kept free to salute.

*The Mexican rein hold*

The Mexican method of holding the reins has several advantages over the normal one. For example, taking up, shortening or lengthening the reins is easier done. This is because it is unnecessary to bring both hands together, which alone is often enough to upset a nervous horse. One does not lose contact with the horse's mouth because one can easily gather the reins when shortening them. Lengthening is done by just letting the reins slip through the fingers.

With the normal rein hold one uses the strongly developed "upper" arm muscles (the biceps). But with the Mexican rein hold the less well-developed "lower" arm muscles come into play. This is reflected in a relaxation throughout the whole of the upper body, which, in turn, induces a "finger tight" rein hold.

From experience I know that many riders feel hopelessly lost when using the Mexican rein hold at first. Without their normally strong hold on the mouth they become insecure and unsteady and consequently lose their balance. These riders evidently do not have an independent balanced forward seat, therefore they balance themselves out of the horse's mouth. The Mexican rein hold is particularly recommended to correct riders with hard hands. Many riders take a stronger hold with the right hand, creating a horse with a "one-sided" mouth. In such a case one should use the Mexican rein hold with the right hand only in order to acquire equal feeling. The same applies to a rider who has the bad habit of checking with one particular hand.

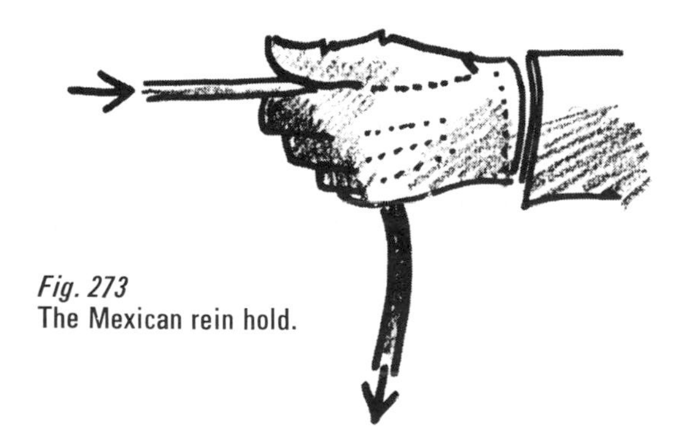

*Fig. 273*
The Mexican rein hold.

It is not necessary to use this rein hold in competitions, although it would not do any harm. If the rider has the habit, while jumping, of sticking out his elbows or fixing his hands on the neck of the horse then the Mexican rein hold ought to be used with both hands.

The Mexican rein hold influences the rider to bring the muscles of his thigh, lower legs and ankles into stronger action to ensure a firmer grip in order to remain in balance. In time this will aid the rider to develop a more independent balanced forward seat position.

The Mexican rein hold should be used not only in jumping and riding over cavaletti but also on the flat – in all paces in the forward seat.

However, no matter which rein hold one uses, rein aids should be applied only by means of guiding the horse into a particular direction and not as an aid for the rider to stay in balance.

## THE HERD INSTINCT

A horse is a herd animal. Therefore, in the early stages of schooling, when the horse does not as yet understand the rider's aids, it is common sense to take advantage of his herd instinct. The young horse should be led by a quieter older horse who does not kick. Preferably the lead horse should be a stable mate of the young horse. This company will be of great advantage because the young horse will feel more at ease, hence quicker and better results will be obtained.

The first "loose" riding should ideally be done in an indoor school as the young horse will find it easier to concentrate here. If there is no indoor school available both horses should be taken into a small paddock, riding the young horse between the railing and the lead horse. At the same time the older horse should go slightly

*Fig. 274*
Captain Mark Philips in excellent style. Light hands and looking for the next fence.

in front to give the young horse confidence and to urge him to follow his leader. If the young horse is impetuous, allow him to go slightly in front and keep the lead horse back.

It is completely wrong to ride in the middle of the field, especially without a lead horse. The young horse would feel lost, because before being ridden he used to cross the field in any direction at will. For this reason one can hardly expect discipline when he is suddenly *not* allowed to do so any more. Do not be surprised when the young horse all of a sudden becomes bold, takes the bit and tries to run off when riding in the *middle* of the field, because he may be remembering his previous freedom.

## LEG AIDS

(i) In equestrian art we distinguish two different leg aids: *The forward driving leg aid.* This should be applied straight behind the girths with equal pressure from both legs. This is to request the horse to increase his propulsory force and lengthen his stride.

(ii) *The lateral driving leg aid.* This should be applied slightly further behind the girths. In the initial stage of schooling it is used to request the horse to move his quarters *sideways.* At a more advanced stage of schooling it is used to bend the horse's body *laterally* around the rider's inner leg and to control the quarters from deviating sideways.

### *Correct application*

Leg aids should always be applied simultaneously. In other words, the stronger pressure of one particular leg aid (active) should be supported by the pressure of the other leg (passive). The precise region *where* to apply these leg aids and the severity depends entirely on the degree of schooling and the sensitivity of the horse. When touching the horse in different regions one touches different muscles, subsequently one achieves different reactions from the horse.

I emphasise that it is impossible to school a horse up to a higher degree of equitation unless he is taught to respond to and to distinguish between the forward and the lateral driving leg aids. This fact is often not taken seriously enough, especially by riders who are not "interested" in dressage. But sooner or later in the career of a showjumper every rider will realise that it is vital to have the horse responding to the leg aids.

### *Hunting as an aid*

In countries where hunting is a national sport, preliminary education is different. Young horses are often taken out hunting as soon as they are broken and ridden before they are taught to respond to the leg aids. The rider depends solely on the horse's herd instinct and the fact that he will follow more experienced horses. In the heat of the hunt the young horse will jump obstacles which he would never attempt on his own without the company of other horses. The rider has no way of making the horse jump, as he has not yet been trained to obey the leg aids.

It is not my intention to criticise hunting as such, but every young horse should be first taught to respond to the leg aids before he is taken out to hunt. Then careful hunting is used as a preliminary schooling for the showjumper (although there is still the risk of the horse getting injured). The horse that is hunted without being taught to obey the leg aids will learn to lean on the bit and go on the forehand. The rider might mistakenly think that the impulsion the horse seems to have acquired in the hunting fields is sufficient and a substitute for obedience to the leg aids.

In small novice jumping competitions this hunting impulsion might be sufficient, but as soon as the fences become larger and more spread the horse that does not respond to the rider's forward driving leg aids will find himself in serious trouble. If this lack of fundamental schooling is not recognised and improved upon even the most talented showjumper will not realise a fraction of his true potential.

Although careful hunting will improve a

horse's muscles, balance, courage and breathing, and at the same time teach the young horse to look after himself and to use his initiative, it cannot replace basic schooling. Hunting is only a very small part of the basic training of a showjumper and is not really essential. Many horses of Olympic fame have never seen a hunting field.

### FORWARD DRIVING LEG AIDS

The forward driving leg aid is the *first* aid the young horse has to be taught by the rider. The obedience to this aid is most important, as one will appreciate later on in jumping competitions. No matter which type of (reasonable) obstacle one wants the horse to jump, he must willingly obey and jump it, guided by the *forward* driving leg aid. If one does *not* gain the horse's absolute obedience to this aid then all the other schooling would be just a waste of time. At this initial stage of schooling it has to be a combination of three aids:

(i) the rider's voice;

(ii) the forward driving leg aid, applied slightly behind the girths;

(iii) the dressage whip, applied just behind the rider's leg.

Each time the lead horse moves forward the young horse is given these three aids simultaneously. Very soon the young horse will understand these combined aids and move forward freely. Then the voice aid may be dropped and after a while the whip aid may also be omitted. Only the forward driving leg aid will then be necessary to urge the horse to move forward. Nevertheless a rider should always "carry" the dressage whip and this should be used only in situations where the horse does not respond sufficiently to the leg aids.

### HALTS USING KICKING BOARDS

The horse is now taught to slow down the pace or come to a halt. At this stage of schooling this must be achieved only by changing the rider's balance, using the *voice* and the *first rein aid*. During the pre-training (lungeing and liberty exercises "on foot") the horse has learned to respond to the trainer's voice and to the first and second rein aids. The benefit of this pre-training is that it is not necessary to take a stronger hold on the bit in order to slow down the young horse.

Unfortunately there are still trainers who neglect this pre-training and therefore believe that a horse can only be slowed down by taking a stronger hold on the bit. They are convinced that this is the *only* way because their horses have not been taught any other aids.

In every field of education, training principles change and progress with time. In equestrian sport, however, some trainers still use outdated training methods and believe in them simply because they were used by their fathers and those before them.

I sincerely hope that those trainers will *try* the Natural Training Method, because I am certain that they will soon discover how effectively it works on the horse and how much easier it is for the trainer.

How to slow down a *green* horse *without* a backwards pull on the mouth? Ride the horse, while the aids for the transition are given, *towards* the kicking boards at an angle of 45° approximately. The fence around a field can serve the very same purpose. The fact that the horse is facing the kicking boards will indicate to him that he should slow down and help to make him understand the aids for slowing down without a backwards pull on the mouth.

Let us say you are riding on the left-hand rein and want to make a transition from a walk to a halt.

The easiest way to do this is in the beginning, when coming from the short side of the school cut off the corner and ride on a straight line towards the kicking boards of the long side. Sit in dressage seat and while cutting off the corner prepare the horse by shifting your weight to his off hindleg. Breathe in deeply, straighten your body and broaden the chest, move the right

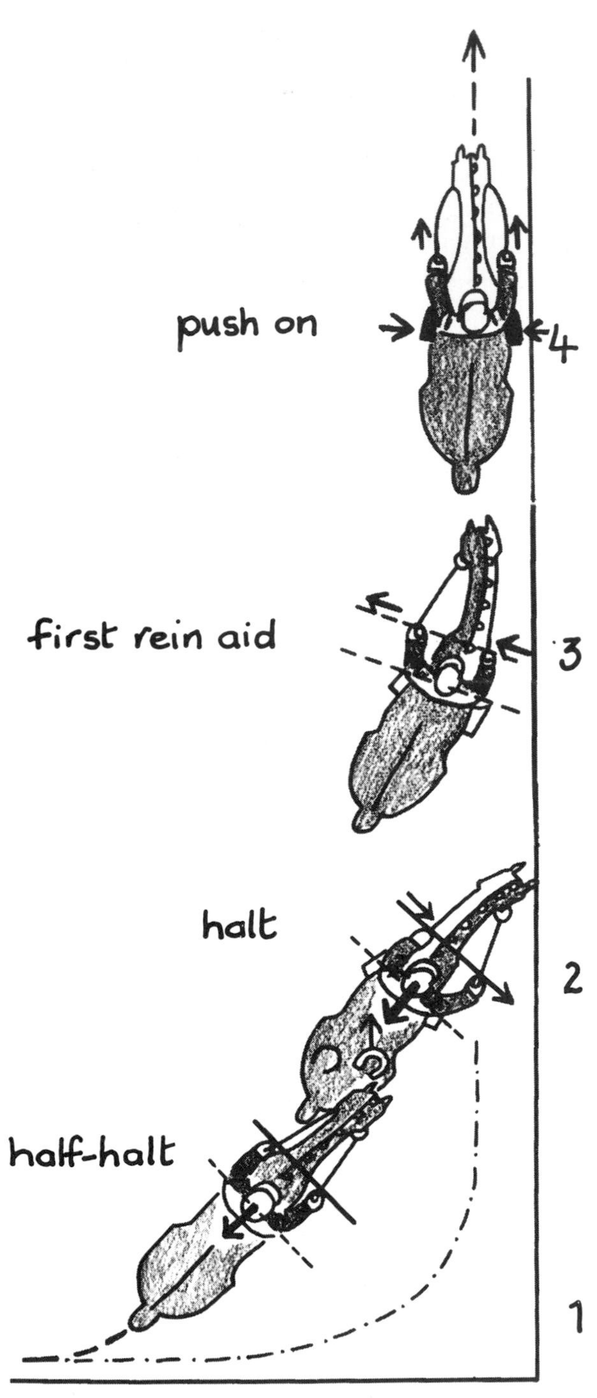


*Fig. 275*
Transition to halt. Start to train this by facing the horse towards the barrier, using the voice and with the rider changing balance. Follow up with the first rein aid.

shoulder slightly backwards and look to the right. *Always* change your balance first before using any rein aids. While preparing the horse like that your hands must stop following the natural nodding movement of the horse's head in the walk (passive hands). At the same time adopt a soothing tone a voice ("whoa") to slow the horse down; the horse learned this when lungeing. Also, at the same time, apply the first rein aid: with the left hand leaning against the horse's neck, *not* crossing the mane, the right hand moves simultaneously out sideways from the neck, *not* backwards. Maintain equal tension with both reins on the bit. The horse's head and neck are bent slightly to the right.

The horse has now reached the track and is facing the kicking boards. This indicates to him that he cannot go any further and helps the young horse to understand the aids to slow down . . . the horse will come to a halt.

Maintain the slight bending of the horse's neck to the right for a few more seconds, then, completing the first rein aid, move the left hand gradually sideways to the left, while moving the right hand against the neck, to such an extent that the horse's neck is now bent slightly to the left. The bit slides over the horse's tongue with the rubber discs pushing against the lip angles. The horse remembers this from lungeing and liberty exercises and will respond by flexing the lower jaw. At once yield the reins completely. The horse will respond by stretching his neck downwards and forward. Make sure *never* to miss this vital moment when the horse offers a submission and reward him by yielding the reins completely. The horse is very green still and one must take every opportunity to improve his confidence in the rider's hands.

After the horse has stretched his neck apply strong forward driving aids. Send him forward at an active walk on a completely loose rein. Make sure the horse lengthens his stride while stretching his neck down, otherwise he may come on to the forehand (riding the horse into the ground). After a few strides pick up the reins gently until the feeling with the bit is re-established.

*Fig. 276*
After coming to a halt, the horse, having made a submission, walks on energetically while dropping the reins.

(while breathing in), and careful forward driving seat and leg aids are applied according to the horse's degree of sensitivity in order not to upset him.

A few seconds before actually coming to a halt do *not* pull backwards, but instead just cease to follow the nodding movement of the horse's head and neck (passive hands). While the near forefoot touches the ground the left rein is brought sideways *out* from the neck and the right rein is brought against the neck. When the off forefoot touches the ground the right rein is brought out sideways from the neck; the left rein is brought against the neck. Keep the same feeling with *both* reins. Continuing in this

Repeat this transition from walk to a halt regularly on both reins. Most horses understand this aid very quickly.

During this initial stage of schooling, approximately the first fortnight under the rider, apply no lateral driving leg aids when doing this exercise. It would only confuse the young horse and would make him increase his pace and lean on the bit. Until now the young horse has only learned the forward driving leg aid. In teaching such a green horse to come back to a halt we may only use the aids explained above: change of balance, voice and first rein aid.

HALTS WITHOUT KICKING BOARDS

Bringing a horse to a halt in the centre of the school is a little more difficult on account of the missing support of the kicking boards. This should therefore be practised only when the horse has performed the preliminary exercise satisfactorily.

The rider should leave the track and turn towards the centre of the school by moving the inner rein sideways *out* from the horse's neck, supported by the outer rein leaning against the neck. In preparing for the halt keep both hands wide apart (open rein) and maintain a steady feeling (with both reins) with the mouth. The rider's weight is transferred slightly backwards

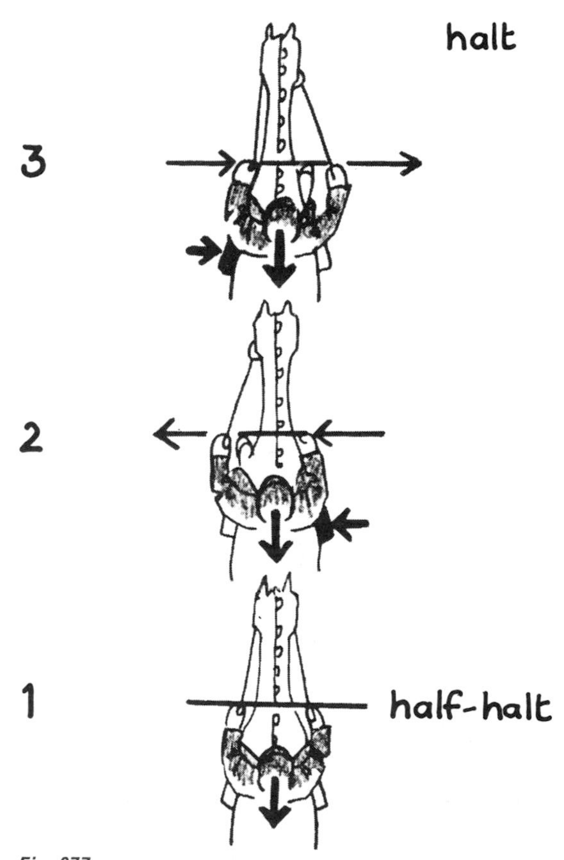


*Fig. 277*
Teaching the horse to come to a halt in the centre of the school.

manner one will find that the strides will become shorter and the horse will finally come to a complete halt.

If the horse does not become excited one can support the rein aids by applying the appropriate diagonal leg aids which corresponds with the sequence of the strides. When the near forefoot touches the ground, the left rein is brought sideways and at the same time pressure is applied with the right leg and vice versa.

Depending on the horse's progress the rider can refrain from keeping his hands exaggeratedly wide apart and from moving them too extremely sideways. In time the shifting of weight and the passive hands will be sufficient. During all the stages of training the rider should also react immediately when the horse makes a submission with the lower jaw by applying one of the three rein aids.

### LATERAL DRIVING LEG AIDS

If the rider is satisfied with the horse's progress he may start teaching him the lateral (sideways) driving leg aids.

The young horse has already learned during the preliminary schooling (work on foot) how to move his quarters sideways and has also developed the necessary muscles. Therefore the horse should not give much trouble when required to perform the same exercise mounted.

The rider should first exaggerate the sideways driving leg aid to make the young horse distinguish the *difference* between *sideways* and *forward* driving leg aids. Therefore, at this stage of schooling, the sideways driving leg aids are applied further *behind* the girths than normal and with the aid of the dressage whip.

Start teaching the horse the lateral driving leg aids by cutting off the corner at the short side in a walk, and while approaching the long side of the school apply the same aids as those used for teaching the horse to come to a halt facing the kicking boards (half halt aids). But in this case, while shifting your weight to the off hindleg, the right leg should be further behind the girths, supported by the dressage whip behind the right leg; the left leg remains on the girths.

While coming to a halt facing the kicking boards the horse will move his quarters slightly sideways to the left and cross with the off hindleg in front of the near one.

Responding to the lateral driving leg aid the horse has engaged the off hindleg and brought it under and crossing, the near hindleg. This proves that the horse has responded to the lateral driving leg aid. The rider should then apply the first rein aid and ride on, following the track in a very active walk, using the propulsive power accumulated by the engaged off hindleg.

This same exercise will be performed later on the track without cutting off the corner. That is a little more difficult, because after cutting off the corner one only has to stay on a straight line and is then facing the kicking boards. When doing this exercise on the track, however, the horse has to be advanced enough to obey the lateral driving leg aid already, because while bending the horse's neck towards the kicking boards the rider's outer leg has to move the horse's quarters away from the track. The horse is actually performing the first one or two steps of a turn around the forehand. The horse should always come to a halt with his off hindleg well underneath his body.

If a horse has not learned to obey the lateral driving leg aid previously he would just keep moving when attempting this exercise. Although his head will be bent towards the kicking boards, his body would stay straight and on the track. This would teach the horse bad habits, therefore it is necessary that the training is carried out exactly step by step as explained.

After approximately six weeks one can follow up the exercise, not only with the first but also with the second rein aid, following the horse's head and neck downwards but maintaining contact with the mouth while creating an active walk.

People who are not familiar with the successive stages of the Natural Training Method may be confused because it advocates practise of the halt with sideways moving quarters. Confused because, in general, a horse should be brought

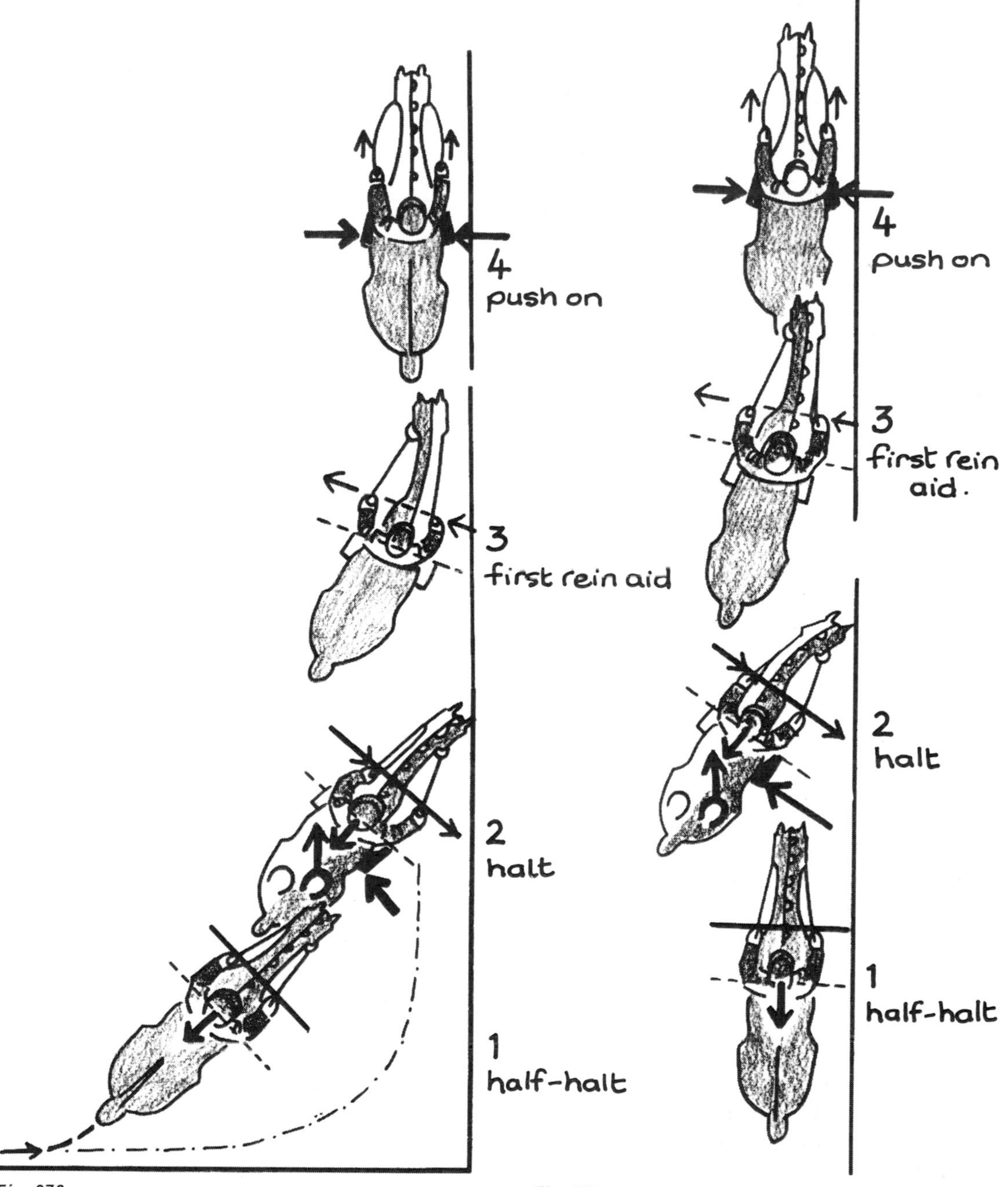


*Fig. 278*
Start teaching the lateral driving leg aid when coming to a halt, by moving the quarters in slightly.

*Fig. 279*
A little more difficult: the same exercise on the track, without cutting off the corner.

to a halt whilst keeping his body *straight* from head to tail with engaged quarters. This theory is, of course, correct. However, one can hardly expect this of a young horse at the initial stages of his training, as he has not yet developed the muscles in his back and quarters which would enable him to engage *both* hindlegs equally at the halt. Force would have to be used, which would obviously be destructive to a young horse. In the Natural Training Method, however, the horse is schooled systematically and progressively. The young horse is *first* taught to move his quarters sideways, which means his having to engage *one* hind leg extensively, an exercise the young horse can do quite easily. This is practised on both reins alternately.

Once the young horse has become supple and muscled enough to engage both hindlegs *alternately* he will then have no difficulty in engaging "both" hindlegs *simultaneously*.

Having learnt this the horse will understand the difference between the "forward" and the "lateral" driving leg aids. *Only then* is it possible to ride the young horse forward and keep him straight from head to tail, because the lateral driving leg aids can control the quarters from deviating sideways.

TURNS AND CHANGES OF DIRECTION

I have already mentioned that there are riders who do not believe in dressage. These riders have difficulty in riding through turns in a competition on account of lateral stiffness in their horses and they soon realise that even the most capable jumper cannot compete successfully without dressage training. A showjumping horse must be able, even at full speed, to bend his entire body according to the degree of the turn. He must do it fluently without any resistance and maintain impulsion, balance and cadence.

*Weight aids in the turn*

When riding a right-hand turn, the aids are:

*In dressage seat*, the rider looks slightly to the right, shifts additional weight onto his right seat bone and onto the right stirrup.

*In forward seat*, the rider also transfers his balance to the right by putting more weight on to the right knee and stirrup.

*Leg aids in the turn*

The right leg (active leg) must be used firmly just behind the girths to maintain forward impulsion.

The left leg (passive leg) is placed slightly further behind the girths to prevent the quarters from moving sideways out to the left.

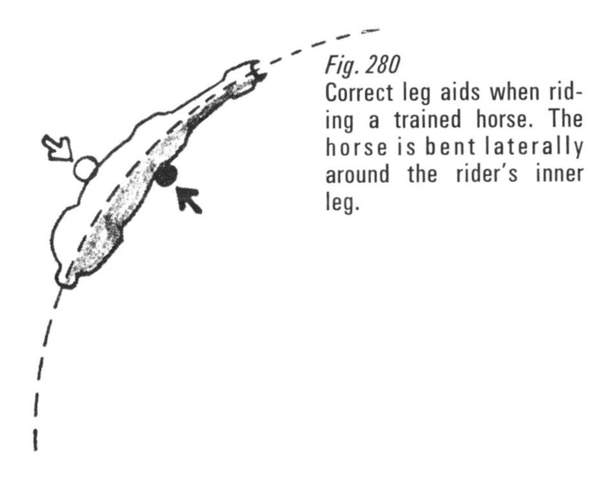

*Fig. 280*
Correct leg aids when riding a trained horse. The horse is bent laterally around the rider's inner leg.

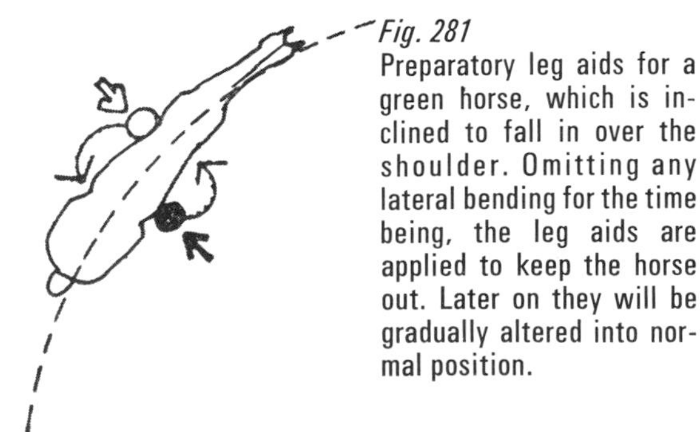

*Fig. 281*
Preparatory leg aids for a green horse, which is inclined to fall in over the shoulder. Omitting any lateral bending for the time being, the leg aids are applied to keep the horse out. Later on they will be gradually altered into normal position.

The horse's body is bent from head to tail laterally around the rider's inside leg (right leg) according to the curvature of the line on which the horse is moving. However the horse will only respond to these aids if he has reached the appropriate stage of schooling. A green horse whose body is not yet laterally flexible in the rib part will find it difficult to bend his entire body, even more so with the additional burden of the rider's weight. He will become imbalanced in the turn, falling, either into the turn or out over the shoulder. One can observe the same imbalanced manner in the early stages of lungeing a young horse. Therefore it is important at the elementary stages of schooling to apply the leg aids in such a way that the horse keeps moving on the *circle* line or turn – even if his body is not bent laterally. One might have to apply the leg aids in a somewhat unorthodox position to achieve this. Later on the horse will become more supple and will then be able to bend his body laterally. Then leg aids are applied gradually in the correct region. It is therefore logical to say that, *when* and in *which* region and how *strongly* the leg aids should be applied, depends on the horse's standard of schooling.

*Rein aids in the turn*

In the Natural Training Method the reins are used merely to *guide* the horse into the turn and to change his centre of gravity in accordance with the direction of the turn. For a right-hand turn the rider's right (inner) hand moves slightly out from the neck *sideways* – not backwards – leading the horse into the turn. This is also called "open rein".

The left rein leans against the horse's neck but should not be moved forwards. This is to support and to prevent the horse from falling out over the shoulder. The *same* feeling with the mouth is kept on both reins.

The fact that the rider's inner hand moves sideways into the turn influences the *balance* of horse and rider. In performing this movement the rider will automatically change his centre of gravity to the right. The horse, trying to stay under the rider's centre of gravity, will be inclined to turn right according to his degree of sensitivity. The sideways moving rein bends the horse's neck laterally to the right (therefore this rein aid is called the "lateral rein aid"). The horse will, in bending his neck to the right, change his centre of gravity to the right foreleg. He is then forced to turn right in order to keep his balance.

However, at the early stages of schooling some horses are inclined to cut the corners and fall *into* the turn. Then the opposite rein aids should be applied.

The degree of sideways rein action required depends on the horse's standard of schooling: from an exaggerated sideways movement in the beginning it may be reduced to a mere sideways turning of the wrists. However, this lateral rein aid can only function if an *equal* tension is always maintained on both reins. Some riders find this very difficult as they have one stronger hand and therefore are not aware of taking a stronger hold with that particular hand. They foster a "one-sided" mouth. To acquire a proper feeling for an even tension on the bit these riders should use the Mexican rein hold. On account of its influence on the balance of the horse the lateral rein aid is of considerable advantage over the rein aids used in "classic" dressage.

In the classic method the rider would turn his right wrist (inner hand) towards his own body. This shortens the right rein and inflicts more pressure on the right side of the horse's mouth, but it does *not* change the horse's balance neither does it cause a change of the centre of gravity. Besides, this shortening of "one" rein might easily encourage the horse to fall out over the shoulder or flex his head sideways at the poll.

The importance of the change of balance for turning can be discovered by taking a snaffle bit in both hands with an assistant holding the reins. Both rider and assistant should then stand with knees and heels close together. The assistant will then move one hand out sideways, as if he was applying a lateral rein aid, keeping both reins tight. One will find it difficult to stand balanced and maintain equal weight on both feet. The automatic reaction will be to move one foot sideways "into the turn" to avoid falling.

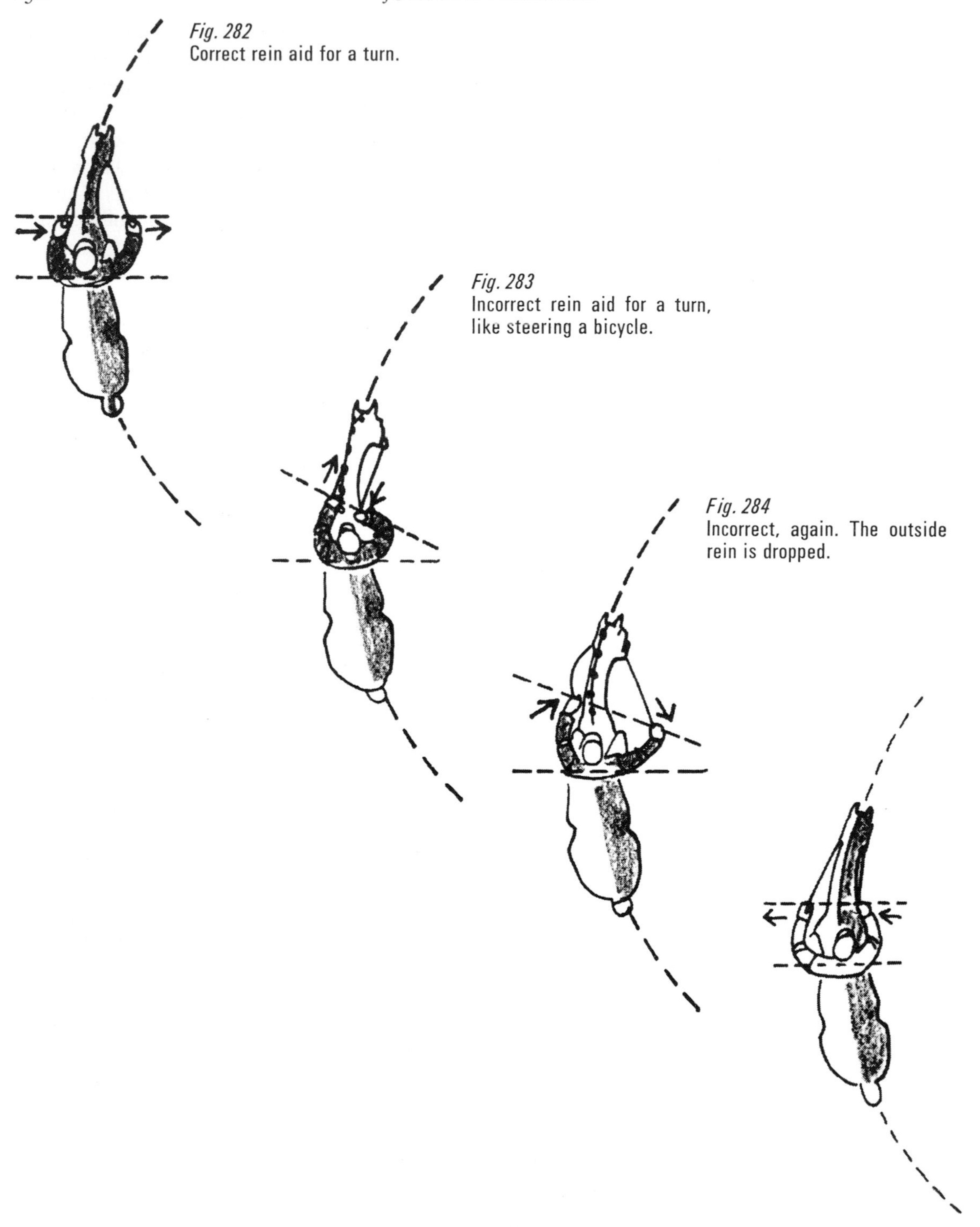

*Fig. 282*
Correct rein aid for a turn.

*Fig. 283*
Incorrect rein aid for a turn, like steering a bicycle.

*Fig. 284*
Incorrect, again. The outside rein is dropped.

*Fig. 285*
Correct rein aid. The horse is inclined to fall into the turn.

*Fig. 286*
Experiencing the sideways shifting of one's centre of gravity on account of the lateral rein aid.

If the horse is schooled with such gentle aids he will keep a soft and sensitive mouth. This will be of great advantage when jumping against the clock. The horse will have no difficulty in cutting the corners and will not run out or rear in the turns. There will be a harmonious partnership between horse and rider because the horse will turn willingly following the natural change of balance.

## THE HALF-HALT

The half-halt aid is a preparatory one, applied to attract the horse's attention before he is given *any* new instruction.

When prepared by a correct half-halt the horse will never be taken by surprise when the aids for a new exercise are applied. That ensures its smooth performance. The horse will also be prepared for the next task by the fact that during the half-halt any excess weight has been transferred to the quarters while impulsion and balance have been animated.

### *In the dressage seat*

When practising the half-halt in the dressage seat the rider transfers his centre of gravity more to the quarters by raising his head, straightening his body (without stiffening it) and expanding his chest. He should contract his loin, seat and thigh muscles and tilt his hip bones backwards. Both legs should apply sufficient pressure to send the horse from the rear into the rider's passive hands.

These combined aids should be applied simultaneously and in harmony with the horse's pace.

If the aids are applied correctly the rider will feel the horse change his centre of gravity to the quarters, which in turn will become more engaged and lowered. The horse, without losing his forward impulsion and rhythm, will become lighter in the rider's hands and he will also round his neck and have more freedom of his shoulder.

In this position the horse is easier to turn and also more alert to any further instructions from the rider.

*Fig. 287*
Later on the sideways movement of the hands can be restricted to a mere sideways turning of the wrists.

*Fig. 288*
Half-halt in the dressage seat.

*In the forward seat*

The same half-halt is practised in the forward seat when training and riding showjumping. The rider sits in the forward seat and applies the half-halt before making a turn, or when the horse is going too much on the forehand, or to make the horse alert when approaching a difficult fence.

Without sitting down into the saddle or taking a stronger hold on the reins, the rider straightens up (raises his chin) and grips a little more firmly with knees and legs. Thus, the rider is transferring his centre of gravity backwards. The horse – made sensitive and obedient through jumping-dressage – will react immediately! The hindlegs come further underneath the horse, and so he will become lighter in the hand, and the canter stride will be more bouncy.

Balance and equilibrium are the secret weapons of a well schooled showjumper. A rider who can give a half-halt only with the reins and who, therefore, always has too much weight in the hands, is missing the finer points and delights of riding over jumps.

### THIRD ("ON THE BIT") REIN AID

There is no problem in riding a horse "on the bit". Only the rider who starts "placing the head" too soon, and in an incorrect manner, will have difficulties.

First teach the young horse to carry the weight of the rider in balance. The horse must be given the opportunity to lower his head and neck so that he can use his back. He must be able to move on his own four legs in all paces on a complete loose rein without losing balance or increasing his speed. If the horse is not able to do this he will, when asked to go on the bit, use the rider's hand as a "fifth leg". The horse must be truly flexible laterally in neck and ribs engaging the inner hock, and he must be able to do this equally well on both sides. If one side of the horse is not flexible enough yet, he will carry the ear on that side slightly higher than the other ear. The more the horse is able to get his hocks under, the easier it will be to teach him to go on the bit.

*Fig. 289*
Half-halt in the forward seat.

*Fig. 290*
Phase I.

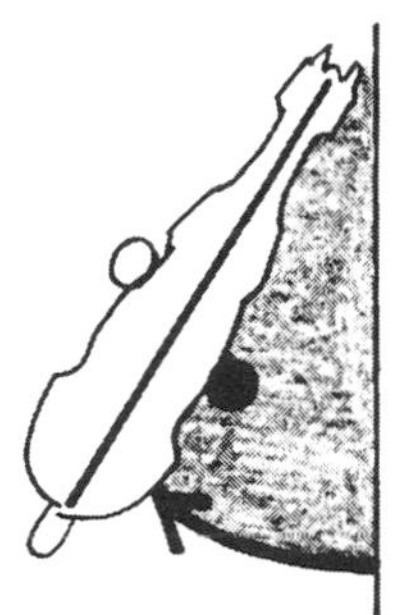

*Fig. 291*
Phase II.

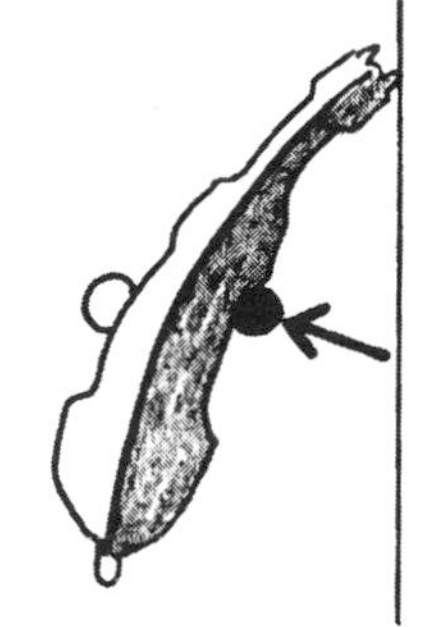

*Fig. 292*
Phasc III.

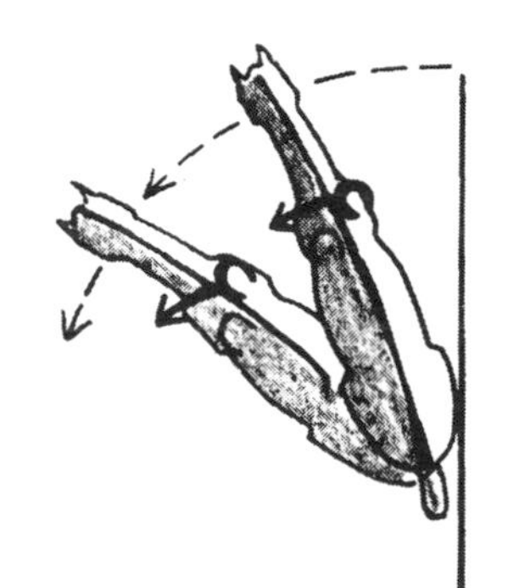

*Fig. 293*
Phase IV.

*Fig. 294*
Phase V.

Only then can one start schooling the horse to go on the bit. There may be no shortcuts. One must start with A, B and C and not with Z.

*The five stages of schooling*

The progressive schooling programme designed to achieve collection, has to be followed step by step.

It is applied to schooling in general, as well as to every single training session. The trainer should subdivide the schooling programme into five distinct and consecutive phases.

These are described below as Phases I to V inclusive.

Phase I:
showing the horse the way to the ground, in all three paces, on a loose rein, maintaining impulsion;

Phase II:
engaging the inner hindleg without lateral bending. Making transitions along the kicking boards from a walk into a halt, moving the quarters slightly away from the track;

Phase III:
moving the quarters away from the track, lateral bending from head to tail, activating the inner hindleg (later the turn around the forehand);

Phase IV:
turning on the haunches. Depending upon the standard of the horse's schooling, this can be either a quarter or a half turn;

Phase V:
riding the horse "on the bit" (collecting the horse). At first in walk then at a trot and at a canter. Increase demands gradually.

*Difficulties*

It should be stressed that there does not exist a standard pattern for the position of head and neck which would fit every horse when going on the bit. Horse conformation and temperament vary so much that it would be illogical to strive for a uniform head and neck position. One must keep in mind the fact that the position of the head also depends on what stage of schooling the horse is at.

An experienced trainer will be able to school every horse, even those who by nature have a difficult head position, to carry the head in such a position that the horse will move in a balanced way and will be under control in all circumstances.

Trying to achieve the same with gadgets which vary according to fashion would not only lead to gross resentment but produce merely superficial results. Too many riders cannot distinguish between the "appearance" of a horse on the bit and one who is genuinely on the bit. When a horse carries his head and neck *too high* he drops his back and his quarters are not engaged. If the rider forces the head down with gadgets then the horse "appears" to be on the bit, which might deceive less knowledgeable riders but not an experienced horseman.

Other riders may have difficulties because their horses have *too low* a head carriage. The horse's conformation could be the cause, as he may be overbuilt and therefore by nature unbalanced and on the forehand. Another reason why a horse is too much on the forehand could be bad riding. (This is also one of the reasons why difficulties arise when trying to re-train racehorses into showjumpers: the former are specially schooled to give the rider more weight in the hand.)

*Fig. 295*
A horse with a too high head carriage.

*Fig. 297*
When the head is pulled down (with a martingale or with running reins), the horse appears to be "on the bit", but the horse's back is still dropped and his hindlegs are trailing.

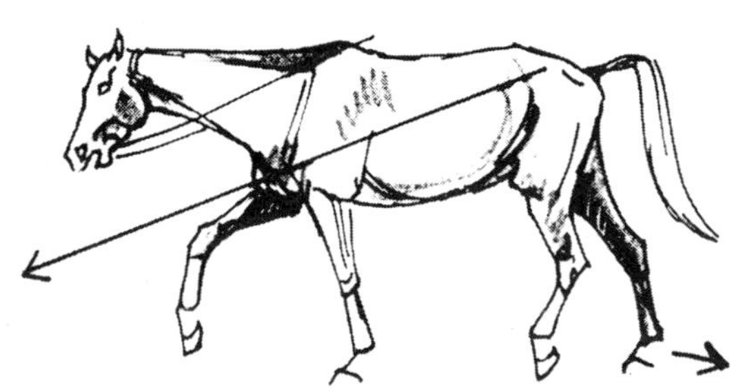

*Fig. 296*
Horse with a low head carriage, on the forehand.

*Fig. 298*
When the rider tries to lift the horse's head (with a gag bridle or by carrying his hands extra high), the horse goes behind the bit, is still on the forehand and the horse's hindlegs are trailing.

Problem horses will "appear" to go on the bit if one uses all sorts of gimmicky tack and bits, or if one carries one's hands extremely high to "lift" the horse's head. In fact they will go overbent, that is, remain on the forehand while the hindlegs are still trailing behind. Whenever one tries to ride these horses without artificial aids one will discover that the problems are just as prominent as before. The horse will be so relieved that he is able to stretch his cramped muscles that he will poke his nose further forward than before.

All gadgets are obviously of negative influence and the time wasted in using them would have been put to better use had it been employed in muscling up the horse properly.

There is always a *reason* for too high or too low a head carriage. We must detect this cause before we attempt to correct it. Sore bars or tooth troubles are often responsible for an incorrect head and neck carriage. It is advisable to have the horse's mouth checked by a veterinary surgeon from time to time. The most common cause, however, is a badly developed back, which makes it impossible for the horse to move in balance. As a result the horse will carry his head and neck (his rudder) in such a position which will enable him to re-balance himself. To get to the root of the problem, exercise and develop the horse's back until it is muscled up and supple. The head and neck carriage will then correct itself.

The best opportunity to correct the back is lungeing with a Chambon. After a fairly long period of proper and regular lungeing sessions one will notice a development of prominent muscles covering each side of the horse's spine. Simultaneously the muscles of croup and buttocks are strongly developed, the latter not only on the inside but on the outside as well. In addition one can further develop these muscles when riding by emphasising the activating of the quarters followed by the first rein aid: that way the horse will use his back actively. Having schooled the horse in the Natural Training Method you will find *no* difficulties in getting him on the bit.

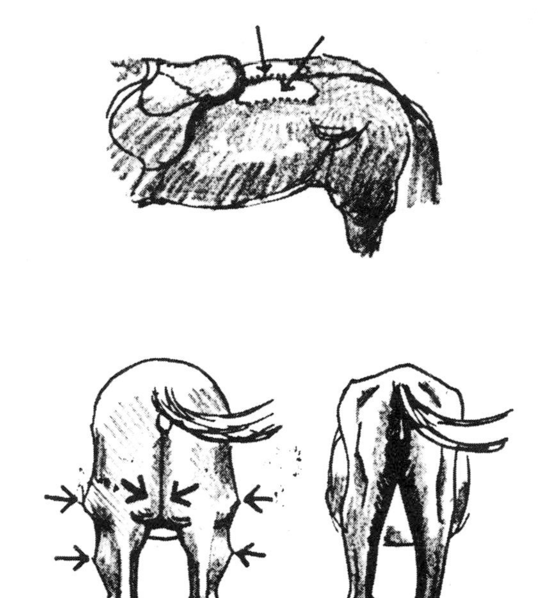

*Fig. 299*
Muscles need to be developed by regular lungeing. The loin muscles *(top)* to enable the horse to go "on the bit"; and the buttock muscles *(bottom)* both inside and outside.

*Aids for riding "on the bit"*

Teach the horse to go on the bit only when his muscles are warmed up at the end of a session, as there is then less chance of resistance. During the preparation one should make many transitions from one pace to another, sending the horse actively forward while applying alternately the first and second rein aid. At this stage of schooling it will not be necessary to keep both hands exaggeratedly wide apart when applying the rein aids. A slight alternate sideways turn of the wrist in rhythm with the horse's step will be sufficient to encourage the horse to flex his lower jaw. The first attempt to ride the horse on the bit should be made during a transition from a walk to a halt. While at a halt the rider maintains adequate seat and leg aids and instead of letting the reins slip through the hands (first rein aid) or following the mouth down and forwards (second rein aid) when the horse flexes his jaw, the immediate reaction of the rider should be: to ease his hands for a few seconds and then tighten them again, like squeezing a sponge. If the rider does not react this way, but has "dead" hands, the horse's mouth will become "dead" very soon. A horse who is taught to respond to the action of the first and second rein aids has gained confidence in the rider's hands. Such a horse will, without any resistance, accept the third rein aid and remain light in the rider's hands while champing the bit.

The neck should form a harmonious unstrained curve, arching from the withers to the poll, which should be the highest point. The nose should be slightly in front of the imaginary vertical line. Such a head and neck position can, of course, only be obtained by applying the third rein aid together with adequate seat and leg aids.

However, if a horse is defending himself and does not accept the third rein aid, and is poking his nose forwards, then he is not ready yet to be ridden on the bit. In the beginning be satisfied if the horse (only at a halt) is on the bit for a few seconds. Always follow this with the first rein aid (the loose rein) and proceed at an active walk (even horses who "offer" themselves to go on the bit from the start will go through this elementary process, even if the trainer is tempted to neglect it). In time increase the number of transitions from a walk to a halt applying the third rein aid (on the bit).

*Increase demands gradually*

If the horse responds willingly to halting on the bit, move forward a few strides at a walk while maintaining the horse on the bit. Follow this up again with the first rein aid. Gradually increase the number of walking strides on the bit. In time the horse will go – in all paces – willingly on the bit for a limited number of strides.

For a young horse it is dangerous to go on the bit for too long a session every day. One takes the risk that the parotid glands may become jammed between the jaw bone and the jowl. The glands may become swollen the next day. Even if not visible they still can hurt the horse, which can lead to resisting the bit. For this reason one should ride the horse on the bit not more than three times a week, which is quite sufficient at the early stage. (Massaging a young horse's parotid glands daily with Vaseline will help to make them supple.)

Only an older, well-schooled and correctly muscled up horse will be able to go on the bit for a longer period without being harmed.

*Accepting collection effortlessly*

Some riders try to get the horse on the bit in an illogical manner: trotting for a length of time, at too fast a pace, pushing him hard onto the bit, hoping that in the end the horse will "give in" and then go on the bit. However, the opposite will be achieved. Owing to the constant pressure on the sensitive bars the horse will fight against the bit instead of flexing his lower jaw. A horse must accept collection effortlessly. As soon as you feel any resistance make a transition, applying the first rein aid while maintaining active impulsion. Send the horse actively forward to encourage the overall important impulsion. The horse should not only lengthen his neck but his stride as well.

Then ride the horse on the bit again for a few strides and repeat. The frequent changes, from collection to relaxation, will make the horse flexible and ensure that he accepts the collection without stiffening. He will seek and maintain with confidence the contact with the rider's sensitive hands.

Whenever the rider shows the horse the way to the ground the horse should obey. If the horse does not respond one will find it very hard to prevent him from creeping behind the bit, evading the rider's aids. This can frequently lead to rearing.

*The danger of losing impulsion*

The frequent lowering of head and neck *could* bring the horse too much on the forehand if impulsion is lost and if the horse is *not* supported by strong forward driving seat and leg aids.

*Fig. 300*
Allow the horse to stretch his head and neck, and then ride him on the bit again. If sent on correctly the horse will not change his centre of gravity.

*Fig. 301*
If the horse is not sent on sufficiently, he might come on to the forehand.

If the horse's entire muscle system is developed correctly and the quarters activated sufficiently one will find no problem riding the horse on the bit. Let him stretch his neck and back and then ride him on the bit again. The horse will not change his centre of gravity to the forehand but maintain his balance without increasing pace or losing rhythm.

Relaxation while maintaining impulsion – that is essential.

### TURN AROUND THE FOREHAND

The turn is performed "around" the horse's shoulders and is of great gymnastic value for a jumping horse. This movement should be performed step by step throughout, but without coming to a half first. This omitting of a halt is to encourage the horse's impulsion and his obedience to the rider's leg aids.

However, the turn is only of value to a jumping horse if executed in a *forward* movement, which means around the forehand and not "on" the forehand. When executed around the forehand the inner forefoot (which forms the pivot) should also describe a small circle.

But when this turn is performed on the forehand the inner forefoot has to turn on the spot, which is very hard on the horse's shoulders and leg tendons. Furthermore, while turning on the forehand the horse may easily brush his hindlegs, because then there is *no forward movement*, and he also may cross his hindlegs *behind* each other instead of crossing them in front of each other (as he should).

In such a case one misses the purpose of the exercise, as the horse does not bring his inner hindleg further underneath his body.

When practising this turn around the forehand in an indoor school one must stay at least 2 metres free from the kicking boards, otherwise, while making the turn, the horse will knock his nose on the boards and he is therefore forced to move backwards (again missing the purpose of the exercise).

The turn around the forehand is called after the direction in which the rider and horse are looking. The quarters move in the opposite direction. For example: when schooling a turn around the forehand to the right the head is leading to the right.

The turn should be executed smoothly, in a slow walk with regularity of the paces. The horse must remain light on the bit.

The horse's body should be bent laterally inwards from head to tail, around the rider's inner leg. The rider has to make sure that the horse's neck is never bent more than his body.

Explanation of the expressions "inner" and "outer" leg are perhaps called for here. When a horse moves on a straight line on the track in the school the legs of horse and rider nearest the kicking boards are called "outer" legs and the ones on the other side "inner" legs. If, however, the horse's body is bent laterally, then the horse's and rider's legs on that side where the horse's body is bent to are called the inner legs, the opposite ones the outer legs.

For instance, when riding on the left-hand rein "shoulder out" (explained later on) then the horse's inner side is the right side (or off-side), because then the horse is bent laterally to the right – although moving on the left-hand rein.

*Aids*

The rider should prepare his horse with the half-halt aids whilst maintaining impulsion.

The aids for the turn vary depending on the degree of the horse's schooling. For example, a green horse needs preparatory aids.

The leg aids, supported by the dressage whip, are applied in such a region where they will indicate to the young horse which movement is required. A rider who has only ridden schooled horses may find this hard to understand, although it is logical and well established with trainers of young horses.

For instance, on a well-schooled horse the rider uses his inner (active) leg on the girths, his outer (passive) leg behind the girths, to control the quarters when moving sideways. The horse's body is bent laterally inwards from head to tail around the rider's inner leg. These aids, however, would confuse a green horse. He would interpret the inner leg aid only as a *forward* driving aid. He would increase his pace, leaning on the bit, since the green horse is not yet flexible enough to bend his body laterally.

At this stage it is important that the horse learns to yield to the leg. It is sufficient if the young horse does this *without* lateral bending. To achieve this the rider uses his inner leg, in conjunction with the dressage whip, far behind the girths. This is supported by the outer leg, which prevents the horse from "rushing" around.

How soon these "preparatory" aids can gradually be changed into the "normal" aids depends on each horse's intelligence and progress in schooling.

All aids – seat aids, leg aids and rein aids – must work in full co-ordination.

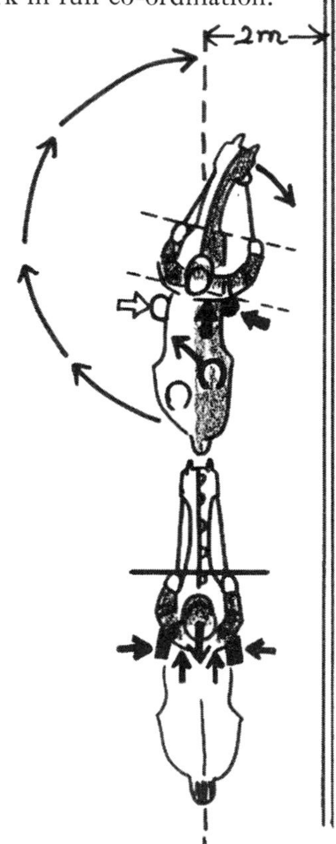


*Fig. 302*
Prepare the horse with a half-halt for the turn around the forehand with lateral bending. The aids for a schooled horse.

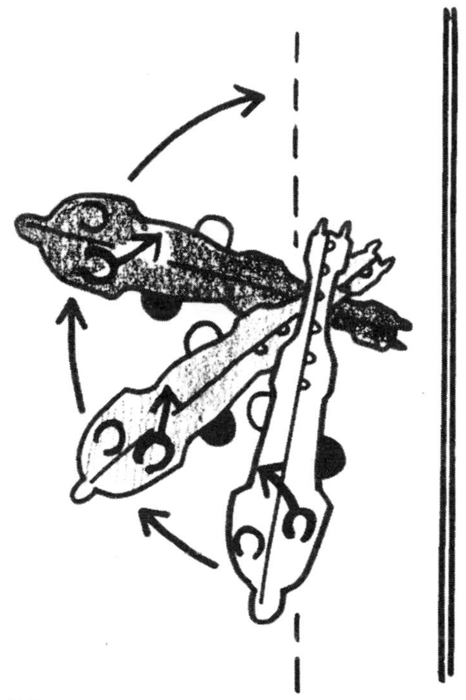

*Fig. 303*
Preparatory leg aids for a green horse. No lateral bending.

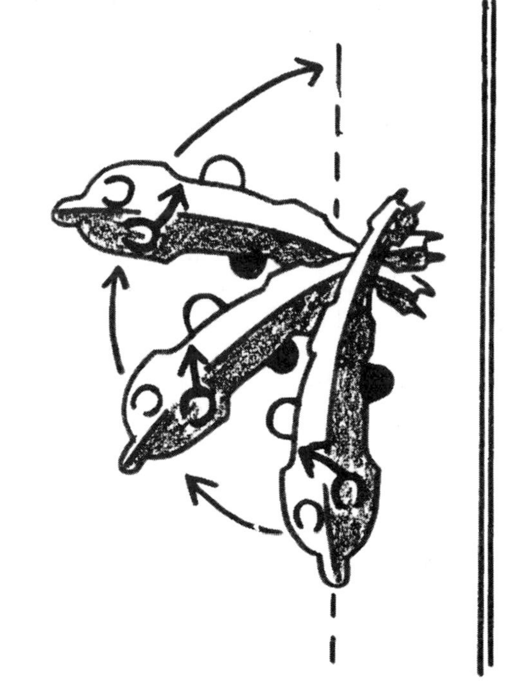

*Fig. 304*
Leg aids for a schooled horse. With lateral bending.

*Seat aids*

For the turn around the forehand to the right, look slightly backwards over your right shoulder, putting more pressure onto the right seat bone.

*Leg aids*

Correct position of the rider's legs is very important in order to apply correct leg aids. Applying the leg aids in different regions, one touches different muscles and consequently receives different reactions from the horse.

How strongly one should apply the leg aids depends entirely on the individuality and sensitiveness of each horse:

(i) for a green horse – the right leg (if necessary with whip) is applied behind the girths, pushing the horse's quarters sideways. This is supported by the rider's left leg on the girths. No lateral bending yet;

(ii) for a schooled horse – the leg aids are opposite to those for a green horse. The horse is now expected to bend his whole body laterally.

*Rein aids*

Maintain equal tension on both reins. The right rein is moved slightly sideways towards the kicking boards. The left rein is leaning against the horse's neck, preventing the horse from falling out over the left shoulder. (Later on a mere sideways twisting of the wrists will be sufficient.) On completion of the turn, where the off hindleg has become actively engaged in crossing in front of the near one, convert the impulsion accumulated into a forward action by walking on actively. Apply the first rein aid (loose rein).

*Advantage of the engaged inner hindleg*

After the young horse has performed the turn

*Fig. 305*
Preparatory rein and leg aids for a green horse.

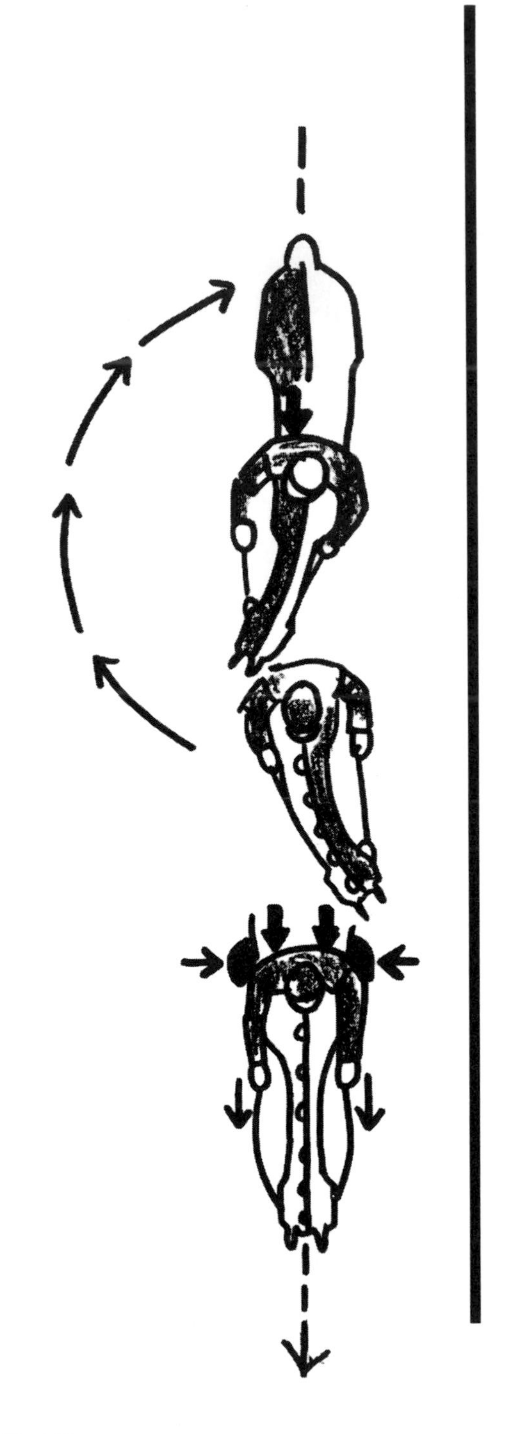

*Fig. 306*
After the turn around the forehand, send the horse on while applying the first rein aid.

fluently on the track and has been allowed to follow it up by lowering head and neck while "marching" on one can now advance a bit more.

Continue with the third rein aid after the turn, keeping the horse light on the bit.

Take advantage of the fact that the horse's inner hindleg has become more engaged in the turn, and call upon the horse to canter on after the turn.

For instance, when turning around the forehand to the right, the horse engages his off hindleg. This is an ideal position to canter on in the left canter, without an intermediate stride, because when the horse strikes off in a left canter he has to stand for a split second on the off hindleg *only*, using it more or less as a spring to canter off on.

Due to the slight lateral bending of the neck to the right during the turn the horse changes

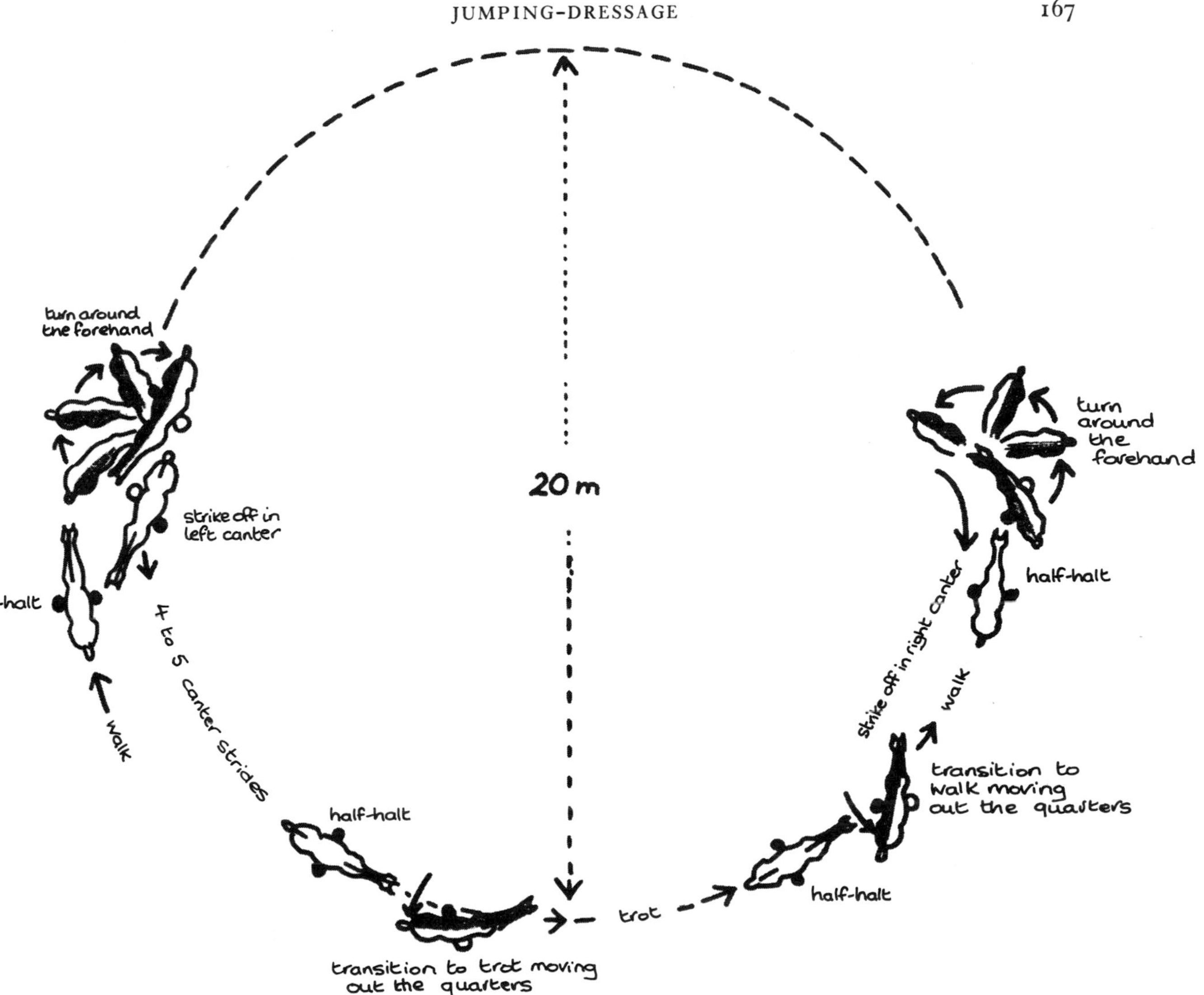


*Fig. 307*
How to take advantage of the turn around the forehand.

his balance to the right, which in turn gives him more freedom in the left shoulder. This makes it easier for him to throw his left front leg freely forward when striking off into the left canter.

The rider's weight, leg and rein aids at this stage of schooling are sufficiently established to let the horse strike off into the *left* canter. The left leg, already on the girths, now applies stronger pressure, giving the order to break into the canter. This is supported by the rider's right leg, which is still behind the girths. The aids for the turn around the forehand to the left are vice versa.

In time one practises this also on a circle, 20 metres diameter (free of the track). Circle to the right in a walk. Apply a half-halt. Ask the horse to move his quarters slightly out to the left (shoulder-in) for a few strides, and without coming to a halt start the turn around the forehand to the right. On completion, canter on in the left canter without an intermediate stride, making sure to keep one's centre of gravity well over the horse's off hindleg. Do *not* bend the upper body suddenly forward, for in doing so one shifts one's weight to the forehand instead of to the quarters. Without realising it one drops the reins as well. This incorrect distribution of one's weight, in conjunction with the sudden surrender of the bit, makes it impossible for the horse to shift his own and the rider's weight to his off hindfoot, and he strikes off on the wrong leg.

If the aids are applied correctly the horse will canter nicely in balance and light on the bit for the first few strides, though after four to five strides one might feel the young horse shifting weight to the forehand, becoming heavy on the bit and increasing his pace. The canter must be discontinued at once. It would be very wrong to ask the young horse to keep on cantering, as he is physically not able to do this in a balanced manner. Soon the horse will become adequately developed so one can gradually increase the number of canter strides. But at any stage it would be very wrong to pass the point where the horse is no longer able to engage his hocks and grows heavy in the hand. There is no point in interfering with the hands the *only* answer is to make a transition back into a trot. This is done after a half-halt by moving the quarters to the right (a shoulder-in movement) and keeping to the circle line with the forelegs. After six to eight strides (sitting trot) make another transition into a walk, again while moving the quarters to the right. After this transition reward the horse with the first rein aid (loose rein).

After an active walk on a loose rein repeat the whole exercise: send the horse onto the bit again and make a turn around the forehand to the left and move off into the right canter. This is a very strenuous exercise for the young horse, therefore repeat it only twice on both reins, allowing the horse to relax at a walk in between.

It is most important during these exercises that the rider prepares his horse correctly with the half-halt aids for each transition.

### THE SHOULDER-OUT

The shoulder-out is the easiest movement on two tracks and the first one the horse has to learn. As soon as the horse understands the difference between the forward and the lateral driving leg aid and responds to, and willingly obeys, the rider's wishes, the trainer can then start to school the horse in the shoulder-out.

In the beginning the shoulder-out may only be attempted for a few strides in a walk. The forward impulsion *must* constantly be maintained. Only then will this exercise make the horse's body laterally flexible, supple all the joints and increase the free movement of the shoulders.

The shoulder-out is the foundation exercise for all movements on "two tracks". There is not any basic difference between the shoulder-out and the shoulder-in exercise if practised in the open field, but in an indoor school the shoulder-out is done *facing* the kicking boards whilst the shoulder-in is done with the *quarters* towards the kicking boards. The horse's movement, the lateral bending of his body and the rider's aids are exactly the same in both exercises.

Nevertheless, one should start by schooling the shoulder-out *first*, because in the school the horse will benefit from the support of the kicking boards, which prevents him increasing his pace and from taking a stronger hold on the bit. If one, illogically, begins the schooling with the shoulder-in then the horse would be facing an open space and would be tempted to move faster, trying to escape the lateral bending of his body and the engagement of the quarters, forcing the rider to take a stronger hold on the bit.

The pre-schooling "on foot" will make it easy for the horse to perform the exercises on two tracks when mounted without any excess effort. At the beginning the *young* horse is obviously not capable of bending his body laterally from head to tail. To prevent tension and frustration one should be satisfied, for the time being, if the horse moves actively forward-sideways on two tracks without lateral bending. As in the turn around the forehand one should begin by applying *preparatory leg aids*, which are easier

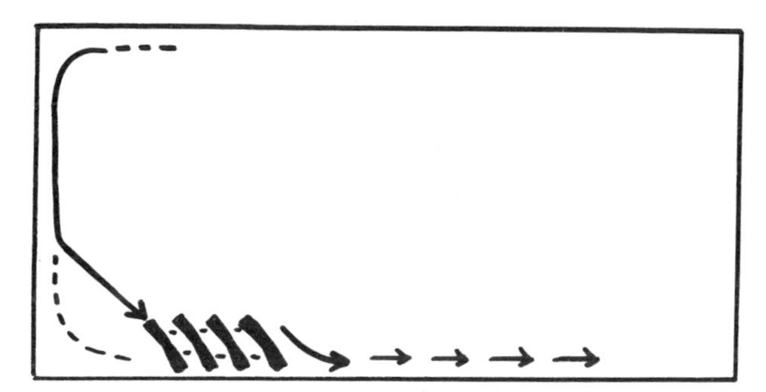

*Fig. 308*
Start the shoulder-out by cutting off the corner and arriving on the track at the correct angle.

for the young horse to understand. When in time the horse has reached a higher degree of flexibility the rider can gradually apply the normal leg aids, bending the horse's body laterally inwards.

Start schooling the shoulder-out as follows: ride on the left-hand rein, sitting in the dressage seat. Come from the short side of the school, cutting off the corner while approaching the long side. Approximately one length before reaching the track prepare the horse with a half-halt. As soon as the horse reaches the track with the forefeet apply the aids for the shoulder-out.

*The aids*

Look slightly to the right, straighten your back without stiffening, bring the right shoulder slightly backwards and shift more weight onto the right seat bone.

(i) *Leg aids for the green horse.* The right leg applies strong pressure *behind* the girths (supported by the dressage whip) to move the horse's quarters sideways away from the track. The left leg on the girths supports the pressure of the right leg, maintaining forwards impulsion (*no* lateral bending).

(ii) *Leg aids for a well-schooled horse.* According to the progress in training, the region of the leg aids is progressively altered, the right (active) leg being on the girths and

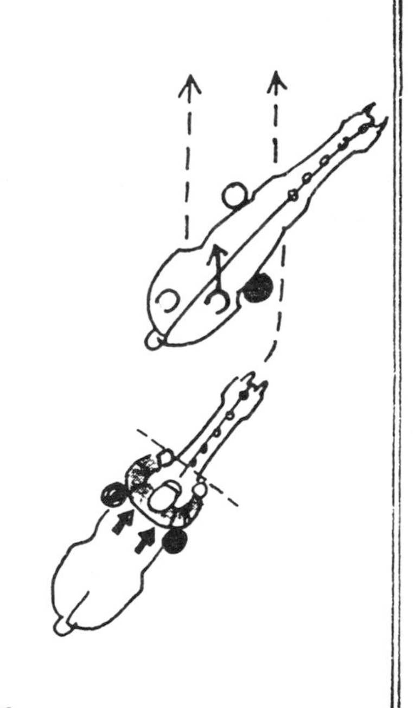

*Fig. 309*
Preparatory leg aids for a green horse. The horse is yielding to the leg without lateral bending.

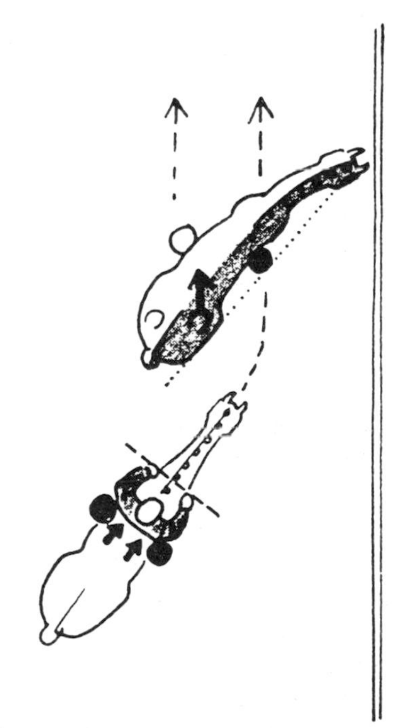

*Fig. 310*
Leg aids for a schooled horse. The horse is moving on two tracks bent laterally.

the left (passive) leg being behind them. This controls the degree of lateral bending. The horse will no longer move only sideways-forwards but will also be laterally bent from head to tail around the rider's right (inner) leg. The horse should move at an angle of not more than 30°. The *right* foreleg and the *right* hindleg must cross the *left* foreleg and the *left* hindleg in *front*.

*Rein aids*

The right rein should move slightly sideways *out* from the horse's neck to the right. The left rein is pushed against the horse's neck, supporting the forehand and preventing the horse from falling out with his left shoulder. Maintain with both reins an equal tension on the bit. Care should be taken to ensure that the horse's *neck* is never bent more than his *body*.

Be satisfied with four to six strides on two tracks. Straighten the horse on the track and apply the first, the second *or* the third rein aid, while walking on actively.

The shoulder-out should be executed on both reins to supple each inner hindleg alternately, but particularly on the horse's stiff side, which will improve in flexibility. If a horse has, for instance, difficulty in striking off in the left canter, then he is trying to avoid bringing his off hindleg under due to stiffness. If that is the case then practise the shoulder-out, especially on the left rein.

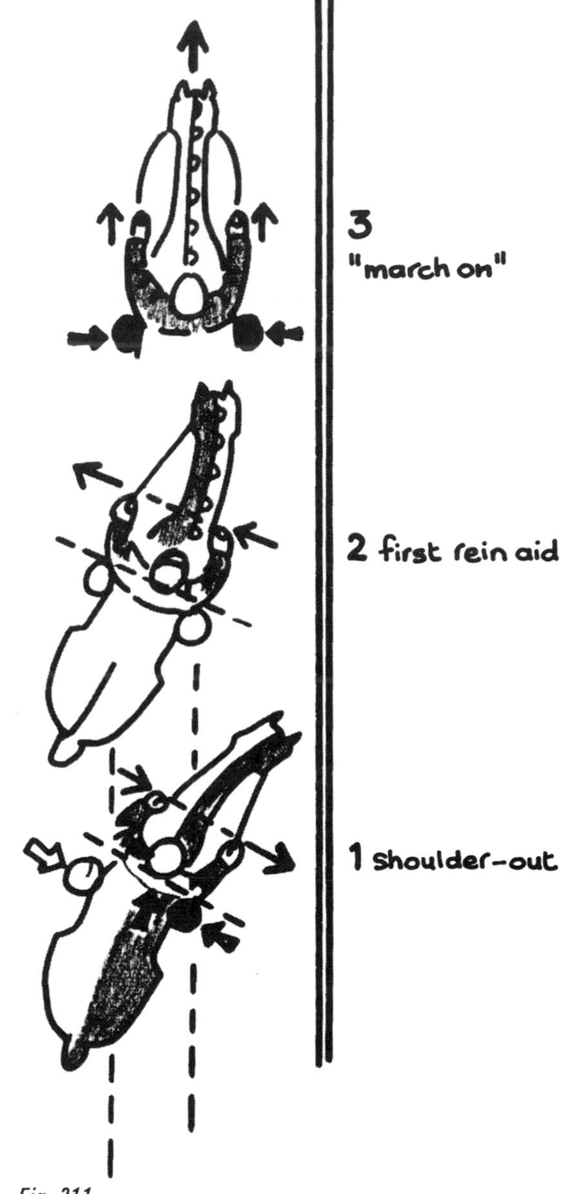


*Fig. 311*
Follow up the shoulder-out exercise with the first, second or third rein aid, while sending the horse on strongly.

LEG YIELDING

Leg yielding is a movement on two tracks similar to the shoulder-out. The rider's aids are the same but the lateral bending of the horse's body is only very slight. Leg yielding is performed *free* of the track, for instance, from the centre line towards the track of the long side, after a half-circle towards the long side or after cutting off a corner.

One starts schooling leg yielding after the shoulder-out has been performed satisfactorily. It is an excellent preparation for schooling the *shoulder-in* as it is not quite as difficult. In leg-yielding the horse is allowed to move slightly more forwards than in other movements on two tracks. This is particularly important for a young horse as it encourages him to maintain his impulsion and to prevent him from coming too much on the bit.

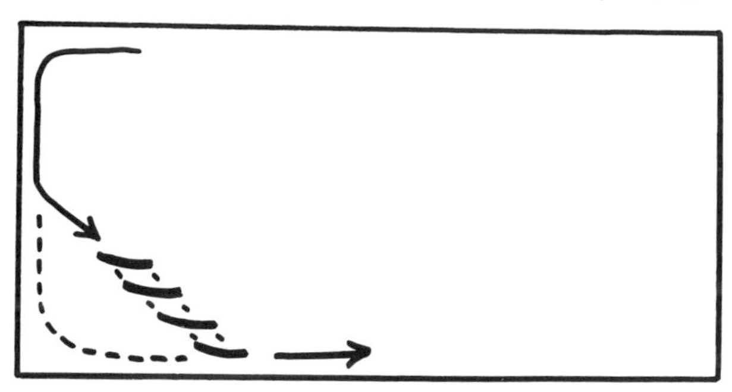

*Fig. 312*
When cutting off the corner move in leg yielding back to the track.

*Aids*

When riding on the left-hand rein, cut off the corner while riding towards the long side in leg-yielding. A horse length after leaving the track on the short side the rider prepares the horse with a-half halt. Rider and horse should look slightly to the left. The rider straightens his back without stiffening and brings his left shoulder slightly backwards and shifts more weight onto the left seat bone.

(i) *Leg aids for young horses.* The left leg aid is applied strongly behind the girths (supported by the dressage whip), asking the horse to move sideways to the right. The rider's right leg is placed on the girths, supporting the pressure of the left leg and maintaining the forward impulsion.

At this stage of schooling only the horse's neck is bent slightly to the left; the body is not yet bent laterally.

(ii) *Leg aids for schooled horses.* Depending on the horse's progress, the rider can gradually change his legs to the normal position. Then the left leg applies stronger pressure on the girths to move the horse to the right and the right leg is placed behind the girths to control the degree of the slight lateral bending of the horse's body around the rider's left leg.

*Rein aids*

The rider moves his left hand slightly sideways out from the horse's neck, bending it slightly to the left. The right rein is leaning against the neck to support the forehand and to prevent the horse from falling out with his right shoulder.

The rider should maintain an *equal* tension on *both* reins.

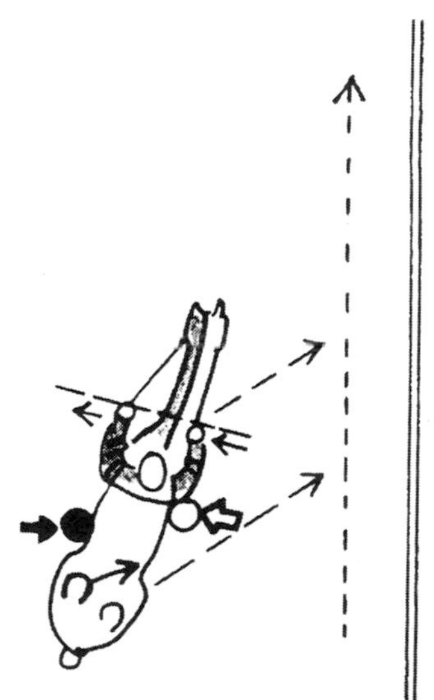

*Fig. 313*
Preparatory leg aids for a young horse.

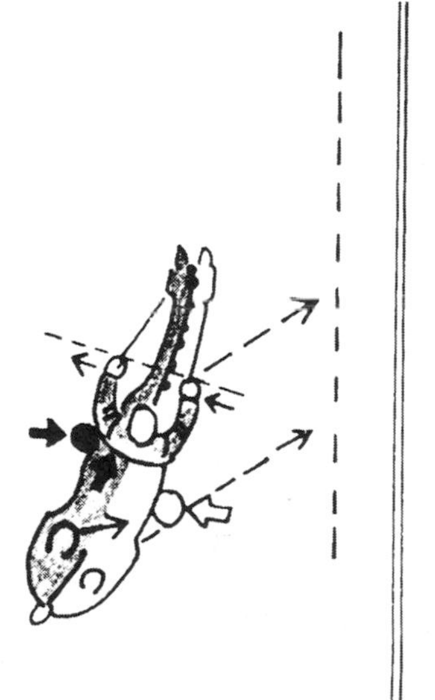

*Fig. 314*
Normal leg aids for a schooled horse.

The forehand *must* always precede the hindquarters. This is the golden rule for all exercises on two tracks.

Therefore, while approaching the track, the horse's off forefoot must touch the track first. If both the off forefoot and the off hindfoot meet the track simultaneously, this shows a complete lack of impulsion.

The rider should use his right leg more strongly and slightly further behind the girths to prevent the quarters from moving sideways too much to the right. His left leg is placed on the girths, which should send the horse more actively forward.

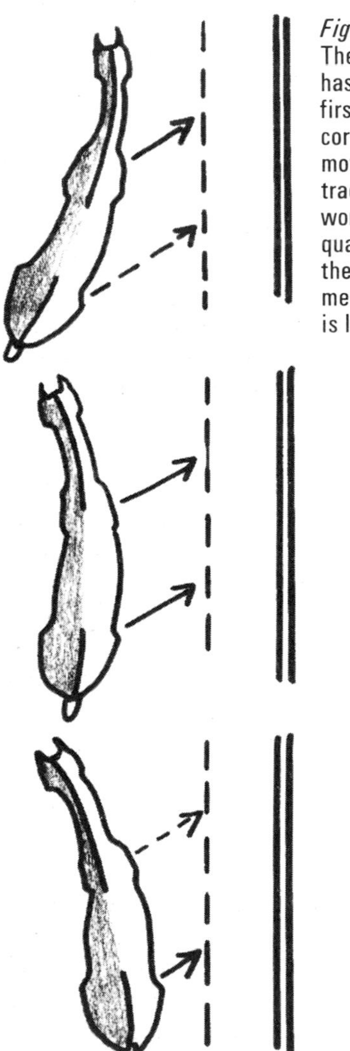

*Fig. 315*
The horse's shoulder has to meet the track first (*left*); it is not correct when the horse moves parallel to the track (*centre*); it is a worse mistake when the quarters arrive first on the track, as it would mean that all impulsion is lost.

A vital mistake is made if the horse's off hindfoot meets the track first. This indicates clearly that the quarters have preceded the forehand and shows also loss of impulsion, missing the purpose of the exercise and ruining the entire schooling of the horse.

After reaching the track, straighten the horse and apply the first rein aid, allowing the horse to stretch his neck and back and ride him energetically forwards.

Later on use the second and third rein aids. It is very important to straighten the horse after the two tracks movement and allow him to relax otherwise one would create tension.

### TURN ON THE HAUNCHES

The main purpose of the turn on the haunches is to reach a higher degree of collection and flexibility. It also improves the free movement of the horse's shoulders.

The forehand performs a quarter or a half circle around the hindquarters without coming to a complete halt first.

The turn on the haunches is most important for the showjumper as it can save valuable seconds in a competition.

In the beginning one should practise only a quarter turn; later on a half turn. At a more advanced stage one can practise a complete pirouette, which in fact is a small circle on two tracks. The turn on the haunches can be performed in all paces, although in the beginning it should only be carried out at a walk.

*Aids*

For instance, on the left-hand rein, the rider prepares his horse with a half-halt. During the half-halt the rider should count the rhythm of the sequence of the forelegs touching the ground: left, right, left, right, and so on. This is vital, because one can only perform the turn to the left smoothly when the horse's near forefoot touches the ground. At *that* moment the off forefoot is free of the ground and can cross in front of the near foreleg unobtrusively.

Should the rider start the turn when the off forefoot is on the ground then the regularity of the paces would be disturbed and the horse could easily brush his legs, or even cross his off foreleg *behind* the near one. Moving backwards and deviating the quarters sideways from the track would indicate loss of impulsion and is strictly to be avoided.

During the half-halt the rider straightens his back and looks slightly to the left. He brings his left shoulder slightly backwards and shifts more weight onto his left seat bone, tilting the pelvis and tucking his seat under. The rider applies strong pressure with his left leg to prevent the horse from moving backwards. His right leg is positioned behind the girths and urges the horse to make the turn on the haunches to the left.

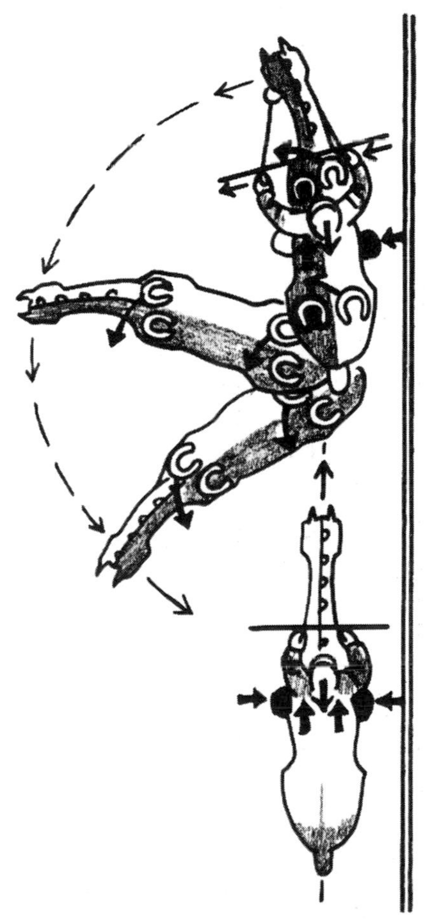

*Fig. 316*
Correct aids for a turn on the haunches. Start the turn at the moment when the inner foreleg touches down.

While maintaining with *both* reins an equal tension on the bit, the rider's left hand moves slightly sideways out from the neck. It is supported by the right rein, which pushes against the neck. The horse's neck is bent slightly to the left. Subsequently there is more weight on the near foreleg, giving freedom of movement to the off shoulder and off foreleg.

When schooling young horses the rider should throughout the whole turn *exaggerate* the transfer of his weight to the horse's inner hindleg and straighten his body rigidly. This urges the young horse to adjust his centre of gravity accordingly, remaining light in the hands. The more the horse obeys the rider's weight and leg aids the less rein aids will be necessary. A showjumper must be taught to adjust himself *immediately* to the slightest shifting of the rider's weight. The turn on the haunches is an excellent exercise to teach this.

Start the turn on the haunches out of a walk *without* coming to a halt. Two to three strides are sufficient in the beginning; also the hindlegs perform a small circle which can gradually be made smaller. (In a dressage test the inner hind-leg should pivot and return to the same spot each time it leaves the ground.)

After this quarter turn straighten the horse and use strong forward driving aids and proceed in an active walk, again without coming to a halt. Use the *first* or the *second* rein aid.

On account of the extreme engagement of the inner hindleg in the turn, which acts as a spring in a forwards direction, the horse will remain in balance when moving off, even while lowering his head and neck.

At the initial stage of schooling the turn on the haunches the horse should be tailed against the kicking boards (which support the horse) and prevented from creeping backwards. Later on the turn can, of course, be practised any-where.

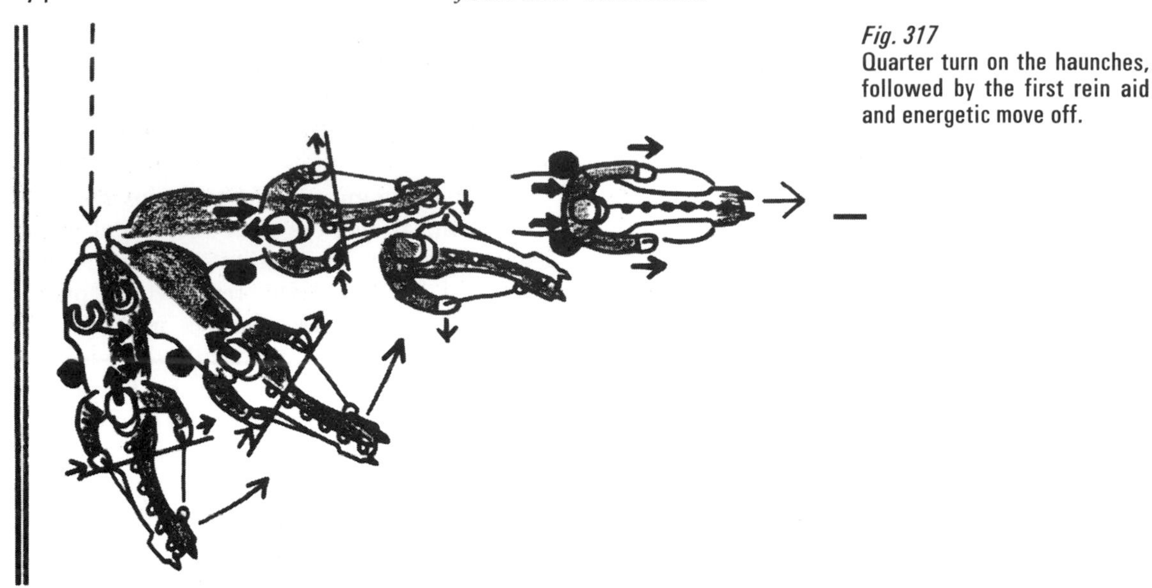

*Fig. 317*
Quarter turn on the haunches, followed by the first rein aid and energetic move off.

*Advantage of the engaged inner hindleg*

The following exercise is an advanced lesson but will be explained here, as it also benefits from the extreme engagement of the quarters and the inner hindleg during the turn.

In a turn on the haunches to the left the horse shifts his centre of gravity to the near hindleg. This makes it easier for the horse to strike off in the right canter. Therefore it is an excellent position to teach the horse to canter on after a turn on the haunches.

After the turn maintain the third rein aid, keeping the horse well on the bit, Without an intermediate step strike off in the right canter. The centre of gravity (of both horse and rider) remains over the horse's near hindleg. The rider keeps his balance well back, applying pressure with his left seat bone.

While proceeding in the right canter one should *not* bend the upper body forward and look down to check if the horse actually strikes off with his leading off foreleg. This sudden movement influences the horse's posture, changing his balance *also* to the off foreleg. The horse does this because to remain balanced he must try to keep his centre of gravity *under* that of his rider. Consequently he will strike off in the *left* (the wrong) canter and increase his pace.

The leg aids for the canter are quite the opposite to those applied in the turn. The rider's right leg (in the turn positioned behind the girths) now applies pressure on the girths and the left leg (in the turn on the girths) moves slightly backwards and applies supporting pressure *behind* the girths.

In the transition into the right canter the horse's left hindleg is so strongly engaged that

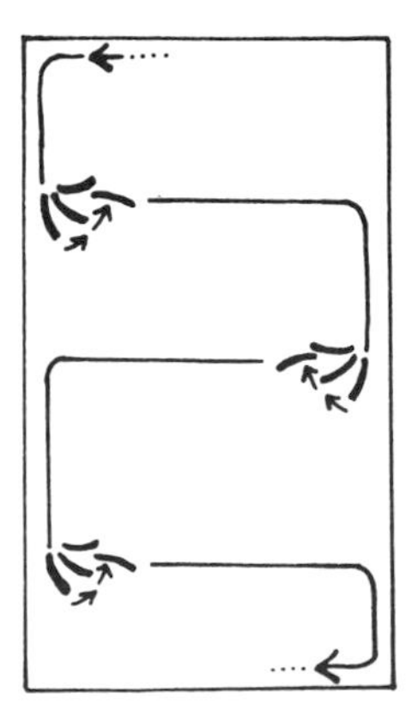

*Fig. 318*
In this manner one can school a quarter turn on the haunches on both reins.

it acts as a spring, which shoots the horse off into the right canter with an enormous force. This is one of the reasons why many young horses are overwhelmed by their own propulsive force created during this turn and, as a result, try to dash off for the first few canter strides. Therefore it is advisable to make the turn at the beginning of the long side, because when cantering on after the turn one faces the corner and the short side. This will discourage the horse from increasing his speed in the canter. For a few strides the horse will canter in a well-balanced manner with engaged quarters. *Before* the horse shifts his balance forwards, increasing his pace and leaning on the bit (which the young horse certainly will do), make a transition into a trot and then into a walk. If the horse is able to remain in balance for a longer period, go on a circle after passing the short side. This will prevent the horse from increasing his pace. Then repeat the whole exercise on the other rein.

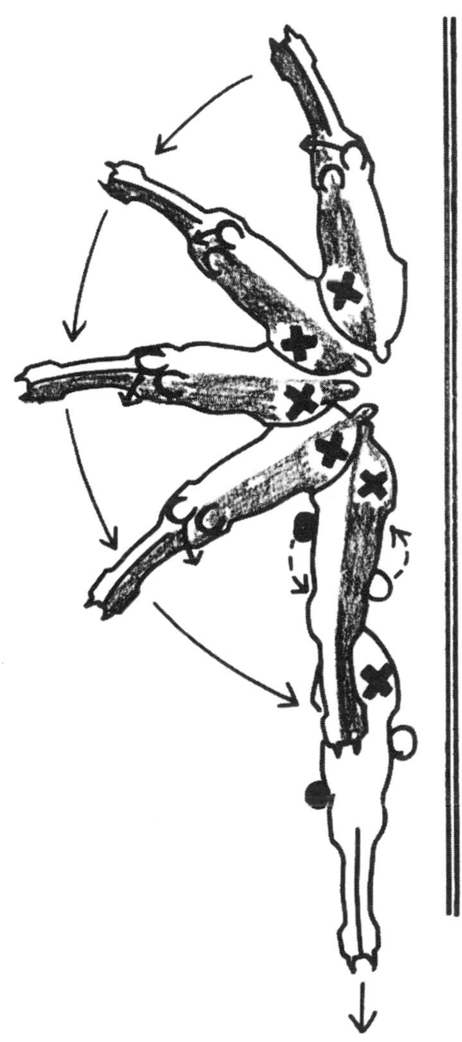

*Fig. 319*
During the turn on the haunches to the left the horse's and rider's weight is shifted to the near hindleg, X, where it should be when striking off in the right canter.

*Fig. 320*
When cantering on in this position the horse's and the rider's weight is shifted to the near hindleg.

*Fig. 321*
If the rider bends forward or looks down when cantering on, the horse's and the rider's weight is shifted to the near foreleg.

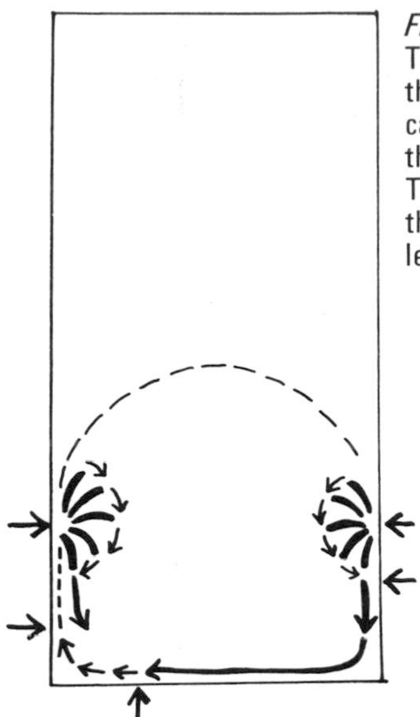

*Fig. 322*
Turn on the haunches to the left, strike off in right canter. On the short side of the school, trot, then walk. Turn on the haunches to the right, strike off in the left canter.

THE THREE PACES

A set pace and rhythm in all three paces is necessary to obtain better control over the horse and his balance and to prevent the horse from unnecessary use of energy. It is often the "too fast" speed of the pace that wears the horse more than the distance he has to cover. Only a rider in complete harmony with his horse is able to apply his aids in full co-ordination with the sequence of each pace. This is important for a showjumping rider, as it will enable him to complete a course effortlessly at an even set pace.

THE WALK

The walk (there are four different walking speeds) is a very important but often a neglected pace. Some riders start a lesson by trotting straight away, or lunge without letting the horse go at a walk first. But in neglecting the walk they automatically spoil the other paces.

This is disastrous for a showjumper because "a horse will canter as he walks". In other words, if he throws his feet out clear and firm at walk he will do so when he is cantering as well.

The walk has a four hoof beat sequence without an interval or a moment of suspension.

*The aids to start walking*

If one wants the horse to start walking, use *both* legs *simultaneously* slightly behind the girths.

*The aids during walk*

The leg aids *during* the walk differ from those used to *start* the horse walking. If the rider

*Fig. 323*
The walk sequence (four phases).

makes the mistake of using both legs simultaneously during the walk, trying to increase the pace, he will achieve the opposite. The pace will become irregular and disunited and the horse will break into a "pony trot".

*During* the walk one has to use the legs *alternately*. To do this at the appropriate moment one has to be able to *feel* the sequence of the walk with one's eyes closed. To learn this: take both feet out of the stirrups but keep the legs in the proper position. One will feel the left hip moving forwards when the horse's near foreleg touches the ground. At the same time the right hip moves backwards, pushing the right lower leg closer to the horse. This is the moment to apply stronger pressure with the right leg because a split second later the horse will lift his off hindleg. Consequently the horse will not only lift this leg higher but will also bring it further underneath his body.

In the same way one will feel that one has to use the left leg when the horse's off foreleg touches the ground. If one has difficulty to feel the rhythm, practise it whilst riding in the forward seat at a walk over cavaletti (flat on the ground). Then the horse will walk with more cadence (lift his legs higher), making it easier to feel the sequence of the hoof beats. Once one has acquired this feeling one will realise that only *alternately* applied leg aids can be in harmony with the sequence of the walking pace and encourage the horse to lengthen his stride and walk actively.

*Ordinary walk*

When walking "on the bit" the horse's neck should be carried long, with the nose in front of the imaginary vertical line drawn from the horse's forehead down. The nose is carried at approximately the same height as the horse's hips. The ordinary walk can be compared to the "march tempo". Before the Second World War the European cavalry schools schooled their horses to walk at a uniform pace, the march tempo. This was executed at a speed of about 100 metres per minute, or 6 kilometres per hour. A walking stride measured approximately 1

*Fig. 324*
Ordinary walk.

*Fig. 325*
Extended walk.

*Fig. 326*
Free walk.

*Fig. 327*
Collected walk.

metre. The march tempo was considered the most "economical" speed, using as little of the horse's energy as possible

*Extended walk*

This is ridden on a long or loose rein. The neck is carried longer and the head lower than in ordinary walk, with the nose further in front of the imaginary vertical line.

The strides are longer than in ordinary walk. The hindfeet should reach well over the imprints of the forefeet without the pace becoming hurried or disunited. Extended walk should not be practised for a length of time as it would force the horse to change his centre of gravity to the forehand.

*Collected walk*

This is ridden on the collected rein. The quarters are lowered and the horse's neck is raised and arched proportionally, remaining light on the bit. The nose is carried slightly higher than the hips and just in front of the imaginary vertical line from the horse's forehead.

The strides show more cadence and cover less ground; this is at a lower speed than in ordinary walk. The hindfeet no longer exceed the imprints of the forefeet.

*Free walk*

The free walk is a pace "at ease" and should be ridden on a loose rein. Nevertheless, the rider must maintain impulsion otherwise the horse could become lazy and stumble.

THE TROT

The trot is a two-time pace, a movement of alternate diagonals separated by moments of suspension. The diagonals are called after each foreleg.

We distinguish three trotting paces: ordinary trot; collected trot; and extended trot.

In all three speeds of the trot the horse should move freely and actively forward without his pace becoming hasty or irregular. The true pace should give an impression of elasticity with great mobility, wherein the hindfeet should follow the same track as the forefeet. To school the horse correctly the rider should always maintain an even regular pace.

*Ordinary trot*

This again, as in the walk, is the march tempo of the trot and is used for normal daily riding. The horse covers approximately 200 metres per minute. The strides are of medium height and length and so is the moment of suspension.

The neck should be carried fairly long without losing the contact with the bit, and the horse's nose must be in front of the imaginary vertical line. Without becoming hurried the horse should move energetically straight forward in a balanced and even stride.

*Collected trot*

This is a very advanced movement, ridden on a collected rein and in sitting trot only.

The horse is collected, his quarters are extremely engaged and lowered and the neck raised proportionally. The strides are shorter and higher, covering less ground than in ordinary trot. The moment of suspension is at its minimum.

The cadence shows more elasticity. Although the speed is slower the horse must maintain an energetic impulsion, whereby the joints are bent more markedly whilst at the same time remaining light on the bit.

*Extended trot*

If correctly executed the horse lengthens his stride and covers as much ground as possible without his action becoming much higher or showing any abnormal elevation of his body.

The moment of suspension is at its maximum. Whilst applying adequate seat and leg aids, the power of the engaged quarters create an extra propulsive force. The rider should maintain the same tension on the bit and not take a stronger hold. Instead, he should gradually follow the lengthening of the horse's neck necessary for extra free movement of the shoulders.

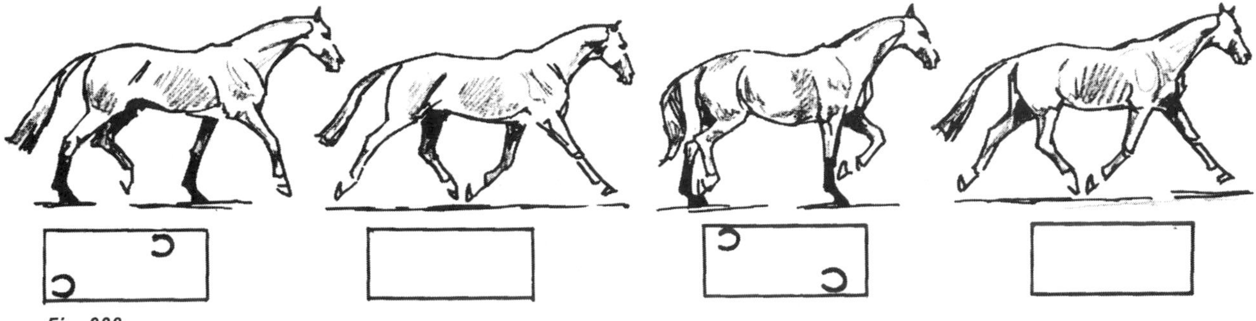

*Fig. 328*
The trot sequence.

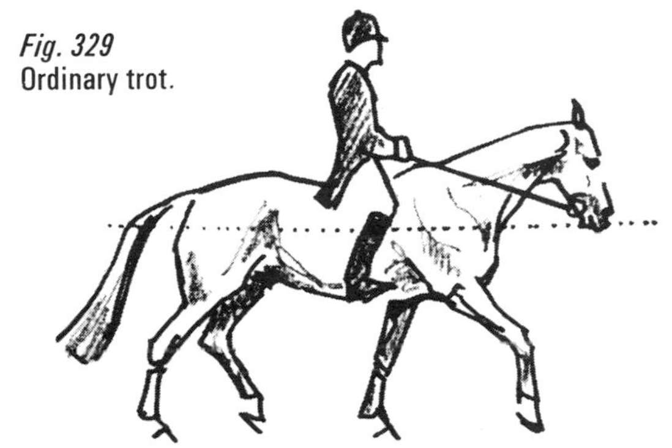

*Fig. 329*
Ordinary trot.

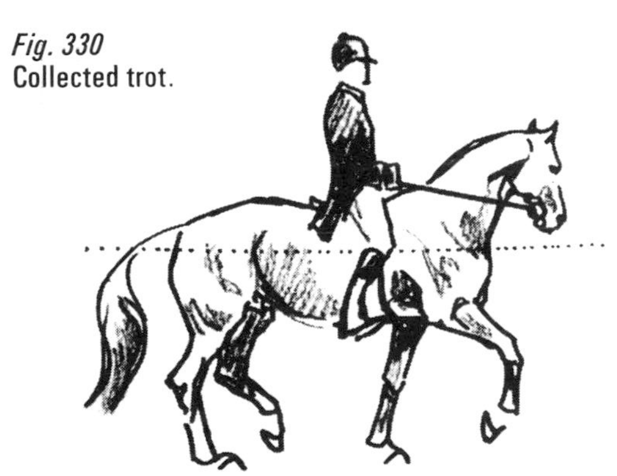

*Fig. 330*
Collected trot.

*Fig. 331*
Extended trot.

The highest point of the neck must be the poll, and the nose should be carried more forward in front of the imaginary vertical line. Although the strides are much longer than in ordinary or collected trot, it still should be performed in an even balanced pace without irregularity in one of the diagonals.

Extended trot should be ridden over a short distance only, otherwise the horse might come onto the forehand and become heavy in the hand.

*Trot seat positions*

*Sitting trot.* One sits in the deep dressage seat. The seat remains in the saddle at all times.

Do *not* ride sitting trot on a young horse. It will put too much weight onto his undeveloped back and loins and he will be inclined to drop his back and raise his head and neck. The stiffening of neck and back will extend to the hindlegs, ruining the action and balance. The horse will not be able to bring his hocks close together, which is so vital for jumping.

At the beginning of each schooling session the horse must first be allowed to lower head and neck and round his back, loosening and developing the back and loin muscles. This should be done at a *rising* trot. During the rising trot one's weight is positioned closer to the withers, thus avoiding any unnecessary pressure on the horse's back. This makes it easier for a horse to retain balance in pace and to round the back as well. It is more comfortable for the horse than *sitting* trot.

Only on a schooled horse, and only after warming up first, should one ride in sitting trot. The rider has to use his own discretion in deciding when this time has come. Even when the horse is ready and allows the rider to sit comfortably, accepting his weight, one should not ride in sitting trot for too long periods.

*Trotting in the forward seat.* This seat position in trot is especially important when schooling showjumpers. The rider is riding on the fork whilst the seat is constantly *out* of the saddle but close to it. This forward seat is used when riding over cavaletti, in hilly country and when approaching obstacles out of a trot.

*Fig. 333*
Trotting in forward seat.

*Rising trot.* In rising trot, one's seat touches the saddle only at every other stride. Starting off in rising trot can be done in two ways:

(i) in the classic method the rider starts off in sitting trot and after a few strides changes over to rising trot.

(ii) in both the Caprilli and the Natural Training Method, the rider does not start off in sitting trot but in the forward seat. This method is very sympathetic to horse and rider, as it avoids unnecessary weight on the horse's back and the risk of the horse stiffening and dropping his back. Using this method of starting the rising trot is important for young horses because their back is still weak and not muscled enough to carry a rider relaxed in sitting trot. At a walk the rider applies forward driving leg aids with both legs simultaneously and changes at the same time into the forward seat. When the horse is trotting the rider changes from the forward seat into the rising trot as soon as he feels the correct diagonal to trot on. An experienced rider will be on the correct diagonal straight away.

*Fig. 332*
Sitting trot on a green, undeveloped horse. He becomes tense, the trot is disunited, the back is dropped.

*Seat positions in rising trot*

One can exercise the rising trot in either of two positions:

(i) dressage seat position: *only* used in dressage competitions. The rider's upper body is nearly vertical; the reins are held longer in relation to this. The rider distributes his weight onto the weaker region of the horse's back, the loin vertebra. This seat position should therefore be executed only on older, well-muscled horses.

(ii) remount seat position. When using this position in rising trot, the rider's upper body being slightly in front of the vertical,

*Fig. 334*
Rider sitting correctly in rising trot.

*Fig. 335*
Rider sitting incorrectly in rising trot.

he will rise a little out of the saddle and return gently to the deepest point of the saddle – not against the cantle.

Proper rising trot promotes the horse's comfort by easing the rider's weight on his back. Therefore execute rising trot *always* in the remount seat. Incorrect rising trot or trotting in the dressage seat will distress a young horse with a sensitive back.

If one rises too high out of the saddle and returns with a thud into the rear of the saddle, then rising trot is a punishment for the horse. Riders who do this hang on to the reins to balance themselves out of the horse's mouth. They have their lower legs and ankles in an unorthodox position, stretched from the knees forwards, positioned in front of the girths. One will appreciate that with this incorrect leg and ankle position it is impossible to apply the correct leg aids. It pushes the rider's seat backwards against the cantle of the saddle. The rider's centre of gravity is not vertically above that of the horse, as it ought to be, but is distributed on the loin, which is not the region to carry the rider's weight. Therefore it obstructs the true movement of the horse. He will drop his back and carry his head and neck too high, which some of these riders then try to correct by the misuse of running reins.

In rising trot in the remount seat, however, the rider's centre of gravity will be located over that of the horse, the rider rising out of his knees instead of depending on the stirrups. This can be improved by practising the rising trot in remount seat *without* stirrups. The rider should fold his arms behind his back (the instructor holds the horse on the lungeing rein) and carry his legs in the same position as *with* stirrups. The rider now must grip with his knees and lean naturally a little forward otherwise he will lose balance.

The forward driving leg aids are applied with both legs together at the exact moment when the rider is sitting *not* when he is rising.

*Diagonals*

One can trot either on the left or on the right diagonal. When trotting on the left diagonal, for instance, the rider returns into the saddle the moment the horse's left diagonal (near foreleg and off hindleg) touches the ground. When riding on the left-hand rein in an arena, or when turning left, the rider should trot on the outer diagonal.

*Feeling the diagonals*

One should close one's eyes while in rising trot and practise *feeling* the diagonals move. While trotting on the *left* diagonal and when the seat returns to the saddle, the left hip and the left lower leg move slightly backwards and against the horse's body, resulting from the horse's *left* diagonal touching the ground (vice versa when on the right diagonal). To learn the difference between the left and the right diagonal, change the diagonals. If you cannot feel at first, practise the same exercise at a sitting trot.

It is often difficult to feel the elevation of the horse's body, particularly on a well-balanced horse. It is easier to distinguish on a horse whose muscles are unevenly developed, as his stronger diagonal will be much more obvious than the weaker diagonal.

The less experienced rider can easily determine on which diagonal he is trotting by looking down at the horse's shoulders. If the right shoulder moves backwards the moment the rider returns into the saddle then he is trotting on the right diagonal and vice versa.

The more experienced rider does not need to look at the horse's shoulders to determine which diagonal he is trotting on. He will feel very much *off balance* when trotting through a turn on the wrong diagonal, because he has been educated and has always paid attention to trot on the correct diagonal. Such a rider should be able to strike off immediately on the correct diagonal when trotting on. This should be practised without looking at the horse's shoulder, but by feeling and counting the rhythm of the diagonal pair of legs. There are three ways to learn how to do this.

*Out of the forward seat position.* This is the easiest method. Ride in the forward seat position at ordinary trot over four poles or cavaletti placed at a trot distance, then the horse is forced to make equally long strides and to lift his legs higher off the ground, with extra cadence. These exaggerated strides make it easier for the rider to feel the diagonal sequence.

When the horse's left diagonal touches the ground one will feel one's hip and left lower leg move slightly backwards. Simultaneously the right hip and right lower leg move slightly forward (vice versa for the right diagonal). If one is able to feel this movement in the forward seat over the cavaletti one should try to feel it also when trotting in the forward seat on the flat, without cavaletti. One should close the eyes and count the diagonals out loud: left, right, left, right, etc. When one feels the sequence of the diagonals with the eyes closed in the forward seat, then one could try to strike off into rising trot – at the first attempt – on the desired diagonal. For instance one wants to trot on the left diagonal. Count the diagonals: left, right, left, right, and while saying "left" the seat should come down into the saddle. From that moment one is trotting on the left diagonal.

*Out of a sitting trot.* In sitting trot the seat is already in the saddle. So one starts the rising trot by *lifting* the seat out of the saddle while the desired diagonal is lifted off the ground. To achieve feeling for the diagonals in sitting trot practise it first without stirrups. Sit relaxed with legs in the correct position, close the eyes and concentrate. When the left diagonal touches the ground one feels the left seat bone and left lower leg move slightly backwards, while the right seat bone and right lower leg move slightly forward (and vice versa).

Pick up the stirrups and practise the same, reciting: left, right, etc. Be careful not to put too much pressure onto the stirrups, as one would then find it difficult to feel the rhythm because one will not sit as deeply into the saddle and the back muscles will stiffen.

If one wishes to trot on the left diagonal one should start to lift the seat out of the saddle when saying "left", because a split second later, when one is out of the saddle, the left diagonal is lifted off the ground. Continue in rising trot and the seat will return into the saddle when the left diagonal is touching the ground and one is trotting on the left diagonal. If one makes it a habit to trot always on the correct diagonal one will not have to count the diagonals any more. One will be able to start the rising trot automatically on the correct diagonal.

*After a transition from canter.* If the rider can

strike off in rising trot out of sitting trot and forward seat without making a mistake he can put this into practise whilst making a transition from canter into rising trot, riding on the desired diagonal at first attempt. The condition, however, is that he must have a good feeling for the canter sequence. If one is, for instance, in the right canter and plans a transition into rising trot on the left diagonal, the most suitable moment is after the moment of suspension of the last canter stride.

If the horse remains in canter the next phase would be the near hindfoot touching the ground. Now, changing into the trot, the horse will not only put down the near hindfoot, but simultaneously the off forefoot as well. This forms the right diagonal pair of legs.

Therefore, when changing from the right canter into trot, the first trotting phase is the right diagonal touching the ground. (When changing from the left canter into trot the left diagonal touches down first.)

The canter is a pace of a three-time hoof beat. During the transition from the right canter into trot (which is executed exactly at the moment of suspension, after the last canter stride) one should count: "one", "two", "three". At the moment one says "two" the left diagonal touches the ground. One should lift one's seat *out* of the saddle the exact moment one says "two", and when the seat returns into the saddle one will be rising trotting on the *left* diagonal.

*Changing diagonals*

When riding in an arena one has to change diagonals each time one changes direction, because only then one will be trotting *always* on the correct diagonal. When hacking one should also change diagonals at least every kilometre (this should become second nature) otherwise one will put too much pressure on *one* particular diagonal. Some riders have the bad habit of always trotting on a particular diagonal and at too fast a pace. They find trotting on the left diagonal, the horse's more flexible side, more comfortable. But if a horse is trotted for months, or even years, as does happen, on the same diagonal his muscles will develop unevenly.

Such a horse will be unable to trot on a straight line, his pace will resemble that of a dog, his hindfeet not moving in line with his forefeet.

If a horse is developed unevenly he will have a particular disadvantage when making a transition into canter. The horse naturally prefers cantering with the stronger foreleg leading, because the opposite (diagonal) hindleg, which is providing impulsion, is the one the horse starts the canter off with when leading with the stronger foreleg. The horse will resent cantering with his weaker legs doing the work.

There are *two ways* of changing diagonals in rising trot:

(i) this one is required for dressage tests. The rider's seat remains *in* the saddle for one more stride. This must be done very gently as it can upset the horse's rhythm and balance.

(ii) this technique I prefer for young horses and showjumpers. The rider's seat remains *out* of the saddle for one more stride. This makes a very smooth change of diagonals and the rider will never disturb the horse's back if he does it correctly, not rising too high out of the saddle and gliding back into the saddle gently.

*Correct timing of the leg aids*

During rising trot the leg aids (and if necessary the whip) should be applied simultaneously – and at the exact moment – when the seat is *in the saddle*. Applying the aids at that moment is most effective, ensures a firm grip and the support of a forward driving seat as well.

Should a rider mistakenly use his legs when rising out of the saddle, he will have little power in his legs, can have no influence with his seat and will push himself off balance.

*Teaching the horse the extended trot*

Some showjumping riders might think that it

is not necessary to teach a showjumping horse the extended trot. This is wrong. The extended trot is an excellent means of teaching a horse respect for the forward driving leg aids. The aids for the transition from ordinary to extended trot and back to ordinary trot also apply for the other paces. A showjumping horse must accelerate his pace at any time willingly and without effort.

During the early stages of schooling never ride a young horse at an extended trot, because the extension forces the horse to change his balance to the forehand, and in order to remain in balance he will lean on the bit. At this stage the extended trot stiffens the horse's back and neck muscles. The diagonal movement becomes irregular and the horse will move with his hocks separated widely. There is also danger of overreaching or forging.

When re-schooling older horses who carry their head too high and are not using their back do not ride an extended trot.

However, when a young horse is ready for this advanced exercise, schooling can start, but for short distances only (never more than 40 to 60 metres). At this stage the schooling has to be done very gradually and in rising trot only. Extended trot, sitting, is *only* required in advanced dressage tests.

When schooling extended trot use *one* long side of the school only and go back to ordinary trot *before* reaching the corner. If the extended trot is continued through the corner one would risk the horse's pace becoming irregular. The horse subsequently would shift his balance to the inner forefoot and break into a canter.

*Preparation*

Prepare the horse correctly for the extended trot. Use the short side and the corners of the riding school. Before reaching the long side, apply stronger pressure with the inner leg when the seat is in the saddle. This creates additional energy and propulsive force for the extension of the trot. Bend the horse's body laterally inwards, go even as far as doing a slight shoulder-in movement. Then the inner hindleg will be extensively engaged.

*Never* make the transition into an extended trot while still in the corner; it would provoke an interruption in the diagonal sequence and the horse could break into a canter.

Proceed at an extended trot *after* the corner when the horse's body is straight from head to tail. Only then is the horse able to bring *both* hindlegs evenly underneath his body and to use all muscles and joints of back and quarters, creating maximum impulsion.

The rider's hands should be absolutely still, because in the trot the horse's head does not make the natural nodding movement as during a walk and a canter, where the rider's hands have to follow this movement.

During the transition into an extended trot the rider should not bend the upper part of his body suddenly forward, which would shift his weight too much to the forehand and ease the feeling on the bit, which in turn would force the horse to change his balance to the forehand. The trot would become hurried and the horse could easily break into canter. While using strong forward driving aids and maintaining the same contact with the mouth, the hands should gradually follow the lengthening of the horse's neck, needed for more freedom of the shoulders.

*Correct transition into ordinary trot*

Having ridden an extended trot from H to K, for instance, *prepare* the horse for the transition into the slower pace with the usual half-halt aid, a horse-length before reaching the marker K.

While changing rein at an extended trot, from H to F, prepare the horse with the half-halt aid, one horse length (3 metres) before meeting the track at F. Still in extended rising trot, one straightens one's shoulders, shifting the weight gently back. Before reaching the letter K – or the track at F – change into ordinary rising trot. If during such a transition adequate seat and leg aids are applied, in conjunction with passive rein aids (*not* backwards pull), then the rider's and horse's balance will be transferred harmoniously to the horse's quarters, which prevents the horse from changing his centre of gravity to the forehand. If a showjumping horse is allowed to come on to the forehand he will make faults, especially with the forelegs.

*Incorrect transition into ordinary trot*

Often mistakes are made during a transition from an extended trot into a slower pace. The most common fault is that the rider neglects the forward driving seat and leg aids, which send the horse into his passive hands, thus engaging the hocks. Some riders are inclined to apply *solely* rein aids. The horse will then lift head and neck and open his mouth. Some will pull the tongue over the bit and/or hold it out of the mouth.

The contraction of neck and shoulder muscles travels down upon the horse's *back*, which will then drop and the hocks will separate widely instead of coming down and under. To ease the pressure and pain in spine and kidneys the horse will move his quarters sideways. In this position the horse cannot engage his quarters and bend his body laterally inwards, which is necessary to be ridden correctly deep into a corner. Instead the horse will shift his weight to the inner foreleg and cut off the corner. For this reason *all* transitions should be made smoothly (whatever the pace may be), never abruptly, whereby the horse remains light in the hand, maintaining a correct position, balance and regular pace.

## THE CANTER

The canter is a pace of a three-time hoof beat, a sequence followed by the moment of suspension. In a gallop (racing speed) this pace has a four-time hoof beat, the moment of suspension being considerable longer than in the canter.

We distinguish the following paces: the ordinary canter; the collected canter; the extended canter; and the counter canter (or false canter). The change from right into the left canter, and vice versa, can be done either by a simple change of leg or by flying change of leg.

*The ordinary canter*

The ordinary canter is the pace between the extended and the collected canter. The speed of the ordinary canter phase is at its medium compared with the other two canter phases, and so is the moment of suspension. The speed is approximately 250 metres per minute. At this speed the horse's posture is in a horizontal position and the tip of the nose is carried in front of the imaginary vertical line and approximately on the level height of the horse's hip. The horse should move freely with long strides, the rider maintaining the rhythm and cadence with forward driving seat and leg aids.

As I have mentioned previously, a young horse should not be requested to canter during the first two months of his schooling. When the canter is introduced in the training one should ride only at the speed of the ordinary canter, either on a long or loose rein, never on the bit. (To prevent bucking at this stage of schooling it is with some young horses advisable to sit only in the forward seat while cantering. This enables the horse to use his undeveloped back freely).

Only at the slow speed of 250 metres per minute is the young horse able to round his back and develop those muscles that will enable him to canter later on collected and extended in balance.

It is a great mistake to gallop a young horse or ride in an extended canter. It would cause the horse to change his centre of gravity to the forehand and to re-balance himself he will take a stronger hold on the bit. The horse would develop the kind of muscles needed for a racehorse. This is opposite to what one wants to achieve for a jumping horse. Therefore *never* canter a young horse faster than ordinary canter.

Regrettably one can often see how young jumping horses are cantered much too fast and how they pull against the rider's hand; and how the riders, leaning forward, pull on the reins in an attempt to slow down the horses, leading to disastrous results.

If, at any time when striking off into a canter or after clearing a fence, the horse should try to dash off for the first few strides, the rider should never bend the upper part of his body forward

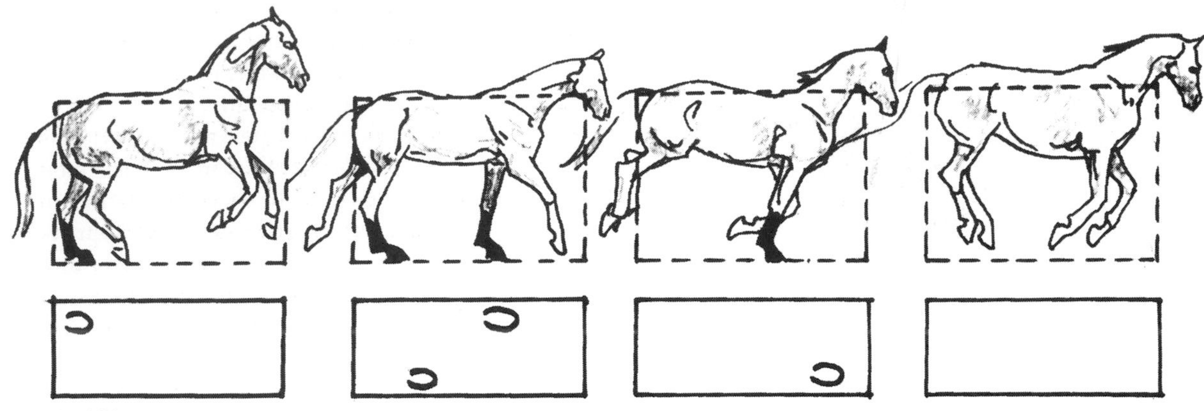

*Fig. 336*
Sequence of the canter.

and pull on the reins to try to slow down the pace. What he should do is straighten his body and lean back, shifting his weight to the quarters. If the horse still goes too fast, ride on a circle, decreasing the diameter of the circle, though not smaller than approximately 15 metres. Once the horse settles down and canters in a slow rhythm increase the diameter of the circle and if he does not extend his pace then go on in a straight line, but if the horse tries to increase his pace again ride at once on a circle again. However, a tactful and educated rider never allows a situation to reach the point where the horse will take the bit and increase his pace. From the very beginning he will never canter faster than 250 metres per minute, giving the horse no chance to pull and dash off. On a young fresh horse the rider will canter on only towards a corner of the school or field, never towards the open field or centre of the school, as the wide space might lead the horse into temptation to increase the pace. A clever rider will not always canter across the same stretch of country, because after a while the horse will anticipate the canter there and try to take off. Also *never* canter towards the stable. An intelligent rider will outsmart his horse, thus saving time and trouble.

*The collected canter*

In the collected canter the horse changes his balance to the quarters, which are lowered and the neck raised in relation to this. The position of head and neck should form a harmonious curve from the withers to the poll, which gives the horse more freedom of movement of his shoulders and makes it easier for the horse to turn in any direction. The highest point of the neck is between the ears; the tip of the nose is carried just in front of the vertical line. The rider must apply strong seat and leg pressure to activate hindlegs and ride the horse from the rear on to the bit. Although the strides are shorter than in ordinary canter, they must become more bouncing. The speed is approximately 200 metres per minute and its moment of suspension at its minimum.

It stands to reason that the horse must have a fairly high degree of schooling before one can practise the collected canter, otherwise the horse will become too heavy on the bit, tense and excited and his pace will become disunited (four-beat canter).

*Extended canter*

In this pace the horse changes his balance slightly forwards, without coming onto the

*Fig. 337*
Ordinary canter.

*Fig. 338*
Collected canter.

*Fig. 339*
Extended canter.

forehand or leaning on the bit. His neck should be lengthened slightly without coming too low. The nose should be carried in front of the vertical line. The rider must follow this lengthening of the horse's neck, while maintaining the same contact with the mouth. He must send the horse strongly forward to develop increased impulsion. The average speed is 300 metres per minute. The horse should not become excited but stay calm, while extending his speed and lengthening his strides. The horse should maintain balance and cadence in his pace, whereby his moment of suspension is at its maximum.

The reason why so many horses dash off and come too much onto the forehand after a transition into extended canter is that some riders suddenly bend their upper body forward. By changing their balance forward they influence the horse to do the same. To regain his balance he will have to take a strong hold on the bit. The canter is called "right" or "left", depending on which foreleg is leading (reaching forward).

The canter is called "disunited" when the horse canters with a lateral pair of legs leading. This pace is most uncomfortable for both horse and rider and should be noticed and corrected immediately.

A rider should *feel* not only in which canter the horse is, or whether the canter is disunited or not, but also he must be sure of the phases of the canter.

If one studies the canter, one will see clearly how the horse changes his centre of gravity in the various canter phases. For example, in the right canter:

(i) In the starting phase, the horse balances himself for a split second on his near hind-leg only. The forehand is raised and the quarters are lowered and engaged. The horse moves his centre of gravity to the quarters.

(ii) The left diagonal is carrying the entire weight; the horse's posture is in a horizontal position.

(iii) In this phase the right foreleg only touches the ground, the horse's balance shifting to the forehand, which is lowered while the quarters are raised.

(iv) This shows the moment of suspension (all four legs off the ground). The horse's body is in a horizontal position. After this moment of suspension the sequence repeats itself.

To acquire a feeling for the sequence the rider should close his eyes and count the rhythm: one, two, *three*, one, two, *three* – with the accent on *three*. Phase one and two are quick-quick rhythms, phase *three* includes phase four, the moment of suspension, and is therefore counted slowly.

The rider should be able to feel with seat and legs the rotating movement in the canter. When the horse is, for instance, in left canter, each time the near forefoot touches the ground one's left hip and seat bone move slightly forward, while the right hip and seat bone move slightly backward. At the same moment one will feel more contact between the horse's body and one's left leg. This is the right moment to apply stronger pressure with the left leg, supported by pressure of the right leg which moves further backwards. If timed like this one will obtain full benefit from the leg aid given because only at this moment the hindlegs are free of the ground and can be activated.

A common mistake when cantering on is that the rider looks down to the leading foreleg. He bends his upper body forward-downwards, shifting his weight to the leading foreleg. This sudden movement influences the horse to change his balance also to the leading foreleg. The horse cannot free the leading shoulder. He will dash forward, lean on the bit, or strike off in the wrong canter.

*The aids*

The "normal" canter aids are well known. They are used to "place" a well-schooled horse into, and at each stride to maintain, the canter. The rider sits in dressage seat, applying a half-halt. For example, when proceeding in the left canter, the rider looks to the right, moves his right shoulder slightly backwards, applying pressure with his right seat bone. He shifts his centre of gravity, in full co-ordination with that of the horse, to the off hindleg. The horse's body is kept straight from head to tail, with a slight flexion to the left. The rider applies strong pressure with his left (inner) leg on the girths, supported by pressure of his right leg behind the girths, to prevent the quarters from deviating. (The aids for the right canter are vice versa.)

The same aids are applied *during* the canter – at each stride – at the exact moment when the leading foreleg touches the ground.

"Placing" a horse into a canter can only be done when these aids are applied at the appropriate moment. The trot is the easiest pace to place the horse into the canter. At the trot during the moment of suspension it is easy for the horse to change from the two-time trotting pace into the three-time canter pace.

Count the diagonals: left, right, left, right; the aids to canter on must be applied *during* the moment of suspension. For example, when proceeding into the left canter the aids have to be applied at the moment of suspension *after* the right diagonal has touched down (counting "right"). Why at this moment? If one continues trotting, the left diagonal (near foreleg, off hindleg) would be *next* touching the ground. But on account of the canter aid being applied during the preceding moment of suspension, *only* the off hindleg will touch down to start the sequence of the left canter.

If the rider is not able to feel the rhythm and does not apply the canter aids exactly at this moment the horse cannot strike off in canter *without* an intermediate stride. Instead of standing on his off hindleg to canter on the horse will shift his balance to the near foreleg, come onto the forehand and increase his trotting pace. After a few extended trotting strides the horse will then *break* into canter, instead of being placed into canter *without* an intermediate step.

These normal canter aids, however, are very hard for a green horse to understand. Therefore one uses "preparatory" aids, which, by law of gravity, make it easy for the horse to *break* into canter. These preparatory aids were practised in the former cavalry schools with remounts before these were advanced enough to be placed into canter with the normal aids.

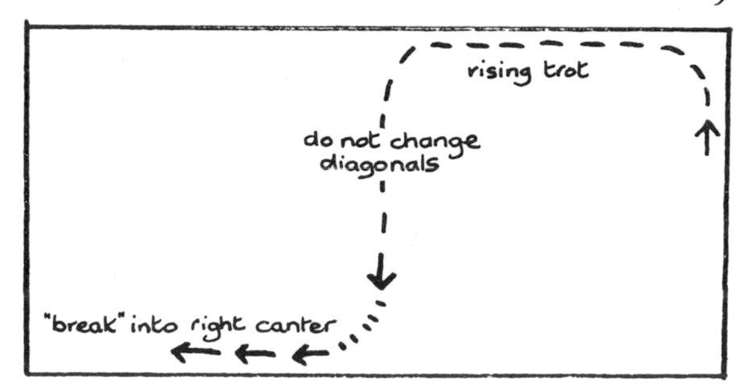


*Fig. 340*
Breaking into canter.

*Breaking into canter*

There are three different techniques used as preliminary aids to teach the horse to break into canter. These are based on the natural change of balance of an unbroken horse.

Watch an unbroken horse in the field "break" into canter. For example, into the left canter: he will lift his head and bend his neck to the right, transferring his weight to the off foreleg. By doing so the gives freedom of movement of his left shoulder to throw his left foreleg freely forward. He will increase the trotting pace for a few strides, changing his balance forward, which will break the left diagonal. This interruption of the left diagonal means that the off hindleg only touches the ground for a split second, while the other three legs are free of the ground. The horse will break into the left canter, because as I have explained previously he stands on the outer hindleg to start the left canter.

This natural behaviour is copied when teaching green horses to canter:

(i) Ride in rising trot on the left-hand rein. Purposely trot on the wrong (left) diagonal. Coming near the end of the long side of the school extend the trot for a few strides by applying stronger pressure with both legs while returning into the saddle.

Bring the right rein out sideways from the horse's neck, the left rein pushing against the neck, maintaining with both reins equal tension on the bit; the horse's neck is bent slightly to the right, giving freedom of movement to the left shoulder, which he needs to throw his left foreleg freely forward in order to break into the left canter.

When reaching the corner, horse and rider transfer their weight to the near foreleg, this extra weight forcing the horse to break the left diagonal and there is no alternative for the horse but to break into left canter. At this exact moment the rider applies stronger pressure with his left leg on the girths, supported by his right leg behind the girths, to urge the horse to break into the left canter.

(ii) Again, ride in rising trot on the left-hand rein. Trot on the right diagonal. Halfway along the long side of the school turn left. Do not change diagonals at the centre of the school, and at a horse length before reaching the opposite long side bend the horse's neck slightly to the left and turn suddenly sharp to the right.

The fact that one is still trotting on the right diagonal and the sudden change of balance in the sharp turn will transfer most of the weight to the off foreleg. This will break the right diagonal, the horse will stand for a split second on the near hindleg and will break into the right canter.

(iii) When no riding school is available, trot on the right diagonal on a small left-hand circle. To make it easier, circle around a fence or a barrel. After trotting around a few times in rising trot, turn suddenly sharp to the right and at the same time urge the horse to break into the right canter. Leg aids are the same as in the first two techniques. While cantering, maintain the normal canter aids to continue in canter and to encourage the horse to engage his quarters.

*Placing the horse into canter*

The young horse has learnt to break into canter at either leg and has shown that he adjusts himself to the rider's change of balance. Most horses understand this technique very soon. Then the time has come to place the horse into canter.

While cantering on the horse stands for a split second on one single hindleg only, for the left canter on the off hindleg and for the right canter on the near hindleg. This first canter phase returns at each canter stride after the moment of suspension. One should realise that that this is always the "starting" phase whether the horse breaks into canter or is placed into canter.

The horse transfers all his weight to this particular hindleg. To be in complete balance and harmony with the horse the rider's centre of gravity has to be distributed vertically above the one of the horse, in other words, the rider must also transfer his weight at this moment to that particular hindleg. To be able to carry this heavy weight this particular hindleg has to be brought well underneath the horse's body.

The young horse, however, has up to now only been asked to break into canter. Although the horse already responds and obeys to the forward and sideways driving leg aids, he will at this stage not be able to engage his outer hindleg sufficiently in response to the normal canter aids (inner leg on the girths, outer leg supporting behind the girths). The horse would most likely strike off at the wrong, or a disunited, canter.

There are various techniques which engage *one* hindleg extensively and bring it further underneath the horse's body. After such an exercise use this engaged hindleg as the outer hindleg to canter on. There are ten such exercises, the more advanced ones being to canter on, out of: a rein-back; a halt; a walk; a turn around the forehand; and a turn on the haunches. In these movements there is not a moment of suspension, consequently there is less mobility in the horse's action.

In the beginning one practises the simpler exercises to bring *one* hindleg further underneath the horse's body.

The exercises described below are all used to "place" a horse into a canter.

*Out of a figure of eight*

This is the easiest way to place a horse into canter. If one wants to place the horse into the right canter, for instance, trot in a slow sitting trot on a small left-hand rein circle, diameter 10 metres. Out of this circle suddenly turn right and canter on immediately. The horse will have to bring his near hindleg under to strike off in the right canter. To encourage him to do this ask the horse to move the quarters out to the right for a few strides. The hindlegs will move on a track beside the track of the forelegs on a slightly larger circle (two tracks, more or less a shoulder-in movement). In doing so the inner (near) hindleg is brought further underneath the horse's body as when just moving on a circle.

The leg aids for this moving on two tracks are contrary to those for riding on the circle: riding on a circle, the inner leg pushes on the girths, the outer leg supporting behind the girths. The horse's body should be bent "laterally" inwards, from head to tail, and the bending adjusted to the curvature of the circle line. The horse's hindfeet must follow exactly the same track as the forefeet.

Moving the quarters out, the inner leg pushes – at this early stage of schooling – behind the girths, supported by the outer leg on the girths. Trot on the left-hand circle for approximately two rounds, now and again moving the quarters out for a *few strides*. Not only will this activate the near hindleg, it will also draw the horse's attention to the rider's left leg, positioned behind the girths.

*Before* changing direction from the left circle

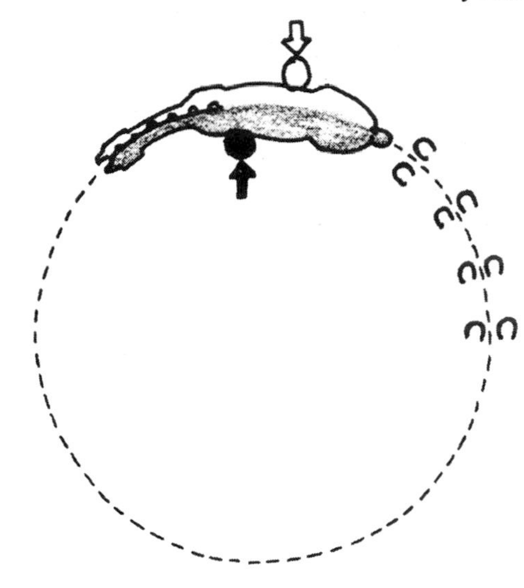

*Fig. 341*
Placing the horse into canter: trot on a small circle.

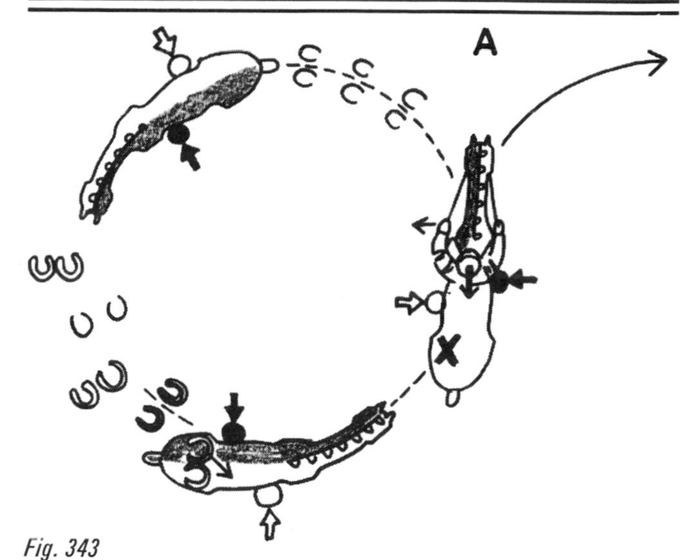


*Fig. 343*
Utilise the engaged near hindleg to strike off into the right canter, weight still shifted to X.

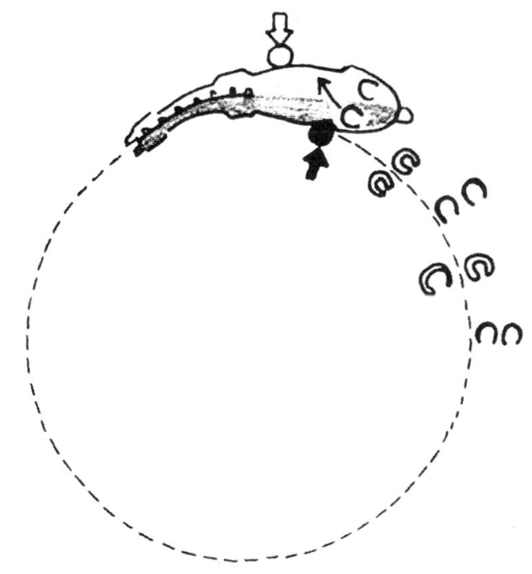

*Fig. 342*
Engage the inner hindleg even more by moving the quarters slightly to the outside.

into the right circle the rider should again move the quarters out to the right. Apply a half-halt aid and turn suddenly to the right, placing the horse into the right canter.

The left leg remains behind the girths, where, after the preliminary exercise, it activates the near hindleg. The right leg applies strong pressure on the girths to urge the horse to proceed into the right canter.

In this early stage of schooling, during the turn to the right, the left hand should remain slightly out from the neck, bending the horse's neck slightly to the left as before when riding on the left-hand circle. This "natural" head position is deliberately maintained when passing from the left into the right circle, as it gives the horse's right shoulder more freedom to strike off into the right canter.

Also, it should be noted that the rider changes from the left to the right circle, facing the kicking boards on the short side. This aids the young horse to maintain balance and will prevent him from dashing forward after being placed into canter. One will feel him cantering the first few strides with well-lowered quarters. Stay on the right-hand circle. Do not canter for a few rounds, but change into a trot *before* the horse reaches the point where he changes his balance and comes onto the forehand. Exercise this on both reins alternately, as this teaches the horse more quickly to distinguish the difference between the rider's aids for the right and the left canter.

To prevent misunderstanding I emphasise that this slight sideways bending of the horse's head and neck to the *left* when placing the horse into the *right* canter should be executed only in the very beginning when schooling the horse to be placed into the canter.

As soon as the horse has reached a more advanced stage of equitation and willingly obeys these preliminary aids, then ,while passing from one circle into the other, one should straighten the horse's body for approximately one horse length.

*Out of shoulder-out*

When riding, for instance, in sitting trot on the left-hand rein, ride four to six strides shoulder-out. In this movement the horse has to bring his off hindleg down and under; head and neck are bent slightly to the right. This is an excellent position to strike off into the left canter. During the shoulder out the rider's weight is transferred to the off hindleg, together with that of the horse – as it should be for the canter on in a left canter. Also, one's legs are already in the correct position: right leg behind and left leg on the girths. One prepares the horse with a half-halt and counts the sequence of the diagonals. A split second after the right diagonal has touched down, apply strong pressure with the left leg on the girths while the right leg remains behind the girths.

If these aids are timed correctly the horse will strike off in a left canter without putting in another trotting stride.

*Out of transitions*

For the first 15 minutes of each schooling session the horse should be loosened up by making frequent transitions and moving the quarters sideways.

This alternate engaging of one hindleg offers a good opportunity to place a horse into canter. If trotting on the left-hand rein, make a transition into a walk, moving the quarters to the left. To achieve this the right leg has to apply strong pressure behind the girths, the horse's off hindleg being brought down and under, ready to carry the full weight of horse and rider in the first canter phase.

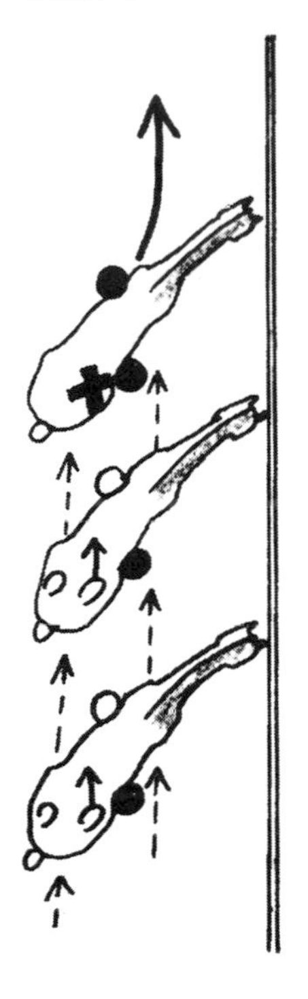

*Fig. 344*
Canter on out of shoulder-out, weight remaining on X.

One is already sitting more on one's right seat bone, one's legs being also in the proper position and the horse's head and neck are bent, slightly to the right. Count the diagonals and apply stronger pressure with the left leg after the right diagonal has touched down, placing the horse into the left canter. In time one can also canter on after transitions from a walk to a halt and from a trot to a halt. This exercise is a good remedy to re-school horses who dislike cantering on on one particular leg.

The cause of the horse disliking striking off in a left canter is that his right (or off) hindleg and whole side are stiff and the right side of the mouth a little harder.

Therefore to teach a horse to strike off in

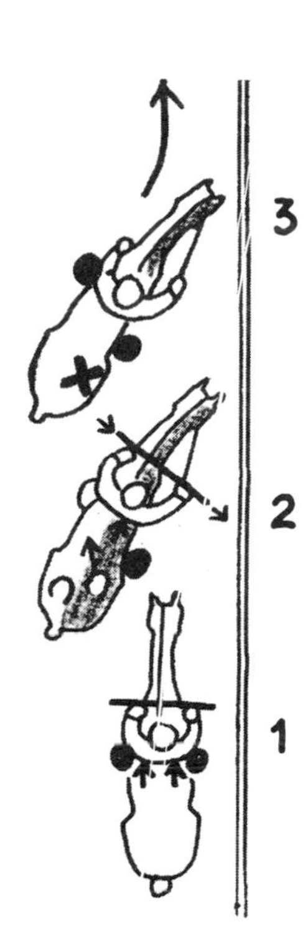


*Fig. 345*
Make a transition from trot to walk, moving in the quarters and transferring weight to X. Use the engaged outer hindleg to strike off in the left canter.

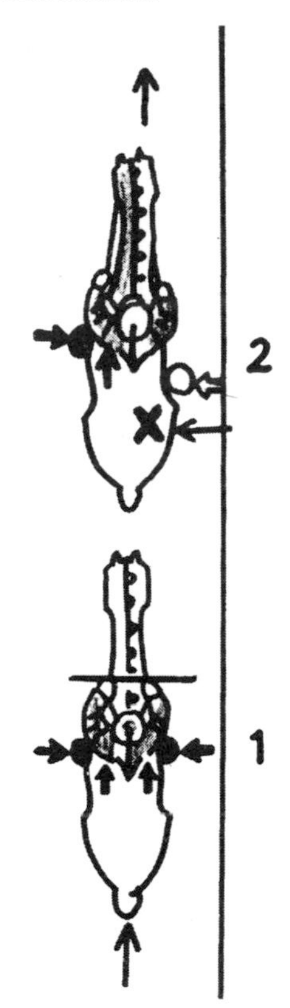


*Fig. 346*
Canter on on a straight line: prepare the horse with a half-halt, transfer weight to X, apply the left canter aid during the moment of suspension after the right diagonal has touched down.

canter properly one has to exercise the opposite, stiff side, especially the hock. Practise the transitions with the horse's stiff side along the kicking boards.

*On a straight line*

When a horse willingly strikes off in either canter after a preparatory exercise he should be supple enough to be placed into canter on a straight line. The schooling of this movement should commence at a sitting trot.

Apply the aids during the moment of suspension, as explained before. The horse will be able to canter on without an intermediate stride. While cantering on, on a straight line, the rider must keep the horse straight from head to tail (no sideways movement of the quarters) with a slight flexion to the inner side.

*Out of a walk*

As this is an advanced exercise it may only be practised when the horse has achieved a fairly high degree of collection. The horse must lower and engage his quarters while remaining light on the bit, maintaining flexibility at the poll and at the lower jaw.

Start the exercise on a figure of eight by walking on a small left-hand rein circle (6 metres diameter) in the corner of the school. While cantering on and changing direction (out of a walk on the figure of eight), move the quarters out for a few strides (a shoulder-in movement), engaging the near hindleg. Count the forelegs touching the ground: left, right, left, right . . . apply the canter aids immediately the moment one counts "right". The next walking phase would be the right diagonal touching the ground. Instead, the near hindleg only will touch down, while the off foreleg is raised simultaneously with the left diagonal to canter on. If the horse obeys willingly without dashing off after the transition, one can practise this exercise later on, on a straight line, controlling the quarters with the outer leg behind the girths, avoiding any deviation.

*Out of a halt*

This is a very advanced exercise based on a high degree of collection. It should therefore be practised only in the second year of schooling. Before coming to a halt one applies the leg aids slightly further behind the girths than normally. The horse should be sent into the rider's passive hands, flexing the jaw while champing the bit and lowering the quarters well. At this stage the horse is so well schooled that he obeys the slightest seat and leg aids. When halting, the horse must stand square on all four legs and rock still. The engaged hindlegs must be kept in readiness to strike off in canter without an intermediate stride or any deviation of the quarters.

*Out of rein-back*

Normally, in a dressage test, when finishing the last diagonal stride of the reining back, the horse should stand square on all four legs, regardless of which pace one will choose to proceed with next. As a schooling purpose, however, when placing the horse into canter one should proceed at the exact moment when *one* of the diagonal pair of legs are still further underneath. For example, while lifting simultaneously the other three legs off the ground (and vice versa for the left canter).

*Out of two tracks*

Cantering on out of two tracks is an excellent schooling exercise for showjumping horses. It increases the lateral flexibility in the rib parts and engages the quarters. This degree of equitation, however, belongs also in the second schooling year.

THE "SIMPLE" CHANGE OF LEG

*With a few trotting strides in between.* Normally the "simple" change of leg is done with a

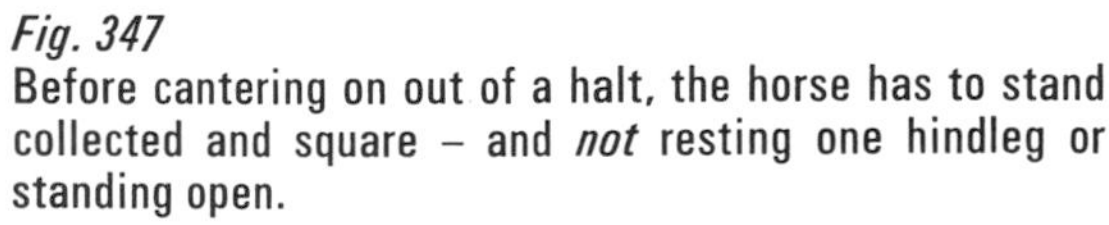

*Fig. 347*
Before cantering on out of a halt, the horse has to stand collected and square – and *not* resting one hindleg or standing open.

few walking strides in between the change of canter. In the beginning, however, practise the simple change with a few collected trotting strides (sitting trot) in between the change of leg. The young horse will then be able to make a smooth balanced transition from a canter to a trot, and the transition from a trot into a canter is simplified by the moment of suspension in the trot when the horse is airborne for a split second. It is easy to school the simple change of leg when changing rein through the diagonal of the school. Riding, for example, in the left canter on the left-hand rein, change rein through the diagonal. The canter change should be made approximately two horse lengths before reaching the track. During the last three to four strides in the left canter prepare the horse with a half-halt, sending him actively into the resisting hands. Do not pull back on the reins, just stop following the nodding movement of the horse's head.

The horse will lower and engage his quarters while making the transition into a collected trot. During the few trotting strides the horse must also be sent on actively to create a distinctive moment of suspension, which will be an advantage when cantering on. (Four to six strides collected at the beginning, to only two strides later on.) Again apply a strong half-halt aid and urge the horse to canter on during the moment of suspension after the left diagonal has touched down.

*With a few walking strides in between.* Prepare the horse by making a simple change of leg with approximately two trotting strides. Then introduce a few walking strides before cantering on, on the other leg. Only when the horse remains calm and light on the bit may one gradually omit the trotting strides and make the transition from the canter "directly" into a collected walk. Apply the aids for the right canter after a few walking strides immediately as the off foreleg touches the ground (vice versa for the left canter). While the horse is advancing in his schooling gradually reduce the number of walking strides until one can make the simple change with *only one* walking stride in between.

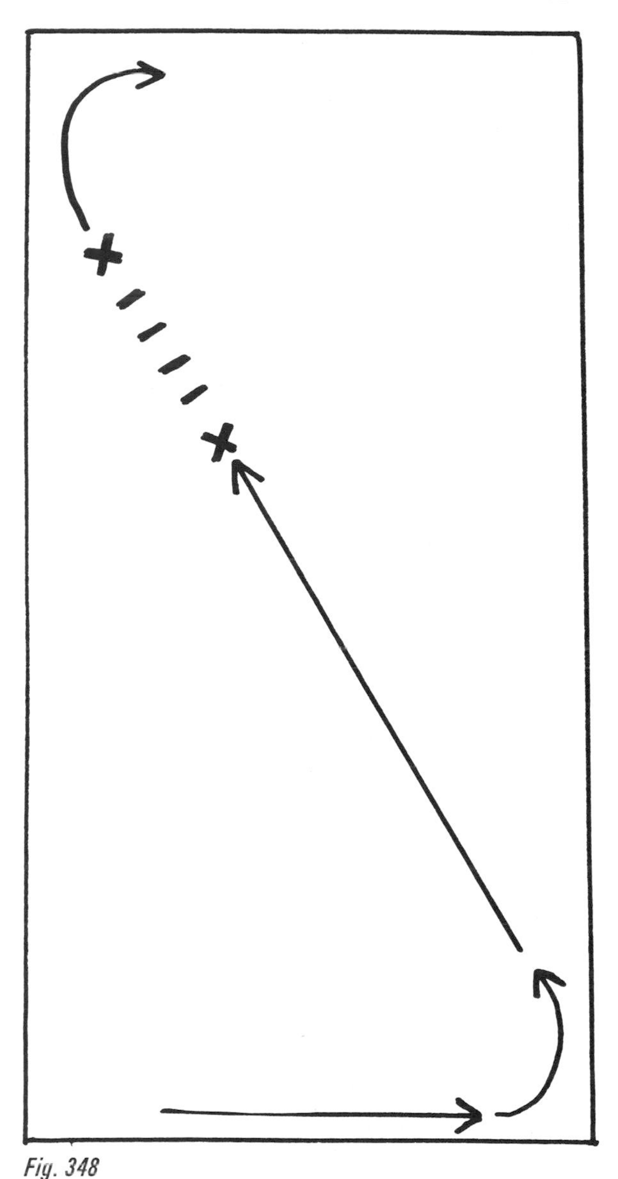

*Fig. 348*
The simple change of leg. Ride in the left canter on the left-hand rein, change through the diagonal. Prepare the horse with a half-halt at X then make a transition to collected trot, trot approximately four strides, apply another half-halt and at the second X proceed into right canter.

It is important that one never looks down (out of force of habit) while schooling the simple change of leg at canter to check if the horse is cantering on the desired leading leg. This would severely interfere with the horse's balance and make it impossible for the horse to make a proper change. If the rider is not able to *feel* the sequence of the trot and walking paces, or with which leg the horse is leading in canter, then he should not attempt to teach his horse a simple change. It would not only upset the horse and bring him onto the forehand but the pace would become disunited as well.

The transition of the simple change of leg must be made smoothly and never abruptly, maintaining impulsion and good collection, with a slight flexion of the lower jaw. The horse's body should remain straight from head to tail with a slight flexion at his inner side.

If the horse is able to perform this fluently, only then has he reached the stage to teach him the *flying* change of leg in the canter.

### THE (MOUNTED) REIN-BACK

Backing is an unnatural movement for the horse. Therefore it is up to the trainer to teach the horse this movement with patience and understanding. The aim is that the horse moves backwards under the rider with regular and long diagonal strides. The horse's posture should be the same as when moving forward. His hocks should be close together and engaged and the forelegs must follow the tracks of the hindlegs.

It is only possible to achieve this if the horse responds to the forward driving leg aids. They push the horse forward against the resisting hand. This results in the horse reining back. The horse has to respond equally well to the sideways driving leg aids. They keep the horse straight in the rein-back, which can *never* be achieved by *pulling* a horse backwards.

A young horse who has learnt from the exercises on foot to rein-back correctly will know the diagonal backwards leg movement and will therefore bring the necessary muscles into action. It is now that one will receive the full advantage of pre-schooling, because the horse will co-operate willingly and should have no problem.

Regrettably, some trainers ask their horses much too soon to rein-back without preparing them with work on foot and without teaching them the two different leg aids first. They can, therefore, only force the horse backwards by pulling on the reins, which is ruining the horse's mouth and back. These trainers create a lot of problems by either being impatient or by not knowing the logical steps which lead up to the point where the horse can be "pushed" backwards with *forward* driving leg aids (as it ought to be done).

#### *The aids*

Prepare the horse properly at a walk by applying strong half-halt aids and make first (five or six times) transitions from a walk to a halt, without reining back, in order to engage the quarters. In doing so, send the horse strongly forward into the "passive" hands. When the horse comes gradually to a halt he will offer a slight flexion with his lower jaw (submission). The rider immediately eases the tension on the bit by opening his hands, similar to un-squeezing a sponge. Third rein aid. The horse should stand square and light on the bit while champing it.

Now the horse is prepared properly. The next time when coming to a halt do *not* ease the tension on the bit when the horse flexes the jaw, but *now* the hands remain passive. Continue with the same forward driving aids. The obedient horse will attempt to go forward but will meet the barrier of the passive hands and move backwards. To continue the rein-back, maintain the forward driving aids. One will feel that the horse is making a submission with the lower jaw at each backing stride and one's immediate reaction should be to ease the tension on the bit and keep the contact with the mouth only finger-tight. Never have more tension on the bit while reining back than while riding forward. If one makes the mistake of maintaining the resisting hand, even without actually *pulling* backwards, one will create resistance and excitement. The horse will hurry backwards, go over or behind the bit, stiffen his neck and

*Fig. 349*
The mounted rein back. The horse stands collected, the rider pushing the horse from the rear against the passive (resisting) hand.

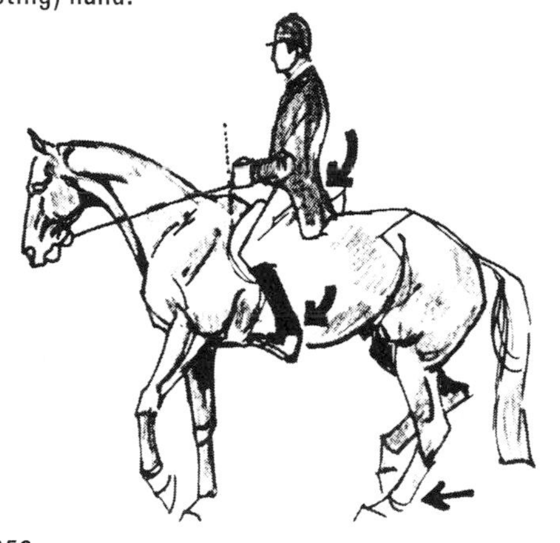

*Fig. 350*
This will cause the horse to rein back rythmically with engaged quarters.

*Fig. 351*
After a few strides utilise the accumulated impulsion to send the horse forward, while allowing him to stretch his neck downwards.

back muscles and move his quarters sideways to ease the pain in his back.

The aids have been applied correctly when the horse moves backwards, the legs of the two diagonal pairs being lifted simultaneously and equally high. The strides should be as high as when moving forward at a walk. The diagonals should move backwards with long and regular strides on a straight line without hurrying.

The highest point of the arched neck should be at the poll. The nose is carried slightly in front of the vertical line, head and neck in the same position as when moving forward, the quarters lowered and engaged.

Before starting to rein-back, decide on the number of strides, and do not allow the horse to move backwards more or fewer strides than desired. At the beginning do not rein-back more than two to four strides in order not to strain the joints of the hindlegs.

After the horse has completed the correct number of backing strides, move forward *without* coming to a halt, because the exercise is a means of testing the horse's responsiveness and ability to maintain balance and impulsion during the changes from forward to backwards and to forward again.

In the beginning, move on immediately after reining back in an active walk on a loose rein. During the rein-back the horse's quarters are lowered and engaged, with all the muscles and joints acting as springs providing impulsion when moving on again. This extra impulsion will encourage the horse to lengthen his stride and preserve his balance, even when he is lowering his head and neck on the loose rein.

In a more advanced stage of schooling one should, after the rein-back, apply also the second or third rein aid (long or collected rein) and proceed immediately in a trot or a canter, without an intermediate stride or any deviation of the quarters.

*When difficulties occur*

If at the beginning, when reining back mounted, a young horse does not respond immediately to one's aids, one should not

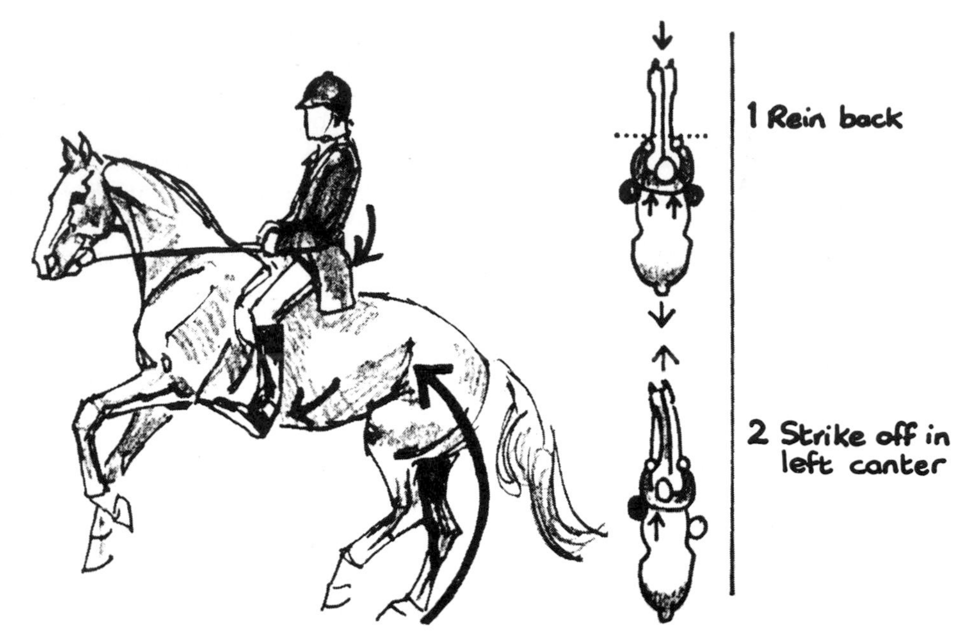


*Fig. 352*
Out of rein back strike off in left canter without coming to a halt first.

become impatient and try to pull the horse backwards. The horse has learnt to rein-back on foot willingly, therefore an assistant should be used to bridge the change from the rein-back unmounted to mounted. The assistant should stand in front of the horse while the rider applies the aids to rein-back. The position of the assistant reminds the horse of his pre-schooling on foot, and in most cases it is sufficient if the assistant simply stands in front of the horse. However, if the horse still refuses to rein-back then the assistant should touch the coronet with the dressage whip, as has been done on foot. When there is no assistant available one should ride the horse at an active walk towards the kicking boards of the school or the railing surrounding a field, applying adequate seat and leg aids. In this case, apply both legs slightly further behind the girths to prevent the quarters from moving sideways. During the last few strides before reaching the kicking boards one's hands should stop following the nodding movement of the horse's head and neck. One sends the horse strongly into the passive hands and against the boards. This will leave the horse no alternative but to move backwards. One will find that the kicking boards will support the passive rein aids, and when one con-

*Fig. 353*
In case of any difficulties ask a helper to remind the horse of the rein back "on foot".

*Fig. 354*
When the horse resists the rein back, ride forward straight against the wall of the school. When reaching the wall apply the aids to rein back (pushing strongly forward) and the horse will respond willingly.

tinues to push with seat and legs the horse will submit and flex his lower jaw and move willingly backwards.

Certain horses have the habit while reining back of moving the quarters sideways. The cause is usually a stiff hock. The deviation always occurs towards the side of the stiff hock. To exercise and improve the hock, practise the rein-back on the track, with the horse's stiff side along the kicking boards. The horse cannot deviate with the quarters and is made, without force, to use the stiff hock.

To keep the horse on a straight line while reining back it is sometimes sufficient to apply the leg aid on the horse's stiff side, further behind the girths.

Spreading of the hocks and deviation or inactivity of the quarters is a sign of insufficiently developed muscles. Supple the horse up by means of lungeing with the Chambon and work on foot on the horse's less flexible side.

*Use of force* is detrimental to the horse's mouth and the joints of the hindquarters. To evade any violent influence the horse may rear, move backwards with irregular strides, hurry, or move the quarters sideways. He might also injure the coronet band of his hindfeet with the fore shoes.

CHAPTER TEN

# FIRST YEAR JUMPING TRAINING

## CAVALETTI WORK

BEFORE actually starting schooling a young horse over cavaletti I would like to remind the trainer of the following proverb:

> When all is said and done,
> when all is taught which can be taught,
> and all is learned which can be learnt,
> anything to do with horses, will still
> retain it's intrinsic element of danger.

It is astonishing that some people do make grave mistakes, merely because of ignorance. Many accidents in the riding and handling of horses could be prevented if more care was taken. Therefore, never ride or jump without a hard hat for protection. Most riding schools will never give a horse to a pupil if he or she is not wearing one because the accident insurance will not cover them if proper precautions are not taken. I have known of cases where, rather than upset her newly-fashioned hairstyle, a woman has preferred not to use a hard hat and has ended up in hospital with concussion as a result.

For safety reasons it is unwise to jump on one's own because an accident can happen any time. One should be warned not to use reins that are too long when jumping because one's feet can easily get tangled in them. One should always make sure that the safety clip of the stirrup bar is *open* and, better still, "movable" – as on the Saumur saddle for example. In the event of a fall, the stirrup leather will then slide out easily and the rider cannot get dragged. One should also never forget to use a surcingle when jumping.

The training of showjumpers is only possible if one has a certain amount of fence material at one's daily disposal. These should include: 12 cavaletti; four uprights; three poles; eight wings; and one straight fence (gate). These are all necessary and sufficient for basic schooling at home.

Later on, when the horse is more muscled and has more experience, one should take the young horse to different jumping training fields. This will get the young horse used to travelling in a horse box and to various kinds of fences and different surroundings. Then, if some day the horse starts competing in a novice jumping competition, he will not be surprised and frightened by the sight of strange surroundings and varied obstacles.

Before one can start schooling over cavaletti the young horse should, of course, obey the rider's aids willingly and must have reached the stage where his muscles are well developed and be in good physical condition. The horse should be in the right frame of mind: attentive; observant and bold; but first of all calm and relaxed. One should be able to ride the young horse in all three paces on a completely loose rein without the horse increasing his pace or leaning on the bit.

The schooling over cavaletti can only be fruitful if it is done in the *forward seat position*, no matter in what pace.

It is because of a lack of understanding that some people ride in a rising or a sitting trot over cavaletti.

Not only when riding over cavaletti, but particularly when approaching the row of cavaletti one must ride in the *forward seat position*. If the cavaletti were approached in *rising* or *sitting trot* or *sitting* in the saddle at a walk, one's weight would be distributed wrongly, Owing to the rider's nearly vertical seat position he has to bend his upper body suddenly forward over the first cavaletti in order to allow the horse to lengthen his neck. This sudden forward shifting of one's weight disturbs the horse's balance and brings him onto the forehand. In trying to stay under the rider's centre of gravity the horse increases his pace, which becomes irregular and hasty.

*Fig. 355*
Over cavaletti ride *only* in the forward seat, and allow the horse to stretch his neck.

For these reasons it is vital that one should ride constantly in the *forward seat*, not only over the cavaletti but also in the approach.

While riding over the cavaletti one must look straight ahead and distribute equal weight on both stirrups in order not to interfere with the horse's balance.

Some riders have the bad habit of looking down and to the *left*, and without realising it

*Fig. 356*
Rider unbalancing his horse.

*Fig. 357*
Many riders, even those of international standard, have the bad habit of leaning to the left side of the horse's neck while airborne over every fence. (Some lean the opposite way, as here). After jumping a round, a distinct grey patch can often be seen on the right upper front part of their coat where it has continuously touched the horse's mane. Shifting of a rider's weight to the left forces a horse to land continuously into the left canter. This, of course, is completely wrong, if one has to make a right hand turn, after landing, while the horse is in the left canter. Since most courses have as many right as left hand turns, the rider's coat should show similar patches on right and left front – or better still none at all.

they shift their entire weight onto the left stirrup. This, of course, unbalances the horse and forces him to land always in the left canter.

Other riders exaggerate the forward bending of their bodies when jumping cavaletti. This is not necessary because the training jumps are small and any excess movement unbalances the horse.

*Every beginning is difficult*

Although the young horse has gained experience in the jumping lane *unmounted*, one cannot expect him to give at first the same good performance when *mounted*.

Even if one should sit still without influencing the horse in any way, the mere additional weight of the rider will influence the horse's balance. It takes a considerable time before the young horse is accustomed to it. Give the horse a fair chance to re-establish his balance in the same manner as when getting used to the rider's weight on the flat. Therefore the exercise over the cavaletti (flat on the ground) is done in the beginning only at a walk and later on at a trot. This period also gives one the opportunity to improve one's forward seat position.

After training the horse over cavaletti, there will be another difficult beginning. This time when starting to jump a row of fences or a small course. Most young horses will again lose their balance. When cantering from fence to fence they might easily come onto the forehand. If the rider then sits in the forward seat, the horse will come even more onto the forehand and will start running.

Therefore, one can only sit perfectly in the forward seat on a well balanced horse.

When jumping an impatient, unbalanced horse, or when the horse becomes excited in new surroundings, is shy or nervous, one will have to sit in the remount seat between the fences.

Over the fences the rider should always sit in a perfect forward seat, which also applies in landing when the horse's forelegs touch the ground. Next, the horse's hindlegs touch down, his forehand is raised. At this moment the rider also straightens up to stay in balance with the horse. When jumping the unbalanced horse, the rider will remain in this upright position, seat slightly in the saddle, riding in the remount seat until the take-off at the next fence.

In extreme cases, where the horse is unbalanced to the extent of leaning heavily on the bit, the rider might even have to sit in the dressage (deep) seat between the fences. This, of course, is most undesirable, as it involves a lot of movement of the rider's upper body when changing from dressage seat to forward seat at take-off. There is no pleasure in jumping such a badly schooled horse.

So, do not misunderstand me. The aim is to school a horse so perfectly that the rider can ride the whole course in perfect forward seat. This, however, is not always possible. Depending on the horse's training, sensitivity, the mood he is in or the surrounding atmosphere, the rider might have to refrain from the ideal and change to remount or even dressage seat.

*Placing the cavaletti*

One starts at a walk over one single cavaletti, flat on the ground. One by one another cavaletti is then placed behind until there are four altogether in a row. The exact distance in between the cavaletti depends entirely on the natural length of the individual horse's stride. Horses should have, *at walk*, a distance of approximately 1 to 1·1 metres, ponies approximately 0·9 metres.

Horses should have at trot a distance of approximately 1·3 metres and ponies 1·1 metres. These are "normal" distances. *Eventually all* horses should be able to walk and trot over cavaletti at normal distances. Likewise, every schooled horse should eventually be able to jump the jumping lane at normal distances or he will be in trouble at shows.

But if these normal distances at the beginning of the training do not suit a horse one will have to adjust them; for a horse with a very short stride first shorten the distances slightly. Gradually increase the distances, starting with the last distance – never the first one. In time the length of the horse's stride will improve and he will then be able to cope with the normal distances.

For a horse with an extremely long stride, first make the distances longer, and in time shorten them gradually until they are of normal length.

One can check whether the distances are suitable for each horse by examining the imprints of the horse's hooves when he has gone over the row of cavaletti. They should be printed at the centre, between the cavaletti. If the horse constantly has to reach for the next cavaletti, or gets too close to the following cavaletti, one should alter the distance accordingly. When the horse walks without hurrying, remains relaxed over the cavaletti on a *loose* rein and lengthens and lowers his head and neck, then one can turn the last cavaletti up to its highest position. When the horse remains relaxed, while lifting his legs higher than before, one can turn the second one up, then the third and then the first cavaletti. This makes the horse attentive without upsetting him. It teaches the young horse to lift his legs, bend his joints and use his muscles properly, while rounding his back. One should not heighten the cavaletti at all the first day but over a period of time. When approaching the cavaletti, as well as when riding over them, one *must* keep the rhythm. If one feels the horse is losing impulsion one has to apply forward driving leg aids. Already during the approach one should count the sequence of the hoof beats. This makes it easier to feel if the horse is losing impulsion.

In schooling the young horse over cavaletti he will already learn to find his correct take-off point. He should never be allowed to shorten his last strides or to put in an extra short stride, but if necessary he should lengthen his strides to meet the first cavaletti correctly. If the horse learns this at such an early stage of his training he will do the same later on when approaching the row out of a trot, or when jumping fences out of a canter.

The young horse's schooling over cavaletti should take about three months. For the first month only walk and trot over the cavaletti *flat* on the ground. The second month turn up the cavaletti to the highest position alternately. The third month the horse must be able to walk and trot relaxed over all four cavaletti standing up at the normal height.

*Fig. 358*
**Perfect balance in both horse and rider. Sonja Paalman, the author's daughter, riding Mrs. Gisela Holstein's horse, Fresko.**

Riding over cavaletti must be divided into several sessions evenly spread over the whole schooling hour, each session comprising approximately four to five rounds over the cavaletti row, either at a walk or a trot. Do not forget to alter the distance when starting the work in a trot. If the horse at any time should get excited when trotting over the cavaletti, go at once back to a walk, changing the distance accordingly; or have two sets of cavaletti, one for walk and another for trot.

Only if the horse is calm and completely relaxed again may one go back to a trot, starting over one single cavaletti only and gradually adding the others, all flat on the ground.

Each time one starts a schooling session commence from the very beginning and never with the positions achieved at the end of the previous session.

*Fig. 359*
Fresko again, winning at Aachen in perfect style, with the German rider, G. Wiltfang, up.

The next step in schooling over cavaletti is to place one cavaletti (normal height) at a distance of 2·5 metres behind the row of four cavaletti at trot distance. Ride this row three to five times in a trot. After this, place another cavaletti on top of the last single one and trot over the row. Clearing the set of two cavaletti at the end of the row, the horse will land into a canter. Having gone over the row three to five times, now place another two cavaletti on top of each other at a distance of 3 metres behind the row. Ride over this three to five times. Again place another set of two cavaletti on top of each other behind the row at a distance of 3 metres.

After having ridden over this, place another cavaletti on top of the last two and widen the last distance to 3·5 metres. Ride over this three to five times.

Only if the horse stays calm and does not increase his pace or become hasty then place a third cavaletti on the second last set and widen this distance also to 3·5 metres, bearing in mind that one has to move also the last set of three cavaletti to maintain their distance of 3·5 metres.

Having ridden over the row three to five times, place *one* pole behind the last set of three

*Fig. 360*
Approach the row at a trot.

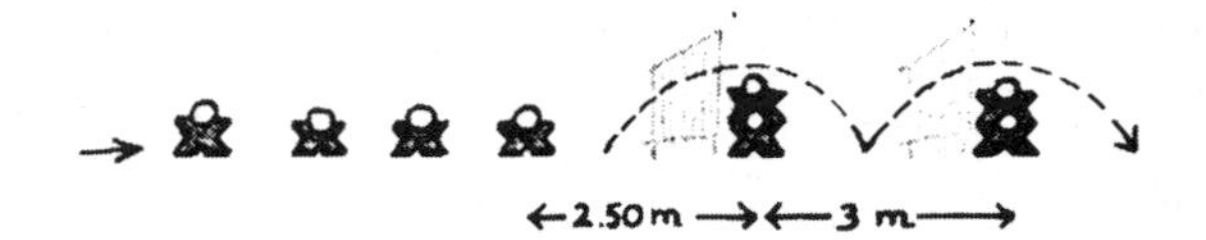


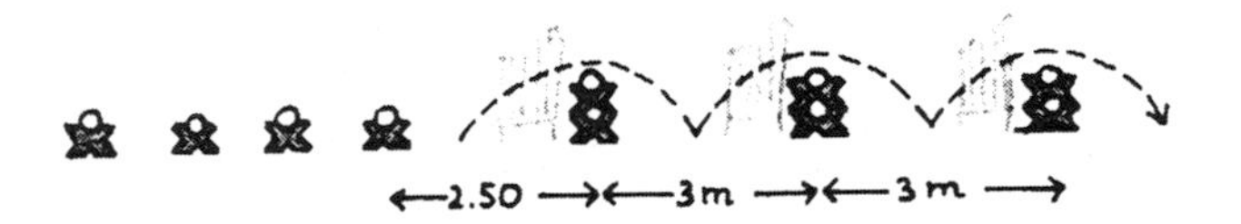


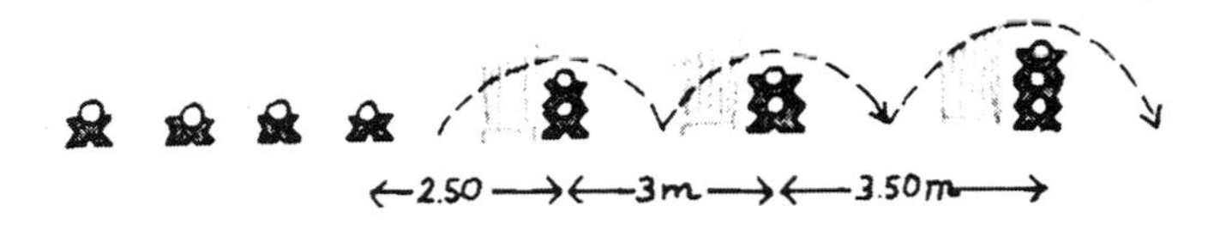


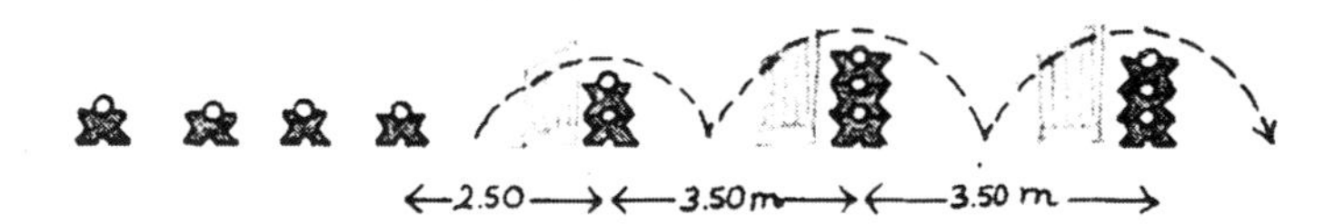


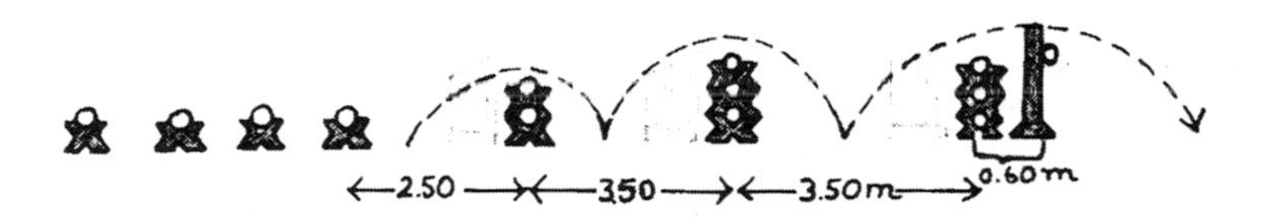


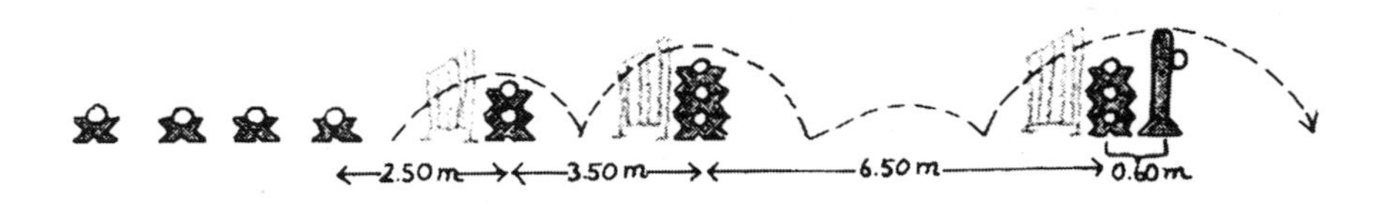


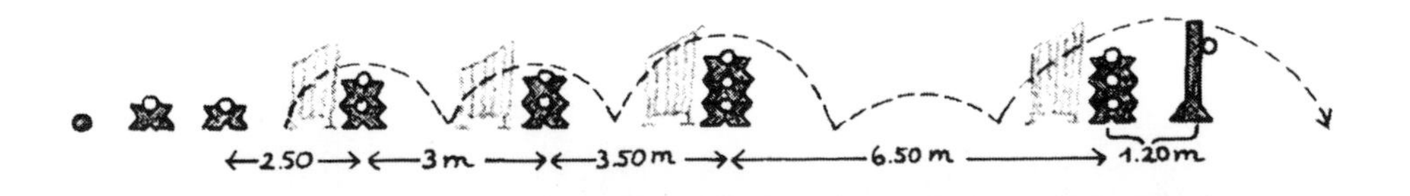

*Fig. 361*
Mrs. Sheena Mardon with her Anglo-Arab mare, Strathon, demonstrate the major influence of weight and leg aids and the fact that the rein aids are only secondary when one is riding a well-schooled horse. No tight rein, no short martingale, no unkind bit, no tight cross noseband, not even a bridle, or any kind of force is used. Mrs. Mardon is applying the correct weight and leg aids, in mid-air, for a following left hand turn. She is looking, and her weight is slightly shifted, to the left and her right leg pushes well behind the girths. The horse, forced to shift its weight also to the left in order to remain with its centre of gravity under that of the rider, will not only turn to the left, but its left near fore foot will touch the ground first as well. In other words the horse will land into the left canter. Such a performance is, of course, based on a true and sympathetic relationship between horse and rider – one of the main ingredients of the Natural Training Method.

cavaletti, making it a small oxer. It should not be wider than approximately 0·6 metres and the single pole at the far end should be slightly higher than the three cavaletti. (For safety reasons never use a plank at the far end of an oxer or triple bar because a plank does not have as much flexibility as a pole. When knocking the plank the horse can easily injure his legs.)

Having practised this jumping row a few times, lengthen the distance in between the oxer to 6·5 metres.

To bring more variety into the jumping row, one replaces at the start of the row two cavaletti by poles on the ground and use these two cavaletti to make another set in the row.

After approximately five months of cavaletti schooling one should gradually spread the oxer to 1·2 metres, but the height should not be much higher than three cavaletti. Particularly when schooling a young horse one will notice that when the oxer is widened some horses may be inclined to "over-jump", in other words they will jump the oxer much higher than is really necessary.

Owing to lack of experience some young horses put in too much effort at this early stage of schooling. Therefore one might find it difficult not to drop the seat into the saddle over the oxer, become left behind and pull the horse's mouth. If one has this difficulty one uses a neck strap, but this can only be a temporary measure. Try to improve the forward seat.

### SLOWING DOWN AFTER LANDING

The correct landing and continuation of the pace after the last obstacle of the jumping row is just as important a part of the schooling as the jumping itself.

During schooling the horse becomes stronger and his muscles develop. He will be more playful, which shows he is enjoying his work. He may play around and give a buck. Some horses may try to run off for a few strides after landing over the last obstacle of the row. This reaction is quite natural, because when the horse is landing his centre of gravity shifts to the forehand. Depending on his temperament and physical fitness, a young horse may need up to ten canter strides after landing to re-balance himself. When in balance again the horse will automatically slow down. The more the horse's loin muscles and quarters develop, the sooner he will be able to slow down after landing, needing fewer and fewer strides.

It is regrettable that some riders are not aware of these facts. The normal reaction of these riders is to pull on the reins and to try to slow down the horse. At the same time they lean forward and pull their hands to their stomach. The horse has then no chance to re-balance himself after landing in a natural manner. He will instead come on the forehand and pull against the rider's hands. It not only ruins the horse's mouth but it also has a psychological effect. It builds up the association in the horses mind, that the fact of clearing a fence means receiving a pull in the mouth. The horse becomes a puller and will try to run off even more. This can be very costly later on in competitions. The horse will take the bit after each landing, make too wide turns (losing valuable seconds) or come too close to the next fence, which can result in a refusal or knocking down a pole. Once the horse has learnt to run off after landing it is indeed very hard to cure him of this habit. One would never get into all this trouble if the horse had not been taught to pull against the rider's hand.

*Fig. 362*
**Pulling on the reins teaches the horse to pull. Pressure creates pressure.**

When re-training older horses who have this bad habit, place a cavaletti, with a wing on either side, at a distance of 6·5 metres or 9·5 metres behind the last fence of the row. While airborne the horse will notice the cavaletti and concentrate on the distance between the landing and the cavaletti to adjust his stride. Subsequently he will slow down the canter by himself without any rein aid from his rider.

After landing the rider must maintain the forward seat, absorbing the landing jolt with his knees *not* with his seat, no matter whether the horse bucks, increases his pace, or both. The rider must have patience and understanding if his horse tries to dash off. Give him time to shift any excess weight from the forehand to the quarters. The rider should neither pull nor drop the reins in landing, but an even contact should be maintained while approaching, jumping, landing and proceeding. In other words: *no* interfering with the horse's head and neck.

Another powerful help in slowing down a horse after jumping is the voice. The horse learned to obey the rider's voice when loose jumping in the jumping lane, where he might take only *one* stride after landing and stop in response to a word spoken in a soothing voice.

Apply the same voice aid when jumping mounted. If a horse has been trained in the Natural Training Method correctly he will not try to run off. The well known soothing voice, even in an emergency, will slow down the horse immediately. If necessary the horse will come to a halt, even at full speed, without any backwards pull on the bit. The horse's response to the aid of the trainer's voice can reach such an extent that it will sometimes even surprise the rider. If the trainer, while free jumping, talks to his assistant, the horse might stop in misunderstanding or, when in a competition the rider talks to his horse out of force of habit, the horse slows down more than intended so that the rider has to push him on.

A trainer who understands the effect of the voice aid, will be able to gain the horse's confidence and co-operation to such an extent that it will take over from many muscular aids.

After landing, apply a half-halt in the forward seat in order to slow down the horse. Keep your head well up, straighten the shoulders and put extra pressure onto the stirrups. The rider's change of balance to the quarters will influence the horse to do the same and is generally sufficient to slow the horse down. However, if a horse is not schooled or sensitive enough to react quickly one should, after a few canter strides, change fluently from the forward seat into the dressage seat. It must be done smoothly without putting much weight onto the horse's back. This should have the desired effect and slow down the horse.

*Slowing down*

The jumping row is built in an indoor school on the track, for instance, on the left-hand rein. One should take advantage of riding along the kicking boards. They play a very important part during the transitions when facing the horse towards the boards.

While still in canter after clearing the last fence of the row move the right hand out sideways towards the boards, bending the horse's neck slightly to the right. This must be supported by pushing the left rein against the horse's neck. On both reins maintain an *equal tension* on the bit.

Apply strong pressure with the right leg behind the girths to move the quarters sideways to the left and out from the track (not more than 45°). The horse's off hindleg is brought down and under and crosses the near hindleg in front. Seat, and leg aids must send the horse fluently into the passive hands (which only discontinue to follow the nodding movement of the horse's head in canter).

When these combined aids are applied simultaneously the horse will make a smooth transition from a canter into a trot, because the horse has learnt these aids on the flat and at an early stage of schooling.

After a few strides of slow trot, first rising then sitting trot, apply the same combination of aids again and make a transition from a sitting trot into a walk.

*Fig. 363*
The author, riding his Irish-bred horse Prospero, demonstrates the airborne turn and is already looking ahead to the next fence. (This horse had unusually long jawbones and was therefore ridden in a special bit.)

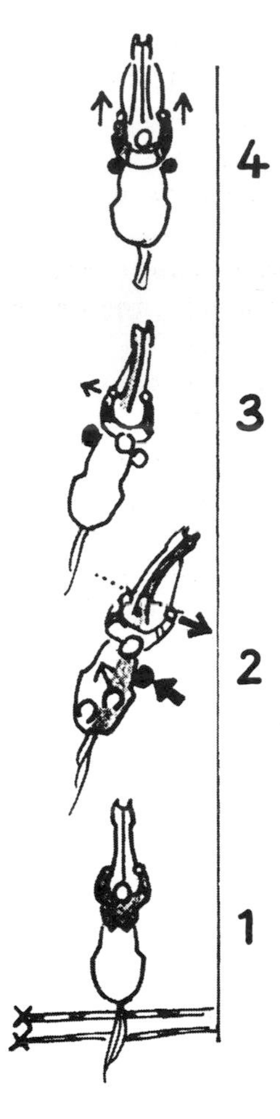


*Fig. 364*
Slowing down correctly. After landing make a transition to trot moving the quarters in, engaging the outer hindleg. Use voice, weight, leg aids and resisting hand. Then continue using the first rein aid.

Again, after a few brisk walking strides, repeat the same aids to make a transition into a halt.

I emphasise that one should make *three* fluent transitions to come to a halt and not try to miss out on one or try to come from a canter abruptly to a halt.

As soon as the horse is at a halt, apply the first rein aid and take advantage from the engagement of the off hindleg to exert impulsion and proceed at an active walk.

The kicking boards are important for these transitions. If there is no indoor school available, build the jumping row along the railing surrounding the field. Building the row without the support of the boards would provoke the horse to lean on the bit and ruin his mouth.

If a horse is less flexible laterally on one particular side, build up the jumping row so the horse faces towards the boards with his stiffer side.

In time one will find that the number of canter strides after landing will become fewer and fewer. Soon the horse will make the transition into a trot after only two to three canter strides. The horse has become so supple and strong that he is able to shift his weight to the quarters very quickly after landing.

Only when the horse has reached this stage of schooling can one build the jumping row in the centre of the school or field, free of the kicking boards. At the beginning, however, one should never continue in a straight line after landing over the last obstacle, instead, while still airborne, turn alternately to the left or to the right. This technique teaches the horse to land into the desired canter and prevents him from taking the bit and increasing his pace. Ride on a circle of approximately 20 metres diameter and make the three transitions into a slower pace in the same manner as when the row was built on the track, moving the quarters to the outside of the circle.

It is vital that one has endless patience, and bear in mind that it is purely a matter of muscle development before any horse will be able to slow down with engaged quarters after only two to three strides. Then there will be no more need to change from the forward seat into the dressage seat. On the contrary, after landing, the horse will wait for the rider's aid to go on again. Then one remains in the forward seat after landing and will have to push to continue in canter. That is the essence of proper schooling. The rider should have to push instead of having to pull. Immediately after taking a fence and landing, the horse is in an even, balanced rhythm, with strongly engaged quarters, remaining lightly on the bit, ready to take the next jump or to make a tight turn.

## AIRBORNE TURNS AND LANDING

There is another important subject the horse will learn now when jumping cavaletti. That is to turn *while airborne* and land in the desired canter. This is a matter of *balance*. Horse and rider are both in balance when the rider's centre of gravity is located exactly above the one of the horse. If the rider shifts his centre of gravity to the right, the horse schooled in the Natural Training Method will adapt himself and do the same. In moving his centre of gravity to the right, the horse will *turn right*. If the rider, still airborne over the fence, shifts his weight to the right, the horse will adjust himself accordingly and shift his weight to his off foreleg, landing in the right canter.

This simple and *logical* fact seems unknown to many riders. From force of habit they always look to the left when jumping and landing, even when going on straight or turning to the right. They bend their upper body sideways-downwards, with their head on the *left* side next to the horse's neck and shift their centre of gravity on to the horse's near foreleg. Often the rider is not aware of it. This not only unbalances the horse over the fence but forces the horse to land *always* into the *left* canter. This is particularly visible when such riders ride novice horses. After landing in the wrong canter the horse will obviously have to go through the turn in the wrong canter or disunited canter. He will make an extra wide turn and lean on the bit while trying to regain balance.

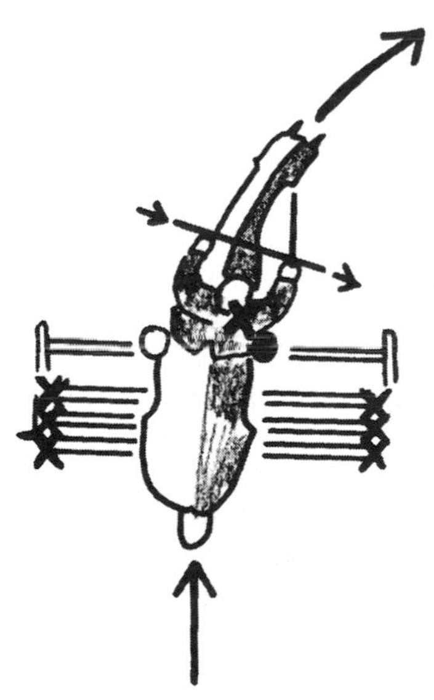

*Fig. 365*
Airborne turn to the right and landing in the right canter.

An older horse might become accustomed to his rider's habit, and after landing in the wrong canter make a flying change of leg.

Schooling the horse to land in the desired canter after clearing a fence should begin as soon as one starts jumping over the jumping row (free of the track). Before starting to jump the row, decide in which direction to turn at the end of the row. Do not leave this decision to the horse.

Approach the row and jump the fences *whilst looking straight ahead only till going over the last fence*, where one gives the aids to turn into the set direction. For instance, to turn to the right one should:

(i) look to the right;

(ii) move the upper part of one's body slightly to the right, transfering more weight onto the right stirrup;

(iii) apply the right leg aid on the girths supported by the left leg behind the girths;

(iv) move the right hand sideways out from the horse's neck (how much depends on the degree of the horse's schooling) so that the horse's neck, while airborne, is bent to the right. Guide the horse into the right-hand turn;

(v) the left rein is pushing against the horse's neck to prevent the horse from falling out with his left shoulder;

(vi) the *same contact* with the horse's mouth must be kept on both reins.

This equal tension on the bit with both reins is vital. Do not pull on the right rein and drop the left one. This would provoke the horse to fall out with his shoulder to the left.

These aids should be applied simultaneously. They shift the rider's weight to the right, forcing the horse to change his centre of gravity to the off foreleg and land into the right canter.

One should ride on a large figure of eight, with the jumping row in the centre, approaching the row out of a left-hand circle, turning right after clearing the last fence, and approaching the row the following time from a right-hand circle, turning left after clearing the last fence. If the horse becomes excited on account of this continuous riding on a figure of eight do not use it anymore, but make a break after each time jumping the row and calm the horse down. Wait until he breathes normally and takes a deep breath, a sign that the horse is relaxed.

With an excited horse do not approach out of a straight line but turn sharply into the row at a *walk* and change gradually into a trot while riding over the first cavaletti. This technique will soon settle the horse, because then the horse is forced to bend his body laterally inwards. In this position he is able to bring only *one* hindleg (the inner) further underneath his body. With one engaged hindleg only the horse cannot create the same impulsion as if both hindlegs were engaged, which would be the case if one would approach the row out of a straight line. On the other hand, if a horse is lazy and not over-keen to jump, one approaches the row out of a straight line.

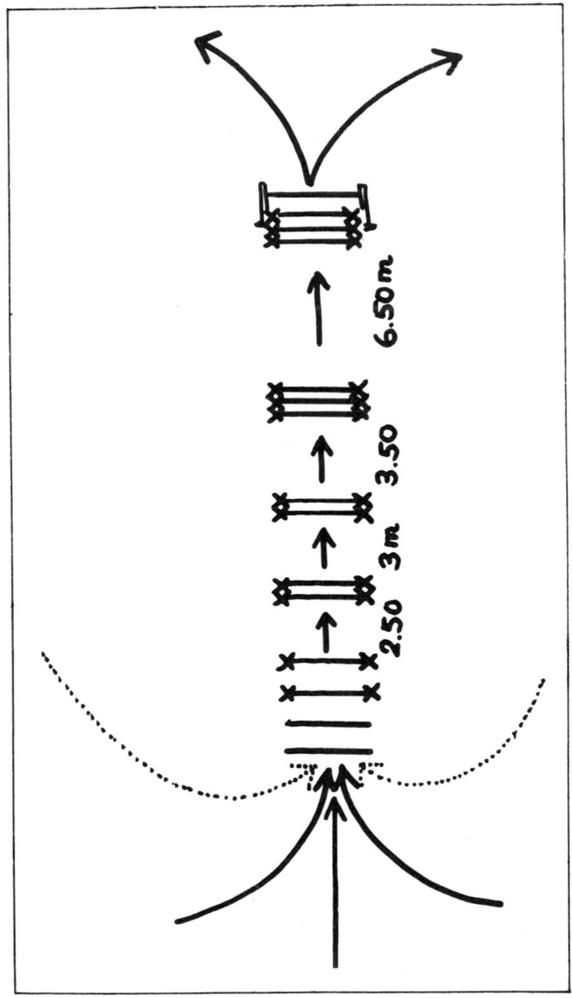


*Fig. 366*
Approach the row at a trot. With a horse which is inclined to rush the fences take the course indicated by the dotted line and turn, alternately, right and left when airborne over the last fence.

### THE JUMPING LANE

When a good result is obtained from the horse's performance over the cavaletti and single fences, proceed by introducing the jumping lane and its variations. At this stage, however, more fence material, especially wings, are needed. If wings are not available use sloping poles. Wings, placed at intervals along the jumping lane, create the impression that the easiest path through the lane lies straight ahead and eliminates the temptation for the horse to run out.

The placing of the four cavaletti (at trot distance) and the technique of raising them alternately is the same as done previously. One now places four poles in a curved V formation on the approach side of the cavaletti. In this way one can approach the cavaletti from either direction. On the inside of the turn, where the poles lay close to each other, the distance should

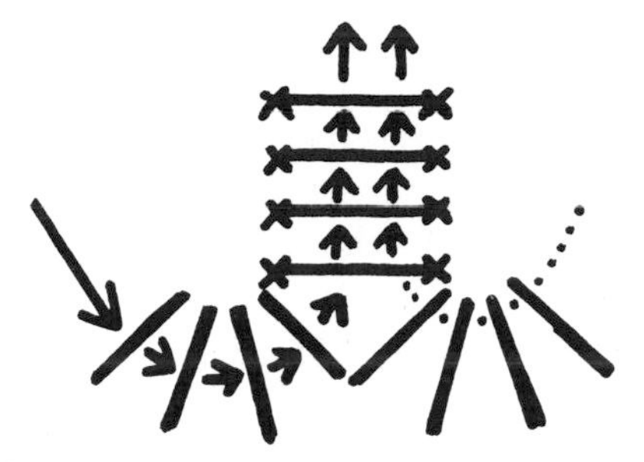

*Fig. 367*
Add four poles on the ground, on the approach line. If the horse tries to rush, follow the dotted line at a walk.

be approximately 1 metre (walk distance). At the centre of the turn the distance of the four poles should be 1·3 metres at a trot distance. On the outside of the turn this distance is even wider. The advantage of the V formation is that a horse with a short stride can, at the beginning, trot on the inside of the turn and gradually take a wider turn across the poles in order to lengthen his stride. A horse with a long stride can trot more on the outside of the turn across the wider distance between the poles. The four additional poles are placed on a turn also, because they force the horse to trot with more pronounced steps in a turn, thus increasing the lateral flexibility.

When the horse is trotting over the poles and cavaletti confidently on a long or loose rein one can introduce a small jump of two crossed poles at a distance of 2·5 metres, height at centre approximately 0·5 metres. The crossed poles teach the horse to jump the fences at the centre, as this is the lowest point.

If at any time the horse tries to rush over the poles and cavaletti, go at once back to approaching the row in a walk on the inside of the turn until he is calm and relaxed again.

Then build the second crossed poles fence at a distance of 3 metres, then the third fence at a distance of 3·5 metres. The distances in between the various fences of the lane gradually increase, along with the height of the fences and the speed of the horse, which also increases.

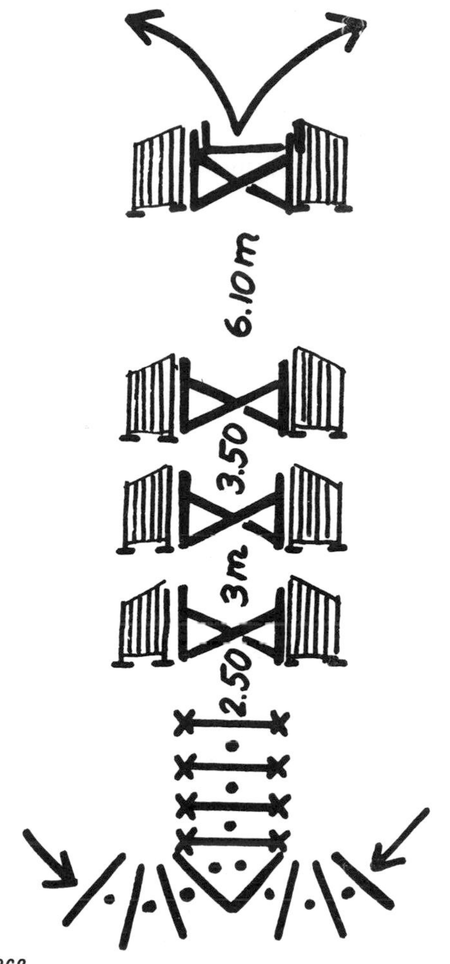


*Fig. 368*
Gradually add some fences and the horse will break into canter over the first cross pole fence.

The fourth fence is placed at a distance of 6·1 metres. It consists of two crossed poles with a single pole behind it. This jump is intended to be a small spread. At the beginning the spread should not exceed 1 metre.

The next additional fence should be a straight fence (gate or poles) at a distance of 6·5 metres, followed up by a low oxer (spread 1 metre height 0·9 metres) at a distance of 10·2 metres.

After the last obstacle of the jumping lane build a small upright fence on a fair right-hand turn at a distance of 15 metres and a triple bar on a left-hand turn at a distance of 14·75 metres.

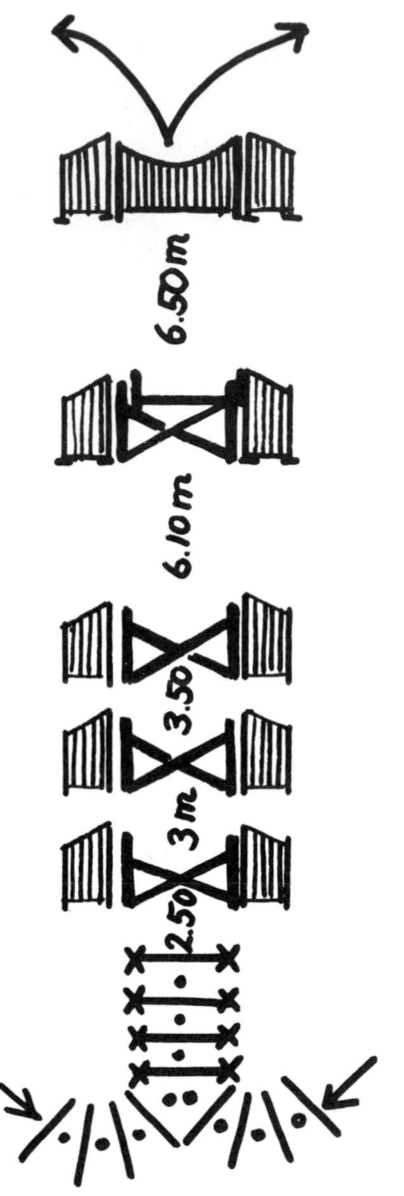


*Fig. 369*
Adding another fence, this time a straight gate.

The distances in between the elements of the jumping lane are shorter than in combination jumps in competitions. This is because the speed in which the jumping lane is being ridden is much slower and the fences smaller, hence the strides are much shorter.

After the previous schooling over the cavaletti, horse and rider should now have no problem in landing after the last fence of the jumping lane in the desired canter for either turn. Approach the single fences in the leading canter and in a balanced pace. Jump over these fences, again either going to the right or the left after landing in the appropriate canter.

The exercise in the jumping lane is an excellent schooling for horse and rider. It teaches the horse self-initiative and increases his propulsive force.

After the first cross poles, the horse will break into a canter and jump the whole row by himself, the rider playing a more or less passive role. The rider develops not only a great take-off feeling but his forward seat position becomes firmly established as well.

Throughout the entire jumping lane the rider should move the upper part of his body as little as possible and take great care to ensure that the horse does not lose impulsion. He must be very alert to apply forward driving aids instantly if he feels that the horse is not maintaining his rhythm by himself. When applying forward driving aids he must avoid touching the saddle with his seat. Falling back into the saddle at any stage in the jumping lane interferes with the horse's balance.

Under no circumstances should the rider *fix* his hands on the horse's neck, but instead he should keep them separated and free from the neck. Only then can he maintain the same contact with the horse's mouth – from start to finish – throughout the entire lane and follow the lengthening of the horse's neck over each element. It would be desirable if the rider could hold the reins at the same length throughout the whole jumping lane. Many horses become upset when the rider lets the reins slip through his hands and gathers them up again. A nervous, tense rider creates the same frame of mind in his horse, who then also becomes tense and upset. Out of self-defence the horse starts to pull or develops some other bad habit.

A cool and intelligent rider would give the horse no chance to take the bit in the first place.

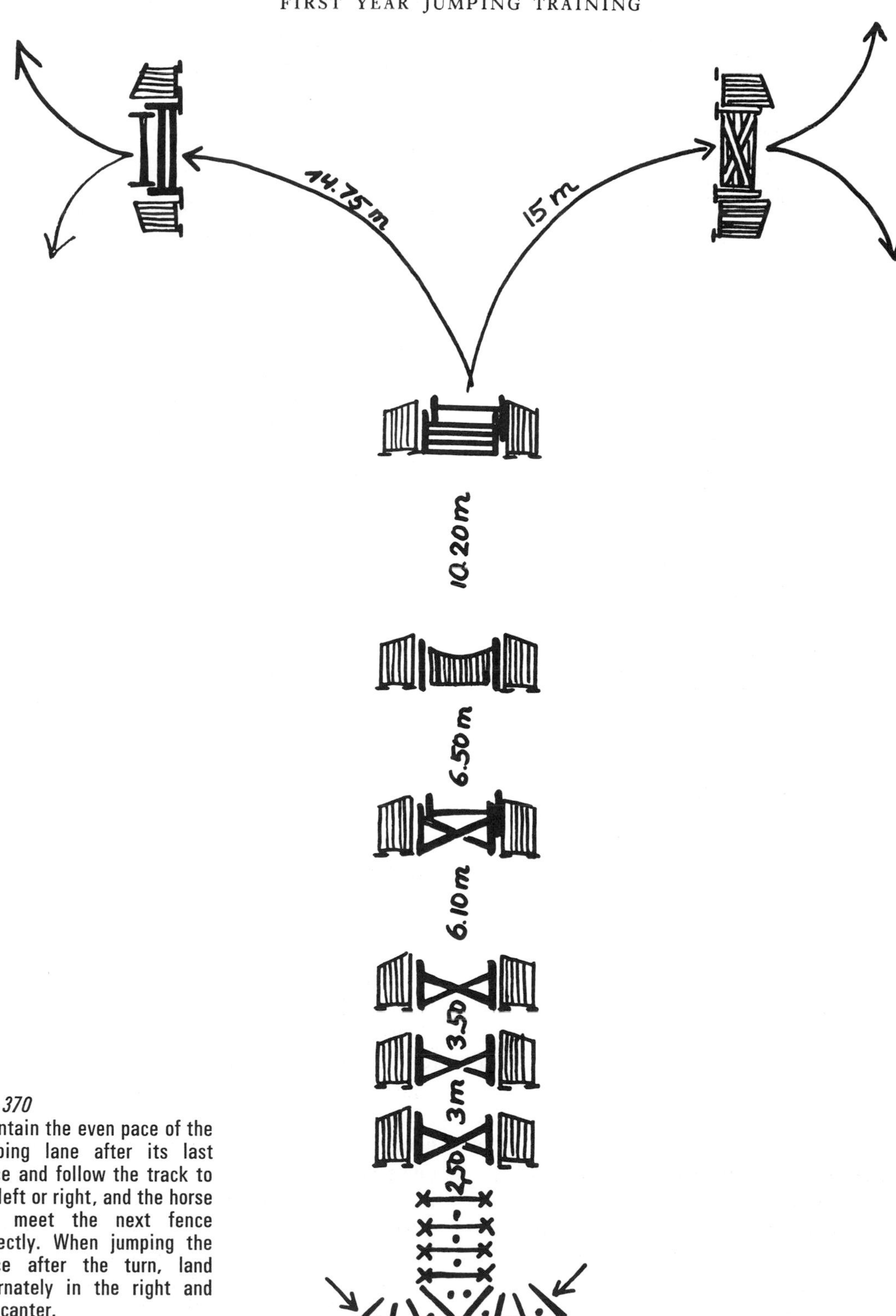


*Fig. 370*
Maintain the even pace of the jumping lane after its last fence and follow the track to the left or right, and the horse will meet the next fence correctly. When jumping the fence after the turn, land alternately in the right and left canter.

*Fig. 371*
Note the enormous gymnastic effect of the in-and-out jumps. The horse has complete freedom, while folding his hindlegs well under.

*Fig. 372*
Hindlegs folded perfectly.

As soon as he feels the horse taking a stronger hold he will ease his hands and try to yield the reins gradually and calm the horse with his voice.

Only when exercises in the jumping lane are executed in this correct manner will one obtain a relaxed horse who needs *pushing* instead of pulling. When the rider reaches this point he will have better control over the horse and gain a higher standard of obedience, which helps to build the horse's future career.

Just as one cannot teach a rider to jump correctly unless he is relaxed, neither can one teach a horse to jump consistently well unless he is relaxed and supple.

In time one will notice that after the last obstacle of the lane the rider really has to *push* to maintain the canter while approaching the next single fence after a turn, because the horse will slow down his pace immediately after landing all by himself.

One of the purposes of the exercise in the jumping lane is to develop the horse's muscles (particularly of quarters and back) so that he will be able to transfer more weight from the forehand to the quarters. The engagement of the quarters in the jumping lane could, to an extent, be compared to the extreme engagement of the quarters in high-class dressage, in the *piaff* or *levade*. The difference is that in the movements of the high-class dressage, like *piaff* or *levade*, the highest degree of collection is performed on

*Fig. 373*
**Note the horse's engaged hindlegs and quarters and the head and neck in the same position, with or without reins.**

the spot; the forward movement is blocked. For a showjumper, however, a similar high degree of quarter engagement has to be achieved, but *without* blocking the forward movement. Promoting propulsive power is essential as the showjumper will have to bascule over big spread fences, using the full length of his neck. In the jumping lane the horse is confronted repeatedly with fences without a non-jumping stride. The horse has no alternative but to transfer his weight to the quarters and engage his hocks to the extreme every time he takes off and after landing, with complete freedom of head and neck. As soon as the horse jumps the entire row correctly and has no problems at take-off one can, *at the end* of the jumping session, gradually take away an element of the row. Start with the second element; the *first* element has to stay and act as a "placing fence" to assist the horse to strike-off at a canter.

After a while the horse will be able to take the row in a free forward manner, with only the first and the last element remaining, without difficulties at take-off. The horse should lengthen the last few canter strides in order to find the correct take-off point. This must be encouraged by the rider who should use forward driving leg aids. Horse and rider must make the distance to the last element fit, not by going faster or rushing but by lengthening the last few strides gradually, as if the fence was a magnet attracting horse and rider.

*Fig. 374* (across two pages)
The whole jumping lane ridden in perfect forward seat – and without reins, a great way to train a firm grip and balance. Demonstrated during a Paalman training course by Otto Nielsen, Kiltallagh Riding School, Ireland.

*Fig. 375*
Standing naturally, the horse carries more weight on the forehand than on the quarters.

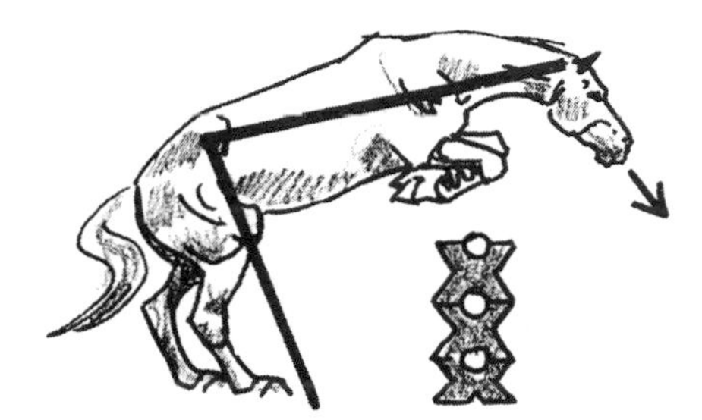

*Fig. 376*
The horse engaging his quarters.

*Fig. 377*
Note the engaged quarters in the *piaff,* while the forward movement and freedom of head and neck are blocked.

*Fig. 378*
In the levade the horse takes, to a certain extent, the same position as a jumping horse in the last phase of his stride, before take-off at a fence. The similarity in the two completely different performances is that, in both cases, the horse's muscles are developed in the same way, hence he is able to shift his centre of gravity to the quarters, which are lowered and engaged. This posture enables the horse to free his forelegs from the ground. Note how the hocks are close together and well underneath, in order to preserve the highest degree of balance. In every equestrian branch one of the vital points in training is the accomplishment of complete balance in the horse's movements.

*Different designs*

(1) The next step in the progressive schooling method is that the trainer increases his demands, not by suddenly building the fences higher or wider but by approaching and jumping them from an angle. Again, the use of wings is essential, particularly on the right-hand side of the last obstacle. After setting up the whole design remove the poles from the fences, leaving only the uprights. The distance between the last two obstacles, measured at ground level from centre to centre, is 6 metres.

Again, first use only the four cavaletti, then put in gradually the poles of the three fences. Approach the row from either direction at a slow trot. After the horse has jumped this a few times correctly build the *first* part of the small oxer (the last fence), which is now only a straight fence. After the horse has jumped this a few times complete the *second* part to make it into an oxer, which may be widened as required.

Due to the diagonal approach the horse is forced to engage the off hindleg extensively and to bend his off foreleg accurately at take-off, because this off foreleg reaches the fence sooner than the near foreleg. While jumping the three fences in the approaching line to the oxer, the rider should look to the right and apply the correct aids to encourage the horse to land in the right canter and approach the oxer in the right canter. The same aids apply when airborne over the oxer. In order to develop the horse's muscles evenly practise this schooling on alternate diagonals.

To improve a horse who is stiff on one particular side (the side where he is careless with his foreleg and has a stiff hock) school that side extensively. The exercise is also particularly useful for horses who rush into fences or bolt after landing. Due to the lateral bending at take-off and after landing, the horse's propulsive force is restricted.

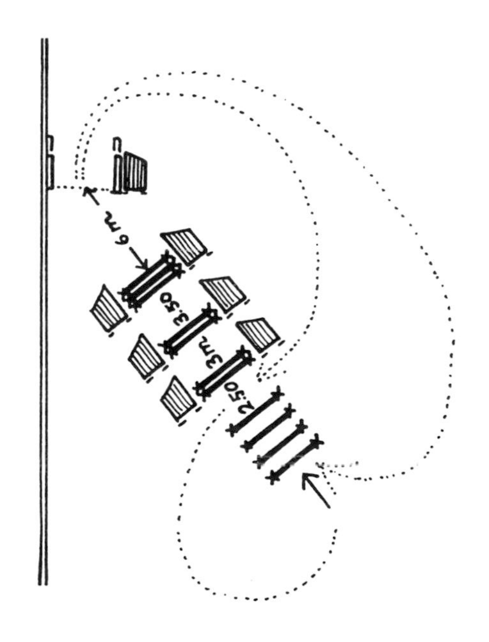


*Fig. 379*
Design (1). At first build up only the diagonal, but so the distance to the oxer is correct. Approach at a trot.

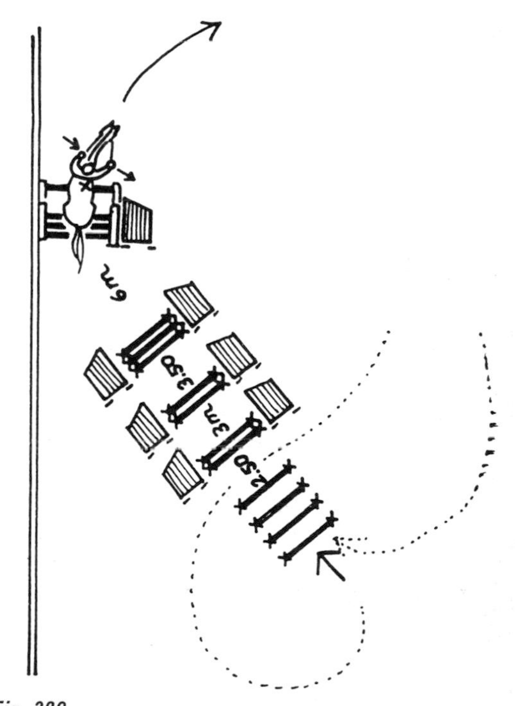


*Fig. 380*
Then build up the oxer as well. If later on the spread of the oxer exceeds 1·2 metres, then the distance of 6 metres has to be increased to 6·5 metres.

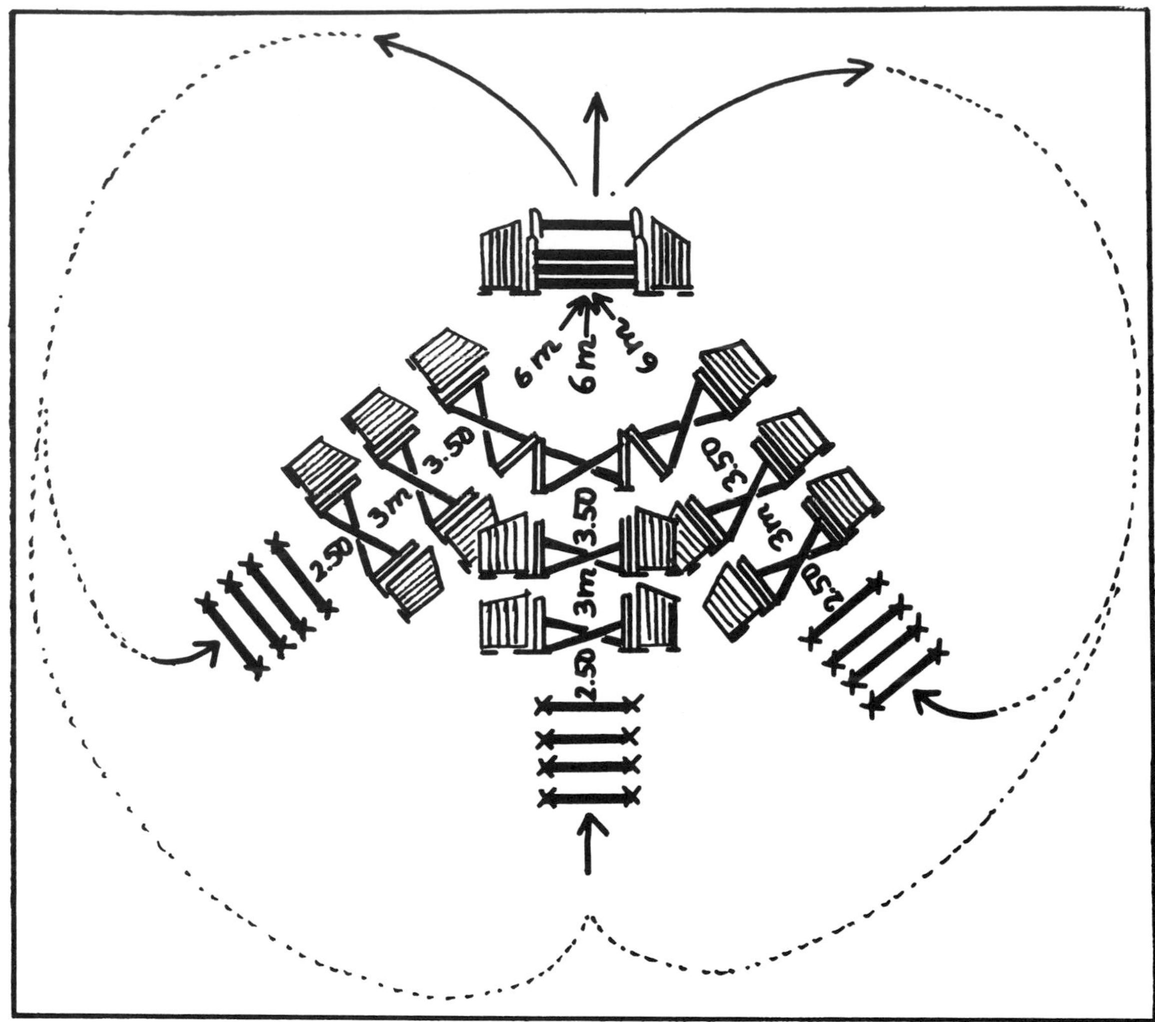


*Fig. 381*
Design (2). In this design the fence can be approached at an angle or on a straight line. Again, widen the last distance if the oxer is considerably widened.

(2) This design differs in that it is built in the centre of the school and should be used only at a more advanced stage. The horse, missing the support of the kicking boards, is more tempted to run out.

Approach the fences from alternate tracks: from a figure of eight and from a straight line. Again, at the start, dismantle the last fence and leave only the uprights and wings standing. After the horse has jumped the other obstacles from either approach, build the centre jump gradually up and make it higher and wider, according to the horse's capabilities and progress.

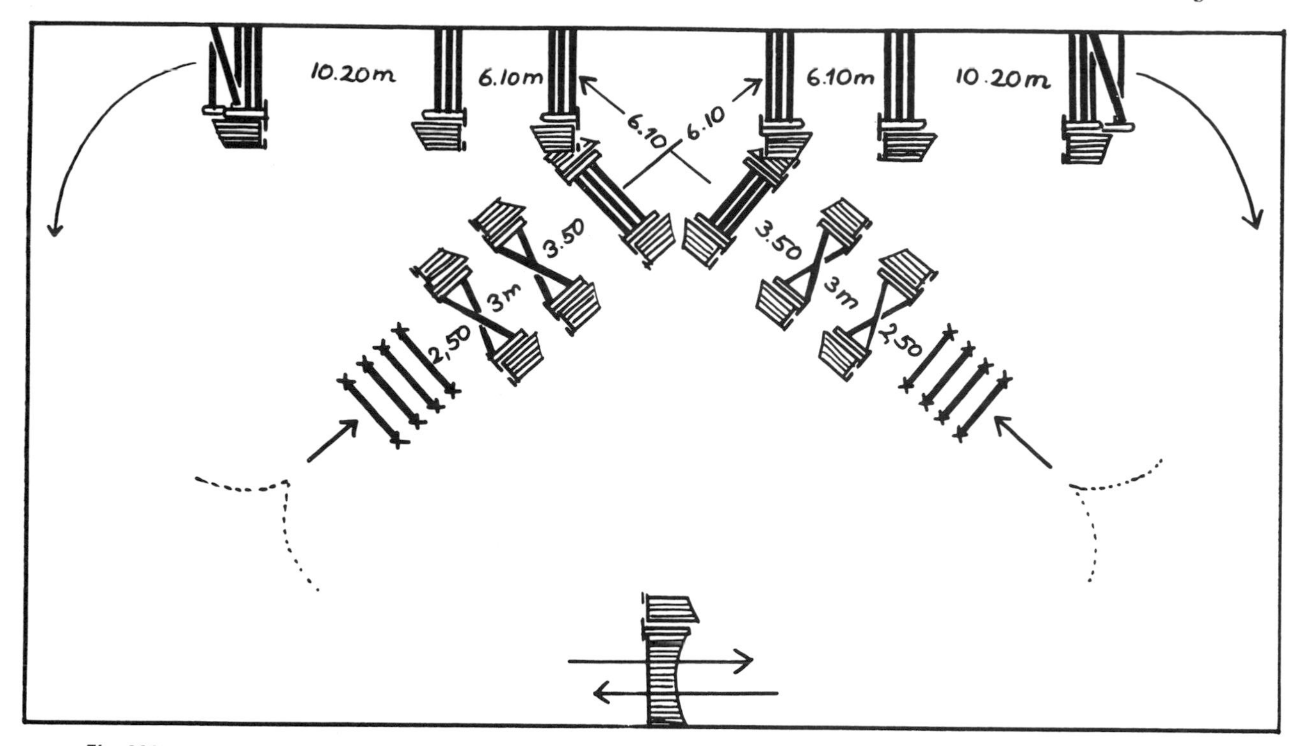


*Fig. 382*
Design (3). A very good design to teach a rider to use his legs firmly.

(3) For this design we need the support of the kicking boards again. When there is no indoor school available build it along the boundary hedge or railing of a field.

It is an excellent plan, particularly for the rider who will learn to use his leg aids. For the horse it is more difficult than the first design because he has to negotiate three obstacles instead of one after approaching from a diagonal. Some horses are inclined to lose impulsion in approaching the three fences on the track. The rider should sense this and send the horse forward accordingly.

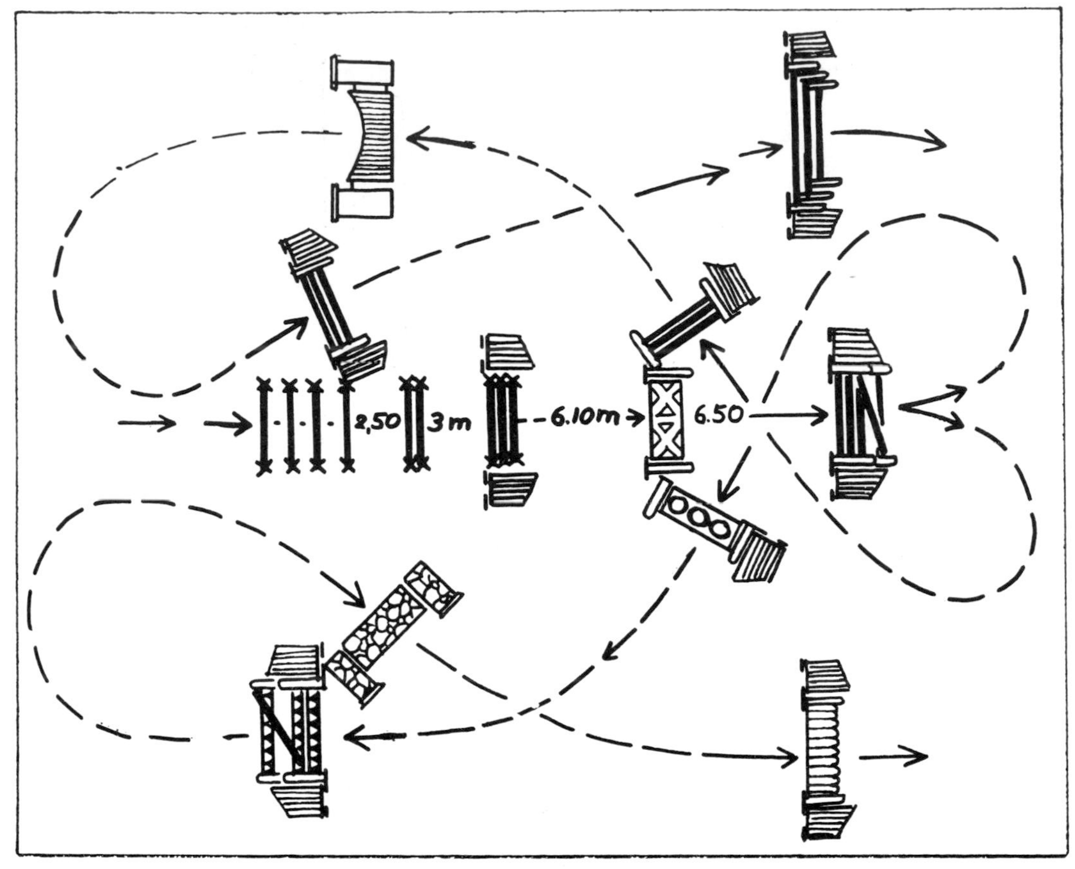


*Fig. 383*
Design (4). This design contains frequent changes of direction, teaching the rider to land in the desired canter every time.

(4) The rider trots over the cavaletti. After clearing the first obstacle the horse breaks into canter and an even canter pace should be maintained throughout the entire course, following the course line as stated on the plan.

While airborne the rider should apply the correct aids so that the horse lands in the correct leading canter, which is necessary to ride balanced through the corners and to approach the next fence.

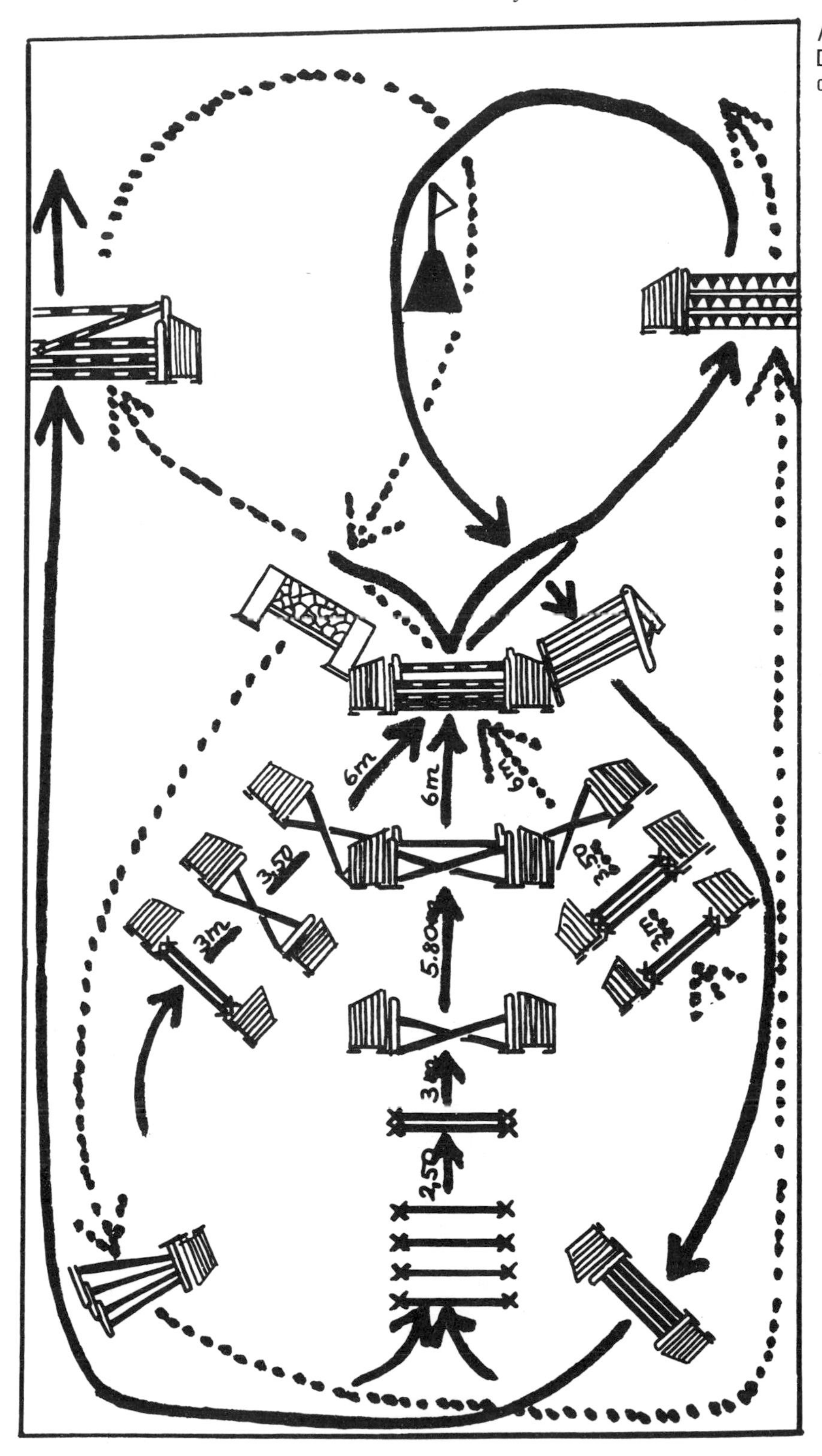


*Fig. 384*
Design (5). A fairly advanced course.

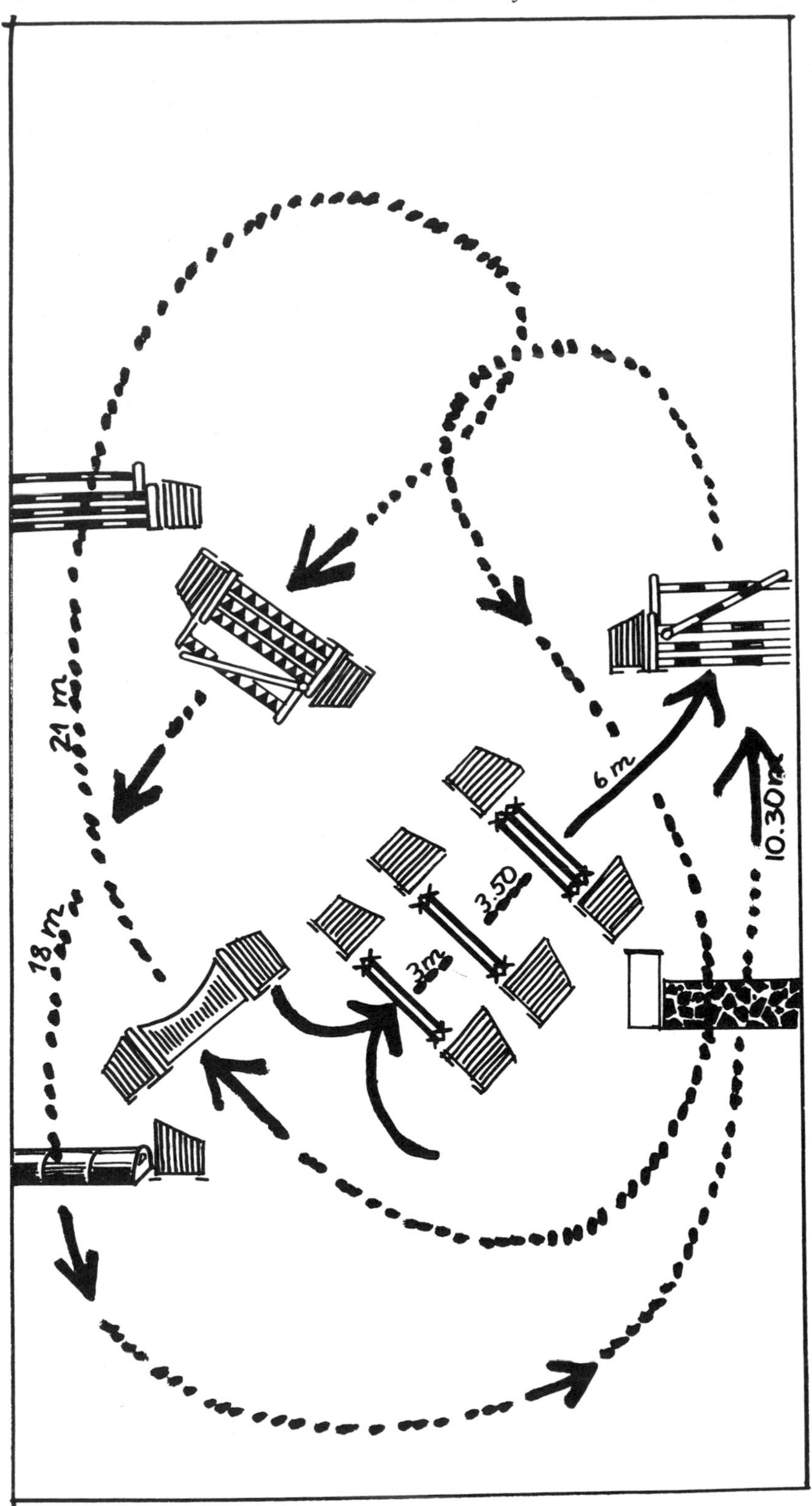


*Fig. 385*
Design (6). Horse and rider learn not to slow down while riding through turns.

(5) This design should be practised only in a more advanced stage of schooling. It serves to engage either *one* hindleg in case of a diagonal approach or *both* hindlegs in case of the direct approach. As the drawing shows the oxer at the centre should be jumped from three directions. To establish the horse's confidence begin by approaching on the straight line at a slow trot and in forward seat. Decide beforehand in which direction one wants to turn after jumping the oxer and follow that track, jumping the fences on the course line. To avoid cutting the corners, ride around a barrel or boundary flag placed on the centre line of the school.

The distances between the single fences should be divisible by 3 metres. A horse with a normal stride who maintains the suggested even pace of 300 metres per minute should meet all fences correctly. But one has to be constantly aware of the fact that the horse is bound to lose impulsion because of the many turns and changes of directions on this plan.

Generally when approaching an oxer diagonally, to deter the horse's temptation to run out, one should apply the following aids: if approaching the oxer on a left-hand rein, transfer more weight onto the right stirrup, bringing the right hand sideways out from the neck, supported by the left rein pushed against the neck. Apply stronger pressure with the left leg further behind the girths. When approaching on the right-hand rein the opposite aids apply.

Build up the centre oxer and the whole course very gradually in order not to confuse the horse but to encourage him to gain confidence and to maintain his impulsion.

(6) Start off with only three cavaletti jumps on the diagonal line. These must be approached at a slow trot and alternately on the left- and the right-hand rein.

When the horse is rushing into these small jumps and becomes excited, turn in sharply at a walk. This extensive lateral bending of the horse's body in turn not only slows down the pace but also will lower his head and neck position.

After jumping these three fences correctly, first build on the track a small upright fence and later alter it into a small oxer. This oxer should gradually be widened and a pole should be placed diagonally over the oxer, to conceal the gap and to encourage the horse to jump with more confidence. After clearing the oxer on the track the horse must land in the left canter. Follow the course line as stated on the plan.

The schooling purpose for horse and rider is to maintain one uniform pace throughout the entire course and *not* to slow down while riding through turns. There should be no severe checking or increasing the pace in approaching a fence. Speed: approximately 300 metres per minute.

Even when the horse lands in a disunited or wrong canter the rider should not correct this. With experience the horse will learn to do this by himself. Pulling the horse up would interrupt the even speed and rhythm. Particularly indoors, the distance and time available between the obstacles is inadequate to change the canter and regain the speed necessary to approach the next fence.

(7) This is a very special design. After each fence there is ample room for the rider to go on to a circle and still approach the next fence out of a straight line. The design has many other advantages as well.

Many riders find it difficult to ride a whole course in a uniform rhythm. Therefore I suggest this design is built out of doors in the speed course to teach the rider to approach a jump and to proceed after landing in a uniform pace. This design can, of course, also be built indoors and used as an "indoor speed course". It is an exceptional opportunity to improve horses and riders who normally during a competition "heat up". They start a course nicely in rhythm, but with each fence they jump becoming more and more excited and tense. They start rushing and run into trouble. Also, those riders who break the fluency of a course by checking and placing the horse too much can improve themselves a great deal in this course.

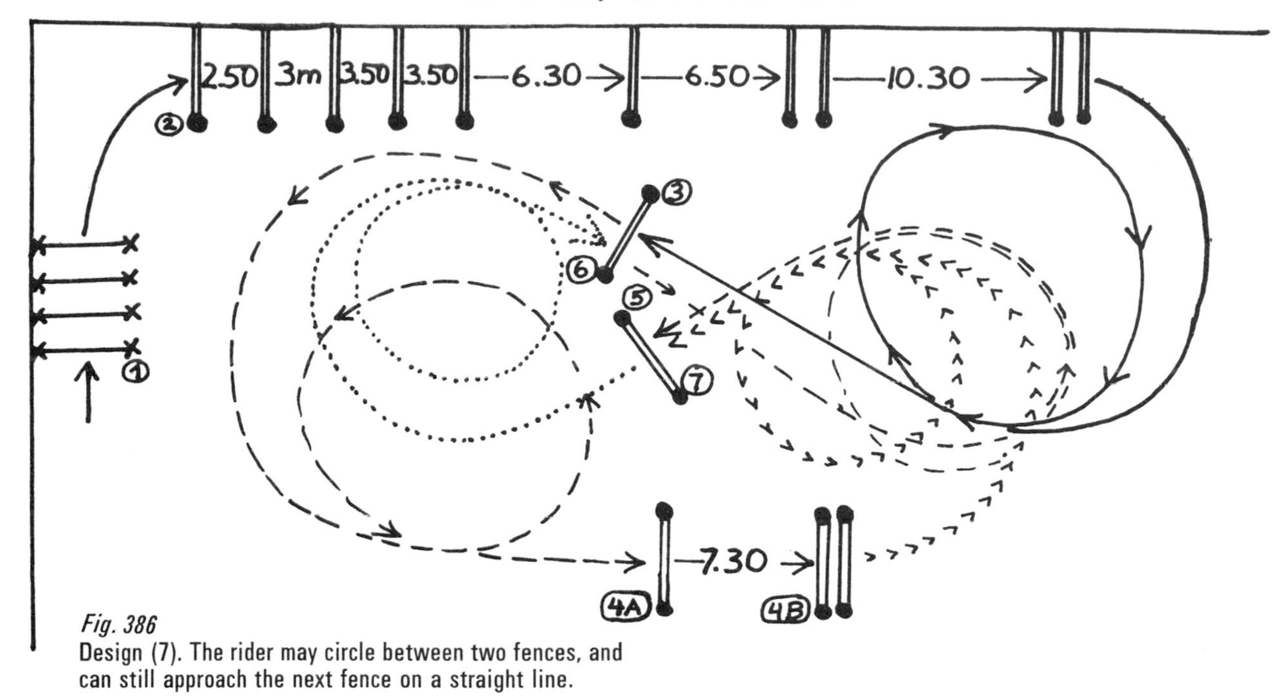


*Fig. 386*
Design (7). The rider may circle between two fences, and can still approach the next fence on a straight line.

The rider has to ride constantly at 300 metres per minute, as in the speed course. I ask my pupils to go on a circle after each fence and stay on the circle, maintaining speed and impulsion until they feel that the horse (and themselves) are relaxed and ready to approach the next fence. The circle has to be ridden as on the course plan, because then there is a straight approach from it towards the fence. If the circle is ridden too wide the horse has to make an S turn in approaching the fence and will be thrown off balance, the pace becoming disunited.

It is *most important* that while still on the circle the rider "warns" and prepares the horse that this time he intends to go straight on. This has to be done without upsetting the horse, otherwise the exercise will be pointless. The horse must not anticipate that *now* the jumping starts again, because then he would rush into the fence. He must only be made alert enough not to be taken by surprise. The rider applies a half-halt and moves his outer hand a little out from the horse's neck and shifts a little extra weight towards the outer side of the circle. This indicates to the horse that the rider intends to leave the circle and to approach the fence.

The rider learns a great deal: to remain cool and not to concentrate on the fence alone, but to observe his horse and to feel whether he is relaxed and ready to approach a jump. After practise the rider may only need to circle once between the various fences, and later on he will be able to ride the course without riding any circles and in a steady uniform pace.

CHAPTER ELEVEN

# FIRST YEAR SCHOOLING SCHEDULE

I EMPHASISE that it is impossible to school all horses in *one* uniform system. This training schedule is meant merely as a guide. The trainer must decide which part of the schooling programme the individual horse needs most.

## INDIVIDUAL SCHOOLING

The trainer will have to find out how to classify the young horse according to his character, potential, intelligence, temperament, mental and physical condition, conformation, age and degree of schooling. Consideration of these facts is essential in programming a horse's schedule. For example, if a horse has, by nature, not much impulsion and is lazy or timid, he needs more lungeing and a lot of free forward riding in the open country in company of other horses.

At the initial stage of jumping *mounted* (in the jumping lane) such a horse needs for a few times the lead of an experienced horse. This will recall the horse's herd instinct and increase his impulsion.

Most horses like to work in company. However, an excitable horse works better on his own or in front of other horses because otherwise he becomes nervous, obstinate and will work unco-operatively. In time he will lose condition as well.

A horse with a stiff, weak or dropped back needs more lungeing. Horses with a weak or "cold" back are inclined to buck straight after mounting. (This can also occur in horses who are tacked up with a badly fitting saddle or who have girth galls.)

Horses who carry their head unusually high when nervous and excited should be lunged with Chambon.

Horses who toss their heads about or lean on the bit and try to dash off will be cured if use is made of the Chambon in daily lungeing.

The horse with a one-sided hard and dry mouth should be lunged extensively on this particular side.

Horses who are overbent, go behind the bit or poke their nose forward need daily exercises on foot, especially the reining back exercise. This will supple the loin muscles and will make it easier for the horse to transfer weight to the quarters and distribute it evenly over his four legs.

The same exercise should be executed with horses who carry their head too low and lean on the bit. In most cases such horses are overbuilt and by nature unbalanced.

Kicking horses are not only unpleasant but also dangerous in company. Before kicking the horse suddenly lowers his head to shift his centre of gravity to the forehand, which allows him to free his hindlegs from the ground and kick. The rider must quickly lift up the horse's head and at the same time send him on strongly with leg and whip aids.

When mares are in season they may kick against the spurs. Therefore ride a mare when in season *without* spurs but with a whip, otherwise the mare would learn to kick, even when she is not in season. At the same time she would not respond to the rider's forward driving leg aids.

The horse's physical condition can influence the training schedule considerably. Condition will depend on the horse's daily amount of exercise and a great deal on the correct feeding. Overworked horses will rapidly lose their appetite, condition and interest in their work. Underworked horses become fat and lazy or too frisky and difficult to handle.

The horse's well-being and health are essential for the training progress; his lungs and heart should never be strained.

The progress should be almost unnoticeable. If the schooling is interrupted for a long period, resuming the training must be done very carefully in order not to strain the horses heart and lungs.

There are countless aspects the trainer should take into consideration when formulating a correct and individual schooling schedule. The first schooling year schedule is the basic preparation for the horse's future jumping career, therefore it is essential that the schooling is not done with undue haste. The horse needs time to grow up in his work, and short cuts can lead to disastrous consequences later on. However, the schooling progress depends not only on the horse but also on the temperament and the capabilities of the trainer himself. He must bear in mind that he can never afford to lose his temper.

*Daily exercise*

I strongly believe that the horse should be exercised *every* day. One day off a week is usual in most stables, but it affects not only the horse's frame of mind but also his physical condition. If for one day one cannot exercise the horse I suggest turning him out in the field (weather permitting) for an hour, or for a while let him loose in the school. Remember that a little exercise is better for the horse than none at all, as all horses enjoy stretching their legs and muscles freely. It stimulates both the horse's mind and his blood circulation, preventing filled legs. At the same time the horse will not get bored in the stable and develop stable vices. On a day when the horse gets less exercise his food must be restricted.

*Free exercise*

The expression "free exercise" occurs repeatedly throughout the training schedule. I want to explain why I consider it so important that every horse should be turned loose before being ridden.

Every rider knows from experience that during the first 20 minutes of the schooling session most young horses play around and try to work off high spirits. The horse is not concentrating and the rider is wasting time. Therefore free exercise before each schooling session is most important. It has an enormous suppling-up effect and settles the horse down. The horse can loosen and stretch his muscles without the encumbrance of the rider's weight. One will soon notice how much all horses enjoy their freedom; they will buck and play around. It makes life for the horse more interesting, gives him variety and prevents him from getting bored with his daily schooling. The horse is warmed up in a most natural manner and will concentrate on his work straight away. The rider can start the training session with a supple and relaxed horse.

This is the condition for a fruitful training. I would even go so far as to say that one should first have the horse relaxed to the extent of laziness, especially a highly strung horse. Then the rider will have to send the horse onto the bit instead of having to pull. The same goes for lungeing. The horse should be so calm that the trainer should have to use the whip instead of having to calm down a fresh horse who is flying around the ring completely out of control.

For the same reason one should start breaking and schooling a young horse in the spring, because in most cases he has spent the winter out on grass and his vitality is at the lowest level. The young horse will be easy to handle. According to the progressive daily schooling feeding must be gradually increased.

When giving the horse free exercise protect his legs with four brushing boots and overreach boots, because while playing around he could easily knock and injure his legs.

*On the leading rein*

As a pre-schooling exercise lead a young unmounted horse in the company of an older and quieter horse. If possible have two horses going in front and another one or two behind. This way the young horse learns to behave correctly in the company of other horses and gains confidence in strange surroundings, traffic and so on.

If the horse later on (when mounted) is taken out on his own he will obey more willingly the rider's aids because he will not be distracted by all kinds of strange objects. Also the risk of an accident is considerably reduced.

The leading rein, which should be attached to a cavesson and *never* to the snaffle ring, should be long enough in case of any difficulties.

At the initial stage when taking the young horse out unmounted on the leading rein it is advisable before going on the road to go in the field alongside the railing, keeping the young horse next to it.

### AFTER DAILY SCHOOLING

*Closing the top door*

Trainers in Australia close the top door of the box for 30 minutes after each training session, the windows being kept open for ventilation. They believe that after schooling the horse should not be distracted and he should be given an opportunity to "think over" what he has learnt during his schooling. The Australians are particularly careful to make certain that when a horse is stabled the sun cannot shine directly into his eyes.

*Bandages*

After every strenuous exercise the horse's legs should be bandaged with a Sandown bandage.

*Massage*

It is quite normal, not only in the early stages of schooling but also later on in intensive jumping training or after competitions, that one will find the horse a little stiff the following day.

On such a day do only light work with the horse, giving him a chance to loosen-up his muscles. After the light exercise massage the stiff parts of the horse's body with diluted Radiol. In most cases these stiff parts will be the horse's shoulders, spine, loin muscles and legs. The massage should be repeated for a few days until the stiffness disappears. (Do not rub too much as that would irritate the horse's skin.)

*Rugging up*

After every training session the horse should be covered with a well-fitted blanket to keep the muscles warm and to protect the horse from flies and dust. The rug should, however, be placed on the horse upside-down (inside-out). Straw should be put underneath the blanket on the spine and shoulders to increase ventilation.

After about 30 minutes the horse is groomed and the blanket turned, then the dry inside of the rug is nearest the horse's body.

### THE TRAINING SCHEDULE

*First and second month*

*Monday.* Free exercise, 30 minutes lungeing, 10 minutes work on foot. As most horses get less exercise on a Sunday it is not advisable to jump the horse on a Monday; he might be too playful and injure his legs.
*Tuesday.* Free exercise, 10 minutes free jumping – only a few times over small fences out of a trot.
*Wednesday.* Free exercise, 30 minutes lungeing and afterwards leading the young horse out in company of an older, quiet horse (walk only).
*Thursday.* Free exercise, 30 minutes lungeing, 10 minutes work on foot.
*Friday.* Free exercise, 30 minutes lungeing, 10 minutes free jumping.
*Saturday.* Free exercise, 30 minutes out on the leading rein.
*Sunday.* Free exercise.

*Third month*

*Monday.* Free exercise, 30 minutes, starting to ride indoors for 20 minutes in company of an older horse, afterwards 30 minutes out on the leading rein in walk and slow trot (unmounted).
*Tuesday.* Free exercise, 10 minutes free jumping, 10 minutes work on foot.
*Wednesday.* Free exercise, 30 minutes lungeing, 20 minutes riding indoors in company of an older horse, 30 minutes out on the leading rein in walk and slow trot (unmounted).

*Thursday.* Free exercise, 10 minutes free jumping, 10 minutes work on foot.
*Friday.* Free exercise, 30 minutes lungeing, 20 minutes riding indoors, 30 minutes out on the leading rein in walk and slow trot (unmounted).
*Saturday.* Free exercise, 10 minutes free jumping, 10 minutes work on foot.
*Sunday. Free exercise.*

*Fourth month*
*Monday.* Free exercise, 30 minutes lungeing, 30 minutes riding indoors in company, afterwards 30 minutes out on the leading rein (unmounted).
*Tuesday.* Free exercise, 30 minutes lungeing, 10 minutes free jumping, 10 minutes work on foot.
*Wednesday.* Free exercise, 30 minutes lungeing, 30 minutes riding indoors in company, afterwards 30 minutes out on the leading rein (unmounted).
*Thursday.* Free exercise, 30 minutes lungeing, 30 minutes riding indoors in company, 30 minutes out on the leading rein (unmounted).
*Friday.* Free exercise, 10 minutes free jumping, 10 minutes work on foot.
*Saturday.* Free exercise, 30 minutes lungeing, 30 minutes riding indoors in company, 30 minutes out on the leading rein (unmounted).
*Sunday.* Free exercise.

*Fifth month*
*Monday.* Free exercise, 30 minutes lungeing, 30 minutes riding indoors, afterwards 30 minutes riding out of doors (mounted) in walk only and in company of quiet horses.
*Tuesday.* Free exercise, 10 minutes free jumping, 10 minutes work on foot, 30 minutes riding indoors.
*Wednesday.* Free exercise, 30 minutes lungeing, 30 minutes riding indoors, afterwards 30 minutes out of doors in walk only and in company.
*Thursday.* Free exercise, 30 minutes lungeing, 10 minutes work on foot, 30 minutes riding indoors.
*Friday.* Free exercise, 10 minutes free jumping, 30 minutes riding indoors.
*Saturday.* Free exercise, 30 minutes lungeing, 30 minutes riding indoors, afterwards 30 minutes riding out of doors in walk only and in company.
*Sunday.* Free exercise.

*Sixth month*
*Monday.* Free exercise, 30 minutes lungeing, 30 minutes riding indoors, afterwards 30 minutes riding out of doors in company in walk and slow trot.
*Tuesday.* Free exercise, 10 minutes free jumping, 10 minutes work on foot, 30 minutes riding indoors.
*Wednesday.* Free exercise, 30 minutes lungeing, 30 minutes-riding indoors, afterwards 30 minutes riding out of doors in company in walk and slow trot.
*Thursday.* Free exercise, 10 minutes free jumping, 10 minutes work on foot, 30 minutes riding indoors.
*Friday.* Free exercise, 30 minutes lungeing, 30 minutes riding indoors, afterwards 30 minutes riding out of doors in company and in walk and trot only.
*Saturday.* Free exercise, 10 minutes free jumping, 10 minutes work on foot, 30 minutes riding indoors.
*Sunday.* Free exercise.

*Seventh month*
*Monday.* Free exercise, 30 minutes lungeing, 20 minutes riding indoors, 60 minutes riding out of doors – only walk without company.
*Tuesday.* Free exercise, 10 minutes free jumping, 10 minutes work on foot, 30 minutes riding indoors.
*Wednesday.* Free exercise, 90 minutes riding out of doors – walk and trot only – including 15 minutes road work at a walk only.
*Thursday.* Free exercise, 10 minutes free jumping, 30 minutes riding indoors.
*Friday.* Free exercise, 30 minutes lungeing, 20 minutes riding indoors, 60 minutes riding out of doors (walk only).
*Saturday.* Free exercise, 10 minutes free jump-

ing, 10 minutes work on foot, 30 minutes riding indoors.
*Sunday.* Free exercise, 60 minutes riding out of doors – walk and trot – including 15 minutes road work (walk only).

* Which type of exercises should be practised indoor and out of doors at this stage of schooling is explained in the chapters concerned.

*Eighth month*
*Monday.* Free exercise, 30 minutes lungeing, 30 minutes riding indoors, 30 minutes riding out of doors – walk and trot only.
*Tuesday.* Free exercise, 10 minutes free jumping, 10 minutes work on foot, 30 minutes riding indoors.
*Wednesdays.* Free exercise, 90 minutes riding out of doors, up and down hill in all three paces, including 15 minutes road work at a walk only.
*Thursday.* Free exercise, 60 minutes riding indoors introducing cavaletti schooling.
*Friday.* Free exercise, 30 minutes lungeing, 30 minutes riding out of doors, up and down hill in all three paces, including 15 minutes road work at a walk only.
*Saturday.* Free exercise, 60 minutes riding indoors, including cavaletti schooling: as Thursday.
*Sunday.* Free exercise, 90 minutes riding out of doors. Same exercises (up and down hill, etc) as Wednesday.

*Ninth month*
*Monday.* Free exercise, 30 minutes lungeing, 30 minutes riding indoors, 30 minutes riding out of doors in hilly country in all three paces.
*Tuesday.* Free exercise, 10 minutes free jumping. 10 minutes work on foot, 30 minutes riding indoors.
*Wednesday.* Free exercise, 90 minutes riding out of doors, 15 minutes road work – walk only – introducing speed course.
*Thursday.* Free exercise, 60 minutes riding indoors, including cavaletti.
*Friday.* Free exercise, 30 minutes lungeing, 60 minutes riding out of doors: same as Wednesday.
*Saturday.* Free exercise, 60 minutes riding indoors, including cavaletti as Thursday.
*Sunday.* Free exercise, 90 minutes riding out of doors: same as Monday.

* Riding indoors, including cavaletti exercises, should be arranged as follows:
Divide the schooling session between dressage and cavaletti exercises. During the first 30 minutes ride approximately 10 minutes over cavaletti at a walk only. For the next 30 minutes place the cavaletti at a trot distance and exercise the horse over the cavaletti, also for approximately 10 minutes.
The 10 minutes walk and trot exercises over cavaletti should be spread out over each 30 minutes. Do not ride continuously for 10 minutes over cavaletti but pause frequently, doing dressage exercises in between.
To prevent confusion or misunderstanding I would like to point out that the word "Speed course" does not mean riding at a fast speed. Its purpose is merely to train horse and rider to maintain a uniform rhythmic tempo in pace, whatever speed it may be.

*Tenth month*
*Monday.* Free exercise, 30 minutes lungeing, 30 minutes riding indoors, 30 minutes riding out of doors in all paces.
*Tuesday.* Free exercise, 10 minutes free jumping, 10 minutes work on foot, 30 minutes riding indoors.
*Wednesday.* Free exercise, 90 minutes riding out of doors, including speed course and 15 minutes road work, at a walk only.
*Thursday.* Free exercise, 30 minutes riding indoors, including cavaletti and introducing in-and-out jumps.
*Friday.* Free exercise, 30 minutes lungeing, 90 minutes riding out of doors: same as Wednesday.
*Saturday.* Free exercise, 60 minutes riding indoors: same as Thursday.
*Sunday.* Free exercise, 90 minutes riding out of doors, *no* speed course.

*Eleventh month*
*Monday.* Free exercise, 30 minutes lungeing, 30 minutes riding indoors, 30 minutes riding out of doors on level ground in all paces.

*Tuesday.* Free exercise, 10 minutes work on foot, 30 minutes riding indoors, 30 minutes riding out of doors on hilly countryside in all paces.
*Wednesday.* Free exercise, 90 minutes riding out of doors, including speed course, and 15 minutes road work at a walk only.
*Thursday.* Free exercise, 60 minutes riding indoors, including 20 minutes cavaletti work and in-and-out jumps.
*Friday.* Free exercise, 90 minutes riding out of doors: same as Wednesday.
*Saturday.* Free exercise, 60 minutes riding indoors: same as Thursday.
*Sunday.* Free exercise, 90 minutes riding out of doors on hilly country in all paces.

*Twelth month*
*Monday.* Free exercise, 30 minutes lungeing, 30 minutes riding indoors, 30 minutes riding out of doors on level ground in all paces.
*Tuesday.* Free exercise, 60 minutes riding indoors, introducing the jumping lane and single obstacles.
*Wednesday.* Free exercise, 90 minutes riding out of doors on hilly country, including speed course and 15 minutes road work introducing a slow trot.
*Thursday.* Free exercise, 60 minutes riding indoors, including jumping as Tuesday.
*Friday.* Free exercise, 90 minutes riding out of doors: same as Wednesday.
*Saturday.* Free exercise, 60 minutes riding indoors, including jumping as Tuesday.
*Sunday.* Free exercise, 90 minutes riding out of doors on level ground.

### SUMMARY

In the olden days many trainers, in particular on the European continent, made the mistake of schooling young horses for too long *indoors.* When the young horses finally were ridden out their mind was so distracted that they did not take much notice of their rider's aids and demands because they were too pre-occupied with the strange surroundings and objects. Frightened, the young horses became obstinate and excited and worked unco-operatively. This, of course, resulted in rearing, bucking, pulling and trying to run off. Accidents were quite frequent.

In other countries horses are schooled mostly from the very beginning in the "open" and behave much more relaxed and are better behaved out of doors. For exampe, the young horse in the English or Irish hunting field settles down after a few outings and behaves himself in a correct manner. There are very few horses biting or kicking. Also in Australia most horses are quiet and relaxed with perfect manners. Due to the climate there are very few indoor schools and most horses are schooled only out of doors.

Nevertheless, it stands to reason that the young horse, before being ridden out on his own, should *first* be taught to obey the basic aids to a certain extent.

The training schedule for the first six months shows clearly how much variety there should be in the daily training. Variety is essential to keep the horse interested in his work and to develop his co-operation, which leads to quicker results in his education.

During the first half year the trainer has taken full advantage of the horse's natural herd instinct by taking him out of doors in the company of older horses, first on the leading rein and later on mounted. By now the horse has developed complete confidence and obedience to the rider's aids. The rider can now take the horse out *on his own* without taking too much risk.

From the sixth month on the training is done *more out of doors.*

When difficulties arise while riding out alone do *not* start a fight with the young horse. The next time when riding out give him a lead with another horse.

Give your horse a chance, but do not make an issue out of it. In time the young horse will learn to overcome his shyness. Because most horses are over-anxious to imitate each other, the young horse will follow the example set by the older horse, who will lead the young horse when passing a strange object, a bridge, a small bank or ditch in the field. The "danger" will pass unnoticed and the next time the problem might not even arise.

Therefore *never* start a fight with a young horse. It mostly turns out that the rider is the loser. But winning or losing the fight might have left a scar on the horse's mind which could remain for the rest of his life.

During the first month, ride in hilly country only at an active walk and trot only when riding on the flat. Always ride straight up and down hill (never at an angle). This enables the horse to use both hindlegs equally and it teaches him to obey the rider's will by following exactly the set direction. If the horse's development of muscle and balance progresses according to the training schedule, one should be able to walk and trot up and down hill within eight months. During the ninth month one can introduce a slow canter when riding in hilly country, but only for very short periods.

When riding in hilly country it is essential that the rider sits in all three paces in the *forward seat* position. Only then will the horse be able to round his back and use his muscles freely to balance himself. If the rider's seat would be *in* the saddle when riding up or down hill then his weight would *not* be situated vertically above the horse's centre of gravity and would interfere with the horse's balance. One should bear in mind that the up and down hill exercise with the encumbrance of the rider's weight is extremely hard on a young horse. One must therefore avoid any unnecessary movement with the upper part of one's body.

The young horse must be handled very cautiously, especially when the going is deep and heavy, in order to avoid losing a shoe or over-reaching.

Because the young horse has to struggle to maintain balance, protect his legs with four brushing boots and two over reach boots. A breastplate should also be used, particularly when exercising in hilly country. It will keep the saddle in position and at the same time the rider could take a hold on the neck strap if he fears to get left behind and jerk the horse in the mouth.

When riding out without the company of other horses the young horse might meet a strange object and shy. Do not use the whip. Dismount and lead the horse to the object which frightened him whilst using a soothing voice. Mostly the horse will regain confidence after he has been allowed to smell and touch the object with his lips. The next time the horse will pass the same object without shying.

*Change route* as often as possible when leaving the stable and when returning home, otherwise the horse will sooner or later work unwillingly when requested to take a strange route. If one takes the same route home all the time the horse will undoubtedly increase his pace or even "pretend" to shy, which would give him an excuse to take the bit and dash off homewards. When riding towards the stable *never* trot or, even worse, canter, but walk the horse for at least 15 minutes.

In general, bring a lot of variation into the daily exercise, keeping the horse's mind occupied and interested in his work. If trouble arises it is symptomatic of either having too little variety or having repeated the same thing too often. For instance: the horse takes off as soon as one enters an open field; the horse refuses to pass a gate; he leans over the shoulder at certain places; or will not leave a certain route. Taking precautions is much easier than having to cure a bad habit.

Road work toughens the horse's leg tendons and prepares the young horse for the jumping on hard going. The vibration on the hard going works as a massage and prevents windgalls. In countries like Australia and Mexico, where the ground is hard the whole year round, I have noticed that the horse's legs are drier and harder. There one will find fewer horses with windgalls than in countries where the going is deep.

Road work is practised also in a slow trot. I emphasise that this must be done at a very *slow* rate only, and not, as one can often see, at an extended trot or sometimes even at a canter. These paces on the hard road will ruin the horse's feet and legs. While doing road work hold for a moment one hand flat on the horse's

*Fig. 387*
**Place your hand flat on the horse's croup to feel how hard going affects the horse's tendons and joints.**

croup, just to realise the enormous vibration which the horse's whole body absorbs on hard going.

Never forget to put on kneecaps when riding on the road. To give confidence and security for both horse and rider Mordax non-slip studs or non-slip horse shoe nails should be used.

I am convinced that a showjumping horse needs 12 months of basic schooling before participating in any jumping competition.

Basic schooling is *not* a waste of time but vital to establish a sound equestrian foundation. It pays dividends because it saves enormous time in the following schooling years, as there will be no set backs caused by short cuts in the basic training. Owing to the progressive basic schooling in the Natural Training Method results will be obtained amazingly quickly.

The initial schooling is a major asset to the horse's future jumping career. In nearly all countries on the European continent a 12 months basic schooling is considered normal and necessary.

After this preliminary schooling year the young horse may begin competing in small jumping events, although the training of the horse may in no way be considered as "complete".

The schooling principles of the Natural Training Method prepare the young horse for a future *jumping career* and they will be continued even when participating in jumping events of the highest standard. Even horses of international standard need continuous schooling and gymnastic exercises between competitions, not only to keep them fit but also to correct faults in technique as soon as they arise.

PART THREE

# THE SECOND SCHOOLING YEAR

CHAPTER TWELVE

# NOVICE COMPETITIONS

During the second schooling year the young horse should start to participate in novice jumping competitions, if possible the first few times indoors, because in the confined space of the indoor arena the horse will be easier to control. If the course rides fluently it will teach the horse obedience to the rider's aids because of the many changes of directions the horse is often faced towards the kicking boards. This will slow down his pace, preventing the young horse from taking a strong hold.

Taking part in competitions is an important part of schooling. Particularly on the European continent many trainers make the mistake of schooling their young horses too long at home only. When finally taken out to a show the young horses are surprised and frustrated by the sudden change of environment. A young horse may jump well at home in the security of his familiar surroundings, or even at various training fields to which he has become accustomed, but he cannot be expected to give the same performance in his first competition . . . even if the fences are lower than the ones he jumps at home.

One should realise that every young horse must first learn to overcome his "stage fright". The change to the showjumping arena starts a completely new chapter in the young horse's life and a new stage in his education. He will in the beginning put in too much effort and "over-jump", therefore it is not really necessary to jump big fences at home when training. Any difficulties at this initial stage (like running out at a fence or refusing a strange looking obstacle) need not necessarily be a lack of basic schooling but are mostly caused by excitement or lack of confidence and experience. If the young horse at the beginning is a little difficult in passing the exit or entrance of the enclosure, being bold or nappy, it is better to give him a lead or follow another horse than to make a lot of fuss about it. This would only make the horse more aware of his misbehaviour, because a horse is very quick to sense an atmosphere. In time he will grow out of it and the less fuss one makes in the beginning the quicker the young horse will settle down.

From now on the young horse must compete regularly (once a week) in small competitions as part of his schooling. The more the horses' jumping in competitions improves, the less one should jump at home. By "improvement" I do not mean winning rosettes or getting placed each time out, but that the horse improves his jumping technique and gains confidence in jumping strange obstacles.

In principle, the competitor must enter the arena with the will to win. However, one should not be a pure ribbon hunter. In the first season the rider should regard every smooth round with his novice horse as a winning round, whether or not he wins ribbons. Of course, the temptation is great, especially if the horse is jumping very promisingly, but taking part in these novice competitions must be considered only as part of the training programme. Only then can it be of benefit. Trying too hard to win at this early stage is short sighted as it would spoil and overface the young horse. Some riders are hard to convince. In their struggle for honours they do not realise that the horse's initial good performance will not *last* and that they are not giving their horse a fair chance to upgrade progressively to compete on big occasions later on.

By upgrading too quickly many young horses with great potential are spoilt, exhausted and disheartened. Such a horse will not jump willingly later on because he will feel insecure.

In general I would say that during the first year in competition one should not be too enthusiastic when a young horse jumps "big" nor be too disappointed when he has not performed as expected. There are always ups and downs on the long hard road to success – "it's all in the game". It is a matter of time before the horse grows out of his childish habits and eventually begins to show his true form.

## PREPARATION

### *Transport*

Before actually participating at shows it is advisable to take the young horse a few times to showgrounds in the company of a quiet stable mate. This way the young horse will get familiar with travelling and the show atmosphere. Also when taking the young horse to a new training field is it advisable that he is accompanied on the journey, especially on the first few occasions. The driver of the horsebox should be an experienced man and should take great care when slowing down and when stopping, so that the horse does not become upset. If a groom is travelling with the horses (they greatly appreciate the company) a bell should be installed so that he can signal the driver, should difficulties arise.

### *Protection*

To avoid horses acquiring any injury or catching cold, protection is necessary during transport. Depending on the climate, either a thick woollen or a light linen rug is necessary to keep the horse's muscles warm.

When travelling in a half-open box, a full facehood with a warm woollen lining is necessary. A head protector made of soft felt can prevent head injuries. The head collar should be covered with sheepskin and leather tail guard prevents damage to the tail. This should be tied to a loop at the back of the blanket and *not* to the blanket roller. On a long journey a blanket roller is most uncomfortable for the horse and causes unnecessary distress, more so when the tail guard is tied to it. Therefore avoid using a blanket roller.

When using a tail bandage, particularly an elastic one, great care should be taken to see that the tapes are not tied too tightly. This can impede the blood circulation to the tail and the whole tail dock main necrose.

*Fig. 388*
A warm hood should be used when travelling a horse in a half-open trailer.

All four legs must be protected, even on a short journey. When loading and unloading try to avoid accidents; slipping off the ramp might cause irreparable damage to the legs. Use either Sandown bandages, covering the fetlock joints, or travelling boots made of felt, which also cover the horse's coronets. Four overreach boots are also advisable. Kneecaps protect the knees if the horse should slip. Hock protectors are ideal for horses who kick against the rear ramp as they prevent capped hocks.

Following the journey remove the leg protectors immediately. Massage the legs and the tummy vigorously but gently to stimulate circulation to the limbs, thereby avoiding stasis.

*Fig. 389*
Head protector.

*Food when travelling*

The horse's normal diet is not interfered with when on a short journey. Keep the horse's mind occupied by giving him a filled hay net. It should be tied as high as possible to prevent the horse's forelegs becoming caught up in it, which can easily happen when the hay net is empty and dangles too low. A release knot should be used.

However, if the horse has a long journey of several days or more, without any exercise being possible, then considerable care should be taken with regard to his feeding and digestion. Very little oats should be given, replacing this with a mash (warm). Damp his hay to avoid colic. Take plenty of food along which the horse is used to, particularly hay. Willow tree branches are an appetite stimulant. Keep the branches fresh for several days by submerging them in a bucket of water.

*Travelling accessories*

*Do not forget to take the following items:* the horse's own drinking bucket and plastic feed manger; first-aid kit; an extra set of rugs; an extra set of shoes; tool kit (hammer, nails, pliers); a grooming kit; and all necessary tack, including a spare head collar and ropes.

Daily massage of the horse's legs and stomach is essential. Following this bandage all four legs (loosely) with Sandown bandages.

Also essential on any long journey is good ventilation in the horsebox without creating draught.

*Horseboxes*

One is independent if one has one's own transport facilities. Make certain that the horsebox is a well-balanced vehicle, stable in turns and does not sway, otherwise every horse will dislike travelling. Therefore, when purchasing a horsebox, make sure that it serves its purpose.

The single horsebox I would not recommend because the wheelbase is too narrow and the box is not stable enough, especially if the horse is a bad traveller. The two or three horsebox is preferable. Firstly, they have four wheels. Secondly, the wheelbase is wider, producing a better balance, more stable turns and there is less sway when it is in motion.

A front unloading ramp is very useful, making the unloading much easier for the horse. Also the horse will not learn to run backwards before the ramp is closed when loading.

*Bad travellers*

Bad travellers get more support and grip in the horsebox if the standing area of the floor has wooden catches (grips).

It is particularly important that the ramp is as low as possible and covered with a fibre mat to prevent the horse from slipping, especially when wet. When the horse kicks he cannot injure his legs if the ramp is covered with a fibre mat, as it offers better protection than wooden catches.

The front window should be covered with bars for safety. The window should be fairly big because horses are more relaxed when travelling if they can look out.

If the horse is a bad traveller widen the partition, which gives the horse more travelling space at the rear end. Then the horse can widen his hindlegs for better support and to balance himself.

Some horses prefer to travel backwards instead of facing forward. From my experience I have found that really bad travellers are completely happy and relaxed when travelling back to front.

Most horses dislike entering a box in the dark. Therefore an inside light should be pro-provided. It keeps the horse calm during the journey. A radio has the same effect, as all horses like soft music.

*Loading the horse*

There are horses who, right from the beginning, walk into the horsebox without any trouble. On the other hand there are horses who dislike being loaded. This can be very annoying, particularly if one is in a hurry or when the weather is bad. The well meant advice from people gathering around does not improve the situation if one has unsuccessfully tried to load

*Fig. 390*
How not to load a horse.

an unwilling horse. The person trying to load the horse easily loses his temper and becomes even more upset than the horse. Rough and ignorant handling is chiefly the reason why so many horses behave badly. Never blindfold a horse; this will frighten the already upset horse even more and can lead to him injuring his head. Shouting or raising the voice or sending the horse on with the whip or broom has also the wrong influence because the horse will look only backwards and his mind will be driven to distraction. He raises his head and risks knocking it against the roof. As a result the horse will run backwards off the ramp.

However, the experienced horseman will never allow his horse to reach such a state of excitement. If the horse, for any reason, should become upset one should forget the loading for a short period altogether, lead the distressed horse around quietly and let him eat some grass or oats before attempting to load the horse again, and one should ask the unsolicited advisers/on-lookers to "please leave the scene".

There are many things which make loading a horse easy and all kinds of precautions should be taken (even if the horse is easy to load) to avoid the horse hurting himself. If he learns to dislike travelling it will take a very long time to overcome his fear. Therefore ensure the following precautions are taken:

(i) Let down the horse box stands or supports to keep it steady when loading and have two large wings attached on each side of the ramp.

(ii) Put some straw on the ramp and give the horse some oats when he is on the ramp or let an experienced horse give him a lead.

(iii) Move the partition to widen the space before entering.

(iv) Always have the groom door of the trailer closed when loading, because when in a nervous state of mind a horse might try to escape through the small door. (This experience gives some weight to the theory that the horse's eyes can envisage objects seven times larger than they in fact really are.)

(v) If the trailer has a front ramp, open it to let the light in and lead the horse through the trailer a few times, possibly after a lead horse.

(vi) Never look directly into the horse's eyes when leading him into the trailer. One should walk with one's back towards the horse (not facing him).

(vii) Hold the lead loosely. Do not pull as that provokes the horse to pull and to raise his head.

(viii) *Important*. Attach a lungeing rein on each side of the horsebox. Place the horse straight in front of the ramp. The two assistants, holding one lunge each, walk slowly towards each other, closing the horse in a V position. If the horse still resists, they pass each other (changing position, crossing the two lungeing reins) and closing the horse in even more. This way the horse cannot slip sideways off the ramp and is pushed in gently with the aid of the combined lunges. This method is also very safe because the horse can not kick anybody.

(ix) A horse (or foal) which does not kick can be loaded easily if two assistants take each other's hands and cross their arms around the horse's gaskins, while a third assistant leads the horse.

(x) To cure horses who raise their head too high one can use the Gogue Independent attached to the roller and bridle.

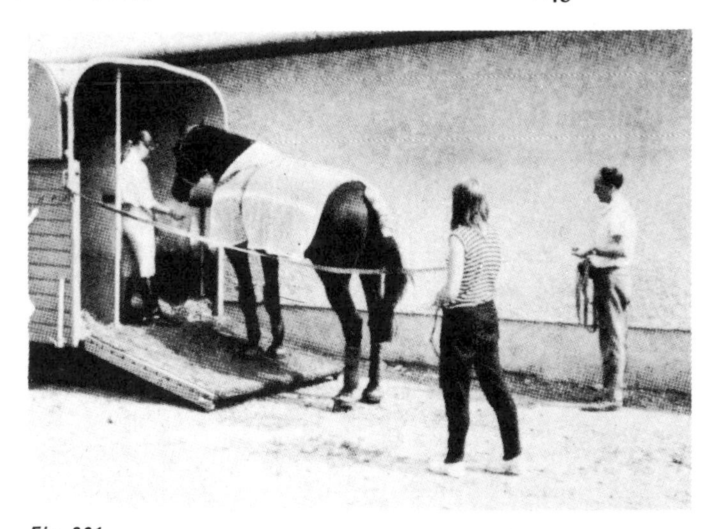

*Fig. 391*
This is the best and safest way to load a horse. Close the horse in with two lunges and "push" him in.

Alternatively, one can take a lungeing rein, attach it to the head collar and pass the lungeing rein in between the forelegs through the roller. This method enables one to control the height of the horse's head as the assistant leads the horse into the box.

(xi) If the horse is finally loaded do *not* tie him up but close the rear ramp first, and as quickly as possible. Then secure the division and the rear bar. *Only then* should one tie up the horse. It is very dangerous to tie up the horse while the rear ramp is open; the horse might suddenly decide to back out of the trailer and could injure his legs or even strangle himself. Only when the rear bar is secured can the ramp be opened again to load another horse.

The main requirement when loading horses is to stay calm under all circumstances. Be patient, never use force or shout at the horse. Instead try to gain his confidence.

VISITING SHOWS

If the young horse jumps quite well at home and at various training fields do not expect him at the beginning to jump as well at shows. The show atmosphere, to say the least, is tense; it disturbs the novice horse and makes him upset. The collecting ring is generally overcrowded with horses approaching from all directions.

In all this excitement one can hardly expect the young horse to stay calm, even if he normally remains relaxed at his home ground in the company of strange horses. To accustom the horse to the show atmosphere take him first several times to a show without actually participating in the events. This will give the young horse a chance to absorb the new impressions and gain experience travelling. If possible, take a quiet stablemate to the showground and ride the young horse around in his company to give him confidence.

Do not bully the horse, but give him time to settle and time to observe all the strange objects and activities. If he halts and raises his head, do not push him forward immediately but leave him alone for a few seconds. If the horse has taken it all in he will heave a deep breath (a sign of relaxation), and he will then want to move on again to find another strange object which may interest him.

If one arrives early at the showground, the pocket may not be too crowded and one can jump the practise fence a few times. First, out of a figure of eight at a slow trot and, if the horse remains calm, then do the same out of a slow canter.

At small local shows it is often permitted to ride into the jumping enclosure after the show is finished. This is an excellent opportunity to show the strange fences to the young horse (if the chief steward agrees even jump a few small fences). This experience will be of great benefit later on when the horse actually starts to compete. Often the novice horse pays more attention to the crowd surrounding the jumping enclosure than to the aids of his rider. The horse's mind is pre-occupied in observing the strange fences and colours.

*Fig. 392*
Showing the fences to the young horse.

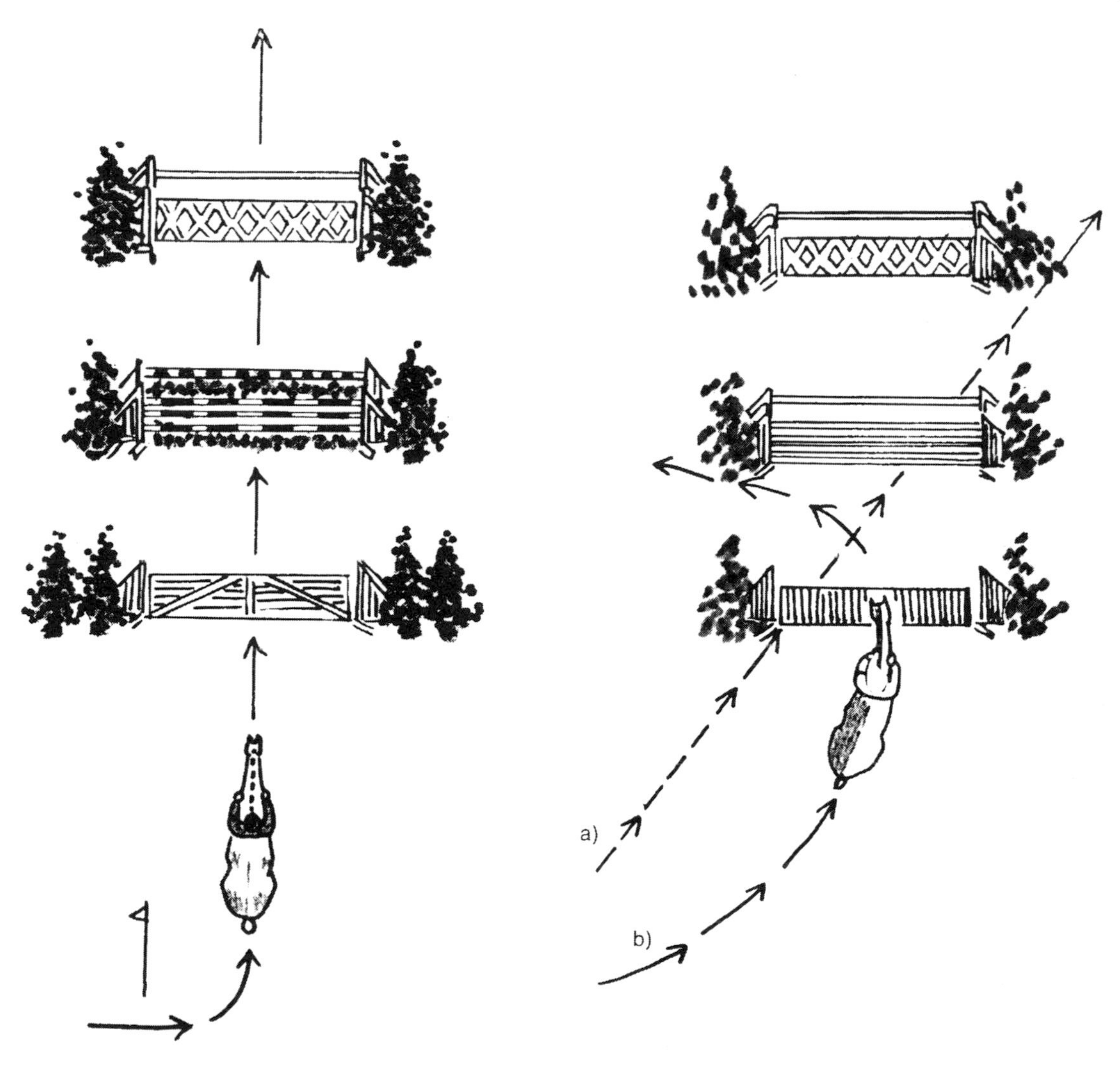


*Fig. 393*
The correct approach to a combination fence, straight and at the centre. This approach is essential when competing with a novice horse.

*Fig. 394*
Two incorrect approaches:

a) Making an approach diagonally means that the distances between the elements of the fence are extremely long. The horse will experience difficulty in finding a suitable take-off point and will try to run out at the second or third element;

b) Making an approach out of a circle, the horse will continue on this line and will, therefore, try to run out to the left at the second element.

In Ireland, where people by nature have "horse sense", it is customary that competitors in novice events are allowed to ride their horses in the jumping enclosure and *show* them the fences before the competition starts. This has enormous educational value for the young horse, because he will not be taken by surprise when entering the arena to start his round. The young horse will learn more in his round.

*Walking the course*

Before the rider walks the course he should first study very carefully the conditions of the competition, which are stated on the plan of the course.

Depending on the type of competition, the conditions can include: a compulsory course line, whole or part; boundary flags; compulsory turning points; jump-off; and so on. Walking the course is just as important as the actual riding of the course. The rider must walk the course from start to finish and he must follow the exact track on which he intends to ride. He should not worry too much about the height and width of the fences, as the standard of the course is, after all, the same for every horse and rider participating.

Special attention should be paid in case of a compulsory course line or turning point because riding a wrong course means elimination. The rider should be particularly observant when studying the turns and how to approach the combination jumps, if possible giving his horse at least four strides on a straight line before take-off. He should pace out the distance in between the single fences to check if they are placed on a "related distance".

The distance in between the elements of a combination jump will tell the rider whether his horse will need to take one or two non-jumping strides. Whether distances are normal, long or short will decide the speed in which the horse has to approach the combination. When competing with a novice horse it is essential to approach all fences straight and at the centre, because only then is the young horse able to engage both hocks equally to ensure sufficient power at take-off. It also allows the young horse to maintain his balance after landing, which is an important factor after clearing the first element of a combination jump. Loss of balance after landing over the first element could mean running out at the second element. Therefore take special care to approach a combination straight and at the centre. If the first element is approached and jumped at an angle the young horse is not able to regain his balance to jump the rest of the combination on a straight line. He will continue the line on which he approached the combination and run out at the second element.

If the young horse is bold and does not run out or refuse he will certainly knock a pole. Jumping from an angle at this stage would not be a fair task to ask of a young horse on account of the excessive strain put on his inner hindleg. However, later on when the horse has developed the necessary muscles and gained more experience, he then will also jump fences from an angle. For instance, in speed competitions or in a jump-off against the clock, but asking a young and inexperienced horse to do this would be looking for trouble. For all these reasons the opportunity to walk the course should never be wasted. It must not be regarded as an occasion to have a pleasant chat with friends in the arena.

The rider must know the course "by heart" and make sure that he remembers the conditions of the course, the nature of the fence (including their colours) and their proper order. Standing with his *back* to the jumping arena he should repeat from memory – in words – the course layout to a friend. Only then can the rider concentrate completely on his horse while competing and will not take the wrong course. If the rider loses his way in the competition he has to pull up his horse, breaking the canter pace. This distracts the horse's attention and disturbs his impulsion. Refusals or jumping faults are often the result. The rest of the course is mostly done in a "steeplechase speed" to regain the time lost. This again will lead to jumping faults. Try to have plenty of time to watch several other competitors riding the course. Knowing the stride of one's own mount, look at other horses and try to compare. If one's horse has a long stride, watch a few other competitors whose horses also have long strides. If they are coming too close to a combination or a certain single fence located at a short related distance then one knows that one will have to ride one's horse there on a shorter, bouncing stride. On the other hand, if one's horse has a short stride, and another rider on a horse with a similar stride has problems in covering a distance, one knows that at that point one will have to ride strongly forward. If there is a problem posed in the course, watch closely how other competitors tackle it and try to learn from them.

It is not good enough to examine the course from the stands alone, because only if the rider has walked the course and studied all its problems seriously will he be able to give the competition his full attention.

*Warming-up*

How to warm-up a horse before a competition depends entirely on the horse's nature and temperament. Some horses need more exercise than others; some need slow and relaxing exercises, others need steaming up. Never should the warming-up time be considered as a last minute schooling. If the rider thinks this to be necessary then the horse has not completed his "homework" and should not compete at all yet. One also should never compete with a horse who has just arrived at the showground and who has not had any warming-up at all. In general a horse should be schooled in such a way that he does not require a long warming-up time. The warming-up time for novice horses, for instance, should be reduced gradually throughout the first jumping season to a minimum; this applies also to the use of the practise fence.

I prefer to arrive at the showground at least two hours before the competition commences. This gives the horse a break after a long and weary journey in the box. Because the horse may be stiff he should be led around, allowed to stretch his legs and see the surroundings.

The rider should not rush his horse over the practise fence. If the rider is in a hurry he will, without realising it, project his nervous tension to the horse. A difficult horse I lunge for 30 minutes with the Chambon. This can, of course, only be done if there are no delays on the journey and if lungeing facilities are available. The warming-up ring could be overcrowded or too muddy. At indoor shows the warming-up ring might be very small, and at night the practise fence is sometimes out of doors in poor light. For all these reasons the horse should not need too long a warming-up time.

Never make the grave mistake of starting the warm-up with an extended trot or canter. Even when arriving late at the show and time may be tight it is essential to start off with an active walk in order to loosen the horse's muscles. Otherwise the horse will get tense. During the walk make *several transitions* to a halt, rein back and make turns on the haunches, move the quarters alternately sideways in either direction to flex the horse's body laterally inwards and to engage the hindlegs. This loosens up the muscles and makes the horse alert to the rider's aids. After the walk session proceed at ordinary rising trot and afterwards change into a slow canter (extending the pace now and then). Repeat the transitions in all paces *frequently* to increase action and engagement of the quarters.

With a lazy horse, or one which is reluctant in approaching the practise fence, one should extend the trot and the canter to the utmost degree over a very short distance, then make a transition into a halt and rein back and repeat the extended paces again. This improves the horse's impulsion.

*The practise fence*

At first approach the practise fence out of a slow trot, so the horse has to jump more from his hocks. When jumping out of canter go as slowly as possible. If the horse tends to increase the pace and takes a stronger hold on the bit, approach the practise fence out of a figure of eight, first at a trot and then in canter. This method will settle the horse very soon.

Do not jump continually over the same fence, but alternately over a low spread and an upright fence. Aim at getting the horse to jump with confidence, rather than to jump too big fences.

It is most important between the jumping to make frequent transitions at all paces, including a halt and reining back. Also walk "at ease" on a loose rein, giving the horse a break to relax. Do not forget to stand still now and then and wait for the horse to take a deep breath, a sign that he is relaxing.

In general, riders make too much use of the practise fence, jumping it over and over again, each time raising it a few holes. They misuse the horse's energy, finishing up with an exhausted and sour horse who does not like to enter the jumping enclosure. They can hardly expect a co-operative horse and a smooth performance. Such senseless warming-up is done mostly to hide the rider's lack of confidence.

The competitor should arrange his time so that he can give the horse a short break after warming-up, but still have him warm when entering the competition. Should the weather require it cover him with a rug to keep his muscles warm. This break before competing should, however, not be too long, otherwise the horse and rider's top condition acquired in the warming-up would fade away.

In hot countries, before competing, the horse should not stand for any length of time in the sun. Bring the horse back into his stable during the intervals between competitions. Otherwise put him back into the horsebox or take him into a shaded place which is not draughty.

Great care should be taken to ensure that the horse is never supplied with a large quantity of food or water shortly before competing.

*Provoking faults*

I am reluctant to make suggestions on how to provoke faults or refusals because they could be misunderstood and misused. But they may be useful and necessary to an experienced rider whose old horse becomes careless and makes faults or refuses when competing; or to a rider whose horse is plainly not caring.

"Rapping" used to be the best known remedy to make a careless horse more attentive. I am glad that rapping is forbidden today, but those riders who used to rap their horses have found less obvious but more cruel and harmful methods to make their horses jump "clean", for instance, jumping unjumpable fences, or using medical remedies hidden under bandages and so on.

Such methods are cruel and ruin the horse's health and confidence in man. I condemn these methods. A rider has to be qualified to improve a horse's jumping style correctly and should not have to resort to any rapping methods.

But if a horse, due to lack of proper schooling, needs a reminder before competing, it should be done very cautiously and only once and in the fairest manner possible.

(1) *Provoking faults with the forelegs.* If the horse is careless with his forelegs, approach an upright fence in a slow collected canter, sending the horse well onto the bit with strong forward driving leg aids – not with the whip.

During the last stride, just before take-off, drop the reins suddenly, surrendering the contact with the horse's mouth. This sudden missing contact with the bit brings the horse off balance and instantly onto the forehand. In this position the horse will knock the top pole of the upright fence with the forelegs.

(2) *Provoking a fault with the hindlegs.* Build from the practise fence an oxer parallel, which should have extra spread but is not too high. Place a pole diagonally across the fence. Approach the oxer in a slow, collected canter, applying strong forward driving leg aids, sending the horse well onto the bit. Approach and take-off should be ridden normally, but as soon as the horse is airborne do not follow the lengthening of the horse's neck with the reins. Take a strong hold on the bit and move the upper part of the body slightly backwards (be left behind). In this position the horse is forced to change his centre of gravity to the hindquarters. He raises his head and his back will be

*Fig. 395*
Provoking faults with the forelegs. This may *only* be done with an old, careless horse. No faults, of any kind, should ever be provoked with a young horse.

*Fig. 396*
Provoking faults with the hindlegs.

*Fig. 397*
Provoking a refusal.

dropped instead of rounded. In such an unnatural position the horse is not able to lift and bend his hindlegs sufficiently and he will knock the far pole of the oxer with his hindlegs. Don't overdo this however. If a careless horse knocks his legs *once* this is more than sufficient.

(3) *Provoking a refusal.* If one has reason to believe that the horse might refuse in the competition, one can provoke a refusal at the practise fence before entering the jumping enclosure.

Place a coloured rug or a pink coat over the practise fence. When approaching the fence the first time do not ride too energetically but in such a way that one can be certain that the horse will refuse the fence.

Refusal will be encouraged by the strange colour of the fence and the weak manner of riding. However, after this refusal the horse must not be given a chance to refuse again. The second time he must jump the fence. Approach the fence with determination and exactly at the centre. Ride in a slow collected canter, increasing the pace strongly in the last few strides before take-off.

It is important to apply strong forward driving leg aids. Send the horse very well onto the bit and maintain the tension *until* the horse takes off. When the fence is approached in this second attempt so determinedly the horse is then given no alternative but to jump the fence correctly.

It is much better to teach the horse a lesson *before* than during the competition, because a horse will very soon recognise the sound of the bell and will realise that after three refusals his work is finished and he may leave the arena. For the same reason one should never leave the arena after three refusals without jumping one of the easier fences.

Now the reader will probably realise that jumping faults or refusals are often provoked unintentionally in the actual jumping competition. Riders use, unknown to themselves but habitually, the same technique as used at the practise fence, causing the horse to make a jumping fault or to refuse a fence.

In general do not make too much use of the practise fence in between competitions or before the jump-off as it will only use up the horse's energy and might make him sour.

*Entering the jumping arena*

When the horse is warmed up for the competition do not stand with the horse at the entrance because this makes many horses dislike entering the arena. One can hardly blame the young horse that hesitates to leave the other horses who are waiting for their turn at the entrance.

When waiting one should keep the horse moving at a walk and then enter the jumping arena without pausing.

When a horse refuses to enter the enclosure, reins back or rears, and at the same time turns away from the entrance, one should not become impatient or lose one's temper and make a lot of fuss about it, because then one would make the young horse aware of this unpleasant situation. The horse becomes more obstinate and one can be sure that the next time he will try it again. In order not to spoil the horse the rider must stay calm without upsetting the young horse further. An assistant or another horse should give him a lead. In time the horse will overcome this habit and forget all about it.

*How* one should enter the arena depends on the horse's temperament and stage of schooling. If a horse is lazy or pays too much attention to the spectators, etc., do not hesitate to enter the arena at full speed, otherwise there will be difficulties at the first fence. However, if the horse is a sensitive or a nervous type, enter the arena calmly and relaxed at a walk, if possible on a long rein. Speak to the horse and pat him in order to give him confidence.

*Riding the course*

When saluting the judges the horse should stand rock-still and attentive, ready to move off at the slightest indication from the rider.

A nervous rider should try not to transfer his stage fright to the horse or to take up the reins too roughly and too abruptly as soon as the

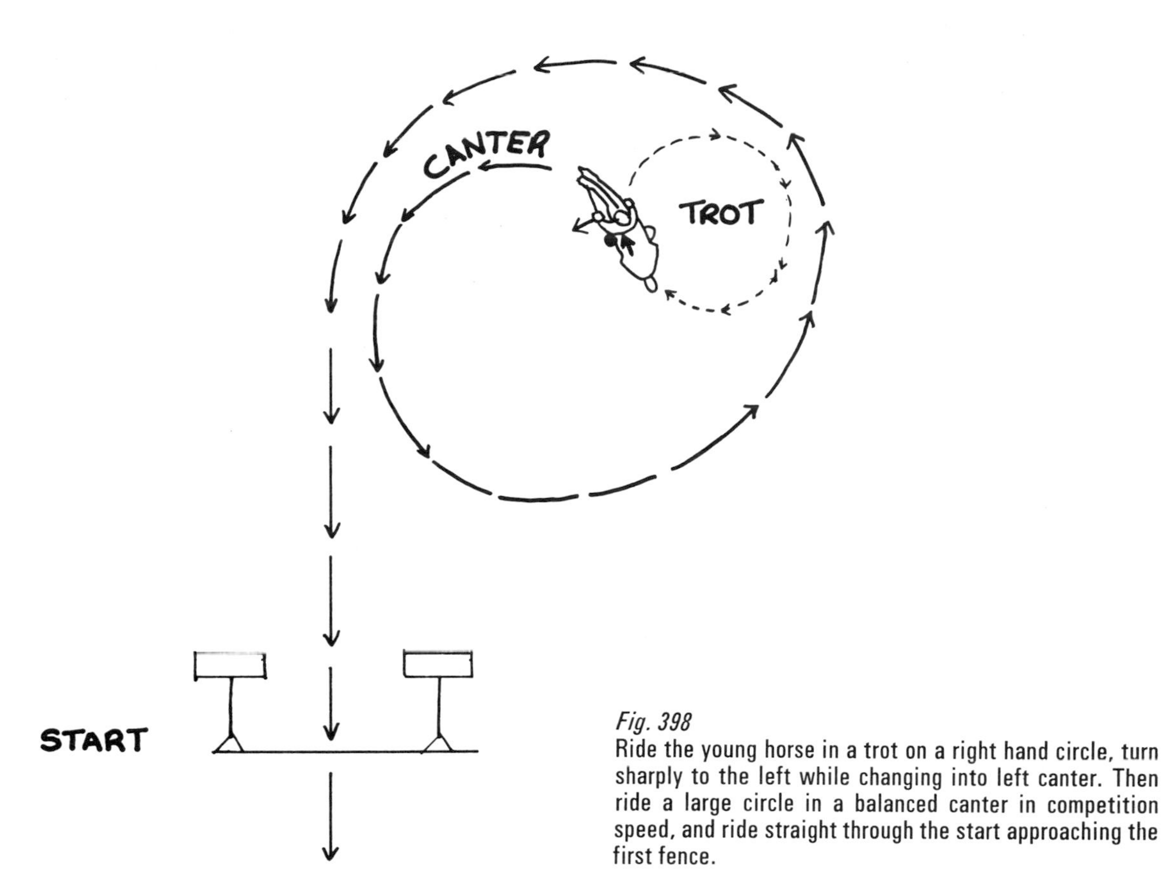


*Fig. 398*
Ride the young horse in a trot on a right hand circle, turn sharply to the left while changing into left canter. Then ride a large circle in a balanced canter in competition speed, and ride straight through the start approaching the first fence.

starting bell has gone. This would surprise the horse and create unnecessary excitement.

There is no reason to hurry, because after the starting bell has gone the rider is allowed *one* minute, during which he must cross the start line. If he takes longer, he will be eliminated. During this minute the rider has plenty of time to prepare his horse for the start and the approach to the first fence. This includes time for the rider to decide in which canter he has to approach the first fence. For instance, if the first fence has to be jumped out of a left canter, ride in canter on a left-hand circle, pass through the starting line and approach the first fence.

All novice competitions in English-speaking countries are jumped at a speed of 300 metres per minute. During training at home one acquires a feeling for this speed. When cantering on the circle before crossing the starting line, canter exactly at a speed of 300 metres per minute. Maintain this speed while passing through the start, approaching the first fence and throughout the entire course. A uniform pace is especially important when riding through turns and when approaching a combination jump.

The entire course has to be ridden in the given speed as stated on the course plan from start to finish. Any deviation, going faster in the approach of a fence or slowing down in a turn, will break the rhythm of the ride.

If the first fence is to be jumped in the direction of the entrance or exit most novice horses clear it without problems, because they are anxious to return to the other horses in the pocket.

However, the rider should be very cautious when the first fence is jumped away from home. The same applies when passing the exit and approaching the next fence away from the exit or entrance. Not only novice horses but many older horses are very reluctant to do so.

Most young horses at this stage of competition approach fences with considerable hesitation. Therefore the rider must approach *every* fence of the course with the same determination, as if it was his last attempt after two refusals. Approach every fence at the centre, sending the horse well onto the bit and maintain this feeling in take-off, while airborne and in landing. Never trust a young horse when approaching a strange fence, especially if the horse tries to slow down during the last few strides. One has to expect a refusal or running out, but determination to clear the fences and the iron will of the rider will give the novice horse confidence. In time the young horse will jump in competitions with the same confidence and impulsion as at home in his familiar surroundings.

I always emphasise that it is wrong when schooling jumping at home to regulate the horse's strides and to place him for take-off. It would ruin, right from the beginning, the horse's initiative. He would perform more or less like a machine, not having learned to assess a difficult situation and cope with it. But in competition it is different. Under the circumstances the horse might be excited and increase his pace too much, come onto the forehand and too close to the fence. Then, of course, it is *necessary* to regulate the horse's strides and pace. Apart from such a situation, do not interfere by suddenly over-pushing or checking in approaching a fence.

I repeat (because this point is so important), in principle the rider must maintain set pace throughout the entire course. If the horse should slow down the rider must send him on energetically. He also has to adjust the pace in case the horse increases his speed too much.

For example, one should regulate the pace after clearing a spread fence or water jump, because then horses are inclined to go on the forehand for a few strides, particularly when required to jump immediately afterwards, at a short distance, an upright fence. Then it is essential to regulate the horse's pace between the two jumps otherwise the horse would come too close to the upright because the horse is not given much space to shift his weight from the forehand to the quarters to take-off. However, when regulating the horse's stride make sure to do it correctly so that the horse will not lean on the bit.

Apply, in the forward seat, half-halt aids, not when the horse is landing but during the next, and if necessary the following, canter stride at the exact moment when the leading foreleg touches the ground, *not* during the moment of suspension. When applying these aids the rider should:

(i) raise his head and breathe in deeply;

(ii) straighten his shoulders, the back slightly hollowed, and bring the upper part of his body slightly backwards. He should not drop his seat into the saddle. His weight is now slightly behind the horse's centre of gravity, which will make the horse slow down;

(iii) push down the heels strongly without touching the horse with ankle or spurs;

(iv) grip firmly with the knees and bring more weight onto the stirrups;

(v) apply strong forward driving leg aids at the same moment;

(vi) the hands are passive during the half-halt.

By applying the half-halt, as explained above, the rider sends the horse from the rear into his passive hands. The horse will shift excess weight to the quarters, thus shortening his stride to the normal length. The horse will move on a *bouncing stride* and will be light on the bit.

In competitions one can observe the most unorthodox rein aids to check and place the horse for the take-off. For example, one hand fixed on the mane and the other one pulled high

*Fig. 399*
In competition regulate the horse's stride by sending him on or by taking back a rushing horse. But in doing so apply correct half-halt aids – in the forward seat, when the leading foreleg touches the ground.

*Fig. 400*
Unorthodox method of taking back a rushing horse.

up to the rider's chest; or, one hand across the mane pushed down on the opposite side of the horse's neck, while the horse is roughly checked with the other hand. At the same time no forward driving leg aids are applied. The resultant pain in the horse's mouth will cause him to stiffen his neck and raise his head and neck unnaturally high. That is why such riders need a martingale or a severe bit. The horse will drop his back, move with his hocks wide apart and trail his hindlegs. The canter stride will become irregular or disunited.

A horse which is forced into such an unnatural position will be stiff and tense and can hardly be expected to engage his hocks for take-off. The result is, mostly, a refusal or a pole knocked down.

When competing the rider should take no chances. Maintaining the horse's (especially the novice's) impulsion even justifies keeping going if the young horse lands in the wrong, or disunited, canter for the next turn.

If the young horse is in the wrong canter while going through a turn, the rider should bend the horse's head and neck for a few seconds to the outer side of the turn and simultaneously apply strong pressure with the outer leg. In most cases the novice horse will change canter. If not, it is still better to continue at normal speed than to interrupt the round.

*Jumping a combination*

Combinations on the whole are very testing for a young horse, even if they are approached correctly.

When approaching a combination after a left-hand turn most horses are inclined to move slightly to the right, therefore one should point the horse slightly to the left side of the first element. One will then find oneself at the centre when taking-off. If one, after a left-hand turn, approaches the centre of the first element one will find that one meets the fence too far to the right and risks that the horse may run out to the right on the second element of the combination (vice versa for the approach out of a right-hand turn).

With an experienced and very honest horse one can approach a combination slightly at an angle in order to gain time in jumping against the clock. If the first element is jumped slightly on the left-hand side and the second and third element on the right-hand side, then the distance in between the elements is increased.

This approach at an angle would lead to disaster with a novice horse. If one attempted to jump the combination on a straight line at a very fast speed then the horse's stride would be too long to suit the distances in between the elements. The horse would certainly get into trouble.

Particularly with a novice horse the rider must approach the first element of a combination very accurately. If the horse makes a mistake at the take-off and puts in an extra stride he may still be able to clear the first element, but will land too short and will lose too much impulsion to reach the next element of the combination. The only solution to clear the second element is to give plenty of rein and use all one's power to send the horse forward straight after landing over the first element. This sending on, however, should be done only with leg aids and *not* with the seat. This is because when one drops into the saddle, one shifts one's weight to the horse's quarters, behind the horse's centre of gravity, which makes him lose impulsion, instead of *increasing* it. On the other hand, if the horse lands too far out over the first element he will come too close to the second element. An experienced horse should be able to pick himself up by engaging his quarters. A novice horse can only cope with this problem if one supports him by sending him strongly on into the passive hands.

Do not concentrate only on the first element of the combination, remember whilst airborne to look straight ahead at the last element. If built correctly this is slightly higher than the first and second element. By looking straight ahead one will distribute one's weight equally on both stirrups. Some riders do not do this and when landing over the first element they look down to the left (out of force of habit), shifting their entire weight onto the left stirrup. In doing so they are forcing the horse to change his centre of gravity to the left. The horse has no alternative but to land into the left canter, and this often causes the horse to run out to the left in between the elements of the combination.

Instead of jumping the elements one by one, treat the combination as a unit, jumping in a balanced pace.

If the horse loses impulsion after the first or second element, send him strongly forward on a straight line.

It is vital that the normal speed of the competition, whatever it might be, is maintained throughout a combination.

*Conclusion*

Before leaving the arena one should make it a habit to ride a circle in front of the exit. The horse will learn to pass it normally in the competition without feeling the urge to run out of the jumping enclosure.

After the horse's first few performances, do not come to a conclusion too soon as to whether or not he has potential. His performance, bad or good, will often change and is dependent on various factors such as the schooling at home in between competitions and the planning of the programme, which keeps the horse keen and improves his confidence and co-operation.

The going of the jumping enclosure has a determining influence on an individual horse's performance. For example, a horse with a short stride has less elasticity in his action, subsequently he covers less ground; or a horse who drags his feet over the ground has less mobility and spring at the moment of suspension. Therefore such horses more easily leave the ground when jumping on hard going because the hard ground supports them. Consequently they jump better on hard than on soft going; a horse with a long stride, or one whose actions show great mobility, will have greater spring and therefore will perform better when the going is deep and heavy. On hard going they are inclined to over jump, which can cause jumping faults, particularly in combinations.

### PRIX CAPRILLI COMPETITION

Riders who are schooling their horses for showjumping or three-day event competitions should first prepare their horses for Prix Caprilli competition. When the horse has received fundamental schooling in dressage and over cavaletti and small jumps, the Prix Caprilli competition is an excellent preparation for jumping or three-day events.

The competition is named after the late Italian, Captain Caprilli. Unfortunately very few of his principles and techniques were appropriately documented before his death. However his ideas and training methods are still very much alive the world over, especially in Italy.

The Prix Caprilli competition is a combination of both jumping and dressage which is performed simultaneously in the same arena. The competition is of great interest to competi tors and spectators alike.

The purpose of the Prix Caprilli is to test whether the horse has had a sound basic schooling. This is proved by the horse's freedom and ease of movement and his complete obedience to the rider's aids. The horse should be relaxed but full of confidence and attentiveness.

According to the rules of the Federation Equestre International (F.E.I.) the Prix Caprilli competition is a test of simple horsemanship, therefore demands have been kept very modest.

There are different grades:

(i) *Novice tests.* For juniors under 18 years of age and also for senior riders mounted on horses not older than six years. This test may be commanded, although it is preferable to learn the test by heart.

(ii) *Medium and open test.* For senior riders only. The competition is held (preferably) out of doors in an arena of 40 × 80 metres. The markers M, F, K and H should be placed 8 metres out of the corners, and *not* as in a dressage test where the markers should be 6 metres out of the corners.

Under F.E.I. rules the maximum height and spread are:

Novice competition:
Maximum height 0·8 metres
" spread 1·5 "
Medium competition:
Maximum height 1·0 metres
" spread 2·5 "
Open competition:
Maximum height 1·1 metres
" spread 3·0 "
Minimum height 0·8 "

The front width of the fence must not be wider than 4 metres; wings are prohibited. Ground lines are allowed in the Novice competition but prohibited in the Medium and Open.

It is recommended that fences are fair, inviting and with as much variety as possible. An upright fence should be followed up by a spread fence and should be positioned alternately in the arena, because it provides a deliberate problem for horse and rider. Only when the fences are in the correct position can the test be performed smoothly. When fences are placed near the track they should be approximately 2 metres away from the kicking boards.

If a fence has been knocked down, and if according to the test the competitor had to jump that particular fence again, then the rider can finish the phase of the dressage which he is performing, but has then to interrupt the test at the bell signal so the fence can be rebuilt.

The competition should be ridden in the *forward seat.* However, paces on two tracks in a trot or riding on a small circle should be performed in a sitting trot.

All transitions from one pace into another must be performed progressively. For example, if a transition from a canter into a walk or halt is required, one should first make a transition into a trot and then another into a walk, and from a walk into a halt.

The same applies when one is cantering on: proceed in a walk, then trot on, and then proceed into a canter.

*Fig. 401*
What the judge looks for. Horse and rider in perfect style.

*Judging the dressage*

Since it is very difficult for one person to judge the dressage and jumping at the same time it is advisable to have at least one judge for each section.

The judge for jumping judges the horse from the moment he is approaching a fence before take-off until a few strides after landing, when the next movement commences. The remaining performances should be judged by the judge for dressage.

The main points of his judging are: that the horse moves in a natural free balanced pace and carries his head in a natural position. His neck should be long, the highest point at the poll and the nose being always in *front* of the vertical line. It is considered a very grave mistake if the horse carries his nose behind – or even in a vertical – position. The horse has to perform in a balanced manner in all paces, having a light contact with the rider's hands. The horse's movements should be lively and easy and his back should give an elastic impression.

When performing a circle in front of a fence the rider should do this in such a way that the horse is still able to approach the fence in the centre and out of a straight line.

If requested to ride a circle around a fence, then the fence should be in the centre of the circle. The diameter should be 10 metres, the front width of the fence plus 3 metres on either side.

Circles on the track and in front of a fence should be ridden with a 6 metres diameter. These small circles are ridden in a *sitting* trot, proceeding from a horse length before until a horse length after the circle.

When the rider, according to the programme, has to approach a jump in a trot, then it is *not* considered a mistake if a horse extends his trot or breaks into a canter a few strides in front of the fence (approximately 7 metres), but it must be done smoothly and without any stiffness.

If the rider, after clearing a jump, has to make a transition into a trot or a walk, this should be done gradually and without any rough aids. If the rider has to continue in canter but has landed in the wrong canter for the next dressage movement it is *not* to be considered a fault, providing the rider notices the mistake, makes a transition into a trot and strikes off in the correct canter.

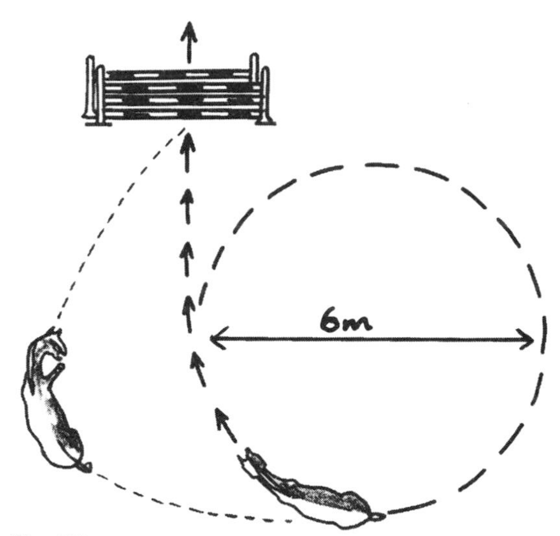


*Fig. 402*
Riding a circle in front of a fence. The correct course (arrowed) and the incorrect (dotted line).

If, according to the programme, the canter has to be changed after clearing a fence and the horse has already done so during the jump, then the rider should continue his test in that canter. Nevertheless, if the rider does not feel that the horse has already landed in the correct canter and makes a transition into a trot to continue again in the same canter, then he has shown that he lacks feeling and points will be deducted by the dressage judge.

*Judging the jumping*

The task for the judge for jumping is an extremely difficult one and demands a very experienced eye, because during the very short moment of the actual jump the judge has to not only observe the horse's jumping technique but also the rider's seat, leg and the position of his body and hands. What he is looking for:

(i) *In the horse.* The horse should move in balance, with a rhythmic tempo in pace and be light on the bit. If the horse rushes into the fences it shows he is nervous. This mistake has to be accounted for in the final adjudication.

After clearing the fence the horse should continue in an even rhythm without extending his pace or leaning on the bit. The style with which the horse jumps the fences, is more important than how high he jumps. The horse should jump as if he were jumping loose (without the encumbrance of a rider) with a long neck, a low head position and a well rounded back.

When trotting over the cavaletti (trot distance approximately 1·3 metres) the horse should carry his head and neck low, the nose well forward and he should lift his legs higher than when moving on the flat. Ride over the cavaletti in a slow trot in forward seat, not in a rising or sitting trot.

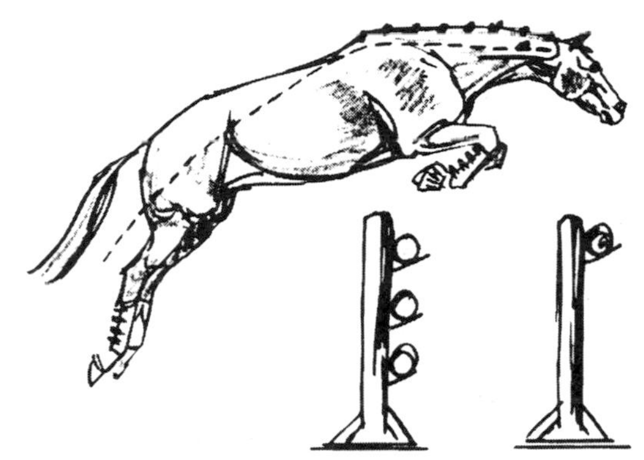

*Fig. 403*
A beautifully executed *bascule* (rounding his back).

(ii) *In the rider.* The performance of the rider while jumping is even more difficult to judge. The judge should take special notice of the following points: the rider has to keep his heels down and knees and calves close to the horse, showing a correct lower leg and heel position; in all three phases of the jump the legs should remain in the same correct position; if the heels go up, the knee will go up as well and the balance of the forward seat will be disturbed.

If the lower leg moves forward, the rider's seat moves backwards and the rider is left behind, disturbing the balance of the horse.

*Fig. 404*
Judging the rider's seat. Correct leg position, hands free of the neck following the horse's mouth.

*Fig. 405*
Incorrect. The rider left behind, legs too much forward, hands fixed on the mane and no contact with the mouth.

*Fig. 406*
Incorrect. The rider falls forward, legs slip backwards, hands fixed, no contact with the mouth.

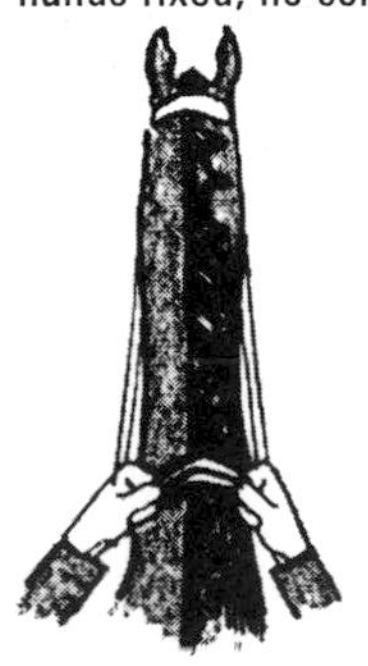

*Fig. 407*
Incorrect. Making a "bridge" with the reins means the hands are fixed.

*Fig. 408*
Incorrect. The rider sits down while landing, thus disturbing the horse and causing jumping faults with the hindlegs.

*Fig. 409*
Perfect. Even when landing the rider's seat does not touch the saddle.

*Fig. 410*
The rider has been left behind, but is trying to save the situation by letting the reins slip through, thus giving the horse a chance to use his neck and reach for the spread of the fence.

If the rider rounds his back and drops his head it also shows that he is left behind.

In neither jumping phase, not even in the third one, should the seat bones touch the saddle. It would put too much weight on the horse and prevent him from using his back.

The rider's hands should follow the movement of the horse's mouth, alongside and *free* of the horse's neck. The lower arm and reins should form *one* continual line towards the horse's mouth. Fixing the hands on the horse's neck or using the so-called "bridge" limits the freedom of the horse's neck. This is one of the biggest mistakes the rider can make.

While jumping, especially combinations, the rider should maintain a light contact with the horse's mouth. Dropping the reins suddenly before take-off, thus losing contact, brings the horse off balance instantly and is completely wrong.

The hands should never be pushed forward on top of the mane towards the horse's ears. It shows that the rider's seat is not balanced because he is looking for support.

Even in the third phase of the jump, when landing, the rider is not allowed to fix his hands on the horse's neck. The reins should always have the same length and not slip through the fingers, except if the horse lost balance or if the rider is left behind. Then the rider has to give as much rein as possible so the horse can help himself out of the difficult situation.

These are the most common faults of the rider's seat position when jumping. However, an experienced judge will observe many more mistakes.

*Marking*

As laid down in the regulations of the F.E.I., the marks awarded for dressage and jumping of horse and rider are in a relation of 2:1:1 – 100 points given for dressage = 50 points given for jumping of the rider + 50 points given for jumping of the horse.

Every judge can award from 0–10 marks: 0 being the worst mark and 10 being the best mark. In the test are the following abbreviations:

DR = dressage

JR = jumping rider

JH = jumping horse

JF = jumping faults

From the points awarded for the jumping of the horse, penalty points for jumping faults have to be deducted:

| Penalties – jumping | |
|---|---|
| Obstacle knocked down | 1 point |
| Refusal (run out, etc) | 3 points |
| Fall of horse and/or rider | 5 points |

Whip and spurs may be carried. The use of bandages, brushing boots and overreach boots are allowed. As a rule the test should be ridden in a plain but thick ordinary snaffle, the same one as used in a novice dressage test. If the competitors want to compete with a different bit the rule is that a fixed number of points should be deducted beforehand.

There are at least 12 original Prix Caprilli competitions available. In case there are difficulties in obtaining the originals one can easily compose a competition oneself. It is, however, most important that the test is well balanced, equally difficult on both reins and, on the whole, the purpose of the competition must be considered.

PRIX CAPRILLI NOVICE TEST

| | | DR | JR | JH |
|---|---|---|---|---|
| 1. | Enter at B at ordinary walk; at X halt and salute; proceed at ordinary walk; at E turn right; between E–H ordinary trot; a circle around fence No. 1 | 10 | | |
| 2. | Past B turn right; trot over four cavaletti (forward seat position); fence No. 2; at E halt; immobility four seconds; proceed ordinary trot | 10 | 10 | 10 |
| 3. | Change rein from M to K; at X change diagonal (leg); circle around fence No. 1; at H turn left and jump fence No. 3 (landing in the right canter) and arriving on track turn right; between B and F rising trot; between F and A walk | 10 | 10 | 10 |
| 4. | Halt at A; rein back four strides; proceed at ordinary trot | 10 | | |
| 5. | From K to H extended trot; in the corner after H proceed at ordinary canter right | 20 | | |
| 6. | Circle around fence No. 1; past A turn right and jump fence No. 4 (landing in the right canter); at C ordinary trot; from M to K change rein; at X change diagonal (leg) | 10 | 10 | 10 |
| 7. | From F to M extended trot; in the corner after M proceed at ordinary canter left | 20 | | |
| 8. | Circle around fence No. 4; past A turn left and jump fence No. 1 (landing in the left canter); at H turn left and jump fence No. 3 (landing in the left canter); arriving on the track turn left | 10 | 10<br>10 | 10<br>10 |
| 9. | At C ordinary trot; halt at E, rein back four strides; proceed at ordinary trot | 10 | | |
| 10. | Past E turn left; trot over the four cavaletti (forward seat position); fence No. 2; at B turn left; at X halt and salute; proceed at ordinary walk; turn right at E and leave arena on a *loose* rein | 10 | 10 | 10 |
| | TOTALS DR | 120 | 60 | 60 |
| | JR | 60 | | |
| | JH | 60 | | |
| | | 240 | | |
| | JF | 0 | | |
| | TOTALS | 240 | | |

### PRIX CAPRILLI MEDIUM TEST

Maximum points: 240. Time: 9½ minutes. Fences 1, 2 and 3 consisting of two cavaletti each. Distance between fences 6 and 5 is 6·5 metres.

| | | DR | JR | JH |
|---|---|---|---|---|
| 1. | Enter at B in ordinary trot; at X halt and salute; proceed at ordinary trot; at E turn left; at K ordinary walk; at A ordinary trot | 10 | | |
| 2. | F–M extended trot; at M ordinary trot | 10 | | |
| 3. | At C halt; four seconds immobility; proceed at orindary trot; turn left and in a serpentine over fences 1, 2 and 3 (in forward seat) | 10 | 10 | 10 |
| 4. | Ride a circle around fences 4 and 7, then jump fence 4; arriving at the back turn right; at E halt; rein back four steps; proceed at ordinary trot | 10 | 10 | 10 |
| 5. | Turn right and jump fences 5 and 6, land in left canter; arriving at the track turn left, still in canter | 10 | 10 | 10 |
| 6. | H–K extended canter; K ordinary canter | 10 | | |
| 7. | Circle around fences 4 and 7; change rein F–E; on the centre line transition to ordinary trot; at E ordinary canter right | 10 | | |
| 8. | M–F extended canter; F ordinary canter | 10 | | |
| 9. | Circle around fences 4 and 7; at E halt (progressive transition); four seconds immobility; proceed at ordinary trot; in the next corner ordinary canter | 10 | | |
| 10. | After B turn right; jump fence 7; land in right canter; arriving at the track turn right; at C halt; rein back four steps; proceed at ordinary trot | 10 | 10 | 10 |
| 11. | Change rein M–K (change diagonals at X) canter on in next corner; after B turn left and jump fences 6 and 5; land in left canter; arriving at track turn left | 10 | 10 | 10 |
| 12. | After E turn left; jump fence 4; land in left canter; transition to trot and walk; at B turn left; at X halt and salute; proceed at ordinary walk; at E turn right; leave arena on a *loose* rein | 10 | 10 | 10 |
| | DR | 120 | 60 | 60 |
| | JR | 60 | | |
| | JH | 60 | | |
| | TOTALS | 240 | | |
| | No jumping faults | 0 | | |
| | TOTALS | 240 | | |

PRIX CAPRILLI OFFICIAL TEST

Maximum: 200 points. Time: 11½ minutes

| | | DR | JR | JH |
|---|---|---|---|---|
| 1. | Enter at A; ordinary canter; at G halt and salute; proceed at ordinary walk; at C turn left | 5 | | |
| 2. | As S turn left past letter I; a figure of eight around fences No. 1 and 2 | 5 | | |
| 3. | At letter I direction X in ordinary trot; at L turn left and a figure of eight around fences 3 and 4 | 5 | | |
| 4. | At D canter right | 5 | | |
| 5. | At A turn right; past A turn to the right and jump fence No. 4; arriving on the B–E line turn right; at X change into the left canter; after X turn left and jump fence No. 1; proceed in ordinary trot; arriving on the track turn left | | 5<br>5 | 5<br>5 |
| 6. | At C halt; rein back four steps; proceed ordinary walk | 5 | | |
| 7. | At H ordinary trot; at S turn left; past letter I and turn right; ordinary canter right; jump fences No. 3 and 5; arriving back on the track turn right | 5<br>5 | 5<br>5 | 5<br>5 |
| 8. | From K till a horse length before M extended canter; at M ordinary canter and immediately turn right; before arriving the track half circle right | 10 | | |
| 9. | Past G and turn right; jump fence No. 1; arriving on the B–E line turn right; at X change into the left canter and turn left and jump fence No. 4; arriving on the track turn left at an ordinary trot | 5 | 5<br>5 | 5<br>5 |

| | | | | |
|---|---|---|---|---|
| 10. | At R half circle and (appuyer) on "two tracks"; sitting trot to B; immediately half circle and (appuyer) "two tracks"; sitting trot to R | 5<br>5 | | |
| 11. | At C ordinary canter left; from H – K extended canter; at K ordinary canter; at F turn left; before arriving the track half circle left | 10 | | |
| 12. | Past D and turn left; jump fences No. 5, 3 and 1; arriving on the track, turn right ordinary trot | 5<br>5 | 20 | 20 |
| 13. | From M – E extended trot; at E ordinary trot; at C ordinary walk | 5 | | |
| 14. | From M - K change rein at an extended walk; at K ordinary walk | 5 | | |
| 15. | At A turn down centre; at G halt and salute; leave arena on a *loose* rein | 5 | | |
| 16. | Position and seat of the rider and correct application of the aids | 5 | | |
| | | 100 | 50 | 50 |
| | JR | 50 | | |
| | JH | 50 | | |
| | TOTALS | 200 | | |
| | JF | 0 | | |
| | TOTALS | 200 | | |

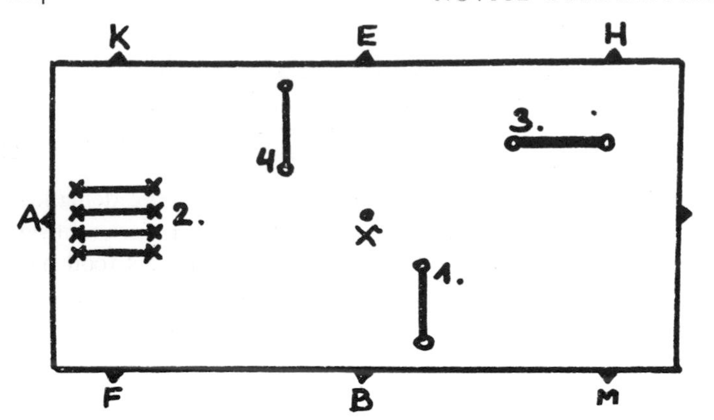


*Fig. 411*
Prix Caprilli Novice Test.

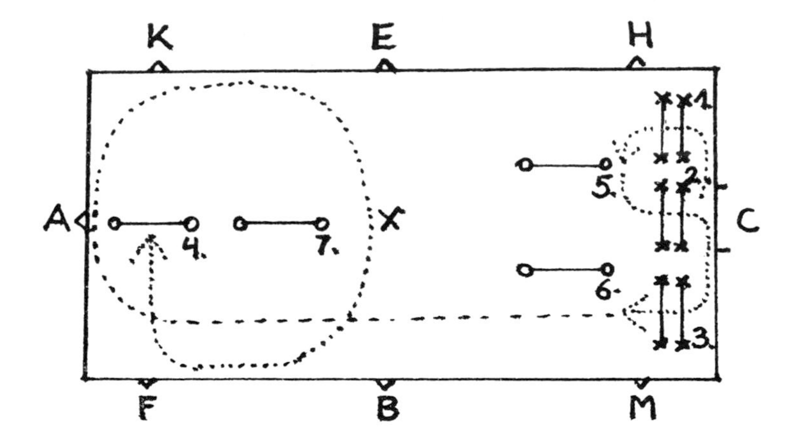


*Fig. 412*
Prix Caprilli Medium Test.

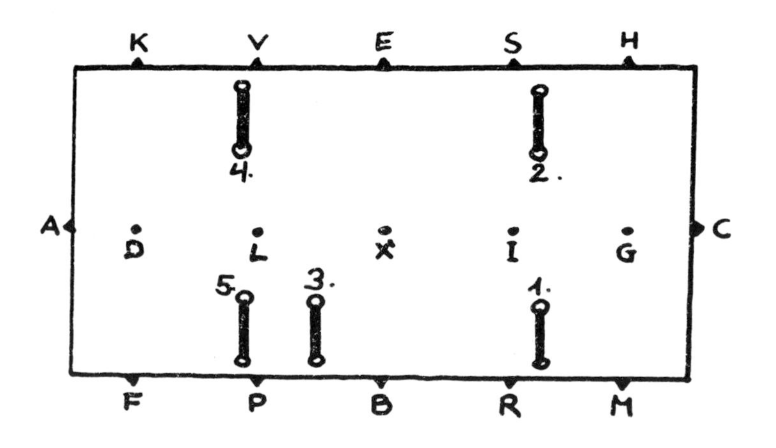


*Fig. 413*
Prix Caprilli Official Test.

SCHOOLING BETWEEN COMPETITIONS

Which type of schooling the horse needs in between competitions depends entirely on the performance he gave in the previous competitions. If the horse competes regularly and successfully one should jump at home as little as possible, particularly when the going is hard or very heavy.

One should practise only those fences at which the horse is not yet good enough, perhaps an upright, an oxer, a water jump or a combination. If the horse has difficulty in finding the correct take-off point at certain obstacles it is advisable to practise these *unmounted* in the jumping lane, but not more than twice a week.

Should the horse jump well while schooling at home, stop immediately after a good jump; do not go on and on, thinking that by doing so the horse will remember the lesson better. The horse would only get exhausted, knock his legs, run out or start refusing. Should one make the mistake of arriving at such a point, one cannot finish and bring the horse into the stable with this unpleasant memory. One has to give the horse a break and afterwards ask him to jump an easier fence so that one can be sure that the horse will jump well and that the lesson can be finished with a happy end. Besides it being a waste of time and energy on the part of the horse and oneself, such overschooling has a bad mental effect on the horse. Knowing when to stop is one of the secrets in schooling show-jumpers.

In addition to a minimum of jumping, the horse needs more advanced dressage between the competitions. Quiet roadwork should not be neglected either in order to harden the horse's legs in preparation for jumping on hard ground during the summer. The horse's jumping technique should also be improved, any disobedience corrected in between competitions and the speed course should be used regularly to keep the horse fit.

In order to increase the physical condition of horse and rider, build a small upright fence, an oxer and a combination on the speed course. Now and again the horse should jump these fences in his stride at a regular speed of 300 metres per minute without increasing the pace in approaching the fences or after landing over them.

During the jumping season, as the demands on the horse increase, his physical condition becomes very important. The horse's food has to be changed, the amount of oats increased and the hay must be reduced in proportion, because overloading the stomach could interfere with the horse's wind.

The intelligent and experienced trainer will avoid upgrading the horse too soon but leave him for the first year in the same grade. Taking advantage of the horse's great potential during the first season is a great mistake. If there is a danger that the horse may upgrade too soon, compete once a week and if the horse has jumped clear in the first round, retire – leaving the horse with a happy memory.

It is not advisable to stop competing for weeks because this would interfere with the systematic education and development of the horse.

It is sensible that the novice horse competes regularly and ends his first season improving gradually. He should have won only so much in order that he still qualifies to start the second season in low grade competition. It is wrong management to upgrade a novice horse too quickly, because the horse is then forced to start the second season (after the winter break) in the higher grade.

After the outdoor jumping season ends, in most countries at the end of September, the young horse should not be requested to jump for the following three winter months. During these three months one should ride the horse daily and do alternately a little hacking, lungeing and dressage.

One should also exercise the horse in the speed course. The exercises should be varied from day to day in order that the horse keeps an interest in his work, remains in good condition and stays right in the wind. Weather permitting, one should also turn the horse out for a couple of hours a day.

*Do not overwork the horse*

This warning cannot be repeated often enough. An apple on a tree needs time to ripen. Similarly, when schooling a horse much time is necessary. Improvisations and short cuts lead to chaotic performances and good results can only be accidental. Today everyone is in a hurry, and most people are over anxious to see quick results. They have a tendency to push a young horse in *half a year* through a *two year* schooling programme.

This cannot work because each and every day of the two year schooling programme is meaningful and part of a system which has to be complete to enable the young horse to grow up in his work.

If a horse is pushed in the beginning of his schooling the harmful effects may not be immediately obvious, because the willing young horse is doing his best and showing great promise. Some riders give in to the temptation and jump the young horse again and again. This is very shortsighted. A horse, over jumped to exhaustion, will not keep on winning year after year. It is a pity that some riders do not realise what they are doing wrong until it is too late. Particularly in the jump off against the clock, the pace becomes unbalanced, it flattens the horse, he comes too much onto the forehand and it will not take long before he will make jumping faults.

I have seen so many promising young horses upgraded too soon, and after two or three seasons many of these potential showjumpers were still at the same level or even lower.

One is also overfacing a young showjumping horse if one asks him to compete in all kinds of competitions: in point-to-point races, hunting, three-day events . . . and in showjumping.

Each branch of equitation requires a development of special muscles in the horse; it is impossible to perform with the same horse equally successfully in various fields of equitation.

CHAPTER THIRTEEN

# ADVANCED JUMPING-DRESSAGE

DURING the second year of schooling (the first jumping season), in between competitions, the horse is schooled further in jumping-dressage. Repeat the dressage exercises of the first year of schooling.

Depending on the horse's progress one can gradually introduce more advanced exercises. The horse should constantly be improved in dressage in order to improve his athletic ability, his obedience and to obtain absolute control over the horse's mind and action.

In time a perfect understanding between horse and rider should be achieved and the various dressage movements should be obtained with unnoticeable aids without apparent effort of the rider.

## COLLECTION

A skilled trainer will only start to collect a young horse when the horse is able to move in a perfectly balanced manner.

The horse has undergone the various progessive phases of the Natural Training Method, he has been allowed to loosen up on a long rein to find his balance and he has been made laterally flexible alternately on both sides. Therefore the horse will now enter the last phase well prepared and will collect easily.

This is most important for a showjumper, as it can be achieved in the forward seat as well without waste of energy of either horse or rider.

### *The aids*

(1) *Weight aids.* During the transition straighten the shoulders, "grow" in the saddle, transfer your weight slightly behind the horse's centre of gravity; this will slow down the horse.

(2) *Leg aids.* The horse in the earlier stages has been taught to move the quarters sideways during transitions when the rider applied stronger pressure with *one* leg behind the girths. At the same time, and on the same side, the horse brought *one* hindleg further underneath his body. The engaging of one hindleg alternately has made the horse gradually stronger and supple in the rib part and developed those muscles which will enable the horse now to bring *both* hindlegs under simultaneously, without effort, tension or strain.

The "one-sided" aids are now applied on "both" sides simultaneously, in conjunction with strong seat pressure. In the very early stages apply the leg aids extra far behind the girths to make the horse more attentive and to prevent any deviation of the engaged quarters. (To obtain extra engagement of the quarters one can later on touch the croup gently with the dressage whip to emphasise the aid.)

After a while, depending on the horse's sensitiveness, there will be no more need to apply exaggerated leg aids behind the girths. The leg aids, applied in the normal region, will then be sufficient to bring the horse into collection.

(3) *Rein aids.* As the horse has been taught to respond to the half-halt aids he will, when sent into the passive hands, make a submission and flex his lower jaw, whereupon one immediately should apply the third rein aid, slightly opening and closing one's fingers like squeezing and unsqueezing a sponge.

Developing this sensitive equestrian feeling is so important. One actually eases the passiveness of the hands as soon as one feels the horse's "*intention*" *to slow down.* Then one repeats this movement, if necessary a few times. In other words, one gives a series of half-halt aids.

Do *not* wait with easing the hands until the horse has actually slowed down. It might take the young horse a few strides to achieve this, and if one should wait until the horse has actually slowed down one's hands would be "dead", without feeling, giving the horse a dead mouth, teaching him to lean on the bit and poke his nose. Remember: *Pressure creates pressure.*

The expression "passive hands" means that the hands stop following the natural nodding movement of the horse's head as they should do in walk and canter. The hands do not pull backwards but just become "passive" and do not move at all. Because they are not moving anymore they are slightly restricting the natural nodding movement of the horse's head.

Practise collecting the horse *first* after coming to a halt from an active walk. The horse should stand well on the bit, square, with his weight distributed evenly over all four legs, his quarters engaged. The horse should champ the bit while the rider is maintaining a light contact.

At the initial stage it is sufficient if the horse only *stands* collected for a few seconds. Afterwards, one yields the reins completely and moves forward in an active walk.

The second phase is now – after coming to a halt from an active walk – not only to stand still, but to proceed at a walk, maintaining the collection for a few strides. After this one again yields the reins completely and moves forward at an energetic walk.

The strides in a collected walk, after the halt, are gradually increased in number. If the horse responds smoothly without tension or resistance one should apply the same aids during a transition from a slow sitting trot into a collected walk, and later from a slow canter into a collected sitting trot. At the beginning, always for a few strides only, all transitions should be made smoothly and never abruptly.

Collecting a horse during and after a transition into a slower pace ensures at this stage of schooling a smoother collection, because one takes advantage of the propulsive force of the faster pace which forces the horse automatically to bring his hocks underneath his body. At this stage it would be more difficult to collect a horse during one of the three paces.

This would be the next logical phase in schooling a horse to collection. First at a walk *only*, which is more than sufficient, and never for too long a period, as that would certainly create resistance and tension. In all collected paces the horse's mobility should be increased without losing impulsion or regularity in the

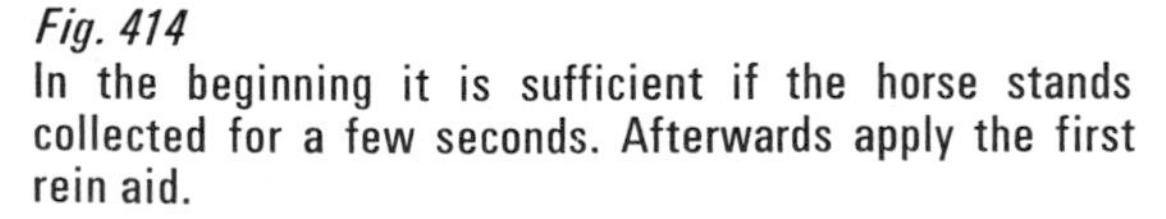

*Fig. 414*
In the beginning it is sufficient if the horse stands collected for a few seconds. Afterwards apply the first rein aid.

pace or leaning on the bit. This proves that the horse has reached proficiency in collecting.

In time every horse will go collected easily in all paces when it is done without any kind of force or increasing the tension on the bit.

The slight flexion of the horse's lower jaw (without nervousness) is the criterion of obedience and harmonious distribution of the horse's energy and weight. Any excess weight from the forehand is transferred to the quarters, which will be lowered and engaged. The horse will arch his neck more, which will form a harmonious curve from the withers to the poll. The poll should be the highest point. The nose must be, under all circumstances, slightly in front of the vertical line. When the horse is forced into collection with running reins he is often behind the bit, which, of course, is a grave mistake.

Collect a young horse only towards the end of a schooling session. Also the advanced horse should first be warmed-up and ridden well forward before one collects him.

After each session in a collected pace the horse should be "rewarded" by being ridden actively forward on a completely loose rein, supported by strong forward driving aids.

Many people start too soon to collect their young horses, forcing them into an unnatural position for their stage of training. The young horse stiffens and instead of lowering and engaging his quarters he will drop his back, widen his hocks and become heavier on the bit, thereby losing his rhythmic tempo in pace and balance. He will increase his pace and either go behind or over the bit.

If difficulties arise when collecting a horse one has started too soon without having the horse properly prepared. One has to go back to the basic training programme and improve the horse's lateral flexibility first.

The well schooled showjumper must be so responsive to the rider's aids, that he can also be collected easily in the forward seat. The rider applies the same aids, as explained, with the only difference being that he is *not* sitting in the saddle, or riding sitting trot. Instead, he remains in the forward seat applying a series of half-halts. The rider transfers weight to the horse's quarters by straightening up in the forward seat. Leg, and rein, aids are the same as in the dressage seat.

### SHOULDER-IN

The movements on two tracks (lateral movements) include the shoulder-out, leg yielding, shoulder-in, travers, renvers and the half-pass. All movements on two tracks improve the horse's lateral flexibility, supple the quarters and give more freedom of movement to the shoulders.

The easiest of the movements on two tracks is the shoulder-out. While doing the shoulder-out the horse is facing the kicking boards and is, thereby, prevented from taking a stronger hold on the bit.

Next, the horse has learned leg yielding, which is similar to the shoulder-out movement, only that it is performed free of the track allowing a little more forward movement. Both these exercises are learned during the first year of the horse's schooling.

Now the horse is well prepared to learn the shoulder-in movement. This is exactly the same as the shoulder-out, the *only* difference being that when performed in an arena the horse is now facing the open arena while the quarters move along the kicking boards. This fact makes the shoulder-in movement more difficult than shoulder-out, because the kicking boards are no longer restricting the horse's forward movement and the horse has to be so well schooled that the rider's hand can restrict the forward movement without having to take a stronger hold.

When starting to teach the horse shoulder-in it is only natural that the young horse will try to move more forward than sideways, this to evade the lateral bending of his body and engagement of this inner hindleg. Do *not* try to prevent this by taking a stronger hold on the bit, but maintain this forward-sideways impulsion. At this initial stage be satisfied with only four to six strides of shoulder-in, during which the horse may move about 2 metres forward, away from the track. Be patient, because in time, when the horse is able to engage his quarters and inner

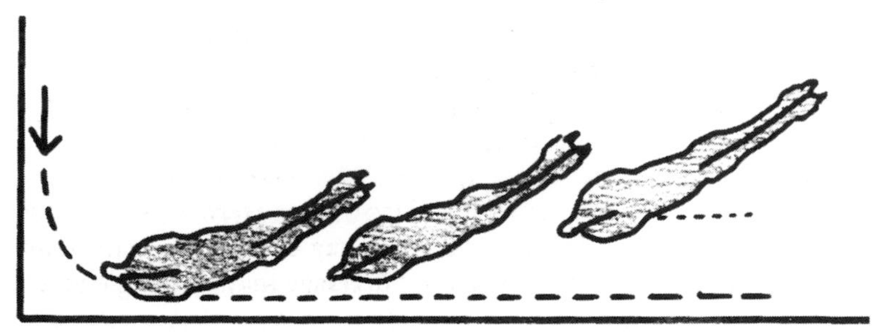

*Fig. 415*
When starting the shoulder-in exercise, the horse is allowed to move slightly more forward.

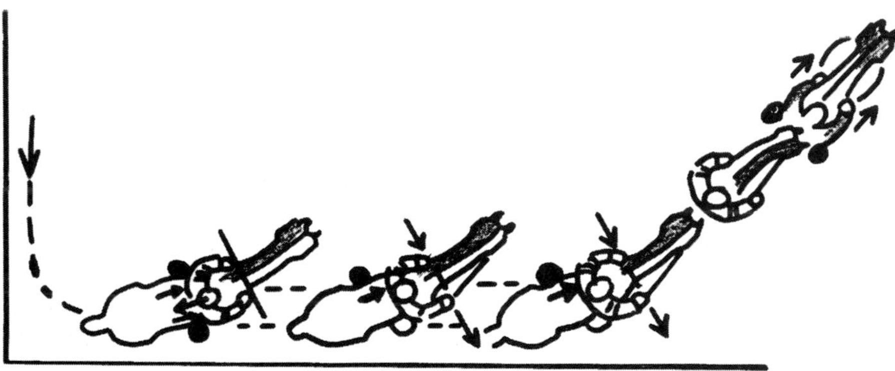

*Fig. 416*
Preparatory leg aids when teaching the shoulder-in movement. No lateral bending in the ribs.

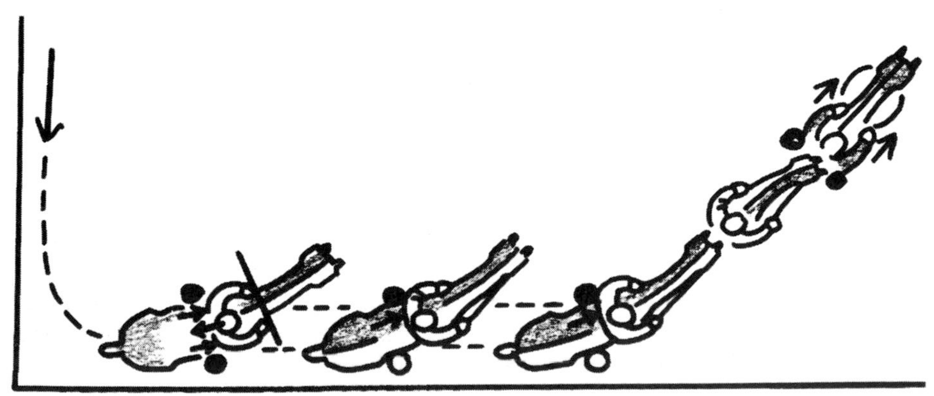

*Fig. 417*
Gradually change over to the normal leg aids, with lateral bending from head to tail.

hindleg and is more flexible laterally, he will then also be able to move on two tracks without moving forward towards the centre of the school.

There is a distinct difference between the *preparation* for shoulder-out and for shoulder-in.

Preparing the horse for shoulder-out one has *to cut-off the corner* coming from the short side of the school, so that the horse is at the correct angle when arriving at the long side.

Preparing for shoulder-in one rides *as deep as possible into the corner*. When coming out of the corner proceed with the shoulder-in when the horse's forelegs are free of the track and his hindlegs still on the track.

This is a suitable position to begin the exercise because the horse is already at the correct angle.

*The aids*

For shoulder-in the aids are exactly the same as for shoulder-out, except that *the preparation*, as mentioned previously, is different. When riding on the left-hand rein prepare the horse with a half-halt aid after leaving the corner. Look slightly to the left in the direction from where you came. Shift your weight to the horse's inner hindleg. Depending on the horse's sensitiveness and intelligence, *lead* the horse with the right hand, moving sideways out from the neck, supported by the left rein pushing against the neck. Maintain the *same* contact with *both* reins.

The leg aids at this stage are again preparatory aids and slightly different than when riding a well-schooled horse. To indicate to the horse the sideways movement of the shoulder-in it may be necessary to apply a stronger pressure with the left leg slightly further behind the girths than usual. The right leg is on the girths to maintain impulsion. At this stage the shoulder-in is more or less *only* a sideways movement without a significant lateral bending of the horse's body.

In time, however, the leg aids are "normalised", in other words applied in the appropriate region. The horse's whole body will then be bent laterally inwards from head to tail around the rider's inner leg, which will then be positioned *on* the girths supported by the right leg *behind* the girths.

The horse's body should only be at an angle of 30° to the track, otherwise the horse cannot maintain impulsion, balance and rhythm and will brush his legs. The exercise should be executed at the same angle of 30° on both reins. Only in high-class dressage may this angle reach 45°. But when schooling a young horse anything more than 30° would ruin the horse's balance and impulsion.

If the shoulder-in exercise is correctly executed then the horse's inner lateral pair of legs pass *and* cross in front of the outer lateral pair of legs. The horse's body is bent *away* from the direction in which he is moving. After some four to six strides shoulder-in, straighten the horse and apply the first rein aid.

Take advantage of the impulsion acquired by the engaged quarters and inner hindleg by sending the horse energetically straight forward on a loose rein, riding towards the centre of the school. Change rein and repeat the exercise on the right-hand rein.

Practise the shoulder-in alternately on both reins but only for a few strides. Stop immediately in case the horse becomes tense, irregular in pace and heavy in the hand. It is a sign that the horse is not ready yet to perform the shoulder-in and one will have to go back to the shoulder-out for a while.

One should remember to always ride an energetic extended trot on a straight line in between *all* movements on two tracks in order to maintain impulsion and to prevent a horse from turning sour.

## TRAVERS

This is a movement on two tracks, where the horse moves forward-sideways with the head towards the kicking boards, similar to shoulder-out, but with the difference that in travers the horse is bent laterally into the direction where he is going.

*Preparing* the horse for shoulder-out on the left-hand rein, one cuts off the corner and the

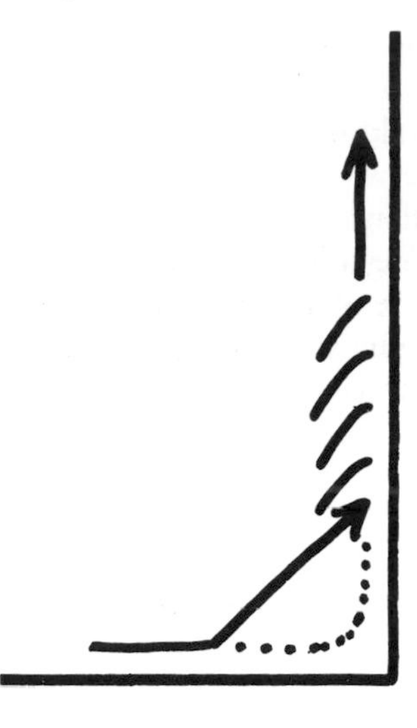

*Fig. 418*
When doing shoulder-out, cut off the corner, then move on two tracks to the left – bent to the right.

*Fig. 420*
When doing *travers,* cut off the corner slightly, then move on two tracks to the left – bent to the left.

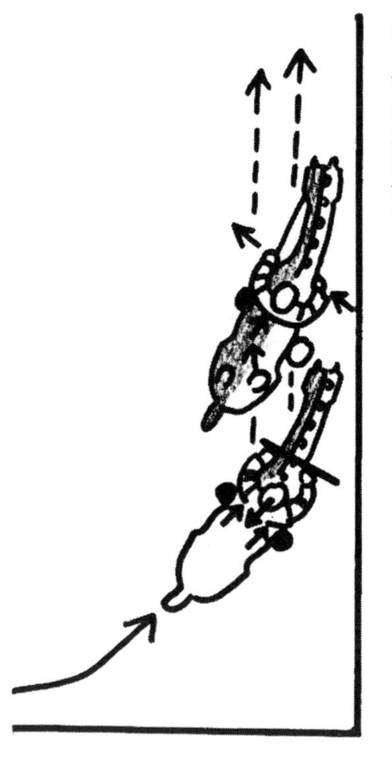

*Fig. 419*
*Travers.* After cutting off the corner apply a half-halt when arriving on the track. Apply *travers* aids and the horse will move on two tracks to the left, bent laterally to the left.

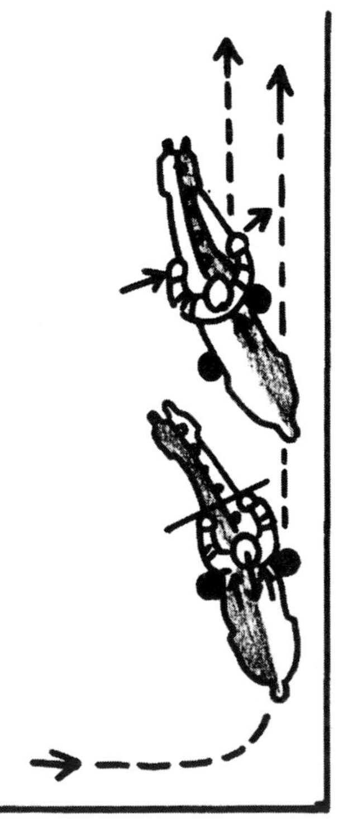

*Fig. 421*
*Renvers.* After riding deep into the corner apply a half-halt when coming out of the corner, the quarters still on the track. Apply *renvers* aids and the horse will move on two tracks to the right, bent laterally to the right.

horse moves on two tracks to the left, while his body is bent laterally to the right.

*Preparing* for *travers*, one also cuts off the corner slightly, but the horse maintains a slight flexion to the left and moves on two tracks to the left. The horse's whole body is bent laterally around one's inner leg. The neck should never be bent *more* than the rest of the horse's body. The forehand should precede the quarters. When riding on the left-hand rein the right lateral pair of legs pass and cross in front of the left lateral pair of legs.

*The aids*

One commences the exercise with the half-halt aids when the horse's head reaches the track, shifting one's weight towards the left in the direction where one is moving.

One's left (inner) leg is positioned on the girths to maintain impulsion. One's right leg is behind the girths, bending the horse around the inner leg and moving the quarters slightly away from the track.

One brings the left-hand (more or less) sideways away from the horse's neck to guide the horse and to obtain a slight flexion of the neck to the left, supporting this by pushing the right rein against the neck. At the beginning, *travers* should be executed only at a walk and one should be content with only four to six strides at a time. Whatever the pace may be later on in a more advanced stage it must always be regular, maintaining balance and impulsion in spite of the sidewards movement.

### RENVERS

In theory, just as with shoulder-in and shoulder-out, there is no difference between *travers* and *renvers* if either are performed along the margin of the school. When performed along the kicking boards, however, in *travers* the horse's forelegs move on the track and in *renvers* the horse's hindlegs move on that track with the tail towards the kicking boards. In both movements horse and rider look in the direction where they are moving. When riding on the left-hand rein, for instance, the left lateral pair of legs pass and cross in front of the right lateral pair of legs. The horse moves at an angle of up to 30° with the track.

Preparing the horse for *renvers* is to a certain extent similar to preparing a horse for shoulder-in, one also rides deeper into the corner. Coming out of the corner, apply half-halt aids and straighten the horse. When his forelegs are beside the track and the hindlegs still on the track commence the *renvers* movement.

*The aids*

One shifts one's weight into the direction where the horse is going. Bend the horse laterally around one's inner (right) leg, which is positioned on the girths, maintaining the impulsion, while the left leg is behind the girths to control the degree of lateral bending and to prevent the quarters from moving sideways.

At the beginning of schooling *renvers* bring the right-hand slightly out – sideways – from the horse's neck in order to obtain a slight flexion of head and neck and to lead the horse sideways. This is supported by the left rein pushing against the neck. Equal contact should be maintained on both reins. The aids for the *renvers* are therefore the same as for the *travers*.

I repeat, to clarify the difference between the difficult movements on two tracks the differences are:

(i) in shoulder-out and shoulder-in horse and rider look in the direction from where they are coming and the horse is bent laterally in that direction;

(ii) in travers and renvers horse and rider look in the direction in which they are going and the horse is bent laterally in that direction. That is what makes this exercise so difficult.

### HALF-PASS

The half-pass movement (in French, *appuyer* =to lean) is an exercise which insists that the

*Fig. 422*
The half pass.

horse moves obliquely forward and is flexed towards the direction in which he is moving.

The half-pass is similar to *travers* and *renvers*, only this movement is performed free of the track. The difference is that the lateral flexion of the horse's body in the half-pass is very slight when compared with *travers*, *renvers*, shoulder-in and shoulder-out, in which the lateral bending of the horse's body is more evident. When schooling half-pass, commence the exercise first at a walk and at the far end of the long side of the school.

If the horse has succeeded in performing leg yielding at the walk and the trot without difficulty, and if he has accomplished the *travers* and *renvers*, then the half-pass movement will be undemanding.

One prepares the horse for this movement. For instance, when on the left-hand rein ride on a circle of approximately 6 metres diameter, then circle once or twice and emphasise that the horse's body is flexed laterally inwards around one's inner (left) leg on the girths. The right leg is positioned behind the girths. Before leaving the circle, half way round, apply a distinct half-halt aid to create that extra activity and engagement of the quarters.

From this point the horse should move at an angle in half-pass back towards the track.

*The aids*

Maintain a slight lateral flexion of the horse's body towards the direction in which the horse is

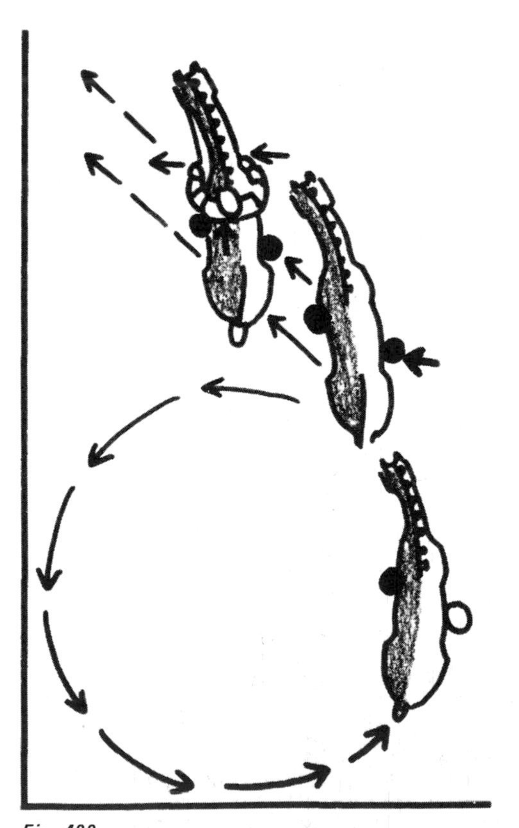

*Fig. 423*
The half pass is similar to the *travers* and *renvers*, but is performed free of the track, and with less lateral bending.

moving, giving the horse increased freedom of movement of his right shoulder. Horse and rider should both look in the direction to where the horse is moving – to the left. The rider should shift his weight in the same direction in harmony with his horse. Bring the left hand slightly out sideways from the neck, guiding the horse to the left, and push the right rein against the neck, preventing excessive flexion. Apply increased pressure with the right leg further behind the girths to move the horse sideways, while the left leg remains active on the girths, reinforcing the all important impulsion. The forehand should be slightly ahead of the quarters. While on the left-hand rein the horse's near foreleg touches the track first. This proves that the forehand is ahead of the quarters. The right lateral pair of legs should pass and cross in front of the left lateral pair of legs without losing impulsion.

It is a grave mistake if the impulsion is neglected. This can happen if the rider is too much pre-occupied with the sideways movement of the horse and does not apply pressure with the left leg. Then the horse will move sideways with his body parallel to the track and the near foreleg and near hindleg will touch the track simultaneously. There is then the risk of the horse brushing his legs.

An even greater mistake is made when the horse's near hindleg touches the track first. This not only shows that the hindquarters are ahead but it also entails the total loss of impulsion.

One can increase the diameter of the circle

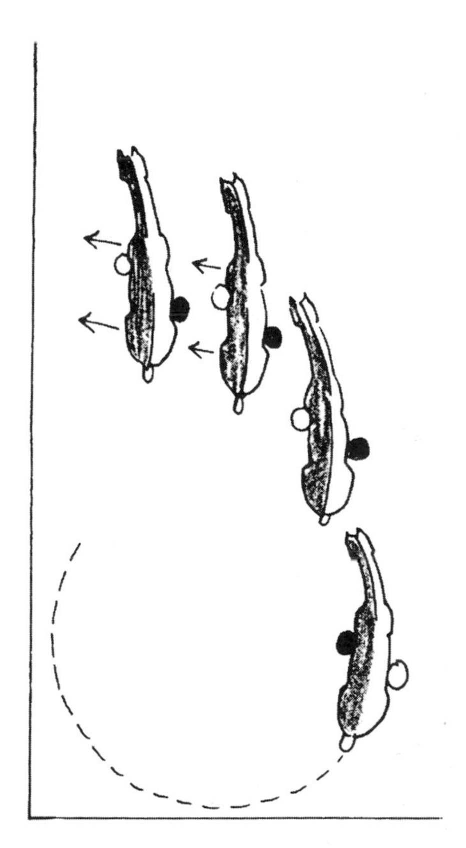

*Fig. 424*
Incorrect half pass. The forehand is not leading.

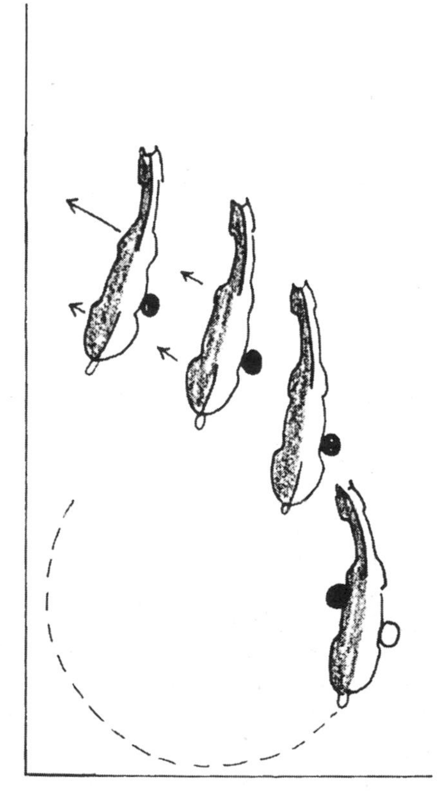

*Fig. 425*
Worse still. The quarters are leading.

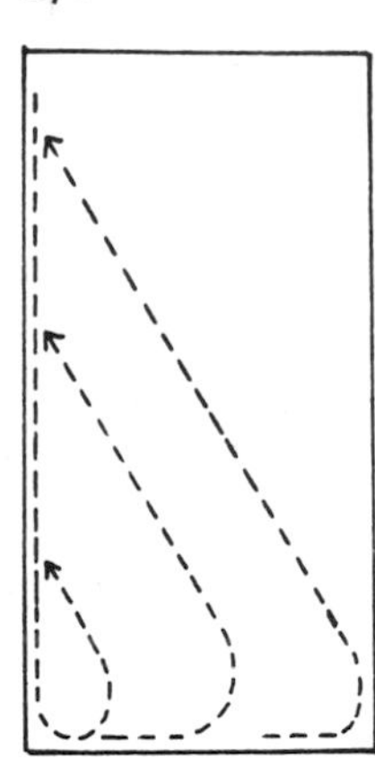

*Fig. 426*
Gradually increase the diameter of the circle, and thereby the number of strides, in half pass back to the track.

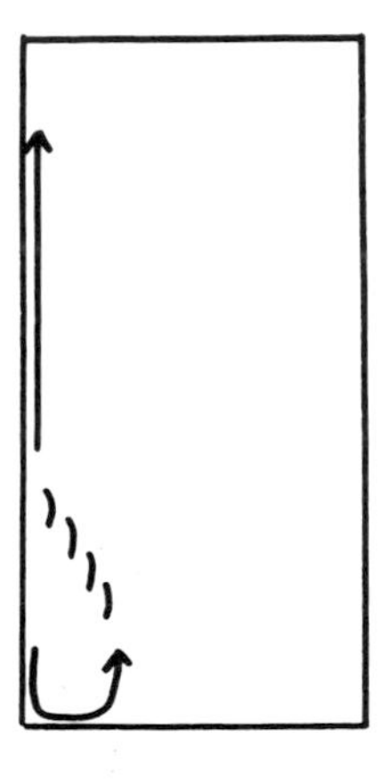

*Fig. 427*
Half pass in canter. Canter on a small circle, ride in half pass back to the track. Arriving at the track make a simple change of leg and continue in the other canter.

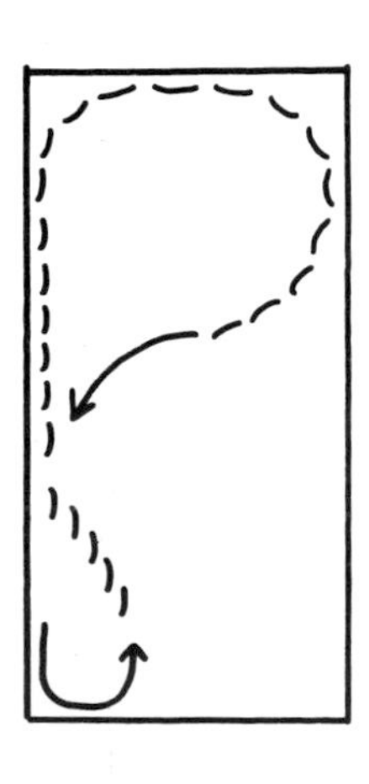

*Fig. 428*
Half pass in canter. Start the exercise the same way, but when arriving at the track after the half pass, do not change canter, but continue in counter canter, then change through the diagonal and continue in ordinary canter.

gradually, whereby the way back to the track will become longer until a point is reached where the horse will, with the greatest of ease, perform the movement through the diagonal of the entire school.

Later on, school this movement also at a collected sitting trot or canter. Always initiate the exercise with a circle and a short way back to the track. Gradually increase the diameter of the circle, as formerly done at the walk.

When riding half-pass at the canter one can make a simple change of leg or a flying change of leg when approaching the track. With the more advanced horse one can continue the left canter after changing rein through the diagonal in half-pass and follow the track on the right-hand rein at the counter (false) canter. Then ride, at the end of the long side of the school, a large half circle, changing rein through the diagonal to follow the track at the left canter.

Remember to make the horse attentive by applying a strong half-halt before trotting or cantering in the half-pass. It will improve the mobility and fluency of pace.

The half-pass movement is an excellent exercise to improve the horse's overall flexibility, necessary to achieve total engagement of the hocks and true collection. It is important that the movement is relaxed but active and performed in complete obedience.

If the horse demonstrates any signals of distress, like tail swishing, ears laid back, grinding teeth or open or dry mouth, then the rider has to realise that the horse is resisting and must try to restore the horse's confidence.

### THE COUNTER HALF-PASS

This time the half-pass is ridden on a zig-zag line.

Start with the first half of the zig-zag line. For example, when on the left-hand rein prepare the horse by riding deep into the second corner of the short side. On emerging from the corner, apply a firm half-halt and maintain the left lateral flexion of the horse's body. The horse is now prepared for the half-pass to the left.

Ride forward-sidewards in half-pass towards

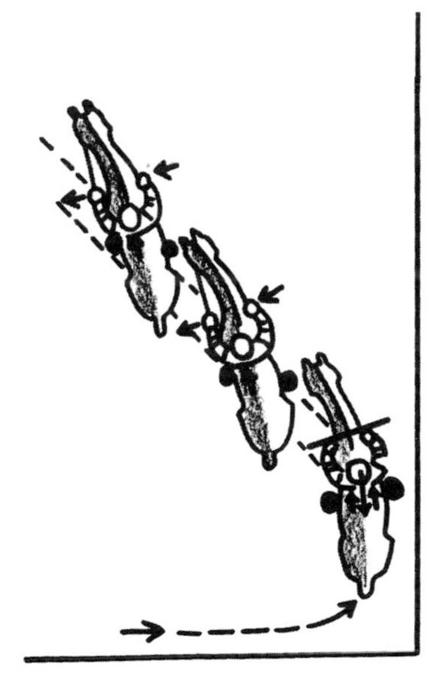
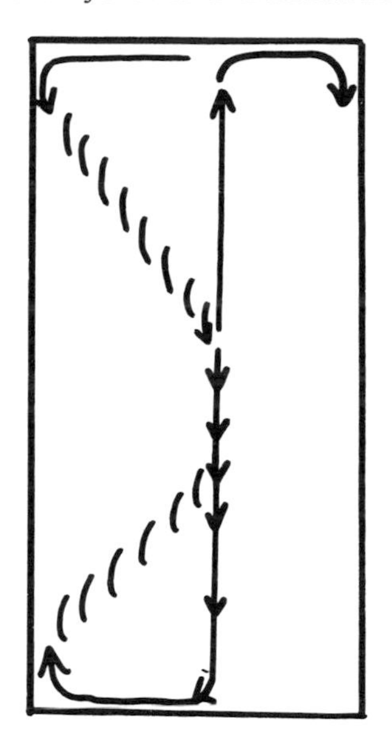
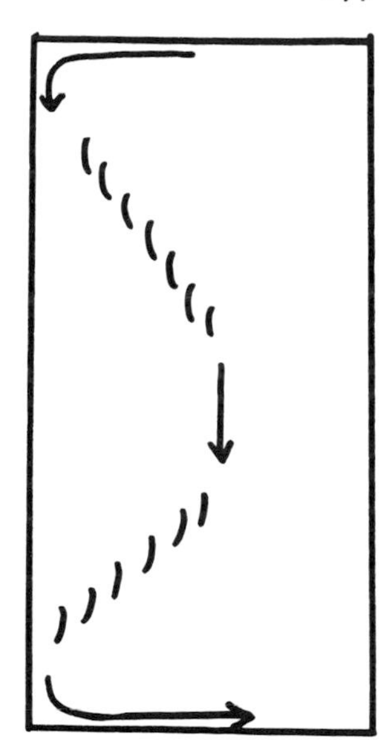

*Fig. 429*
The counter half pass. *(left)* emerging from the corner; *(centre)* at first, only up to the centre line alternately on both reins; *(right)* next a full zig-zag line.

the centre of the arena. There apply half-halt aids, straighten the horse and send him vigorously forward on a straight line towards the centre of the opposite short side. Proceed on the right-hand rein. Approaching the next long side, prepare the horse and repeat the exercise, this time to the right.

The next step would be to perform the full zig-zag line: when reaching the centre of the school straighten the horse for two horse lengths only. Then apply strong half-halt aids and ride in half-pass back to the track. On the track straighten the horse and send him forward. Apply first rein aid. Relax after the collection in the half-pass.

When the horse can perform this exercise correctly in a walk, ride it also at a collected trot and at a collected canter. Again begin with a half zig-zag only. At the canter the first flying change of leg must be executed on reaching the centre line of the school and the second one on the track. One can, of course, also continue on the track at the counter (false) canter.

THE FLYING CHANGE

A showjumping horse must be able to make a flying change of leg at the canter, because in competition it will be necessary to do so. If the horse is able to perform all the movements on two tracks to perfection one can commence to school the flying change of leg at the canter. The flying change should first be executed at the changing points of directions, just as when schooling the simple change of leg at the canter. For example, changing out of the circle on the figure of eight when riding a serpentine while changing direction from one loop into another. Later on it may be performed before reaching the track, after having changed rein through the diagonal, because in the following corner the horse's body will be bent laterally inwards, which makes it easier for him to change the canter.

At a more advanced stage one will make the flying change in the centre of the school, which is more difficult because it has to be done on a straight line.

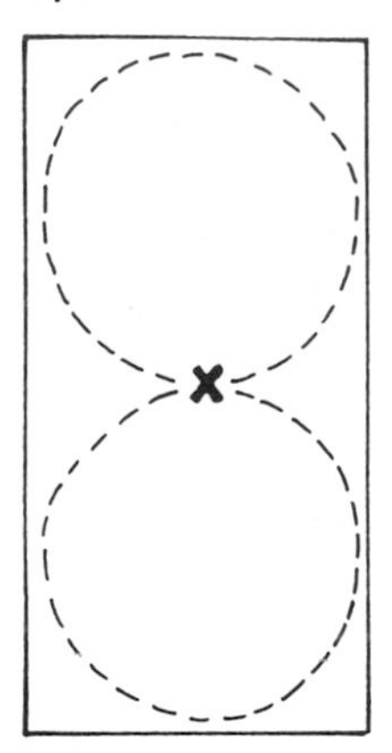

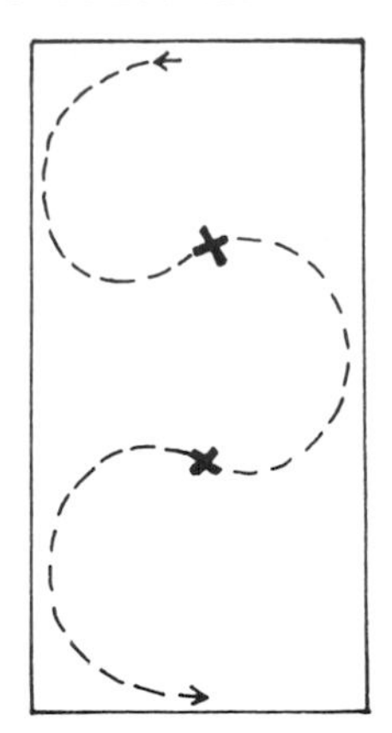

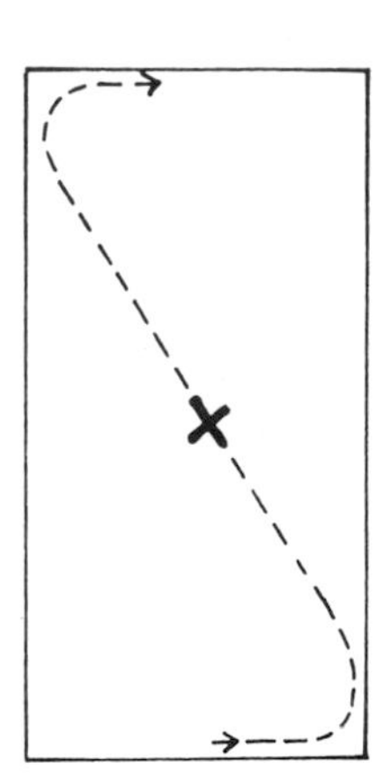

*Fig. 430*
Start training the flying change at changing points X from one turn into another. Later on also perform it on a straight line.

*Preparation*

As a preparation for the flying change, practise the simple change of leg at the canter with only one or two walking strides in between them. While changing the canter the horse should remain light in the hand and champ the bit, and in order to keep the horse straight one brings one's outer leg slightly further behind the girths and applies strong support to prevent deviation of the quarters.

The horse must be able to make the simple change of leg, not only at all the changing points but also on a straight line. First, at the centre of the school and finally on the long side of the school, after every six canter strides, one changes the canter.

Spread over a period of time one can reduce, step by step, the number of canter strides to three and even to one. When the horse gets accustomed to this technique of changing the canter and remains calm then there will be no problem for him in making the flying change.

It stands to reason, of course, that the rider must master the necessary feeling for the sequence of the canter stride to be able to apply the aids for changing the canter at the correct moment. The exact moment is when the leading foreleg touches the ground, because the next phase is the moment of suspension when all four legs are free of the ground. This is the *only* canter phase where the horse is in a position to make a flying change (the leading foreleg in the left canter is the near foreleg; in the right canter the off foreleg is leading).

*The aids*

For example, when in the left canter during the last canter stride, (before the flying change), when the *near* forefoot touches the ground, one prepares the horse strongly with the usual half-halt aids. Simultaneously, one changes the region of one's leg position and distribution of one's weight and applies the aids for the right canter. The flying change will then be executed during the following-up moment of suspension. The rider must place his weight (or centre of gravity) above the horse's near hindleg. This is necessary to stay in balance with the horse; because of the right canter being started with the left hindleg the horse has to shift his centre of gravity to the near hindleg as well.

Only if the rider's centre of gravity stays above that of the horse can the horse throw his off foreleg freely forward while proceeding into the right canter.

The horse can hardly do this if the rider commits at this moment the common fault to bend his upper body forward and look down to the off foreleg, thus changing his centre of gravity to the off foreleg.

Apply increased pressure with the left leg slightly further behind the girths (to prevent any deviation of the quarters to the left). Support this with strong pressure of the right leg *on* the girths, while maintaining the same tension on the bit. The right leg urges the horse to change the canter and to strike off at the right canter after the moment of suspension.

When the horse is inclined to deviate the quarters to one particular side during the flying change, practise it with this side along the kicking boards. Only when the horse is able to perform the flying change without any deviation of the quarters while passing from one turn into another will he be advanced enough to perform the flying change on a straight line without the support of the kicking boards. For example, when changing rein through the diagonal.

It is essential that the horse keeps straight from head to tail, maintains collection, impulsion, balance and rhythmic tempo in pace while light on the bit.

Precaution should be taken not to execute the flying change too often at the same point in the school, because after a few times an intelligent horse would anticipate it, which could lead to the horse stiffening his muscles and taking a stronger hold on the bit.

The schooling of the flying change can only be successful if it is executed systematically step by step without rushing, which would confuse and upset the horse.

One must take into consideration that the horse does not seem to have a very high degree of intelligence but a very good memory. Of course this varies a little from one individual to another.

Therefore before starting a new lesson one has to repeat the last one often enough until it is firmly established in the horse's mind and performed correctly. If a horse has difficulties to learn a new task it need not necessarily be that the horse is unwilling. More often the horse just did not understand what was asked of him. Repeat the lesson often enough, but make sure the training does not become monotonous.

For the same reasons introduce only *one new* lesson at a time into the training programme. Anything else would be unfair to the horse and only confuse him. The horse would not be able to understand, would become excited and unwilling and resist the rider.

### COUNTER (FALSE) CANTER

The counter canter is a very advanced training because the horse has to canter on a bend (through a turn or on a circle line) while his body is flexed in the opposite direction. Therefore the counter canter has an extreme suppling effect.

First practise the counter canter on one short side only. For instance, riding at left canter on the left-hand rein, change rein through the diagonal of the school. Do not change the canter but continue in the left canter on the next short side of the school.

To prevent the horse from changing into the right canter or the pace becoming disunited, apply at every stride strong seat and leg aids to maintain the left canter, impulsion and rhythm. Maintain distribution of the rider's weight on the right seat bone in co-ordination with the horse's balance, the left leg being on the girths, maintaining impulsion, and the right leg slightly further behind the girths than usual.

With these aids the horse's left flexion is maintained in spite of the right-hand turn.

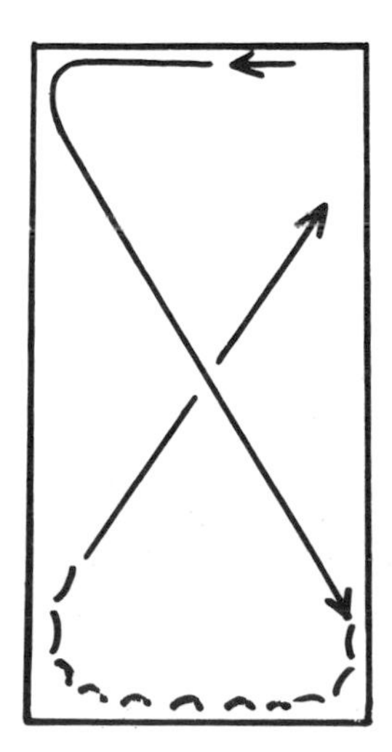

*Fig. 431*
Counter canter on one short side.

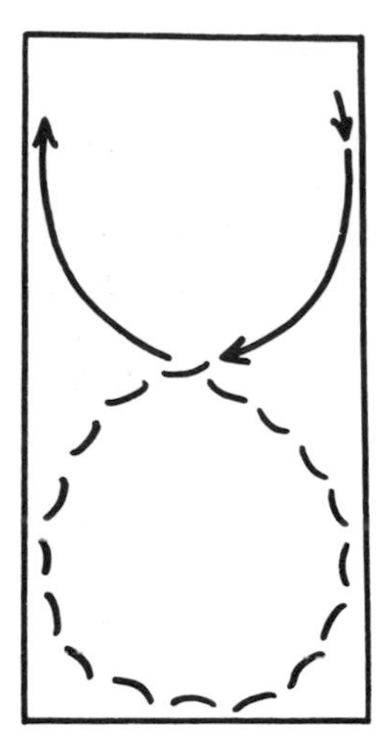

*Fig. 432*
Counter canter on a circle.

*Fig. 433*
Counter canter on a serpentine.

Change rein again through the diagonal and continue in the left canter. At this stage it is sufficient to practise this exercise only twice on both reins as it is very strenuous for the horse.

If the canter pace becomes disunited or the horse changes canter during counter canter, apply stronger pressure with the right leg, and position it further behind the girths to ensure that the horse's off hindleg will be brought further underneath his body, which is necessary to continue the counter canter.

In time the horse will be able to do one short side in counter canter correctly, remaining calm, right on the bit and in balance.

When the horse masters the difficult two corners of the short side in counter canter one can continue after the short side on a circle of 20 metres diameter. Now, on the circle, the horse is on a continuous turn, his body flexed continuously contrary to the curvature of the circle. This will be very difficult and strenuous and should therefore only be tried when the horse's training has reached the point where he is completely supple and obedient.

Begin with only one circle round (on both reins). Then change rein out of the circle and continue in the normal canter. Remember the strain put on the horse and often make a break between the exercises.

At a more advanced stage of schooling one can add more variety by practising the counter canter on a figure of eight or on a serpentine without a change of leg at the changing points.

An even more advanced task would be to ride in counter canter on a figure of eight or a serpentine with a simple or a flying change of leg at the changing points, changing from counter canter to counter canter.

### THE PIROUETTE

The *pirouette* is a full 360° turn on the haunches and can be performed in walk, trot and canter.

In classic dressage this turn is performed with the inner hindleg returning to the same spot after each step of the pirouette. The inner hindleg is called the pivot. The outer foreleg and hindleg pass and cross in front of the inner foreleg and hindleg. The horse must be collected to a high degree and perform the pirouette smoothly with a regular sequence and cadence of pace. The pace is no longer regular if the inner hindleg is not raised as high as the outer one. This is especially noticeable when the pirouette is performed in canter.

Coming to a halt, moving backwards or sideways is a fault, as then the purpose of this exercise is missed.

First practise the pirouette as a half 180° *pirouette* at a walk, which means ride a turn on

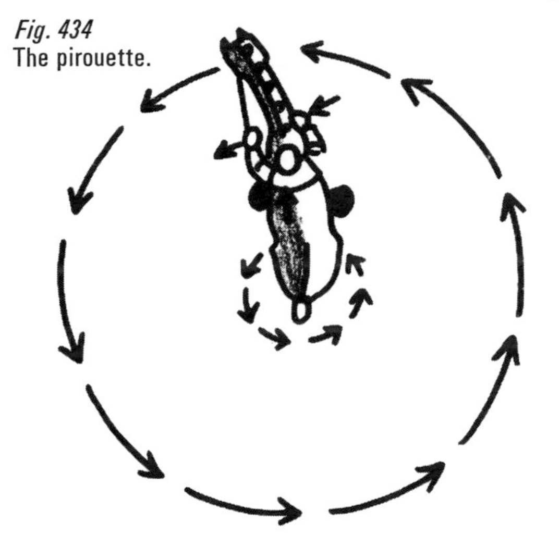
*Fig. 434*
The pirouette.

the haunches at a walk. Start this exercise away from the track and increase the number of strides gradually until a full turn of 360° (the *pirouette*) is performed. When attempting the pirouette at a trot or canter start again as in the walk and increase the number of strides step by step. Finally the horse will be able to perform the complete turn of the pirouette with ease in all paces.

*The aids*

The aids are the same as for the turn on the haunches.

When starting to train the pirouette exaggerate the aids slightly, that is transfer your weight to the inner hindleg and lead the horse with the inner hand into the turn a little more pronounced.

For a showjumper the pirouette is particularly important. He should be able to master this movement in all paces without much effort. When jumping against the clock it can save valuable seconds in a tight turn.

Nevertheless, for a showjumper the impulsion is of supreme importance. Therefore a showjumper should perform the pirouette with a slightly larger radius; the quarters are not turning on the spot as in dressage but move on a small circle. This way the horse is able to maintain his impulsion more easily.

If the horse's pace becomes irregular the impulsion has deteriorated. Then perform the pirouette on a fairly large circle giving the horse more room to move forward on two tracks. In time, when the horse has gained more flexibility, decrease the radius of the circle gradually. In all circumstances the impulsion must be maintained. Together with the regularity and suppleness of the performance it is more important than a very small pirouette radius.

After each pirouette, no matter in which pace, ride the horse actively forward on a straight line to transform the propulsive power accumulated through the collection into increased forward impulsion.

THE SPEED COURSE

The speed course for a showjumper should not be mistaken for the gallop track for a racehorse. Schooling in the speed course is vital for the education of the showjumping horse and rider, for the *rider* because he will develop a feeling for the rhythmic tempo in pace and the length of the stride in the various paces and speeds and because he has to maintain a uniform pace throughout the speed course. This is essential, as in different standards of competition different speeds are requested; for the *horse* because he will learn to maintain an even balanced rhythm and the particular speed in which he has to perform in his standard of competition. The speed course also improves the horse's physical fitness (heart and lungs) considerably. Particularly in the beginning of the jumping season one can often see horses halfway round the course making jumping faults or refusing because they are too unfit to finish the course, which takes barely two minutes.

It is very easy to make a speed course if a large field with suitable ground is available. With sticks or flags mark out a large circle or track which is 600 metres long and approximately 3 metres wide. Mark out one line for start and finish.

Use the speed course for schooling the horse in the following exercises as:

One round (600 metres) takes 6 minutes when *walking* at 100 metres per minute; or 3 minutes when *trotting* at 200 metres per minute; or 2 minutes when *cantering* at 300 metres per minute.

*Only* when training experienced horses for open and international competitions one needs to train at a canter speed of 350 or 400 metres per minute. Then make an additional finish line, 200 metres further up the track and use the speed course at canter.

Two rounds and 200 metres (1,400 metres) takes 4 minutes when *cantering* at 350 metres per minute.

Two rounds (1,200 metres) takes 3 minutes when *cantering* at 400 metres per minute.

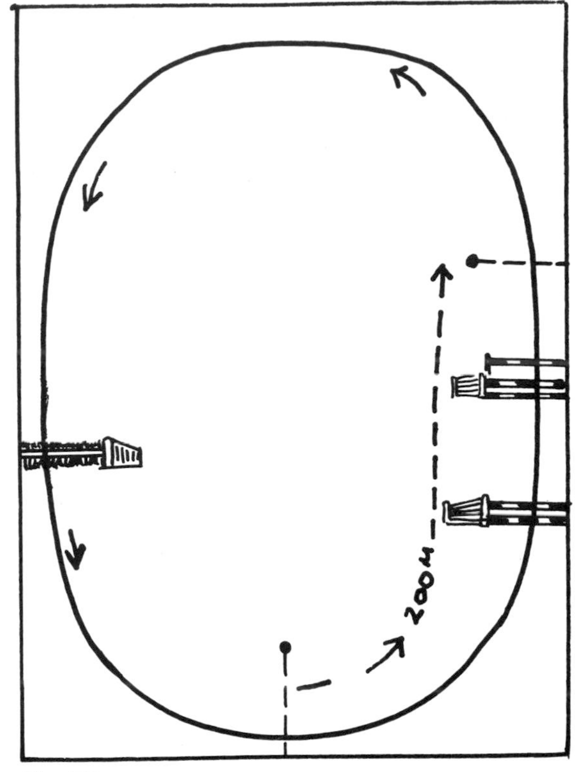


*Fig. 435*
The speed course, 600 metres long with one line for the start and finish at the short side. Mark out an additional finish line a further 200 metres up the long side (only needed when training at 350 metres per minute).

The exercises in the speed course (except walk and trot) should, of course, be ridden *only* in the forward seat. Before crossing the starting line the rider must already ride at the speed in which he intends to complete the circle.

To develop the feeling of rhythmic tempo during the canter pace the rider should count every canter stride at a set pace. The rider should carry a stopwatch to be able to check the speed. He has to maintain the same speed from start to finish evenly, only then will the rider learn to feel the length of each stride and the rhythm of the various speeds.

In time the rider will feel, even with his eyes closed, at which speed the horse is moving and so will develop an in-built timepiece and has less need to rely on the stopwatch.

To master this feeling for rhythm and speed is essential when competing, because a course should be treated as *one* operation and ridden in a uniform, set pace, without breaking the horse's pace by checking, placing and jumping the course in bits and pieces.

*Training young horses*

Even during his first year of schooling the young horse should be trained in the speed course. It goes hand in hand with the normal basic schooling. According to the training schedule in the ninth month the schooling includes work twice a week in the speed course.

Start the exercise at a walk, six minutes at a speed of 100 metres per minute (one round = 600 metres of the track). After this start the trot session at a speed of 200 metres per minute. This means one has to cover the 600 metres track in exactly three minutes. Then, to give the horse a break, repeat the walk session on a loose rein (at ease) but maintaining impulsion.

After the break canter slowly for two minutes at a speed of 300 metres per minute. One has to cover the 600 metres track *once*. Make a break again, at a walk, and repeat the whole exercise session again on the other rein.

It is most important – and I repeat it – that all paces are ridden at the exact speed and at a set pace. Particularly with novice horses, *never* canter faster than at a speed of 300 metres per minute. Training at a faster speed would unbalance and flatten the horse and shift his weight on to the forehand, teaching him to lean on the bit.

After schooling in the speed course walk home on a loose rein. When the schooling of the young horse is progressing systematically over the first 12 months he should be so fit that a few minutes after the canter session his breathing should be normal.

*The second schooling year*

In preparation for the jumping season the canter sessions are gradually increased, although still at a speed of 300 metres per minute. After the normal walk and trot sessions, canter 600 metres on one rein and, after a break at a brisk walk on a loose rein, canter 600 metres on the other rein at the same speed. Altogether the horse has covered 1,200 metres at the canter in four minutes. Depending on the horse's fitness one can gradually increase the length of the canter sessions to four minutes on each rein, cantering eight minutes over 2,400 metres.

Do not forget the walking sessions in between the rounds in order not to strain the horse's heart and lungs.

If, during the jumping season, there are only competitions at weekends, then the horse should be schooled in the speed course two or three times per week in order to keep horse and rider fit.

If the horse tries to increase his pace, comes onto the forehand and leans on the bit, it shows that the rider has used the speed course incorrectly. These symptoms always occur if the rider has trotted or cantered too fast or did not maintain an even balanced rhythm in the paces.

To correct this the rider should count the sequence of the canter strides and apply stronger driving leg aids, thus sending the horse into his hands and transferring any excess weight from the forehand to the quarters. But maintain the same speed and check on this with the stop-watch.

It is vital that one practises *only* at the exact speed at which the horse has to complete. A speed of 400 metres per minute, for example, is only required in a Nation Cup competition and in the Olympic Games and should therefore be practised only if horse and rider have to compete in either. Ride two rounds in three minutes.

In addition to the usual speed course training, one can build a few fences in the speed course. For example, an upright, an oxer and a combination, the height and width depending on the horse's speed and degree of schooling. Ride the speed course as usual at the set pace and maintain this pace while approaching the jump and after landing. Ride the same set pace as if the fences were not there at all.

Riders who have the bad habit of checking or placing their horse too much during jumping competitions and who suddenly increase their speed while approaching the take off will learn to take the fences "in their stride".

### TAKING A WATER JUMP

Some horses and riders, even at international level, have problems when clearing a water jump, despite the fact that the horse by nature jumps a spread fence with greater ease than a high upright jump.

Nevertheless, for many riders and horses the most difficult jump in a competition is the water. The reason is that horse and rider have more experience and practise over normal obstacles. A course consisting, for instance, of 18 obstacles has seldom more than *one* water jump. I believe that it is chiefly lack of experience and incorrect schooling which contributes towards this problem. The insecure feeling while approaching a spread water jump is often exaggerated in the rider's mind and transferred to the horse. Those riders should realise that in fact the average canter stride during a speed of 350 metres per minute has a length of 3·5 metres. If while approaching the water jump the horse should increase his speed to 400 metres per minute, then the last few strides before take-off should be 4 metres long. Therefore the horse will only have to make one extended canter stride to jump a water of 5 metres spread. Even in the Olympic Games the width of the water jump may not exceed 5 metres.

*Fig. 436*
A water jump with large wings. Very suitable for training.

During the first period in schooling a horse to jump water, the spread of the water jump should not exceed 1·5 metres, and this includes a brush fence, which is 0·45 metres in height and sloping at an angle of 45° marking the take-off base. This brush fence is moved progressively as the spread is increased. The free space between the brush fence and the water is covered by additional brush fences set at a more acute angle to fill the gap. All the brushes must overlap and the last one must be level with the water's edge.

The water jump should be rectangular in shape and must have a front of 5 metres width. The obstacle should have large wings on each side, which must be extended towards the approach side so as to form a passage way to prevent the horse from running out.

To assist the horse in finding the correct take-off point at the initial stage of schooling a white pole is placed on the ground close to the brush fence. The correct take-off point is close to the pole.

A triple bar is built over the water jump, preferably of rustic poles, giving him greater confidence than would brightly painted poles. This rustic triple bar camouflages the spread into a better known ordinary jump. If a horse clears a triple bar correctly his body describes a semi-circle, of which the highest point is exactly over the last pole. Therefore the highest pole of the triple bar (the last one) should be over the centre of the water jump. The first pole should be about 0·5 metres high, the centre one 0·7 metres and the last one 0·9 metres. The purpose of the triple bar is to teach the horse to *bascule* over the water. This ensures that the horse learns from the very beginning to *get off the ground* when jumping water and will leave no room in the horse's mind for the idea of galloping straight through the water without becoming airborne at all.

Most young horses will clear this type of obstacle with ease, as they are already airborne before they realise that they are negotiating a water jump.

If the horse has jumped the obstacle two or three times correctly and with confidence be satisfied.

The next step in training is to begin leaving the obstacle as arranged previously. Having cleared this two or three times correctly, remove the last and highest pole of the triple bar (0·9 metres) and rearrange the triple bar so that the

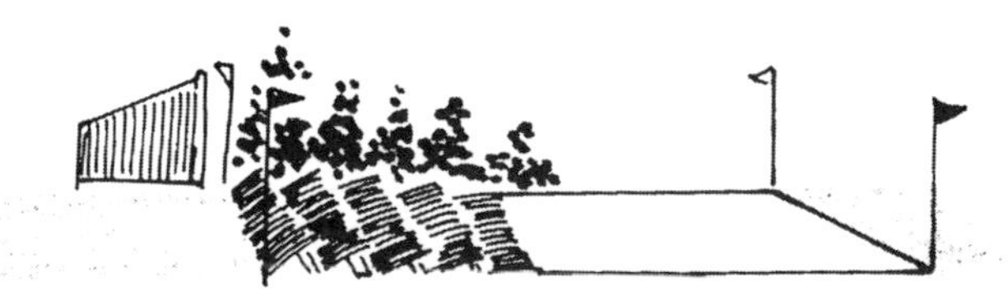
*Fig. 437*
Increasing the spread of the water jump by adding sloping brush fences.

second pole (0·7 metres) is now at the centre of the entire width (this is inclusive of the brush fence).

If there are no further problems in overcoming this obstacle, remove the pole at 0·7 metres height, which leaves the remaining pole of 0·5 metres. This pole should now be positioned at the centre of the width of the entire jump. In time this pole may also be removed, which leaves only the "open" water. The horse will accomplish the jump in perfect style without the slightest difficulty. Nevertheless, schooling young horses to clear a water jump properly takes time – at least six months.

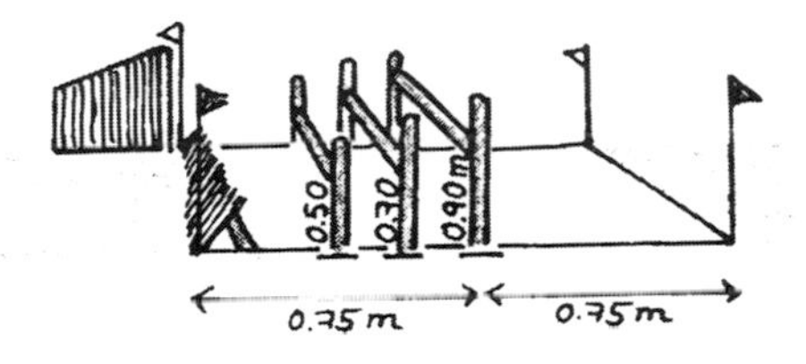


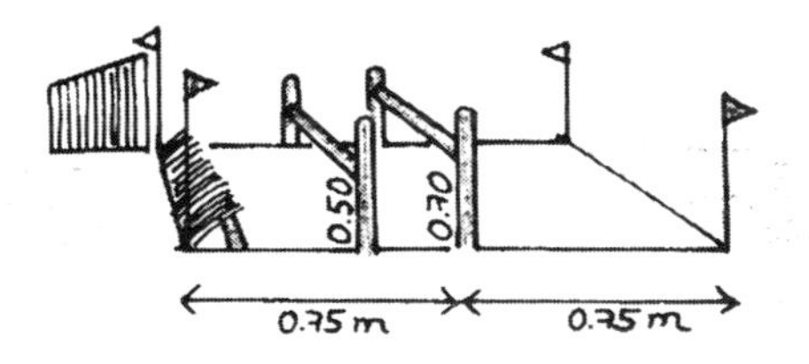


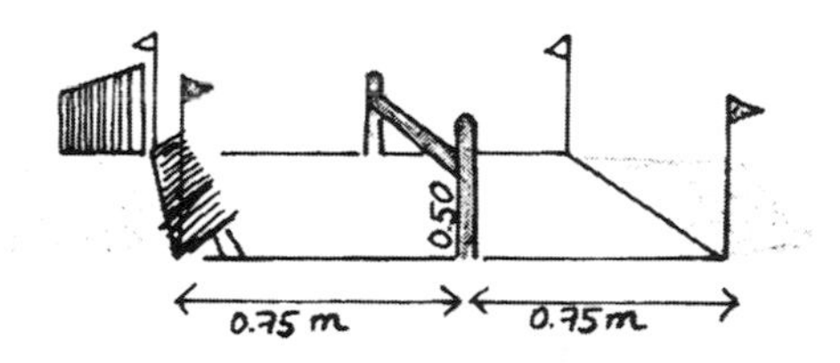


*Fig. 438*
The triple bar over the water jump *(top)* will teach the horse to jump the water well and confidently. Then the number of poles can be gradually reduced *(centre)*, until *(bottom)* finally there is only one pole left.

*The aids*

Approach the water jump at a normal canter pace and only extend the last few strides before take-off, preferably by applying determined forward driving leg aids rather than whip aids.

(1) *On the bit.* The horse must remain well on the bit in order to prevent him flattening and coming on the forehand which results from the increased extension of pace. By maintaining the *same* contact with the horse's mouth, with the reins in *both* hands, the horse will approach in a balanced pace, both hocks well under.

If one feels the horse becoming lighter on the bit in the approach apply stronger leg aids, creating more contact with the mouth, which will achieve greater equilibrium for the take-off.

By losing the tension on the bit during the approach one takes the risk that the canter stride will flatten, that the horse will stand back too far at take-off and will land in the water. The horse is obviously not able to get *off* the ground, which will make the curve of the jump too flat. Also, after landing, the pace would be too fast and flat. The horse will move over-burdened on the forehand for the next couple of strides. This must place the horse in a very difficult position if he has to jump a straight fence following the water jump, particularly if it is placed a short distance ahead. Then the horse might not have time to re-establish his balance to take-off at the next jump with accuracy.

Therefore, remember: *never drop the reins* during the approach to, take-off at, while airborne over, or when landing beyond the water jump.

(2) *Wrong approach.* Many riders make the great mistake of accelerating the pace much too soon in the approach. The horse becomes unbalanced, drops on to the forehand, flattens and is unable to propel himself free off the ground at take-off.

Another mistake is common. In the approach the rider suddenly takes both reins into *one* hand and sends the horse on with the whip instead of with the legs. In doing so contact with the mouth

*Fig. 439*
Over the water jump *(top)*, the horse's forelegs are extremely stretched . . . but the horse should fold his forelegs when jumping the spread oxer *(bottom)*. The Mexican rider, Gerardo Rodriguez Pozos photographed during a Paalman training course.

is lost for a moment, with the result as above. The horse transfers his weight to the forehand, flattens, incurs a fault or simply runs out. Should the horse run out then, of course, apply the whip aid when approaching the next time. Do so on the horse's shoulder, on the side to which he ran out, while holding the reins in both hands.

To avoid the "do or die" attitude of some riders, I place the water jump in such a position that this mistake becomes impossible. For example, by placing an upright fence at a distance of four to five canter strides in front of the water jump, or by making the rider approach the water jump out of a turn with a straight approach line of four to five canter strides only. This technique of course building prevents a rider from rushing. It also forces riders to increase the momentum of the pace over the last few canter strides. In doing so they will get the best from the horse over the jump.

To correct a horse who has the bad habit of taking the bit and trying to dash off after clearing a water jump, build a small upright fence or oxer at a distance of 21 metres beyond it.

In time the distance can gradually be reduced, but always in such a way that this distance will be divisible by 3 metres but should be never shorter than 12 metres.

If it is a novice horse one should extend the distance by *one* extra metre, which makes it more convenient for the young horse to re-establish his balance in between the two jumps. This method will teach the horse to collect and to pick himself up again in between the waterjump and the following fence and cure him from dashing off on landing.

## PROHIBITED REINS

There are *disadvantages* associated with the use of the standing martingale, running reins and double bit. The F.E.I. prohibits the use of standing martingales and running reins in international jumping competitions. For the horse's sake I am delighted about this decision and I would like to see it introduced also in all national jumping competitions.

There is a good reason for this rule. Running reins and standing martingales prevent free movement of the horse's head and neck, thereby interfering seriously with the horse's balance. And interfering with a showjumper's balance can have disastrous results.

Using a standing martingale or running reins with the intention of placing the horse's head is completely wrong and shows lack of equestrian knowledge. Both reins can force the horse's head and neck into a certain position, but at the same time they tighten the muscles of neck and shoulders. This changes the centre of gravity to the forehand. In this unnatural fixed position the horse is unable to use his back; he will stiffen his spine and widen his hocks.

### *Placing the head*

All over the world people have difficulties with what is termed "placing the head". Only because they do not know that placing the head is not done by trying to fix the position of the horse's head, but in the *only logical* and natural way. This is to first bring the horse into balance, allowing him to re-establish his natural balance with the additional weight of the rider. Secondly, to ride the horse from the *rear to the front* into the rider's hand, activating the quarters. If these fundamental rules are followed the horse's head *is* placed automatically.

Yes, it is as simple as that. The more the horse engages his quarters the more he will move in balance. The quarters will be lowered, which in turn brings withers slightly higher. The entire vertebrae, in back and neck, is rounded and the neck will be slightly flexed at the poll. Develop and supple the horse's back and quarter muscles . . . as a result the horse's head and neck will be placed.

People with difficulties do not realise this or want to take short cuts. They try to hide the horse's lack of training by forcing the head into a fixed position. Thereby they create the false impression of a schooled horse. Of course the results can never be the same, just as reducing a patient's temperature with drugs does not remove the cause of the illness. To achieve such

*Fig. 440*
Allowing the horse *(top)* to re-balance himself with the rider up; and then pushing him *(bottom)* from the rear into the hands, thereby engaging the quarters and "placing the head" automatically.

a false impression people use all sorts of equipment either to "lift" up a horse's head or to "bring it down". One only has to look at any saddlery shop and the wide selection of artificial aids to realise that people find it hard to learn.

*The standing martingale*

This is a connection between the girths and the ordinary noseband. Some people even attach it to a drop noseband, which is even more cruel to the horse.

The only advantage of the standing martingale compared to running reins or a running martingale (if adjusted too short) is that the standing martingale does not give the horse painful pressure in the mouth but on the nasal bone only. When jumping, the standing martingale is

*Fig. 441*
A standing martingale cannot ever achieve a satisfying result.

dangerous because it will interfere considerably with the natural movement of the head and neck, which plays the most important role in the horse's balance, particularly when jumping. The horse's neck might be compared with a parasol or rod of a tight-rope walker. The right-rope walker would not be able to retain his balance if he was forced to perform with his arms tied to his side. This is, in fact, what one does by tightening down a horse's head while jumping.

*The running reins*

The running reins have the same dangerous effect on the horse when jumping. There are three different types of running reins:

(i) the so called "Kohler–Zugel", widely used in Germany. It is attached to the girths like a running martingale, has a V-form and its ends run through the snaffle rings and are attached with clips onto the normal reins;

(ii) the "normal" running rein, approximately 4 to 5 metres long, is attached on each side of the girths and runs through the snaffle rings (from inside to outside) into the rider's hands, together with the normal snaffle rein;

(iii) the same running rein is sometimes used in a different way, being attached to the girths underneath the horse, instead of on each side, running up between the horse's forelegs. Positioned in this way it works even more severely on the horse's bars. Some "experts" claim to be able to "show the horse the way to the ground" with the artificial aid of the running rein. A real expert, however, will be able to bend the horse's neck "directly" and lower his head and neck without artificial aids at any time. There are even riders who school their horses on a running rein *only* without using the snaffle rein at all, forcing the horse to carry his head nearly between his forelegs. This ruins the horse.

*Fig. 442*
Running reins may pull a horse's head momentarily into place (mostly even behind the bit) but cannot achieve a result, because the back is dropped and the hindlegs are trailing.

If a rider does not have the knowledge and experience to school the horse correctly in a natural manner and is really unable to show the horse the way to the ground and to place his head, he might see no other alternative than to use running reins. He should only use them, however, in co-ordination with the snaffle rein. He should ride the horse on the snaffle rein and use the running rein *only now and again* on the horse's stiffer side.

*The running martingale*

A running martingale cannot do much harm, provided it is correctly adjusted and used. It is adjusted correctly when the rings of the martingale reach a horizontal line at the height of the horse's hip. Then the rein can still maintain one straight line from the bit to the hand.

When this straight line is broken by the force of the martingale then the martingale is too short and has to be readjusted, because it hinders the horse in the use of his neck and back while jumping.

It also interferes with the rider's rein aids because the "direct" contact between rider's hands and the bit is disturbed, and some horses

*Fig. 443*
A loose running martingale does not disturb the horse much, only in turns when using the "open rein" aid.

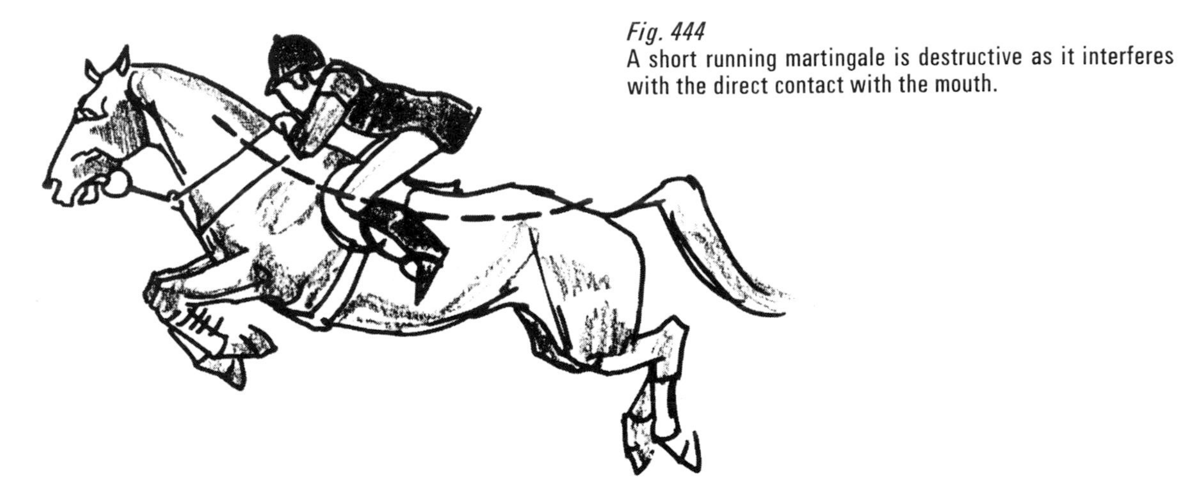

*Fig. 444*
A short running martingale is destructive as it interferes with the direct contact with the mouth.

take advantage of this by leaning on the bit. It pulls downwards on the horse's mouth so that the crown piece becomes tight behind the ears. A running martingale which is adjusted too short can do much harm and the horse will be more difficult to control, particularly while riding turns. The horse learns the bad habit of running out over the shoulder when going through turns, or will rear and sway around sharply on his hindlegs and get completely out of control.

*The double bit*

Since running reins and standing martingales are prohibited in international jumping competitions it is surprising to see how many riders have changed over to using the double bit.

It seems to me that the double bit is now the last refuge for those riders unable to control their horses.

Today, even in international jumping competitions, one can see riders who even with the double bit are still unable to control their horses and have to use, in addition, a martingale. If riders are convinced that they have to use both then only the snaffle reins should run through the martingale rings, but never the curb bit reins. However, even the curb bit reins running through the martingale rings does not satisfy some riders and they put *both* snaffle and curb bit reins through. These riders should think about the following verse from Pecavi:

Pelham or snaffle,
Liverpool double,
What a commotion,
What's all the trouble?
Dozens of letters
From horse-loving lads,
It isn't the bridle my boys,
It is the hands!

Unfortunately for the horse, many riders learn to jump before they learn to ride properly. When jumping they stand in the stirrups without proper grip and balance themselves out of the horse's mouth. As a self-defence the horse will learn to pull or some other bad habit.

But does the rider blame himself? No, instead he resorts to more and more severe bits. Riders who do not have an independent balanced seat use a severe bit because they think that their horse has a hard mouth and might otherwise run away. Running away, however, is the horse's self-defence against the hard bit.

A tactful rider will not try to pull harder than the horse but will ease his hands instead and yield the reins in time and try to calm the horse with his voice rather than with muscular action. Most horses are taught to pull. In many cases it is not the horse who starts pulling but the rider. If one is observant one will notice that nearly always the same riders have horses with bad mouths and difficult tempers, and surely this proves that it is the rider who is the cause of the hard mouth and badly mannered horse. These riders make their horses mentally exhausted as well as physically and I am convinced that if the same horse was ridden by a cool and relaxed rider the horse would be able to put up a completely different performance.

I have nothing against a double bit provided it is used on an older, experienced horse and only in the hands of a well-educated rider. The rider must have a firm seat and be able to use his hands independently from his body.

If the double bit is used by an inexperienced rider who uses the reins to balance himself then it is as sharp as a razor blade.

Having trained horses and riders on three different continents I have found that each country has its own fashion as regards to bits, saddlery and schooling methods.

In English speaking countries the standing martingale is most popular, whereas in Europe running reins have more adherents, especially in Germany. I found that in Germany, Austria and Australia side reins are used extensively in training young horses. In Mexico it appears that double bits, pelhams, martingales and hackamores are in fashion.

In Europe riders earn extra points by showing horses in classes, novice dressage tests and Prix Caprilli tests in an ordinary thick snaffle, because this displays better horsemanship.

In England and Ireland, young and relatively green horses are shown and jumped in double bridle. Many of these horses are shown before they have received any basic schooling or physical development. Trying to escape the action of the double bit such young horses will go with an open mouth or with the tongue over the bit or hanging out of the mouth. Some of them will develop the bad habit of never having a relaxed lower jaw, nor will they accept the bit with confidence. They lose points later on when participating in dressage tests on account of grinding teeth and flapping lips.

Of course, a horse is easily collected by means of the force of a double bit, but this kind of collecting does not reach further than the neck; the hindlegs are dragged far behind. When young horses are ridden too soon in a double bit they are forced to drop their back and develop incorrectly.

In France there are special showjumping competitions held which are open only for French bred horses from the age of four to five years. In these competitions one is only allowed to use an ordinary thick snaffle and no martingale. This is a national rule to prevent young horses being spoiled at an early age.

CHAPTER FOURTEEN

# IMPROVEMENT AND RE-SCHOOLING

### WRONG FORELEG TECHNIQUE

NEARLY all horses who are schooled systematically in the Natural Training Method will jump willingly with confidence and with good technique. However, even when one is schooling a young horse right from the beginning, which is ideal, the horse can have difficulties while jumping due to bad conformation.

There are specialised schooling techniques which will improve the horse's jumping style, no matter whether the horse has a naturally bad jumping technique or a deficient one due to bad schooling. Rapping is not only against the regulations but utterly useless, especially as a long-term remedy. The best and most natural way to improve the young horse and to correct the older one is to use the jumping lane *unmounted*. The distances between the various elements of the jumping lane should vary, depending on the horse's length of stride and fault in technique. Remember to use brushing boots, overreach boots and knee caps to safeguard the horse's legs.

Some horses do not fold their forelegs correctly. They bring the forearm forwards and leave the lower leg hanging down. In young horses this is mainly due to weakness or inexperience. Older horses mostly use their back and shoulder muscles incorrectly on account of bad schooling.

This wrong foreleg technique can be corrected by gradually shortening the normal distances in between the elements of the jumping lane.

The reason for shortening the distances until the required result is achieved is that when these distances are shortened the horse is forced to bring the hocks under. While doing so the horse has to shift more weight from the forehand to the quarters, which are lowered and engaged. With less weight on the forehand the horse is now in a better position to use his muscles in the forehand with greater ease and freedom. The horse is also forced to fold his forearm correctly, otherwise he would knock the obstacle. This will certainly happen in the beginning. Therefore do not forget to protect the horse's legs.

*Fig. 445*
Wrong foreleg technique. The forelegs should be folded.

*Changing the nature of the oxer*

The top front pole of the oxer at the end of the lane should be two to three holes higher than the single pole at the far end. This teaches the horse to bend his forearm further, to the extent that his forefeet nearly touch his elbows. If the far pole is higher then the oxer will be sloping upwards and the horse will still be able to clear it easily without bending his knees correctly.

Shorten the distances in between the fences very gradually and spread the oxer until the

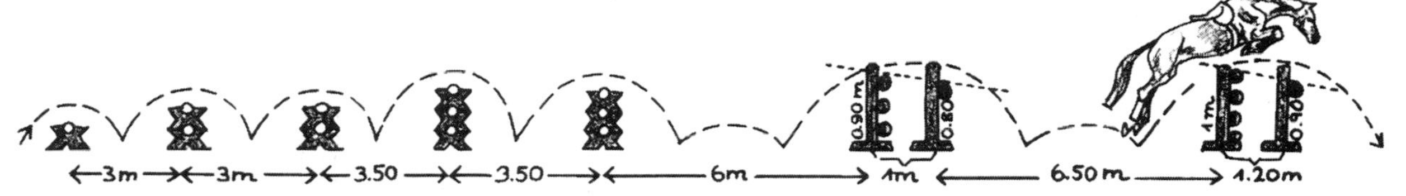


*Fig. 446*
Teaching a horse to fold his forelegs

horse has gradually corrected his wrong foreleg technique completely.

One should, of course, have *patience* and spread this specialised re-training over a length of time, otherwise the horse will become upset, lose confidence and refuse. Realise that improving the foreleg technique requires a slow muscle development, which can take quite some time. And even if the re-training is done correctly it will still take roughly three to four months before good results are obtained. After this period the horse should be able to jump not only the jumping lane *unmounted* at the normal distances but also single fences with a perfect foreleg technique.

Some people use solid fences to improve their horse's foreleg technique. This is, of course, worse than rapping. I have too often seen promising young horses lose their confidence on a solid fence and/or carry big knees for the rest of their life.

TRAILING FORELEGS

A common fault in thoroughbred horses is the trailing of the foreleg. This is because, by nature, they move with their forefeet low over the ground. A horse with a natural knee action will automatically fold and lift his forelegs correctly.

Horses who allow their forelegs to trail when jumping are often unsafe in landing and give the rider a most unpleasant feeling, because while landing they put their forelegs forward at the very last moment, in some cases one by one. This is often the cause of a so-called "peck on landing" and subsequently a nasty fall.

Horses with this dangerous foreleg technique usually bring the hocks too far under at take-off (often to an extent of overreaching). The horse's body is in too vertical a position. This shortens the horse's base of support and in this position he has difficulty in finding his balance and cannot use the muscles in his forelegs at take-off.

*Fig. 447*
Wrong foreleg technique. Trailing forelegs.

*Fig. 448*
The wrong foreleg technique will cause a nasty fall (peck on landing).

*Fig. 449*
Normal jump curvature.

*Fig. 450*
Curvature too steep, forelegs trailing.

To improve this too vertical position of the horse's body, *widen* the distances between the various elements of the jumping lane gradually. In order to clear the next element the horse will have to reach forward. He will no longer be able to raise the front of his body as high and will automatically bring his knees forward and lift and fold the lower foreleg correctly.

*Changing the nature of the oxer*

Widen the oxer and change its nature by raising the pole on the far end two to three holes higher than the top front pole. This makes the oxer slope upwards, which forces the horse to bring his knees into a forward position while jumping the oxer. His knees will be well bent and his forefeet will come closer to his elbows. By practising this system correctly and by spreading this schooling over three to four months the horse will undoubtedly improve his bad foreleg technique.

HINDLEG FAULTS AND USE OF THE BACK

Tense and nervous riders, who constantly interfere with the horse's mouth and pull his head up, cause the horse's back to drop. This creates an excited horse who leans on the bit and, in many cases, one who will incur jumping faults with the hindlegs.

It is amazing to see that the same horse, when jumping *unmounted* in the jumping lane, performs relaxed and in a much better manner than when being ridden by his usual rider. Instead of rushing the fences he will jump unmounted so calmly and slowly that one has to send him on with the whip.

If the horse gives such a different performance when unmounted then it is advisable that the horse should be ridden by a more experienced and calmer rider who has better hands.

However, if the horse also performs with a bad technique unmounted then the fault lies in the horse himself. Horses are only careless with their hindlegs if they are not using their back and neck muscles correctly. One notices this when the horse is clearing the elements in the jumping lane unmounted. The horse is unbalanced over the jumps because he is not stretching the neck and lowering the head position, but instead lifts up his head and drops his

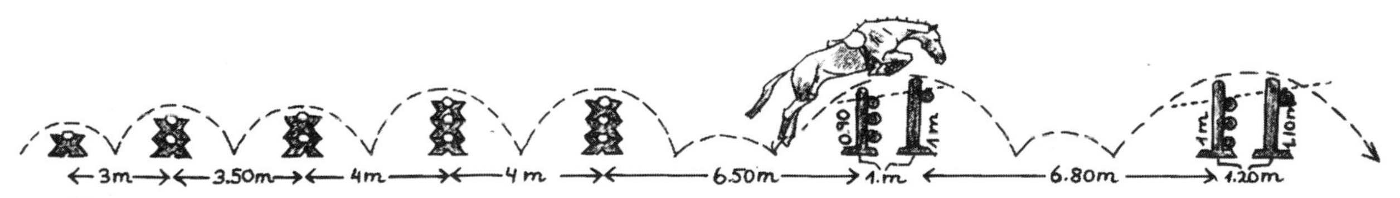


*Fig. 451*
Correcting the horse from trailing his forelegs.

*Fig. 452*
Wrong technique. The horse is not using his back, thereby making faults with his hindlegs.

back at every element. This raised head position, in conjunction with the hollow back, forces the horse to change the centre of gravity too much to the hindquarters. As a result the horse is unable to fold and lift his hindlegs sufficiently.

To correct this one has to develop the horse's neck, back and quarters by extensive gymnastic exercises on the flat, lungeing with the Chambon and schooling on foot.

*Changing the nature of the oxer*

Apart from these exercises the horse needs a specialised jumping re-training. This is done by shortening the distances in the jumping lane gradually. It forces him to bring his hindlegs further underneath his body at take-off and to round and use his back over the fences to the utmost degree, with head and neck in a low position and his nose well forward. Now the horse's highest point, whilst airborne over a fence, will be the withers instead of the head.

At the end of the jumping lane build two oxers fairly high and spread, depending, of course, on the horse's experience. The distance in between should be approximately 6·5 metres. Both oxers should be completely parallel. These parallels should be widened gradually, maintaining the distance of 6·5 metres. The fact that both oxers are completely parallel encourages the horse while jumping to round his back in such a way that the highest point of the semi-circle line the horse's body describes is situated exactly over the centre of the width of each oxer. In the beginning, when retraining, the horse might certainly knock the far pole of the oxer with his hindlegs, but soon he will correct this carelessness himself.

To prevent the horse putting one foreleg in between the oxer or from losing confidence one should place a pole diagonally across each oxer. This conceals the spread of the oxer.

During the re-schooling one will notice an improvement in the horse's jumping technique. According to this I bring the distances step by step back to the normal ones. At the end of this re-training period of three to four months the horse should be able to jump the whole lane at normal distances in the newly acquired good style. If at any time the horse should show the tendency to jump in the bad style again, alter the distances again as described in the pre-schooling programme above.

In general one can say that carelessness with the legs when jumping always has a particular *reason*. Find it out, then decide upon a specialised training programme and have endless patience to see it through. This is the only cure.

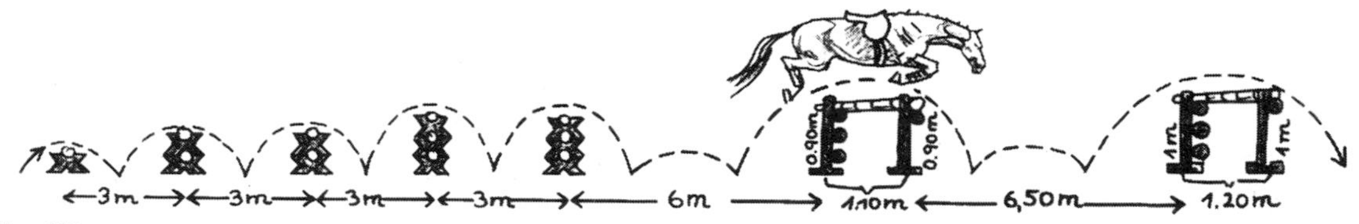


*Fig. 453*
Teaching the horse to use his back and fold his hindlegs properly.

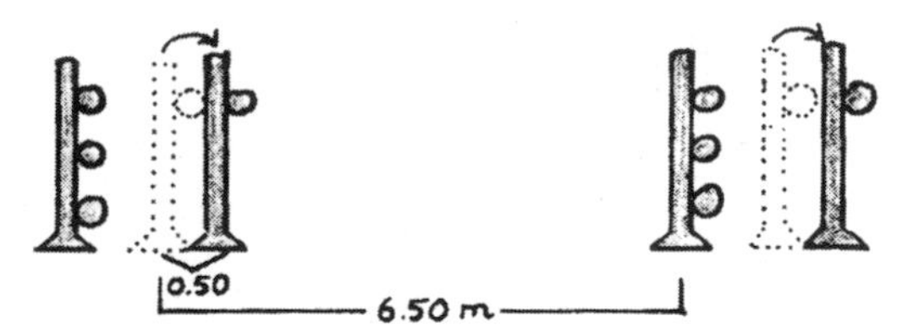


*Fig. 454*
By spreading the first oxer the distance between the two oxers becomes shorter, which would be very wrong.

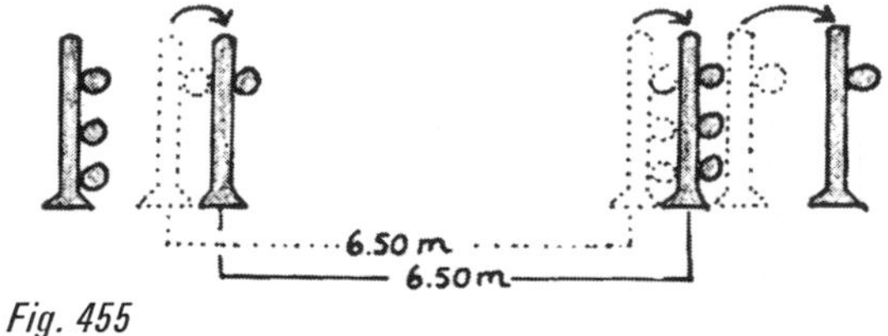


*Fig. 455*
Therefore, when spreading the first oxer never forget to move the complete second fence further away by the same margin, as well as spreading it.

Rapping or jumping the horse over higher or solid fences is not only cruel but unwise as well, because it does not work. It is of no lasting value and often worsens the situation.

Training must be logical, systematic and natural. All artificial training methods cause pain if the horse resists.

He who has a knowledge and love of horses will agree that cruel training methods are completely wrong, cause unnecessary frustration and suffering to the horse and have no educational value. The horse will become upset, lose confidence in his trainer and himself and will become unco-operative.

### DIFFICULTIES AT TAKE-OFF

A young horse, which has from the beginning been correctly schooled unmounted in the jumping lane, will have no problem later on when mounted to judge the take-off point. The horse has confidence and is able to assist himself. This becomes obvious, especially in a difficult take-off position, providing that the rider does not interfere.

If a horse is not as surefooted as one schooled in the Natural Training Method he is probably in general uncertain in approaching a fence. He will either reach for the fence from too far away or will come too close to it, putting in an extra short stride before take-off. Such a horse needs re-schooling unmounted in the jumping lane.

However, if a horse has take-off difficulties only at certain obstacles this can be corrected by a special re-training method. Condition is, of course, that the trainer knows exactly where the correct take-off position for the various types of fences is.

Generally speaking, fences can be divided into three categories:

*Upright fences*

The correct take-off position is at a distance approximately equal to the height of the fence. At a gate of 1 metre high the horse should take-off 1 metre in front and land about 1 metre behind it.

*Parallel oxers*

The correct take-off position is at a distance approximately equal to the height plus half the width of the oxer.

*Staircase fences*

This category includes the triple bar, the hog's back fence and the fan fence. The position of the take-off is at a distance equal to the height of the first pole or part of the fence. A fan fence has at one side only one wing; it is at this side an upright fence. At the other side the fence has four wings; at this side it is a triple bar fence. If the rider approaches the fence on the side with the one wing the horse has to take-off at a distance equal to the height of the fence at that side. If the rider approaches the fence on the other side he will be jumping a triple bar and can therefore come closer to the fence. The distance between take-off position and fence should be equal to the height of the first and lowest pole of the fan.

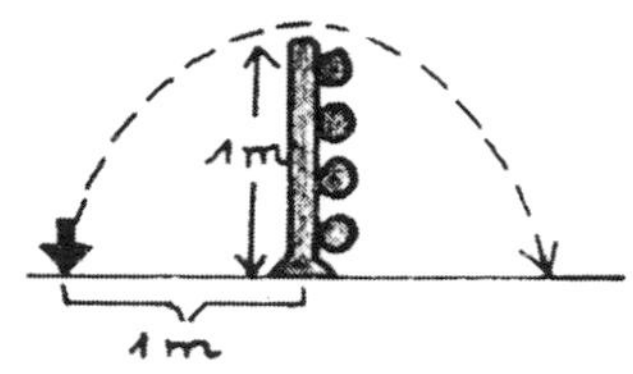


*Fig. 456*
Correct take-off point at a straight fence.

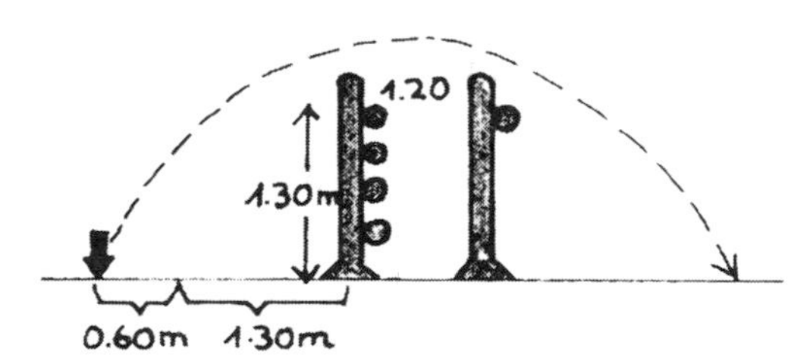


*Fig. 457*
Correct take-off point at an oxer.

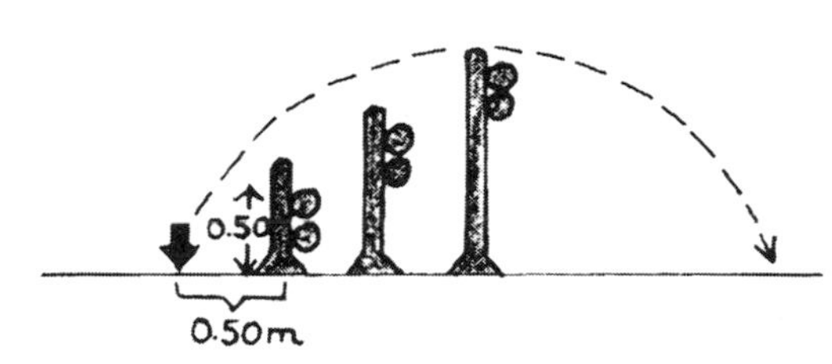


*Fig. 458*
Correct take-off point at a triple bar.

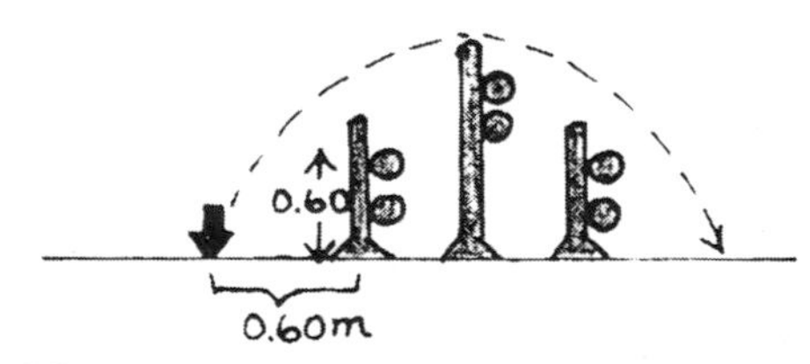


*Fig. 459*
Correct take-off point at a hog's back.

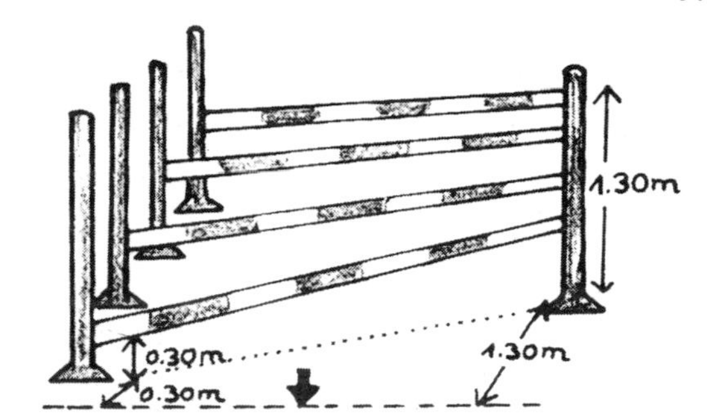


*Fig. 460*
Correct take-off point at a fan fence.

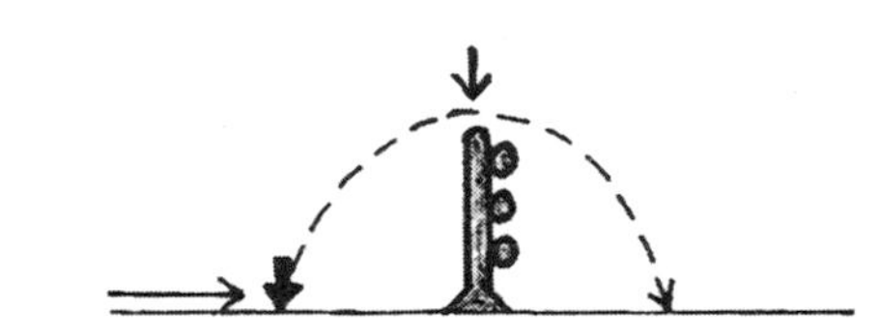

*Fig. 461*
Correct jump curvature.

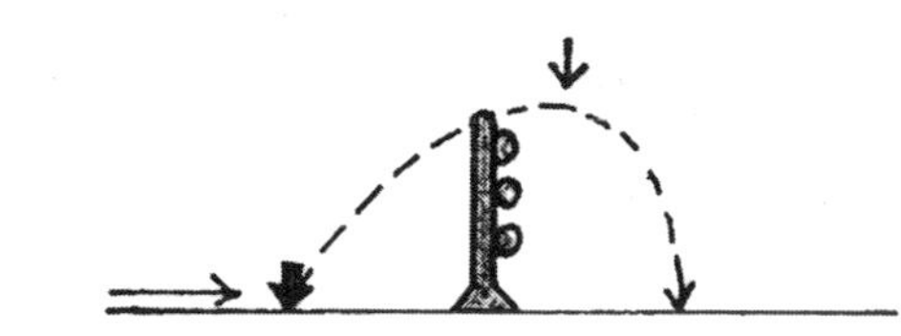

*Fig. 462*
Incorrect jump curvature.

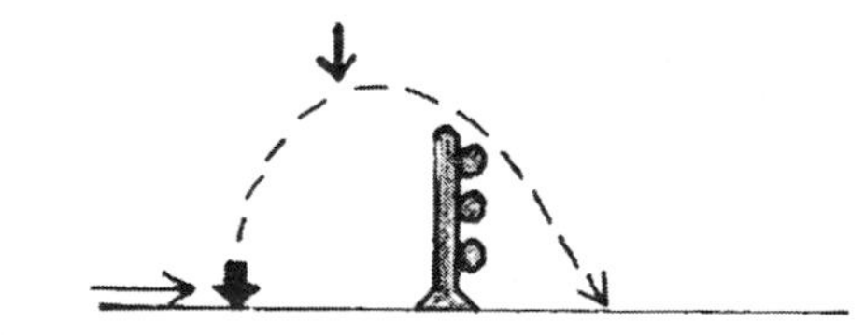

*Fig. 463*
This jump curvature is also incorrect.

Nevertheless, even if the horse takes-off at the correct point he still can incur faults if the curvature of the jump is not correct. As mentioned earlier, the correct curvature is a regular semi-circle line and one which is too steep or too flat will most likely incur faults. This will be most obvious at a combination jump, where the horse will be in serious trouble at the second, and even more so at a possible third element.

Various other take-off difficulties are described overleaf, with suggestions as to how the difficulties can be overcome.

### COMING TOO CLOSE

Horses with a short stride are inclined to come too close to a fence, which makes it very difficult to take-off correctly, particularly at a spread fence. At combinations the horse finds the normal distances problematic and there is a tendency for him to put in an extra short stride. This makes it quite impossible for the horse to clear a large spread because he comes too close to the fence and would have to take-off nearly vertically. Some clever horses may still be able to clear an obstacle from that position if it is a single fence, but if it is the first element of a combination the horse will find himself in a serious situation. Because he took off too close to the first element he will not only land too close behind it but will also lose considerable impulsion. The distance to the second element of the combination grows too long and the horse has therefore to reach for it.

A really bold horse will battle on even if he stands too far back from the second element. If this is an oxer parallel then he is likely to knock the far pole. If the timid and reluctant horse has to cope with such a difficult situation he will either put in an extra short stride, which will cause him to knock the front top pole of the oxer, or he will try to not jump at all, refuse or run out at the second element.

Coming too close to an obstacle is often caused by the rider himself, who has forced his horse to do so and whose ambition is out of proportion to his ability.

Some riders, from force of habit, try too hard to regulate the speed of their mount when approaching an obstacle. They interfere by incorrectly adjusting the horse's stride. They impair the rhythmic tempo of the horse's pace and disturb his concentration. The result is a refusal or a knock down.

Such a rider should practise the exercise in the jumping lane, without reins, to correct his own bad habits.

*Re-training in the jumping lane*

Commence re-training a horse who habitually comes too close to a fence at take-off in the jumping lane unmounted. Reduce the distances in between the elements of the lane by approximately 0·3 metres if the horse has a natural short stride.

The distances are now tailored to his requirements, allowing him to take-off without inserting an extra short stride. In time this will become established and the horse's confidence will grow.

Then, starting at the far end of the lane, gradually increase the distances until they are

*Fig. 464*
The horse coming too close to the wall has to take off at an extremely steep angle.

*Fig. 465*
At a straight fence the situation can be saved by jumping the fence at an angle.

not only normally long but extra long. This necessitates that the horse during the non-jumping strides in between the elements maintains impulsion. The horse must be sent on sufficiently so that he is not tempted to go back to his old fault and put in an extra short stride just before take-off. This uniform pace, coupled with the increased distances, compels the horse to lengthen his strides and to stand further back at each take-off. Once good results have been achieved unmounted, repeat the same exercise when mounted. The rider, however, must be very alert, applying strong leg aids to prevent his horse from slowing down the pace in between the elements of the lane. The rider must drive his horse energetically once he realises that the horse is losing heart or impulsion.

*If unmounted*, the horse should approach the lane out of a relaxed but active canter.

If *mounted* the rider should approach the lane out of a trot and, of course, in the forward seat.

*Re-training over single fences*

To train the horse to stand further back at single fences use a "take-off pole" in front of the obstacle.

(1) *At an upright fence* of 1 metre high, theoretically the horse should take-off at a distance of approximately 1 metre in front of the fence. To assist the horse in locating his correct take-off point, place a take-off pole on the ground in front of the fence at a distance of 0·7 metres. This leaves the horse 0·3 metres for a take-off position and he has no alternative but to stand back correctly.

If re-training a nervous horse who dashes flat out into a fence, arriving too close for take-off approach the fence with the take-off pole out of a figure of eight at a slow trot in the forward seat. Once the horse has settled down comfortably at a trot then proceed with the exercise in a slow canter.

(2) *At an oxer parallel* 1 metre high and 1·2 metres spread, theoretically the horse should take-off at a distance of approximately 1·6 metres (being 1 metre of the height and half of the 1·2 metres width of the oxer). Place the take-off pole at a distance of 1·3 metres in front of the oxer, leaving the horse 0·3 metres for his take-off position. This will necessitate that he stands well back.

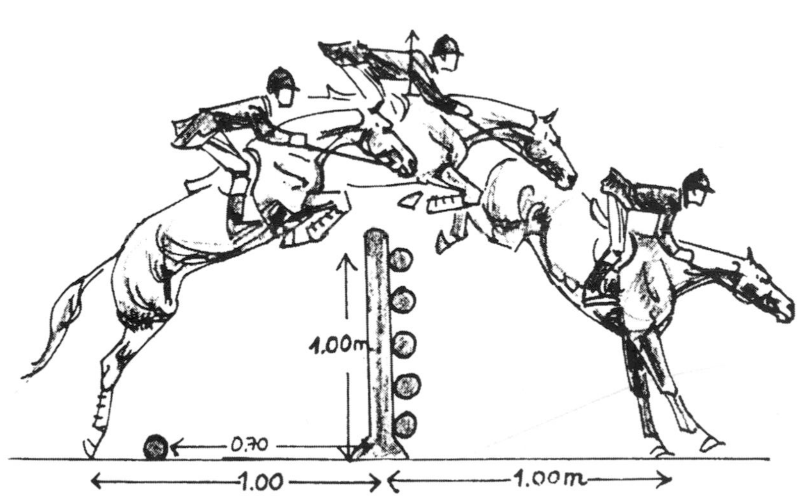


*Fig. 466*
Teaching a horse to stand back more by using a take-off pole, here at a straight fence.

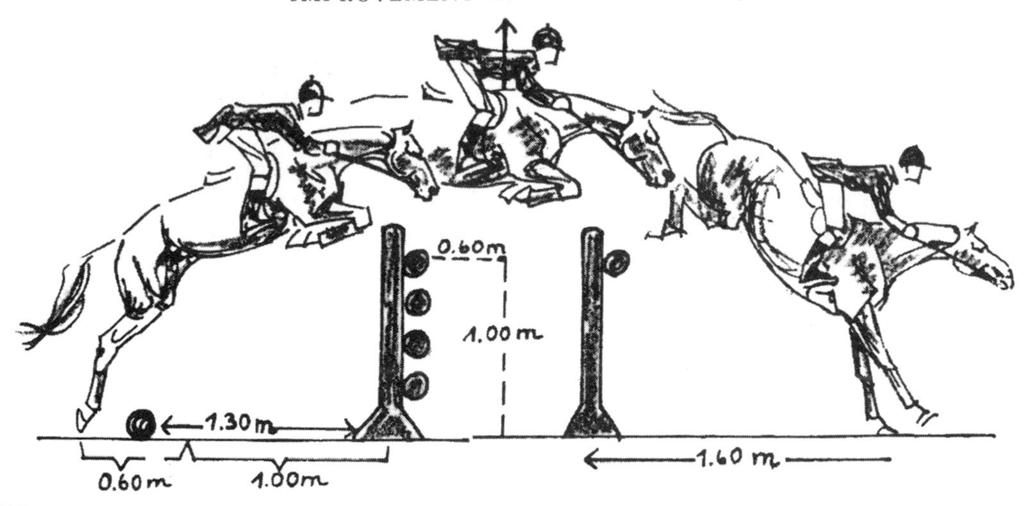


*Fig. 467*
Using a take-off pole at an oxer.

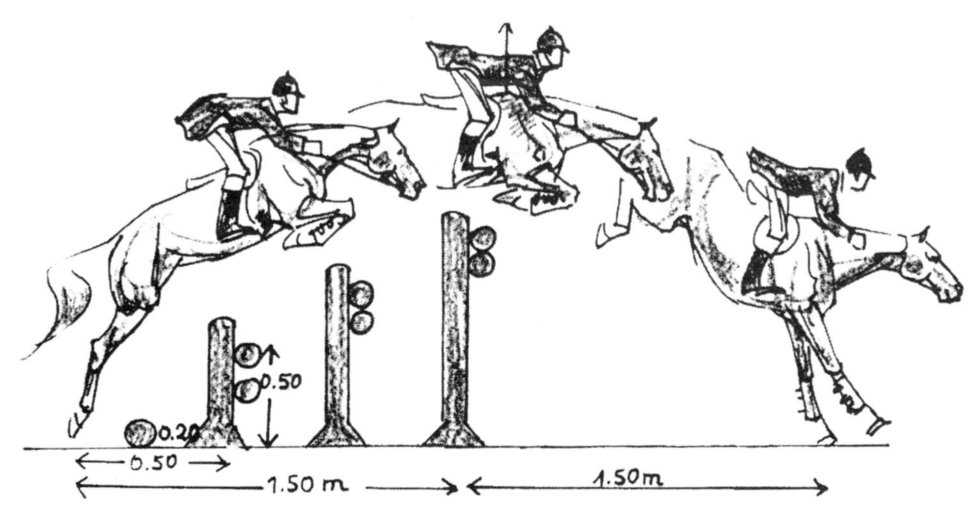


*Fig. 468*
Using a take-off pole at a staircase fence.

(3) *At a staircase fence* where the first front and lowest pole is, for instance, 0·5 metres high, the horse should take-off at a distance of approximately 0·5 metres from the obstacle – the height of the first pole. Therefore the take-off pole is placed only 0·2 metres out from the fence, which leaves 0·3 metres space for the take-off. When the horse *bascules* over the staircase fence the highest point of the semi-circle line will be exactly over that of the fence.

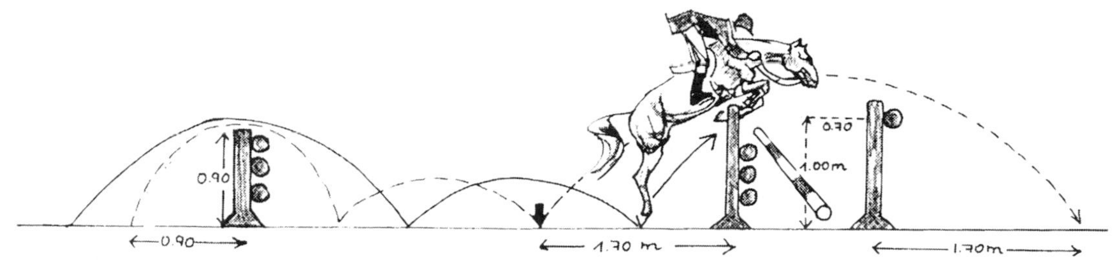


*Fig. 469*
At a combination fence the horse is in trouble. Having stood too far back at the first element he therefore comes too close to the second. Dotted line shows the correct take-off course which should have been followed.

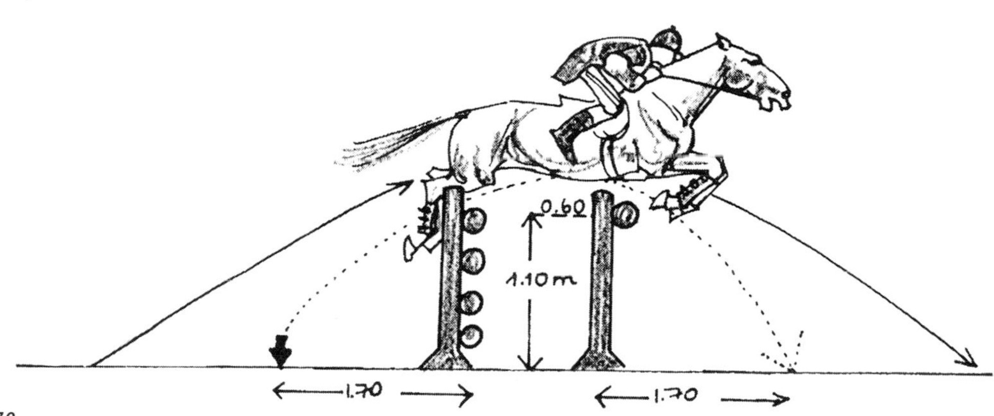


*Fig. 470*
The horse that stands back too far will knock the front pole of an oxer with his hindlegs. Dotted line shows correct take-off and jump curvature.

## STANDING BACK TOO FAR

Horses who have a naturally long and "bouncing" stride are inclined to stand back too far out from the fence when taking off. This will produce difficulties, not only at a spread oxer but in particular when jumping a testing combination. On account of standing back too far at the take-off the horse will tend to land too far over the first element and will then meet the second element uncomfortably close. The horse will either knock the front pole with his forelegs, refuse or run out at the second element.

Standing back too far at a single fence will also be costly. The horse will incur faults by knocking the far pole of a spread oxer with his hindlegs.

However, there are some imaginative and agile horses who take-off too soon yet are able to readjust their equilibrium instantly by extending their moment of suspension while airborne. In doing so they avoid rapping their hindlegs and incurring faults.

*Fig. 471*
At a single straight fence a clever horse will – having stood too far back – prolong the jump curvature to clear the fence.

*Re-training in the jumping lane*

The jumping lane, once again, is the most efficient means of re-schooling the horse. Start the re-training by lengthening the normal distances between the elements by approximately 0·6 metres. These increased distances will suit the horse's long stride better and he will no longer come too close to the second and following fences in the lane.

When the horse jumps these distances with a correct take-off position, gradually shorten them until they are extra short. The reduced distances force the horse to shorten his canter stride accordingly. This exercise will teach the horse to engage his quarters more efficiently and to round his back extensively. He will transfer more weight to the quarters and will jump with more balance and control. He will no longer find it necessary to take an obstacle by standing back too far out from it, nor to extend his moment of suspension while airborne, in order to avoid rapping his hindlegs.

*Re-training over single fences*

This is done mounted and with the aid of a take-off pole. In this case place the take-off pole further out from the obstacle to regulate the horse's take-off in a "natural" manner. This should be done without use of the rider's rein aids as a means of checking and placing the horse for a take-off position, the horse being in a position to regulate his strides himself. The take-off pole should be placed in front of the fence and so far out that the horse takes-off between pole and fence. The hoof imprints should be exactly centred in between the take-off pole and the fence.

(1) *At an upright fence* of 1 metre high, place the take-off pole at a distance of 3 metres when approaching the fence out of a trot and at a distance of 3.5 metres when approaching out of a canter.

(2) *At an oxer parallel* 1 metre high and 1 metre spread, place the take-off pole at a distance of 3·5 metres when approaching out of a trot and 4 metres when approaching out of a canter.

(3) *At a staircase fence*, where the first and lowest pole is 0·5 metres high and the highest pole 1·2 metres, with a spread of 1·5 metres, place the take-off pole at a distance of 2·5 metres when approaching out of a trot and 3·5 metres when approaching out of a canter. All these distances are, of course, average. An experienced trainer will make adjustments if necessary.

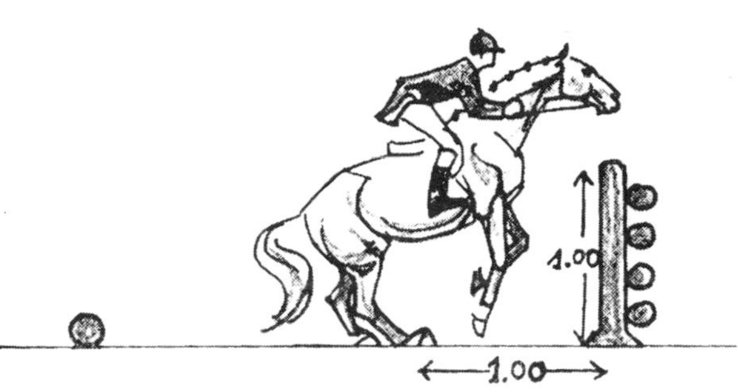


*Fig. 472*
Re-training a horse from standing back too far, with the use of a take-off pole. When approaching a straight fence out of a trot, place the pole 3 metres in front of the fence. When approaching in canter, place the pole 3.5 metres in front of the fence.

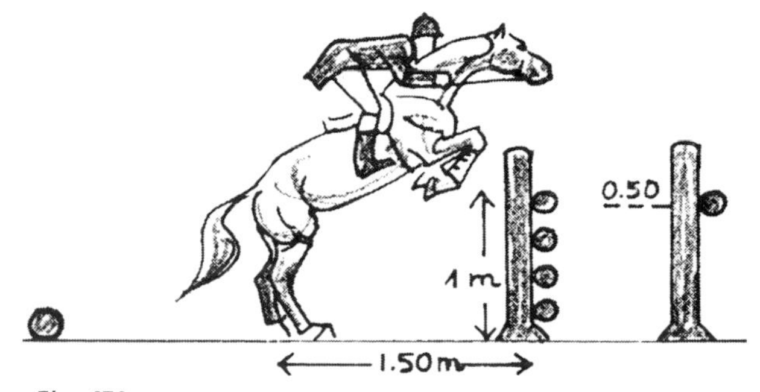


*Fig. 473*
When approaching an oxer parallel out of a trot, place the pole 3.5 metres in front of the fence. When approaching out of a canter, place the pole 4 metres in front of the fence.

During a jump-off against the clock some well-schooled horses display an amazingly intelligent take-off technique when jumping a combination fence. In the jump-off the horse has to travel at a much faster speed than that stated on the course plan. The distances of the combination fence, however, are unaltered and suitable for the competition speed stated on the course plan. For the faster jump-off speed these distances will be uncomfortably short. The horse has jumped the first element of the combination at the faster speed and has therefore landed further out over it. The well-schooled horse realises that he will be coming too close to the second element. Therefore he will approach and take-off at the second element slightly at an angle, in other words diagonally. This way he lengthens the distance between the elements and will be able to take-off correctly in spite of the faster speed.

During the *unmounted* schooling sessions in the jumping lane the horse acquired the ability to judge such a difficult take-off situation and displayed the initiative to cope with it. These qualities must be preserved during the whole of the horse's jumping training, because then the rider can, when actually taking part in competitions, rely on his horse's skill and full co-operation.

FORELEG CARELESSNESS

If a horse is careless with *one* or *both* forelegs, the trainer should set up fences and distances which will make the horse less so.

The rider should trot over four cavaletti. When clearing the first fence – the two cross poles – the horse will break into a canter.

Having cleared the second cross pole fence the horse is allowed only *one* non-jumping stride before take-off.

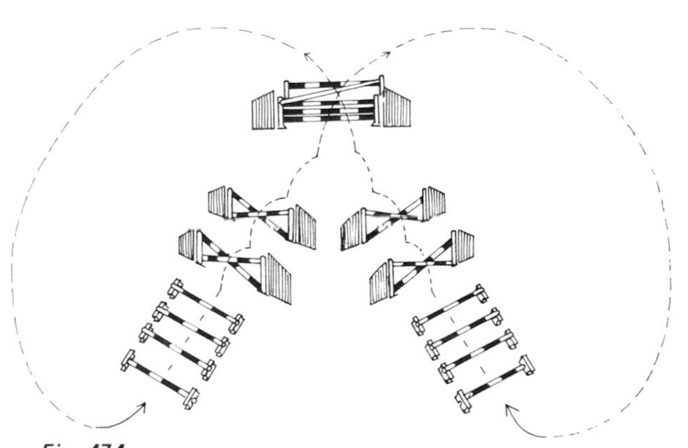

*Fig. 474*
Cavaletti at trot distance. To the first cross pole fence is 2·5 metres; to the next cross pole fence 3 metres and to the centre of the oxer 6 metres. The oxer measures 1 metre in front, 1·05 metres behind with a spread of 1·2 metres.

The purpose of this particular set-up of fences forces the horse to jump the last fence at an angle and it teaches him to exaggerate the flexion of *one* particular foreleg more than the other. When approaching the last fence at a left-hand angle the horse will reach the fence with his near foreleg first. In this position he will have no alternative but to flex and tuck his near foreleg well up to avoid knocking the pole.

At first the horse might knock his legs before he will learn better. Therefore always protect the horse's legs. In particular use kneecaps.

Horses who are habitually careless with *both* forelegs should be ridden over this course alternately on both reins. This is done simply by riding on a figure of eight.

If one has not the necessary fence material at one's disposal to build the complete course, one can improvise as follows:

First build a low upright fence, no higher than 0·5 metres, and place two take-off poles in V formation on the ground at the take-off side of the fence.

One should approach the fence out of a slow trot – never out of a canter – and only at a particular angle, depending on with which foreleg the horse is most careless. Do not approach out of a straight line. A proper well-planned approach is most important.

Make sure to present the horse squarely at the take-off pole and exactly at the centre of it. All four hooves must leave their imprints midway between the centre of the take-off pole and the centre of the fence.

Guiding the horse correctly is important, as the diagonal approach and jump is very difficult. Any swaying can make the fence into a very big spread.

According to the length of the horse's natural trot one crosses the take-off pole more towards the point of the V, where the distance is longest, or more towards the side of the fence, where the distance is shorter than at the centre. The distance between pole and fence may seem short if compared with those for re-training over single fences. But remember that there the pole and fence were approached on a straight line, where the horse can only engage the inner hock and will have considerably less impulsion, hence the shorter distance.

Supposing the horse is negligent with both forelegs, make the approach out of a figure of eight. This will improve both forelegs. While airborne one must urge the horse to change rein and land in that specific canter. For instance, when approaching the fence on the left-hand rein one will have to change rein over the fence to the right. The horse has to land into and

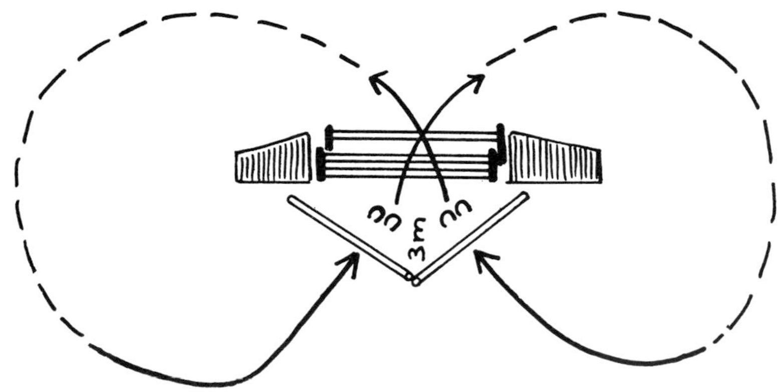


*Fig. 475*
Another excellent method of training an experienced horse to be careful with the forelegs. Approach at a trot only. The poles in V-formation – at the centre a good 3 metres away from the fence, at the sides about 1 metre.

continue on the right-hand turn in the right canter.

The aids for changing rein while airborne over a fence are as explained earlier.

Having jumped the upright a few times one can now alter it into a small low oxer which can be widened gradually. The oxer should not be higher than 1 metre and not wider than 1 metre, and should now be approached more towards the point of the V, where the distance between pole and fence is 3 metres. Since the oxer is jumped diagonally, which increases the spread considerably, and is jumped out of a slow trot, it is quite difficult for the horse, who must jump it completely from his hocks.

This build up is an excellent method, not only in re-schooling horses which are careless with the forelegs but is also valuable in making a horse flexible in the rib cage, as it has to jump on a figure of eight. It also teaches the horse to use his hocks and engage his quarters extensively. One will also find that a horse who is inclined to rush his fences will soon settle down.

To increase the effect use two additional fences, both upright ones. Having cleared the oxer, land into the appropriate canter and continue the turn to jump the additional straight fence. While airborne over this fence change rein again and land into the other canter and turn sharply into the new direction.

In changing direction over every fence, and in changing from one turn into another, the horse will become very supple because the lateral bending of the horse's body will change constantly according to the turns. There will also be less risk of the horse dashing off and coming onto the forehand, because by moving on a turn continuously the horse can only engage the inner hindleg. Therefore he creates only half his propulsive force, unlike a horse moving on a straight line with full engagement of both hindlegs.

There is an additional means to steady an excitable horse who rushes his fences too much: change the nature of the oxer. Instead of building an oxer parallel, lower the pole at the far end two holes. The horse will notice this lower back pole *only* when airborne over the fence. The surprise will subconsciously steady the horse and induce him to round his back and bascule well.

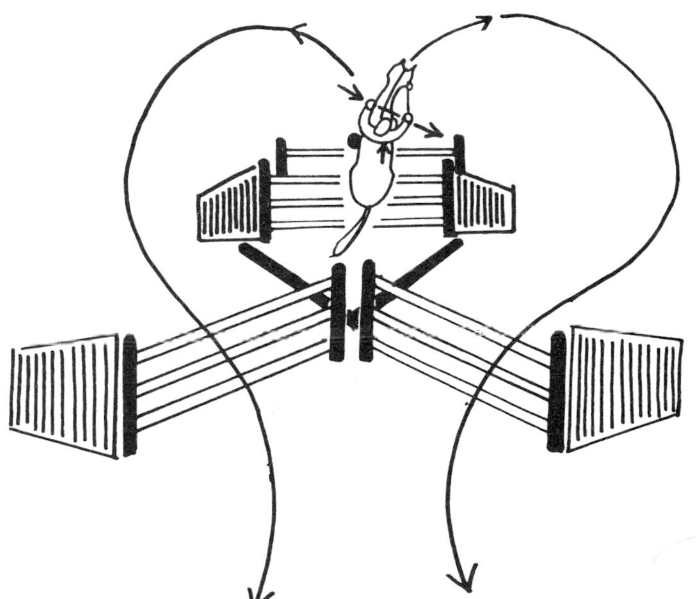

*Fig. 476*
Adapting the V-formation already used; later on also use two upright fences.

Never forget the powerful aid of a soothing voice when trying to calm an excited horse.

I stress that the above method of re-training is not recommended for a very young horse and should not be overdone with older ones. Jumping at an angle is extremely strenuous for the inner hock and loin muscles. A young horse would not stand up to it and would easily incur a stiff or even injured hock. That is also the reason why I am strictly against jumping on the lunge, as mentioned previously.

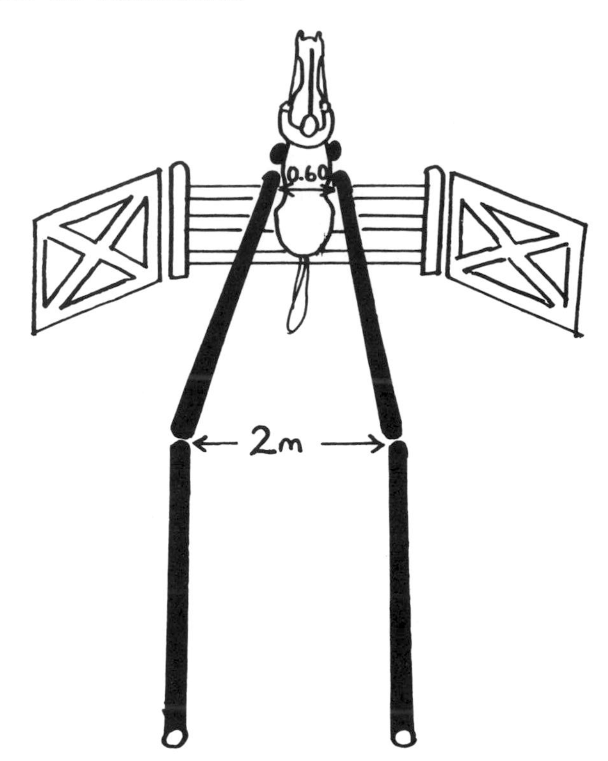


*Fig. 477*
Re-training a horse from a zig-zag approach.

### CORRECTING A ZIG-ZAG

There are horses, mostly novice or timid ones, who lack confidence at take-off. Instead of approaching fences in a straight line they move in a zig-zag line during the last four to five canter strides, searching for a suitable take-off position. When doing so the horse loses impulsion, and his flowing forward movement deteriorates to a bad take-off position, a refusal or a run-out at the fence.

*Re-training in the jumping lane*

To re-train these timid horses, at first lunge daily with the Chambon and also use unmounted exercises in the jumping lane.

In the jumping lane the horse has to approach the many elements all on a straight line. This fact alone will in time re-train the horse from a zig-zag approach. I mentioned that it is also necessary to increase the horse's impulsion and the length of canter stride. This is achieved by widening the distances in between the elements of the lane gradually.

To increase the horse's impulsion when mounted, and to eliminate hesitation at take-off, take advantage of the horse's herd instinct. Use an experienced horse to give the reluctant one a lead over the fences.

An additional means to give the horse confidence is to commence each re-schooling session in the jumping lane by putting all poles of each element together on the ground. Ride the horse through the lane over the poles. When the horse moves forward freely build up each element gradually, one by one. Start with the *last* fence in the lane. The next time round build up the second last as well, and so on. Everytime the horse jumps the lane he meets the new additional fence first. Once the horse jumps it the rest of the lane will be well known; the horse will jump it confidently and fluently. It would be an error to build up the elements starting with the *first* one. While building up all the fences gradually the "new" fence would always be the additional last one in the lane. When the horse is starting to jump the fences in the lane he will notice the strange fence ahead and, as he is a reluctant jumper, will slow down. He will then no longer be able to cope with the distances between the elements, will incur faults, refuse or turn around.

The horse should be ridden three times a week in the speed course – at a speed which is 50 metres per minute *faster* than the speed in which the horse normally competes in a jumping competition. This will improve the horse's impulsion and he will learn respect for the rider's forward driving leg aids.

An additional technique to correct a spooky horse, or one who habitually tries to run-out at a fence (both cases reflect the insecurity in the horse when he calculates the take-off point), is to place two poles 5 metres long in a V shape with their ends on the top front pole of a fence 0·6 metres apart. Their other ends should be placed on the ground. These poles are extended by two more poles placed *on* the ground.

The purpose of the position of these four poles is to form a passageway to guide the horse into a straight approach line and pulling the horse as a "magnet" towards the centre of the fence. When approaching the fence the rider should send the horse well on to the bit. While requesting a lengthening of his last three strides before taking-off, the rider should count these canter strides (when the leading forefoot touches the ground). The rider should count one, two, three, and the horse should take-off. If the rider ensures that the horse really lengthens the last three strides while remaining on the bit every horse will improve by this method. At first one should make it an easy fence, gradually increasing the size of it in accordance with the horse's confidence and progress made.

### THE ONE-SIDED HORSE

Most horses are stiffer on the right-hand side from birth. Also, most riders are right-handed and subconsciously apply stronger aids on this side. Because the right side is often the stiffer one it is more difficult to loosen and therefore is often neglected in the daily routine and when lungeing.

The one-sided horse is not only laterally stiff but also has a stiff hock on the same side and a one-sided hard mouth. To most riders the only and most obvious aspect of a one-sided horse is the one-sided hard mouth. They try to overcome it by using a more severe bit. This of course, is wrong. To a knowledgeable trainer it is logical that the whole stiff side of the horse must be suppled in order to give the horse a better mouth on that side. And that is not the only reason. It is also absolutely necessary that a horse is equally flexible on both sides in the rib cage, the quarters and the hock, because only then will he be willing to strike off and land into the leading canter on that stiff side and to do equally smooth and fast turns to both sides.

The re-training of a one-sided horse is achieved by daily lungeing with the Chambon by exercises on foot and by jumping fences at an angle. Rewarding results will be produced in about three months. The horse's body muscles will develop evenly over his frame and the flexibility will improve. As a result of this the horse's habit of taking the bit on one particular side will have gone completely.

If, for instance, a horse is stiffer on the right-hand side, place on the right-hand rein a cavaletti on the track. Place a take-off pole at an angle of 45° in front of the cavaletti. The kicking boards of the indoor school on the left side, or the railing surrounding a field, play a vital part in

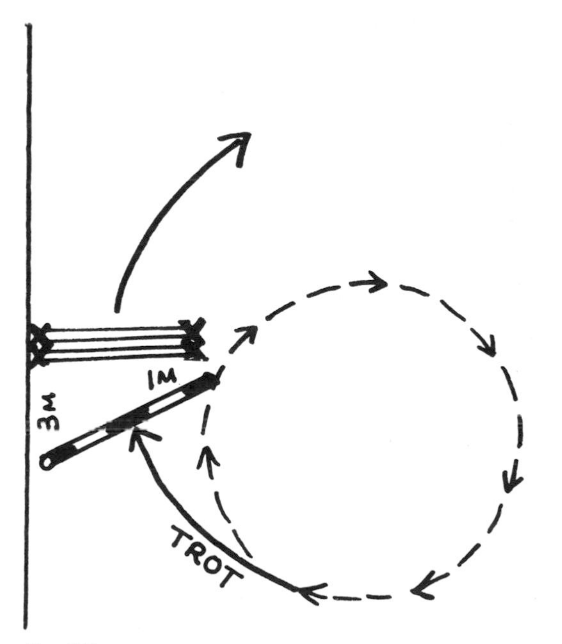


*Fig. 478*
Trot slowly on a circle, cross the pole in a slow trot and jump the fence. The pole is on the right-hand side 1 metre – on the left-hand side a good 3 metres – away from the fence.

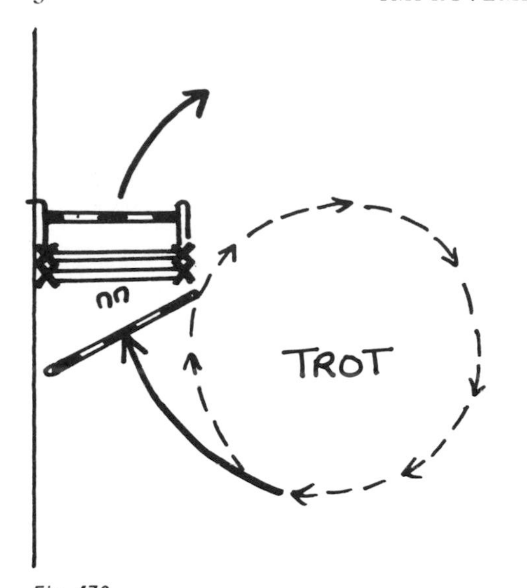


*Fig. 479*
Trot slowly on the circle, trot over the pole and jump – this time an oxer.

preventing the horse from running out to the left. Trot slowly in forward seat on a circle on the right-hand rein, close to the cavaletti. When the horse has settled down, trot him over the centre of the take-off pole and the cavaletti.

Place a second cavaletti on top of the first one. When this has been jumped correctly, and the horse lands in the right canter a number of times, place a pole behind the set of two cavaletti so that it forms a small oxer. This fence should not be more than 0·9 metres wide and 1 metre high.

Approaching this fence out of a right-hand turn, the horse's body is now bent laterally to the right. In this position the horse is forced to bring his right hindleg unusually far under, excellent to supple both body and hock.

Having jumped this small oxer a few times, place an upright fence 0·9 metres high ahead of the oxer at a distance of 6·3 metres.

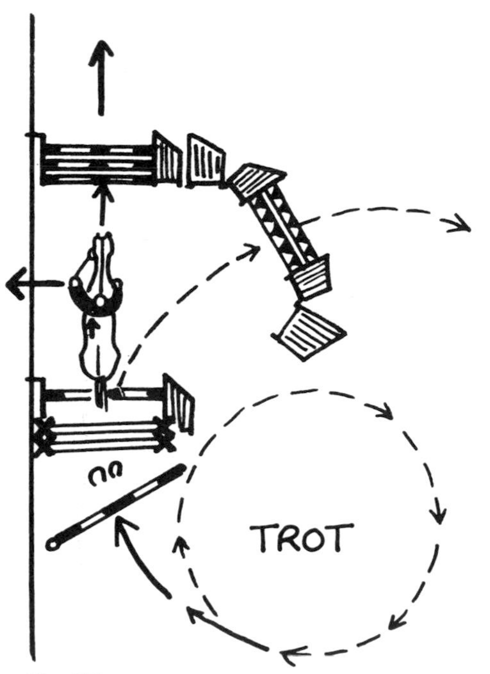


*Fig. 480*
Start the same way, but add an upright fence straight ahead at 6.3 metres, and on a fair right hand turn at 6.5 metres a straight fence. Jump both directions alternately. Note the open rein aid to remain on the straight.

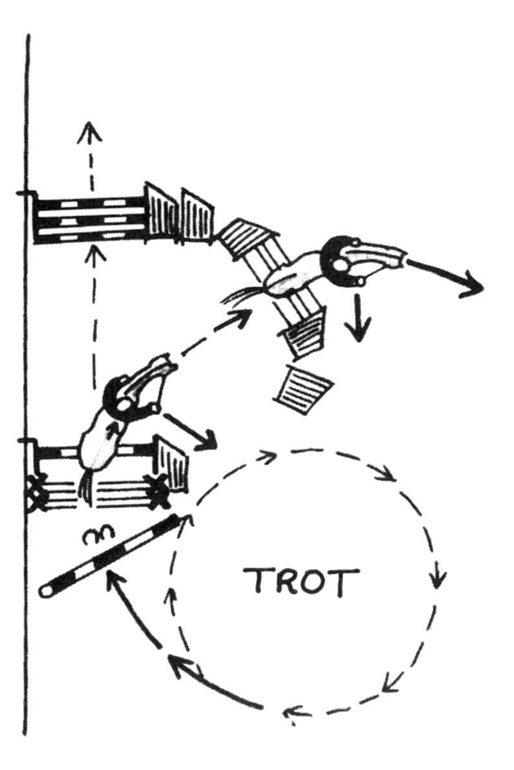


*Fig. 481*
Note the open rein aid when turning right.

If the horse is jumping relaxed and without rushing, build another small oxer with similar dimensions to the first one on the track at a distance of 10·3 metres. Further ahead, at a distance of 6·5 metres, build the final upright 0·9 metres high.

After the first fence an additional small fence (with wings) can be built on a right hand-turn at a distance of 6·5 metres, measured from the centre of the first oxer.

Now jump, alternately, the jumping lane on the track and the single fence on the circle to the right, continuing the right-hand circle from the approach of the whole set-up. It is *most important* to remember that when turning in alternate directions over the first fence one is very careful to apply *decisive* aids, whether one intends to continue on straight or to turn right.

On account of the fact that one is approaching the row out of a right-hand circle the horse might be tempted to continue on that line and run out to the right in between the first and second fence on the track. This tendency will be even stronger when one intends to go straight on *after* having previously turned right and jumped the single fence. A similar situation often arises in a competition if the horse in the jump-off has to make a left-hand turn after clearing a fence where he had to turn right in the first round. In most cases the former right-hand turn is still in the horse's mind. This will cause the horse to land into the previous right canter and try to follow the right-hand turn, a very important point to be remembered when jumping against the clock, where it is essential to land every time into the correct canter in order to save vital seconds by doing a smoother turn.

*The aids*

If one intends to go straight ahead after the first fence, look straight ahead to the *last* element of the lane while airborne over the first oxer. Transfer more weight on to the *left* stirrup, the left leg on the girths now being supported by strong pressure from the right leg *behind* the girths.

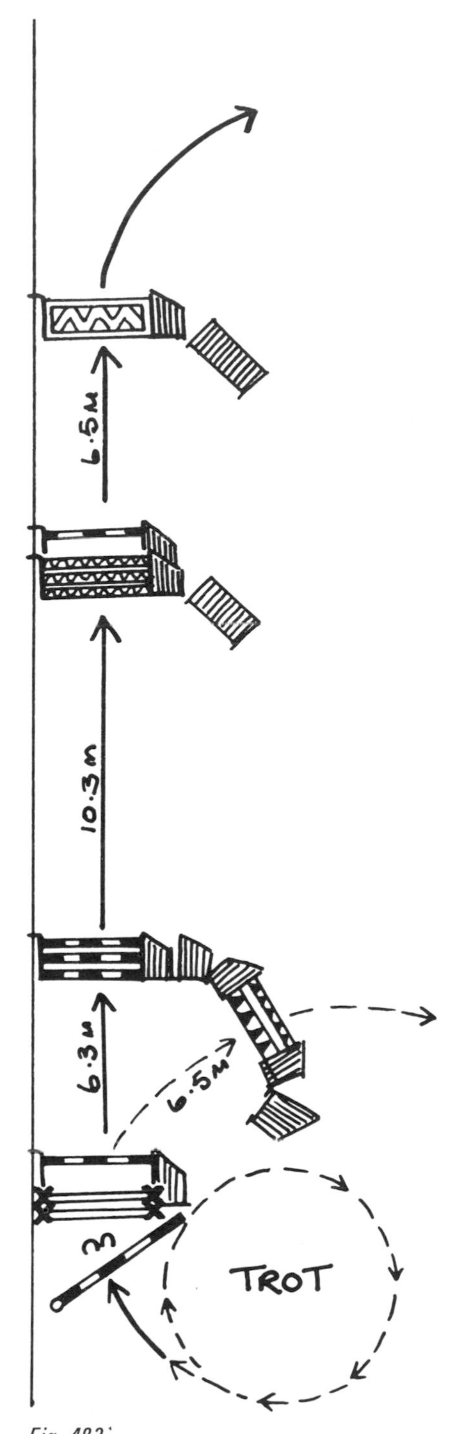


*Fig. 482*
Now add another oxer at 10·3 metres and a straight fence at 6·5 metres.

The left rein should be brought sideways out from the horse's neck, supported by the right rein pushed against the neck. Maintain the same tension on *both* reins. These combined aids will explain clearly to the horse that this time the rider wants to go straight ahead instead of turning right, as formerly. If necessary use these aids not only for the second but also for the following jumps of the lane to keep the horse from running out to the right.

If one intends to jump the single fence on the right-hand turn, and continue on a right-hand circle, one should look to the single fence on the right while airborne over the first fence. Approach the centre of this second fence, because only then is the distance between the two fences correct.

Transfer more weight on to the right stirrup with the right leg on the girths and the left leg pushing strongly behind the girths. Maintian with both reins the same tension on the bit, but bring the right hand sideways out from the horse's neck. Support this with the left rein pushed against the neck. Guide the horse into the right-hand turn.

These combined aids over the first oxer of the lane and again over the single fence compel the horse to land in the right canter. The same aids should also be applied when clearing the last element of the jumping lane.

If one's horse is stiffer on the *left*-hand side, build the whole set of fences on the left-hand rein, where the opposite technique in every detail applies.

### REFUSALS AND REASONS WHY

*Why* a horse refuses seems a great mystery to many riders. Riders in such difficulty have often asked me: "Why did he refuse? He has never refused before and now he is getting worse and worse. I cannot rely on him anymore. He always stops at a certain fence. He stops when the going is slippery or hard".

I will explain what is widely considered as an equestrian "mystery" in the hope of preventing horses from becoming habitual refusers. The reason I use the word mystery is that some riders just do not understand why their horses start to refuse fences and how this fault must be corrected.

#### *Lost confidence*

One can never be reminded enough about the importance of this word *confidence*. Lack of confidence is the most common reason for a horse refusing. "One can lead a horse to the water, but cannot make him drink". One can ride a horse to a fence, but it is very hard to make him jump once he has learnt to refuse. The best advice is that one's horse should never *learn* how to refuse. However, a horse schooled in the Natural Training Method has confidence in his rider, he will always obey, and jump well and willingly according to his ability because he has never learned to refuse.

If a horse loses his confidence it will be more evident in jumping than in any other field of equitation. To re-establish lost confidence may take months of patient and careful training, and even then the distrust may not disappear entirely.

It is quite possible that a young horse might refuse out of inexperience, simply on account of a misunderstanding, or because the horse is physically unable to cope with a certain fence. Therefore, if a horse refuses a fence or runs out, it is certainly not always disobedience. There may be a good reason for a refusal.

It is a grave mistake to make a scene out of a young horse's refusal. It will draw the horse's attention unnecessarily to the fact.

Rough punishment of a horse after a refusal, using spurs and rough rein aids and so on, is utterly useless and even damaging. Even more damage is done if the rider has to have an assistant sending the horse on over the fence with a whip. When a horse refuses in the jumping enclosure because fence stewards are standing too close to the fence, it reveals what bad experiences the horse has had and how little he trusts men.

Horses who take the bit after landing and run off, refusing the next fence, also lack confidence in their riders. They are afraid and therefore are trying to escape the rider's rough actions.

The use of force will create additional fear and self-defence. To cure such defects correctly one should avoid jumping single fences for the time being, but build several in-and-out fences without a non-jumping stride in between.

Because the elements follow so closely one after another the horse is unable to run off but has to come back by *himself* after every landing. In this position the horse has no alternative but to engage his quarters each time when taking off at the next element. The horse should not be pulled in the mouth after clearing the last element of the lane but come to a halt facing the kicking boards in the corner of the school *without* taking a stronger hold on the bit.

Another rule to prevent refusals is that horses who rush into fences should never be jumped in the direction of the exit or stable. Conversely, if the horse is not overkeen to jump and therefore refuses he should be jumped in the direction of the stable. This psychological aspect saves unnecessary problems. Always think and try to outsmart the horse.

It is important to put very high wings on each side of the fence. The wings must be higher than the fence to give the horse the impression that the jump is the lowest part and the easiest way out. A few bales of straw in front of the fence make a good ground line and make it more inviting for the horse.

Many young horses are taught to refuse before they have learned to jump. For example, a person buys a young horse and is not satisfied until he gets a chance to try out how high the horse can jump. Such people have no understanding for the horse's psyche anyhow, so it would be wasting time to tell them anything about confidence. They are careless in demanding more and more from the trusting, honest, young horse, going beyond his present capacities and in effect they are asking him to refuse. Such demands are almost criminal, as the horse certainly will completely lose all confidence in himself and his rider and become frustrated from this illtreatment. His first refusal will, from now on, surely not be his last one, as it will leave a mark in his mind for the rest of his life.

Nevertheless, even if one does not act so irresponsibly and the young horse is *not* tried out in this manner, one might overface the horse by surprising him and cause him to refuse. The young horse will be taken by surprise if he is faced suddenly with a strange fence. For example, a colourful wall. Show the obstacle to the horse first. If he is very shy, cover the approach side of the wall with bales of straw. After having jumped the wall a few times, gradually remove the straw from the wall. Using this method his confidence grows gradually and he will, later on, jump the wall like any other fence with comparative ease and confidence.

Another reason for a refusal is if the fences during a schooling session are suddenly put up a few holes. The willing young horse does not refuse on account of the height of the fence but because of the *sudden* rise in height. Fences should only be raised one hole at a time and never two or three holes at once, otherwise one is asking for refusal and undermines the horse's confidence.

If a young horse has refused a fence do not punish him but reduce the fence completely. Put the poles on the ground and ride the horse over them at a walk and later at a trot. If the horse is relaxed, build up the jump gradually and his confidence will return.

*Do not overwork* the horse when training over jumps. If the horse's legs swell up the following day it is a sign that the horse has done too much on the previous day.

Not having enough experience to find the correct take-off point is often the reason for a refusal. Apply strong leg aids when you feel the horse slowing down and try not to interfere with the hands. When the horse carries his nose right up in the air on account of the rider's rein actions he cannot get a clear picture of the take-off position and will subsequently refuse.

All in all, one can say that a well-schooled horse has confidence in himself and his rider and will not easily refuse.

*Pushing too hard*

A refusal is sometimes caused when the horse

is surprised by being suddenly pushed too hard during the last few canter strides up to the fence. At that exact moment the horse is calculating the distance to the fence and searching to find a correct take-off position. This unnecessary and exaggerated pushing brings the horse instantly off balance, hence the pace becomes irregular due to the sudden increase in speed. The horse is forced to shift his weight suddenly to the forehand and is not able to transfer the excess weight back rapidly in order to engage his quarters sufficiently, enabling him to free his forelegs off the ground in time to take-off. As a result the horse is unsure at take-off and will either refuse or, if he is a real trier, go right through the fence. Overpushing might also cause the horse to stand too far back, dropping into the middle of a fence and hurting his legs. He will remember this pain and will be not too keen to repeat the experience, refusing the next time. When approaching an obstacle make sure that the horse keeps an even pace without losing impulsion. Apply *even* support with forward driving leg aids and send the horse well onto the bit, slightly lengthening the last strides. This is how one should approach a fence, not by suddenly overpushing just before take-off and thus causing the horse to refuse.

*Dropping the reins*

Other riders make the mistake of suddenly dropping their reins either during the last few strides when approaching the fence or just at take-off, which brings the horse instantly off balance. The horse suddenly loses all contact with the rider's hand and is forced to change his centre of gravity to the forehand. This prevents the horse engaging his quarters sufficiently for take-off and as a result he comes too close to the fence. Once the rider has dropped his reins there is nothing to prevent the horse from running out at a fence or refusing.

On the other hand, there are horses who during the last few strides before take-off slow down their pace and lose impulsion. Then the rider might be inclined, mistakenly, to drop the reins or ease the feeling on the bit. Instead, he should send the horse strongly forward and push him energetically well up to the bit. These horse's mostly lack obedience to the rider's leg aids. The respect for the leg aids should be increased at home by schooling the horse with spurs and whip. Later on the horse will be more obedient to the leg aids without the spurs and whip being used. Only then will the rider be able to send the horse well on to the bit to maintain a steady contact with the mouth in approaching a fence and in take-off. Obedience to the leg aids is of vital importance if one hopes to obtain good and consistent results in showjumping.

*Slowing down the pace*

This is a bad habit and one which in effect is asking for a refusal.

Instead of riding the course in an even set pace there are riders who make the mistake of going too fast in between the fences and slowing down when approaching a fence. Hence, they make too wide turns, being unable to bring the horse straight into the fence for take-off. Such riding is looking for refusals and trouble, especially if the obstacle is a spread or a combination jump.

*Approaching too far left*

One can often see in competitions how riders cause the horse to refuse by approaching the fence too much to the left-hand side. Of all horses, 99% will run out to the left if they are running out at a fence because most horses are by nature more laterally flexible on the left-hand side.

Besides this, many people when breaking a horse lunge only on the left-hand rein, developing the horse one-sided. Such a horse should approach the fence slight'y more to the right instead of at the centre.

*Newly shod*

This reason for refusing is often overlooked. Often horses are shod a day before, or even on, the morning of a competition. This may cause refusing because the new shoes usually take a few days before they feel comfortable. In landing over a jump the horse may find them very uncomfortable, particularly when the going is hard. Therefore I suggest one has one's horses shod at least a couple of days before a competition.

*Jumping facing the sun*

When I am building a course I always try to place the fences in such a way that the horse does not have to jump facing the sun, because it may cause him to refuse, especially at combination jumps. But sometimes the course builder cannot avoid a situation where a fence must be jumped facing the sun. Therefore, to prevent refusals in a competition, I suggest jumping brightly coloured fences at home facing the sun. When the horse gets accustomed to jumping against the sun he will not be taken by surprise in the jumping arena.

*Too much checking*

When approaching a fence some riders check and place their horses to such an extent that the horse refuses. By calculating the size and nature of the fence the rider can regulate the approach and adjust the length of the horse's stride. But if the rider lengthens or shortens the stride too much he interferes with the horse's rhythmic tempo in pace, which will become irregular and unbalanced. A horse ridden and schooled in such an unnatural manner will depend totally on the rider's initiative, and if the rider makes the slightest mistake in his judgement in finding a correct take-off point the horse will find it impossible to cope with the situation and has no other alternative but to refuse.

However, a horse schooled in the Natural Training Method develops his initiative in searching for the correct take-off point. He will not let his rider down and will be able to cope, even with a difficult situation, just as he had to do when he was jumping unmounted.

*Martingale*

A young horse will be excited by the strange surroundings and the atmosphere of a show. Everything is new to him and out of curiosity he will lift his head and look around. That is why most young horses in the beginning of their first season carry their head a little high. This is normal and natural; a horse turned out into a strange field would react the same. The rider should understand and accept this. Should he try to force the horse's head down with a martingale the horse would feel hindered and unhappy. He would stiffen himself, fight it and most likely refuse. Therefore ignore the horse's high head position at this stage and do not try to correct it.

When approaching a fence the horse will lower his head and neck automatically in order to see the take-off point. As time goes by the horse will gain more confidence, will concentrate more on his jumping and will lose interest in surroundings which had so much attraction for him in the beginning.

*The tense rider*

Refusing can be considered as a result of the rider's wrong state of mind, which he, unknown to himself, projects onto his horse. When the rider is either too anxious or too hesitant, and therefore, interferes too much with the horse's natural behaviour, it will provoke the horse to refuse. This is because nerves and fear are the first thing that the horse senses about the rider.

The tense and insecure rider must try to control himself, keep calm and trust the horse's ability. The rider should ride the course as if there were no strange or difficult fences and most horses will then not even think of refusing.

*Overworked*

Halfway through the jumping season, more and more horses who had originally started the season keen and full of confidence, start to refuse. One of the reasons is that the horses are overjumped, tired, stiff and no longer in top condition. They are exhausted, turn sour and lose all interest and confidence in jumping. For these reasons it is most important that if the horse has to compete nearly every weekend he is *not* jumped at home.

Relax the horse by hacking daily. This should

include long walking sessions on a loose rein, as this gives the horse, after all the excitement of competition, some peace of mind. Weather permitting, turn the horse out on grass for a few hours every day so that he can exercise his muscles freely.

If there is no paddock available, turn the horse loose in the indoor school and lunge him every other day. Keep the horse interested in his work and prevent monotony in his daily exercise.

To avoid a horse refusing and to keep him interested and keen on jumping the first requirement is to keep him in top form throughout the jumping season. This, of course, requires highly skilled horsemanship, particularly during a long hot summer when the horse is subject to a great deal of sweating, because one must realise that if the horse sweats extensively he may lose weight and along with it energy and condition.

If a horse gets tired towards the end of a season, remember that a showjumping horse in full competition leads a hard life. With this realisation those of us who demand so much from the horse should be both humble and grateful.

Therefore, think first before making an unfair judgement on the horse's performance and possible refusals.

*Fig. 484*
Stopping.

*Fig. 485*
"Putting on the brakes".

*Fig. 483*
Running out to the left at a fence. When re-approaching on the same left-hand circle, the horse will most likely run out again to the left. You stand a better chance when re-approaching on a right-hand circle.

*Fig. 486*
Suddenly raising the head.

*Running out sideways*

The most common kind of a refusal is that the horse, one or two strides before take-off, starts to run out to the left without coming to a complete halt. The horse takes the bit and runs off, because he knows from experience that punishment will follow. The horse was created fleet-of-foot to be able to get himself out of danger quickly. Therefore, when running out sideways, the horse is afraid and more fleeing than refusing.

*Stopping*

Some horses refuse at exactly the moment they should take-off. They suddenly turn their head and neck (mostly) to the left and come to a halt, with the right side of the body facing the fence. The rider might land on top of the fence or on the other side of it. A horse refusing in this manner reveals insecurity in the take-off, lacks confidence in his rider and stiffens himself on the right-hand side.

For re-training give the horse relaxation exercises. Daily lungeing with the Chambon, especially on the right-hand rein, in conjunction with free jumping, the latter in the jumping lane (unmounted), fences at normal distances, three times per week, to again establish the horse's confidence at take-off. Commence later on the same exercise in the jumping lane (mounted) and over small single fences. Approach these mainly out of a right-hand turn from a trot with a take-off pole in front of the fence at an angle of 45°.

*Putting on the brakes*

Young horses, as well as older ones, refuse by "putting on the brakes". The moment one expects the horse to take-off he suddenly lowers head and neck and sticks both forefeet into the ground and refuses to jump. Some horses put on the brakes a few strides away from the fence. With young horses the rider has probably approached the fence too fast in the last few strides and has brought the horse too much onto the forehand. Older horses will also refuse in this manner because they always carry too much weight on the forehand, either naturally or due to bad schooling.

The similarity in both cases is that the horse's posture is in a position which makes it impossible to shift excessive weight to the quarters in time for take-off. Even if the horse makes an effort to clear the fence he will still make a fault with the forelegs, because in such a situation it is very difficult indeed to get his forelegs off the ground.

Lunge the horse daily with the Chambon and work on foot, particularly the rein back, to make the spine more supple. And three times per week work unmounted in the jumping lane with shortened distances to teach the horse to shift weight to the quarters before take-off.

*Suddenly raising the head*

Some horses who carry their head naturally high have a bad habit of suddenly lifting the head even higher while approaching the fence. This raised head position makes it sometimes impossible for the horse to get a clear view of the fence in order to calculate the take-off, which again ends up in a refusal.

Because of the high head position the horse drops his back and transfers too much weight on to the quarters, forcing the quarters into such a low position that the hindlegs come too far underneath his body and slide between, or even beside, his forelegs. As a result the horse is sitting with his hocks on the ground and may slide in this position into, or right through, the fence. These horses make jumping faults generally with the hindlegs.

Again, lunge daily with the Chambon to lower the head position and to improve the arching of the back and rein-back (unmounted). Also, three times a week, exercise in the jumping lane over parallel oxers to lengthen the horse's stride.

I have explained in detail many reasons for, and manners of, a refusal, because only when one is able to analyse the reason for a refusal can one attempt to cure it. Do not forget to consider the horse's health: heart and leg troubles could make a horse unreliable. Bad eyesight can be suspected, especially if the horse shys from all sorts of objects, not only fences.

Every horse might refuse on occasions, but one should never allow it to become a habit.

*Approaching a fence after a refusal*

Whatever may be the reason which causes a horse to refuse, do not give him a chance to repeat it. First of all, after a refusal, do not use the whip to punish the horse while moving *away* from the fence because this will only upset him. The refusal has already taken place so there is no need to upset him further. Also, from a psychological point of view, this action is completely incorrect, because in such a situation the horse is overkeen to get away from the fence by himself. Use the whip, if necessary, only while approaching the fence.

If the horse has run out to the left, as usually happens, it would be a grave mistake to approach the fence for the second time out of a left-hand turn and in the left canter. This would provoke the horse to run out again to the left. The correct second approach would be out of a right-hand turn and at the right canter, going for the right-hand side of the fence. If the horse should attempt to repeat his error, be disobedient and try to move sideways to the left, he still finds himself facing the fence at the centre. If the horse ran out to the right-hand side of the fence the opposite method would apply. Some riders are unaware of this simple rectifying technique. They approach the fence for the second and a third time in the same wrong manner, ending up by being eliminated.

When approaching the fence after a refusal the correct speed is most important. It is wrong to approach the fence for the second time at a faster speed. Instead one should approach it out of the opposite turn (as explained previously) in a slow, collected canter. Only in the last few strides before take-off should extra strong forward driving leg aids be applied, sending the horse well on to the bit until the take-off. In this manner the horse is not given any other alternative but to jump the fence. Remember, do not drop the reins before take-off. Always carry the whip in the left hand, and if one anticipates that the horse might run out to the left again, touch the horse's shoulder with it in the approach.

REARING

Rearing is a vice and a very nasty one. A horse starts rearing for various reasons. It can be due to bad schooling and it can be found in excitable horses who are overfed and underworked. A horse which goes behind the bit can easily develop rearing, because he does not respond to the rider's forward driving leg aids.

When trying to determine the cause of rearing one should never forget that the horse has an exceptional memory. Because of this he will, once he realises that when he rears his rider is no longer in control, repeat the habit again and again. Once he has adopted this nasty vice he will take advantage of it by using it to defend himself and to resist the rider's aids and wishes, sometimes at the most unexpected moments.

Rearing horses have no respect for the rider because the rider is no longer master over them. On account of stubborness and bad temper, rather than fear, the horse will refuse to move forward, especially in jumping competitions, will rear and refuse to enter the arena, pass the exit correctly and so on. If the horse gets away with it a few times it will be very hard indeed to cure him. In the arena the horse will indulge in

*Fig. 487*
Rearing.

turning, running away, running backwards or even running out of the arena altogether.

If the horse rears, the rider should never bend the upper part of his body backwards and pull on the reins, because he could easily pull the horse completely off balance and cause him to fall backwards on top of the rider. Instead the rider should bend his body forward and hold himself in balance by putting one arm around the horse's neck. The other hand should be brought sideways and out as far as possible from the horse's neck, bending the neck sideways-downwards. This brings the horse off balance instantly, because it forces him to change his centre of gravity sideways. Subsequently, the horse will come down forward-sideways onto his forefeet.

The rider must now establish his authority straight away. As soon as the horse's front feet come to the ground, the rider must keep the horse's head and neck bent and circle the horse around violently, nearly on the spot, about two or three times. Then send him energetically forward on a straight line.

### STUMBLING

Stumbling is a symptom observed in both young and old horses. Most suffer from it when they commence schooling. It arises most frequently during the initial stage, as soon as the horse has to carry the additional weight of the rider, which disturbs the horse's natural balance. Therefore a decisive factor in his schooling will be to reinstate, his balance, otherwise this early stumbling phase could develop into a permanent habit. Later on, when the horse commences his schooling in jumping when mounted, the same procedure of re-adjusting his natural balance may be continued. At this stage, while jumping mounted, it is important that the young horse *bascules* over the fences without any restriction of the rein aids and without the slightest interference by the rider's weight. The horse must be completely free and independent, otherwise he may be spoiled and develop into a habitual and inveterate peck-on-landing horse.

Habitual stumbling in older horses may be caused by various factors:

(i) badly shod feet, with toes left too long;

(ii) forefeet too hard and too dry;

(iii) pastern joints which are too straight, particularly those of the forelegs;

(iv) badly ridden – too much on the forehand;

(v) physical weakness or laziness;

(vi) being overworked or just plain clumsy;

(vii) nervousness, stumbling out of impatience when regularly ridden by a tense, impetuous rider. If such a rider constantly pulls on the horse's mouth it will learn to lean on the bit, using it as a "fifth" leg. The horse's stride becomes hasty and irregular. As soon as the rider yields the reins the horse loses balance and stumbles. The horse will become so dependent on the support of the rider's strong hold on the bit that he is not able to move on his own four legs without stumbling.

*Curing stumbling*

Firstly, consider the cause of the habit. Find out whether the rider or the horse is at fault. If the rider has defaulted the stumbling can indeed *not* be cured by taking a stronger hold on the bit in order to hold up the horse's head. Believing it can is a natural, but wrong, reaction in many riders. The chief concern of the rider should be the unloading and transference of the horse's excess weight from his forehand to his quarters. Once this is obtained the horse can be ridden freely at all paces (jumping as well) on a long rein without further stumbling.

The horse should be lunged daily with the Chambon, as well as being exercised on foot, especially reining back. He should also do regular free jumping.

These suppling exercises are valuable in the

development of the elasticity of the back and quarters muscles required for pure movement.

## IMPROVING THE RIDER

*Heavy hands*

Heavy hands apply rough rein aids. Bad hands are nearly always the result of an unbalanced seat, either forward or dressage. The rider lacks a firm grip because his muscles, especially the leg muscles, are underdeveloped. On account of this the rider balances himself out of the horse's mouth and feels uncertain and tense. The horse senses this and takes a stronger hold on the bit.

Many riders could improve their method of applying rein aids. To achieve an improvement they have to acquire first of all a completely independent seat. This cannot be done overnight. It takes much practise and perseverance to develop strong and firm muscles of pelvis and legs. They are the foundation for achieving a "soft" hand.

*Jumping without reins*

This is an excellent exercise to improve the rider's independent seat, his feeling for balance and rhythmic tempo.

The exercise is carried out over a row of low fences in the jumping lane. The rider should be mounted on a quieter and more experienced horse. The reins are knotted over the withers beforehand.

The rider sits in the forward seat with his hands on his hips. This position encourages holding his head up high, broadening his chest and the small of his back is pushed forward. To ensure a firmer grip the rider presses his heels down further and thus exercises all the muscles required to reinforce his seat.

To obtain a perfect feeling for the horse's cadence and rhythmic tempo between the elements and whilst basculing over the fences the rider should close his eyes while jumping through the lane.

By closing his eyes and jumping in this way he will learn to feel the tempo of the horse's pace and the take-off. Those riders who particularly "overact" when jumping will have to sit still and refrain from any excess movement, because now, without reins, they are compelled to use their muscles solely to grip and balance themselves.

This exercise helps and often surprises riders who believe their horse would never get over a jump if the take-off was not dictated by the rider. Having spoilt their horse's initiative by prolonged use of the wrong method, they will be amazed to feel how the horse is able to manage without the rider's "help". With growing confidence in the horse's ability the rider will in time refrain from constant interference.

Jumping without reins and with hands on hips makes many, even highly successful, riders feel helpless at the beginning. They lose balance and are often left behind the movement. They are probably surprised by this fact, as they did not realise how much they depended on the reins for balance. They are in this way reminded of what they know to be true but forgot to practise: that the reins are solely a means of communication with the horse.

*Riders who drop the reins*

Exercises in the jumping lane are also excellent for correcting those riders who drop the reins during take-off and gather them again on landing. Such a rider loses contact with the horse's mouth and thus interferes with the horse's balance and pace.

This becomes obvious between the elements of combination jump: by suddenly losing contact with the rider's hands the horse shifts his balance to the forehand. To regain his equilibrium the horse has to increase his speed and stride. He cannot come back in time for the take-off at the second element and refuses, runs out or knocks a pole.

To keep the horse in balance one has to maintain a consistent contact with the horse's mouth. This rule applies not only to riding on the flat but also over cavaletti and when jumping, during the approach, the take-off, while airborne and on landing.

Therefore it is so vital that the rider *never*

fixes one or both hands on the horse's neck but that his hands are free of the neck during all jumping phases. Only then will the rider "feel" the lengthening and lowering of the horse's head and neck and will his hands be able to follow this movement smoothly and without interruption.

The jumping lane is ideal to teach a rider not to lose his reins. When my pupils make this mistake I give them a small branch to hold in each hand, together with the reins. If the rider drops a branch it proves that he also drops his reins. I do this not only in training but also in competitions. Most riders are cured very quickly and begin to realise that the fault of dropping the reins is the outcome of a badly developed forward seat.

Another interesting observation I have made in regard to rein control is that in most countries female and junior riders have fewer difficulties with the rein aids. Their arm muscles are less well developed than in a man and tend to enhance the sensitivity of their hands and fingers. These riders use less force and, in my opinion, are surprisingly better in many cases at riding and handling those strong horses known as a "man's horse".

### DISOBEDIENCE

When schooling horses the trainer should always bear in mind that he is handling a sensitive, living animal. By nature the horse is a trusting and honest animal. If not, he has become so by unskilled handling, abuse and ill-treatment at the hands of human beings.

A discerning trainer will put his horse through a well planned and complete training course in order to eliminate as many causes for disobedience as possible. He will constantly observe and consider the frame of mind of his horse. He will convey only reasonable demands to his horse clearly and exactly. A horse, trained so wisely, will obey willingly and has no reason to become disobedient.

Nevertheless, horses have, just like humans, good days and bad days. One day the trainer will notice that his horse is unco-operative. The intelligent trainer is sensitive to the horse's state of mind and will never let a situation deteriorate to the extent that the horse becomes disobedient. The trainer will "sense" disobedience and will try to avoid it before it actually develops.

But when a situation does get out of hand and the horse is disobedient the first law is to avoid a fight with the horse. This would only make matters worse, because one would draw the horse's attention to his disobedience and establish it in the horse's mind.

The first thing to do is to think: "Where did I go wrong?" It is more than likely that one has contributed to the horse becoming disobedient. In any case, first of all it has to be decided whether the horse's action was caused by disobedience or just by a *misunderstanding*.

One will find that, in most cases, the cause was a lack in communication: either the horse did not understand the demands at all or became confused and took the command to be a similar one. Perhaps the horse did understand but was simply incapable of complying with the demands made. If such a misunderstanding is mistaken for disobedience and dealt with accordingly then it can easily develop into disobedience. Therefore try to express your demands as clearly and simply as possible, and never ask too many different things at the same time in order not to confuse the horse. If a misunderstanding occurs be fair and agree that it most likely was your own fault. Ignore the horse's behaviour and try to express yourself more clearly the next time.

A *disobedient* horse, however, poses a difficult problem. Every experienced trainer knows that. Before he will attempt to correct it, without conflict, but restoring the horse's confidence, he will try to find out *why* the horse became disobedient.

The reason can be one of many. If misunderstanding as a likely cause is eliminated one has to judge whether the horse was "overfaced" and therefore not able to fulfil the task. Disobedience in a horse can also be caused by a feeling of debility or of discomfort from aching muscles as a result of overtraining the previous day. This, of course, should never happen, as a horse should never become wet with perspiration, either from over excitement or excessive training. A horse, steaming from sweat, is an example of bad horsemanship.

A horse can also be just bored with the ways of an unskilled trainer who repeats a certain exercise over and over again until the horse is exhausted and in a frame of mind where he cannot take any more: the horse becomes disobedient.

Disobedience can also be caused by the trainer ignoring the horse's nervous disposition, particularly in a highly bred one. Such a horse has to be treated with considerable consideration, patience and kindness. To prevent disobedience and to gain the horse's co-operation the trainer will reward the horse warmly and speak to him every time he responds to the demands made. Not only with nervous horses but with horses in general, remember to "make much of the horse". You cannot reward your horse often enough. The principles of the Natural Training Method are based on gaining the horse's co-operation and confidence. Bear in mind the advice of Colonel Avisi: "The horse always remembers a kindness and to whom he owes it." Should a trainer lack the feeling for a horse's frame of mind, many horses will become sour, obstinate and nervous wrecks.

Apart from all these reasons, disobedience is often plainly asked for by incompetent or ill-tempered trainers. Training showjumpers is a highly specialised task and if a person attempts it who is unsuited, or too uneducated, rushing the training and cutting corners here and there, then the horse will soon become disobedient. It always seems to be the same people who have "difficult" horses. A horse merely mirrors the qualities of his trainer. A well mannered, skilful trainer will always turn out well mannered and intelligent horses who perform willingly and to the best of their ability, whereas an unqualified trainer will produce unwilling, sour or frightened horses, who perform only under pressure and display disobedience whenever possible.

Before blaming a horse remember the proverb "Let me ride your horse and I will tell you who you are."

### PUNISHMENT

Even the best trainer will encounter situations where punishing a horse is obligatory.

But if a horse has to be punished it has to happen *instantly*, at the very moment the horse is misbehaving. If the trainer's reaction to a disobedience is too slow, or if he does not have the opportunity to punish the horse *instantly*, he has to refrain from punishment altogether. On account of the horse's small brain he cannot relate punishment to passed misdeeds. It is *criminal* to beat a horse because he kicked someone ten minutes earlier. Such unjust punishment will leave a deep and lasting scar on the horse's mind. With it fundamental damage is done. It can take a very long time to regain such a horse's confidence if he is not completely ruined altogether. We often take advantage of the horse's exceptional memory during training, but this fantastic memory also works to a disadvantage because the horse will also memorise unjust punishment or another mistake the trainer might make. Most "problem horses" became difficult because at some stage they have been indiscriminately punished.

Having punished one's horse one is still often troubled by conscience, even if the punishment was properly and justly executed. One may well reflect that whoever created the frame of mind in the horse which led to punishment is the real culprit and the one who should accept it.

PART FOUR

# THE THIRD SCHOOLING YEAR

CHAPTER FIFTEEN

# SECOND SHOWJUMPING SEASON

## PREPARATION

THE third schooling year is the *second* show-jumping season. The *first* year of competition should be considered only as one where the novice gained experience, confidence and learnt to control his "stage-fright".

During the second season the horse's up-grading should be carefully managed and prepared.

*January*. During this month exercise the horse in the jumping lane *unmounted* three times per week. Following his well-deserved winter rest (non-competing period) this free jumping will produce an increasingly stronger and more supple horse and renew his confidence.

*February*. Continue the exercises in the jumping lane, but now *mounted*, Approach the row of fences out of a trot and on finishing the last obstacle jump a single fence, alternately on the left and on the right rein.

*March*. During this month progressively increase the jumping schooling to strengthen the horse's muscles and to prepare him for higher grade competition.

The training covers not only the jumping of higher obstacles but also the increased speed with which these obstacles must be jumped. In the *first* jumping season the horse has been trained on the speed course and competed in novice competitions at a speed of 300 metres per minute. In the *second* jumping season, however, if he has been upgraded steadily, the horse will now be required to jump at a speed of 350 metres per minute in accordance with the rules of these competitions. Jumping at this faster speed is often the reason that a young horse suddenly gives disappointing performances, although showing great promise in a lower grade at a lower speed.

If the horse's muscles are not fully developed and prepared for this faster speed he will become unbalanced in pace, flatten and will come too much on the forehand. He will subsequently come too elose to the fence for take-off, with the result of faults with the forelegs, running out at a fence or refusals.

For this reason one should in *March* school the horse on a speed course at a speed of 350 metres per minute. In addition, place an upright fence, an oxer and a combination jump so that the horse will get accustomed to jumping at this new and faster speed of 350 metres per minute.

Furthermore, before competing out of doors, participate in a few small indoor jumping competitions. Providing a good course is built these indoor competitions teach the horse great obedience to the rider's aids. Owing to the restricted area and the surrounding kicking-boards the horse will be easier to control during the many changes of direction of the course.

Systematic preparation during the first few months of the *second* jumping season is necessary to develop the horse. The increasingly strenuous demands encourage the horse to enjoy his work and co-operate with his rider's wishes. Together they even out any bad habits possibly collected during his *first* jumping season.

During the *second* jumping season the horse will compete more often than in his first season. Therefore jump as little as possible at home in between competitions in order not to turn the horse sour.

Should the horse need correction at particular

obstacles confine him to schooling *unmounted* over these only. The correction should be done in the jumping lane.

Between competitions it is important that the horse is schooled in advanced dressage to improve his obedience and to obtain finer control. To keep the horse fit in wind, heart and lungs continue in between competitions with schooling in the speed course, hilly countryside and roadwork. Variety in his daily routine keeps the horse keen and interested in his work.

After participating in a competition, and having had a long tiring journey in the horsebox, the horse should not spend the next day standing in his box. He would stiffen up, his digestive system would suffer and his legs might show filling. Much better than a day at complete rest is a little exercise. Weather permitting, turn the horse out in the field for an hour, not longer or the horse might overeat; or turn the horse loose in the indoor school for a time or take him out for a quiet hack at a walk. But under no circumstances leave him standing in his box after the very active previous day.

### TESTING JUMPING ABILITY

Halfway through the *second* jumping season one can test the horse's jumping ability. At first we ask the horse to jump unmounted to give him a chance to use himself fully over the larger obstacles of increasing difficulty.

Place a fence (an upright one) in the jumping lane, about 1 metre in height. After the horse has jumped it twice raise the fence to 1·2 metres. After jumping this reliably and in good style two or three times, raise it again to 1·3 to 1·4 metres and let the horse jump this also two or three times. Now give the horse a break, make much of him and reward him with oats or carrots.

Next place a pole behind the upright, changing it into an oxer, which at first should be about 1 metre wide. The pole at the far end should be slightly higher than the top front pole.

When the horse has no difficulty in clearing the oxer after two or three times widen the oxer gradually to 1·5 to 1·8 metres spread. To cover and conceal the gap in between the oxer place a pole diagonally across, which makes it more inviting for the horse.

If the horse should have difficulty at first in finding the correct take-off position – as the obstacle becomes larger – then put a small "placing fence" in front of the oxer at a distance of about 6·8 to 7 metres, depending on the size of the oxer, and, of course, on the length of the horse's canter stride and also on the speed of the approach. The placing fence, which can be made of three cavaletti, should not be higher than approximately 0·9 metres.

The horse should approach the fence calm and relaxed with an even balanced rhythm in the pace, not rushing into the fence and not too slow. The correct speed is approximately 300 metres per minute.

If the horse, with the aid of the placing fence, finds no difficulty in locating the take-off point, the placing fence can be removed and the horse is then allowed to jump the single oxer alone.

When the horse has jumped this single oxer satisfactorily, *stop* jumping at once, because to

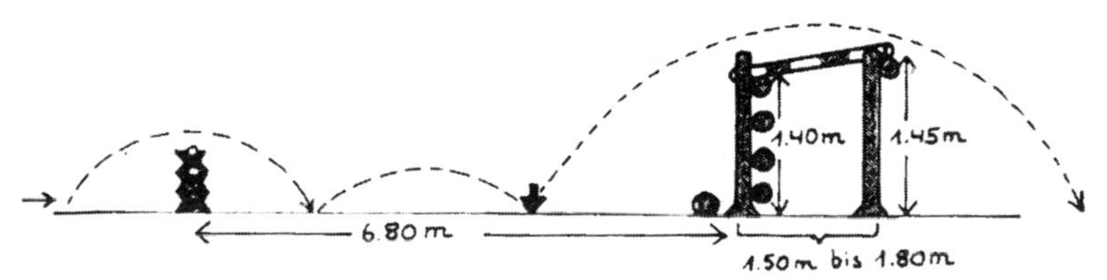


*Fig. 488*
During the third year of training one may test the horse's jumping ability.

demand more from the horse at this stage of schooling could easily have disastrous results. If the horse at any stage of the jumping test has difficulties with the height of the upright, or later on with the spread of the oxer, immediately reduce both and do not increase them again. For the time being be satisfied and use commonsense, because this test has clearly shown that the horse is not really up to standard. Such a jumping test should not be requested from the horse during the first half of his *second* jumping season; only do so halfway or near the end of this season.

Something which cannot be overstated is that there are too many riders who are too impatient to find out how high their horses can jump. It is very dangerous to give way to such impatience. Any tests should not be done any sooner than in the *second* season.

Nevertheless, if the jumping test is executed correctly, without any rushing or unnecessary excitement for the horse, he will gain tremendous confidence in clearing larger obstacles. At the same time it will give his rider satisfaction and confidence in his horse's jumping capabilities. It has been demonstrated during the test that the horse has the courage, power and correctly controlled jumping technique to clear these formidable obstacles.

This *unmounted* test is the most objective way to discover the horse's true capabilities. Here he has to do everything himself without the help of a rider and without a rider's interference.

It is advisable when purchasing an older experienced showjumping horse to use the same jumping test *unmounted*. Many an older horse is so used to the trick riding of his usual rider that when jumping unmounted he will find it very difficult indeed to locate his own take-off point. This could lead to serious problems when sold to a rider who is not used to trick riding.

If good results have been obtained from the first test then repeat the whole exercise, unmounted, two weeks later.

When the horse has gained the experience and self-confidence to jump larger obstacles one should start to practise the same exercise *mounted*. Particular attention should be paid by the rider to the speed at which he approaches these larger obstacles – no slower than 300 metres per minute. Therefore it is advisable to jump the obstacles when built in the speed course.

Jumping a few larger fences occasionally, for example, an upright, spread oxer and a triple combination jump, is essential at this stage of schooling, but not too often and *only* when the horse is not regularly participating in competitions.

## SPECIALISING

These test sessions enable the rider to make a decision in regard to the future jumping career of his horse. Now, at the end of the *second* jumping season, the rider is in a position to decide what type of competition his horse is most suitable for.

Unless the horse proves the exception it would be wrong to expect that he can be equally successful in *all* types of jumping competitions (whereas an accomplished jumping rider must be capable of riding every type of competition from a *puissance* to a speed competition). If a horse, during his second jumping season, shows that he has, for example, the potential to become a *puissance* horse, then it is not advisable to let him participate in speed competitions as well. To be successful in speed competitions the jumping horse has to stand extra far back while taking-off, and has also to land far out over the fence.

This style of jumping is necessary in a speed competition in order to save time while airborne over the fence. But as a "preparation" for ordinary jumping competitions, and in particular for *puissance* obstacles, it would be detrimental. It flattens the horse considerably and destroys his real jumping ability.

In general, do not make the horse specialise too early and not before the end of the second season. In the beginning of every horse's career there are many ups and downs. By being too impetuous in judging a horse's qualities one could make an irreversible mistake.

### JUMPING AGAINST THE CLOCK

To become successful in jumping against the clock the horse has to learn to jump fences at an angle. In spite of the faster speed he still should be able to take-off correctly. A special set-up is used to train the horse to do this. Proceed with four cavaletti, the first one flat on the ground and the three others at normal height and at a trot distance of 1·35 metres approach at a trot out of a figure of eight and change reins alternately.

Use two crossed poles (centre height 0·5 metres) added as a small fence on each track at a distance of 2·5 metres behind the last cavaletti. This fence is followed by a second small fence, placed at a distance of 3 metres (two crossed poles, height at the centre 0·9 metres). After this fence place a small oxer at a distance of 6·6 metres, measured from the centre front base of the oxer. This oxer should not be higher than 1 metre with a spread of 1·2 metres, which should gradually be heightened and widened.

At the beginning one places only the two wings of the oxer and later on one builds up the first part of the oxer only, so that it is an upright fence.

Having jumped this row a few times, alter the upright fence into a small oxer. When clearing the first element the horse breaks into a canter. Do not interfere with the horse by regulating his stride in between the elements but leave the take-off completely to the horse. If the horse should slow down then he should, of course, be sent on to maintain the impulsion.

The distances in between the last crossed poles fences and the oxer is shorter than normally in combinations, because the training speed is much slower than in a competition and the cavaletti are approached at a trot speed of 200 metres per minute.

In this row of fences the horse's canter speed will be approximately 250 metres per minute. The purpose of the short distance and the slow

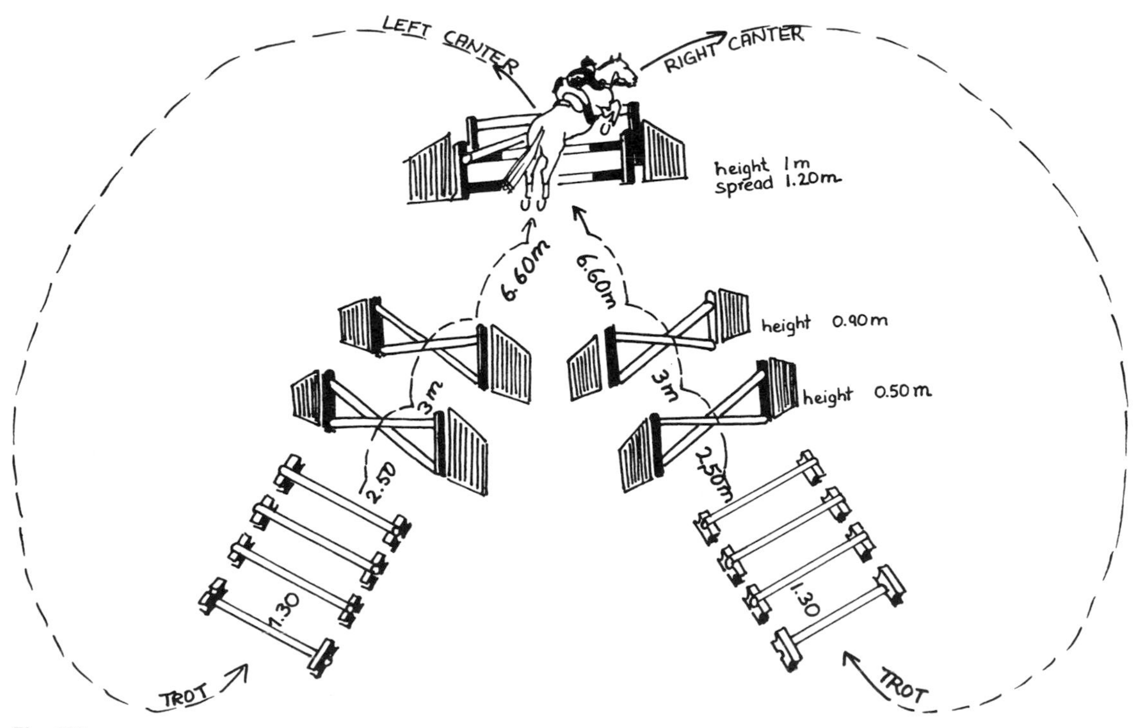


*Fig. 489*
Training a horse for speed competitions.

speed at the beginning of this special schooling for jumping against the clock is to teach the horse to engage his hocks at take-off to the utmost degree. This position enables him to raise the forehand excessively and lift and fold his forelegs extra high, which is vital in jumping obstacles at an angle.

In time, when the horse has developed the necessary muscles to master this technique, take away the cavaletti and lengthen the distances in between the elements. The speed should then be increased in correspondence with the length of the canter strides.

At first, after removing the four cavaletti, approach the elements still out of a slow trot. Having practised this a few times, widen the distances in between the first two elements to 4 metres and approach out of a slow canter.

Then remove the first element and widen the distance to the oxer to 7 metres. Jump these two elements a few times out of a canter.

Then remove the second element and jump the single oxer a few times from both directions at a speed of 3·5 metres per minute. When the oxer is made gradually wider and higher, place a pole diagonally across the oxer. This makes the oxer more inviting to jump because it conceals the gap of the spread. Particularly at the beginning stage do *not rush* the schooling or go *too fast*, because the horse has not developed strong enough muscles yet nor fully mastered this technique of jumping a spread at an angle. Otherwise the horse would easily run out or refuse.

When the horse is able to jump the oxer at an angle on a figure of eight with correct take-off, which he is taught aided by the use of the placing fence, he will be able to do the same at a much faster speed when jumping against the clock.

Together with the horse the rider learns to jump at an angle to beat the clock.

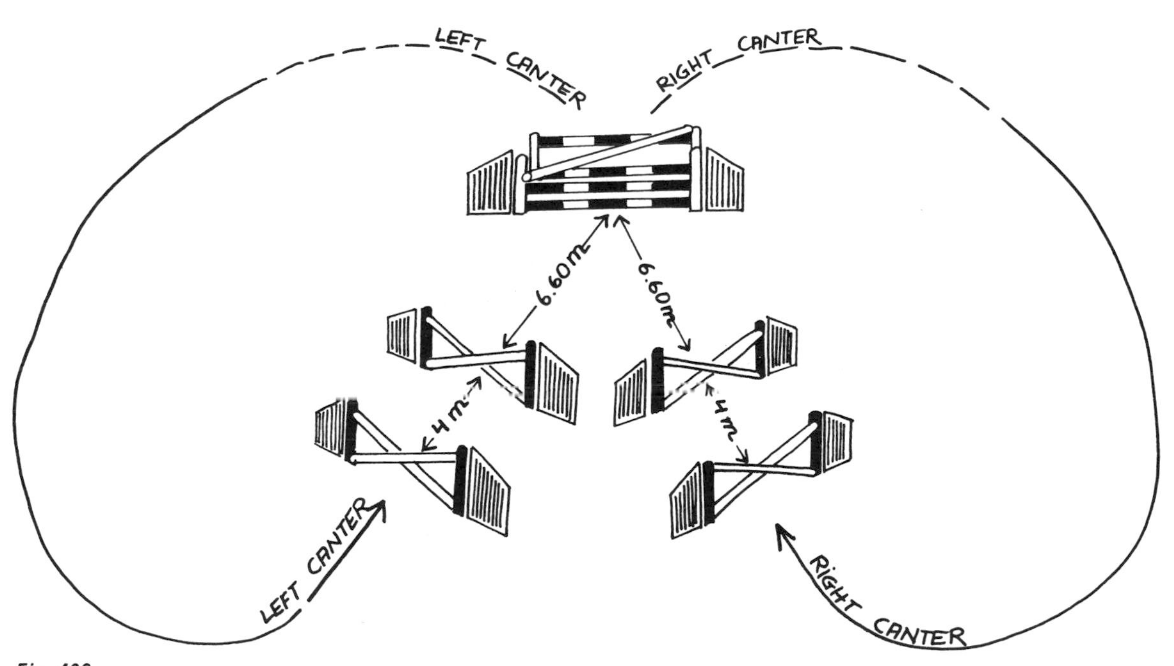


*Fig. 490*
Approach in canter, increase the distance between the two cross pole fences to 4 metres.

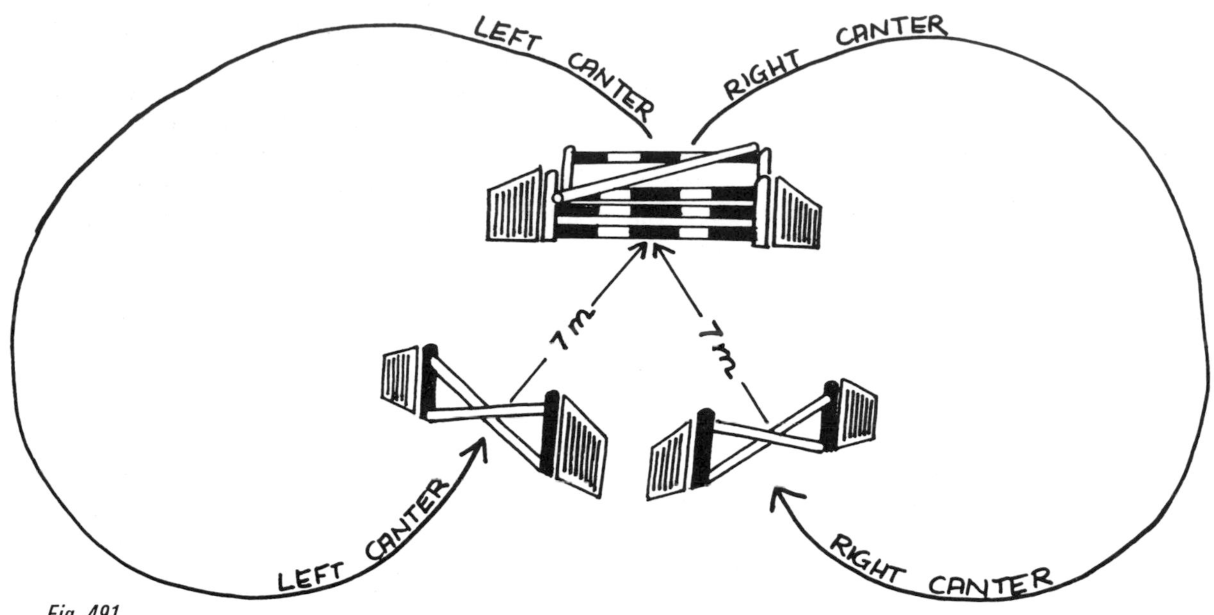


*Fig. 491*
Take away one cross pole fence and increase the distance between the two remaining fences to 7 metres.

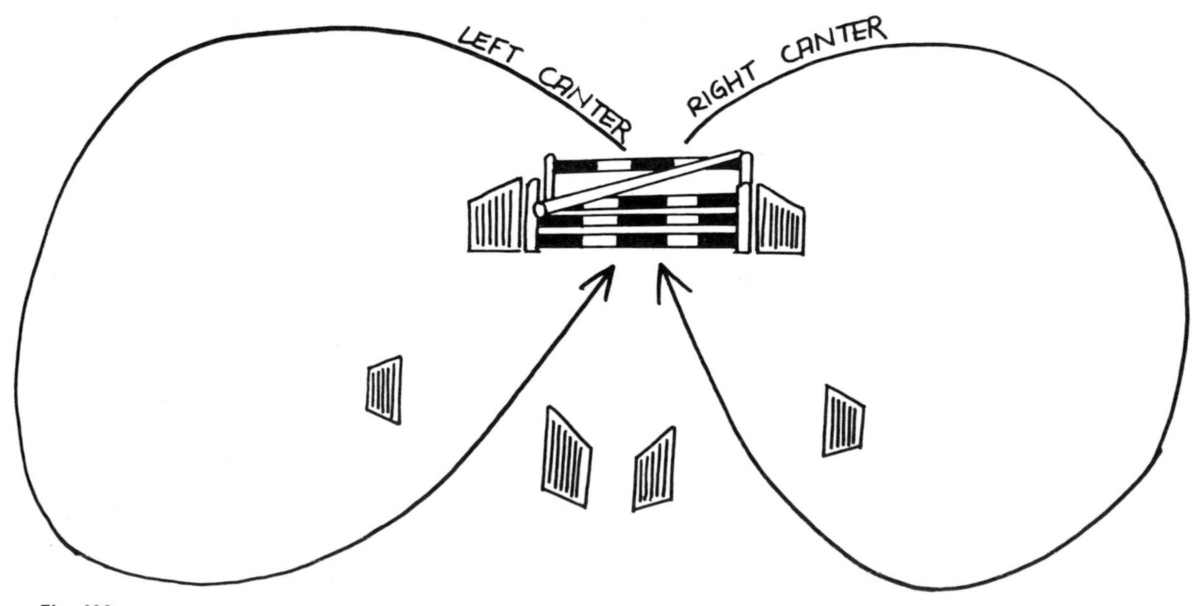


*Fig. 492*
The last fence remaining is the oxer. Jump it at alternate angles.

To make sure that my pupils apply the correct aids while airborne and land each time in the appropriate canter when jumping an oxer on a figure of eight, I position myself at the end of the row of fences on that particular side in which I want the rider to turn on landing. I hold up one hand, showing a varying number of fingers. I ask my pupil to tell me how many fingers I am holding up while he approaches each element and while airborne. This teaches the rider to keep his head well up, to look in the direction in which he is going on landing, to shift extra weight onto the stirrup on that particular side and to guide the horse into that turn by moving his hand *sideways* (not backwards) into the turn. The rider's attention is distracted from the approach and take-off and he will thereby acquire a safe feeling for the rhythm and speed of the non-jumping strides in between the elements. This method brings both horse and rider into perfect balance and complete harmony, because the rider's weight is at all times distributed exactly above the centre of gravity of the horse.

## THE HORSE'S CAREER

If, during the first three years, a horse has received a sound and systematic basic schooling, and if this competitive schedule has been carefully planned with suitable jumping events, then the long hard road toward becoming a good international showjumper has begun in the correct manner.

Even if the horse has the potential of a first-class showjumper, and even if he received a skilful and specialised training, it is still dependent on many factors whether the horse's performances can improve further to reach the top of his capabilities. The main factors are discussed below.

### *An experienced rider*

The performances of many promising young horses only reach a certain level, where they seem to come to a standstill in their upgrading. This may be due to their rider's lack of experience, courage or will to win.

Often the horse progresses, by systematic schooling between competitions and participation in suitable events, more rapidly than his inexperienced novice rider. Of course, the rider accomplishes a great deal by bringing the young horse successfully up to a certain grade of jumping but he may lack the experience to support the horse in his up-grading in big open or international competitions. A horse starting to participate in these competitions can hardly be expected to look after his inexperienced rider.

Nevertheless, if a rider has the right temperament, character and determination to win it is quite possible that both horse and rider may upgrade together which, of course, would be ideal. But these are more or less exceptions. Ordinarily it would be much more advisable that a young horse is ridden by an experienced rider. His firm determined aids and his whole hearted efforts to win will give the young horse confidence to jump the obstacles encountered in big competitions.

I believe that a rider who lacks international jumping experience would be more successful if he arranged to compete for a couple of seasons on an older horse with experience of, and expertise in, international competition. Such a horse will become the rider's teacher and will give the rider confidence and the experience needed. In time such a rider will be qualified to jump on big occasions on a younger horse that he has schooled and upgraded himself.

### *Carefully planned participation*

This is a very significant factor to ensure that a promising young horse also becomes a top international showjumper.

To achieve this the horse should participate in jumping competitions most suitable to him.

For example, a horse who by nature has not got a great deal of impulsion should be considered for entry in speed competitions every now and then, as this will improve his free forward movement.

On the other hand, a nervous or highly strung horse should be held back as long as possible from speed competition.

*Fig. 493*
Photographed at the Dublin International Horse Show, Miss Iris Kellett rides her Irish-bred horse Morning Light to win the European Ladies Championship. Miss Kellett schooled this horse herself from the very beginning and was rewarded by winning not only the European Ladies Championship with him, but many other major prizes as well.

Whilst Miss Kellett is experienced in planning a horse's career, she is also an expert in "making" a rider. One such is Eddie Macken, one of the best and most stylish showjumping riders in the world.

Even when jumping such a horse against the clock in a jump-off it is better to try and save time by cutting corners than by increasing the overall speed. To do so would be too soon for this type of horse and upset him. He would lean on the bit, flatten, refuse or make jumping faults.

In time, when this horse has gained more competition experience and is relaxed and cool, he will have a calmer approach and more control over his muscular actions. He could turn out to be an excellent speed specialist. Years ago time was *not* a deciding factor in every important championship. Then there were many more good *puissance* horses about than today, where nearly every important class is decided on time. I am sure there are as many potential *puissance* horses being born today as years ago, but they do not come to prominence because they have to jump so often against the clock to win a big competition. They are not given a real chance to develop the power and technique necessary for puissance fences.

*Well planned homework*

The reader will note that in this book many chapters are concerned with the basic schooling of the horse and his preparation for, and actual participation in, competitive jumping events rather than with the horse's final upgrading from national to international competition. This, of course, is logical because it takes years of concentrated schooling before the jumping horse has graduated to the highest standards.

These first years are the most important and the really difficult ones, with all the ups and downs of the horse's performance. They are the foundation for the horse's further successes.

During these years the horse has to overcome childishness and stagefright in the jumping enclosure. Once he has competed successfully in national events for a few years the actual step to international standard is a very short one. Therefore all those years of gaining experience are the actual *homework* to reach international level.

One should never underestimate the wealth of experience the horse gains from the routine of regular participation in competitions. It is a worthwhile lesson for him, more so when he is ridden by an experienced rider.

Some riders are convinced that a horse should be schooled for bigger occasions by persuading him to jump enormous obstacles in between competitions. Quite the opposite. Nothing courts disaster more than harshly disciplined jumping of the horse over increasingly larger obstacles. This is wrong and dangerous and calculated to ruin his capability and keenness.

It is neither educational nor interesting if the horse, while schooling, jumps 2 metres high. More important is his performance while competing, and for how many years to come will he be in such top form?

I would like to stress that with his schooling in jumping the advantages of jumping dressage should not be omitted. The combination of both will add finesse in his progress from national to international standards.

*Systematic upgrading*

There are exceptional horses who are more or less upgraded overnight without much preparation. The danger is that such an exceptional horse may at first give his rider the impression that all preparation and groundwork is a waste of time, since he is jumping superbly. It is lamentable that his rider does not realise that he is taking advantage of the honesty of his superior horse. In most cases the horse's perfect performance will not continue because he is physically and mentally not matured enough.

Experience shows that quite often such a splendid horse disappears just as suddenly as he was upgraded. This, of course, is a great pity. A horse who by nature has such potential could easily have become a top horse if prepared properly.

THE GRAND PRIX COURSE

To prepare a horse for international jumping competitions, such as a Nations Cup or the Olympic Games, is a formidable challenge. It is vital that the horse is in the peak of condition.

Not only his physical but also his psychological condition must be systematically prepared.

The Olympic Grand Prix, for instance, is for many horses participating the biggest course they have ever jumped. Olympic courses are built in such a way that a clear round can only be achieved by a superior horse. That is a horse which can pass the most searching test of stamina, courage, power, jumping talent and suppleness. No matter if he should knock his legs he must remain calm and battle on as if nothing has happened. To cope successfully with such an extremely severe course at the fast speed of 400 metres per minute a horse must be an expert. Not only must he be able to jump *puissance* obstacles but he must have the skill to turn swiftly, absolute balance and obedience.

This Grand Prix course must be tackled at the first attempt, a circumstance that creates apprehension in many riders and horses. At every international horse show horse and rider are given the opportunity to compete first in "warming-up" competitions in the same arena prior to the more important events, so that horse and rider may familiarise themselves to the new setting, obstacles and surroundings. This is not permitted prior to the Olympic Grand Prix.

Besides this handicap, the usual pressures which are imposed on the rider's nerves, such as that of the responsibility in representing their country, is further aggravated by the advance publicity before the Olympics. Even the most experienced and hardened rider who has previously proved himself in top competition may find the pressures too great. To overcome them the rider needs to be the complete master of himself, have the right sort of competitive spirit and be able to make the supreme effort needed to win. It is a challenege he may well never have met before. To meet it and to surpass it is his reward and one which time will never eradicate.

CHAPTER SIXTEEN

# JUNIOR RIDERS

THE training of junior riders, even if they are still very young and mounted on ponies, is based on the same principles as those described in this book for senior riders and their horses. I emphasise again that it is the responsibility of the instructor to see that all his pupils – from the first lesson on – should wear hard hats for protection.

It is very encouraging to note that over the past few years more and more children in Europe receive tuition mounted on ponies. Formerly they had to ride horses, because most continental instructors did not encourage pony riding as such. This was a disadvantage and also wrong for the development of the child's body, especially for the legs. For a small child to ride a big horse is almost the same as for an adult to ride an elephant. It is the height and width of a horse which so often frighten a child.

It is impossible for a child, mounted on a horse, to have a proper grip or to apply the proper leg aids. Sometimes the child's legs are so short that they do not reach beneath the saddle flaps.

Children should not only ride ponies but should also do so in a pony saddle and not, as often happens, in an adult size saddle.

Every year more and more ponies of different breeds are exported to all parts of the world for the child rider, Shetland, New Forest, Welsh and the Irish Connemara pony being examples. I find the Shetland pony the least suitable as a riding or jumping pony, they are no comparison to other breeds. Most of all I favour the Irish Connemara pony.

In Ireland there is a deep love for good ponies and horses for which the Irish always have been noted. Ireland is often associated with the thoroughbred, but no horseman can fail to be entranced by the magnificent Connemara ponies which can be found in the western parts of Ireland. They are hardy ponies from a hard land where rocks frequently occupy a larger area than soil.

To improve quality while maintaining hardiness Connemara mares were very successfully crossed with thoroughbred stallions. The ponies are strong and fast and have equable temperaments. They are very seldom tricky and are quite easy to train. This characteristic makes the Connemara pony particularly valuable for children. The height of a Connemara varies, though the bigger pony is more in demand because children of a far larger age range can ride them. This is not always the case with most ponies.

### HANDLING THE PONY

There are many urban riders who have ridden all their lives but have never learned to tack up a horse. Such a ridiculous situation should not be allowed to arise. Therefore instruction for children should commence with elementary stable management. This will bring urban children closer to their ponies. They should be taught to treat their ponies as a friend, with kindness and sympathy.

Riding tuition alone will not make the children good riders. It is, in fact, more important that children first learn how to groom and handle their pony. Handled calmly but decisively the pony will obey and gain confidence in his young rider. This is the only method to establish a friendly and happy relationship, so that pony and child can rely on each other later on when jumping in competition.

A great deal depends on which type of pony the child receives his first lesson. In the first place, children must be mounted on ponies with pleasant tempers. For beginners the ponies must be very quiet and reliable; they should not have a hard mouth and their movement should be smooth. The instruction can only be successful if the pony is schooled in such a way that he walks, trots and canters willingly on the lunge in a slow and balanced rhythm. His manners must be perfect and easy to control. This will give a child confidence. They feel they are master of the pony and are able to stop whenever they want to.

### FEEDING

Even a good tempered pony can easily become a difficult, naughty and bad tempered one if he is fed too much and exercised too little. The feeding of a pony must relate to the amount of daily exercise. Unfortunately, too many ponies are spoiled by wrong feeding and too little exercise.

If a pony is used for hacking only the only remedy to keep him quiet is to feed him very little oats. If the pony is kept out on grass during the summer he will only need a small feed when he has finished his work. In the wintertime, when the pony is in the stable, he must have good hay, fed in small portions, three times a day. In this manner the hay will not be wasted and it keeps the pony occupied.

He will also appreciate some old bread and carrots, a warm bran mash and pony nuts. One should make sure the pony always has a thick warm bed of straw and plenty of fresh water.

Naturally, the feeding of a jumping pony who competes regularly is completely different. It is not advisable to turn a jumping pony out daily for longer than an hour, otherwise he will get a "grass tummy" and this would interfere with his wind and his action. If a pony is too fresh he must be lunged using the Chambon, before being ridden.

### INSTRUCTION

It is quite normal to find that some children are frightened in the beginning, but this can be overcome by gentle tuition. To gain a child's full confidence the instructor leads the pony during the first few lessons. When the child is able to halt, walk on and trot, then the lead (lunge) can be gradually lengthened. In order to have better control, take the pony on the lungeing rein on a circle of 12 metres diameter. It is advisable to make a barrier (lungeing ring of straw bales) around the lungeing circle, as this prevents the pony from pulling on the lungeing rein and it will ensure that he moves smoothly on the circle.

To keep the pony quiet he is tacked up with the Gogue Independent, which should not be too tight. Use a rubber snaffle so as not to harden his mouth.

Gymnastic exercises are most important for the child and must be practised during each lesson. They develop the child mentally and physically, establishing a firm grip and an independently balanced seat. This in turn enables the child rider at a later stage to give independent rein aids. From the very beginning all instruction must be given correctly and never hurried, as this forms the basis of the child's riding. Faults established in the early stages are very hard to correct later on.

The child must be able to mount and dismount alone, and the pony should be taught to stand rock still under all circumstances.

Riding without stirrups is very important. When losing a stirrup, for example, later on during a competition, the child rider should be able to control the pony without the use of stirrups. During the beginning, 30 minutes

*Fig. 494*
To break the rough rein action of a beginner, thread the reins through under the neck strap of the breastplate.

*Fig. 495*
A junior training session in Ireland. Horses and riders are relaxed, natural and content. All horses are standing on a loose rein.

tuition is sufficient to avoid stiffness of the muscles and should consist mainly of walking and very little trotting. One should realise that the bones and muscles of a young child are not strong enough yet to stand up to the strain of a full 60 minute lesson at this early stage.

The most important part of training is gaining the child's confidence, and this can be achieved only by an experienced instructor who loves teaching children. Because the instructor has a great influence on the child's frame of mind the instructor must have the right temperament and personality to educate a child rider in the correct way. Children are generally very quick in following an example set by others. Once they have gained confidence in their instructor the children will place their trust in him and he can make them believe they can do anything, although he must never forget how *fragile* this confidence is and take advantage of it. He must never give an inexperienced child a difficult pony to ride or one which might run away, nor should he allow an inexperienced child to jump big fences.

Children are usually overkeen once they have gained confidence and some are in the beginning even too brave, not knowing the danger of possible accidents. However, the experienced instructor will study the capabilities of his pupil at the various stages. He must think carefully about what he can ask from his young pupil.

In the first 20 minutes of each riding lesson practise gymnastic exercises. In the early stages carry these out when the horse is standing still and later on make the horse walk, trot and canter, depending on the improvement of the child and on his age. It is advisable that the reins should be threaded underneath the breastplate during the first few trotting sessions, then the child cannot hurt the pony's mouth should his hands move excessively.

At the beginning the child does not know that rough rein action can hurt and spoil the pony's mouth. When the child's riding improves then the lunge may be taken off at the end of each riding session and the child may ride loose, under supervision, in the lungeing ring or in the indoor school.

When the child gets stronger and has gained confidence he can be taken out on a leading rein, by the instructor, who should be mounted on a quiet horse. In time, when the child is able to control the pony completely by himself, the leading rein can then be taken off. When the child has a firm grip, can do rising trot without stirrups and is able to give independent rein aids, the instructor should also introduce cavaletti placed flat on the ground, at which stage he may then teach his pupil the balanced forward seat. The elementary cavaletti lessons are gradually increased into jumping lessons.

### TRAINING

The training used when schooling a pony is the same as that used for his bigger relation, the horse. Therefore, lungeing with the Chambon, the work on foot exercises, which include reining back, free jumping in the jumping lane and cavaletti work, are all the same, only the distances are tailored to the shorter stride of the pony.

In England, Ireland and Australia it is always a pleasure to watch those brave children with their fighting spirit and courage, coping with big courses as if the fences were only cavaletti. They approach testing obstacles in a free forward style of riding without complicating matters by checking and placing their ponies at take-off. Some senior riders could learn from these junior riders. Pony jumping competitions have an enormous educational value for junior riders in these countries because they pick up a lot of experience and "ringcraft".

In comparison with children on the European continent, these children have a much closer and friendlier relationship with their ponies, having grown up with them. The relaxed, cool and easy manner with which they handle their ponies is unbelievable. I have seen children riding big thoroughbred horses without any difficulty on a plain snaffle and ordinary cavason noseband. On the whole, people in England, Ireland and Australia are both relaxed and courageous, qualities which they subconsciously project onto their horses. I believe that this is one of the reasons why their horses and ponies are calm and so well mannered. They are good tempered and lion hearted!

My experience has convinced me that the character and mentality of people has a determining influence on their horses and ponies. I have noticed that people in several countries in Europe and also in Central America are generally rather tense, which is perhaps mainly due to their hectic way of life. This attitude reflects itself in their horses. Bad temper, grinding of teeth, swishing tails, ears back, biting and kicking are fairly common faults. As a result people are forced to ride with various types of unkind bits, crossed nosebands, running reins and so on.

It stands to reason that a quiet relaxed pony will turn in no time into a nervous wreck in such a frustrating atmosphere. One should never forget that most of the "difficult" horses or ponies become that way as a result of wrong handling, especially the clever pony. With his exceptional memory he does not easily forget rough treatment and pain, though fortunately he will also remember kindness and sympathy.

### STARTING YOUNG

It has given me great pleasure and satisfaction to have trained several junior international jumping teams. In general I prefer to start training pupils from an early age because young children are so anxious to learn and have an open mind for suggestions. Similarly, it is much easier and more satisfactory to school a *young* horse or pony than re-train older or spoiled ones. It is also much more difficult to instruct and correct a senior rider. Some riders

*Fig. 496*
The Irish Junior Team, trained by the author, after winning the European Junior Championship at Hickstead. Left to right: Kevin Barry on Costo, team captain Paul Darragh on Woodpecker, Marilyn Dawson on Clare Cottage and Charles Curtis on Feltrim.

feel it is below their dignity to ask for advice. They only turn to an instructor when they are in a complete muddle with their horse, and then still with a considerable amount of suspicion and hesitation. They have developed bad habits and the wrong muscles over months or even years and the best instructor cannot change this overnight.

These riders are inclined to blame their horses for their poor performances. They use the worn out "bad luck" story as an easy way out.

I teach juniors to understand that to become a successful national or international rider a great deal of serious work and a lot of patience is necessary. It is they who will be responsible for

*Fig. 497*
An Italian pupil of the author, thirteen-year-old Lilian Bryner, riding her Anglo-Arab mare Begonia.

continuing progress in the art of riding and that they will, therefore, need to study the secrets of the Natural Training Method seriously and constantly work to improve themselves and their horses.

### BEGINNING COMPETITION

When a child is ready to compete in public should be the decision of his instructor. Often the instructor's carefully planned training schedule for a child rider is interfered with by over ambitious parents who are too keen to show off their children in jumping competitions. In so many cases both pony and child still lack the necessary experience to compete. Both are over faced and as a result of this the child often ends up in tears. I have many times seen promising children being pushed by their parents to compete to such an extent that instead of enjoying it they lose all interest. Many parents are not aware that by doing this, apart from asking too much of a child's limited riding experience, they also impose a great strain on the physique of the child. Children should never be forced to participate in jumping competitions.

Performing in the public eye makes many children, in the beginning, nervous and tense, and for some it takes a long time to overcome their stage fright. For this reason many children

*Fig. 498*
Paul Darragh again, riding Woodpecker at Hickstead during the European Junior Championship, where he took the individual silver medal.

act completely differently in the jumping enclosure than while jumping at home. When falls occur in the arena, even not serious ones, they easily lose their nerve and are ashamed. I have experienced instances when, after a fall, the children were even too ashamed to stand up again and face the crowd. At this early stage confidence is easily lost and it takes a very long time to regain it. There are also cases where confidence entirely disappears and the child is completely discouraged from riding at all. For this reason parents should never force their children to jump. Many children pretend to enjoy jumping lessons to please their parents and to show that they are not frightened, but when they grow up they will probably hate everything connected with horses.

### HOMEWORK

To prepare a really experienced junior team is a long term policy. To send a jumping team abroad means that a great deal of money is involved. Sponsors will be more interested if the team is successful.

In the past many young riders have had little or no systematic training. They lacked experience at home over the type of fences and courses which they had to face in international championships. This often had disastrous results. It was not the juniors' fault as none of them lacked

*Fig. 499*
An ideal pony, the Connemara, for the young rider to start his jumping career with.

courage, but in international jumping courage and determination alone are not enough. They must be combined with horsemanship and the necessary experience to lead to success.

Today, in most European countries, it is the objective of training committees to see to it that a well trained junior team is selected for the European Jumping Championships. Usually an experienced instructor is engaged who is responsible for seeing that the juniors are properly educated and prepared for the big occasion, giving them every possible opportunity, support and encouragement beforehand.

In Britain it has proved to be most successful

*Fig. 500*
Dundrum, winner of many international jumping competitions, including *puissance* competitions, was out of a Connemara mare by the thoroughbred Little Heaven.

to train junior teams at home over European championship standard courses, ridden at a speed of 400 metres per minute. As a result, the British team have won, up to 1970, 11 European championships out of the 13 they have contested.

These championships were inaugurated in 1952. In 1956 a British junior team was entered for the first time. A string of victories ensued, mainly achieved because of Britain's introduction at home of the Young Riders Competition. This gave the juniors the necessary experience to cope with the European Championship Course without too much effort. The instructor not only taught his team a correct uniform jumping style

*Fig. 501*
Sonja Paalman, then only thirteen years old, riding the Irish-bred horse, Killarney. This photograph was taken in 1956, when pony competitions were fairly unknown on the Continent. If children wanted to compete, they had to ride horses instead of the ponies which would have been more suitable.

*Fig. 502* (left)
A more usual scene today. Miss Carola Williams on the champion pony, Pendly Statuette. Note the attentive and cool expression of both pony and rider. Carola's father is Mr. Dorian Williams, the internationally known equestrian expert and television commentator.

but all the tricks of the trade as well, such as knowing by heart all the international jumping rules and regulations, studying a course plan, realising the vital importance of boundary flags, compulsory whole, or partly, course lines and so on. All these rules were used and practised at home, because it is far better to make a mistake in a competition at home than later on while representing their country abroad – and without the risk of letting the entire team down.

Junior riders who hope to represent their country successfully in the future must not regard their training courses just as a holiday pastime. They should be aware that the junior jumping team of today must gain international experience to form the senior team of tomorrow, remembering that it will not be possible to rely on the same international senior riders year after year.

In all fields of sport there must be an incentive to get to the top. The top for the young show-jumping rider is to be able to represent his country *successfully*. It is no longer good enough to only "compete and show the flag". It is the result that counts.

However, there are no short cuts to the top. Quick results breed conceit. Therefore, coaching and guidance should commence at an early age and must be continued even at the highest standard of participation.

PART FIVE

# DESIGNING AND BUILDING COURSES

CHAPTER SEVENTEEN

# COURSE DESIGN

ALTHOUGH this book is primarily concerned with the training of horse and rider for showjumping, it would be incomplete if a chapter on designing and building jumping courses was omitted.

The history of showjumping is brief compared with that of racing, dressage and hunting. At the turn of the century hunting as a sport proved how well a horse could jump. This encouraged selective breeding of hunters, whose requirements were to overcome natural obstacles with courage and dash. Highly skilled craftsmen, farriers, saddlemakers and professional course designers have contributed to make showjumping emerge as the sport it is today.

Showjumping began with the organisation of obstacle races. Soon afterwards shows with simple fences in arenas were established. Artificial obstacles were constructed to resemble natural obstacles, as found in the hunting field, and new demands were made in the approach to overcome them without penalties. The events became competitive, more difficult, more varied and fast.

A whole new field was established in course design and construction. This led to a requirement for the more powerful and better balanced horse and an increasingly perfected skill in the rider. Domestic shows graduated from national events to international Grand Prix and to the highest achievement of participation, the Olympic Games. The first ever jumping competition at an Olympic Games was that held at Stockholm in 1912, when 11 nations took part. From year to year since, it is encouraging to note the tremendous popularity of showjumping sport throughout the world.

Competitors should know the difference between a correctly built course and a bad one, if only to help them distinguish between fair difficulties and unfair problems.

The rider should be able to build a good training course at home, including combinations with correct distances in between the elements. Unless the training course and the fences are built up in a professional manner considerable harm can be done in the schooling of the horse. It can lead to refusals and ruin the horse's confidence. A badly built course at a show can destroy the carefully planned home schooling and preparation of many months, to say nothing of the confidence of the young novice showjumper. A well designed course in competition however, is part of, and completes, the education of the showjumping horse.

Even if the showjumping rider has no intention of building a course at any time he should study this chapter.

## PROFESSIONAL COURSE BUILDING

Professional course building is no secret, nor something beyond ordinary comprehension – merely hard work. It is the privilege of those with an equestrian background. It requires much time, knowledge and study to build a carefully planned and perfect course which will provide the horse and rider with confidence and increase their experience and technique.

However, I have not the slightest intention here, indeed there is no need, to address my suggestions to leading and world-famous professional course builders. Their courses are works of art, greatly admired at international shows the world over. They have fence material of endless variety and they can build a much higher standard of course, because only the highest grade of horse and rider participate at their shows. Regrettably many of these great masters are not always able to attend the smaller local shows. My suggestions are, therefore, merely meant for that grade of show and for its assigned course builder.

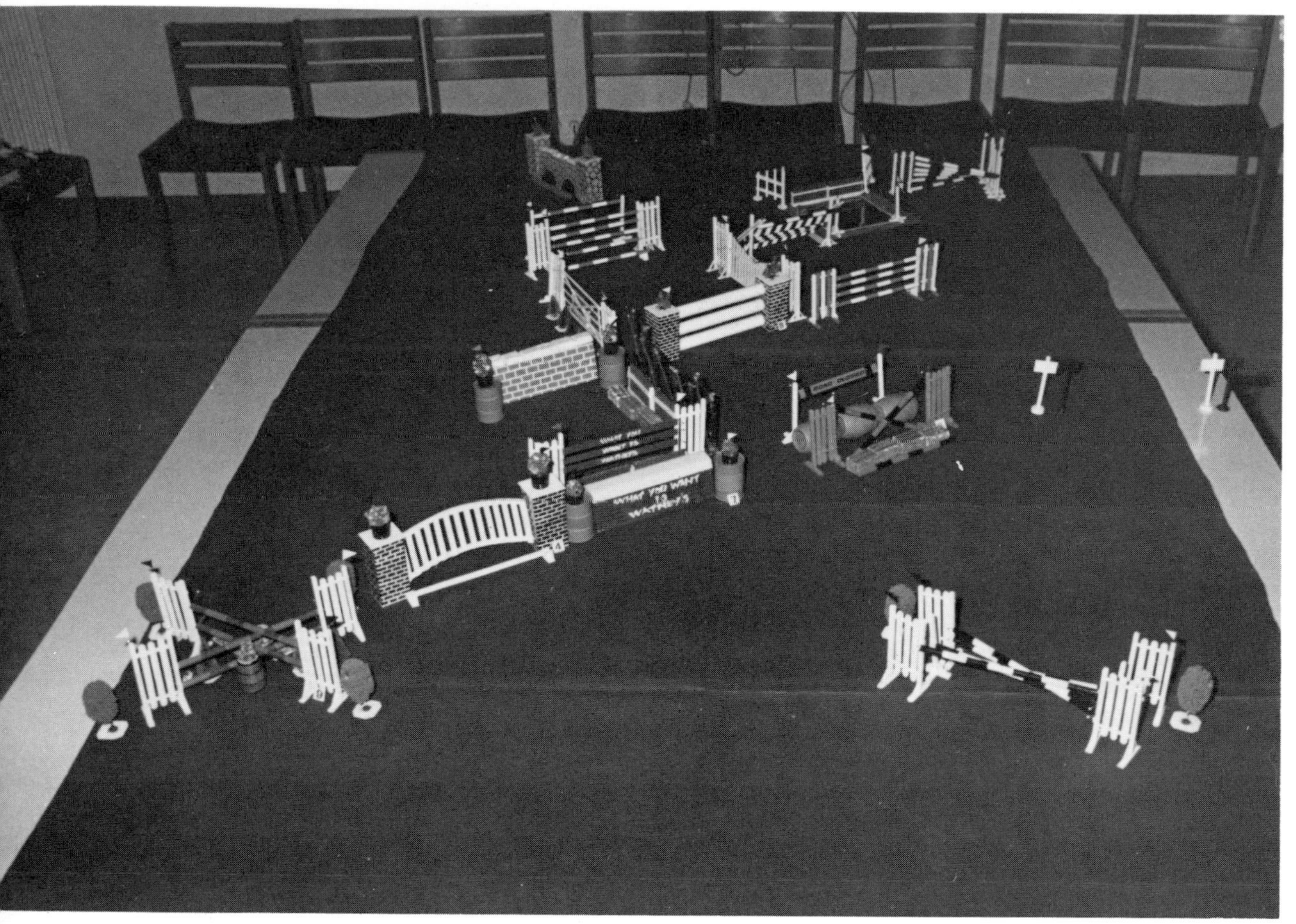

*Fig. 503*
The author's miniature set of fences which he uses in his lectures on course design and building, and in showing his pupils how to ride a course.

One should not underestimate the great importance of the small local show, and in particular the novice competitions, as these shows (often with insufficient fence material) still provide basic schooling for many future international horses and riders.

When building courses, in various continents, I have always been very impressed by the enthusiasm of so many people to improve courses. In spite of their lack of knowledge and real understanding of the principles involved they realised that expertly built courses and well-constructed fences always induce jumping of a high calibre, giving greater pleasure to competitors and spectators alike.

### INSPECTION

The course builder's first duty prior to designing the course is to inspect the location and the conditions of the actual jumping arena or field.

The following factors are vital and should be carefully taken into consideration.

(i) the actual size of the jumping enclosure. The ideal size is approximately 70 × 120 metres, even if the outer track must be left temporarily free for the use of harness horses or showing classes. (If it happens that a few fences have to be removed to facilitate these classes then the course builders should mark the ground with chalk and a large paint brush, indicating the position of the removed fences, so that they can be rebuilt swiftly on the same location);

(ii) whether the terrain is level or sloping;

(iii) whether the going is hard or soft;

(iv) inspect where the softest spots in the enclosure are situated in the event of weather or other abnormal conditions necessitating adaption of a course;

(v) the northern aspect of the course and the assessment of direction of the sunshine during the most important jumping competition of the show. This is important so horse and rider will not have to face the sun when jumping the more formidable fences. This applies particularly to combinations and the waterjump;

(vi) the above also applies when choosing the location for the judges box. Avoid direct glare of the sun, which will hamper the judges;

(vii) where the grandstand will be situated so that most spectacular obstacles will be placed in front of it;

(viii) separate entry and exit at the jumping enclosure;

(ix) if there is no permanent water jump then a suitable location to construct one should be found. This should have sufficient space for a long straight approach line, especially if the waterjump is built in conjunction with a single fence or a combination (in front, or behind, or both);

(x) the size and location of the warming-up ring, practise fences and their distance away from the actual jumping enclosure;

(xi) inspect the type and colours of the fence material and assess the quantity of material available to design the course. Make sure that one has the necessary spare parts of fence material available in case damage occurs during the show;

(xii) check which type of competitions are being held and in what order. In case a show covers several days build the courses on the first days in such a way that the ground surface is not cut up for the more important events on the following days.

At most country shows the course builder has only a field at his disposal, which he has to transform into a showground, involving making a complete layout. This includes providing parking facilities for horseboxes, which should be situated not too far from the warming-up ring and the jumping enclosure. He has also to take into consideration that in many cases there are just as many pony competitions as there are competitions for horses. Then the course builder has to complete the entire layout twice, building one course for the ponies and one for the horses. If both arenas are to be built on the same field one should leave plenty of space between them so as to facilitate accommodation for the two groups of spectators and their cars.

The pony warming-up ring should be kept separate from the one for the horses, because with children on ponies one must not take any chances.

*Conclusion*

Having considered all the various facts and conditions, a course plan should now be made based on the list of fence material available. This course plan should be submitted to the show organisers, enabling them to deposit beforehand material for each fence at the required location in the jumping enclosure.

### PLANNING

Having completed the inspection personally, or according to the information supplied by the show committee, the course builder can now start his homework, planning the courses for the various competitions. His chief objective in designing a course is to test the horse's training and the rider's technical ability. In novice courses he will not ask too much, yet he will encourage free riding and assist the horse's education.

The course builder aims at producing the best combination of horse and rider as the winner. His course is designed with this end in view, rather than with placing a few "catch" fences to reduce clear rounds and to give the lucky ones a chance to win.

He must have some idea of the horses taking part and their capabilities. With these aspects in mind he plans his courses. He should know exactly the number of horses competing in each jumping competition, especially in the novice events. His most difficult job is to produce a fair result from a big field of novices.

All the above information enables the course builder to decide on a shorter course, which is time saving, efficient and successful. In novice competitions, for instance, each round should not take longer than approximately one minute. It is justifiable to shorten these courses to save time and to prevent the show from running late. On occasions, due to the length of the first round novice course for example, the competition runs much too late, which makes some judges bored and tired. The same applies to the jump-off course. For quick results some judges raise the fences too high for the jump-off, which is criminal, because the young novice is over-faced, loses confidence, incurs jumping faults and refuses. This method of obtaining quick results is ruinous.

Therefore, the shorter course in the first round is the fairer and the most efficient manner of saving time.

A competent course builder can predict approximately how many clear rounds will be produced over a particular course. His problems cover the size of the fences, the distance between them, the smoothness of the route with no abrupt checks for the horses, the weather, terrain and the use of the natural contour of the arena or field in question so that his design follows a logical pattern.

He is human and can err as such with the occasional miscalculation, but the experienced man rarely errs because he knows that the responsibility for a given schedule rests fair and square on his shoulders.

### TERRAIN

The terrain is another important aspect which should carefully be considered when planning a course.

*Downhill gradient*

If the surface is sloping then the course should be designed so as to avoid the horse having to jump downhill. If a horse is forced to jump downhill he will tend, just as when the surface is slippery, to come too close to the fence in his take-off position. In such a position it is indeed very difficult for the horse to get his forelegs free of the ground to become airborne, and in many cases instead of taking-off the horse refuses or slides right through the fence.

This downhill gradient lengthens the canter strides in the approach to a fence. The fault becomes strikingly apparent when a *combination jump* is built downhill. Refusals occur, not only at the first element but in particular at the second and the third element. Owing to the lengthening of the stride the horse is unable to cope with the distance in between the elements of the combination jump.

Hard going also lengthens the horse's strides. When building courses in Australia and Central America, where the going is usually hard, I made the distance between the elements for combination jumps approximately 0·3 metres longer, which made matters easier for the horse.

*Uphill gradient*

An uphill gradient, as well as a deep and heavy going, will shorten the horse's strides. This should be considered when erecting and positioning a combination jump and when assessing the distances between the elements. The distance should be slightly reduced if the going is not perfect. In general, when the going is bad, the height and the spread of fences should be reduced from those obtaining under normal circumstances.

FENCES

Imagination and flair are important in providing a variety of obstacles within the scope of a good horse. Broad and high wings on each side of the fences make the jumps look smaller and more inviting for the horse.

All obstacles must be capable of being knocked down, but not too easily. On no account should any obstacle be tricky or an unfair surprise for the horse.

The front base of the fences should be as wide as possible, generally not smaller than 4 metres. The preferable width is 5 metres. The higher the fence the broader the front base should be.

The fences should have a "full" appearance, rather than appearing empty with too much daylight shining through. Even at small local shows, which often have insufficient material, one can, with goodwill and imagination, still build quite an attractive and inviting course when using plenty of straw bales. These make an excellent ground line, which is important to encourage novice horses to locate a correct take-off point. They also provide a good filling. With a further supply of greenery, such as pine trees and flowers, the course will be given a pleasant appearance. Artificial green grass mats provide a good variation. They can be used to cover planks or a wall. Out of doors the mats should be fastened so as not to frighten the horse should they flap in the wind. To make some fences more effective in appearance the ground beneath a triple bar or a "fan" fence can be covered with white sawdust. (This novelty is *not* recommended for use in novice competitions, as it may frighten the young horse.) Each fence should have *one* dominant colour.

Have fences painted if necessary. All paintwork should have a gloss finish and painted poles or planks should be painted both ends in the brighter colours (black, Windsor green, signal red, cornflower blue, sunlight yellow), the remainder divided by sections of white. These bright colours carry an air of distinction and good taste (poles with too many colours are ineffective; soft colours are not suitable for a sports arena). A tip for the do-it-yourself painter: divide the sections on the poles with rubber bands when painting; this ensures a neat looking border between the colours.

*Fig. 504*
In a novice competition all fences should have a full appearance, straw bales and some green branches can be used as filling.

*Fig. 505*
An empty looking fence, no groundline, difficult for a young horse.

### SURFACE

Precautions should be taken in regard to the surface at the take-off and landing side of a fence in case the going is extremely hard during a dry spell, or when it becomes slippery, which can happen very easily if there is a sudden shower of rain on hard going.

When the going is hard I prefer to put down a mixture of coarse sand and shavings as a shock absorbent substance and to prevent slipping. Sand *only* does not have the same effect and can cause overreaching on landing. Shavings alone and peat moss or sawdust should never be used. These substances are not sufficiently shock absorbing and on a windy day it will be blown, not only all over the place, but it increases slippery conditions still further when the going gets wet. One should put the mixture of coarse sand and shavings on both sides of the fence and *not* on the landing side only. Putting it only on the landing side distracts the horse's attention prior to the take-off. This frequently leads to jumping faults. This problem does not, of course, occur when the fence has a close front base, such as a wall, but it may when the horse can look right through the fence, because he is then paying more attention to what has been put on the ground *behind* the fence than on the actual fence itself. (It is amusing how the horse pays attention to all objects that are positioned on the ground. I have seen horses making a jump over an electric wire from timing equipment which had been buried into the grass but had become partly visible during the competition.)

For these reasons the course builder should take the horses' reaction into consideration if he is forced to put the mixture on the landing side *only*, and reduce the height of the fences accordingly.

### COLLECTING POCKET

Provide a special collecting pocket at the entrance to the jumping enclosure so that there will always be two horses in the pocket waiting for their turn to enter the arena. This saves an enormous amount of time should the previous competitor be eliminated and finish his round sooner than normal. The next competitor can then enter immediately.

*Entrance and exit*

It is practical and time saving to have a separate entrance and exit at the jumping enclosure. A young horse coming into the arena will not be tempted to turn around and follow a horse leaving the arena through the same gate. Horses in the collecting pocket will dislike entering the jumping enclosure and will possibly rear if a horse leaves the arena through the collecting pocket. It also calls for smooth operation and will cut seconds by allowing the next competitor to enter the jumping enclosure before the previous competitor leaves, having completed his round. The jumping enclosure gate should be closed after a horse has entered in case a fall has occurred and the rider has become separated from his horse. Then the horse cannot run out of the arena, which would mean elimination.

### AN INVITING COURSE

When planning a course remember one psychological aspect. Build the first two fences so that they are not only easy to jump but are also jumped towards the collecting pocket as well. This encourages reluctant young horses, or spoilt ones, to start their round with increased confidence. Once they have jumped the first few fences the battle is half won. If a horse is forced to jump straight out of the collecting pocket *away* from the other horses he will dislike starting his round. He will rear, refuse or knock the first fence, because most horses naturally do not like to leave their comrades.

I am fully aware that course designers differ in their approach to the subject. This is essential to avoid monotony in courses. Nevertheless, I disagree with the method of some course builders who design a course pruposely so that the first fence is jumped "away" from home in order to save time. This, in my opinion, is unfair and a miscalculation. Adding up all the time for refusals, reapproaches and rebuilding the first fence will prove more costly in minutes than a fluently ridden full course. The first two fences

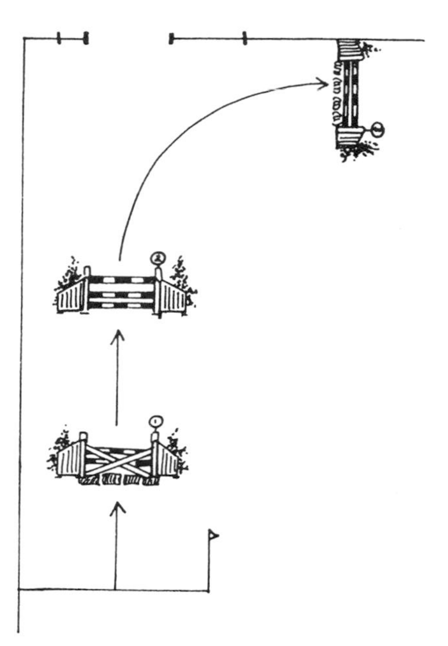

*Fig. 506*
This is a good design. The first two fences are jumped "towards home", with an easier fence after passing the exit.

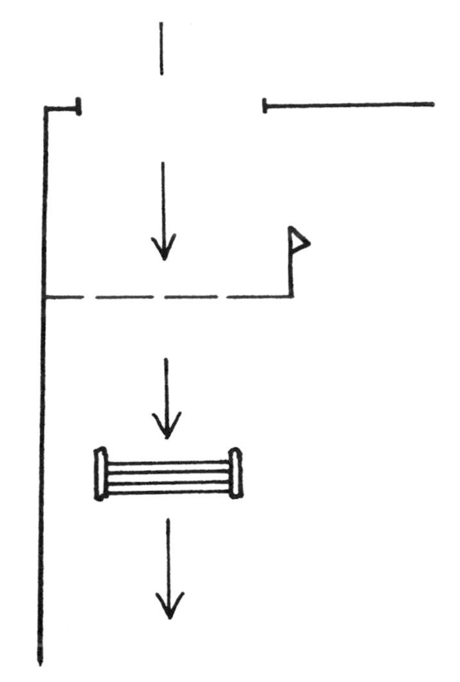

*Fig. 507*
A very badly planned course, causing a lot of trouble to young horses. The first fence has to be jumped straight out of the pocket.

of the course should be at a moderate level, inviting and encouraging the horse to speed onwards with confidence. The remainder of the fences should increase in difficulty towards the finish of the course.

In general, each fence should provide a definite problem, and the more intricate the course the more searching the questions asked of horse and rider.

If the first two fences are placed in the direction of the pocket then the third fence – after a fair turn – should be jumped in a different direction. It should not be placed too close to the pocket gate and at least 42 metres away from the second fence. This gives the rider a chance to ride a balanced turn and to prepare the horse for the third fence. As this is the first fence away from home it should be inviting and simple. Such considerations are most important for novice horses, especially at the beginning of the season. It builds up confidence and teaches the horse to enjoy the game. Remember that this is the main purpose of novice competitions.

This also applies when locating the combination jumps. They should never be built too soon on the track of the course and they should be in the direction of the collecting pocket, ensuring better jumping and less refusals. The first element of the combination should be at least 60 metres away from the preceding single fence. This will give the rider plenty of space to approach the combination correctly.

When combinations are positioned in this manner they will have a greater educational value for novice horses. A further important point to make a combination more inviting is to present the first element well. It could cause novice horses a lot of unnecessary trouble if the first element was an oxer parallel or an upright, such as a gate or a wall. Instead, build a simple

*Fig. 508*
An inviting first part *(left)* of a combination fence, for use in a novice competition; this can be altered without trouble *(right)* into an oxer parallel for the following open competition.

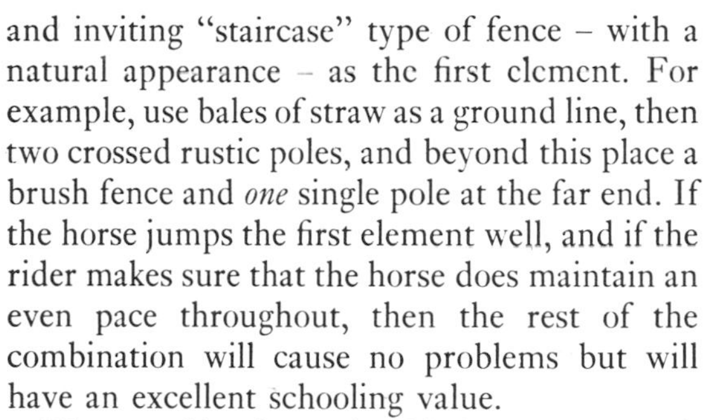

and inviting "staircase" type of fence – with a natural appearance – as the first element. For example, use bales of straw as a ground line, then two crossed rustic poles, and beyond this place a brush fence and *one* single pole at the far end. If the horse jumps the first element well, and if the rider makes sure that the horse does maintain an even pace throughout, then the rest of the combination will cause no problems but will have an excellent schooling value.

The combinations should be spaced at a suitable distance in accordance with the simplicity of the elements and with a view to the slower speed in which these novice competitions are jumped. Building the first element is also time saving because firstly it will ensure less refusals and, secondly, from the same material an oxer parallel can be built for the following higher grade of competition.

One should also consider that the more spectacular fences, combination jumps and so on, are positioned so that from the grandstand or the Royal Box a good view can be had, giving spectators an exciting outlook.

### COURSE LENGTH

The total length of a course depends on the type of competition and the grade of the horses participating. However, the total length of the course should never exceed its number of fences multiplied by 60. For example, if a course consists of ten fences the total length must not exceed 600 metres.

In novice competitions, however, the course should not be longer than 300 to 350 metres, because even if it takes a competitor only *one* minute to complete his round one can be sure that two horses will take three minutes, including entering and leaving the jumping enclosure. The most efficient starter at the entrance cannot cut down this time. Therefore if a course builder is faced with an entry of over 100 horses in a novice competition he cannot afford to build too long a course without taking the risk that the more spectacular competitions later on during the day will commence far behind schedule. Besides, if a novice course is too long, the young horse becomes tired halfway through which causes refusals and jumping faults. The rebuilding of knocked down fences further imposes on precious time.

### COMPETITIONS

The public needs innovations. To ensure an interesting jumping programme it is worthwhile to have as wide a variety of obstacles and cometitions as is possible. Their effect will have added impact, pleasure and excitement for spectators and competitors alike.

Which type of competition is chosen depends on which country the show is being held in, on the preferences of riders and spectators, on the grade of horses participating, on the going and so on.

For example, in a "horse breeding country" such as Ireland, there are many horses at shows of novice standard, but few of open or international standard. Most promising young horses are exported and only a few good ones are kept "at home" to compete in open competitions. Therefore competitions for older and experienced horses are of the *puissance* or six bars variety, or instead there are typical Irish competitions, held under special rules over natural stone walls and double and single banks.

Other countries specialise in upgrading horses. In these countries there are many horses of international standard at shows and these are catered for with a wide selection of various types of open competitions.

An "open" course should be a fair test of horsemanship, skill and ability. In a well balanced course, the questions asked of both horse and rider should be evenly distributed over the whole course. The uprights and spread fences should be placed alternately. Too many clear rounds become tedious. On the other hand too few clear rounds show that the course is too demanding for the standard of the horses participating. It is ideal if there are in the first round three to four more clear rounds than prizes available, as this will ensure an exciting jump-off to round off the competition.

A fair test, but quite a difficult one, is, for instance:

(i) an upright fence, oxer parallel or a combination jump placed in front of or behind a waterjump;

(ii) if a single fence or a combination jump is placed behind the waterjump, at a minimum distance of 11 to 12 metres, than the whole sequence of jumps is considered as *one combination*. However, such a combination belongs only to international competition.

In ordinary open competitions the distance from the landing side of the waterjump to the single fence or combination jump should be 18 to 21 to 24 metres and so on, depending, of course, again, on the grade of the horses participating.

In spite of the fact that a horse lands much closer behind a waterjump than behind a normal obstacle, one can make it somewhat easier for the horse by lengthening these distances by one extra metre. Less experienced horses will flatten and be on the forehand immediately when the waterjump is cleared. Therefore this one additional metre will give the horse more space to re-establish his balance and to locate his correct take-off position for the jump placed behind the waterjump.

When a single fence or combination is placed in front of the waterjump the distance will again be influenced by the grade of horses participating and the width of the waterjump. I do not like these distances to be shorter than 18 metres and this still demands "some riding". To ease the problem one lengthens the distance so that the total length is divisible by 3 metres. The shorter the distance the greater the effort the horse must make to accelerate in order to have sufficient speed to clear the oncoming spread of the waterjump.

As a horse should take-off much closer to a waterjump than to a normal fence, one should *not* extend the distances in between the fence prior to the waterjump. Because the horse has to come closer to the waterjump than to an ordinary fence, the distance is already longer than normal and suitable for the faster speed in which the water will be approached.

*Related distances*

The term "related distance" means that distances in between two single fences are divisible by 3 metres, ergo 15 to 18 to 21 metres and so on. After 30 metres the relation of the two fences has no longer any real influence in relation to the length of a horse's canter stride.

There are course builders who favour placing a large number of single fences at short related distances. This gives the impression that the whole course consists of a series of combination jumps. For the following reasons I am strongly against too short a related distance, especially in novice and indoor competitions:

(i) Essentially the novice horse requires more space in between the single fences to encourage free, fluent and bold jumping. If these distances are too short the young horse has neither sufficient space nor time in between two single fences to collect and rebalance himself and to reorientate himself for the next take-off position. Consequently he loses impulsion. To prevent this happening the distance in between the single fences for novice horses should *never* be shorter than 18 metres. Rather, they should be longer.

(ii) Particularly with indoor competitive events or in a small out of doors arena do not use too short related distances, as it is difficult anyway to maintain a controlled even pace owing to the many changes of direction, the shorter turns and the restricted space. When the horse is also required to jump single fences at too short a related distance, more particularly if they are positioned behind or in front of a combination, then I feel the question asked is an unfair one for both horse and rider, since it not only ruins the competition but interrupts free forward riding. These deliberate and unnecessary severe distance problems are an even more taxing test for the horse at a faster speed when riding against the clock. The faster speed involves a longer canter stride then the related distance does no longer correspond with the extra length of the stride.

Of course, some horses are clever enough to jump at a faster speed the two related fences at a slight angle, increasing the related distance by several feet, but the majority of horses will come too close to the second related fence, which leads to refusals and unnecessary jumping faults.

*Three-in-one*

A further fact to be considered in designing a course is, for example, if there are three different competitions being held on the same day, then the three different courses should be designed in such a way that they all can be built just by slightly altering the one course. First novice, second open and third a speed competition. These designs are suitable for an indoor arena of 20 × 60 metres.

This saves an enormous amount of time and delay during the day of the show, since it will not be necessary to rebuild each course in between the different competitions other than swiftly adjusting the different heights, spreads and, of course, the different course lines. It also prevents a hold up where spectators are subjected to watch boring course changes. This method is especially important at indoor shows due to restricted space.

*The course line*

A carefully planned course line always provides an interesting jumping competition. The customary figure of eight course line is boring for the spectators as well as for the competitors.

I prefer a stimulating track, with fair turns and many changes of directions. Such a track will be of the highest educational value for both horse and rider.

*Compulsory course line*

It is up to the course builder to decide whether or not to introduce on part, or on the whole of the course a compulsory course line. If he does decide to do so then the track, or part of it, will become the line which every rider *must* follow when competing. It is also the line on which the course builder has measured the total length of the course.

Should the rider not follow the compulsory course line he is penalised by elimination. The main purpose in introducing the line is to prevent riders negotiating turns so that they approach fences out of an incorrect angle. This spoils a young horse and, furthermore, teaches the rider to think. A few good riders will disregard the course line and be eliminated, which will save time and keep the competition from running late.

*Compulsory turning point*

Instead of a compulsory course line the course builder may introduce a compulsory turning point. This again will prevent riders from taking unnecessary and unfair short turns, as they must

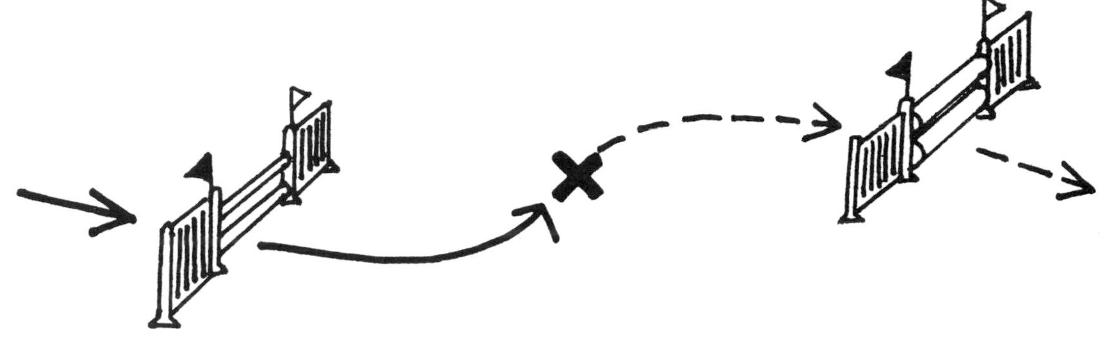

*Fig. 509*
An unfair course line: the two fences are not in line. The horse has to land over the first fence in the left canter for the left hand turn. At X, only an experienced horse will be able to make a flying change of leg at the canter. A novice horse will instantly lose balance and go through the right hand turn in counter canter or disunited. This will cause take-off problems at the next fence.

ride around the marker on the prescribed side. For example, a boundary ground flag is placed at a correct distance, say from four to five canter strides away from the first element of a combination jump. This forces the rider to approach it in a straight line.

Once the rider passes the compulsory turning point on the wrong side to that stated on the course plan, without rectifying his error, he will be eliminated.

*The practise fence*

In each warming-up pocket (for horses and ponies) place two practise fences, of which one should be an upright fence and the other an oxer, both constructed from poles. Do not use a wall or a gate.

Both fences should carry two boundary flags on the approach side which must be clearly marked and from which side only the fences *must* be jumped. This rule should be strictly enforced and checked by the pocket steward to prevent riders from jumping an oxer from the opposite direction and thus using it for illegal rapping.

The wings of the practise fences in the pocket should have holes only up to a height of 1·20 metres, then these fences cannot be built higher than approximately 1·25 metres. In this way one can stop certain riders from jumping their horses insensibly high while warming up.

TOOLS

In planning, designing and constructing courses, good tools are essential. The course builder's equipment will include:

(i) measuring stick to measure the dimensions of obstacles;

(ii) measuring tape to measure the distances in between the elements of combination obstacles;

(iii) measuring wheel to measure the entire length of a course;

(iv) the working plan of the designs, stating the nature, colours and the exact measurements of the various obstacles of each competition and the jump-off, distances in combinations and the total length of each course;

(v) crayons of chalk and/or drawing pins.

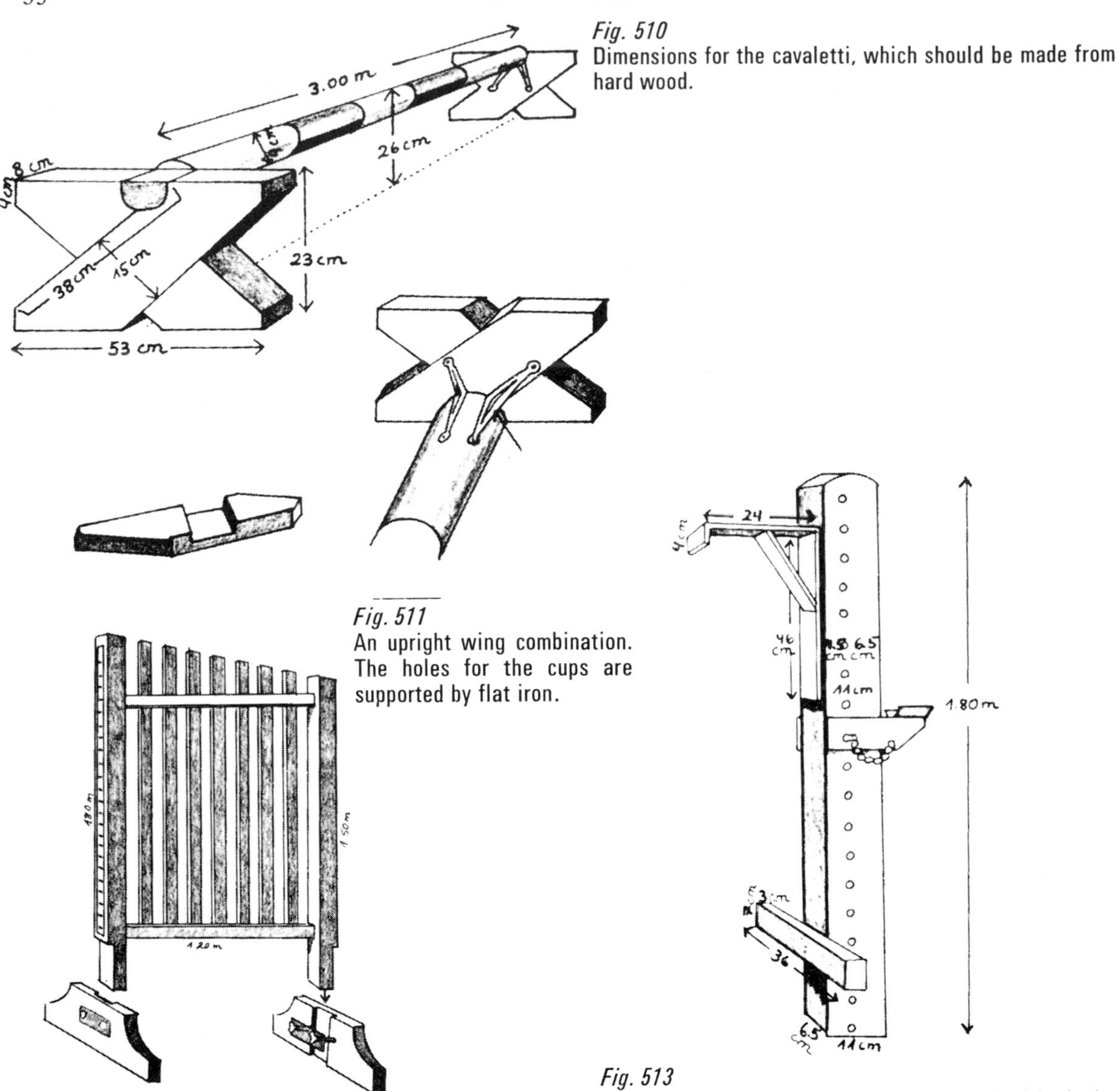


*Fig. 510*
Dimensions for the cavaletti, which should be made from hard wood.

*Fig. 511*
An upright wing combination. The holes for the cups are supported by flat iron.

*Fig. 513*
A wall hanger for use in the indoor school, with sloping kicking boards.

*Fig. 512*
The upright. Note the practical square number block on the top.

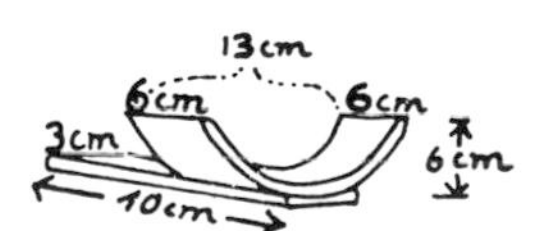


*Fig. 514*
A simple cup to fit all uprights and fences.

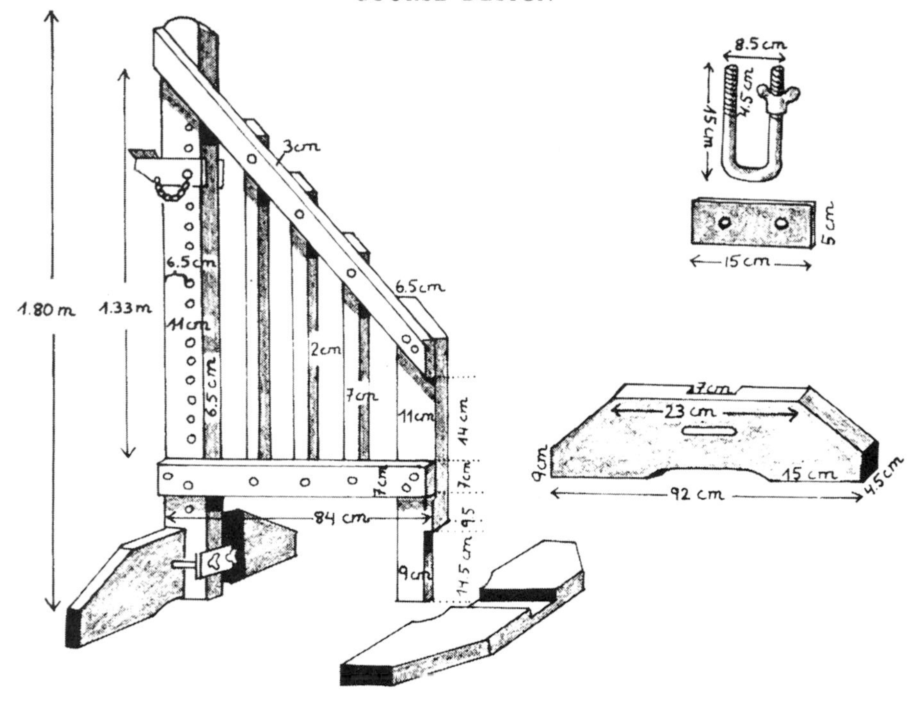


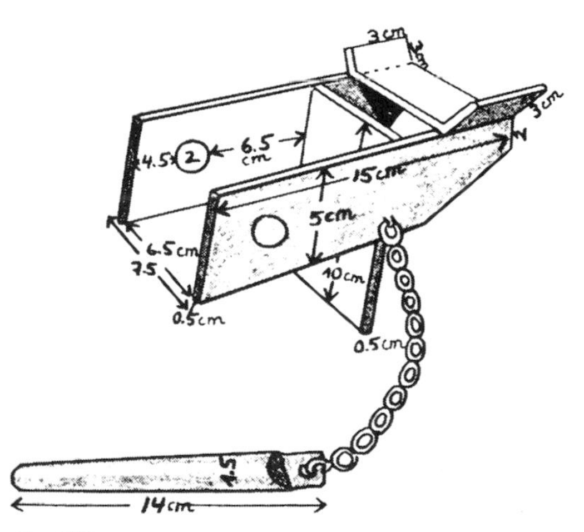


*Fig. 515*
An upright wing *(top)*, standard for the British Horse Society. The wing can be dismantled for transporting. The cup *(bottom)* for the upright wing, should *not* be used with round poles as they will fall too easily. Use eight-sided poles only.

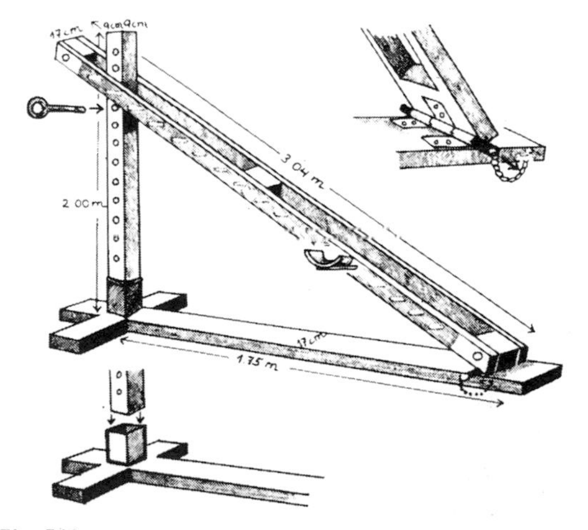


*Fig. 516*
An upright for a triple bar. This can be folded together, the posts slide down into a steel casing, when transporting.

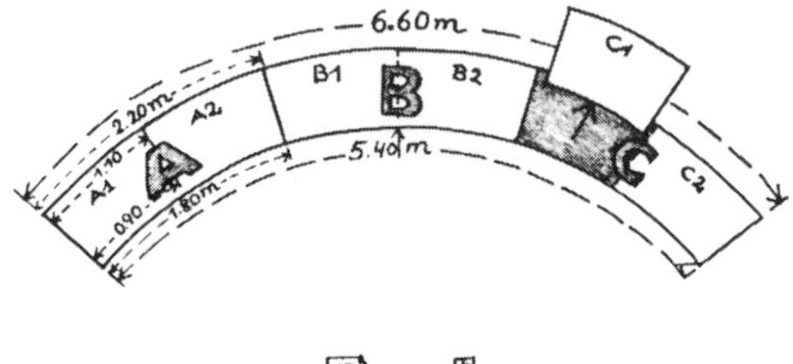


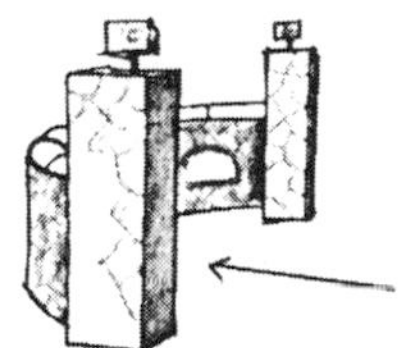

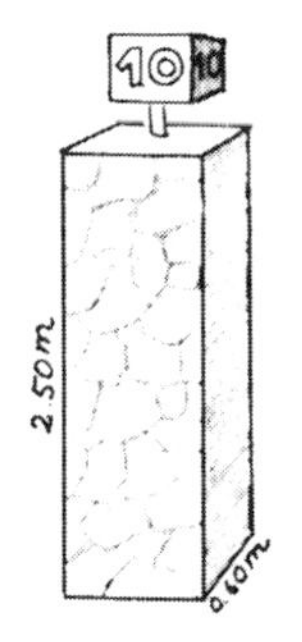


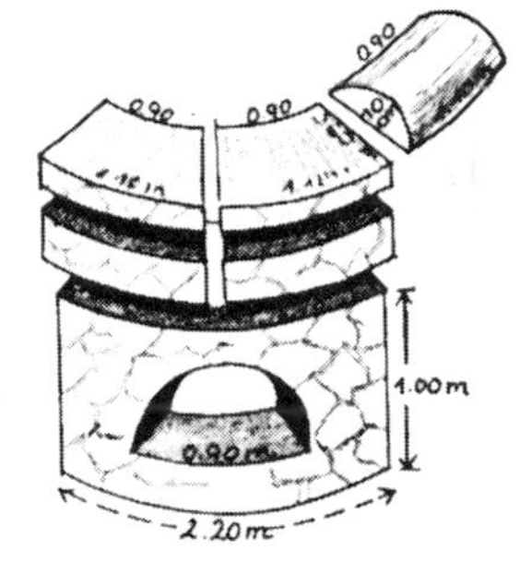


*Fig. 517*
The London Wall.

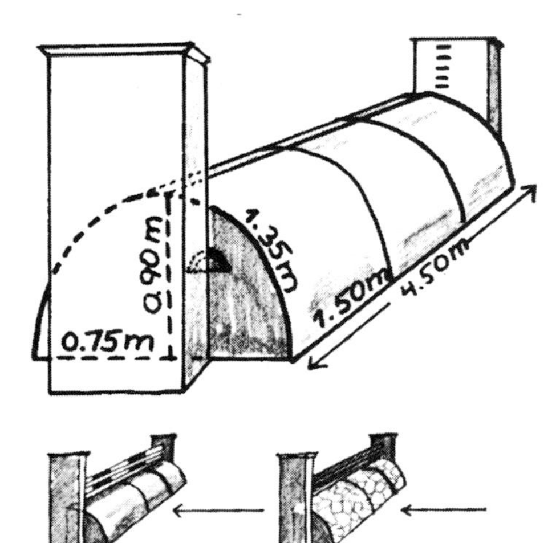


*Fig. 518*
A very practical, half-round, "Mexican" wall in six sections.

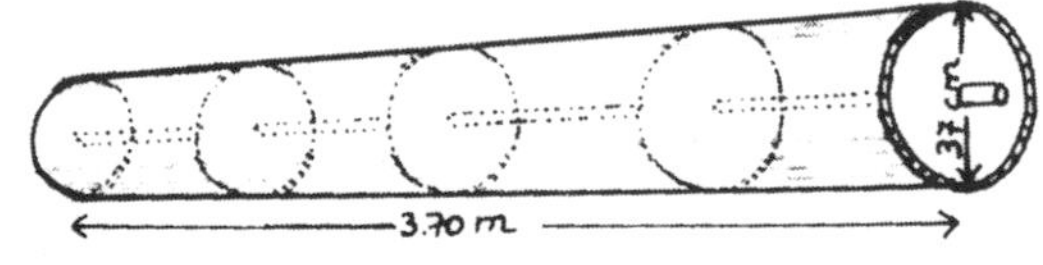


*Fig. 519*
The Elephant pole makes an impressive fence. As it is very heavy, it needs a steel pipe fitted through the centre of the supports which keeps the pole in shape. The ends of the pipe serve as hangers.

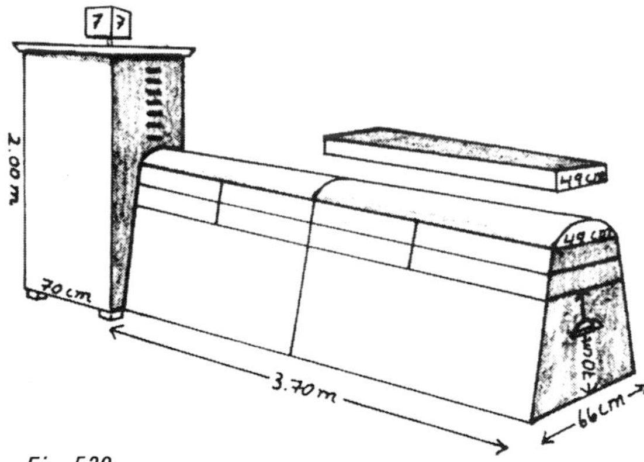


*Fig. 520*
A wall. There are holes in the pillars for poles over the wall or to make the fence into an oxer.

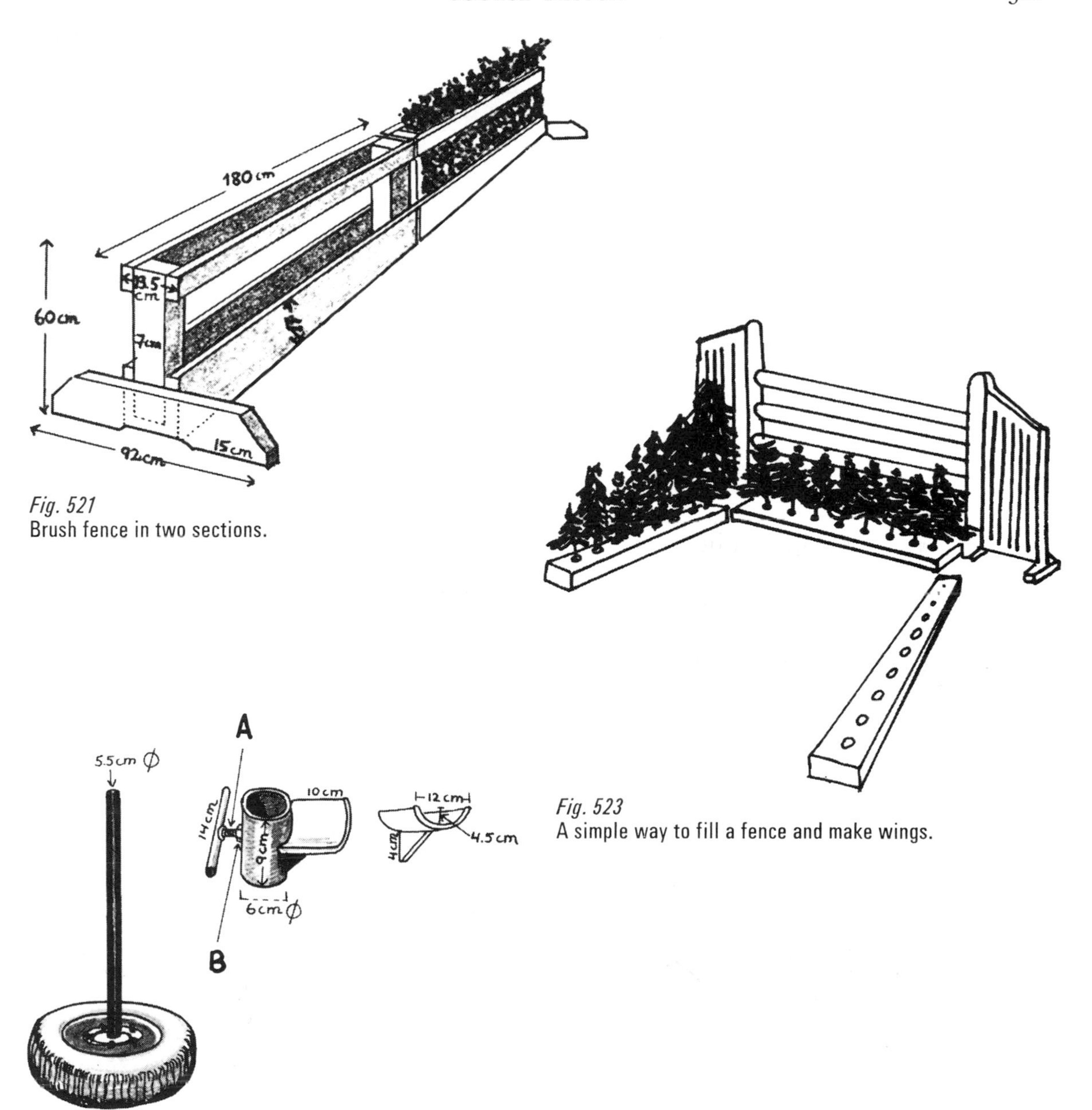


*Fig. 521*
Brush fence in two sections.

*Fig. 523*
A simple way to fill a fence and make wings.

*Fig. 522*
For training at home, an inexpensive and indestructable upright and cup can be made quite easily. The cup can be a piece of pipe and can be made adjustable. Weld a handle to the head of a bolt (A); then drill a hole in the pipe and weld a nut over it (B). Screw the bolt into the hole. The cup can then be slid up and down the upright and fixed, by turning the handle to tighten, at whatever height is desired. Holes in the upright itself are therefore not required.

Both should be of different colours and are required for marking the heights of the fences for each different competition and jump-off on the uprights

The holes in the wings should be numbered and the marking should be done exactly at the number of the hole where the cup of the fence is situated. This method saves considerable time, because not only will the fence stewards know the heights for the jump-off and for the next competition but they will also be able to rebuild a fence quickly and correctly in case an obstacle is completely demolished during a round and the cups fall out of the wings. The cup can then easily be replaced into its previous position.

PROVISIONAL COURSES

When building the course nothing is more aggravating for the assistants than lugging a heavy fence to a spot indicated and then to be told to move it somewhere else. Therefore, before erecting a complete obstacle, place first two wings with a single pole – as a temporary fence – exactly on the spot where each fence is intended to be built. Do this throughout the entire course. Mapping the course in this manner will provide a clearer picture of the "frame" of the course.

Bear in mind that the spread fences, oxer, waterjump and combinations need a longer approach line than a single upright fence and that the turns are fair and easy to ride.

I design all my courses so that the rider can follow a smooth track, with plenty of room to balance and to encourage free forward riding, eliminating any necessity to pull a horse up.

One measures the distance between the single fences. They should be under the "three metre rule". These distances are convenient for the horse in locating an easy take-off point if he follows the track correctly.

*Flags*

Each fence should have a red boundary flag on the right-hand side and a white flag on the left-hand side – or more flags if it concerns a spread fence.

These flags should be placed independently of the fence and remain undisturbed should the fence be knocked down. The same flags can be used to cross out a fence which is not used during a round.

*The finished course*

When the provisional course is built and the course builder has checked that the course rides fluently, all the fences can now be erected properly. Each fence must be clearly *numbered.* I prefer number blocks which display the

*Fig. 524*
Garden wall with pole.

*Fig. 526*
American triple bar.

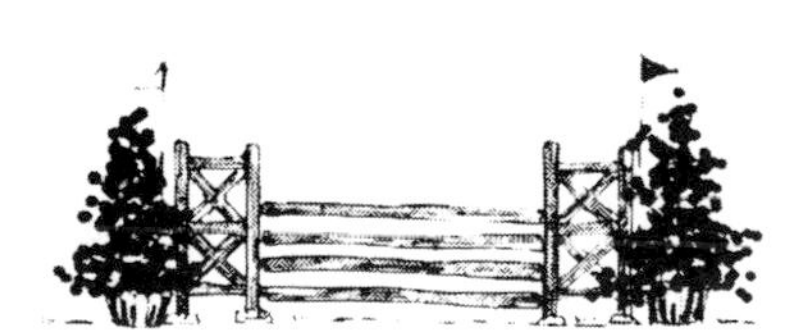

*Fig. 525*
Rustic pole fence.

*Fig. 527*
Brush fence with poles.

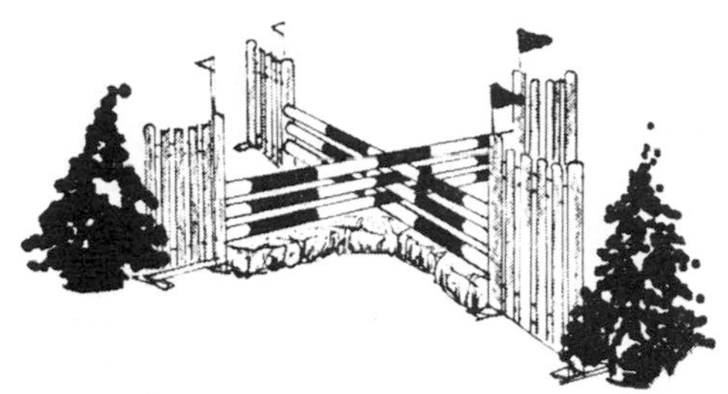

*Fig. 528*
Spider fence.

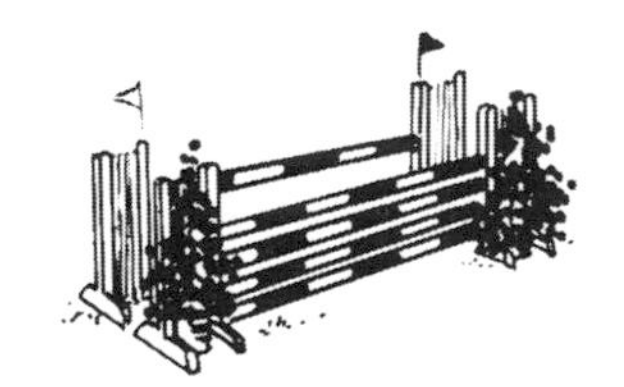

*Fig. 529*
Oxer.

*Fig. 530*
Hog's back.

*Fig. 531*
Triple bar.

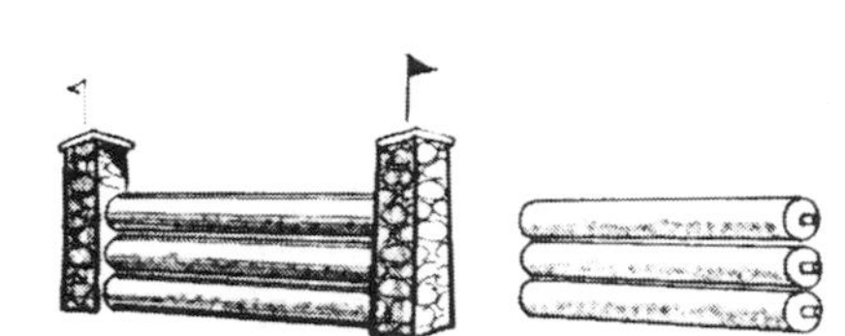

*Fig. 532*
Elephant poles.

*Fig. 533*
Triple bar with elephant poles.

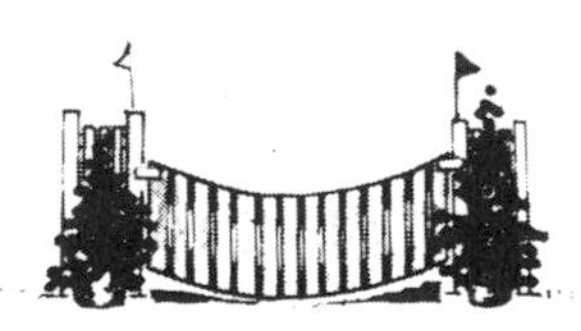

*Fig. 534*
A Stockholm gate for novice competitions.

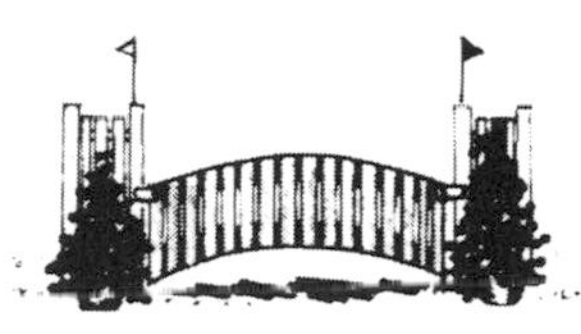

*Fig. 535*
Same gate used upside down for open competitions.

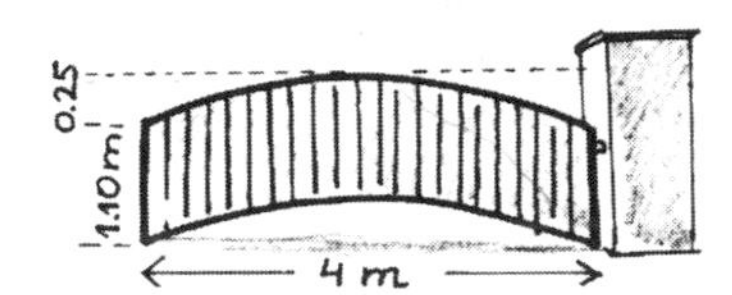


*Fig. 536*
Diagram for Stockholm gate.

*Fig. 537*
Brick wall.

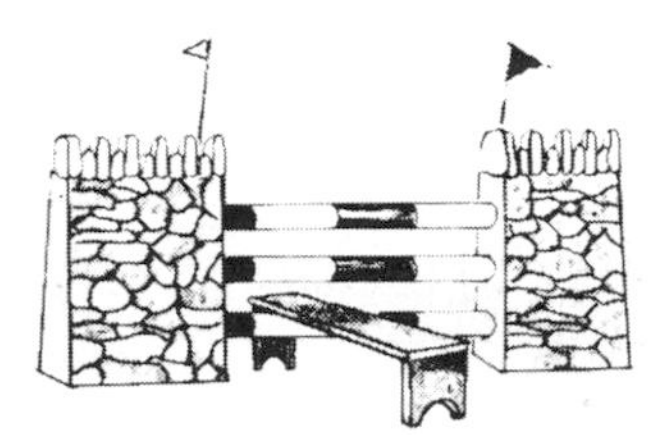

*Fig. 538*
Stile.

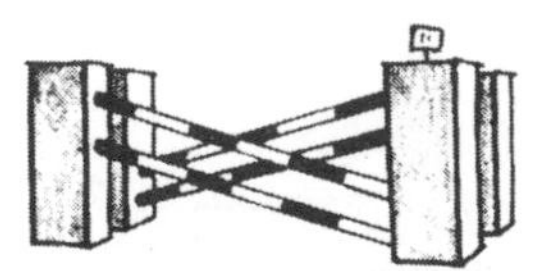

*Fig. 539*
This oxer is not suitable for novice competitions as it has no groundline and is difficult to judge. It is more difficult still with a wall in the middle, as then the fence has a false groundline.

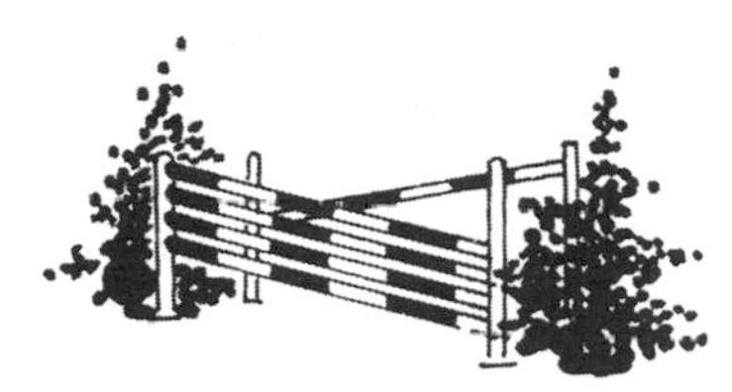

*Fig. 540*
Another difficult oxer.

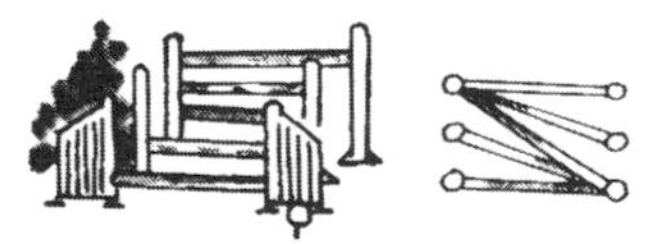

*Fig. 541*
The ''twister'' fence.

*Fig. 542*
A difficult oxer, which can be jumped from both directions.

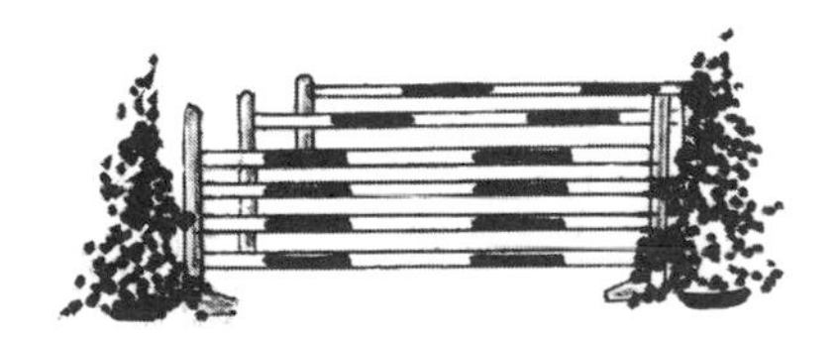

*Fig. 543*
An extra spread oxer.

*Fig. 544*
A fan fence, to be placed in turns only. The one illustrated is for a left hand turn.

number on four sides. They should be positioned on the *top* of the right upright or wing of each fence. (During my stay in Mexico I introduced these number blocks; they were also used in the Mexico Olympic Games of 1968.)

These numbers are clearly visible, not only for the competitors, who might have lost the track of the course, but for the spectator and judge alike. If the number of the fence is positioned on the ground their only value is to riders when walking the course. Once mounted the rider can barely see these numbers and they lose their value as signs if he has lost his way.

When all the fences are erected, measure the course with the measuring wheel and follow exactly the track through the turns. The total length is measured from start to finish with the wheel; distances in combinations are measured with the tape.

The distance from the starting line to the first fence should be a minimum of 6 metres and a maximum of 25 metres.

The distance between the last fence and the finishing line should be at least 15 metres but no longer than 25 metres. This rule also applies for the jump-off course. The jump-off course is measured in the same manner and should never have less fences than half the number of fences of the original course. In any case there should never be less than six obstacles.

## TIME AND SPEED

When the total length of the course is measured, the element of time in each course is calculated in accordance to the standard, type and purpose of each competition:

(i) novice competitions should be jumped at a speed not faster than 300 metres per minute;

(ii) open competitions should have a speed of 350 metres per minute;

(iii) international competitions may be ridden at 375 to 400 metres per minute;

(iv) Nation's Cup competitions, international championships and the Olympic Jumping Grand Prix are ridden at a speed of 400 metres per minute.

It is very important that the different grades of competition are ridden at the correct speed as laid down by the rules. With experience and age the horse grows into the higher grades of competitions and the speeds are accordingly increased. Nevertheless, in some countries these rules are neglected, which is highly damaging for novice horses.

In Germany and Switzerland, for instance, all novice competitions are decided in the first round on jumping faults and time. To upgrade a horse the rider has to win prizes. He is forced to ride his novice horse at too fast a speed in order to win. Therefore these novice competitions are more like a hurdle race than a jumping competition. In Mexico an even worse system is used in deciding novice competitions. The courses are much too long, take about two minutes to complete and, as a rule, the riders must jump these comparably small fences at a speed of 400 metres per minute. In the timed jump-off they use the full course again instead of shortening it to safeguard the horse's legs in view of the usual hard going.

The result of this unsatisfactory system is that young inexperienced horses are unable to jump off their hocks but come too close to the fences. Their balance is changed too much onto the forehand and their trajectory is flattened. The outcome is usually faults incurred with the forelegs or refusals.

Even if a horse has received a correct basic schooling at home and jumps in perfect style, the fact that he has to compete under such appalling conditions will give the horse no chance to develop his abilities. The young horse will be ruined before he has an opportunity to upgrade and jump in bigger competitions where his jumping ability would be of more significance than his speed.

The show organisers in countries using such unworthy methods of deciding novice competitions should review their traditional ideas with these facts in mind. I would strongly advise them to consider the methods for upgrading young horses used in Ireland and England.

There, novice competitions are not jumped against the clock. Instead all horses who have jumped clear in the first round will jump again over a shortened course, which may be raised. Should there be more than one clear round the prize money and rosettes will be divided equally as first prizes. A "time allowed" and a "time limit" is, of course, used.

This system is ideal and gives every horse a chance to develop naturally and exhibit his real jumping ability. Only in the higher grade competitions will the first or the second jump-off be held against the clock. Time and jumping faults will then decide the result of the competition.

I am convinced that this is the most satisfactory and justified way of running novice competitions. Young horses are not asked to run before they are able to walk.

*Time allowed*

In every course a time allowed and a time limit should be in operation. The time the competitor takes to cover the course from start to finish is recorded accurately in seconds and in fifths of a second.

The time allowed is set according to the speed required:

(i) if the speed in a competition is 300 metres per minute and the length of the course is

300 metres, the time allowed to complete the course is one minute;

(ii) exceeding the time allowed is penalised normally at the rate of a quarter fault for every second or part of a second;

(iii) in speed competitions the time allowed depends on the length of the course and the number of fences.

In novice competitions I generally allow a few additional seconds to prevent the rider from upsetting his horse unnecessarily by rushing the course. To simplify the tiring job of timing, the course builder should round off the time allowed upwards to a round figure.

To a certain extent the time allowed also prevents a competition from running late, since many competitors in novice competitions make their turns unnecessarily wide or make transitions into a trot, sometimes even into a walk. Should these competitors have a clear round they risk time penalties and are prohibited from the jump-off. This weeds out the unpolished performers and reduces the number of competitors in the jump-off, thus saving time.

*Time limit*

In all jumping competitions the time limit is twice as long as the time allowed. Exceeding the time limit means elimination.

FINAL COURSE PLAN

Having completed these preparations the course builder may well take a satisfied look at the finished course before drawing the final course plan. He will have to make four copies, one for the judges, one (waterproof) for display in the collecting ring for the competitors, one for press and television reporters and one for himself. The course plan will state the following conditions:

(i) the number of the competition concerned;

(ii) under which "table" or rules the competition will be judged;

(iii) the length of the course;

(iv) the speed required;

(v) time allowed and time limit; rate of time penalties;

(vi) the number of obstacles and jumps on the course;

(vii) position of start, finish, entrance and exit;

(viii) compulsory, partly compulsory or free course line. The first two will be indicated on the plan of the course as one continuous line;

(ix) compulsory turning points;

(x) arrows indicating the direction in which each fence should be jumped;

(xi) two arrows should the fence be jumped from both directions;

(xii) position of the judges box and timekeeper;

(xiii) the fence numbers – on each single obstacle and on the first element of a combination. Letters are placed on the remaining elements of the combination, A, B, C and so on;

(xiv) details of subsequent rounds as defined by the "table". Number of fences in the jump-off, their order, the degree to which they will be raised, time allowed and time limit, time penalties, free or compulsory course line.

The course plan should be on display in the collecting ring at least one hour prior to the start of each competition.

One course plan is given to the (chief) judge who should walk and inspect the course. He is to judge the height, spread and fairness of the fences and their suitability for the competition concerned. He will also check the time allowed and the time limit, the compulsory line, turning points and so on. He will confirm the going and, if necessary, arrange with the course builder to make appropriate adjustments. The course is then open for inspection by the competitors, usually to riders only, though in novice competitions it is preferable to allow the horses in as well so that they also can view the fences and get confidence with the new surroundings.

### BUILDING WATERJUMPS

The waterjump is the fence that causes most problems in a competition for the simple reason that there are too few opportunities for the riders to jump this fence. Too few shows include a waterjump because (a) only a very few arenas include a permanent waterjump, and (b) to most show organisers it seems unjustified in costs and labour to erect one and dig up the ground for just one show a year. Often it is not even allowed to do so if the field is rented from a sports club, for instance.

But the waterjump is the fence most appreciated by competitors and is of high educational value for horse and rider. Every jumping enclosure should include a waterjump and use it not only in open but also in novice and advanced events. It is absolutely necessary that horses and riders get many chances to familiarise themselves from the early stages on with the waterjump. In the novice events, of course, it should be a small waterjump, with a fence over it to hide the open spread and introduce the water successfully to the novice horses.

This is the only way to take the problem out of jumping water. If this point is neglected the horse will be faced with a standard waterjump for the first time in an open competition. They will be surprised and frustrated. Many will refuse or even be eliminated. When this happens once or twice the problem becomes even greater. The horse will realise the next time he meets a waterjump that he will be the winner when he refuses three times. Then the horse is on the way to becoming a habitual refuser at waterjumps. Therefore we have to find, first of all, a waterjump which is *easy* and *cheap* to erect, so that not only every show but also every rider, when training at home, can afford a waterjump.

#### *The Australian waterjump*

In Australia I saw a waterjump which is easy and cheap to build and therefore the answer to the problem. It is built *on top* of the ground rather than dug into the ground. My experience is that horses jump it not only as well but often better than a permanent one which is built into the ground. Because the water level is above the ground, horses tend to jump it higher, which makes it easier for them to get over the spread of it.

An additional advantage is that the course builder can place this waterjump wherever he wishes and, therefore, it allows him to build most interesting courses.

The frame is made of six pieces of foam plastic.

One can, of course, alter the width of this waterjump easily by using more or less sections of the frame. This is another very important advantage of the Australian waterjump: the sections on the landing side are graded down.

Next, one needs a sheet of *heavy* waterproof material, painted light blue. A piece of 6·5 × 6·5 metres is large enough to cover the whole area of the jump, including the frame. The edges of the sheet are folded around the outside of the frame. To make it look realistic, cover the sidebanks with artificial grass mats.

The ground underneath the waterjump must be covered first with a thick layer of sawdust. This gives support to the plastic sheet and will prevent it being holed in case a horse with studs lands in the water. It also helps to make the surface underneath the sheet level.

On the landing side the sheet and frame under it should be covered with fibre mats, width approximately 0·5 metres. They have to cover the complete width of the waterjump on the landing side. Position half the width of the mats into the water and the other half sloping down to the landing surface.

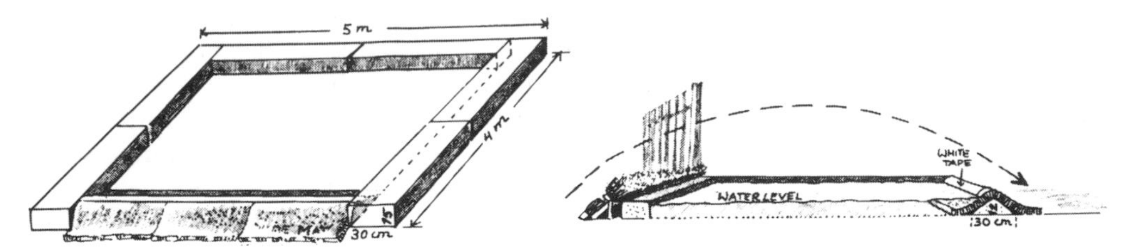


*Fig. 545*
The Australian waterjump, easily erected on top of the ground.

Mark the edge of the water on the landing side with a white tape. It must be one piece and should be positioned on the fibre mats on the edge of the water, not in the water. Secure the tape to the ground at both ends, not in the middle as it is often done. This can be very dangerous to a horse's feet in case he lands on the tape. A piece of a fire hose, painted white, is safe to be used as tape because it is soft and cannot injure a horse. Do not use a timber lath, as it would break too easily and possibly do damage to the horses' legs. The F.E.I. rule to simplify the judging of the waterjump is to have a strip of white rubber-coated plasticine used at all official international shows to mark the landing edge of the water. The coating will show the imprint clearly if a horseshoe has touched the tape.

Mark the two sides of the waterjump with small railings, 0·25 metres high, decorated with flowers or shrubs. Place a flag at each corner of the waterjump, a red flag at each right-hand corner and a white flag at each left-hand corner.

At the take-off side place a brush fence of 0·45 metres height leaning at an angle of 45° towards the water. The total width of the water includes this brush fence.

The capacity of this size waterjump is approximately 700 litres.

On the day of the show keep handy a few drums filled with water for refilling the jump. Two large wings should be placed on the approach side of the waterjump to make the fence more inviting and to prevent horses from running out.

*Novice waterjumps*

At the beginning of each jumping season in novice events I place a small triple bar over the waterjump. When approaching the waterjump the young horse will, at first glance, only notice the take-off brush fence and the triple bar, which should be built of rustic poles. Because it is a very natural looking fence the young horses will approach it without hesitation and without slowing down the pace. Mostly the young horses are already over or on the other side of the fence before they realise that there was water under the triple bar. That is why one should also adopt this method when introducing the waterjump at home in training.

During a lengthy novice competition the triple bar over the waterjump is also time saving, because otherwise many young horses would refuse and need extra time for another approach. Also the triple bar safeguards the waterproof sheet because without the poles over the water many young horses would land in the water on the sheet.

The triple bar also emphasises the effect this waterjump has on teaching the horse to jump *high* over the waterjump.

Gradually, about halfway through the season when the novice horses have gained experience and confidence, I take first one pole and, later, another one away until there is only one pole of the triple bar left over the centre of the total spread of the waterjump. Towards the end of the season I can remove this last pole also, because I can be satisfied that, by then, all novice horses have had a solid schooling and will approach the fence correctly and jump it on the curve of a semi-circle, which is essential when asked later on to clear an open waterjump of 4 to 5 metres spread.

*The indoor waterjump*

It is difficult to have a standard waterjump at an indoor show. Even the Australian waterjump, which could be built on top of the floor cover of the indoor arena, is unsuitable.

Because of the large amount of water which it holds it is stationary and the course builder would have a difficult task to design, in the restricted space of the arena, all his courses around the waterjump, especially if it is a two-day show. Besides, as the competition progresses the water surface gets dusty and is then camouflaged against the surface of the arena. Horses will jump badly or go right through it.

In order to bring more variation to my indoor courses I designed an "artificial" waterjump which is very suitable for indoor shows but is not permitted under F.E.I. rules.

To construct this artificial waterjump, lay down a piece of sandpaper to the same dimensions as those of the required waterjump. Cover the sandpaper with a thick sheet of transparent cellophane which gives a very good impression of clear water, especially under floodlights. Should dust or sand accumulate on the cellophane during the competition it can easily be brushed away. To finish the construction you need a brush fence on the take-off side, a white tape on the landing side, four flags and rustic poles for a triple bar to be built over the waterjump.

It is advisable to build a triple bar over this water in any case, whether it is a novice or open event. Without it there would always be the danger that a horse might land "in the water" onto the cellophane. The horse would realise that it was not jumping water at all and might lose the necessary respect of, and become careless at, a real waterjump.

In any case, no matter if it concerns an "artificial" or a "real" waterjump, as long as there are poles over the water the obstacle is *not* considered to be a waterjump. That means a horse will only be penalised for knocking down a pole but not for touching the tape or the water.

COMBINATIONS

In jumping competitions held under F.E.I. rules the distances in between two elements of a combination jump (whether it is a double, treble or a multiple combination) may be of any length between a minimum of 7 metres to a maximum of 12 metres, except in speed competitions (*parcours de chasse*) where the distance may be less than 7 metres, for example, in an in-and-out jump without a non-jumping stride in between two elements (where indoors it could be 3·5 metres and out of doors 4 metres).

All distances of combination jumps (including six bars) must be measured from the base at the landing side of the first element to the base at the take-off side of the second element, and so on.

Within this limit there are no fixed rules for the distances in combinations. Therefore it is up to the course builder to decide on the distance he will use. His decision will be influenced by various conditions:

(i) the standard of the competition;

(ii) the height, spread and nature of fences;

(iii) the order in which the various elements are placed;

(iv) the speed in which the competition has to be ridden;

(v) the number of non-jumping strides the horse is expected to take in between two elements;

(vi) if the going is deep, good or hard;

(vii) if the surface is level or sloping upwards (downhill gradient would be incorrect);

(viii) if the combination is built towards the

entrance or exit of the jumping enclosure or at a short distance away from it;

(ix) if the combination is built at a related distance preceding a single fence or a waterjump;

(x) the length of the straight approach line to the combination;

(xi) whether the combination is built indoors or out of doors, particularly in connection with novice competitions.

Considering all these different facets, which have a determining influence on the distances in a combination, one will realise why there can be no fixed rules.

Therefore it takes a highly competent course designer to take all these points into account.

To test the horse's abilities and the horsemanship of the rider the course builder may deliberately cause difficulties, without being unfair to the horse, by means of slightly widening or shortening the distances of the combinations. In such a case it is up to the rider to decide how to deal with the problem set when approaching the difficult combination and in order to jump it clear. Depending on whether his horse has a long or a short stride, he will either try to lengthen or shorten the stride accordingly.

To make combination jumps not only more interesting but more educational as well they should have different distances in between the elements. In other words, when there is a double, a treble or a four-element combination jump, they should all vary in the number of "non-jumping" strides. This, of course, applies also to the arrangement of the elements themselves, for example, the first element being a spread, followed up by a straight element or vice versa.

If a single fence precedes a combination on a short related distance, the combination can become as much of a problem as if it was built on a short distance following a turn. In such a case the distances in the combination should be shortened slightly, because the rider will find it very hard indeed to maintain sufficient impulsion.

This is also noticeable when a combination is built so that it must be jumped away from the entrance or exit, because most horses dislike jumping in this direction, hence they shorten their strides and lose impulsion.

In such a case the distances should be slightly shortened because a combination with normal distances would cause trouble.

However, if the combination is placed towards the entrance or exit, and in particular when it is used also in the jump-off against the clock, then the distances can be slightly longer than normal because jumping towards "home" will increase the horse's pace, thus lengthening his stride. Also in the faster speed when trying to "beat the clock" the horse's stride is considerably longer than normal.

In open competitions the course builder can pose fair problems by placing the combination elements in a different order in comparison to the combination in novice competitions. For example, he builds first a treble, and further on the track a double combination jump. To make it even more testing he builds the first element as an oxer parallel and the second element as an upright fence, with only *one* non-jumping stride in between. As the third element of the treble combination he builds again an oxer parallel, allowing now two non-jumping strides. Between the first two elements the horse must not lose any impulsion, otherwise he will not have sufficient speed to cover the following two non-jumping strides and to cope with the third element of the treble, the oxer.

Another good test is to build a multiple combination jump consisting of four elements. For example, make the first element an upright and the second an oxer parallel with two non-jumping strides in between. As the third element build again an oxer parallel with only *one* non-jumping stride between it and the second element. As the fourth element, again an upright, with two non-jumping strides between it and the third element. Another alternative is to build a multiple combination in the following manner. Build the first element as an oxer parallel, the second element as an upright, with only one non-jumping stride between these two elements. The third element is an upright with two non-jumping strides between it and the second element. The fourth element is, again, an oxer parallel after only one non-jumping stride.

A further test is to vary the length of the non-jumping strides between the elements of a combination jump.

*In novice competition* the order of the combinations and its elements should be placed in an easier manner. At the commencement of the jumping season I build first a very inviting "double" combination. Not only the nature of the two elements are simple and easy but also they allow the horse to make two non-jumping strides in between the two elements. These two non-jumping strides make it more convenient for the horse to maintain his impulsion and normal speed.

Halfway through the season, when the horse has gained more experience in jumping a combination, I will then introduce also a simple treble combination jump. Again, in order to make it easier to jump, I give two non-jumping strides in between the first and the second element, and between the second and the third element only one non-jumping stride. When building a treble combination in this order, even novice horses will be able to maintain their impulsion and cope with the one non-jumping stride in the last part of the combination owing to the two non-jumping strides in the first part.

If the rider supports his horse by means of applying strong forward driving leg aids then a treble combination should not pose problems to most novice horses. Quite the opposite will be achieved as it will give the horse courage and confidence for further difficult questions set in the course.

On the other hand, if a treble combination for novice horses was built the other way round (one non-jumping stride in the first part and two in the second part) the young horse would certainly lose impulsion and would have to struggle to regain his normal speed in the two non-jumping strides to reach a correct take-off position to jump the third element of the treble. This would cause the horse to put in an extra short stride just before take-off at the last element. Only the really bold horse will be able to cope with it. A horse with less courage will either refuse, run out or go right through the last element of the treble combination.

*Fig. 546*
An example of a combination designed for a novice competition.

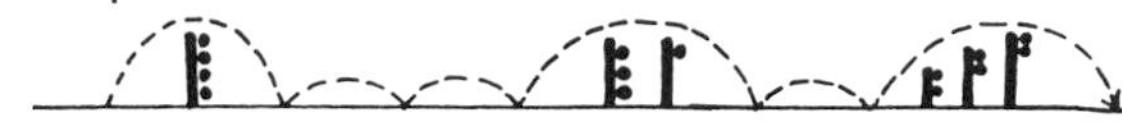

*Fig. 547*
A simple treble combination.

*Fig. 548*
This treble would be unfair for a novice competition. The horse would lose impulsion on account of the first part having only one non-jumping stride.

It is also unfair to the novice horse to build as the first element of a double or of a treble combination an oxer parallel followed by an upright as a second element. When approaching the oxer the horse is forced to increase his speed in order to clear the spread. In the very short distance between the first and the second element he has to collect himself and stand well back to take off and clear the second element, the upright. For novice horses this is too difficult and most unfair and should therefore not be used.

*Distances and relative speeds*

When calculating the distances in between the elements of combinations it is, of course, essential to also take the speed in which the competition has to be ridden into consideration.

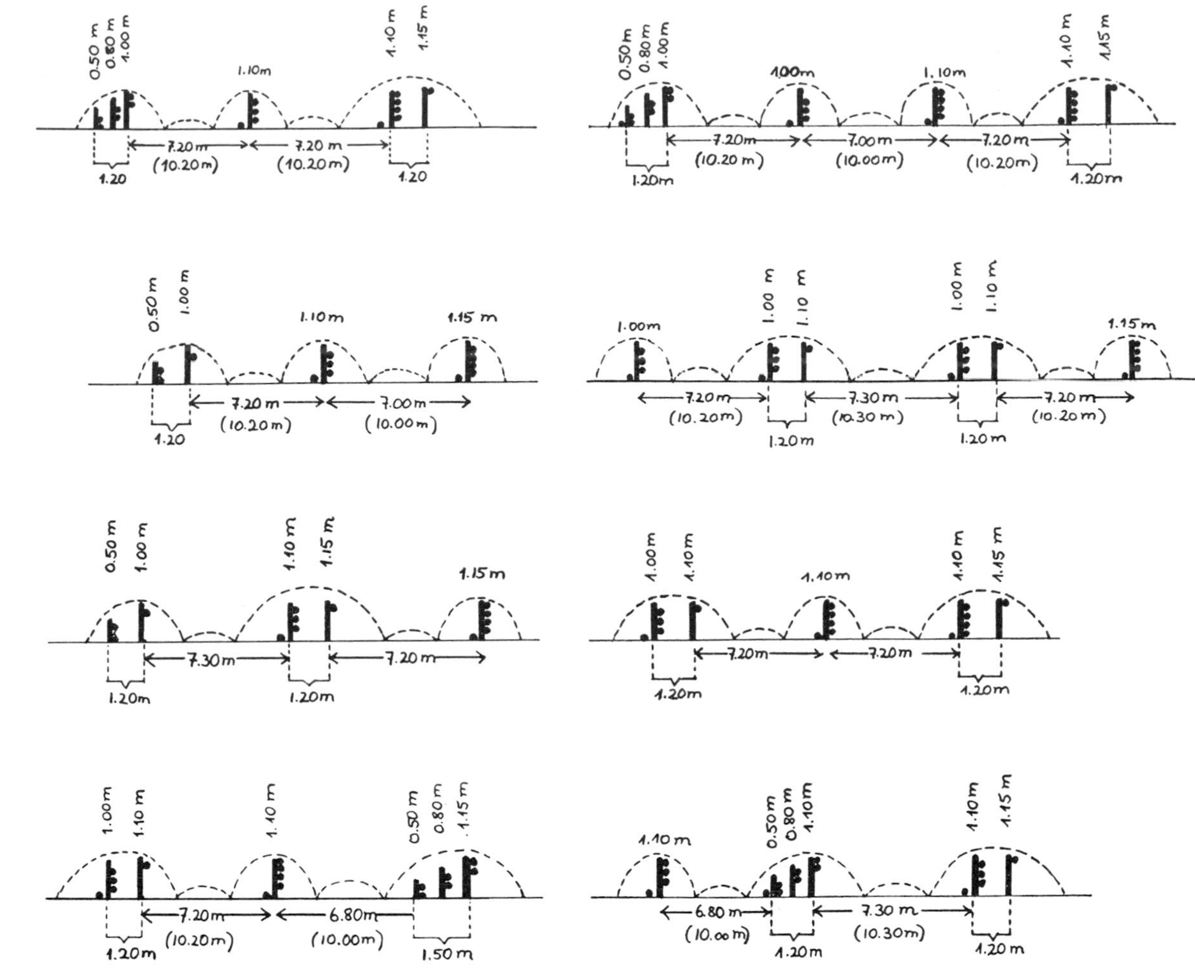

*Fig. 549*
Eight examples of combinations for novice competitions. Speed 300 metres per minute. Maximum height 1·3 metres. Maximum spread 1·35 metres.

This is because the speed at which the horse is cantering on has a determining influence on the length of the canter stride. For example, when cantering at a speed of 300 metres per minute the average stride will be approximately 3 metres. *Under* this speed it may be less.

However, at a speed of 350 metres per minute the stride will be approximately 3·3 metres and at a speed of 400 metres per minute it will be approximately 3·6 metres, or even more, depending on the length of the horse's natural stride and the many other aspects which have a determining influence.

For all these reasons it is logical that the distance in novice combinations (particularly indoors) should be shorter than in open or international competitions, where the required speed is 350 to 400 metres per minute. Therefore it is not only the height and the spread or the nature of the elements and their order which influences the distances in combinations but also in which speed the combinations have to be jumped.

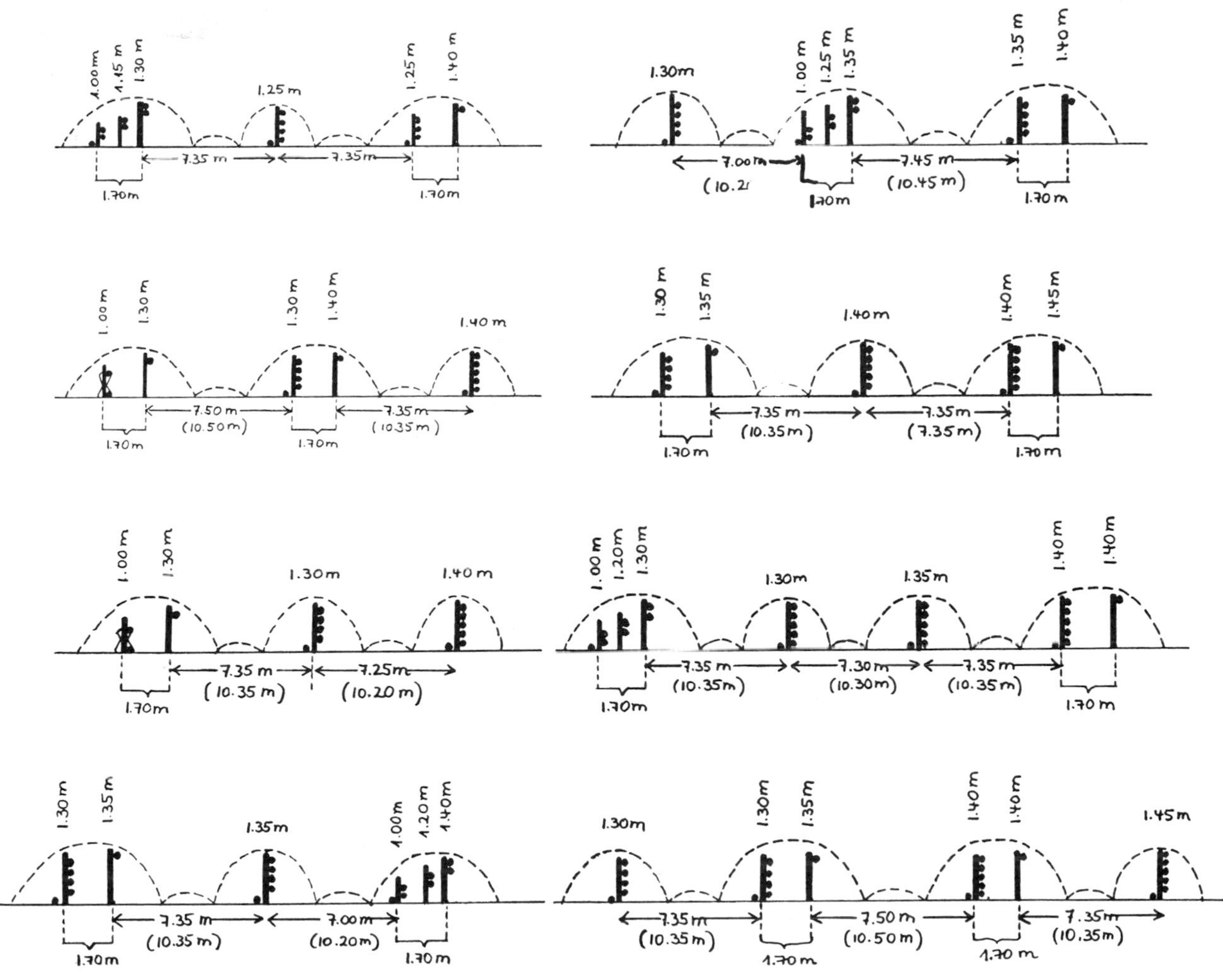


*Fig. 550*
Eight examples of combinations for open competitions. Speed 350 metres per minute. Maximum height 1·5 metres. Maximum spread 2 metres.

As the correct length of the distances is so important it is necessary too that distances in combinations must be measured with a tape.

Having built a combination, stand in front and look at it to ensure that it should in itself be an upwards sloping gradient – the first element the lowest, those following increasing in height.

### INDOOR COURSES

The preparations for designing an indoor course are the same as those for designing one outdoors. Designing and building an indoor course is in fact more difficult. It requires expertise, since every foot within the restricted area is that much more important. In a small arena a badly built course with hairpin turns is a hazard, and to negotiate tightly packed fences may have a destructive effect on a young horse. I dislike speed competitions indoors because it is harmful for the horse's fetlock joints and hocks and abuses the mouth.

The smaller the arena the more difficult it is

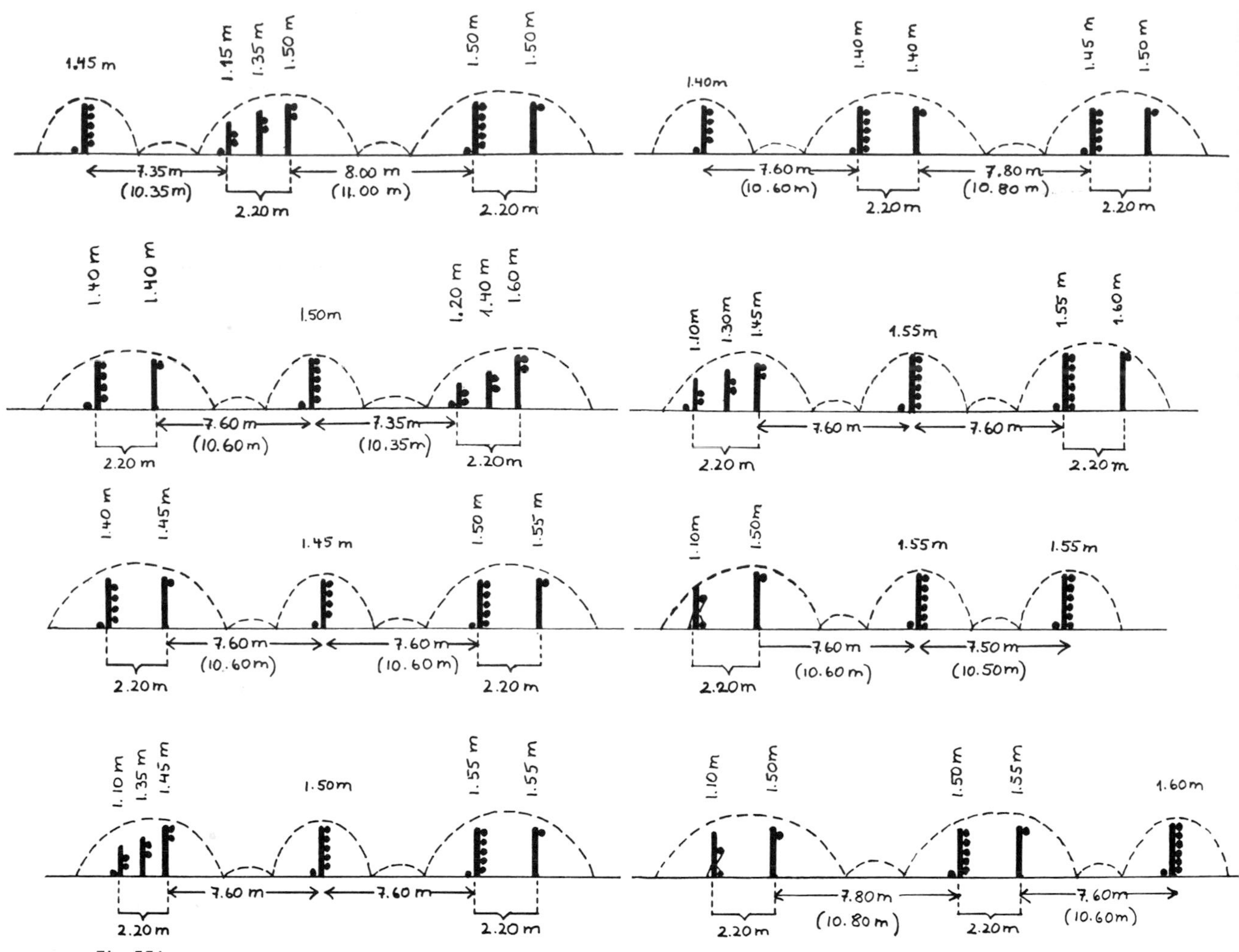

*Fig. 551*
Eight examples of combinations for Nations Cup and Olympic Games competitions. Speed 400 metres per minute. Maximum height 1·6 metres. Maximum spread 2 metres

to build an interesting course which can be ridden smoothly at an even pace. The rider must be able to approach each fence correctly by making the most effective use of the corners and should not have to pull up his horse abruptly. Therefore *never* erect fences on *both* long sides of the track which is so often done at indoor arenas. It will force the rider to apply a series of severe checks and the course will then have to be jumped in separate bits and pieces.

A well planned course will give the rider – even in a small arena – at least three canter strides on a straight line to approach a single fence and at least four canter strides on a straight line to approach a combination. Therefore the combinations should be built through the diagonal *only* or on *one* long side *only*. Once the rider has used the corner in the arena he will then have ample room to approach and jump the combination smoothly.

Regrettably today, even in large international indoor arenas, one can often observe fences

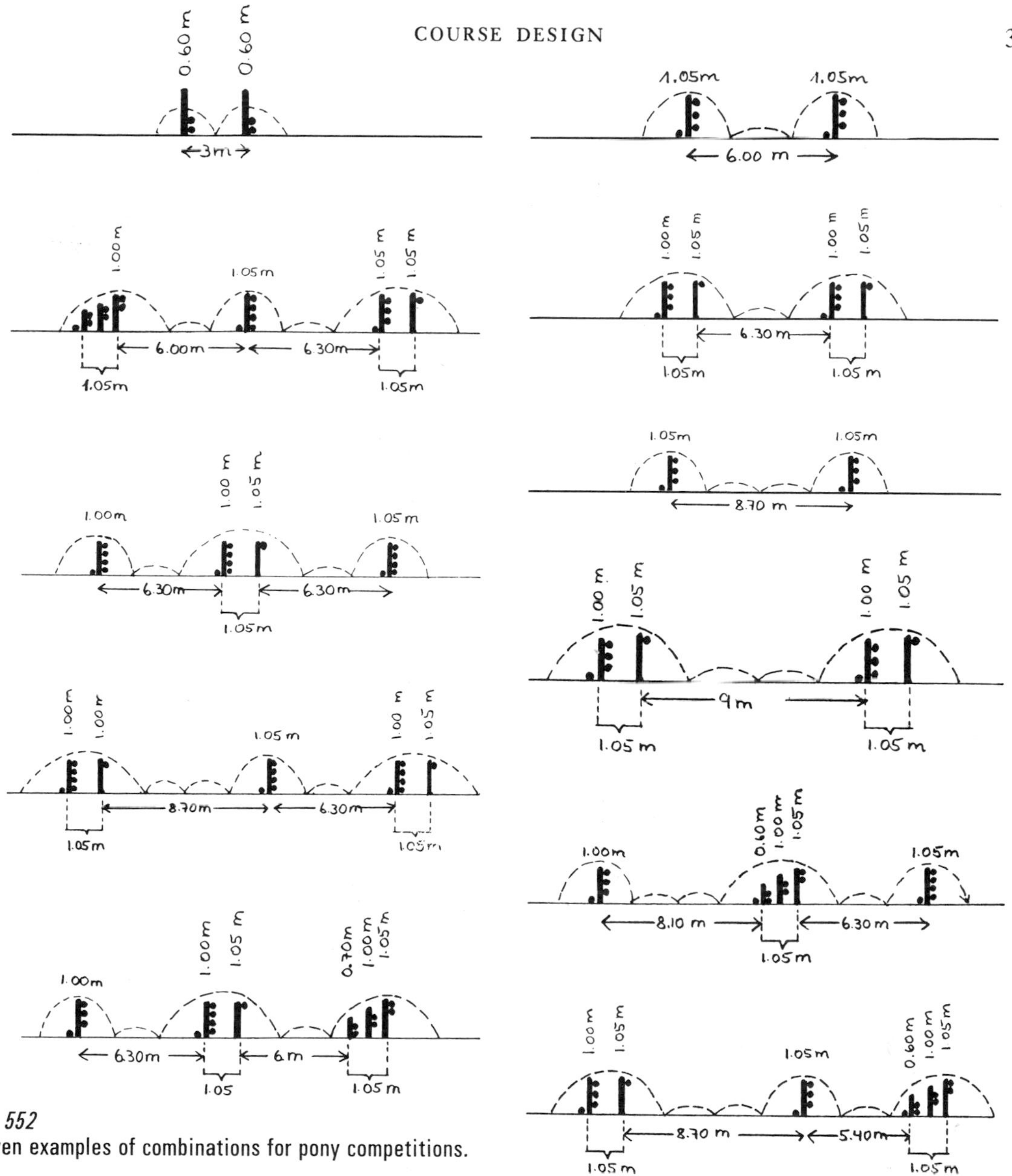


*Fig. 552*
Eleven examples of combinations for pony competitions.

crowded together, for example, where combinations are built on either long side of the arena in conjunction with a single fence placed either in front or behind the combination at a too short related distance.

This method of erecting a sequence of fences on one long side prevents a rider maintaining his horse's impulsion and a rhythmic tempo in pace.

*Distances for indoor combinations*

The size of the indoor arena determines the speed at which the competition can be jumped. In the customary sized indoor school, about 20 × 40 or 20 × 60 metres approximately, the speed should be 300 metres per minute but *never* faster, as it would be impossible to ride a smooth safe course with an even set pace throughout.

In internationally sized arenas, a speed of 350 metres per minute is possible. A speed of 400 metres per minute is most inconvenient for both horse and rider and tends to make the horse rush over the course.

With the above in mind, an outdoor competition, ridden at a speed of 300 metres per minute, enables the horse to lengthen his stride and slightly increase his pace with ease when approaching the fences, especially if the jump is positioned on a straight line.

Owing to the many changes of direction necessary in, and the restricted dimensions of, an indoor arena it is easy for a horse to lose his impulsion. The rider must push more vigorously to compensate for this, particularly so in the approach to fences, to maintain energy and speed. It is certainly necessary when approaching a combination jump out of a turn, which is in marked comparison to jumping out of doors. It is an essential point for the course builder to consider when assessing the distances in between the elements of the combination jump indoors.

Should the course plan state a required speed of 300 metres per minute it will be impossible for the rider to ride well into the corners of the arena and still maintain this speed. He will not manage anything faster than 250 metres per minute. This means that when approaching a combination jump after a turn in the corner of the arena the rider has to regain the competition's speed of 300 metres per minute in the four strides of the approach line to the first element. This can only be achieved by applying very strong leg aids, which should be continued throughout the entire combination, to maintain the speed.

Without the necessary speed of 300 metres per minute the horse will not be in a position to cope with the distances in between the elements. Even in international indoor competitions the combinations are always a very severe test.

It is most interesting to watch horses and riders of international standard tackle the problem of distances in combinations and related speeds. These riders are used to tight time-allowed competition and their experience gives them the necessary expertise in how and when to regain speed. This ability is particularly useful in the indoor arena, saving them incurring time penalties and enabling them to cope with both spread oxers and enormous combinations in the correct speed. Such ability cannot be expected in the young horse and rider. So when building a combination for novice horses indoors the course builder should shorten the distance in between the elements by 0·3 metres. I deplore the method of some builders who, for novice horses, use exactly the same distances for indoor and outdoor competitions. They claim, incorrectly, that a horse with a long stride will cope with an outdoor distance equally well indoors and that a horse with a short stride will manage by putting in an extra short stride.

This is a ludicrous theory and in practise is a sure way of ruining many a young horse. The prerogative of schooling showjumping horses is that the horses be taught to lengthen their stride whenever it is necessary in their efforts to jump freely and fluently. It is equally important that they are taught never to insert an extra short stride in between the elements prior to take-off of a combination.

To insert this short stride is definitely wrong. It can cause disastrous results when the second or third element of a combination consists of an oxer parallel. With that extra short stride the horse will come too close to the oxer, unable to find his correct take-off position. He refuses or knocks the front top pole of the fence with his forelegs. Therefore the distance in combinations indoors in novice competitions is approximately 0·3 metres shorter than that out of doors. This factor should be taken into all assessments made by the course builder.

When smaller indoor shows are held at night time there may sometimes be difficulties in providing the competitors with sufficient opportunity to warm-up their horses. The warming-up ring may be ill-lit or soaking wet, the practise fence inadequate and the risk for both horse and rider of catching colds be high.

The best thing to do in such a case is to let the competitors warm-up their horses in the indoor jumping arena prior to each competition. If there are fences set on one long side of the track then the poles should be taken out for the time being so that the riders have the use of the complete track. Meanwhile, while the riders are exercising their horses, the course builder can go ahead and change the course as planned for the next competition.

Just before the competitors leave the arena a practise fence should be built on the track. (This fence may *not* be included in the competition later on.) All riders should be allowed to jump first an upright fence, which is later on altered into an oxer. Each competitor may jump the oxer once, after which they should leave the arena, except the first competitor to jump.

I am fully aware that this method is not ideal. However, in certain circumstances, it is better and safer than jumping out of doors, in darkness or in mud. To do so could easily lead to the confusion and frightening of the horse which, in turn, could be the cause of refusals or of accidents.

### HORS-CONCOURS

In some countries the splendid opportunity to compete *hors-concours* – "participation without competing" – is, regrettably, unknown not only to competitors but even to some show organisers.

*Hors-concours* has many advantages because it is meant as a schooling exercise, either for the horse or for the rider. At the beginning of a new jumping season it allows a competitor to enter a horse in a lower grade competition than the horse is allowed to compete in. This, of course, is an excellent opportunity to start off the new jumping season and to get the young horse going again. It also gives the trainer the opportunity, at any time during the jumping season, of entering a Grade A horse in a lower grade of competition. For example, where a horse has lost his confidence over big fences, or where he has had to start all over again after being laid off.

On the other hand, however, a horse is *never* allowed to compete *hors-concours* in a competition *above* his own grade, as this would lead to overfacing the horse.

*Hors-concours* also allows the rider to participate with an experienced Grade A horse in a lower grade competition where, under normal circumstances, the horse is not eligible to jump. This opportunity enables the young rider to gain competition experience, because in such a case he will be learning from the horse who is now the rider's teacher.

#### *Rules and conditions*

As a rule, on the continent a rider who competes *hors-concours* usually enters the horse on the entry form and pays the normal entry fee, although there will be no prize rewards for him. Riders are only allowed to start with that particular horse at the end of every round, including the jump-off, in order to prevent causing confusion to the judges and spectators. As these riders do not compete for prizes their jumping faults are not important, except if those faults include three refusals, when they are eliminated as usual.

If a competitor has permission from the show committee to compete *hors-concours* with a horse in one particular competition he is not eligible to compete with the same horse on the same day in another competition for prize awards. Neither can the *same* horse be ridden by another rider for normal prize awards in any competition during the *same* day. A course builder is not allowed to compete on the continent in a normal prize awarding competition over courses which he himself has designed or built. In such a case (should he wish to do so) permission may be granted by the show committee for the course builder to compete *hors-concours*.

The number of entries accepted for *hors-concours* is up to the show committee, though usually there are not too many applicants. It is completely different, however, if the acceptance of entries involves a special training plan, for example, for a European junior championship. I emphasise how important it is that junior riders should be given all possible support in their equestrian education. Training for an important event should include competing *hors-concours* only at the *end* of the shows, for the simple reason that then there is no hurry. If the judges and other show officials, after a long and tiring day, want to leave the showground they can do so, because this training jumping does not have to be judged for jumping faults. However, the style and jumping technique of the riders competing should be judged by other young riders.

I use the following method. When one of the young riders is jumping his course the other riders stand close to me in the centre of the jumping enclosure. There I am in a position to explain to them the technical mistakes made by the rider who is completing his round. The young riders will learn to be observant and judge the mistakes of their fellow riders and will try to do better.

### SIX BARS

It is regrettable that the spectacular six bar competition has in recent years lost its popularity, since it is not only a searching test of ability for both horse and rider but a thrilling and exciting sight and entertainment for spectators.

In Europe the six bar competition consists of six upright elements placed in a straight line.

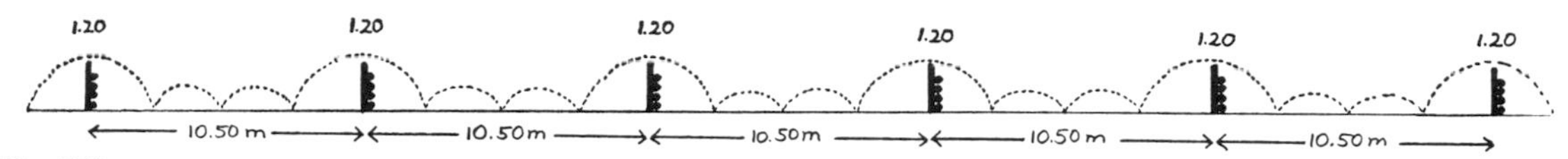


*Fig. 553*
Six bars competition. All six fences are at the same height.

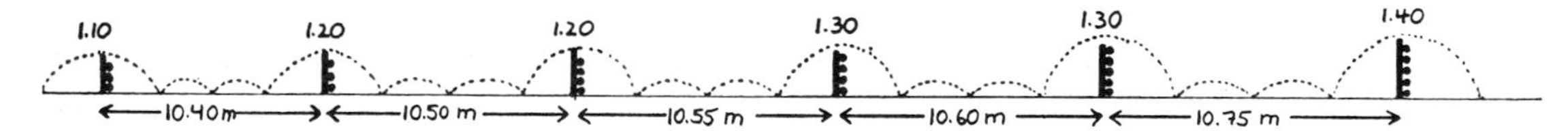


*Fig. 554*
Six bars competition. Fences increasing in height, distances increasing accordingly.

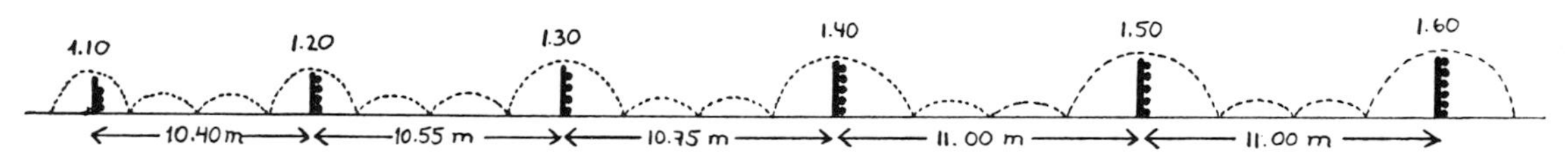


*Fig. 555*
Six bars competition. Fences increasing in height more rapidly, distances accordingly.

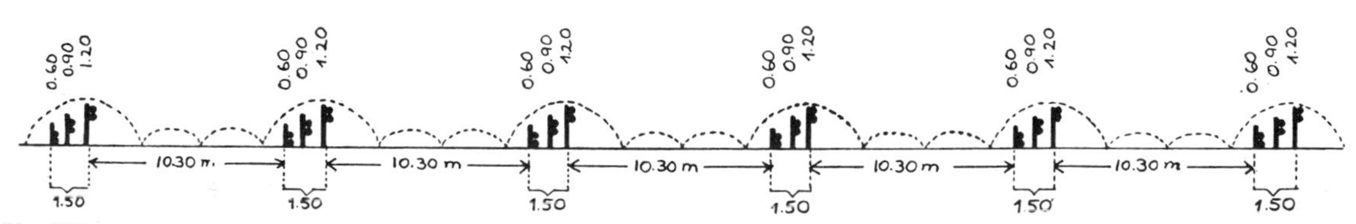


*Fig. 556*
American six bars competition. Six treble bars, all at the same height.

In fact it is a multiple combination jump of six fences, all similar, and constructed of poles. The distance in between the six elements must be – in accordance with the rules of the F.E.I. – approximately 11 metres.

The distances in between the elements of the six bars depends largely on the fact whether the elements are placed all at the same height or at progressive heights. If they are all equally high then, accordingly, the distances in between the elements must be of exactly the same length. However, if the fences are built at progressive heights, similarly the distances between the elements must be progressively lengthened according to the increasing height of the elements.

The course builder knows the standard of the horses competing, therefore he has a fair idea of at what heights the competition will be decided. He will, therefore, put the elements at distances which will be suitable to that expected finishing round. This means that in the first rounds the distances will be too long for the fairly low fences. The riders can make good this by riding energetically forward to prevent the horse from reaching for an element and putting in an extra short stride. In turn they will have the privilege of jumping later on the difficult high fences at correct distances.

If a horse refuses or runs out, or if the rider and/or the horse falls, for instance at the second last element, the rider does not have to re-start at the beginning of the row but can continue at the same element where the fault occurred. In every round the height of the elements should be increased. In connection with the standard of the horse competing the judge can end the competition after a few rounds in order not to overface the horses. If the competition is stopped the riders who were eligible to jump again are placed equal first.

In America the six bars elements consists of triple bars, all of equal height. An "American" triple bar consists of five poles, two in front, two in the centre and, for safety reasons, only one pole at the far end. This gives the triple bar a "full" appearance. After each round all triple bars are raised equally. The distances are all equally long and calculated beforehand to suit the height of the fences of the excepted last round.

### PRIZE MONEY

The secret of the success of top showjumping riders in the world is that they safeguard their horses, whenever it is possible, from unnecessary jumping, particularly in between competitions. It may sound simple but it is, in fact, a long way from it.

The prestige and the value of big prize money has its greatest attraction at the international shows. A prelude to these events is the work and time of seasons on the road, travelling a country up and down from show to show and from prize event to still more attractive prize event. The temptation is clearly there and even top international riders will succumb to the risk of overjumping their horses and will take chances which spell victory if they come off and trouble if they do not.

I believe that the F.E.I. ruling on prize money in jumping competitions is indeed a help to the rider. It has cut down the great gap between the first prize and the lower awards. It will give the rider the opportunity to win a lower prize and still receive a substantial amount of money without being forced to rush his horse to win first prize.

### SHOW PROBLEMS

For one reason or another many shows, and in particular the small shows, frequently run behind schedule. Disgruntled spectators leave the showground often before the main event has started, which is poor encouragement for the sponsors of these events.

At such small shows the judges usually have several jumping competitions to judge, which is both an exacting and painstaking job, voluntarily accepted to support the show and the sport. Show officials, if fatigued following a long and tiring day, are often anxious to leave a show which is already running a couple of hours late.

Fence Material required for: Rathfarnham Castle Show

Date : 27. 7. 1977

| Fence Nr. | Type of Fence | Wings | Poles | Gates | Walls | Planks | Barrells | Brush-fences | Tripple Bars | Cups normal | Cups flat | Pillars | Elephant Poles | Boundary Flags | Feet |
|---|---|---|---|---|---|---|---|---|---|---|---|---|---|---|---|
| 1 | Staircase Fence | 4 | 3 | 1 | | | 4 | 1 | | 4 | 2 | | | 4 | 8 |
| 2 | Planks | | | | | 4 | | | | | 8 | 2 | | 2 | |
| 3 | ROM Oxer | 4 | 4 | | | | | | | 8 | | | | 4 | 8 |
| 4A | Oxer | 4 | 5 | | | | 4 | 1 | | 10 | | | | 4 | 8 |
| 4B | Tripple Bar | 6 | 5 | | | | | | | 10 | | | | 4 | 12 |
| 5 | Scissors | 4 | 5 | | | | | | | 10 | | | | 4 | 8 |
| 6 (15) | Hogs Back | 6 | 8 | | | | | | | 16 | | | | 4 | 12 |
| 7 | Fan Fence | 5 | 5 | | | | | | | 10 | | | | 3 | 10 |
| 8 | Wall | | | | 1 | | | | | | | 2 | | 2 | |
| 9 | Oxer | 4 | 1 | | | 4 | | | | 2 | 8 | | | 4 | 8 |
| 10 | Gate | 2 | | 1 | | | | | | | 2 | | | 2 | 4 |
| 11 A | Oxer | 4 | 5 | | | | | 1 | | 10 | | | | 4 | 8 |
| 11 B | Upright | 2 | 4 | | | | | | | 8 | | | | 2 | 4 |
| 11 C | Oxer | 4 | 5 | | | | | 1 | | 10 | | | | 4 | 8 |
| 12 | Tripple Bar | 2 | | | | | | | 1 | | 6 | | 3 | 4 | 4 |
| 13 | Water Jump | 2 | | | | | | 1 | | | | | | 4 | 4 |
| 14 | Oxer | 4 | 5 | | | | | 1 | | 10 | | | | 4 | 8 |
| 16 | Stockholm Gate | | | 1 | | | | | | | 2 | 2 | | 2 | |
| | | 57 | 55 | 3 | 1 | 8 | 8 | 6 | 1 | 108 | 28 | 6 | 3 | 61 | 114 |

Also required: Material for Practice Fence 6 Wings
12 Feet
8 Poles
16 Cups

Start 2, Finish 2, Fence Numbers 1–16, 2×A, 2×B, 1×C, Sets 1.

*Fig. 557*
The course builder sends this pre-printed form to show organisers before the course is designed, asking by use of this form for availability of fence material. After receiving this information the course builder then designs his courses and uses the same form to mark down what material he will use and at which fences. This makes the building of the courses much easier.

Course Plan for: Rathfarnham Castle Show, Date: 27.7.1977

Competition Nr.: 5 ( Open Jumping Competition
Fences Nr. 1-10 (lowered) used as Novice Competition

1. Round: Table A, Rule 238 — Course Length: 764 m — Speed: 350 m/min.
Time Allowed: 131 sec. — Time Limit: 262 sec. — Time Penalties: 1/4 pt. /sec.
Obstacles: 16 — Jumps: 19 — Compulsory Courseline from Fence Nr.: 9 to Finish

2. or Subsequent Rounds: Fences Nr. 6, 7, 8, 9, 4A - 4B, 5

Table A, Rule 238 — Course Length: 338 m — Speed: 350 m /min.
Time Allowed: 58 sec. — Time Limit: 116 sec. — Time Penalties: 1/4 pt./ sec.
Obstacles: 6 — Jumps: 7

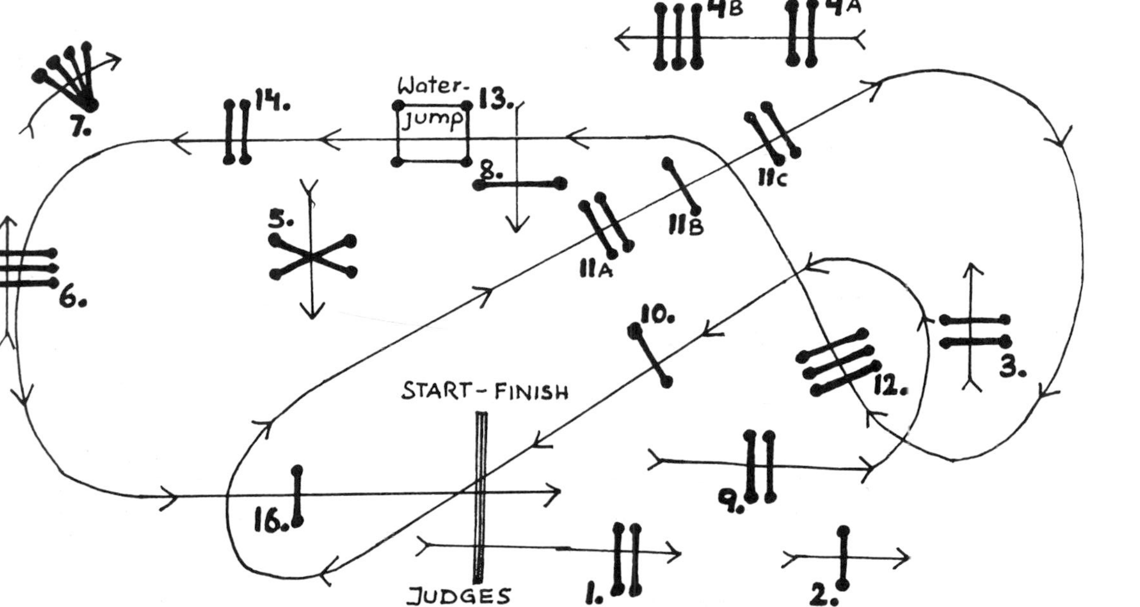


| 1. Round | | |
|---|---|---|
| Fence | Max.Height | Max.Spread |
| 1 | 1.20 m | 1.35 m |
| 2 | 1.20 m | |
| 3 | 1.30 m | 1.60 m |
| 4A | 1.30 m | 1.40 m |
| 4B | 1.30 m | 1.90 m |
| 5 | 1.30 m | 2.00 m |
| 6, 15 | 1.30 m | 1.80 m |
| 7 | 1.20 m | 2.00 m |
| 8 | 1.35 m | 0.75 m |
| 9 | 1.35 m | 1.75 m |
| 10 | 1.35 m | |
| 11 A | 1.30 m | 1.70 m |
| 11 B | 1.35 m | |
| 11 C | 1.35 m | 1.80 m |
| 12 | 1.35 m | 2.00 m |
| 13 | 0.60 m | 5.00 m |
| 14 | 1.35 m | 1.50 m |
| 16 | 1.35 m | |

| Subsequent Rounds | Raised | | Widened | |
|---|---|---|---|---|
| Fence | 2. Round | 3. Round | 2. Round | 3. Round |
| 6 | 0.05 m | 0.05 m | 0.10 m | 0.05 m |
| 7 | 0.10 m | 0.05 m | 0.10 m | |
| 8 | 0.10 m | 0.05 m | 0.05 m | 0.05 m |
| 9 | 0.10 m | 0.05 m | 0.05 m | 0.05 m |
| 4A | 0.05 m | 0.05 m | 0.10 m | 0.05 m |
| 4B | 0.10 m | 0.05 m | 0.05 m | 0.05 m |
| 5 | 0.10 m | 0.05 m | 0.10 m | |

*Fig. 558*
Example of a correct course plan. The organisation and running of a small show is greatly improved by use of pre-printed forms which can generally be obtained from relevant showjumping associations. This form is used by the course builder to show the course plan and all the necessary information appertaining to it. Copies are distributed to the judges, television commentators and so on.

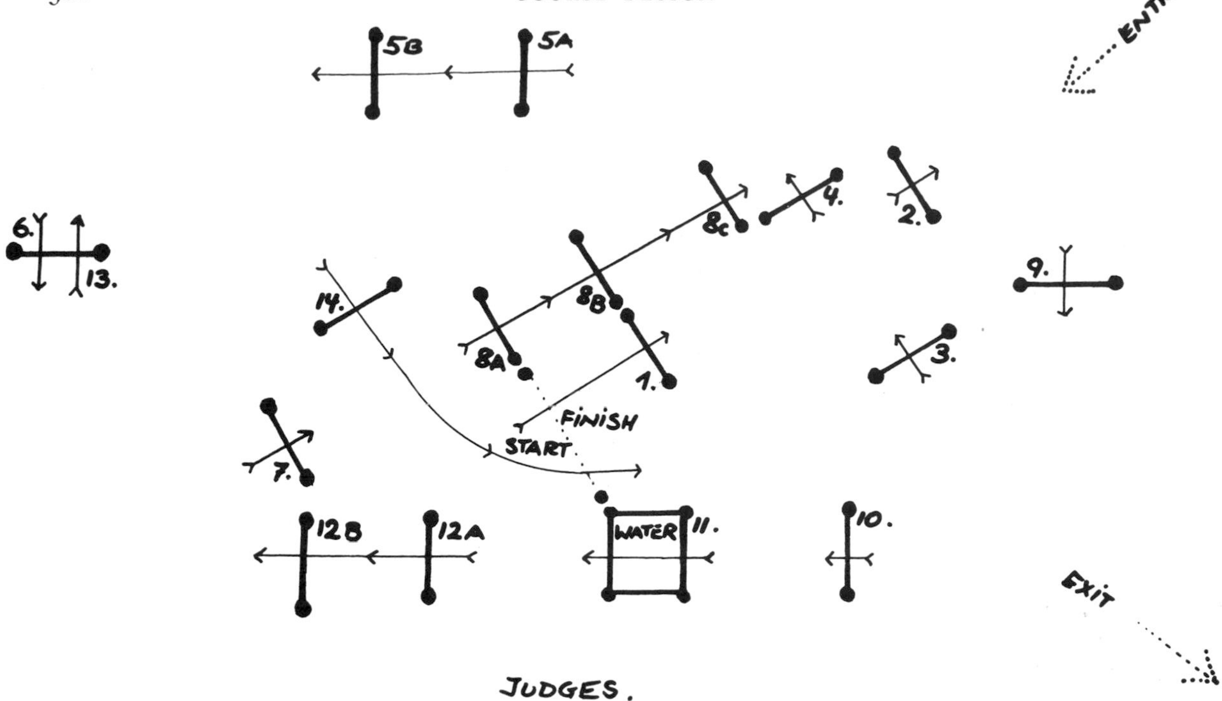


*Fig. 559*
Outdoor course for Novice and Open competitions.
Novice competition: 7 obstacles, 8 jumps.
Open competition: 14 obstacles, 18 jumps.
Novice jump-off: Same course.
Open jump-off: 1, 5A-B, 8A-B-C, 9, 10, 11, 12A-B, 14.

*Fig. 560*
Outdoor course for Novice and Open competitions.
Novice competition: 9 obstacles, 12 jumps.
Open competition: 13 obstacles, 16 jumps.
Novice jump-off: Same course.
Open jump-off: 5, 6, 7A-B-C, 8, 9, 10, 11, 12, 13. (9 obstacles, 11 jumps).

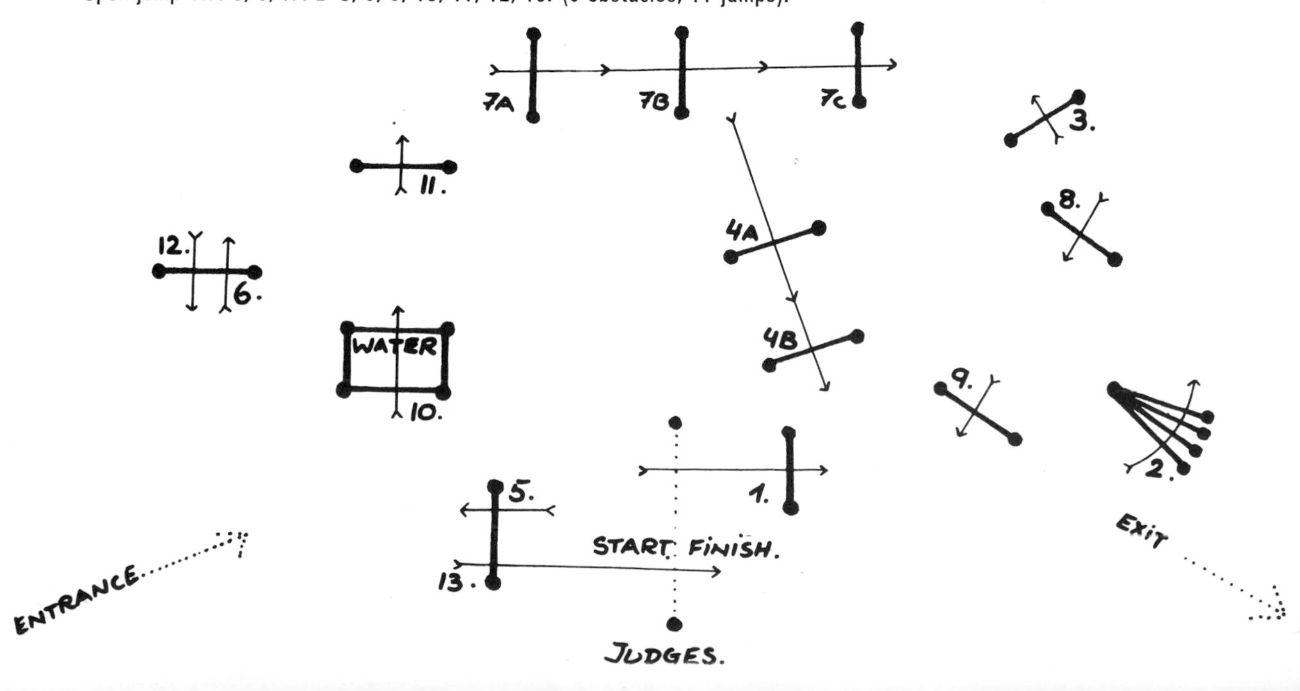

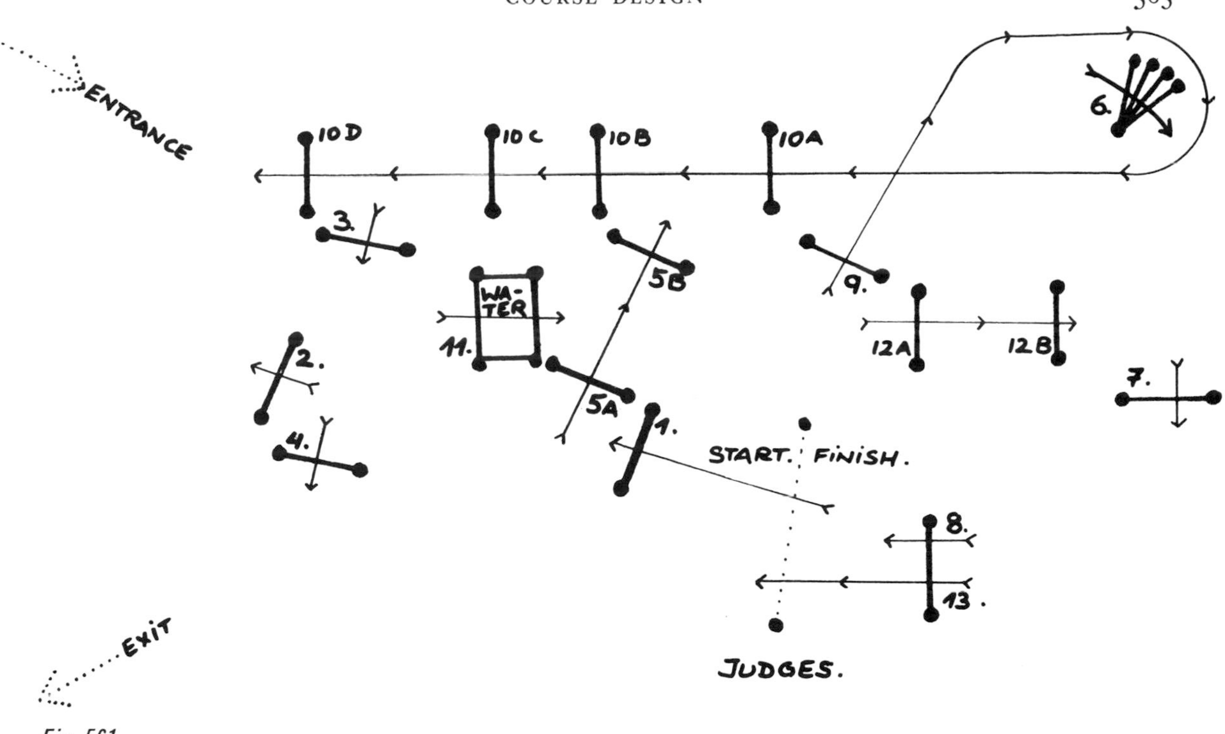


*Fig. 561*
Outdoor course for Novice and Open competitions.
Novice competition: 8 obstacles, 9 jumps.
Open competition: 13 obstacles, 18 jumps.
Novice jump-off: Same course.
Open jump-off: 1, 2, 3, 4, 5A-B, 10A-B-C-D, 11, 12A-B, 13. (9 obstacles, 14 jumps).

*Fig. 562*
Outdoor course for Novice and Open competitions.
Novice competition: 9 obstacles, 10 jumps.
Open competition: 14 obstacles, 18 jumps.
Novice jump-off: Same course.
Open jump-off: 1, 2, 3, 4, 12A-B-C, 13, 14. (7 obstacles, 9 jumps).

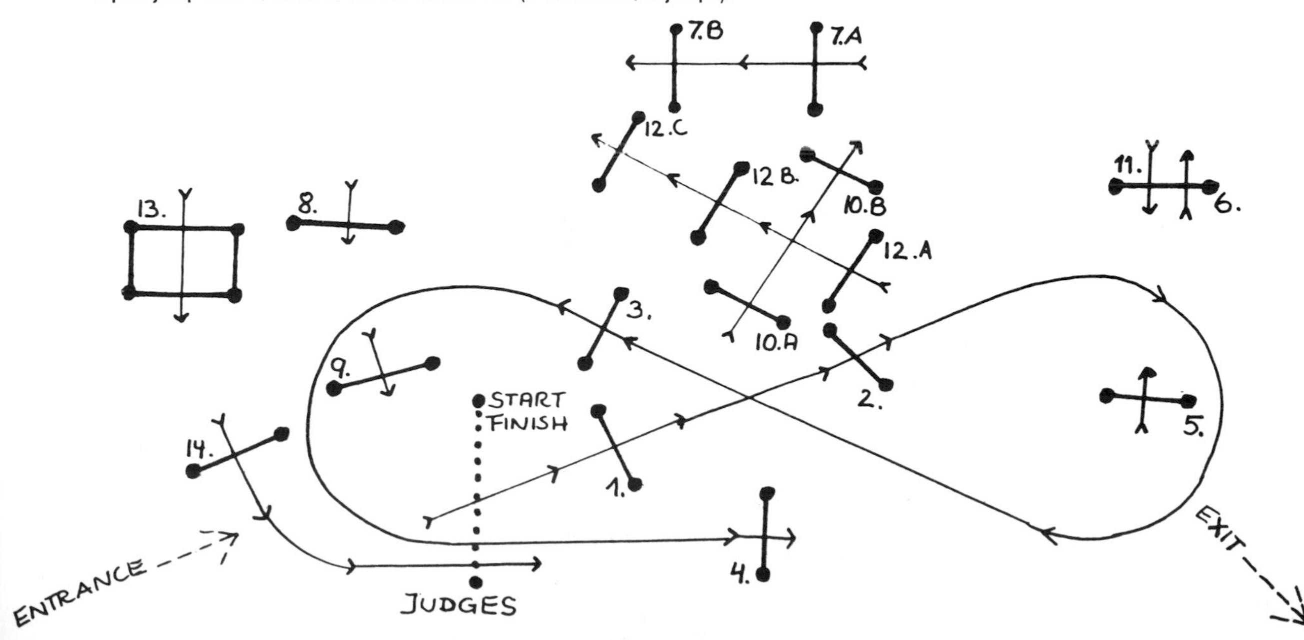

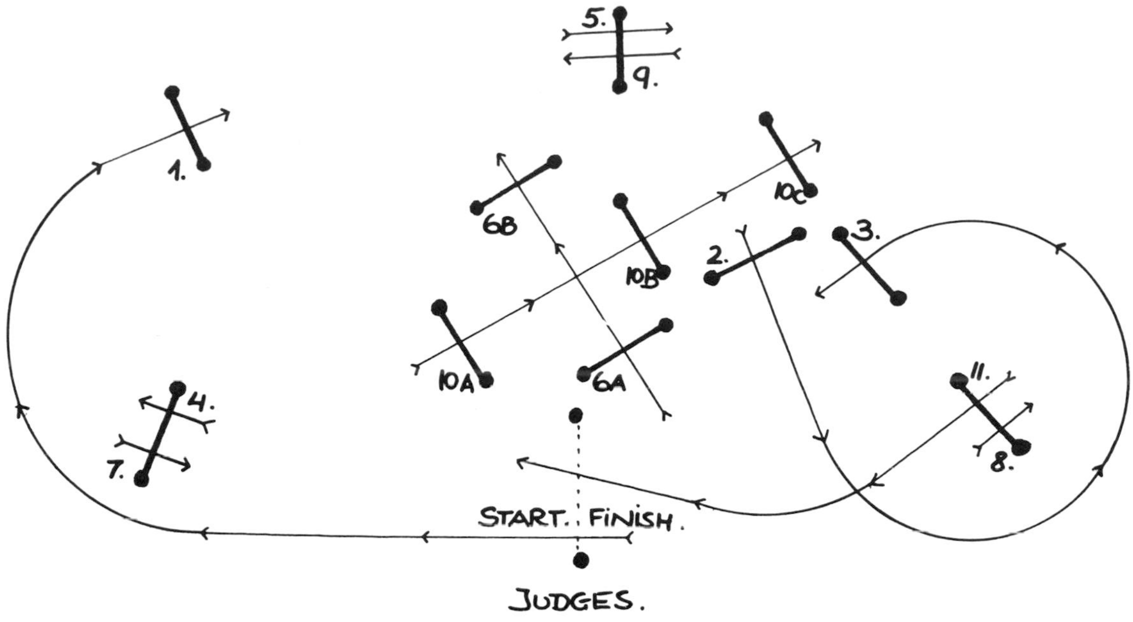


*Fig. 563*
Indoor (20 x 60 metres) course for Novice and Open competitions.
Novice competition: 7 obstacles, 8 jumps.
Open competition: 11 obstacles, 14 jumps.
Novice jump-off: Same course.
Open jump-off: 3, 4, 5, 6A-B, 10A-B-C, 11. (6 obstacles, 9 jumps).

*Fig. 564*
Indoor (20 x 60 metres) course for *Puissance* competitions. (Using remains of course in *Fig. 563*).
*Puissance* competition: 6 obstacles, 6 jumps.
Jump-off: (Fence 3 optional) 4, 5, 6.
Third (or subsequent) round: 5, 6.

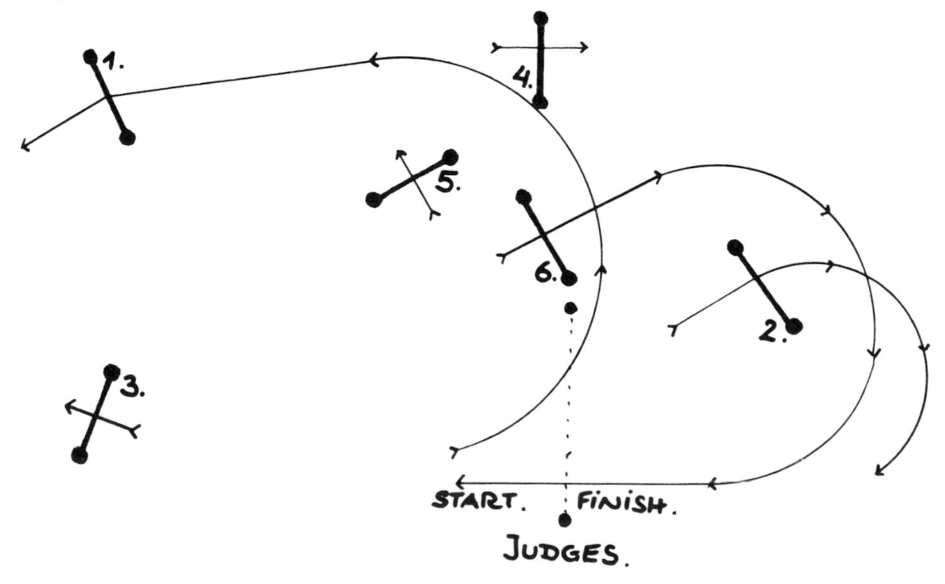

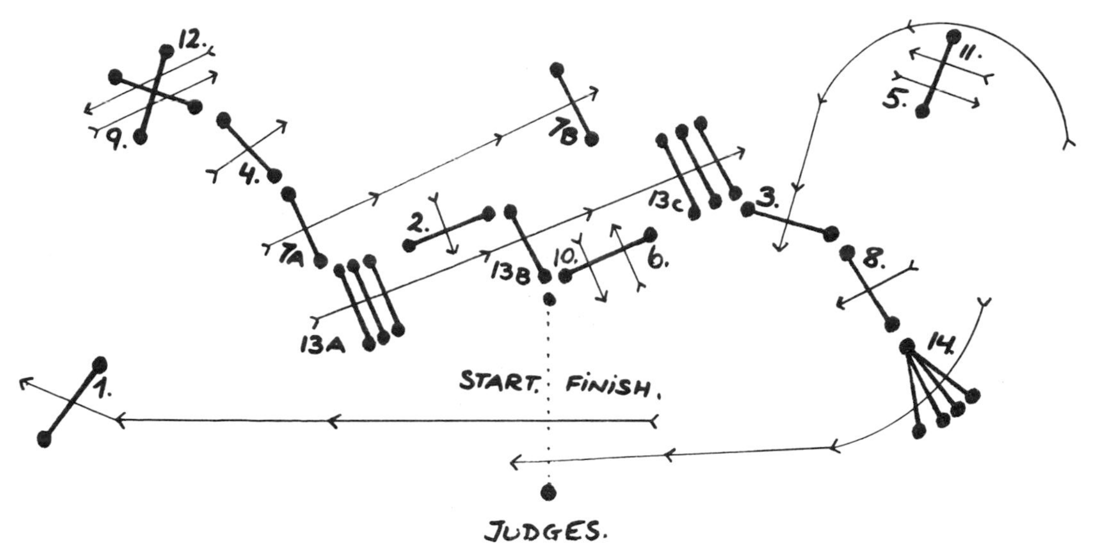


*Fig. 565*
Indoor (20 x 60 metres) course for Novice and Open competitions.
Novice competition: 8 obstacles, 9 jumps.
Open competition: 14 obstacles, 17 jumps.
Novice jump-off: Same course.
Open jump-off: 1, 10, 11, 12, 13A-B-C, 14. (6 obstacles, 8 jumps).

*Fig. 566*
Indoor (20 x 60 metres) course for Novice and Open competitions.
Novice competition: 7 obstacles, 8 jumps.
Open competition: 12 obstacles, 15 jumps.
Novice jump-off: Same course.
Open jump-off: 8, 9, 10A-B-C, 11, 3, 4, 6A-B, 7. (8 obstacles, 11 jumps).

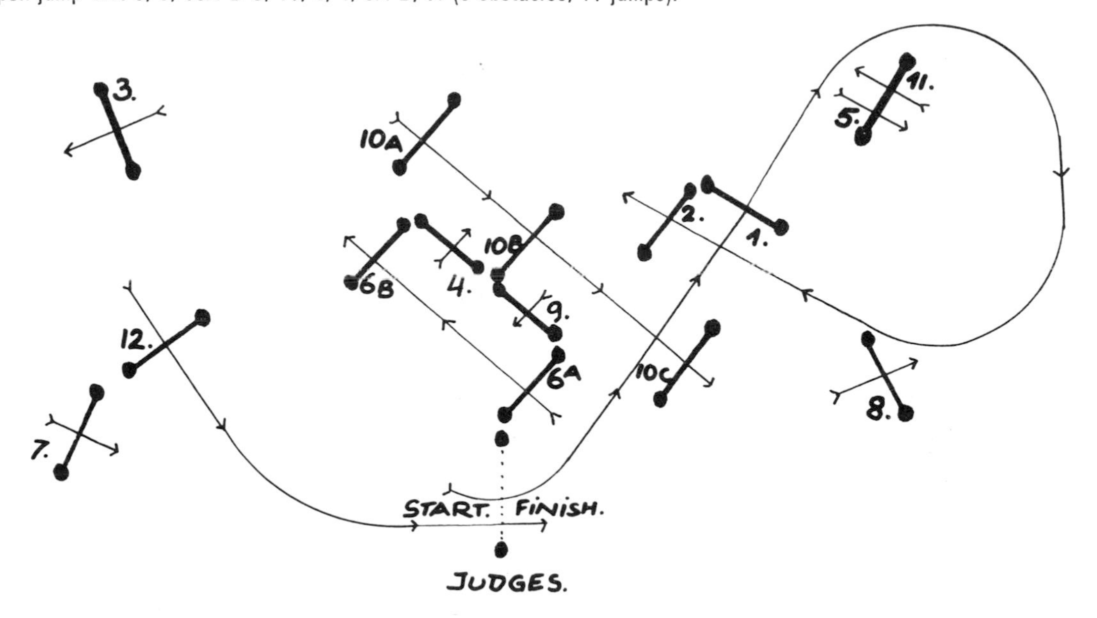

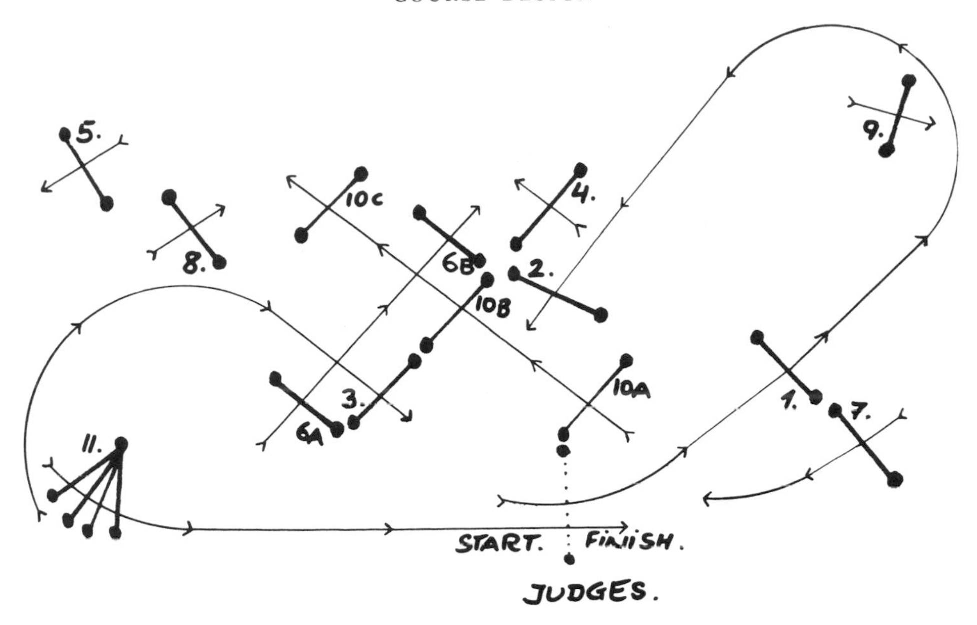


*Fig. 567*
Indoor (20 x 60 metres) course for Novice and Open competitions.
Novice competition: 7 obstacles, 8 jumps.
Open competition: 11 obstacles, 14 jumps.
Novice jump-off: Same course.
Open jump-off: 4, 5, 6A-B, 9, 10A-B-C, 11. (6 obstacles, 9 jumps).

*Fig. 568*
Indoor (20 x 60 metres) course for Novice and Open competitions.
Novice competition: 7 obstacles, 8 jumps.
Open competition: 11 obstacles, 14 jumps.
Novice jump-off: Same course.
Open jump-off: 3, 4A-B, 5, 9, 10A-B-C, 11. (6 obstacles, 9 jumps).

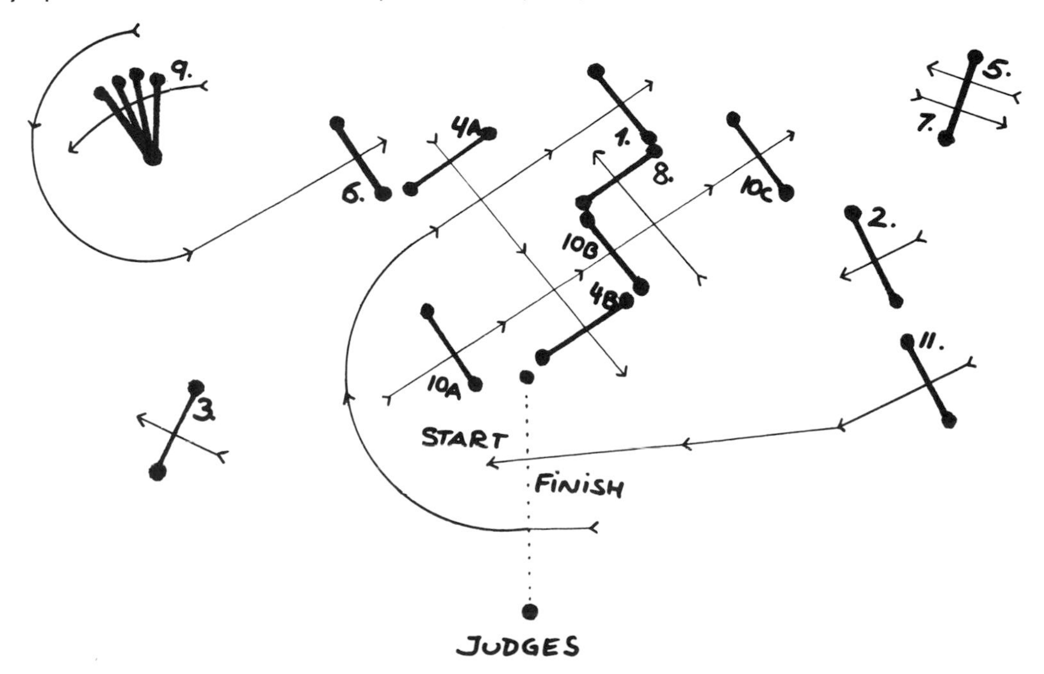

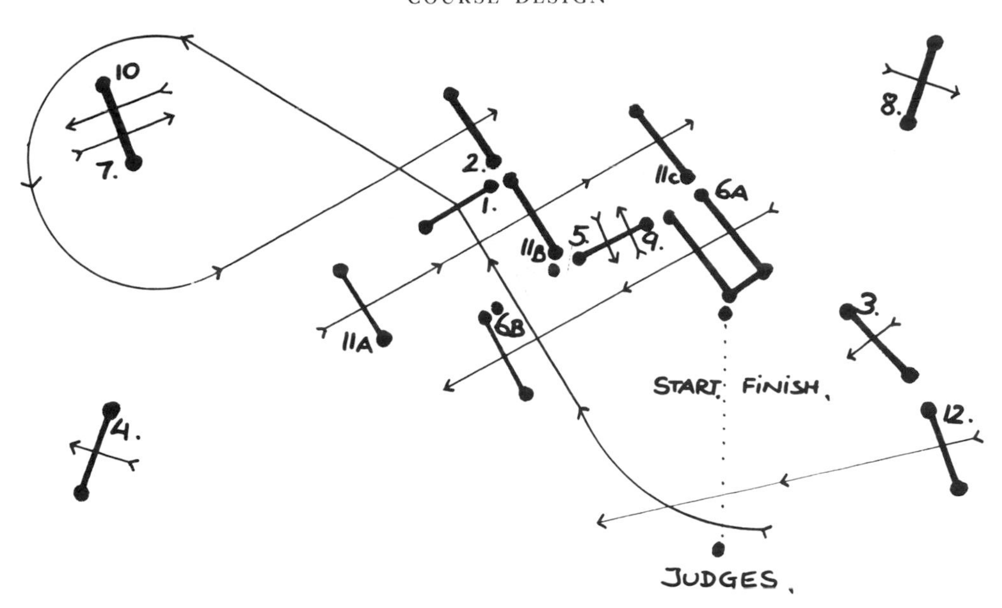


*Fig. 569*
Indoor (20 x 60 metres) course for Novice and Open competitions.
Novice competition: 8 obstacles, 9 jumps.
Open competition: 12 obstacles, 15 jumps.
Novice jump-off: 3, 4, 5, 6A-B, 7, 8. (6 obstacles, 7 jumps).
Open jump-off: 4, 5, 6A-B, 7, 8, 9, 11A-B-C, 12. (8 obstacles, 11 jumps).

*Fig. 570*
Indoor (20 x 60 metres) course for Speed competitions. (Using remains of course in *Fig. 569*).
Speed competition: 9 obstacles, 11 jumps.

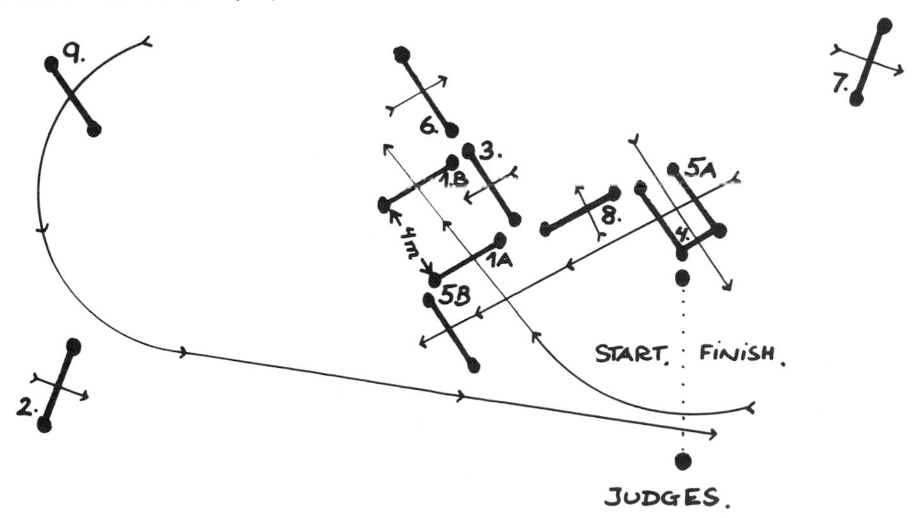

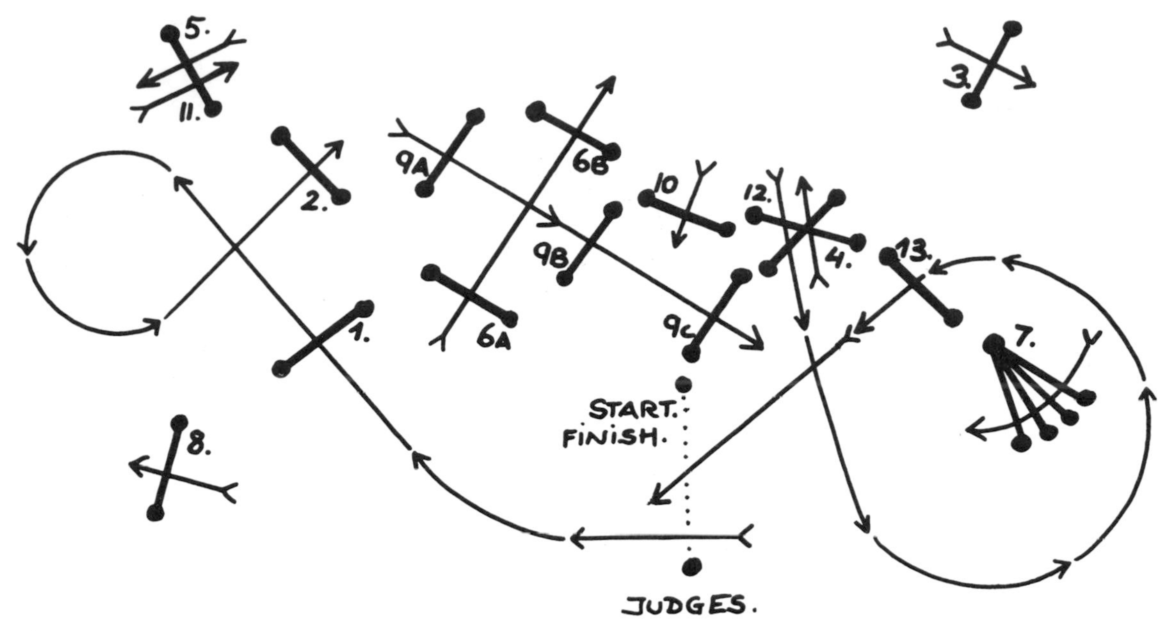


*Fig. 571*
Indoor (20 x 60 metres) course for Novice and Open competitions.
Novice competition: 7 obstacles, 8 jumps.
Open competition: 13 obstacles, 16 jumps.
Novice jump-off: 2, 3, 4, 5, 6A-B, 7. (6 obstacles, 7 jumps).
Open jump-off: 4, 5, 6A-B, 13, 8, 9A-B-C, 10. (7 obstacles, 10 jumps).

*Fig. 572*
Indoor (20 x 60 metres) course for Novice and Open competitions.
Novice competition: 13 obstacles, 14 jumps.
Open competition: 15 obstacles, 18 jumps.
Novice jump-off: 8, 9, 10, 11A-B, 12, 13. (6 obstacles, 7 jumps).
Open jump-off: 1, 15, 10, 11A-B, 12, 13, 14A-B-C, 15. (8 obstacles, 11 jumps).

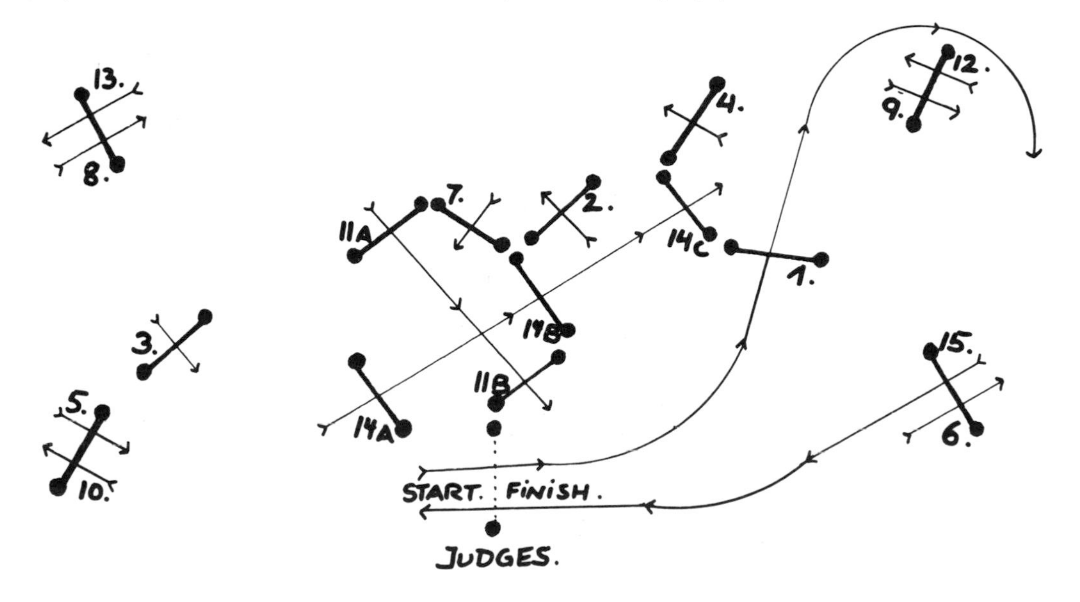

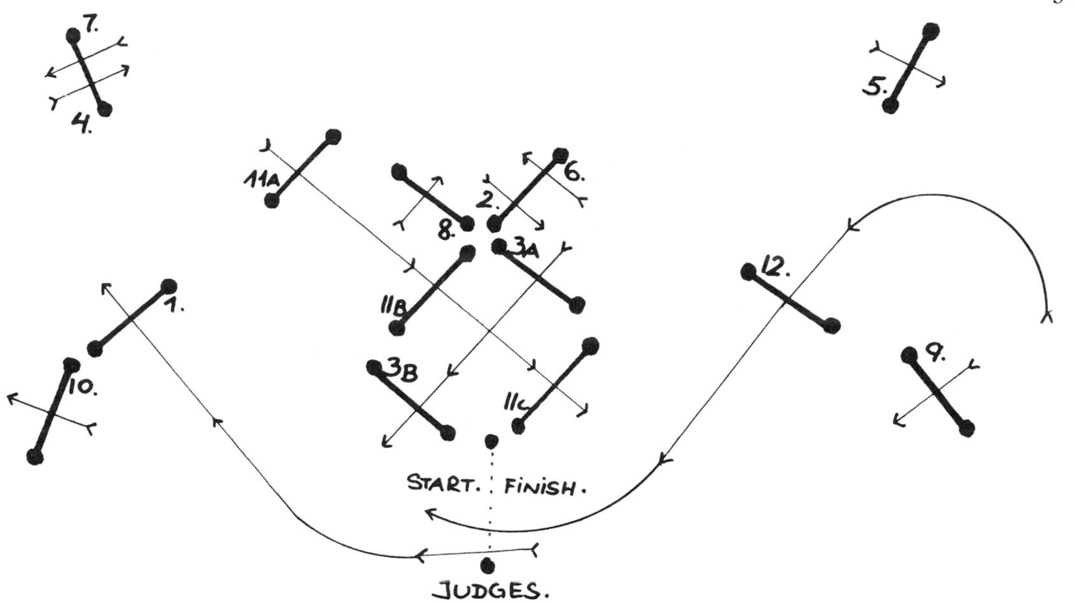


*Fig. 573*
Indoor (20 x 60 metres) course for Novice and Open competitions.
Novice competitions: 9 obstacles, 10 jumps.
Open competition: 12 obstacles, 15 jumps.
Novice jump-off: 1, 2, 3A-B, 4, 6, 6, 7. (7 obstacles, 9 jumps).
Open jump-off: 6, 7, 8, 9, 10, 11A-B-C, 12. (7 obstacles, 9 jumps).

*Fig. 574*
Indoor (20 x 60 metres) course for "Take Your Own Line" Speed competitions. (Using remains of course in *Fig. 573*).
"Take Your Own Line" competition: 8 obstacles, 8 jumps.

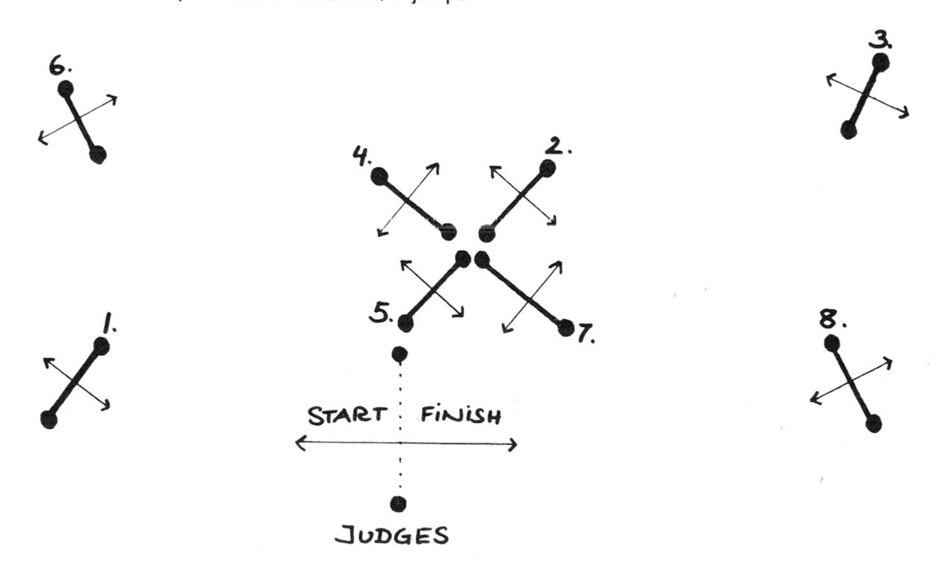

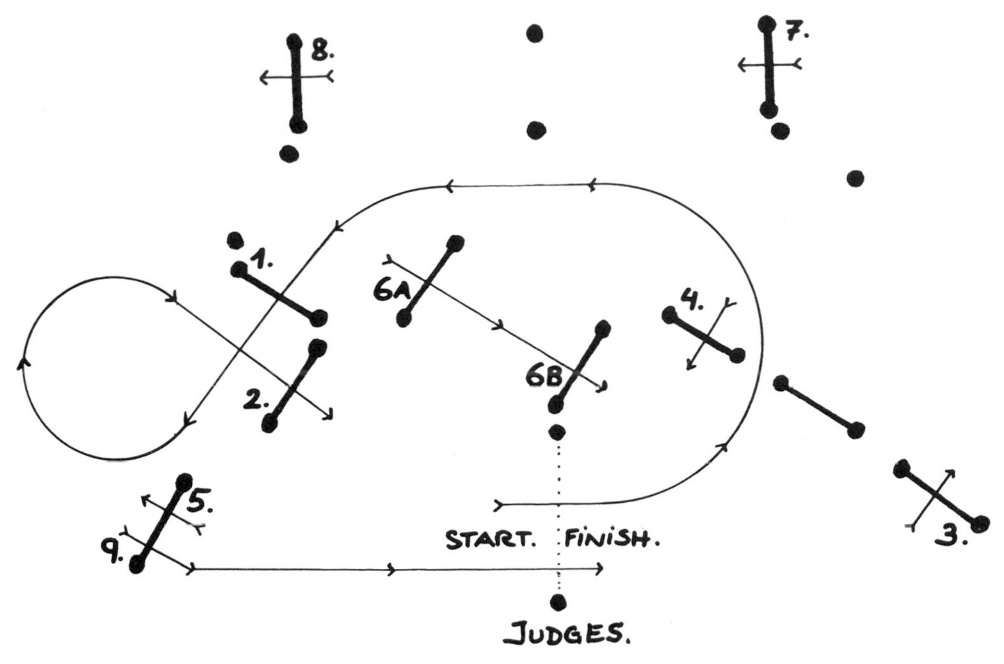


*Fig. 575*
Indoor (20 x 60 metres) course for Novice competitions.
Novice competition: 9 obstacles, 10 jumps.
Novice jump-off: 3, 4, 5, 6A-B, 7, 8, 9. (7 obstacles, 8 jumps).

*Fig. 576*
Indoor (20 x 60 metres) course for Open competitions. (Using remains of course in *Fig. 575*).
Open competition: 12 obstacles, 20 jumps.
Open jump-off: 1, 2, 3A-B, 5, 6A-B-C, 7A-B-C, 8. (7 obstacles, 12 jumps).

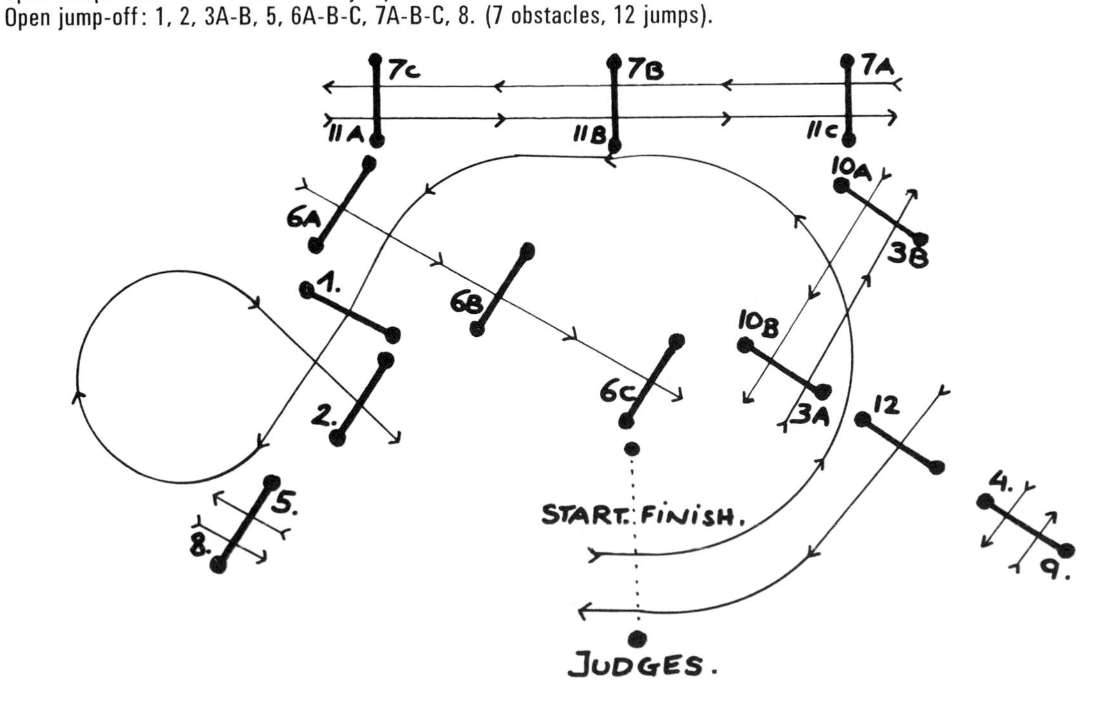

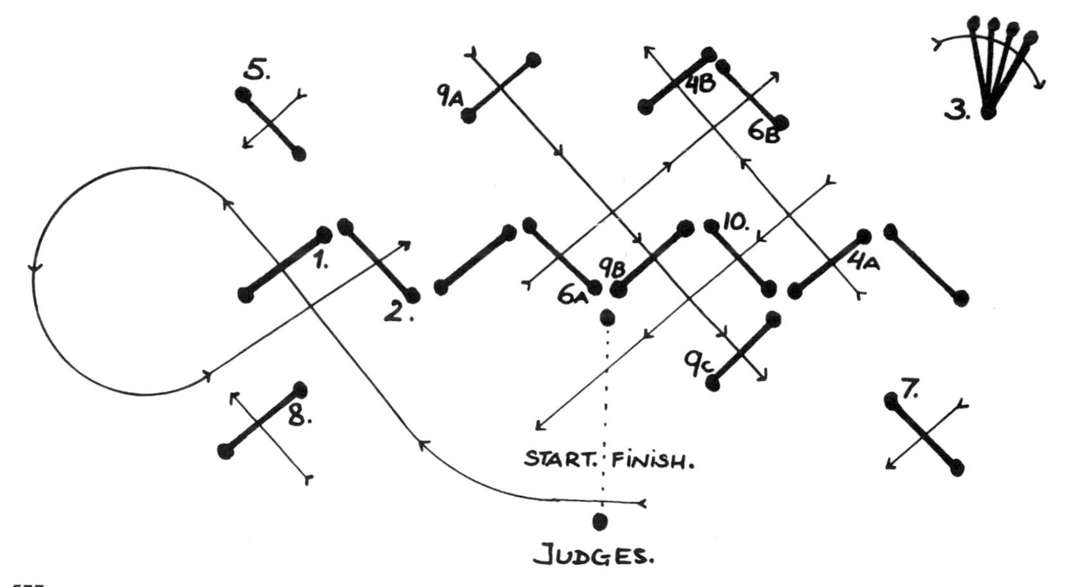


*Fig. 577*
Indoor (20 x 60 metres) course for Novice and Open competitions.
Novice competition: 7 obstacles, 9 jumps.
Open competition: 10 obstacles, 14 jumps.
Novice jump-off: Same course.
Open jump-off: 1, 6A-B, 7, 8, 9A-B-C, 10. (6 obstacles, 9 jumps).

*Fig. 578*
Indoor (20 x 60 metres) course for "Take Your Own Line" Speed competitions. (Using remains of course in *Fig. 577*).
"Take Your Own Line" competition: 8 obstacles, 8 jumps.

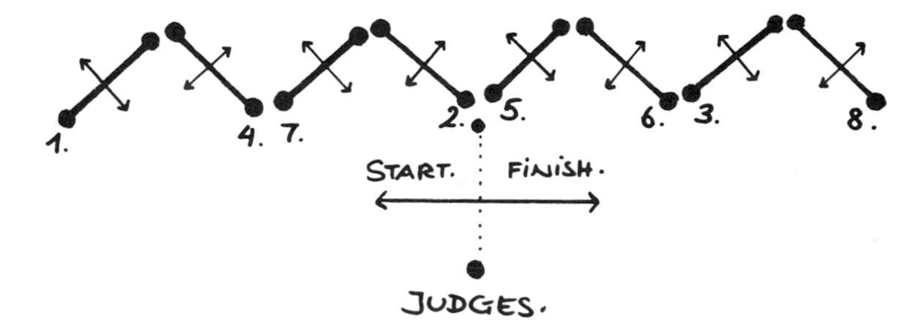

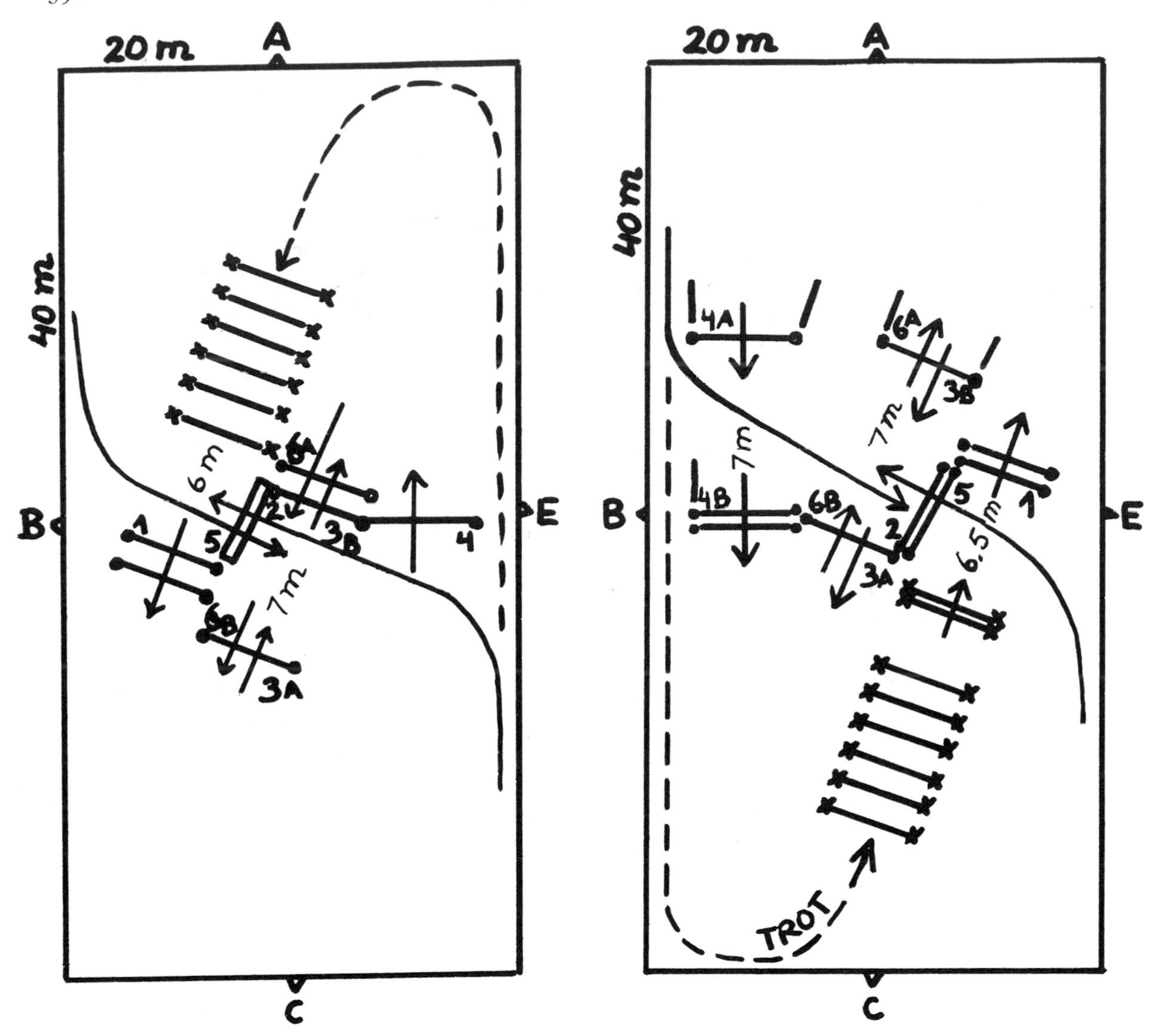


*Fig. 579*
Training course in an indoor school of 20 x 40 metres.

*Fig. 580*
Training course in an indoor school of 20 x 40 metres.

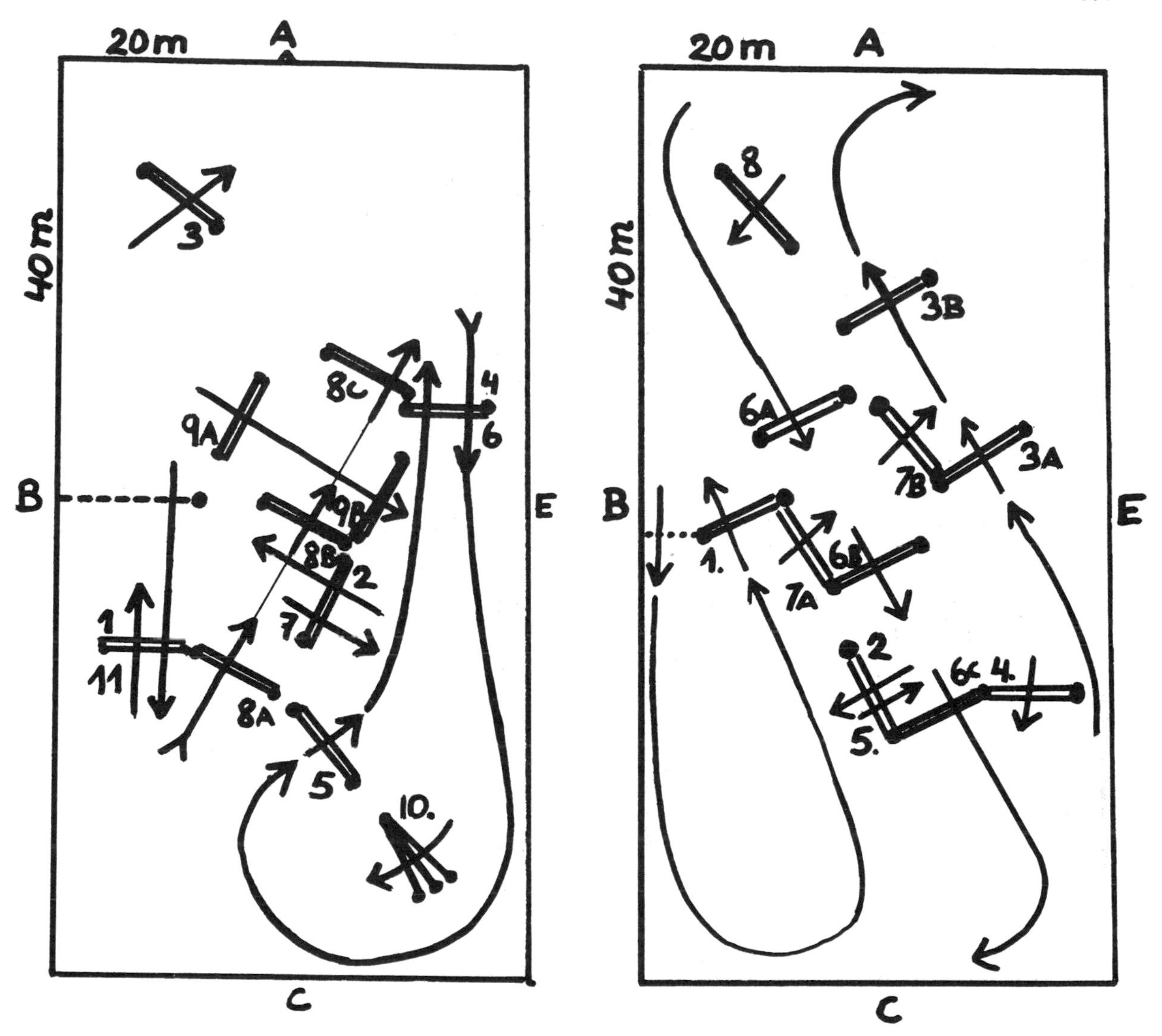


*Fig. 581*
Competition course in an indoor school of 20 x 40 metres.

*Fig. 582*
Competition course in an indoor school of 20 x 40 metres.

In such cases some judges attempt to remedy matters by making the jump-off course too severe for a quick final result. This is disheartening for many a young horse and rider.

*Preventive measures*

These are some suggestions which the show organiser may adopt in order to prevent his planned programme from running behind schedule:

(i) require the course builder to plan a short novice course, approximately 300 metres, with no more than eight obstacles and ten jumps in the first round;

(ii) fence stewards (mostly inexperienced) must be instructed by the course builder prior to the commencement of the show how to rebuild a fence efficiently and quickly should it be knocked down completely;

(iii) at least one steward should be assigned to each obstacle. To prevent unnecessary refusals which means, again, losing time, the fence stewards should stand perfectly still and not too close to the fence when the horse is approaching it because this might distract the horse and make him shy away;

(iv) *two* stewards are required if a fence has to be jumped in either direction. If demolished it has to be reconstructed quickly so as not to delay the competitor;

(v) each steward should receive written instructions for "his" fence. The holes in the uprights (wings) should be numbered and clearly marked with colours to indicate the position of the cups for each round;

(vi) a separate entrance and exit is vital;

(vii) a roped-out collecting pocket will prevent any serious hold up. Two horses should always be waiting to enter the arena. A steward should be assigned to ensure that the *right* competitor enters the arena and at the *right time;*

(viii) an efficient starter will announce every competitor to the judges prior to their entering the jumping enclosure;

(ix) the first few fences should be jumped towards the entrance. This arrangement will avoid resistance and refusals at the first obstacles, which again would mean further loss of time;

(x) a "time allowed" and a "time limit" should be adopted, especially in novice competitions;

(xi) a compulsory turning point or a compulsory course line also saves time;

(xii) the judge's box and the timing apparatus must be positioned with a commanding view of the start and finish line. I consider it very convenient to have both in *one* line and in front of the judges box. If the timing apparatus should fail then the timing can easily be done by stopwatch;

(xiii) fence stewards should signal jumping faults to the judges box. This is especially important at fences which cannot be viewed clearly from the judge's box. A red flag should be hoisted when a fall occurs. Once the fence is rebuilt the reverse-side (white) of the flag is then raised to inform the judges that the course is ready again.

*Conclusion*

One will have noticed that several points are to be taken into consideration. When carefully planned and executed they will have the dual effect of a smoothly run show and a programme effectively timed.

Finally, a personal note. Competitors must be meticulously attired. In Australia and Central America competitors may *not* participate unless they are correctly dressed (a pink or black jacket must be worn), irrespective of the climate. This is in contrast to countries with a cool climate, who permit their competitors to participate dressed in a shirt, even with rolled up sleeves.

I feel that a show should not be organised by a committee who are so permissive as to ignore slapdash exhibitions of riding attire. Better the committee who firmly insist – as it should be – that a compulsory ruling on dress be stated on their programme which each competitor, when competing, must comply with, or be penalised with elimination.

The weather should be of no concern, wet or fine, because each candidate remains in the ring no longer than *two* minutes.

### THE OUTDOOR JUMPING PADDOCK

The floor in the outdoor jumping paddock must provide a non-slip and springy "all weather" surface. The most important factor is to prevent the surface from becoming hard, deep, heavy and dusty. Neither should it become soaking wet during a long rainy spell.

The locality can, of course, have a determining influence on the all weather surface. Therefore, various factors should be taken into consideration. These include: the type of sub-soil; the location and if it is surrounded by trees, bushes or existing buildings; if the location is exposed to wind or sun and if there is the possibility of arranging sufficient drainage. Also check that there are no underground springs

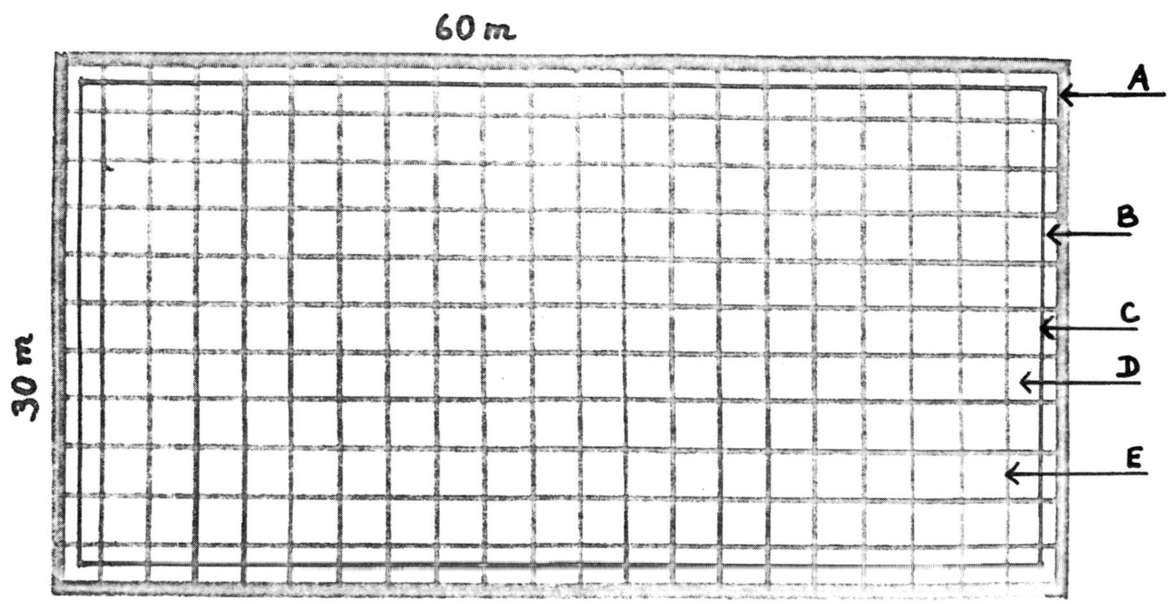


*Fig. 583*
Drainage plan for an all-weather outdoor jumping paddock. **(A)** Main drain outside arena, 1 metre deep by 0·5 metre wide; **(B)** kicking boards; **(C)** track; **(D)** track; **(E)** surface drainage.

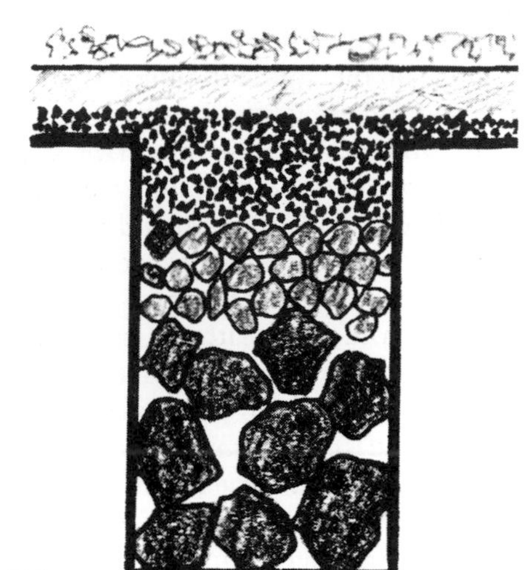

*Fig. 584*
Layers of filling material for the drains.

which might cause trouble in the winter. The jumping paddock should be level and situated on the highest piece of ground available. A slope or humps in the surface provide bad jumping. While turning on such places there is the chance that the horse either might stumble and fall or cause strain on his legs and feet. If the field is not completely level one should be careful not to excavate too extensively. If hard core has to be used in building up some slopes it must be covered by at least 3 centimetres of soil, after which these places should be thoroughly rolled.

*Size*

The principal object of the jumping paddock will be for training purposes. However, it should also allow the jumping of a full course. A size of 30 × 60 metres is perfectly adequate, even to run jumping competitions.

*General drainage pattern*

The main drainage ditch should be dug at a distance of 50 centimetres on the outside of the paddock on all four sides. It should be 1 metre deep and 50 centimetres wide and has two vital functions: first to absorb the water from the working surface drainage; and second to isolate the jumping paddock from seepage from surrounding land. It should *not* be filled with stones, but kept open. Only at the entrance put concrete pipes into the open ditch and fill up to make a crossing. The same applies to the main drainage ditches around the all-weather lungeing ring and the indoor school. The drainage system should be sloping from the centre to the main drainage ditch.

*Surface drainage*

One should dig out in the subsoil ten ditches in the length and 20 ditches in the width of the paddock. They carry the water away to the main drainage ditch surrounding the paddock. These ditches should be 50 centimetres deep and 30 centimetres wide. They should be filled up first with 30 centimetres of large natural stones (bricks are not advisable), then covered by 10 centimetres of small natural stones, with the last layer being 10 centimetres of cinders.

*The track*

The first surface drainage ditch should be situated 50 centimetres inside the track and *not* underneath the track. The track will be more in use than the other parts of the working surface. Therefore if a drainage ditch is situated underneath the track the surface becomes depressed and drainage blocked. This means surface water would not be carried away to the main (outside) drainage ditch and the track becomes shallow and humps and/or ridges will appear on it.

*Covering the soil*

The whole working area should now be covered with 5 centimetres of rough cinders and consolidated with heavy rolling, then cover it with 4 centimetres of white sharp river, or coarse, sand. I allow 1 centimetre more sand than for the indoor school floor because it will work into the cinders more than into clay of the subfloor. Finally cover it with 5 centimetres of woodshavings, which is not only to create a springy surface but also keeps the floor moist. It is necessary to water the floor once it is covered by the shavings and to roll the whole area again. Care should be taken in the maintenance of the surface by means of keeping it damp (which makes it free of dust and hence is healthier for the horse's breathing and eyes). Also a daily handrake is advisable to keep the surface flat, not only on the track but particularly at the take-off and landing side of the fences. To keep the paddock free from humps, holes or ridges is vital outdoors, because the working surface has to stand up to all weather conditions. Occasionally it will be necessary to add some more sand and shavings to compensate for wear, but great care must be taken not to increase the depth of the floor, which could lead to disaster in the training of showjumpers.

### THE PERMANENT LUNGEING RING

The permanent lungeing ring is a very common sight in Australia and Central America, particularly at racing stables where the ring is extensively used for breaking. The ring is indeed of great help, provided it has the following characteristics: it must be well drained; it must have a good non-slip and springy "all weather" surface; it must have kicking boards or something similar; it must *not* be larger than 13 metres in diameter.

The general drainage pattern is similar to the one for the outdoor jumping paddock. The only difference with the lungeing ring is that the drainage ditches are dug out in circles and with a cross through the centre. From this cross at the centre the drainage should be sloping towards the main drainage ditch. So the depth of the ditches should be in the following order:

at the cross centre .......... 35 centimetres
at the first drainage ditch...... 50 centimetres
at the second drainage ditch .. 60 centimetres
at the main drainage ditch.... 100 centimetres

To construct the working surface the same material is used as for the outdoor jumping paddock. The kicking boards (or something similar) are essential to support the horse, because without it most horses are inclined to lean on the lungeing rein. If the lungeing ring has a diameter of more than 13 metres, for example, 15 or 18 metres, then it misses the two vital points of the purpose of lungeing.

Firstly, lungeing on too large a circle does not create sufficient lateral bending in the rib parts of the horse's body and it does not achieve the engagement of the inner hindleg.

Secondly, when lungeing with the lungeing *rein* at the correct length of 6 metres in a lungeing ring of 18 metres the horse is then not supported by the kicking boards and therefore is taught to lean on the lungeing rein.

A lungeing ring constructed in the correct manner will be 100% successful in use, because besides the lungeing exercise one can also ride the horse in the ring at all paces. One should realise that the average circus *piste* has the same dimension and it is amazing to see that so many horses are able to perform simultaneously.

For small riding schools or private owners who have no indoor or outdoor school, a good lungeing ring where one can work under all weather conditions will indeed be very helpful, particularly when teaching beginners, because most horses are more at ease when fenced in than in an open field. During a dry spell in the summer when the going is rock hard, or in the winter when the fields are soaking wet and the going is deep and heavy, one will then appreciate the value of an all-weather lungeing ring and be happy to have at least one place where one can work a horse at all times.

### BUILDING AN INDOOR SCHOOL

Indoor schools are costly to build, there is often little return on the investment and technical faults are often made in construction. I hope the following suggestions will be of use.

*Inspecting the surface*

The following four points are vital, and I stress that the surface of the site should be carefully investigated and peculiarities identified before building commences.

(i) building the school on marshy land is not recommended, especially land which has no drainage ditches, so that there is nowhere for the water to drain to. Building on a potential bog has no point, neither where there is any danger of flooding;

(ii) another hazard, and one to discover before starting to build, is if there are any underground springs present below the surface of the school. This could cause serious trouble by water rising through the floor of the school;

(iii) around the outside of the school there should be an open main drainage ditch to isolate the school from seepage from the surrounding land. It will also catch the large quantity of rainwater from the roof, this prevents under running of the walls of the school.

(iv) on the Continent, where indoor schools have existed for many generations, several schools have, as a foundation, a concrete or tarmac subfloor, which I will explain in detail later on. This prevents not only the hazard of underground springs but it also prevents any unevenness in the floor, particularly when the school is extensively used for jumping. If one realises that the weight of a horse is approximately 750 kilogrammes then one can appreciate the forces to which the floor is subjected when in use.

*Location*

It is essential that the site chosen for the school should be as near as possible to the stables in case of bad weather. Personally I prefer school and stable all under one roof, providing there is sufficient ventilation.

*Size*

The size of the school depends on the purpose it will have to serve. For private use a riding space of 20 × 40 metres is sufficient. This is a convenient size for free jumping in the jumping lane, whereas in a very large school it is harder to keep control over a horse jumping loose. A small gallery can be built on to the outside of the centre of the long side of the school to cater for an occasional visitor.

If one intends to run jumping competitions then the size of 20 × 60 metres is more convenient and a large gallery is then essential.

Maximum clearance under the framework of the roof above the track is essential, because jumping will also take place on the track, particularly when free jumping. An approximate height of 5 metres is sufficient.

*The roof*

I recommend having a horizontal *extra* ceiling underneath the original arched roof top. This extra ceiling can be made of light timber or soft board material. It gives a cooler atmosphere in the summer and a warmer one in the winter and it has the same effect in hot or in cold countries. Most important is that there should be a ventilation ridge, in other words an open space of 15 centimetres between the roof and the ceiling, running along the top part of the walls and round all four sides, which ensures sufficient ventilation. This ventilation ridge must be constructed in such a way that it can be closed in case of bad weather conditions and in the winter to prevent the floor from getting frozen. Having sections of transparent sheets on the roof for better light is a hazard which is often overlooked when planning. It gives not only false shadows on the floor, which confuses a horse when jumping, but it creates also a greenhouse temperature, even when the sun is only shining mildly. This humid heat is unbearable, even more so when the school is frequently hosed. This heat is very tiring as it consumes energy, thereby unnecessarily exhausting horses and riders.

*Lights and windows*

The windows should be large and located directly underneath the ceiling, running along the entire length of the building. It must be possible to open the windows for ventilation and fresh air, but in such a way that occasional rain water cannot run into the school. This high location of the windows also prevents false shadows on the floor which, again, is safer when jumping. For the same safety reasons, uncovered mirrors are dangerous. I have witnessed

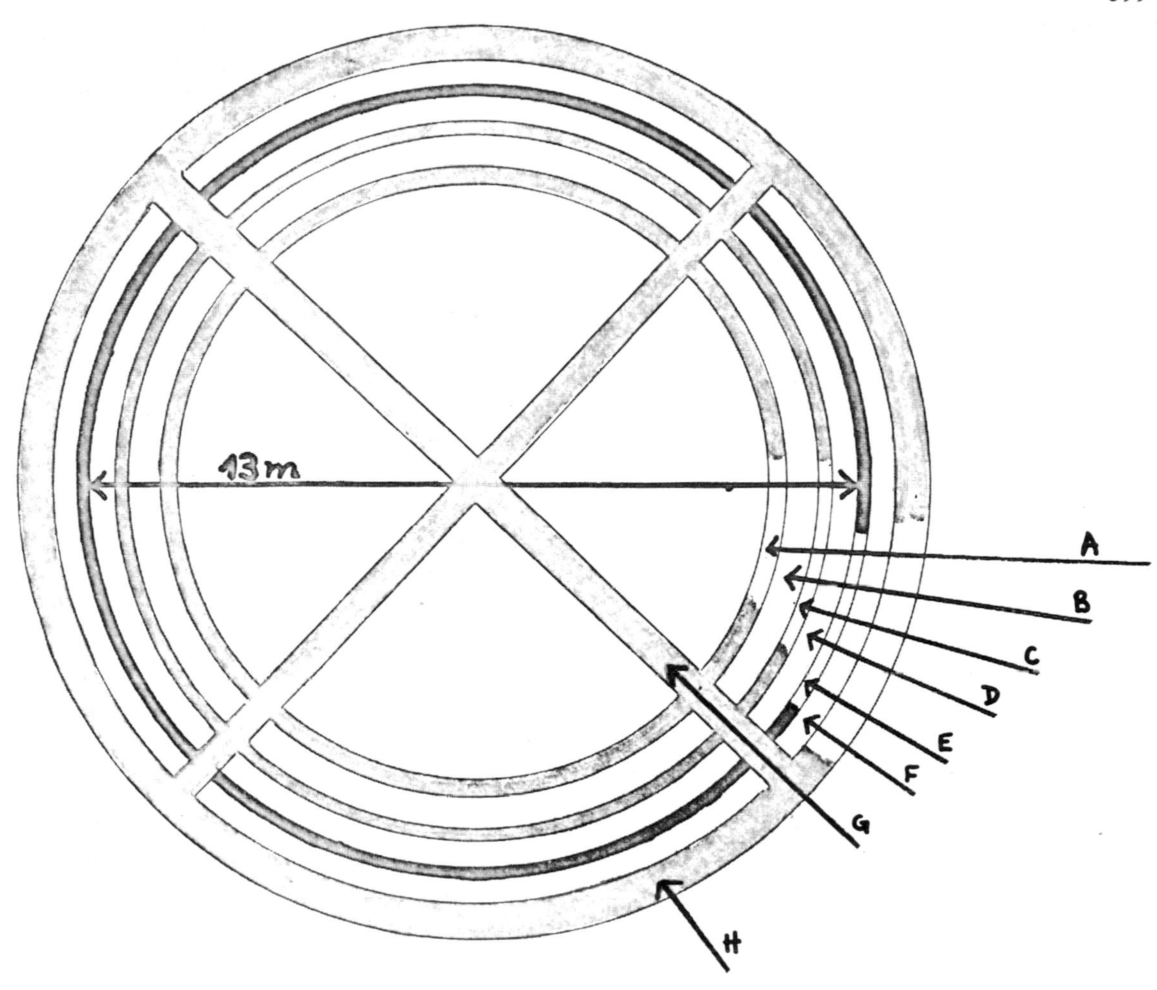


*Fig. 585*
Drainage plan for an all-weather outdoor lungeing ring. **(A)** First drainage ditch, 0.5 metres deep and 0.3 metres wide; **(B)** space between first and second drainage ditch is 0.5 metres wide; **(C)** second drainage ditch, 0.6 metres deep and 0.3 metres wide; **(D)** the track, 0.5 metres space between kicking boards and second drain; **(E)** kicking boards (or railing); **(F)** distance between kicking boards and main drainage ditch is 0.5 metres; **(G)** cross drains through centre of the ring should slope from approximately 0.35 metres at the centre to 0.7 metres at the outside of the ring when joining the main drainage ditch. Use pipes for this drain, otherwise the drain might get blocked where it crosses under the track; also the track might become uneven in these places; **(H)** the main drainage ditch, 1 metre deep and 0.5 metres wide. This should not be filled in but kept open and clean. It collects the water from the drainage and isolates the lungeing ring from seepage of water from the surrounding land.

on several occasions horses who, when free jumping, are inclined to jump right through them. To prevent this happening the mirrors should be covered by a curtain, which should run on a top – as well as on a bottom – rail. When the curtain runs on the top rail only it will move when a horse passes by and will frighten him when free jumping. In the winter, mirrors should be heated so that they are kept free from condensation.

When a gallery is glazed in, for example, for a restaurant with a view into the indoor arena, to reduce dust and dirt the *floor* of the gallery and the floor of the restaurant should be level with the *top edge* of the kicking boards in order to reduce the risk of a horse kicking or jumping through the windows.

Electric lighting should be installed so that it creates no false shadows. Neon lighting is the most economical and is recommended. Tungsten is not bright enough.

*Kicking boards*

The kicking boards are not only safe but they also prevent a horse from leaning against the wall. The vertical part at the bottom is positioned 20 centimetres above, and 10 centimetres into, the floor and should be saturated with creosote. It should rest on concrete with a sheet of damp-proof material in between to protect the timber from rising damp. This vertical part of the kicking boards ensures that the horse keeps well away from the sloping section. A completely sloping kicking board without a lower vertical section is dangerous, not only during jumping competitions but particularly when breaking and schooling young horses.

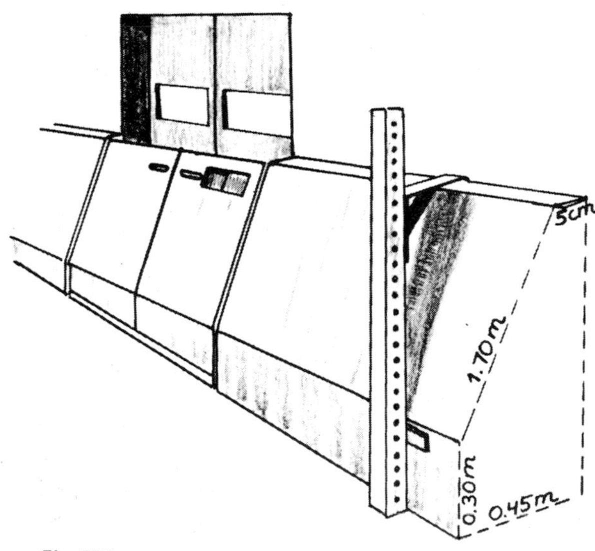


*Fig. 586*
Sloping kicking boards and double doors of an indoor school.

Many young horses are, at an early stage of schooling, a bit clumsy and inclined to lean against the wall. Owing to this the horse can knock his feet against the lower part of the slope, slide downwards along the kicking boards and on to the ground. It has happened that the rider comes in between the kicking boards and the horse. The *planks* of the vertical, and also on the sloping, part of the kicking boards should run vertically. The space between the wall and the kicking boards should be closed at the top edge (flat, not rounded off). The space can then be used to hang movable uprights of fences. These uprights are not only handy when free jumping and in practise sessions but they also take up less space than the normal wings. Space behind the wall of the school and the kicking boards can be used to store fence material. Therefore I recommend having two movable sections in the sloping part of the kicking boards on each long side of the school.

*The doors*

The main double doors are usually situated at the A and C markers. They should be sufficiently high and wide to enable a lorry to pass through them to deliver sand and woodshavings. A separate entrance and exit is most convenient in view of jumping competitions. An emergency bell or a telephone is vital in case of accidents. The main entrance should be situated on the "good weather" side. Furthermore, a small exit to the stables or to the gallery is also essential. All doors should have glazed-in peep holes in order to make sure the track is free before one enters the school. The kicking boards should *not* be attached to the double doors but instead be constructed as two separate doors, each of them opening to the inside of the school. For this reason the vertical parts of the kicking boards doors should not be higher than 20 centimetres to allow free movement over the floor of the school. The advantage of separated doors is particularly noticeable during the summer, because one can open all the double doors to allow fresh air and keep the kicking board doors shut.

*The floor*

The floor is the most important aspect of the whole school. As previously mentioned, and to be on the safe side, a concrete or tarmac foundation as an underfloor is ideal. Nevertheless, if the subsoil is of clay and level then there is no need for an extra underfloor. If not, cover the whole area of the underfloor with 5 centimetres of clay. The clay floor should now be rolled level and given at least one week to dry otherwise it will mix with the second covering of the sand. The whole area of the floor should now be covered with 3 centimetres of white coarse sand. Do not use a dark coloured sand as it absorbs the light in the school. A dark floor is not only inconvenient when jumping but it is also bad if a jumping competition is being televised. After having rolled the sand floor it should now be covered with 5 centimetres of woodshavings. Sawdust is not recommended; it not only balls up in the horse's feet but it is also inclined to create hard humps, which can cause nasty falls when jumping. The whole floor will now have a depth of 13 centimetres which is for the time being sufficient, depending of course on how much the school is being used. To compensate for wear one can occasionally build up with another 2 centimetres of sand and 3 centimetres of woodshavings. One should, however, be very careful with sand because it deadens the floor, which becomes too heavy, exhausting to jump on and causes strain on the horse. About 300 bags of woodshavings three times a year is necessary.

*Maintenance of the floor*

The mixture for the floor, mentioned above, provides a non-slip and springy surface, but it is of vital importance that this surface be kept level – daily – particularly the landing and the take-off places, and not forgetting the track in order to prevent excessive shock to the horse's legs. Hand raking is the best daily solution, although once a week the whole surface should be levelled with a tractor and hydraulically controlled yard scraper.

*Salt*

The application of salt to dampen the floor is definitely wrong. One has only to realise the serious damage it does to our cars when used on icy roadways to appreciate how disastrous it is to the horse's feet. They become hard and brittle and the salt also causes cracked heels. This bad feet condition occurs also in those horses who go regularly into sea water.

*Peat*

Personally I am against peat, although it is used in some schools as a traditional material. In my experience it is not a good substance for a floor. Peat makes the floor extremely dusty, which is not only unpleasant for the rider but it is bad for the horse's wind and eyes as well. If the peat is kept damp the floor becomes slippy, which again is dangerous, particularly when a school is being used extensively for jumping. Peat also darkens the colour of the floor, consequently absorbing the light in the school. Peat also clogs up in the horse's feet and it causes an unpleasant smell when dampened.

*Watering systems*

It is advisable that two water points be located at the centre of each long side (at the E and B markers) of the school for watering the floor. The taps should be situated behind the kicking boards at the lower vertical part and behind a little door whose hinges should be sunk. Hand held hose pipe watering is the best answer to keep the floor moist. It is not time consuming if one installs a high pressure machine and uses the same size hosepipe as the fire brigade. When using a normal hosepipe one should water the school very early in the morning, because at that time very few people are using water, consequently there is more water pressure. In any case, it is advisable to water the floor early in the morning, particularly in the summer, because it makes the school cool and fresh. Overhead water sprinklers are not recommended because they function in most cases unsatisfactorily, particularly when there is a certain amount of lime in the water. This results in some sprinklers becoming completely blocked and supplying no water at all, while others over-water the floor at a certain point. This makes a soft bog at some places and if the water sinks down through the clay sub-soil then it creates great damage to the floor. These soft spots are particularly dangerous when jumping. The horse can easily slip and fall and suffer lameness. The same hazard can occur when lawn sprinklers are being used in the school unless repeatedly removed, for this can easily be forgotten.

However, the composition of the floor, provided care is employed in its maintenance, will ensure a non-slip, springy surface, which encourages good jumping, gives a firm grip in the take-off and reduces the shock to the horse's feet and legs when landing.

## ACKNOWLEDGEMENTS

I am greatly indebted to two of my pupils, Mrs. Gisela Holstein for illustrating the book with her superb linedrawings; and Mr. Arthur Lardner for his help in having my manuscript typed. Lastly, I thank my wife Sonja, without whose assistance, patience, encouragement and care this book would never have been written.